Vocational and Practical Arts Education

Exploration Series in Education

Under the Advisory Editorship

of John Guy Fowlkes

VOCATIONAL AND PRACTICAL ARTS EDUCATION ❧ HISTORY, DEVELOPMENT, AND PRINCIPLES

SECOND EDITION

ROY W. ROBERTS

Head, Department of Vocational Teacher
Education, University of Arkansas

HARPER AND ROW ❧ PUBLISHERS

New York, Evanston, and London

CONTENTS

EDITOR'S INTRODUCTION

When the first edition of this book was published eight years ago, it filled a vital need for a scholarly, comprehensive text that would report past experiments and developments in practical and vocational education, and, equally essential, the present state of this important and expanding field. Professor Roberts saw the desirability of establishing a common "vocabulary" among professional workers and laymen in the field for whom the terms "practical arts" or "vocational education" might have widely divergent meaning. *Vocational and Practical Arts Education* eminently served that purpose and has continued to do so, both in this country and abroad.

The significance of vocational arts in our time was and continues to be so generally recognized that this field of education is supported by substantial sums of money from local and state governments as well as the Federal government of the United States. This volume has provided a useful and informative guide not only for professionals but also for others concerned with the formulation and execution of a truly functional program of educational opportunity.

In the second edition Professor Roberts has expanded the original volume, bringing in the most current and significant developments in the field, new data and ideas, as well as the results of past experiments and a fresh view of the whole field of practical and vocational arts education.

I am very pleased to be able to introduce this significant volume by my long-time friend and colleague, Roy W. Roberts.

JOHN GUY FOWLKES

February 10, 1965

PREFACE

This volume, in its second edition, is concerned with a study of vocational and practical arts education. Emphasis is placed on the origins, development, principles, and relationships of these areas of education in schools of less than the baccalaureate degree level. This new edition became necessary because of the many changes in policies and procedures in vocational education since the publication of the first edition. The high incidence of unemployment in recent years has prompted the enactment of many new laws granting Federal aid to vocational and technical education. Many workers have lost their jobs because of automation, changing consumer demands, and new products and processes. The large number of school dropouts has focused attention on the need for new programs and special financial assistance to youth in need of vocational education. Improvements in health care have motivated new programs of practical nursing education.

Changes in manpower requirements and qualifications in industry and agriculture have brought about a need for area vocational and technical education programs which serve larger geographic areas than the local school district. The impact of world problems and foreign aid has made it necessary for this country to know more about the educational problems and needs of other nations. These and other topics are discussed in this second edition.

This volume also contains an analysis of the Vocational Education Act of 1963. The Act grants state boards for vocational education more discretionary power in the use of Federal funds than was provided in previous acts and authorizes special programs of vocational education for disadvantaged youth. The Act also includes for the first time some basic amendments to previous vocational education laws.

This volume is written primarily for the purpose of providing factual information and general principles concerned with the various areas or fields of study in vocational and practical arts education and their relationship to each other. This is especially important to the new concept of vocational education, which is cooperation and interrelationship among the various fields of study. This type of cooperation is designed to provide the individual student with the kinds of information and skill he needs to accomplish his specific vocational goal.

The topical rather than the strictly chronological approach is used in the parts of the volume dealing with the history and development of the program. The volume is not closely documented. Some citations are shown in the text. The statistical data concerned with economic and social relationships were taken from the publications of the U.S. Bureau of the Census and other government publications. The statistical data relating to the scope and cost of the various programs described were taken from the annual reports of the agencies concerned. The source references given at the close of each chapter contain the documentary information referred to in the chapter.

The author is indebted to many persons for their assistance in the writing of the manuscript. Many of the author's colleagues and friends read parts of the manuscript and provided helpful suggestions in its revision. The author is especially indebted to his wife, Edgar Lyday Roberts, who read, corrected, and reread the manuscript many times during the course of its preparation.

This book is especially designed for use in teacher education programs of vocational and practical arts education and for the education of school administrators who have or may have responsibility for organizing and administering programs in these areas. It should prove useful as a textbook for courses concerned with the history, development, and administration of the programs described. It will be useful as a source of information to administrative personnel and teachers of vocational education and to other individuals interested in programs of vocational and practical arts education.

Roy W. Roberts

Vocational and Practical Arts Education

CHAPTER ONE

INTRODUCTION

This volume is concerned with vocational and practical arts education. Special attention is directed to the Federally aided programs of vocational education and to industrial arts. The term *vocational education* is relatively new in the literature of education. It came into prominence near the beginning of the present century. This term, however, is simply a new name for a practice as old as civilization itself. Man, since the beginning of time, has worked for his livelihood, and this has necessitated that he learn to work. Most educators, both general and vocational, agree that vocational education is concerned with learning to work. However, many divergent opinions arise in determining the ways and means of implementing this learning process. Differences occur in attempts to answer such questions as: What types of learning experiences shall be included in vocational education? What teaching methods and techniques shall be used? In what trades or occupational areas shall vocational education be provided? Who shall pay for vocational education? Who shall administer voca-

3

Students in Culinary Arts Prepare for Positions in Restaurant Operation and Management. (Los Angeles Trade-Technical College)

tional education programs? On what grade levels shall vocational education be provided? What standards shall be maintained in operating programs of vocational education? These and many other questions have given rise to differences not only between vocational and general educators but also among vocational educators themselves.

Acceptable answers to questions such as those shown above involve an examination of many facts, principles and practices in education and in vocational education, and this volume is designed to provide information and data that will be useful in arriving at acceptable answers to the above and other similar questions. The information and data included in this book are concerned primarily with the history and development of vocational and practical arts education below the baccalaureate degree level and their impact on related programs.

The first chapter is an introduction to this volume. It consists of statements and points of view concerning the meaning of vocational education and some of its commonly used terms, the need for vocational and practical arts education and a brief description of some of the present-day programs in these areas. A discussion of some controversial issues and conflicting relationships that affect the operation of the programs is also included. The information in this chapter should be useful in establishing a point of departure for the examination of the remaining chapters of this volume.

Concepts and Definitions

Frequently, differences of opinion resolve themselves into differences in definition. This has especially proved to be true with reference to many differences in vocational education. A review of the literature of vocational education indicates that variations have existed in the meanings of terms commonly used in vocational education and in concepts of vocational education and their implications. A discussion of some of these terms and concepts is presented below. The first of these discussions is concerned with the significance of work.

THE SIGNIFICANCE OF WORK

No force has been more powerful in man's rise from savagery to civilization than work. Work has enabled man to satisfy his ever increasing needs and wants. The savages of early times had few wants and as a consequence spent little time at work. Likewise, present-day individuals with few wants spend less time at work than individuals with many wants. Man needs to spend only a small part of a day at work to escape starvation, but he must work the greater part of the day to provide those comforts and necessities that mean the difference between present-day savagery and civilized living. Man discovered early in his history that he did not wish to remain in savagery and that by work he could obtain more palatable food, more comfortable clothing and more suitable shelter. Through the ages the results achieved by work have stimulated man to seek ways of increasing his efficiency in work. Thus man has learned to work.

Individuals have learned to work by various methods. The first learning was perhaps by accident. The discovery of fire, the results obtained from the application of pressure and the saving of energy by the use of the wheel doubtless occurred in this manner. Each of these discoveries contributed materially to man's progress. Man also learned to work by trial and error and by imitation. All these methods of learning are still in use and have been responsible for many advances in civilization. Learning by accident and learning by trial and error have proved costly, and man has been obliged to seek new and less costly methods of learning to work. As a result, the method of learning through planned experiences has come into use. Apprenticeship, which originated during ancient times and flourished during the Middle Ages, was among the first forms of this planned learning. The organized vocational school, which is of relatively recent origin, is a more modern example of planned learning. Educators are constantly seeking ways of improving methods of learning to work through organized instruction.

Work, which is defined as the continuous application of energy for a purpose, is accomplished by many forces. Water, steam, electricity, gas and chemical reactors are capable of producing work. Individuals also engage in work. From the standpoint of an individual, work consists of exerting physical or mental energy or labor for the accomplishment of a specific purpose or object. When the object is a product or a service for consumer use the work involved is referred to as productive work. Productive work engaged in as the chief means and for the purpose of making a living becomes one's chief gainful pursuit, regular occupation or vocation. As the individual seeks and finds new and improved ways of working he increases his vocational efficiency.

VOCATIONS AND AVOCATIONS

The vocations of individuals are classified in various ways. Workers are frequently referred to as professional men, businessmen, farmers, and tradesmen. The differences between these classifications are not well defined and are the result of tradition rather than of differences in salary, education, type of product, or nature of service. It is much easier to list the vocations classified as professions than it is to distinguish clearly between a professional worker, a businessman, or a tradesman. However, man's vocation does have an important bearing on his status in society. Some vocations lend more prestige to the workers who are engaged in them than do other vocations. These favored vocations are not necessarily those that provide the highest monetary rewards or require the most extensive educational preparation; nor do these favored vocations remain the same for each succeeding generation. These difficulties of definition and the changing status of vocations add materially to the difficulty of selecting and preparing for vocations and in improving in vocational efficiency.

Vocations are also classified as callings, positions, and jobs. These terms also are difficult to define. The term *calling* is frequently used to denote a ministerial position. It may also be used to denote any vocation in which an individual is employed who regards his vocation as an end in itself and one from which he receives a high degree of personal satisfaction. The term *position* is frequently associated with clerical and professional vocations, and the term *job* is frequently associated with the trades. Here the dividing line between the two is vague and is determined more by tradition than by definition. A vocation that is dull, uninteresting, and commonplace to the worker is sometimes referred to as a job by that particular worker. To another worker the same vocation may be a position or even a calling.

Tradesmen are referred to as skilled, semiskilled, or unskilled workers. In general, a skilled worker is one who has completed an apprenticeship program in a trade or is engaged in a vocation in which technical knowledge and the exercise of judgment are required. A skilled worker who has achieved a high degree of proficiency and recognition in his vocation is frequently referred to as a master craftsman. An unskilled worker or laborer is one who performs work that chiefly requires muscular energy and very little judgment. Semiskilled workers are classified somewhere in between these two categories.

Man exerts energy for play as well as for work. The amount of physical or mental energy exerted by an individual may be equally as great for play as for work. The motive for play or recreation is found in the activity itself, and some specific activities are classified as play for one individual and work for another, depending upon the purpose of the activity. Avocations are becoming increasingly important in modern society, and individuals are spending more and more time in avocational experiences. Some of the practical arts are providing learning experiences of an avocational nature.

CONCEPTS OF VOCATIONAL EDUCATION

The world of work presents many problems of concept and definition, most of which arise from tradition and are resolved by common usage. These differences have resulted in various concepts of vocational education. These varying concepts have brought about differences, some of which are fundamental in nature, in programs and practices in vocational education. An examination of some of these concepts will reveal the basic reasons for certain practices and relationships in vocational education and practical arts.

Some individuals have suggested that *vocational education is the education or training of workers*. This concept implies that any type of education or training in which a worker participates is vocational

Vocational Agriculture Enables Future Farmers to Acquire Proficiency in Farming. (Arkansas Association, Future Farmers of America)

education. It doubtless had its origin in early apprenticeship programs in which all educational activities, both general and vocational, were under the supervision of the master craftsman and were included in the apprenticeship program. Individuals who hold this concept are inclined to be critical of pre-employment courses and to suggest that the cost of vocational education should be paid by industry and business.

Another concept held by some individuals is that *vocational education is education for manual work,* which suggests that vocational education is not concerned with work involving mental activity. This concept had its origin in the nineteenth century schools for underprivileged children and has resulted in the present-day practice of placing mentally and socially handicapped students in vocational courses without regard to the learner's interest or ability. The concept that *practical arts is vocational education* emphasizes the importance of the idea of the transfer of training by suggesting that one or two basic courses will provide the needed competencies in vocational education. This point of view had its origin in the manual training movement which some individuals suggested was a feasible way of teaching vocational competencies. This point of view has resulted in the designation by some individuals of industrial arts courses as vocational education.

The passage of the Smith-Hughes Act in 1917, in which Federal funds were provided as a reimbursement for vocational agriculture, home economics, and vocational industrial education, has given rise to a concept that *vocational education is education in certain specified subjects* and more frequently subjects confined to the secondary school. This concept suggests that any person who is pursuing these subjects is in vocational education; whereas, if this same person is pursuing subjects other than those designated as vocational, he is in general education. This point of view disregards many vocations and fails to recognize the purpose of the learner.

Another concept is that of *education for production,* in which vocational education is contrasted with liberal education. Vocational education is designed to make a person an efficient producer, and liberal education is designed to make a person an efficient consumer. Other concepts of vocational education involve the use of such words as *utility* and *practicality,* in which vocational education is confined within narrow limits to subject matter looked upon with less favor than that of a cultural nature. Then, too, there are those who declare that no distinction between vocational and general education should be made, and, as a consequence, no special programs of public education should be maintained for vocational education.

Most vocational educators suggest that the distinction between vocational and general education is based on purpose. If a learner engages in the study of subject matter or other activities for the purpose of increasing his vocational efficiency, he is engaged in vocational education. Similarly, if the content of a course or curriculum is designed for the purpose of enabling the learner to increase his vocational efficiency, such content is classified as vocational. One characteristic of these interpretations is that both the purpose of the learner and the content of the course be classified as socially useful.

This concept suggests that a specified course or curriculum may be vocational to one individual and nonvocational to another enrolled in the same course, depending upon the purpose for which each is enrolled. This concept implies that a person, to be properly enrolled in vocational education, should have made a choice of a socially useful vocation and be making a conscious effort to prepare for or improve in the vocation of his choice. This means that vocational education does not become a part of the educational program of an individual until he makes a decision to prepare for or upgrade himself in his chosen vocation. Vocational education is not designed to take the place of general or nonvocational education but to supplement it. It is not limited to specific subjects or activities, nor is it confined to training for manual dexterity. It has both cultural and utility values and includes the knowledge, skills, and attitudes that fit an individual for entering or progressing in a socially useful vocation.

DEFINITIONS OF VOCATIONAL EDUCATION

The acceptance of the idea that *purpose* is the controlling factor in defining vocational education has resulted in a variety of definitions of vocational education, illustrating again the problem of interpretation. These definitions, some of which are shown below, illustrate varying interpretations and limitations of *purpose* in defining vocational education.

The Federal Board for Vocational Education defined vocational education in 1917 as follows:

To the extent that it is subsidized by the Federal Government under the Smith-Hughes Act vocational training must be vocational training for the common wage earning employments. It may be given to boys and girls who, having selected a vocation, desire preparation for entering it; to boys and girls who having already taken up a wage earning employment, seek greater efficiency in that employment; or to wage earners established in their trade or occupation, who wish through increase in their efficiency and wage earning capacity to advance to positions of responsibility.[1]

This definition recognized the purpose of the learner as a factor in the definition of vocational education and suggested that vocational education has responsibility for both pre-employment and in-service education.

The President's Advisory Committee on Education in its report, published in 1938, defined vocational education as follows: "Vocational education is a very inclusive term and, viewed broadly, may cover all those experiences whereby an individual learns to carry on successfully any useful occupation. These experiences may be organized and institutionalized or unorganized and more or less haphazard. In a narrower sense, vocational education may be defined as a series of controlled and organized experiences arranged to prepare a person for socially useful employment."[2] The report stated that all education is vocational insofar as it prepares for satisfactory living. In this point of view less emphasis was placed on the idea of selection of an occupation as a factor in the definition of vocational education. Then, too, the definition included both planned and vicarious learning. It differed in

[1] Federal Board for Vocational Education, *Statement of Policies,* Bulletin No. 1, Washington, D.C., 1917, p. 9.
[2] John Dale Russell and associates, *Vocational Education,* The Advisory Committee on Education, Staff Study No. 8, Washington, D.C., 1938, p. 13.

this respect from the definition suggested by others in which vocational education was limited to planned experiences rather than haphazard learning.

The Southern States Work Conference, composed of vocational and general educators which met at Daytona Beach, Florida, in the summers of 1944 and 1945 for the study of problems of vocational education, formulated the following definition for vocational education: "In its simplest terms Vocational Education is that aspect of education that aims at the development of human abilities in terms of knowledge, skills and understandings so that the individual may serve happily and efficiently in carrying on the activities in the vocational pursuits of his choice."[3] The conference, in discussing the implications of this definition, suggested that the citizens of the nation were faced with problems of social living, social relationships, and vocations. The task of the school was that of helping students, whether young or old, in school or out of school, to meet these problems. The conference suggested that the problems involved in choosing an occupation, as well as those involved in preparing for and progressing in it, were a part of vocational education. The conference also agreed that public education should assume responsibility for providing adequate programs of vocational education, together with programs of vocational guidance to assist the individual to make a wise choice of an occupation.

The Committee on Research and Publications of the American Vocational Association stated in 1954 that vocational education is "education designed to develop skills, abilities, understandings, attitudes, work habits and appreciations encompassing knowledge and information needed by workers to enter and make progress in employment on a useful and productive basis. It is an integral part of the total educational program and contributes toward the development of good citizens by developing their physical, social, civic, cultural and economic competencies."[4] This statement is substantially the same as the one included in the 1958 revision of the policy bulletin, *Administration of Vocational Education*, published by the Vocational Division, U.S. Office of Education. This definition recognizes purpose, involves various types of outcomes, and includes both pre-employment and in-service programs. The definition suggests that vocational edu-

[3] Edgar L. Morphet (ed.), *Building a Better South Through Education*, Southern States Work Conference on School Administrative Problems, Tallahassee, Fla., 1945, p. 244.
[4] American Vocational Association, *Definition of Terms in Vocational and Practical Arts Education*, Committee on Research and Publications, Washington, D.C., 1954, p. 27.

cation is a part of the total education program and makes its contribution by the development of good citizens as well as proficient workers.

A somewhat different concept used to identify the Federally aided program of vocational education of less than baccalaureate degree level is included in the Vocational Education Act of 1963 (Public Law 88–210). It states that vocational education means:

vocational or technical training or retraining which is given in schools or classes (including field or laboratory work incidental thereto) under public supervision and control or under contract with a state board or local educational agency, and is conducted as a part of a program designed to fit individuals for gainful employment as semiskilled or skilled workers or technicians in recognized occupations (including any program designed to fit individuals for gainful employment in business and office occupations, and any program designed to fit individuals for gainful employment which may be assisted by Federal funds under the Vocational Education Act of 1946 and supplementary vocational education acts but excluding any program to fit individuals for employment in occupations which the Commissioner determines, and specifies in regulations to be generally considered professional or as requiring a baccalaureate or higher degree).

This latter concept of vocational education is used in this volume to identify the Federally aided program of vocational education.

The Need for Vocational Education

The people of the United States by means of continuous and purposeful work have converted the resources of this nation into a quantity and variety of goods and services hitherto unknown in the history of mankind. The products of this conversion have enabled the people of the nation to maintain a standard of living far beyond the most fantastic dreams of their forefathers. And the end is not yet in sight. Scientists are constantly discovering new products and processes, and from these discoveries will come new plastics and chemicals, improved transportation devices, new sources of power, and many other devices and services for the improvement of standards of living. The scientific discoveries of today will develop into the standard goods and services of the immediate future as a result of the dynamics of present-day civilization.

The amazing expansion of the economic system in the United States is due to many factors. Among these are the American system of inventions and patents, the techniques of mass production and increased productivity per worker, efficient business management and the methods of distributing profits. The successful use of most of these factors and techniques is conditioned by educational programs and procedures. Workers and prospective workers who are responsible for, or responsive to, these success factors are in need of education and training that will enable American industry and business to keep pace with the increasing demands for consumer goods.

INCREASING CONSUMER DEMANDS

Some indication of the scope of the educational needs of workers may be obtained by examining business statistics. The disposable personal income that is available for the purchase of goods and services is one indication. The disposable personal income, which is defined as the current income received by individuals, unincorporated business and nonprofit institutions less taxes on individuals, increased from $76 billion in 1940 to $383 billion in 1962. During this same period, the income per capita increased from $576 to $2052. It is recognized that some of this increase in income is due to changes in the purchasing power of the dollar. When these changes are taken into account the increase in income for the 23-year period was about $715 per capita. This means that the people of the United States had an average of $715 more per person in terms of constant dollar values in 1962 than in 1940 for the purchase of goods and services.

This increase in purchasing power was used to purchase various kinds of goods and services; and agriculture, business, and industry were required to increase their production to satisfy the increasing demands of consumers. Many types of new goods and services came on the market during this 23-year period. Among these were transoceanic air mail and air passenger service, television, color photography, computers, dial telephones, radar, diesel locomotives, atomic submarines, and various kinds of synthetic fibers and electrical goods. The more extensive use of discoveries and inventions of previous years resulted in changes in the nation's economy. The increased use of the automobile resulted in the expansion of the petroleum industry and improved and increased the nation's highways. The diesel locomotive increased the efficiency of rail transportation and changed losses to profits on many railways. The improvements in telephone and radio equipment have enabled telephone companies in the United States to establish lines of communication throughout the world and with ships at sea.

INCREASES IN THE LABOR FORCE

The increased production of goods and services which is the result of, and has resulted in, increased purchasing power has been obtained in two ways. More workers have been employed from year to year, and the output per worker has increased. The number of workers in the civilian labor force, which includes persons 14 years of age and over who are employed or who are unemployed and looking for work, increased from 55,640,000 in 1940 to 71,854,000 in 1962. This represents an increase of 29 percent. The increase was not uniform for all classes of workers. For example, during the 23-year period from 1940 to 1962 the number of clerical and kindred workers increased about 130 percent, the number of operative and kindred workers increased 50 percent, the number of farmers and farm managers decreased 49 percent and the number of private household workers increased 12 percent.

The decrease in the number of workers in an industry has not necessarily resulted in a decrease in the output from that industry. For example, the farm population declined 49 percent from 1940 to 1960, but the index of farm output increased 54 percent during this same period. The output per worker in American industry has increased at an average rate of about 2 percent per annum during the past 50 years. This rate of increase has been about 3 percent per annum during the past 20 years. The output per worker varies among the different industries. For example, the index of output per man-hour in synthetic fibers was about 6 times as high in 1960 as in 1940. During this same period the index of output per man-hour in some mining industries increased only about one and one half times.

The increased output per man is due to technological advances and discoveries and the ever increasing use of nonhuman energy in American industry. It is expected that the output per worker will continue to increase. This increase is necessary to provide the goods and services required for the constantly rising standards of living of the American people.

THE NEEDS OF YOUTH AND ADULTS

The success of the nation's economy depends in no small part on the proficiency of the nation's workers. These workers have used various means to acquire proficiency. In time past, proficiency was acquired either by the pickup method or by apprenticeship. The pickup method through the years has proved costly and inadequate, and the apprenticeship system is applicable only to a limited number of occupations and workers. These two methods alone will not provide the number of workers and the quality of workmanship required of the present-day labor force. For this reason, it has been necessary to find other devices and systems for maintaining an efficient labor force. Programs of vocational education have been established to meet this need for education and training.

Students in Cooperative Distributive Education Acquire Information About Goods and Services in Related Training Classes. (Board of Vocational Education and Rehabilitation, Illinois)

Differences exist in the competencies expected of workers in different occupations and in the characteristics of workers themselves. This occasions a need for different kinds of vocational programs. Programs are needed for the group of young people attending the full-time secondary school. These youth are generally from 15 to 18 years of age. The vocational courses designed for a youth who will end his full-time schooling at the secondary school level should provide this individual with the knowledge, skills, and attitudes that will enable him to enter an occupation and plan and carry out the additional training required for advancement.

Programs of vocational education are needed for youth and adults attending a post-secondary school, such as a junior college or technical institute, where they may secure education or training for the more highly skilled trades and technical positions. A third type of vocational education is needed for the group of young people who have left the full-time school for their first regular employment. These youth, as a rule, are between the ages of 16 and 25. Many of them leave school to take positions requiring limited knowledge and skill. Frequently, these positions are of a temporary nature, and the youth in time find themselves unemployed because of limited education. These persons require an educational program that will permit them to spend part time in school and the remaining time in remunerative work for self-support.

A fourth major group in need of vocational education is composed of older adults who have been employed for a number of years. Many of these workers find themselves in need of training due to technological changes in industry or to new discoveries and inventions in agriculture. Unless education is provided, these persons may become unemployed because of their inability to meet trained workers on a competitive basis. Programs of vocational education and rehabilitation are needed for workers who have become mentally or physically handicapped. These workers, because of their handicaps, are no longer able to follow their usual occupations and must be retrained for positions in keeping with their disabilities.

THE NEEDS OF SOCIETY

Society recognizes the fact that every citizen should be equipped to contribute effectively to the welfare of the group. The highest possible welfare is achieved only when each individual produces to the limits of his maximum capacity. For this reason, the necessity for equipping each person for some occupation is a fact that even the most primitive society has recognized. Society has recognized that youth and adults need not only vocational competencies but also general abilities. These vocational and general needs have been well stated by the Educational Policies Commission of the National Education Association. The Commission suggested that a broad program of education including both general and vocational education would accomplish the following:

1. Equip a youth to enter an occupation suited to his abilities and offering reasonable opportunity for personal growth and social usefulness.
2. Prepare him to assume the full responsibilities of American citizenship.
3. Give him a fair chance to exercise his right to the pursuit of happiness.
4. Stimulate intellectual curiosity, engender satisfaction in intellectual achievement, and cultivate the ability to think rationally.
5. Help him to develop an appreciation of the ethical values which undergird all life in a democratic society.[5]

It is also recognized that the education of workers is becoming more

[5] National Education Association, *Education for All American Youth*, Educational Policies Commission and American Association of School Administrators, Washington, D.C., 1944, p. 21.

important and at the same time more difficult in a social order characterized by the highly mechanized process of present-day industry. Consequently society cannot leave to the chance interests of individuals or corporations the provision of this training that is so vital to the general welfare. It seems appropriate, therefore, to assign this responsibility to some agency or institution qualified to provide this instruction, and accordingly this task has been assigned to the school.

Meeting the Vocational Needs

The people of the United States have recognized the need for organized programs of education and training for the workers and prospective workers of the nation and have provided a variety of programs to meet these needs. Some of these programs are sponsored by management and some by labor. Some are in educational institutions, both public and private, of college level and of less than college level. Also included are training and education by extension and by correspondence. These programs are designed for pre-employment training and training on the job, for youth and adults and for semiskilled, skilled, technical, and professional workers. Courses are offered in a wide variety of occupations, both as an integral part of general education institutions and in institutions separate and apart from general education.

THE FEDERALLY AIDED VOCATIONAL EDUCATION PROGRAM

The Congress of the United States, in response to popular demands, passed a vocational education law in 1917. This law provided Federal aid for the reimbursement of salaries and other designated expenses for administration, teaching, and teacher training in vocational agriculture, homemaking, and industrial education. Additional funds have been provided in subsequent acts, and the Act of 1963 authorizes Federal funds for any recognized vocation except those considered professional or requiring a baccalaureate degree. The Federally aided program is limited to education under public supervision and control, and the controlling purpose of such education is to fit persons for gainful employment. Educational programs, under these acts, are required to be below the baccalaureate degree level and designed to meet the needs of persons over 14 years of age who have entered upon or who are preparing to enter an occupation. The Federal funds are designed to promote the organization of state and local vocational programs and are granted with the provision that they be matched by state or local communities or both.

A total of about 89 million enrollments have been reported in 4 Federally aided programs of instruction during the 45-year period of 1918 to 1962 inclusive. The largest enrollments were in vocational homemaking education and in vocational industrial education, representing 39 percent and 32 percent respectively of the total. The enrollment in vocational agriculture was about 22 percent of the total and the enrollment in distributive education, which was not started until 1938, was 7 percent of the total. Enrollments in classes for out-of-school youth and adults accounted for 60 percent of the total and classes for regularly enrolled day school students 40 percent.

The Federally aided program in vocational agriculture is designed to train present and prospective workers for proficiency in farming and allied agricultural occupations. Organized class instruction is provided in various crop and livestock enterprises, farm management, agricultural mechanics, soil conservation, and other fields of agriculture on the basis of the agricultural needs of the students enrolled. Supervised agricultural experience programs in which students put into practice the knowledge and skills learned in class are included as a part of the instructional program in agriculture. Student organizations, especially the Future Farmers of America, provide opportunities for the development of rural leadership.

The vocational distributive education program is designed for preparing and upgrading workers for positions in the distribution of goods and services. Some of the employed workers attend classes during their nonworking hours, and some are permitted to leave their work for parts of a day, or longer, to attend part-time classes. Among the latter are students who attend day school about half time and work half time. Federal aid is also provided for vocational counseling designed to assist school students and adults to make intelligent choices of and satisfactory progress in vocations.

The vocational homemaking education program is for persons who are preparing for or engaged in the vocation of homemaking or occupations involving knowledge and skills in home economics subjects. Organized classes, supervised work experiences, student organizations, and community activities are included in vocational homemaking and home economics. Courses of study are designed to improve home and family living and are arranged to meet individual and community needs and interests. Vocational education in home economics under the provisions of the Vocational Education Act of 1963 is designed to fit persons for *gainful* employment as contrasted to *useful* employment in previous Acts.

The vocational industrial education program provides for instruction in the trades such as machine shop, auto mechanics, the building trades, the metal trades, and printing. Courses are also provided in practical nurse education and in education for fishery occupations. Courses, most of which are for out-of-school youth and adults, are arranged in various occupations and for varying periods of time to meet individual and community needs. Some pre-employment courses are conducted for youth who desire to acquire competencies in some trade prior to graduation.

Technical education curriculums for the education of technicians in industry, business, and agriculture are included in the Federally aided program. These curriculums are in community colleges, technical institutes, area vocational schools, and secondary schools.

OTHER FEDERALLY AIDED PROGRAMS

Federal funds have been appropriated for a number of special programs of vocational education and rehabilitation. These include the civilian vocational rehabilitation program, the program of vocational rehabilitation, and education of veterans of World Wars I and II and the Korean conflict, the war production training programs of World Wars I and II, and the more recent manpower development and training programs. The vocational rehabilitation program for civilians had its beginning in 1920. It was designed for preparing physically and mentally disabled persons with occupational handicaps for employment and placing them in suitable jobs. Federal funds have been provided to the states on the basis of population, need, and ability to pay. Studies indicate that there are about 2 million persons in the United States who need and can profit from vocational rehabilitation. The Federally aided program, which is one of many programs for disabled persons, has been responsible for the rehabilitation and placement of about 1,428,000 persons during the 43-year period ending in 1962.

Responsibility for war production training was assigned to Federal, state, and local agencies responsible for vocational education during both World War I and World War II. The World War I program had just been launched at the time of the armistice, and at that time 61,000 individuals had completed war production training. Two general types of programs were developed for training workers for World

Child Care is an Important Aspect of Day School Vocational Home-making Classes. (Public Schools, Parkin, Arkansas)

War II industries. These involved training for industrial occupations and training for food production. More than 11 million workers enrolled for training in these two programs which were operated at a total cost of about $345 million.

Funds for the rehabilitation of disabled veterans of World Wars I and II and the Korean conflict have been supplied by the Congress of the United States. These were first administered by the Federal Board for Vocational Education, but the administration was later transferred to the Veterans Authority. More than 815,000 disabled veterans of World Wars I and II and the Korean conflict had entered training under the provisions of the various laws by November 30, 1962. Much of the training of these veterans has been carried out in various types of vocational schools and classes.

A comprehensive program of education and training was established by the U.S. Congress for nondisabled veterans of World War II and the Korean conflict. This training was provided to enable the veterans to recapture the educational opportunities lost while in service. The training has been carried out in various public and private schools and colleges and on the job. Most of the training programs and activities have been conducted by vocational educators in various types of vocational schools. About 10,182,000 veterans of World War II and the Korean conflict had entered training by November 30, 1962.

The Area Redevelopment Act and the Manpower Development and Training Act were enacted to help create new jobs, stimulate private investment, reduce unemployment and retrain and upgrade workers. It is expected that these programs will not only reduce unemployment but materially improve the standards of living of a large number of Americans who now are on the fringes of poverty.

NON–FEDERALLY AIDED PROGRAMS OF VOCATIONAL EDUCATION AND PRACTICAL ARTS

There are in the United States several vocational education programs that are not Federally aided. These are conducted in both public and private institutions and on various grade levels. They include vocational education in secondary schools, technical high schools, trade schools, technical institutes, junior colleges, and senior colleges. The products of these institutions are known as craftsmen, tradesmen, technicians, and professional workers. Practical arts courses are offered in many schools throughout the nation. These courses are not included in the Federally aided program of vocational education. Nonvocational practical arts courses include general agriculture, general home economics, general business and industrial arts. These courses are designed to provide knowledge and skill of a general nature needed by all individuals rather than the specific competencies needed for vocational efficiency.

Non-Federally aided technical courses are offered in some of the public and private technical institutes and technical junior colleges. These students are preparing for positions concerned with testing and production, with planning and control and with supervisory pursuits involved in operation and maintenance. Data indicate that the number of technicians needed in industry and business is increasing faster than the facilities required for training these types of workers. Therefore, many workers who are trained for other types of vocations find employment as technicians. Special consideration is needed for the provision of facilities for technical education.

VOCATIONAL TRAINING IN INDUSTRY

Large numbers of industrial and business organizations, both large and small, provide some kind of training for their employees.

Industrial Arts Students Work With Various Materials Utilized in Industrial Processes. These students are making molds and models. (Wide World)

The type of training provided varies from the informal learning of one worker from another to organized instructional programs within the plant under the supervision of the personnel department or of a special education and training division. Training programs are sometimes organized jointly by industry and some outside educational institution. As a rule, the content of training-in-industry programs is limited to the competencies needed to increase production in the occupation providing the training. Some programs, however, especially the cooperative programs, include related information and some instruction of a general education nature.

The training-in-industry programs include extension and correspondence courses, cooperative classes, supervisory training programs, apprenticeship and job training. Supervisors, apprentices, and other workers who are eligible for extension classes comprise about 30 percent of the employed persons in industry. The remaining 70 percent need and can profit from job training. The large numbers involved warrant more extensive planning for the vocational education of workers.

A program known as the training-in-industry program was developed during World War II to "assist industries to meet the manpower needs, by training within industry each worker to make the full use of his best skill up to the maximum of his individual ability, thereby enabling production to keep pace with defense demands."[6] The various laws for the vocational education and rehabilitation of returned servicemen authorized on-the-job training, and more than 18 percent of all veterans, who had terminated training by June 30, 1955, under the provisions of these laws, were in on-the-job training programs. These experiences indicate that properly planned on-the-job training programs, in which both labor and management participate, can provide much needed training for a large segment of the labor force.

Relationships in Vocational Education and Practical Arts

Extensive changes have occurred in the objectives and in the program of studies of the public secondary school during the past seventy-five years. The traditional college preparatory curriculum with its limited offerings, which characterized the secondary school of the 1880s, has developed into the present-day comprehensive high school with its multiplicity of subject matter offerings and activities, both of a vocational and a general education nature. This change has not occurred without differences of opinion among educators and lay citizens of the nation. These differences have been especially noticeable in problems and procedures relative to the introduction of some of the special subjects into the secondary school curriculum.

Vocational education and practical arts are special subject matter areas, and differences have arisen relative to the organization and operation of these areas, more especially in the Federally aided program of vocational education of less than baccalaureate degree level. Some of the more frequently mentioned differences are those concerned with the relationship of vocational and general education, the relative importance of the cultural and the practical in education and the effectiveness of vocational education in reducing school dropouts. A discussion of these relationships is presented below. This discussion, which includes the point of view of this volume, should be helpful in

[6] Federal Security Agency, Office of Education, *Vocational Technical Training for Industrial Occupations*, Report of the Consulting Committee on Vocational Technical Training, Vocational Division Bulletin No. 228, Washington, D.C., 1944, p. 217.

examining the remaining chapters which contain information concerning the history, development, practices, and principles of vocational education and practical arts.

VOCATIONAL EDUCATION AND GENERAL EDUCATION

The relationship of vocational education and general education has occasioned differences of opinion among individuals, more especially educators, since the beginning of the present century. Some school administrators and others in general education have insisted that vocational education is a subject matter field of general education and has the same relationship to general education as do other fields of study, such as social science or mathematics. Teachers, administrators and other personnel employed in vocational education take the position that vocational education and general education are major divisions of the total education program, and one of these divisions does not necessarily include the other. Each of the divisions is of equal importance, and both of them are necessary in the education of workers.

Some of this difference in point of view is due to definition. Ordinarily, the term *general education* has reference to the knowledge, skills, and attitudes needed by all persons for successful living, without reference or application to particular vocations. Frequently, words and phrases such as cultural, liberal, academic, and nonvocational are used to refer to this same kind of education. The term *general education* is sometimes used to mean the total education program, which suggests that it includes both vocational and other types of educational programs. Differences in point of view may, therefore, resolve themselves into differences in definition.

For the most part, however, different concepts of the relationship of general and vocational education are due to differences in educational philosophy. Some educators contend that a general or fundamental course is the best preparation for a vocation. These educators suggest that courses such as industrial arts, domestic science, general agriculture and general business provide appropriate training for both vocational and general education needs and are included in the category of general education subjects. Vocational educators agree that these subjects are in the area of nonvocational practical arts and are useful as such. However, vocational educators insist that they do not provide education for the specific competencies needed in preparing for or progressing in a vocation. These educators contend that courses of a specific nature as well as those of a general nature are needed in the education of workers.

This volume is written from the point of view that vocational education and general education are major divisions of the total education program. Each of these divisions is of equal importance and is necessary in the education of workers. This point of view suggests that programs of vocational education should be organized to meet vocational needs and that standards established by vocational educators should be maintained in the organization and operation of the vocational education program. This concept also recognizes that vocational education and general education have much to contribute to each other and to the total education program and that both vocational and general educators should strive to achieve the proper coordination of these aspects of education in the total education program.

UTILITY AND CULTURE IN VOCATIONAL EDUCATION

The classification of the content of education into the categories *vocational* and *general* has led some individuals to suggest that vocational education is associated with utility and general education with culture. Two alternatives are prevalent among those who accept this point of view. One suggests that the two terms *culture* and *utility* are not antagonistic but that they have nothing in common. The other point of view is that the two terms are antagonistic, and unless vocational courses are severely restricted, culture will perish.

Individuals who hold to the theory that utility and culture are not antagonistic suggest that the curriculum should consist of a proper balance between vocational and general education, and this balance may be achieved by the selection of certain subjects, some of which are narrowly utilitarian and some of which are broadly cultural. The proper balance of these two will contribute to the development of a well-rounded individual. The contention is made that placement of subject matter in a program of studies affects its cultural or utility values. For example, courses in the arts and science division of a college are cultural, but those in the agricultural division are utilitarian. Similarly, the pure sciences are cultural, while the applied sciences are utilitarian or vocational. Those who believe that culture and utility are definitely antagonistic usually classify the language and traditions of the Golden Age and the Renaissance, together with a few other subjects, as cultural subjects.

A more acceptable point of view to many individuals, especially those in vocational education, is that the standards of culture are not wholly derived from the traditions of the past, nor are they due to convention and to conformity. Culture is a process of valuing life and living it according to the values set upon it. The cultured man finds truth and beauty in many activities, and these activities are not static but relative and changing. The sculptor and the painter find truth and beauty in the works of the masters, but they may also find it in their own work, whether it be for pleasure or for profit. The farmer finds truth and beauty in the fields of grain and herds of cattle. Culture is more of an attitude than a product or a symbol of possession. It is not identified with specialized content or activity but may be acquired through many types of activities and pursuits, both of a general and of a vocational nature.

VOCATIONAL EDUCATION AND DEMOCRACY

Some have suggested that it is undemocratic to teach a boy to become a carpenter because by so doing he may be prevented from becoming a lawyer, a doctor, or a statesman. Individuals who propose this point of view contend that it is more democratic to provide each person with a broad general education and leave him to his own devices in the matter of vocational preparation. These individuals usually define the broad general education in the secondary schools as a college preparatory curriculum. This college preparatory curriculum is in reality a preparation for further education in the professions at the college level. Thus, vocational education for the professions is approved but not vocational education for many positions in agriculture, business, or industry.

A second and more defensible point of view with reference to democracy in education is that modern society requires that all workers be educated for their work and that equality of opportunity for obtaining this education be provided. Various studies have shown that individuals differ in interests, needs, and abilities and that no one type or kind of educational program is suited to the needs and capabilities of all workers. This suggests that a variety of educational programs must be provided to meet the needs of the many kinds and types of workers in present-day society. The single college preparatory type of curriculum provides too few competencies for those individuals who graduate from high school but do not enter college. Therefore, it would seem more in the spirit of democracy to provide opportunities for many types and kinds of workers, rather than to limit these opportunities to the few who are preparing to enter the professions.

Educators recognize that it is more difficult and more expensive to provide a variety of vocational courses and activities than to provide one course for all students. This fact has probably encouraged some individuals to accept the one-curriculum-for-all idea. From a practical standpoint, it is recognized that one school or college cannot provide vocational curriculums for all the vocations. In most instances, one school cannot provide training for all the vocations in the community; but a school can provide training in the more important vocations and vocational fields as determined by an occupational survey. Less extensive training, in the nature of short-unit courses for employed workers, may be provided for a large number of vocations. These various types of schools and classes enable the school community to provide the equality of opportunity characteristic of the democratic way of life.

VOCATIONAL EDUCATION AND SCHOOL DROPOUTS

Educators and laymen are becoming more concerned with the large number of youth who leave school before completing the usual twelve grades. Studies show that from 30 to 40 percent of the youth who enter the first grade drop out before the completion of high school. The junior high school grades eight, nine, and ten show an unusually large number of dropouts. The larger schools with a greater variety of course offerings have a higher holding power than the smaller schools.

Teen-age youth are finding it increasingly difficult to obtain permanent employment. The unemployment problem is especially critical for school dropouts. These youth as a rule have no special skills and frequently lack the educational background necessary for training on the job. Many industrial and business concerns require high school graduation as a prerequisite for employment. The unemployment of youth may well develop into a major social problem of the nation.

The seriousness of the dropout problem and its relationship to unemployment of youth has brought forth many suggestions for its solution. Some educators and laymen have indicated that the dropout problem may be solved by increasing the scope of the programs of vocational education and industrial arts in the public schools. This suggestion is predicated on the assumption that youth leave school because of an uninteresting program of studies and that vocational education and industrial arts will interest these school leavers. In some instances the statement is made that youth leave school because they find little or no interest in mental activity but would likely stay in school if more manual activity were provided.

Some provisions of the Vocational Education Act of 1963 are designed to reduce the incidence of school dropouts. The scope of the Federally aided program under the provisions of the 1963 Act is extended to include all gainful occupations except those that require a baccalaureate degree. The Act also authorizes the use of funds for work-study programs in which eligible students may receive pay for part-time employment to enable them to remain in school. The Act authorizes funds for special classes for youth with academic or socio-economic handicaps that prevent them from succeeding in the regular program. It authorizes Federal aid for area vocational programs to enable more youth to concentrate on vocational and technical courses. These provisions should reduce school dropouts due to such reasons as lack of funds, dissatisfaction concerning some parts of the program of studies, and inability to succeed in regular courses.

Industrial arts courses with emphasis on shopwork may provide an inducement for some students who are especially interested in shop skills to remain in school. These courses which are general education in nature should not be confused with the specific vocational education courses. Industrial arts may be offered in the elementary, junior, and senior high school grades. Some schools practice ability-grouping in industrial arts courses with more manual and less mental activity for low ability pupils. Some of the new areas of industrial arts including electronics, plastics, and rocketry will appeal to many youth who are not interested in the more traditional areas of industrial arts.

However, neither vocational education nor industrial arts will eliminate all dropouts. Vocational education has as its purpose the education of individuals for gainful employment. It is designed for individuals who need and can profit from this type of instruction. It is presumed that a person has selected a vocation before he enters a vocational course to prepare for or progress in it. Industrial arts is not confined entirely to shop work nor is it designed for slow learners who cannot succeed in the academic curriculum.

A comprehensive program of education, both general and vocational, has possibilities for reducing the number of school dropouts. Such a program should include industrial arts and other practical arts subjects as well as an adequate program of guidance and counseling. It should be designed for in-school and out-of-school youth and adults, both talented and disadvantaged. Such a program will enable each student to achieve his maximum in the knowledge, skills, and patterns of conduct necessary for a successful and satisfying life.

QUESTIONS FOR STUDY AND DISCUSSION   79524

1. Discuss the significance of work in relationship to vocational education.
2. What are some of the more important characteristics of vocations?
3. Indicate some of the varying concepts of vocational education.
4. What is your definition of vocational education?
5. What are some evidences of the increase in consumer demands, and how is this increase being met?
6. What are some of the needs of youth and adults? Some of the needs of society?
7. What types of educational programs are provided to meet the needs of youth and adults?
8. What are some evidences that these programs are meeting the needs?
9. What are some of the shortcomings of these programs?
10. What is the relationship of vocational and general education in the total education program?
11. What is meant by democracy in education? What is the relationship of vocational education and democracy in education?
12. Discuss the effectiveness of vocational and practical arts education in reducing the number of school dropouts.

SOURCE REFERENCES

Emerson, Lynn A., *Vocational Technical Education for American Industry*, Circular 530, U.S. Department of Health, Education and Welfare, Office of Education, Washington, D.C., 1958.

Federal Security Agency, Office of Education, *Vocational Technical Training for Industrial Occupations*, Report of the Consulting Committee on Vocational Technical Training, Vocational Division Bulletin No. 228, Washington, D.C., 1944.

Hawkins, Layton S., Charles A. Prosser, and John C. Wright, *Development of Vocational Education*, American Technical Society, Chicago, 1951.

Kellar, Franklin J., *Principles of Vocational Education*, Heath, Boston, 1948.

Ogburn, William F., "Technology and the Standard of Living in the United States," *The American Journal of Sociology*, January, 1955.

Reinhardt, Emma, *American Education: An Introduction*, Harper & Row, New York, 1960.

U.S. Department of Commerce, Bureau of the Census, *Statistical Abstract of the United States, 1964*, Washington, D.C., 1964.

U.S. Department of Health, Education and Welfare, Office of Education, *Education for a Changing World of Work*, Report of the Panel of Consultants on Vocational Education, Washington, D.C., 1963.

U.S. Department of Health, Education and Welfare, Office of Education, *Education for a Changing World of Work*, Appendix I, *Technical*

Training in the United States, Report of the Panel of Consultants on Vocational Education, Washington, D.C., 1963.

U.S. Department of Labor, *Manpower Report of the President of the United States and a Report on Manpower Requirements, Resources, Utilization and Training*, Washington, D.C., 1964.

U.S. President, *Economic Report of the President, 1964*, Washington, D.C., 1964.

Willing, M. H., John Guy Fowlkes, and others, *Schools and Our Democratic Society*, Harper & Row, New York, 1951.

CHAPTER TWO

THE ORIGINS OF VOCATIONAL EDUCATION

The history of vocational education is the history of man's efforts to learn to work. Work has enabled man to satisfy his ever increasing needs and wants. Man learned early in his history that he could improve his lot by means of work. He also learned early that the ways in which he worked affected his output and efficiency. These first learning experiences which doubtless came about as a result of some accidental discovery stimulated man to seek new discoveries and new ways of learning.

Sometime during his early existence man developed language and learned to speak. He learned to make tools and weapons. He invented social institutions such as the family and the tribe and discovered that his individual welfare was related to the welfare of his family and his tribe. He transmitted his knowledge and skill to the succeeding generation. Each generation added to the accumulation of knowledge and skill and passed the total accumulation on to the next generation. This learning process enabled man to replace stone implements with those of copper, bronze, and iron; to find green pastures for his cattle and sheep; and to grow grains on fertile fields, all of which contributed to the improvement of his way of life.

As man learned new ways of working he discovered that some individuals had the ability to perform certain tasks better than others. Man learned that the male members of the family or tribe could more efficiently provide the raw materials for food, clothing and shelter and that the female members were more efficient in the preparation and processing of these materials for use. This was the beginning of the division of labor and the age of specialization. Some individuals developed special skills and practiced such trades as woodworking, stonecutting, pottery-making and metalworking. The division of labor enabled man to improve the quality and quantity of the total output and at the same time necessitated the use of new methods of learning to work which involved the selection of youth of special abilities and the assigning of these youth to the vocations or tasks according to their aptitudes and abilities. These youth spent some time as learners, and in this manner the system of apprenticeship, which was the first form of organized learning, came into being.

The Beginnings of Education for Work

Relatively recent discoveries in Europe indicate that man worked with stone implements more than 50,000 years ago. The characteristic handiwork of this period was the fist hatchet with cutting edges sharp enough to shape wooden tools and weapons. During the succeeding 40,000 years he continued to work with stone and passed through what is known as the Early, Middle, and Late Stone Ages. Man, during this period, learned to fabricate sharper implements from flint, construct wooden boats, domesticate animals, manufacture pottery, produce grain, and live in communities. Man continued to make progress through work, and about 6000 years ago he developed civilizations based on scientific knowledge, government and religion in the valleys of the Nile, the Tigris, and the Euphrates rivers.

LIFE AND EDUCATION IN EGYPT

The men of the Nile of 6000 years ago learned to irrigate their fields; to construct buildings of brick and stone; to grow barley, wheat, and flax; and to use domesticated animals for food and for work. The Nile dwellers learned to measure time, and the Egyptian calendar established about 4200 B.C. is said by James H. Breasted, the historian, to be the first dated event in history. About this time the Egyptians learned to reduce copper ore to copper metal. This discovery, the most important since the discovery of fire, ushered in the age of metal and enabled the people of Egypt to construct buildings and monuments

A Fist Hatchet of the Early Stone Age—Man's First Device to Increase His Efficiency for Work. These stone implements were used for operations such as cutting, scraping, boring, punching, and hammering. (University of Arkansas)

of various kinds, many of which are present-day wonders. While there is no record of organized apprenticeship in Egypt during this age, the many accomplishments in the arts and crafts lead some historians to believe that organized apprenticeship programs were in operation at that time.

The Egyptians used a form of picture writing before 3500 B.C. from which an Egyptian alphabet was later developed. This alphabet consisted of 24 characters or alphabetic signs. The Egyptians devised a pointed reed for a pen, compounded a writing fluid, and learned to split papyrus into thin layers for use as writing paper. These inventions led to the establishment of the first organized schools. These schools for scribes were started in Egypt during the period between 2000 and 1200 B.C. Two stages of training were given in these schools. The first or primary stage consisted of learning to read and write ancient literature. The second was an apprenticeship stage during which the learner was placed as an apprentice scribe under an experienced scribe, usually a government worker. Youth of the nobility and middle classes were urged to become scribes, as evidenced by the following quotation from the early writings: "Dost thou not bethink thee how it fareth with the husbandman? The worm hath taken half the corn, the hippopotamus hath devoured the rest. The mice abound in the field and the locust hath descended. . . . But to the scribe, he

Maintenance Console of the AN/FSQ-7 Computer—One of Man's Modern Devices for Increasing His Efficiency. (Massachusetts Institute of Technology)

directeth the work of all people. For him there are no taxes for he payeth tribute in writing and there are no dues for him."[1]

THE CIVILIZATION OF THE ORIENT

The Fertile Crescent, a strip of land extending from what is now the Persian Gulf along the northern border of Arabia to the Mediterranean Sea, was the first home of the people of Western Asia. This crescent-shaped strip of land was occupied in turn by the Babylonians, Assyrians, Chaldeans, Medes, Persians, and Hebrews. This area, frequently referred to in the Bible, was the home of the Christian religion.

The people of this area long before 3000 B.C. had reclaimed the marsh lands and produced harvests of barley and wheat. During the Babylonian Age, which extended from about 3200 B.C. to 2100 B.C., the people of the Fertile Crescent constructed houses of sun-baked brick and fashioned arts and crafts works from stone and metal. Vocations became specialized, and apprenticeship training programs were organized and legalized. The first historical reference to apprenticeship was in the Babylonian Code compiled about 2100 B.C. by King

[1] Adolf Erman and Aylward M. Blackman, *The Literature of the Ancient Egyptians*, Dutton, New York, 1927, p. 198.

Hammurabi of Babylonia. This Code included a collection of ancient and contemporary laws of the times. The Code suggested that: "If an artisan take a son for adoption and teach him his handicraft one may not bring claim against him. If he does not teach him his handicraft that son may return to his father's house."

The peoples of Babylonia carried on commerce with the inhabitants of the Nile Valley and recorded business transactions on clay tablets. A form of postal delivery service was established about 2100 B.C. The various commercial transactions required the services of many clerks for recording agreements. These workers were trained in schools frequently conducted under the direction of the religious leaders. A school house of about 2100 B.C. has been uncovered in ancient Babylon. Some of the clay tablets used by students have been found in the ruins of this school. A reed stylus and a tablet of soft clay were used to record the cuneiform characters. Writing was held in high esteem as evidenced by the following quotation from one of the tablets of this age. "He who shall excel in tablet writing, shall shine like the sun."[2]

The Assyrians who conquered the Babylonians brought cotton and iron to the Fertile Crescent and organized a postal service; but they in turn were conquered in 612 B.C. by the Chaldeans. Commerce and business flourished, religion and literature were cultivated and notable progress was made by the Chaldeans in the science of astronomy. The Chaldean astronomers divided the equator into 360 degrees and mapped the sky into the twelve signs of the zodiac. After the death of King Nebuchadnezzar in 561 B.C. the empire lost its power, and the civilization of the Medes and the Persians came into prominence. The Persians maintained an organization of government controlled by one man. The subject peoples and nations were ruled in provinces and these enjoyed some freedom. Farm lands were divided into large tracts held by powerful landowners. Silver and gold were coined into money, and excellent systems of roads were maintained. The Persian Empire, which lasted until about 330 B.C., provided documents that have enabled present-day man to read the cuneiform inscriptions of Western Asia.

HEBREW CULTURE AND EDUCATION

The Hebrews, originally nomads of the Arabian Desert, settled in Palestine, a country in the Fertile Crescent, about the year 1200 B.C.

[2] James H. Breasted, *Ancient Times, a History of the Early World,* Ginn, New York, 1916, p. 137.

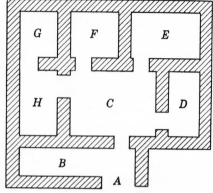

Classes for Scribes Were Conducted in This Babylonian School House About 2100 B.C. The house was about 55 feet square and contained an entrance hall, classrooms, and a court. (Reproduced from James Henry Breasted's *Ancient Times, A History of the Early World,* by permission of Ginn and Company)

The early Hebrews were singers, poets, and tentmakers. They acquired the art of writing from the Philistines who probably had acquired it from the Egyptians. The Hebrews found in Palestine a civilization far advanced in agriculture, arts, and trade. They rapidly adapted themselves to this new mode of life and became skilled artisans as well as poets and singers. The Hebrews, because of their location between Egypt and Babylonia, became traders and merchants. They traded in jewelry, furniture, and bronze from the valley of the Nile; pottery from the islands of the Aegean Sea; and earthenware and woven cloth from Babylonia. The Hebrews, unlike many of the early peoples, held manual labor in high regard. The Talmud suggested that:

When a man teaches his son a trade he should pray to the Possessor of the world, the Dispenser of wealth and poverty; for in every trade and pursuit of life both the rich and the poor are found. It is folly for one to say 'this is a bad trade it will not afford me a living,' because he will find many well-to-do in the same occupation.

Happy the pupil whose teacher approves his words. First learn then teach. He who studies cannot follow a commercial life; neither can the merchant devote his time to study.

Responsibility for the education of Hebrew children was first assigned to the father of the household. The religious teachings were known as the *Law,* and all children were taught to know the *Law* and to follow it. The father also taught each of his sons a trade, usually the trade he followed. The Hebrews in time changed their language from the original Hebrew to the Aramaic language. The original Hebrew language which was used for the *Law* and for religious worship came to be a sacred language. This necessitated a literary class known as scribes to keep and translate the text of the *Law*. Schools for religious instruction were established in the synagogues, and the *Law* was explained to the people of the towns and villages. Schools for children were attached to the synagogues by 100 B.C., and compulsory education of children for the first time in history was ordered in A.D. 64. A youth as a rule attended the church school in the mornings and learned a trade from his father in the afternoon.

The Hebrews evolved a religion involving the idea of one God, that man was a child of God and that man lived after death. Morality and truth were among the essential elements, and all persons, including women and children, rich and poor, were equal in the sight of God. Christ was born to the Hebrew race, and he preached morality, everlasting life, and the importance of the individual. Christian emphasis tended to subordinate the interest of the state. The Christian religion was uncompromising with sin, and conflict between Christianity and paganism was inevitable. Christians were first tolerated, then expelled and finally tortured and persecuted because of their beliefs. These persecutions were of no avail and for the most part had ended by A.D. 300. Christianity soon spread, and pagan worship was forbidden in the Western world. The religion of the Hebrew peoples which has extended throughout the world has had a far-reaching influence on Western culture and education.

EDUCATION IN SPARTA AND ATHENS

With the decline of the Persian Empire, the civilization that had flourished in the Fertile Crescent began to decline and that of the European mainland to advance. The first and most rapid development occurred in that part of Europe nearest to Egypt and the Orient which was Greece and the islands of the Aegean Sea. Tribes of warriors came from the valley of the Danube about 1500 B.C. and conquered the highly civilized peoples of the Greek peninsula and the islands of the Aegean. These conquerors became amalgamated with the conquered to form the Greeks of ancient history. These peoples established small, independent city-states, some of which developed democratic forms of government. Sparta and Athens, two of these city-states, developed two well-known types of educational programs, each having the same general purposes but differing in practices and principles.

Education in both Sparta and Athens was for the purpose of training strong and courageous soldiers and loyal citizens. The chief objectives of education in Sparta were strength, courage, endurance, patriotism, and obedience. The mother had responsibility for the children from birth to age seven. The boy was then placed in public barracks where he remained until he was 18 years of age. His teachers were older men experienced in war, and his education consisted of physical drill. Each youth spent the years between 18 and 20 in professional training and in conditioning his body for war. Dancing and music were provided for mental and moral training. Spartan youth listened to public discussions as a means of political training. The years between ages 20 and 30 were spent at an army post, and at 30 years of age the youth was admitted to full citizenship. Women and girls were given gymnastic training to make them strong and capable of bearing healthy children.

Formal education in Athens began at age 7. The boys were sent to school and the girls were educated in the home. The boys attended the letters school for reading, writing, and arithmetic; the music school; and the gymnastic school. Each of these was a private school supported by tuition. At the age of 18 the boy was presented as a candidate for citizenship and was examined morally and physically. If he passed his tests successfully he became a citizen-cadet and went through 2 years of training after which he became a citizen of Athens.

Education in Athens changed during the Golden Age of Greece (479 B.C. to 431 B.C.). Less strenuous training, new musical instruments, geometry, drawing, grammar, and rhetoric appeared, and a higher or university education was developed. The beginnings of higher education in Greece occurred near the close of the fourth century B.C. Private teachers or Sophists went from city to city and gave a series of lectures for youth who had completed the grammar school. The Sophists recognized the importance of public speaking and organized instruction into sequences of studies with emphasis on clear thinking and clarity of expression. The Sophists organized schools of philosophy, and these schools were later granted public support. The merging of these schools created a form of university life which developed into the university of the Greek world. Universities were established at Athens, Rhodes, Alexandria, and other cities. The study of medicine, architecture, engineering, and other professions was conducted in these universities. Extensive library and laboratory facilities were available as well as a staff of research specialists. Greek culture through these channels continued to dominate the Western world long after Athens was reduced to a Roman provincial town.

SCHOOLS FOR ROMAN YOUTH

The warm, sunny Italian peninsula attracted many peoples. Among these were the Swiss Lake Dwellers, the Italics and the Greeks. One of the tribes of the Italics established a trading post at Rome about 1000 B.C. This post grew and prospered, and by 200 B.C. the armies of Rome had subjugated the other peoples of the peninsula and were well on the way to world conquest.

Augustus Caesar became emperor of the emerging Roman Empire in 27 B.C., and this empire lived at peace for almost two centuries thereafter. The extensive conquests of the Roman armies brought much wealth to Rome. Banks for lending money were established, and leather currency and silver coins came into general use. Shares in commercial enterprises were sold; roads, aqueducts, and drainage systems were installed; and theaters and baths were constructed.

The Roman people were a practical and conservative people. They were especially noted for their codes of law and plans for public administration. Their engineering and architecture were on the practical side, and they excelled in the art of spreading a civilization over wide areas and among many peoples. This civilization, much of which was borrowed from the Greeks, has had a strong influence on our present-day civilization.

The practical aspects of Roman civilization were exemplified in their system of education. Early Roman education was carried on in the family. Obedience to the law and custom, the maintenance of religion and the mores were the important objectives of Roman education. The father provided a practical education for his sons. The sons were taken to the fields and to the forums where they learned by observation and participation. The phrase, "the school is life" is of Roman origin, and the idea of learning by doing was prevalent during the time of Cicero.

The Roman genius for organization was extended to the school, and three distinct levels of schooling were provided. These were the elementary, secondary, and higher. Elementary education, which began at the age of 7, consisted of reading, writing, conduct, and memorization of the laws. At the age of 10 years the child entered the secondary or grammar school where he studied literature in Latin and in Greek. Higher schools for training youth in rhetoric, oratory, and other subjects such as mathematics, music, history, and law were designed to prepare Roman youth for effective public life. Youth who desired further education obtained it by attending the Greek universities and later the University of Rome, which had its origin about A.D. 75 and in time developed faculties of law, architecture, mathematics, mechanics, grammar, and rhetoric. While schools in the Roman Empire were largely private institutions, the practice of paying the salaries of teachers of grammar and rhetoric from public funds was started about A.D. 75. Public competitions which served as qualifying examinations were held for prospective professors. With the fall of Rome in the fifth century, the influence of Roman culture declined, and the teaching in the schools became formal and superficial. This type of education began to have little appeal, and by the sixth century most of the universities were closed. Western civilization at that time entered the Dark Ages of the medieval period.

The Development of Education for the Professions

The three learned professions—theology, law, and medicine—have occupied an important place in higher educational institutions since early times. The Greek universities were started in the fourth century B.C. and remained in existence about 900 years. With the coming of the Dark Ages these institutions were closed, and the monasteries maintained by the Roman Catholic Church became the centers of learning. Cathedral schools designed to train religious leaders were established throughout the Christian world. Many of these developed into elementary or parish schools of the Catholic Church. Charlemagne, a Frankish king who ruled an empire consisting of western Germany, France, Italy, and northern Spain, turned his palace into a school and in A.D. 781 employed Alcuin, an English scholar and teacher, to head the school. The princes and princesses of Charlemagne's family and the sons of the nobility were given instruction in the liberal arts at this palace school.

Two centuries of feudalism, invasion, civil disorder, and religious turmoil followed Charlemagne's rule, and education again went into a decline. There were, however, some signs of a revival of Western learning during this period. Moslem culture, which recognized scientific inquiry as a basis for development, was beginning to find its way into the Western world. The recognition of philosophy as a professional subject separate and distinct from theology led to a spirit of tolerance. Beginnings were made in the study of law and medicine as new professional subjects. These influences led to the establishment of new schools, some of which were free from civil and religious control.

These increased in number, and the need for higher educational institutions became apparent.

THE RISE OF THE UNIVERSITIES

The new spirit of inquiry and the apparent need for an educated professional class led many students to seek higher education in the cities that had become noted as centers of professional education. Students of law from many parts of the world came to Bologna, and Bologna became noted as a city for legal studies long before the University of Bologna was established in the twelfth century. Students interested in theology assembled at the Cathedral School of Notre Dame in Paris, an institution that had become noted for theological studies. Students interested in the study of medicine congregated at Salerno, a city in Italy famed since the ninth century for its medicinal waters and its medical study. By the close of the twelfth century the educational institutions at Bologna and Paris had developed into universities with faculties for a number of professions. The school at Salerno did not develop into a university but remained a medical school.

Bologna and Paris typify the two types of organizational patterns found in universities of the Middle Ages. Bologna was controlled mainly by the students and the university in Paris was controlled by the faculties. The students who assembled at Bologna formed student guilds for protective purposes. These guilds merged into a single student guild which by the year 1411 had both civil and criminal jurisdiction over the university community. The instructors who were citizens of Bologna were not permitted to join the guild. The instructors were required to pledge allegiance to the guild master and to post bond for the performance of their duties. The University of Paris was dominated by a guild of masters. The instructors held their teaching positions under a license from the Chancellor of Notre Dame.

The universities of the Middle Ages were corporate bodies of students and faculties legally free from external control by the church or by the state. Students were subject to the law of the university instead of the law of the land, and the university was authorized by its charter to arrest, try, and discipline offenders. The university had the right to license the instructors and to determine the program of studies. The usual organization included faculties of arts, law, medicine, and theology. Instruction was in Latin, and the methods of instruction were lecture, repetition, and disputation. The university movement spread from the original centers, and by the year 1500 there were 80

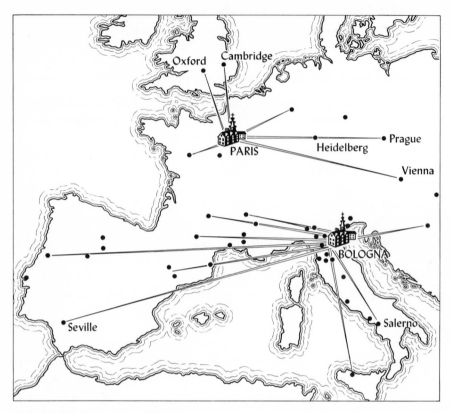

The Universities of Bologna and Paris Influenced the Organization of Other Universities in Western Europe During the Middle Ages. (From *Civilization Past and Present* by Wallbank and Taylor. Copyright 1949 by Scott, Foresman and Company)

universities in operation. These early institutions stimulated interest in learning, developed trained workers for the professions and prepared leaders for the Renaissance movement that was soon to bring new ideas to Western culture.

NEW THEORIES AND NEW SCHOOLS

The transition from medieval to modern times which occurred in the fourteenth and fifteenth centuries is known as the Italian Renaissance. One phase of the transition, the scholarly phase, is referred to as the Revival of Learning. This revival was a return to the ancient literature of the Greeks and Romans that had been discarded at the beginning of the Dark Ages. This revival was coupled with a humanistic movement combining self-realization and self-expression with a classical education. Humanism included a study of the achievements of the Greeks and Romans as a means of understanding present-day living. This was in contrast to previous educational theory which was concerned primarily with the world to come. Humanistic studies included history, literature, philosophy, and social anthropology. Humanistic education was general and cultural rather than practical and vocational. It was for the nobles, ruling classes, merchants, and bankers—not the common man. Its most important contribution was in the transformation and expansion of the school curriculum.

Humanism in the sixteenth century became narrow and formal and soon was in need of reform. The reformation which came was a popular and not an aristocratic movement. The Protestant religion, an outcome of the Reformation, was for all the people. It was based on a faith in and understanding of the Bible, and this suggested the need for a universal education. The reaction against Humanism was responsible for the *Realism movement* of the seventeenth century. This movement resulted in the introduction of science and practical arts into education, the rationalization of methods of teaching and the attempts to relate experience and education. Realism in education was characterized by an enriched program of studies for the school. The curriculums included such subjects as history, geography, the sciences, modern languages, Latin, dancing, trade subjects, and travel.

The eighteenth century, called the Age of Reason, was a period of diverse trends in higher education. Humanism was still prevalent, and Realism was opposing it. The movement for Nationalism was gathering headway, and the church schools were beginning to experience some criticism from those who demanded universal education for citizenship. The new views of the nature of man advanced by Rousseau and implemented by Pestalozzi, Herbart, and Froebel resulted in new schools characterized by realism and democracy. The lecture-recitation method was supplemented by observation, excursions, handiwork, construction projects, demonstrations, and experiments. Pupil self-government, as a means of learning how laws were made and enforced, came into prominence. These changes in educational organization, methods, and materials which at first were more evident in elementary and secondary education later had an important influence on the nature and control of education for the professions in the higher institutions of the New World.

PRIVATE COLLEGES AND STATE UNIVERSITIES IN THE COLONIES AND STATES

The early settlers came to colonial America for many reasons, but none came for educational purposes. With few exceptions these settlers were satisfied with the educational programs of the mother country, and as a consequence the first schools of the New World were similar to those of the country from which the settlers came. Four main types of educational activity were conducted in the colonies during the seventeenth century. These were apprenticeship, religious schools for instruction in reading and writing, Latin grammar schools, and practical schooling in mathematics. The South depended upon private schools, and these followed the classical pattern. The schools of the middle colonies were parochial and neighborhood institutions and followed the medieval practice. The New England colonies fostered the public education idea. The American academy developed from the Latin grammar schools for the purpose of preparing students for entrance into college.

Harvard College, established in 1636 for education in the ministry and other professions, was the first of the colonial colleges. Its early curriculum was composed of three historical strata of materials taken from the Middle Ages, the Renaissance, and the Reformation. Harvard remained a small institution for 50 years after its founding. It began to grow in enrollment and importance in the eighteenth century. A medical school was established at Harvard in 1782, a law school in 1817, a dental school in 1867, a graduate school of business administration in 1908 and a graduate school of education in 1920. Four colonial colleges were established in the New England colonies. These were Harvard, Yale, Dartmouth, and Brown. The people of the middle colonies established the College of New Jersey (now Princeton), King's College (now Columbia), the College of Philadelphia (now University of Pennsylvania) and Queen's College (now Rutgers). The College of William and Mary was founded by the southern colonists.

The private colleges in the early days were given some public financial aid in the form of land or money. The obligation to the state of the institution receiving this aid was never clarified. After the Revolutionary War some states attempted to secure control of private colleges in order that public funds might properly be used in these institutions to enlarge the offerings, especially in law and medicine. However, the Supreme Court in the Dartmouth College case of 1819 ruled that the state of New Hampshire could not legally transform this private institution into a state-controlled college. This ruling convinced state authorities that the states would have to establish their own colleges and universities to provide higher education for the professions at public expense.

Nine state colleges and universities including Georgia (1785),

North Carolina (1789), and Virginia (1819) had been established by the year of the Dartmouth decision. Twenty-one state universities were founded before the Civil War. The early institutions were somewhat below college grade and did not receive regular support from the state. The University of Virginia and the University of Michigan became the leaders in the development of standards of scholarship and teaching. The state university eventually became the highest stage in a general system of public education open to all people.

THE LAND–GRANT COLLEGES

Early in the nineteenth century demands were made for higher education in agriculture and engineering. The need for engineers became more acute during the last half of the century because of changes in industry brought about by the Industrial Revolution. The need for technically trained agricultural workers to develop the agricultural resources was recognized by many leaders in agriculture. This need was met by the passage of the Morrill Land-Grant Act of 1862. This Act provided that public lands should be granted to each state in the amount of 30,000 acres for each senator and each representative a state had in Congress at the time of the passage of the Act; or if later, at the time it was admitted to the Union. The proceeds of the sale of these grants were to provide for the endowment and support of at least one college in each state: "without excluding other scientific and classical studies and including Military tactics, to teach such branches of learning as are related to agriculture and mechanic arts, in such manner as the legislature of the states may prescribe in order to provide the liberal and practical education of the industrial classes in the several pursuits and professions of life."[3]

Congress granted land script to those states which had no Federal land within their borders. As a result of the Federal grant every state has established a land-grant college. Some states founded separate colleges, and some combined the land-grant college with existing state colleges and universities. In some states the land-grant college and state university were formed in the same institution. The land-grant institutions developed slowly because the sciences and the teaching of agriculture, home economics, and engineering were not well developed in the years immediately after the passage of the Morrill Act. The institutions needed facilities other than those concerned with teaching,

[3] Alfred C. True, *A History of Agricultural Education in the United States,* U.S. Department of Agriculture, Miscellaneous Publication No. 36, Washington, D.C., 1929, p. 100.

and the Hatch Act of 1887 provided Federal funds for state agricultural experiment stations. A second Morrill Act of 1890 provided an additional $15,000 annually for each of the land-grant colleges.

The land-grant colleges began to grow rapidly at the beginning of the present century. Most of the land-grant colleges have developed into state universities. This development is due to the fact that the basic preparation in the arts, languages, mathematics, and sciences needed in advanced studies in vocational and technical education is offered in these colleges. These institutions have exercised influence over the high schools by preparing teachers, developing new sciences and materials, and helping the public schools to serve the people's needs.

THE NORMAL SCHOOLS AND TEACHERS' COLLEGES

In colonial times teachers were usually considered sufficiently prepared to teach when they had completed the work of the school in which they were to teach. As public schools increased in numbers and enrollments, however, teachers were expected to show competence in methods of teaching as well as subject matter. Special schools were advocated as early as 1789 for the training of teachers.

The development of method in education as advocated by Pestalozzi and other educators resulted in the formation of special schools for the education of teachers. The first of these in the United States was established in Lexington, Massachusetts, in 1839. It combined instruction in the common branches with work in methods and management in a practice school. A state normal school was opened at Albany, New York, in 1844. A few other states established normal schools prior to the Civil War. After the close of the war the normal school idea grew rapidly, and by the end of the nineteenth century more than a hundred of these schools were in operation.

The first normal schools were housed in a single building which contained the dormitories and the model school. The one-year curriculum consisted of reviews of the common branches, methods of teaching, classroom management, and work with children in the model schools. The normal schools of 1880 consisted of a three-year curriculum including some academy and college preparatory subjects. The practice of providing academy courses in the normal schools continued until the normal schools became teachers' colleges.

Professional courses for elementary school teachers of the normal school type were given in some universities about the middle of the nineteenth century. These courses placed the state universities in competition with the normal schools. The universities later abandoned their normal departments and offered professional education courses for teachers on the college level. By the end of the nineteenth century about half of the recognized colleges and universities reported offerings in professional education for teachers. Enrollments in these courses increased, and departments and colleges of education were established in the universities. In the meantime, the rising standards of certification, competition with universities and increased demands for better-trained teachers compelled the normal schools to develop college level courses. At the present time there are very few institutions of less than senior college level engaged in the education of teachers.

The English Guilds and Apprenticeship Training

Reference has been made to the organized programs of apprenticeship conducted by the peoples of ancient times. It was suggested that apprenticeship, which consists of learning a trade on the job under supervision and according to established specifications, is the earliest form of vocational education. Historical records of ancient times do not show detailed descriptions of apprenticeship programs, but the evidence indicates that apprenticeship was an important part of the educational programs of the early Egyptians, Babylonians, Hebrews, Greeks, and Romans. Apprenticeship, like other educational programs, reached a low ebb during the Dark Ages but experienced an awakening during the Middle Ages. This revival of interest was due in part to the programs of apprenticeship training organized by the guilds of this age.

The guilds were organizations of merchants and of craftsmen formed for the mutual protection of the members of the group. Some of these organizations were in the nature of labor unions and cooperative societies, while others resembled present-day manufacturers' organizations. The guilds also had religious and benevolent features. They kept a fund collected from assessments and fines for feasts, for masses, for the relief of the sick and unfortunate, and for the proper burial of needy members. The guilds carried on a system of vocational education which provided the only educational opportunity for the working people of the Middle Ages.

The origin of the guilds is veiled in obscurity. Some writers have suggested that they were a continuation of the Roman culture while others attribute them to early Germanic and Scandinavian influences.

There is little evidence to substantiate either of these claims. Guilds were mentioned in the enactments made by the synod of Nantes, early in the ninth century. The ecclesiastical ordinances of Rheims of the year A.D. 852 prohibited villeins from forming associations, "vulgarly called guilds." The guilds of Norway, Denmark, and Sweden are first mentioned in the eleventh, twelfth, and fourteenth centuries respectively; those of France and the Netherlands in the eleventh century.

THE ENGLISH GUILDS

The guild merchant came into England soon after the Norman conquest in 1066. The merchant guilds received trade monopolies from the ruling monarch in exchange for allegiance and services. These guilds regulated the buying and selling of goods, the times and places of sales, the prices of commodities, and sales practices. The craft guilds, which came into prominence sometime after the merchant guilds, were concerned with the quality and quantity of goods produced by craftsmen.

It is believed that craftsmen were first members of merchant guilds. They registered as merchants because they bought raw materials and sold manufactured products. Separate societies of craftsmen were formed in England soon after the guild merchant came into existence, but at first they were few in number. There was no clear-cut distinction between the craft guilds and merchant guilds during the twelfth and thirteenth centuries. Many craftsmen belonged to both organizations. With the creation of new craft fraternities, the guild merchant's sphere of power was weakened. The greater the commercial and industrial prosperity of a town, the more rapid was the multiplication of the craft guilds, which was a natural result of the ever increasing division of labor. The increase in the power and influence of the craft guilds marked the beginning of a period of industrial expansion.

APPRENTICESHIP TRAINING

The guilds recognized early the importance of taking apprentices and requiring them to go through a course of training before being admitted to the trade as a journeyman or master craftsman. Records indicate that apprenticeship was practiced in England in the thirteenth century. Guild regulations of this era forbade one master to entice away another's apprentice, required that the names of apprentices be recorded in the guildhall records, provided for written agreements between apprentice and master and prescribed the minimum term of apprenticeship. Other regulations of local guilds and municipalities provided that only qualified master craftsmen or freemen were eligible to take apprentices, that no apprentice could practice his trade until he was approved by the master and the guild members and that no master could take more than two or three apprentices unless he employed journeymen to assist in the teaching of the apprentices. Apprentices were required to pay an entry fee and an exit fee.

The apprenticeship contract bound the apprentice to live with his master for the required time, to serve him diligently, and obey his reasonable commands, to refrain from immoral practices, to remain unmarried, and not to absent himself from his master's service without permission. The master agreed to instruct the apprentice in the trade and in citizenship and to provide him with room, board and clothing. Searchers were appointed by the guild to inspect and report on any violations of the apprenticeship contract. Upon the completion of the prescribed period of apprenticeship, which was usually 7 years, and upon recommendation of the master and guild officers, the apprentice became a journeyman. The journeyman usually lived in the master's house and received a fixed wage for his work. The journeyman, after several years of experience, was eligible to try for the title of master by performing a piece of work known as a masterpiece. The master workman, if he so desired, could establish his own shop, employ journeymen and train apprentices.

The guilds also maintained schools. These were of two kinds: Latin secondary schools and schools for apprentices. The Latin secondary schools provided a literary education for boys who desired to enter a university and prepare for a profession. Among the more important guilds schools were the Merchant Taylors' School, the Mercers' School, and the Stationers' School. Guilds also established continuation apprenticeship schools. The apprenticeship program in the workshop was supplemented and sometimes replaced by trade school classes. Schools of this type were maintained by associations of craftsmen long after the decline of the guilds.

THE STATUTE OF ARTIFICERS AND THE POOR LAW

Prior to 1562 apprenticeship was a general practice in England, but it was regulated by local guilds and municipalities. The Statute of Artificers, passed in 1562, transformed apprenticeship from a local to a national system in England. This Act provided for a readjustment of wage standards and codified the various local laws and regulations relative to employment of servants and apprentices. This action was made necessary by the countless number of local statutes which from time to time had been enacted to adjust the wages of labor to social conditions. Many of these statutes were out of date, and others were contradictory. The need for reform had been evident for some time, and a general law seemed to offer the best possibility for meeting this need.

The Statute of Artificers contained the better practices of the municipalities and the guilds. The apprenticeship clauses of this statute legalized many of the established customs and local regulations. The length of apprenticeship in manufacturing was fixed at seven years with the provision that the term of the apprentice would not expire until he was at least 24 years of age. Householders were required to be 24 years of age before they were eligible to take apprentices. Apprentices in the farming occupations were bound until they were 21 or 24 years of age as agreed between contracting parties. Apprentices who refused to work were subject to the penalty of remaining in jail until such time as they agreed to work. Masters of apprentices were subject to fines and other court action. Each master who had more than three apprentices was required to employ one journeyman for each extra apprentice, in order that proper instruction might be provided and the supply of craftsmen be limited.

The rise in prices and the increase in unemployment late in the sixteenth century created distress among the lower classes and made necessary some measures for the relief of the poor. The leaders of England decided that the apprenticeship system would provide a partial solution to this problem, and in 1601 the English government enacted the Poor Law which permitted church wardens and overseers to apprentice children of the poor to masters who would agree to maintain these apprentices until the boys became 24 years of age and the girls 21 or married. The terms of the contract for the Poor Law apprentices were similar to those of industrial apprentices. The overseers were parties to the contract, and the consent of two justices of the peace was required. While this law was essentially for the purpose of maintaining the poor, many apprentices received trade training from masters engaged in industrial pursuits.

THE DECLINE OF APPRENTICESHIP IN THE GUILDS

The apprenticeship system was established by the guilds as a means of controlling the quantity and quality of goods and services. Since the regulations were formulated by the workers themselves, they tended to keep the supply of workers small. However, the increased demand for goods, the consolidation of guilds, and the increase in the labor force made it extremely difficult to control the supply of workers. Frequently, because of a shortage of labor, it became necessary to import foreign laborers to perform the necessary work in a town. When guildsmen raised the price of their labor, the boroughs of England retaliated by bringing in foreign artisans. Masters, in the early years of the seventeenth century, began to take apprentices contrary to guild rules and to reduce the customary 7 years of apprenticeship. Journeymen frequently became masters without the sanction of the guild. In the year 1753 the courts proclaimed the guild regulations "injurious and vexatious" to the manufacturers and the state.

By the middle of the eighteenth century, the English guilds had for the most part lost their power to control trade and industry. Merchant and craft organizations in many communities renounced their control over local trade. The decline of an industry brought dissolution to the guild. Municipal governments encouraged free trade, and in many communities trade monopolies were declared invalid by law. The passage of the municipal reform bill in 1835, giving to every inhabitant the right to keep a shop for the sale of lawful merchandise in any borough, brought an end to government sanction of guild regulations. Many of the guilds were terminated the following year and their property distributed among the members. Others drifted aimlessly for 40 or 50 years before final dissolution.

The guilds were able to maintain a standard of workmanship by means of craft supervision and by means of a plan for training and examining new workers. The high standards, together with the prevailing idea of work well done, brought about a new point of view toward everything included in the word "learning." The apprenticeship system of the guilds offered an opportunity for learning all branches of a trade, favored the development of artistic ability and provided a general education for many apprentices. This system was well adapted to the social and economic conditions of the times. There was little capital, little machinery, no factory system, and close relationship between employee and employer. The close supervision imposed by the guild was responsible for high standards of workmanship and resulted in the well-wrought and artistic productions of the later Middle Ages. The institution of apprenticeship provided a form of vocational education to a middle-class people at a time in history when all types of education were at a low ebb.

The Beginnings of Apprenticeship in America

Apprenticeship came to the New World in the early colonial period. This type of training in the colonies resembled that of the mother countries, except that it developed directly under the laws of the towns and counties. There were no guilds or similar craft organizations, as such, in colonial America. The English apprenticeship system was modified to suit conditions in the New World, and apprenticeship in colonial America became the most important educational agency of the period of colonization and settlement.

Two kinds of apprenticeship were established in the American Colonies. These were voluntary and compulsory. The voluntary apprentice entered into the agreement of apprenticeship of his own free will. He was motivated in most instances by a desire to learn a trade, and he selected the master who was willing and able to teach him a trade. The compulsory apprentices, who as a rule were children of the poor, were bound out as apprentices by the town authorities primarily for the purpose of providing maintenance for the children.

APPRENTICESHIP LAWS IN THE COLONIES

The General Court of the Colony of New Plymouth passed a law in 1641 adapting the English Poor Law of 1601 to the needs of the Colony. The selectmen of the town were empowered under this law to apprentice the children of the poor to more fortunate families. The apprentices worked for these families and in turn received from them maintenance and education. The usual practice was to apprentice all children whose education was being neglected. The Massachusetts Bay Colony in 1642 enacted a comprehensive apprenticeship law requiring parents and masters of apprentices to teach each child a trade or calling and to instruct him how to read and understand the principles of religion and the laws of the colony. Labor was emphasized because the Puritans believed in the virtue of industry. Any parent or master who neglected to teach these abilities was subject to a fine. The selectmen of the town were required to remove children or apprentices from the custody of neglectful parents or masters and apprentice them to other masters who would follow the law.

The deputies and selectmen of every town in the New Plymouth colony were ordered in 1671 to see that parents and masters taught the children or apprentices a trade, how to read the scriptures, and the laws of the colony. A fine of ten shillings was levied against parents and masters who failed to observe the law. A similar law was enacted in 1650 in the Connecticut colony. Under its provisions all heads of families were ordered to examine and question children and servants at least once each week on the principles of religion. Masters and parents who were not qualified to teach were required to send their children or charges to those who could teach, and many apprentices were sent to schools. These early schools taught reading, writing, and ciphering. Girls as a rule were not taught a definite trade under these laws. They were, however, trained to do housework, including cooking, sewing, spinning, and weaving, all of which were carried on in the home.

The Province of New York made its first provision for education in 1665 with the enactment of a law which required the instruction of all children and apprentices in religion, the laws of the Province and a trade or calling. The essential features of this law were taken from the laws of the New England colonies. The New York law was a compulsory education law, but it did not use apprenticeship as a means of enforcing the law. The Common Council of the City of New York found it necessary to enact legislation in 1694 requiring that apprentices be registered and serve for a term of not less than four years. The minimum length of the apprenticeship was raised to seven years in 1711. The state of New York in 1788 enacted legislation requiring that poor apprentices be taught to read and write. The overseers of the poor were directed to make inspections and report violations of this law. The law legalized a practice that in general had been carried out for more than a hundred years.

THE APPRENTICESHIP INDENTURE

When a master took an apprentice he entered into a contract, usually written, with the apprentice or the overseer. This contract or indenture set forth in detail the conditions of the contract, and when properly witnessed and recorded it became a public document. As a public record it provided protection to both the apprentice and his master. The following apprenticeship indenture made in 1676 illustrates the type of contract used in the New England colonies.

This Indenture witnesseth that I, Nathan Knight, sometime of Black point, with the consent of my father-in-law, Harry Brooken, and Elend, his wife, have put myself apprentice to Samuel Whidden, of Portsmouth, in the county of Portsmouth, mason, and bound after the manner of an apprentice with him, to serve and abide the full space and term of twelve years and five months, thence next following to be full, complete and ended; during which time the said apprentice his said master faithfully shall serve, his lawful secrets he shall keep, and commands shall gladly do, damage unto his said master he shall not do, nor see to be done of others, but to the best of his power shall give timely notice, thereof, to his said master. Fornication shall he not commit, nor contract matrimony within the said time. The goods of his said master, he shall not spend or lend. He shall not play cards, or dice, or any other unlawful game, whereby his said master may have damage in his own goods, or others, taverns he shall not haunt, nor from his master's business absent himself by day or by night, but in all things shall behave himself as a faithful apprentice ought to do. And the said master his said apprentice shall teach and instruct, or cause to be taught and instructed in the art and mystery as mason; finding unto his said apprentice during the said time, meat, drink, washing, lodging, and apparel, fitting an apprentice teaching him to read, and allowing him three months toward the latter end of his time to go to school to write, as also double apparel at end of said time, As witness our hands and seals, interchangeable put to two instruments of the same purpose, November the twenty-fifth, one thousand six hundred and seventy-six.[4]

When the apprenticeship was completed, this fact was acknowledged by the master at a town meeting and duly entered in the minutes of the meeting. If the apprentice had given satisfaction, he was permitted to follow his trade. If the master was not satisfied with the progress made, the apprentice was forbidden to practice the trade and could, if all parties agreed, continue his apprenticeship program.

APPRENTICESHIP SCHOOLS AND APPRENTICEABLE TRADES

The compulsory school laws of the colonies made it necessary for masters and parents who were unable to read and write to send apprentices and children to schools established for this purpose. The Massachusetts General Court required each town having a population of fifty families to maintain a school for apprentices and children. The master or parents were required to pay tuition for the students. The officers of the town were authorized to subsidize masters of apprentices who were unable to pay the tuition. The usual practice was to pay the master a sum of money for educating the apprentice at the time the apprenticeship went into effect. In other instances poor children were permitted to attend school without the payment of tuition. Some towns provided free schools for children and apprentices. These schools at first were limited to reading and writing. Later ciphering and accounting were added.

[4] New Hampshire Historical Society, *New Hampshire Province Records 1680 to 1692*, Concord, 1866, p. 287.

Masters of apprentices in the Province of New York followed the practice of sending their apprentices to evening or night schools. These schools were usually held during three winter months, January, February, and March. This practice of sending the apprentice to a night school was followed because the master was unable or unwilling to send the apprentice to school during the working hours. The records indicate that these evening schools were private institutions, and masters were required to pay tuition for the apprentices. The evening school curriculum consisted of reading, writing and ciphering which included accounting.

The apprenticeship program provided training in many trades. Seybolt stated:

> The indentures show that apprentices were taught such trades as: baker, barber and wig-maker, blacksmith, blockmaker, boatman, brasier, carpenter cooper, cordwainer, currier, farmer, feltmaker, glasier, glover, goldsmith, gunsmith, hatter, innholder, joiner, leather-dresser, mariner, mason, merchant, painter, pewterer, pipemaker, printer, saddler, sailmaker, seamstress, shipwright, silversmith, skinner, tailer, turner, weaver, wheelwright. Girls were usually taught housewifery, which included "to sew plaine work," and "spinning and knitting," occasionally they learned the tailor's and glovemaker's trades.[5]

Apprenticeship was also a means of entering the professions of law and medicine during the Colonial era. The records indicate that apprenticeship in colonial America was not a scheme for the exploitation of children but a means for providing elementary education and trade training for the younger citizens of the colonies.

THE DECLINE OF APPRENTICESHIP IN AMERICA

The period of the Industrial Revolution began in England about the year 1760 with the use of machine methods in the textile industry. Restrictive legislation in England was responsible for a delay in the time the Industrial Revolution reached the United States. However, by the year 1803 there were four cotton mills in operation, and by 1812 manufacturing was well started in the United States. The expansion of trade brought about the invention of new machines and the improvement of others in the agricultural and manufacturing industries. The power loom in 1814, the locomotive in 1829, the mechanical reaper and the telegraph in 1835, the sewing machine in 1846, to-

[5] Robert F. Seybolt, *Apprenticeship and Apprenticeship Education in Colonial New England and New York*, Contributions to Education, No. 85, Bureau of Publications, Teachers College, Columbia University, New York, 1917, pp. 91–92.

gether with the development of the coal and iron mines and the growth of the railroads, brought about rapid changes in the nation's economy. At the close of the Civil War, the nation was well into the Industrial Revolution with its increasing demands for and readjustments of labor.

The rapid development of power machinery and the increased demands for goods led to a greater demand for labor than could be met by apprenticeship. This demand was met in part by the employment for wages of young children and in part by the compulsory apprenticeship of the children of the poor. Too frequently the apprenticeship became indentured servitude. Children of the poor who in previous years were placed under a master craftsman and taught a trade were placed in a factory under a foreman interested primarily in production. These children were required to work long hours under unsafe conditions with little consideration given to related training or general education. Many young children who were not apprenticed were placed in the factories by their parents or guardians to work long hours for low wages.

Factory operators found it more convenient to pay the small wages than to assume any of the responsibilities of apprenticeship, particularly with the development of power machinery and the increased use of unskilled labor. The conditions of employment of children grew steadily worse despite the attempts in some states to remedy these conditions by legislation. The cruelty and wastefulness of child labor gradually began to be recognized, and the states began to enact more and more legislation designed to correct the evils of child labor. The decline of the apprenticeship program and the increasing interest in the educational welfare of children made necessary the organization of new types of schools both vocational and general for the education of the workers of the nation.

QUESTIONS FOR STUDY AND DISCUSSION

1. What types of educational programs were conducted in ancient Egypt?
2. What new educational developments occurred in the Orient prior to the Christian Era?
3. In what ways did education in Sparta differ from that of Athens?
4. What contributions did the Romans make to the organization of educational programs?
5. What were some of the characteristics of the universities of the Middle Ages?
6. What new theories relative to educational philosophy appeared during the fifteenth, sixteenth, and seventeenth centuries?

7. Discuss the development of higher education in the United States.
8. Discuss the origin and nature of the guilds.
9. What were the characteristics of the apprenticeship training programs conducted by the guilds?
10. What factors were responsible for the decline of apprenticeship in the guilds?
11. Discuss the characteristics of apprenticeship in colonial America and in the United States prior to the Industrial Revolution.
12. What factors caused the decline of apprenticeship in the United States, and what were the effects of this decline?

SOURCE REFERENCES

Bennett, Charles A., *History of Manual and Industrial Education up to 1870*, Manual Arts, Peoria, 1926.

Boyd, William, *The History of Western Education*, Black, London, 1921.

Breasted, James H., *Ancient Times, a History of the Early World*, Ginn, New York, 1916.

Erman, Adolf, and Aylward Blackman, *The Literature of the Ancient Egyptians*, Dutton, New York, 1927.

Good, H. G., *A History of Western Education*, Macmillan, New York, 1962.

Kramer, Stella, *The English Crafts Gilds*, Columbia, New York, 1927.

Leake, Albert H., *Industrial Education*, Houghton Mifflin, Boston, 1913.

McCarthy, John A., *Vocational Education: America's Greatest Resource*, American Technical Society, Chicago, 1952.

Mays, Arthur B., *Principles and Practices of Vocational Education*, McGraw-Hill, New York, 1948.

Monroe, Paul, *A Brief Course in the History of Education*, Macmillan, New York, 1912.

Moore, Ernest C., *The Story of Instruction*, Macmillan, New York, 1936.

Seybolt, Robert F., *Apprenticeship and Apprenticeship Education in Colonial New England and New York*, Contributions to Education, No. 85, Bureau of Publications, Teachers College, Columbia University, New York, 1917.

Struck, F. Theodore, *Foundations of Industrial Education*, Wiley, New York, 1930.

True, Alfred C., *A History of Agricultural Education in the United States*, U.S. Department of Agriculture, Miscellaneous Publication No. 36, Washington, D.C., 1929.

West, Willis M., *The Story of Man's Early Progress*, Allyn and Bacon, Boston, 1931.

CHAPTER THREE

THE DEVELOPMENT OF
EDUCATION IN THE
PRACTICAL ARTS

Education in the practical arts which had its origin in the teachings of Pestalozzi came to the forefront during the last two decades of the nineteenth century. The practical arts or manual training movement came into being because of the insistence on the part of some educators that hand work and artistic modeling were as much a part of general culture as mathematics and foreign languages. The practical arts educators stated that education in the practical arts had both a broadening and humanizing effect and contributed to the development of the individual as a whole. The advocates of practical arts education from the beginning of its period of development have insisted that it not be confused with vocational education. The practical arts in education are not designed to prepare a worker for a vocation but to provide him with general knowledge, skills, and attitudes to enable the individual to find a degree of satisfaction in everyday life and meet his responsibilities as a citizen. The more common nonvocational practical arts subjects are industrial arts, general home economics, general business, and general agriculture. Industrial arts has been identified through the years as a practical arts course. The other courses are offered both as vocational courses and practical arts courses, frequently with little or no differences in the course content. Combinations of these practical arts subjects have been made. For example, the early manual training courses included agriculture, home economics, and industrial subjects. One of the first of the practical arts subjects was drawing. This was first offered as a separate subject but is now usually included in the secondary school as a unit in courses of study for industrial arts and other practical arts. This chapter is concerned with the development of the practical arts with special emphasis on industrial arts and the relationship of drawing to industrial arts.

The Introduction of Drawing in Educational Programs

The importance of drawing in the fine arts of painting, sculpture, engraving, and designing was recognized by the ancient Greeks. The drawing school near Corinth, Greece, established about 400 B.C., was responsible for the inclusion of drawing as a necessary subject in a liberal education in Greece. Drawing schools were maintained by the guilds of the Middle Ages as an essential part of the fine arts courses. Schools of design were established to enable nations to compete with each other in the fabrication of arts and crafts. Drawing became an essential part of art education in the American colonies, and later public educators in the United States recognized its value as a school subject.

THE INFLUENCE OF THE FINE ARTS

Italy became noted for the excellence of its arts and crafts about the time of the Italian Renaissance. Other European countries were required to give special attention to ways and means of meeting competition from Italy in the manufacture and sale of arts and crafts such as glassware, mosaics, lace, metal work, carving, and silk weaving. The French people recognized the need for producing better arts and

The Technique of Drawing from Models Constructed by Students Has for Many Years Constituted an Important Area of Instruction in the Practical Arts. (Black Star)

crafts and founded the French Academy of Painting and Sculpture in 1648. This Academy, which was established in Paris, was organized to develop skilled artists. It received support from the French government and included a school of drawing in which many famous French masters served as instructors. Academies were established in other cities of France early in the eighteenth century, and the French government took over the porcelain industry and encouraged the production of high-grade porcelain. The French Revolution caused the closing of the French Academy, but in its place the National Institute of France was established in 1795.

Art instruction in England had its origin in individual effort and did not receive the financial support of the government as in France. The early art schools of England were designed more for the liberal education of the gentry than for the development of artistic talents. Most of the English painters learned by the individual instruction method. A private academy for drawing was opened in Covent Garden in 1724. This school closed ten years later. Other private schools were operated during the eighteenth century, and in 1768 the Royal Academy of London was organized for the purpose of encouraging the fine arts of Great Britain.

Schools of art and design were established in Scotland and Ireland to teach drawing and pattern making for the purpose of improving the arts and crafts industries of these countries. The Dublin Society in 1731 offered premiums to young persons for the encouragement of drawing and the promotion of art. This society in 1741 established a freehand drawing school as a means of improving arts and crafts manufactures. This school was successful in training architects, sculptors, designers, and pictorial artists. Art academies were established in other European countries in the sixteenth and seventeenth centuries. The city of Augsburg, Germany, had a guild of painters in the thirteenth century, and the first art academy in Germany was opened in Nuremberg in 1662.

The concern for the shortcomings of British arts and crafts as evidenced in competitive exhibits at international trade fairs was responsible for the founding of a School of Design which opened in London in 1837. This school was under the management of the London Board of Trade. The course consisted of drawing and the history and application of ornament to the manufacturing industry. Funds were appropriated by the British government in 1840 for starting other schools of design. Later schools of art education were established as a branch of national education for individuals interested in improving the manufacture of arts and crafts. By 1872 there were 122 of these provincial art schools in operation. Instruction in drawing was also provided in elementary schools, and teachers in these schools received salary increases when they passed examinations in drawing and taught this subject successfully. These various efforts were in part responsible for the noticeable improvement in the quality of English arts and crafts shown at the Paris Exposition in 1867.

ART EDUCATION IN THE UNITED STATES

The development of applied or industrial art was limited in colonial America because of the policy of the English government which discouraged manufacturing in the colonies. This policy also had the effect of limiting the development of the fine arts of painting and sculpture although there were no bans on these arts in the colonies. Many American artists received their training in Europe and returned to colonial America to engage in portrait painting. One of these, Charles Willson Peale, started a drawing school in Philadelphia in 1791 and organized an American Academy of Painting, Sculpture, and Architecture in 1794. The principal activity in the Academy was drawing from models of antique sculpture. The efforts of Peale to establish a class in drawing from living models were at first unsuccessful due to the manners and customs of the citizens of the community. The Pennsylvania Academy of Fine Arts was established in 1805 to promote the fine arts. A collection of copies and originals of painting and sculpture was included in the Academy. Professional artists who were members of the Academy established a separate institution in 1810 known as the Society of Artists primarily for the purpose of sponsoring a school to teach the elements of the arts, establish a drawing school, and hold an annual exhibition of art work. These exhibitions were instrumental in developing interest in art in Philadelphia.

The American Academy of Fine Arts was chartered in New York City in 1808. This Academy was composed largely of stockholders who were not artists, and this fact led to differences between young artists and stockholders. As a result of these differences, the young artists organized a Drawing Association in 1825. This Association in 1826 became the National Academy of Design, with Samuel F. B. Morse, the inventor and painter, as first president. The two academies competed during the years prior to 1841, at which time the American Academy of Fine Arts was disbanded. An attempt was made in 1834 by the Academy of Design to start a drawing school, but the project was abandoned because of a lack of interest.

Other organizations in New York City became interested in promoting interest in art. Among these were the Apollo Association and the New York Gallery of Fine Arts. The trustees of Cooper Union of New York City in 1859 took over the management of a school of design for women which had been established the previous year by a benevolent group. This institution became the first school of industrial art in New York City. The need for a museum and art center in New York became evident in the latter part of the nineteenth century, and as a result the Metropolitan Museum of Art was established in 1870. This institution, since its founding, has made outstanding contributions to the promotion of the fine arts in the United States.

An association of literary men known as the Anthology Society was formed in Boston in 1804. This Society established a reading room in 1806, and the Society became the Boston Athenaeum in 1807. The

Boston Athenaeum started an art museum in 1822 and held an exhibition of paintings in 1827. This institution maintained an art gallery for 50 years, and as a result of the interest created by the society, the Boston Museum of Fine Arts was established in 1876. Other early art centers included Charleston, South Carolina, with a number of distinguished painters and Cincinnati with its Academy of Fine Arts and School of Design. The Cincinnati School of Design was established in 1869, and this school provided instruction in the designing of ceramics, metal work and textiles. This school has enabled Cincinnati to establish a number of art industries in pottery, color printing and metal work. Art schools were established in Chicago in 1866, and Yale University in 1864 took the lead among American universities by establishing a School of Fine Arts. These American institutions concerned with the development of fine and applied arts had an important influence on the development of drawing and art in general education.

DRAWING COURSES IN GENERAL EDUCATION

Interest in drawing as a general education activity in the United States came early in the nineteenth century. John Rubens Smith, a drawing teacher in a New York City academy, compiled a drawing book in 1822 designed for use in general education. This book, originally intended as one of a series, was written for the purpose of introducing the simple elementary principles of drawing into the schools. This volume differed from other drawing books of the times by including instructions on how to draw as well as what to draw. The book commenced with mathematical forms such as squares, curves, and triangles and included landscapes, perspectives of buildings, and ornaments. Smith recognized the principle of copying and provided directions in his book for more effective copy work. Instructions were also found relative to the necessary equipment for drawing and its proper use.

Boston pioneered in providing drawing instruction in public schools. William Bently Fowle introduced drawing in a boys' school in Boston in the early 1820s. The course was designed to teach the drawing of geometric figures, architecture, and objects in profile. Fowle was also interested in mechanical perspective and prepared a drawing book with instructions in the principles of perspective. Drawing became a required subject in the English High School of Boston in 1836 but received little attention until 1853, at which time a drawing teacher was provided. A report made by Horace Mann, secretary of the Board of Education of Massachusetts, was responsible for placing drawing in the grammar school studies in 1848. Interest in drawing as a school subject in Boston was stimulated by John Dudley Philbrick who was superintendent of schools during the years 1856 to 1874. A complete graded system of drawing was introduced in the schools for primary, intermediate, and high school grades in 1868. This was designed to help the students gain practical knowledge and skill in the art of representation as well as in the ability to copy.

The type of drawing initiated by Superintendent Philbrick did not satisfy the demands of persons who desired a type of drawing that would ultimately result in the improvement of manufactured articles in Massachusetts. This was uppermost in the minds of many persons because of the rapid development of industry in the latter part of the nineteenth century. More technical education was demanded, and instruction in mechanical drawing was considered an important part of technical education. This point of view was responsible for the passage of legislation in Massachusetts in 1870 providing for free instruction in industrial or mechanical drawing. School committees in towns or cities of more than 10,000 inhabitants were required by this law to provide this instruction in day or evening classes for persons over 15 years of age. The passage of this law resulted in the opening of an evening school of drawing in the laboratories of Massachusetts Institute of Technology. This school was open 4 nights a week and instruction was given in general freehand drawing, in freehand drawing of machines from solid models, in mechanical drawing, architectural drawing, and ship-drafting.

The public school commissioners of Baltimore in 1845 introduced drawing into the high school course of study, and an architect was employed to give instruction in drawing. The report of the president of the Board of Education of Cincinnati, Ohio, for the school year ending in 1843 indicated that experiments in teaching the "art of design" were undertaken successfully in that year. A drawing department as a separate part of the school organization was established in Cincinnati schools, and a supervisor was employed to organize the drawing department. Drawing was taught in the Cleveland, Ohio, elementary and high schools in 1850, and many of the regular teachers took special courses in the teaching of drawing. These facts seem to indicate that the states of Massachusetts and Ohio were among the first states to make drawing an integral part of public school instruction.

The Beginnings of Manual Training

The teaching of drawing courses, first in the fine arts institutions and later in the elementary and secondary schools, was responsible for the development of public sentiment for other types of manual or industrial education in the public schools. As a result of this sentiment and other forces, manual training was added to the high school and elementary school curriculums. Various types of schools in prior years had had some of the elements of manual training or industrial education. The schools of Pestalozzi and Fellenberg provided industrial education as a school discipline as well as a means of vocational training. The manual labor schools of the first half of the nineteenth century had some of the elements of industrial education. However, it was not until the last quarter of the nineteenth century that an effort was made to include an organized course of manual training in a secondary school curriculum.

THE MANUAL TRAINING SCHOOL OF WASHINGTON UNIVERSITY

The first manual training high school in the United States was established in St. Louis, Missouri. The school, which was a part of Washington University, was founded in 1880 by Professor Calvin M. Woodward, dean of the Washington University Polytechnic faculty. Professor Woodward had operated courses in shopwork at Washington University for 2 years prior to the founding of the manual training school. These shop courses were organized for college students and for some academy or secondary students. Professor Woodward, out of the experiences of these courses, saw the need for a combination of shopwork and academic courses for secondary school students as a means of supplementing liberal education with manual activity. It was suggested that this combination of manual and mental activities would improve the educational programs of all prospective workers.

The manual training school was a 4-year institution which had for its purpose instruction in mathematics, science, drawing, and language and literature, as well as practice in the use of tools. The course in mathematics included arithmetic, algebra, geometry, and plane trigonometry. The science and applied mathematics course included physical geography, botany, natural philosophy, chemistry, mechanics, mensuration, and bookkeeping. Penmanship and freehand and mechanical drawing were taught. The language and literature

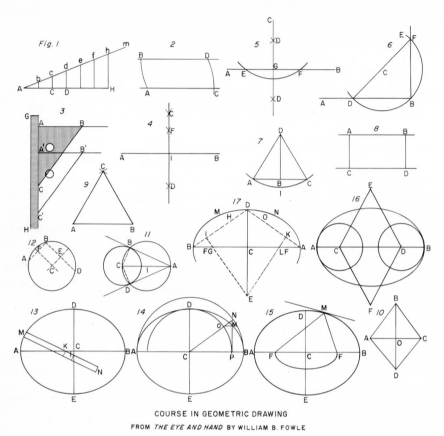

COURSE IN GEOMETRIC DRAWING

FROM *THE EYE AND HAND* BY WILLIAM B. FOWLE

William B. Fowle of Boston Used a Plate Similar to the Above To Teach One of the First Courses in Instrumental or Mechanical Drawing in an American Public School. (From *History of Manual and Industrial Education Up to 1870*, Chas. A. Bennett, by permission of Chas. A. Bennett Co., Inc.)

course consisted of grammar, spelling, composition, literature, history, and political science. Electives in Latin and French were provided. Tool instruction included carpentry, wood turning, molding, brazing, soldering, forging, and bench and machine work in metals.

The manual training facilities in the school included a blacksmith shop, a machine shop, a turning shop, a carpentry shop, a drawing room, a physical science laboratory, and rooms for academic subjects. Each shop was equipped for 20 students to do the same kind of work at one time. Each student was provided with a set of edge tools for which he was responsible, and additional tools were provided as needed. Each student was required to complete a shop project involving planning and construction before he was eligible to receive a diploma.

The school day was divided into six periods. This time allotment provided one period daily for each of the academic subjects and a double period for shopwork. The classes were scheduled so that the shop instructor could teach three sections of shopwork every day. The laboratory method was used in the shopwork. This involved demonstrations and instructions by the instructor with opportunities for students to ask questions and take notes. After this demonstration period, the students proceeded with their work.

The Manual Training School of Washington University Was Housed in This Building Beginning in 1880. (From *History of Manual and Industrial Education, 1870 to 1917,* Chas. A. Bennett, by permission of Chas. A. Bennett Co., Inc.)

The administrators of the school pointed out that the desired end of the manual instruction was that of acquiring skill in the use of tools and materials and not in the production of specific articles. The course of study was not concerned with teaching a trade but rather with the simple mechanical principles of all trades. The shop training was directed by means of a series of graded lessons in the use of ordinary tools. Students were permitted to work on individual projects of interest to them after school hours but were required to follow the established course during the regular school shop period. Students were required to construct and maintain the tables, shelving, tool handles, and other items of the school shop. The school opened in September 1880 with about 50 boys and increased to an enrollment of about 200 boys in 1884. An enrollment of 200 to 300 students yearly was maintained for more than 25 years.

CONFLICTING THEORIES OF EDUCATION

The manual training school met the need of a large group of secondary school students and proved popular among the lay citizens from its beginning. However, it aroused the opposition of many of the professional educators who did not recognize the educational value of any type of manual activity. These educators feared that the manual training idea would break down the standards of the college preparatory type of secondary school which was becoming established at the close of the nineteenth century. These educators contended that the state violated the rights of students when it undertook to prescribe their future careers during their school age. They suggested that whatever energy or strength was used in manual exercises with tools was just so much energy withdrawn from mental training. It was further contended that the business of the school was not to educate operatives but to supply the elements of general culture which are necessary to all men and women alike.

The proponents of manual training contended that instruction in the use of tools was not for its application to any particular trade or trades, but for the development of the skill of hand as a means of both manual and mental development. These manual training educators contended that the school shop stimulated and increased interest in books and provided direct and positive help in the study of the basic sciences. These educators also took the position that while manual training was not designed to fit students for special industrial occupations it was helpful in assisting the student to make a more intelligent choice of a vocation and to arrive at a better understanding of industrial processes and materials. Professor Woodward suggested that the teaching of manual training would enable the school to provide for a more symmetrical development of mind and body than was possible under old systems of general education.

Some educators expressed approval of manual training but suggested that it be carried out in separate manual training schools having no connection with academic high schools. This point of view suggested that manual training was a substitute for apprenticeship, and therefore it should be confined to special schools for boys twelve to fifteen years of age. Others advocated that manual training was not a substitute for apprenticeship and should be included in academic high schools and in elementary schools.

The following remarks made by Dr. Nicholas Murray Butler, president of the New York College for the Training of Teachers, at the 1888 meeting of the Department of Superintendence, National Education Association, represented the thinking of many educators and served to bring a measure of harmony to the controversy.

We are not now discussing the philosophy of manual training. That stage is passed. It has been incontestably established that the powers of thought, expression by delineation and construction, the judgment and the executive faculty must be trained as well as the observation, the memory, and the power to learn. . . . If shopwork is used as a means of manual training, it is because of its disciplinary value, not because of its utility. It is only a means, not an end. It will be discarded whenever anything better adapted to accomplish the end in view is discovered just as an old geography is thrown away when a better one is made. . . .

That part of the training of the expressive faculties which is included in the terms "drawing" and "construction work" is what is meant nowadays by manual training. If the term manual training is used in antithesis to mental training, it is wrongly understood. Manual training, as I use the term, is mental training. It is mental training by means of manual training. It is included in the psychologically determined course of study because it reaches important mental faculties which no other studies reach. It is also a most valuable and important stimulus to the receptive faculty of observation. The child can neither draw accurately nor construct correctly unless he observes acutely.[1]

TYPES OF MANUAL TRAINING HIGH SCHOOLS

The success of the Washington University Manual Training School led to the establishment of manual training high schools in other cities and towns of the United States. The organizational pattern of these first schools followed that of the St. Louis school. That is, the manual training high school was administered and operated separate and apart from the academic high school. For example, the Chicago Manual Training High School was founded in 1884 by the Commercial Club of Chicago. The Commercial Club provided the funds necessary for the construction of a building and took the necessary steps to secure a charter and board of trustees for the school. The plan of instruction was similar to that of the St. Louis school. Schools having somewhat similar patterns of organization were established at Cincinnati, Toledo, New Orleans, and New York.

A change in the pattern of organization was noted in the founding in 1884 of the Baltimore Manual Training High School. This was the first manual training school to be included as a part of the public school system and supported at public expense. The Philadelphia Manual Training High School established in 1885 was also a part of the public school system. The course of study in the school at Philadel-

[1] Isaac Edward Clarke, *Art and Industry, Education in the Industrial Arts in the United States*, Part II, Bureau of Education, Washington, D.C., 1892, pp. 845–846.

phia differed somewhat from that of St. Louis. For example, the daily program called for both woodwork and metal work each year. The school was organized on the basis of three 2-hour periods; one for literary subjects, one for drawing and one for shopwork.

The Toledo, Ohio, school provided for the first time in this type of school courses for girls as well as for boys. The "domestic economy" courses for girls by years were as follows:

First year: Light carpentry, wood carving and care and use of tools.
Second year: Clay modeling, wood turning, introduction to cookery, and garment cutting and making.
Third year: Instruction in preparing and cooking food, purchasing household supplies, and care of sick.
Fourth year: Cutting, making and fitting garments, household decorations, and typewriting.[2]

This school also provided courses in drawing for both boys and girls.

As the manual training high school grew in popularity there was a tendency to provide a wider range of courses and more elective opportunities. This enrichment brought about two important changes in the nature of the organization of the manual training high school. One of these was towards a fusion with the academic high school which ultimately resulted in the cosmopolitan high school. The other change was an increase in technical subjects which resulted in designating some of these institutions as technical high schools. The Peru, Illinois, High School in 1884 was among the first of the academic high schools to offer courses in manual training. The superintendent of schools purchased some shop equipment and secured the service of a carpenter to teach these courses. Later, one of the high school teachers was assigned this responsibility. A one-year course was introduced in the Eau Claire, Wisconsin, High School in 1884, and this was extended to three years in 1887. Similar programs were established about this time in the high schools at Omaha, Minneapolis and Washington, D.C.

The term *technical high school* was used to designate a more specialized school of the manual training high school type. Courses in this school such as shopwork, drawing, and science were prominent in the curriculums. Since this was a separate high school this plan of organization was adapted to the larger cities in which more than one high school was maintained. Among the first of these schools was the Technical High School of Springfield, Massachusetts, established in 1898. This school provided instruction in the usual academic subjects

[2] *Ibid.*, pp. 418–419.

of the high school together with the fundamentals of drawing, of design, and of hand and machine tools. Other technical high schools established shortly after the beginning of the twentieth century included the Stuyvesant High School in New York City (1904), the Cass Technical High School of Detroit (1907) and the Lane Technical High School of Chicago (1908).

The cosmopolitan or comprehensive high school plan of organization was adopted in some of the cities shortly after the beginning of the twentieth century. This plan brought the courses and equipment for general, commercial, and manual training education into one school. Courses were classified as either academic or technical. The academic group usually included general subjects, classical subjects, domestic science, and manual training. These were for general culture and for preparation for college. The technical group consisted of commercial subjects, technical cooperative subjects, art, and music. Students in the cooperative courses spent half of their time in commercial establishments and the other half of their time in school. The comprehensive high school offered an opportunity for a choice of curriculums not available in a specialized school and recognized the growing demand for courses leading more definitely towards a vocation.

MANUAL TRAINING IN THE ELEMENTARY SCHOOLS

An educational experiment was conducted in Boston in 1882 to determine the feasibility of teaching manual training in the elementary grades. This experiment was the result of public sentiment developed during the previous decade by individuals and agencies, including the Whittling School of 1871 and the Industrial School Association founded in 1876. These agencies sponsored classes in carving and tool skills which led to the recommendation by the Boston School Committee that experiments in manual training be conducted in some of the city's grammar schools.

As a result of the Boston School Committee's recommendation one of the rooms in the Dwight School was fitted as a workshop, and a carpenter was employed as a teacher. The experiment started in January 1882 with 2 classes of 18 students each. The manual training —largely woodwork—was given in addition to the regular school work. The students were graded, and records of progress were kept in much the same manner as records in academic subjects. It was found that students were stimulated to do better work in academic classes in order to remain in the shop classes, and shopwork was judged to be a benefit rather than a detriment to work in other classes.

Manual training was introduced into the New York City elementary schools largely through the efforts of the Kitchen Garden Association. This agency, which later became the Industrial Education Association, had for its purpose the promotion of industrial education and the training of industrial teachers. The Association sponsored exhibitions of industrial work constructed by children, and this led to a demand for more of this type of work in the elementary schools. The New York Board of Education in 1888, largely through the efforts of Grace Dodge, one of its members, authorized the writing of a course of study in manual training for the first five grades including knife work, drawing, gluing, making joints, planing, sawing, chiseling, and project construction. This course was an effort to introduce manual methods in teaching the regular school subjects in the elementary school with special emphasis on form study, drawing and modeling.

At a school meeting in 1882, the citizens of Montclair, New Jersey, agreed to provide manual training in the grammar grades provided that such instruction did not interfere with the regular studies. The course consisted of shopwork for the boys and needlework for the girls with two hours per week devoted to these subjects. Manual training was also started in 1882 in the Jamestown, New York, elementary school for both boys and girls. Manual training activities were provided from grades one through nine. One of the New Haven, Connecticut, elementary schools conducted an experiment in 1883 that later resulted in an effective program of manual training. Among the other cities that provided manual training in the elementary schools during this time were Peru, Illinois (1884), Omaha, Nebraska (1885), Springfield, Massachusetts (1886), and Beardstown, Illinois (1887). After 1887 manual training developed rapidly in the grammar schools throughout the nation.

From Manual Training to Industrial Arts

The manual training programs of the nineteenth century have developed into present-day industrial arts programs. During this period of development the nature of manual training programs was influenced by a series of movements or developmental stages. These included the Russian influence, the sloyd movement, the arts and crafts movement, and the industrial or vocational movement. Each of these movements, some of which occurred simultaneously and all of which have overlapped to some extent, was especially prominent during the 40-year period from 1880 to 1920. Some characteristics of each of these movements are found in present-day programs of industrial arts.

THE RUSSIAN MANUAL TRAINING SYSTEM

The organized manual training programs in the United States were first influenced by the Russian system of manual training. This system had its origin about 1868 in the work of Victor Della Vos, director of the Moscow Imperial Technical School. The Russian system as proposed by Della Vos was designed to teach the fundamentals of the mechanical arts to large groups of students in the least possible time. The idea came to the United States through an exhibit of tool instruction shown at the Centennial Exposition at Philadelphia in 1876. The exhibit attracted the attention of John D. Runkle, president of Massachusetts Institute of Technology, and as a result a somewhat similar system of shopwork was organized at the Massachusetts Institute to provide practical training for engineering students. Professor C. M. Woodward of Washington University was also impressed by the Russian exhibit and as a result formulated a shop course for engineering students at Washington University.

The Russian system of manual training was a formalized system based on the principle of a logical method of procedure in which exercises were assigned in order of increasing difficulty and were undertaken by students in this order. Each course of instruction in manual training under the Russian system consisted of a series of graded exercises without special reference to their application in the construction of useful articles. The teaching of the course involved three stages. The first consisted of a study of tools and materials, the second involved the acquisition of skill in joining together the materials under study, and the third stage was the construction stage in which whole or parts of projects were made. Students learned to sharpen, care for, and adjust tools and to know the nature of materials. Emphasis was placed on freehand and mechanical drawing throughout the course.

The Russian system is characterized by the same type of formalism as was present in the academic courses of the early days. The formal class method of instruction provided little opportunity for self-expression and for the recognition of individual differences. Students were told how to proceed in each step of the teacher-selected exercises. The exercise and the demonstration were used almost exclusively. Illustrations and lesson sheets prepared by the teacher were used, and attempts were made to prepare textbooks with detailed instructions for the student. A system of teacher's marks and grades added to the formalism of the course.

THE SLOYD EMPHASIS

The formalism and abstract exercises of the Russian system of manual training had small appeal to elementary school students who could see little reason for developing skill in the use of tools. Consequently, elementary school teachers began a search early in the history of manual training for a system more suitable to the needs and interests of elementary school students. The sloyd method, which originated in the Scandinavian countries and had attracted the attention of American educators, seemed to offer some advantages. Sloyd had its origin in the home industries that occupied the time of the people of northern Europe when they were not engaged in farming. Articles such as handles, rakes, pins, benches, tools, kitchen utensils, and other items were constructed for sale and for home use. Interest in the movement spread to the schools, and sloyd schools were established in the northern countries during the latter half of the nineteenth century.

Sloyd was brought to the United States by Lars Erickson and Gustaf Larsson, both of Sweden. Erickson started a class in Anoka, Minnesota, in 1884, and Larsson organized a class and a training program for teachers in Boston in 1888. An experiment was conducted in Boston in the 1890s to determine whether the sloyd or Russian systems could better meet the needs of the grammar grades. This experiment resulted in the almost exclusive use of sloyd in the Boston schools. Sloyd was recommended for use in the Albany schools by the Committee on Manual Training in 1889, and Chicago tried out this system in 1892. The Report of the U.S. Commissioner of Education for 1893–1894 listed 18 schools in which sloyd was taught. This represented about 25 percent of all schools offering manual training in grades 7 through 12.

The outstanding characteristics of the sloyd system were the individual method of instruction, the useful model, and the encouragement of student initiative and self-direction. This course included not only objects that required the use of the measuring tape but also freehand work which required a sense of form through sight and touch. Special importance was attached to neatness, accuracy, finish and the desire to do good work. Well-trained teachers rather than artisans were preferred as sloyd teachers. American educators made some changes in the Swedish sloyd. Two of these changes were the development of a course in drawing and the improvement in the design of the models.

The sloyd system differed in many respects from the Russian system. The sloyd system involved the use of the completed model rather than an exercise. Sloyd gave greater prominence to the study of form by the use of some models which involved student judgment of shape and proportion rather than the testing of tools. The sloyd system also offered a greater variety of models, exercises and tools which tended to stimulate greater student interest. Some American educators considered the sloyd system too formal and inflexible, criticisms that had been directed against the Russian system.

THE ARTS AND CRAFTS MOVEMENT

The arts and crafts movement which originated in England during the latter part of the nineteenth century as a protest against poor craftsmanship exerted an influence over manual training programs of the United States. This movement placed emphasis on the aesthetic and creative side of the work instead of the skilled side as stressed in the Russian and sloyd movements. The arts and crafts emphasis was introduced into the Philadelphia schools about the same time the Russian system was getting started. Other cities in which the emphasis was prevalent included Chicago, New York, Boston, and Washington. James P. Haney, in an address at the 1903 meeting of the National Education Association, suggested that the term *manual arts* be used instead of manual training as a means of placing more emphasis on artistic elements of manual activity.

The arts and crafts movement stressed the importance of industrial drawing and various types of decorative work. Activities such as drawing, modeling, carving, leather work, and metal tooling made up the major part of the course of study for elementary school students. Formal benchwork and the old system of woodworking exercises were omitted from the arts and crafts course. Students were expected to draw, model, and carve reasonably well before they were allowed to use tools and precision instruments. Teaching devices included demonstrations, notebooks, models, excursions, and discussions.

One of the features of the arts and crafts movement was the principle of rotation of work. Students were usually required to rotate among the four departments of drawing, designing, clay modeling, and wood carving. Then, too, a greater attempt was made in the arts and crafts movement to correlate drawing with other school work. Students were expected to select and design some article of personal

A Rare Old Photograph Showing the Class of 1913, Sloyd Training School, Boston. (From *History of Manual and Industrial Education, 1870 to 1917*, Chas. A. Bennett, by permission of Chas. A. Bennett Co., Inc.)

interest, and some students were encouraged to use various types of material other than wood, iron and steel for planning and design work. The arts and crafts emphasis was responsible for shopwork of a more artistic nature that was better adapted to the interests of youth.

THE VOCATIONAL EMPHASIS

The cultural trend in manual training which characterized the Russian, sloyd, and arts and crafts movements was interrupted during the first decade of the twentieth century by the advocates of a vocational emphasis in manual arts. These educators suggested that the manual arts program should contribute more directly to the vocational preparation of secondary school students. This point of view was popularized as a result of the report of the Douglas Commission appointed by the governor of Massachusetts in 1905 to investigate the need for vocational education. This report deplored the cultural emphasis in manual training and suggested that more practical courses in vocational education were needed.

Manual training educators such as John D. Runkle of Massachusetts Institute of Technology and Calvin Woodward of Washington University had previously suggested that while manual training had some value in training for the mechanical occupations, it was primarily general education. The report of the Douglas Commission caused some educators to suggest that the emphasis be shifted more to the vocational and less to the cultural. Robert W. Selvidge, who later became professor of industrial education at the University of Missouri, suggested in 1913 that the vocational side of manual arts had not been stressed as much as it should have been and that students needed instruction in industrial methods and practices to give them a greater understanding of how consumer goods are produced. Advocates of the vocational emphasis suggested that the school shop be organized on a factory basis and engage in productive work for the school system. This involved the use of group rather than individual projects, the use of foremen over groups of students, an emphasis on the proper routing of materials through the shop and the standardization of shopwork to include essential trade practices.

The passage of the Smith-Hughes law in 1917, providing Federal aid for vocational education, resulted in the organization of special schools and classes designed to carry out many of the principles and practices previously suggested as desirable in manual training programs. As a result, many manual training educators suggested a return to the general education emphasis. There were some, however, who continued to insist that manual training with a vocational emphasis met the requirements of the Federal vocational education act despite the fact that the manual training program was designed for general rather than specific education. The vocational emphasis on manual training proved beneficial because it brought about a re-examination of the purposes of manual training which resulted in a restatement of its values and aims in terms that were more attainable.

THE DEVELOPMENT OF INDUSTRIAL ARTS

Some manual training educators early in the twentieth century objected to the undue emphasis on skill and the formalized instruction of the Russian, sloyd, and arts and crafts movements. These educators suggested that manual training courses should center more attention on a study of the industrial processes that operate in transforming raw materials into usable products. Charles R. Richards of Teachers College, Columbia University, suggested in an editorial in the October 1904 issue of *Manual Training Magazine* that the term *industrial arts* be used instead of manual training or manual arts as more descriptive of this changing point of view. Dean James E. Russell, also of Teachers College, proposed a course in industrial arts in 1909 in which the stages of production, manufacture, distribution, and consumption of such raw materials as foods, textiles, woods, metals, and clays be included for study. Such a course, it was contended, would not only provide for self-expression in the arts but would also simplify the teaching of other subjects in the curriculum.

The industrial arts movement has increased in popularity since the passage of the Smith-Hughes law. This law shifted responsibility for vocational education to separate schools and classes, thereby freeing industrial arts from this responsibility and enabling industrial arts educators to devote their efforts to the aims of general education. As a consequence, the school shop has become more of a laboratory in which the student may get first-hand information about materials and in which he can explore those fields that appeal to his interest. The term *industrial arts* has come into general use, and industrial arts courses are offered in both elementary and secondary schools throughout the nation.

From Sewing to Homemaking

Courses in domestic science were included among the practical arts introduced into the public school curriculum as a part of the manual training movement which occurred during the latter years of the nineteenth century. However, the origins of domestic science as a school subject date back to the colonial era when women were first permitted to attend school. From these early beginnings, during which time progress was slow, the study of homemaking has progressed to present-day homemaking programs extending from the first grade through the graduate school. A study of the early beginnings reflects some of the problems that have confronted home economists through the years.

Education in colonial America concerned itself primarily with training leaders for the church and state, and since women were not considered eligible for positions of this type, their formal education was neglected. The Dames schools were the only organized agencies of the colonial period for the education of women. Boston in 1784 admitted girls to writing schools for a short time each school day, and girls were permitted to attend school at different hours of the day from boys in the double-headed schools of 1789. The school board of Gloucester, Massachusetts, voted in 1790 to allocate two of the eight hours of instruction per day to girls.

Boston in 1825 established a high school for girls, but after one year this school was closed because of the difficulty of financing the venture. Meanwhile, the academies and private schools had increased in importance, and many of them were admitting women students. Among these were Oberlin College, a coeducational institution founded in 1833; Mount Holyoke Seminary, an institution founded in 1837, in which cooperative housekeeping was practiced as a means of self-support for girls while securing an education; and the New England Female Medical College, established in 1842. These institutions were the forerunners of the movement to provide educational programs for women students, which led eventually to a recognition of the need for a homemaking program for women.

THE BEGINNINGS OF DOMESTIC SCIENCE

Records indicate that girls attending the Boston public schools in 1798 spent a portion of their time on needlework, a subject taught by the regular school teacher. Sewing was introduced into the primary grades of the Boston schools in 1820 and in the grammar grades in 1835. A female seminary established by Emma Willard at Troy, New York, taught a course in "housewifery" in the 1820s. Elmira College in 1855 required its young women to take work in domestic science and general household affairs. Lasell Seminary in Massachusetts offered courses in cookery, housekeeping, sewing, dressmaking, and millinery in the year 1877.

The land-grant colleges provided leadership in homemaking in the last quarter of the nineteenth century. Iowa State College started formal instruction in home economics in 1872. The first formal instruction in Iowa State College consisted of lectures to girls in the junior class relative to housekeeping. A kitchen was provided in 1877, and lessons in cooking were added. By 1882, the college offered instruction in cooking, house furnishing, care of children, care of the sick, management of help, dress, physiology, and domestic chemistry. Classes in laundry work and sewing were added, but these were later abolished to provide additional time for foods and nutrition. By 1900 thirty colleges had established departments of domestic science and art. Kansas State College offered courses in sewing in 1873 and fitted up a kitchen for practical instruction in 1877. A Department of Domestic Science and Art was established at Illinois Industrial University in 1874.

Cooking schools were established in New York in 1874 and in Boston in 1879. The New York school was established in the Free Training School for Women. The plain cooks class, which started in 1878, had for its objective "instruction in the principles of plain family cooking for young housekeepers in moderate circumstances, young women employed as domestics and the wives and daughters of workingmen."[3] The Boston school, which was founded by the Committee on Industrial Education of the Women's Education Association, gave practical instruction in cooking to women. This school became a part of Simmons College in 1902.

DOMESTIC SCIENCE IN PUBLIC SCHOOLS

The state of Massachusetts in 1872 authorized schools to offer courses in sewing and other industrial education subjects. The Kitchen Garden Movement which began in 1877 utilized miniature toys as devices for teaching household arts to young children. Each student had a set of toy models of household furnishings and equipment. These models, together with songs and games, were used to teach housekeeping. The Kitchen Garden Association developed into the Industrial Education Association in 1884 in recognition of the fact that domestic science was a part of manual training. This Association was instrumental in developing subject matter and methods of instruction in home economics. The Association was also influential in 1888 in the organization of the New York College for Training Teachers, which has now become the Teachers College of Columbia University.

The Philadelphia High School for Girls offered courses in sewing in 1880, and in 1885 sewing instruction was extended to the elementary and grammar grades. The Board of Education in Washington, D.C., in 1886 included cooking and sewing as a part of the manual training courses. These courses were required in the elementary schools and elective in the high schools. Content based on scientific knowledge as well as handicraft was emphasized. San Francisco provided domestic science courses for girls in 1885. Domestic science was taught in nine elementary schools in New York beginning in 1888, and a director of domestic science was appointed in 1896. At the close of the century, domestic science courses were established in public schools throughout the nation to provide a type of manual training suitable for girls.

THE LAKE PLACID CONFERENCES

A series of 10 annual conferences held at Lake Placid, Chautauqua, and Boston during the years 1899 to 1908 exerted a marked influence on the homemaking movement. These conferences had their

[3] Isabel Bevier, *Home Economics in Education*, Lippincott, Philadelphia, 1924, p. 135.

origin as a result of a need to determine the content of a New York Regents examination in household science. The idea expanded over a 10-year period to include a variety of topics concerned with the economic and social aspects of the home. Such topics as training of teachers of domestic science, courses of study, evening schools, extension teaching, rural school work, home economics in women's clubs and manual training and education for citizenship were discussed.

The fourth conference of 1902 suggested that "home economics in its most comprehensive sense is the study of the laws, conditions, principles and ideals which are concerned on the one hand with man's immediate physical environment and on the other with his nature as a social being, and is the study especially of the relation between these two factors."[4] Considerable discussion was given to terminology in home economics. There was a feeling that the common term *domestic science* was not adequate to describe the various homemaking programs. Therefore, the sixth conference, held in 1904, suggested that to describe the homemaking activities the term *hand work* be used in the elementary schools, *domestic science* in the secondary schools, *home economics* in normal and professional schools and *euthenics* in colleges and universities.

Each of these conferences was directed by Mrs. Ellen H. Richards, a leader in the problems of homemaking. The conference was a semiprivate affair with attendance by invitation. Two conferences were held by special invitation outside of Lake Placid. One of these, held at Boston in 1903, was a joint session with the manual training section of the National Education Association. This meeting served to bring to the attention of manual training educators the necessity for including home economics in the manual training movement. The 1908 conference was held at Chautauqua, New York, at which time plans for organizing the American Home Economics Association were made.

PUBLIC SCHOOL HOME ECONOMICS COURSES
PRIOR TO 1917

Before the passage of the Smith-Hughes Vocational Education Act in 1917 there was little uniformity as to terminology, scope, time allotment, and grade placement of home economics. Such terms as *household science*, *domestic science*, *domestic art*, and *home eco-*

[4] Hazel T. Craig, *The History of Home Economics*, Practical Home Economics, New York, 1945, p. 15.

nomics were in use. Many departments were housed in basements with little equipment other than the minimum needed for cooking and sewing. Frequently the home economics teacher did not meet desired qualifications for teaching home economics. Then, too, she was required to teach a number of other school subjects with inadequate time for home economics. Inferior students were placed in home economics courses, and other school students considered that home economics courses were designed for dull children.

An attempt was made in 1911 to develop satisfactory courses of instruction and related subjects for home economics classes. A committee of the American Home Economics Association published a *Syllabus of Home Economics* in 1913 which attempted to classify in logical order the various topics which can properly be incuded under the term *home economics*. The committee defined home economics "as the study of the economic, sanitary and aesthetic aspects of food, clothing and shelter, as connected with their selection, preparation and use by the family in the home or by other groups of people."[5] The committee suggested that courses in home economics may be cultural, technical or vocational; and they may be offered in the primary and secondary school or in college. The main divisions of subject matter proposed were (1) food, (2) clothing, (3) shelter, and (4) household and institution management. This committee's report served as a guide for homemaking programs for a number of years.

Up to the time of the passage of the Smith-Hughes Vocational Education Act in 1917 every state had some type of home economics in one or more schools, and much of it was of excellent quality. In most of these schools it was given as a part of general education and was usually scheduled for about two periods per week. There was no integrated program of homemaking, and related art and home economics or domestic science for the most part consisted of cooking and sewing. Prior to the passage of the Smith-Hughes Act, comparatively few schools offered well-rounded courses in vocational homemaking designed for the preparation of homemakers. However, within a short time after the passage of the Act vocational homemaking courses were established in all states, and the domestic science of the first decade of the twentieth century was well on the way to becoming the modern-day program of vocational homemaking education.

Present day courses in homemaking with nonvocational practical arts objectives are offered in the junior high school, frequently as cooking or sewing courses. Some senior high school courses in home-

[5] Isabel Bevier, *op. cit.*, p. 167.

making are classified as nonvocational practical arts subjects if they are designed to meet the general education needs of youth.

Practical Arts Education in Agriculture and Business

The practical arts courses in agriculture and business, usually referred to as general agriculture and general business, are designed as nonvocational general education courses. Both of these courses had their origins in similar subjects or activities designed to improve occupational competency. These courses through the years have appeared in school curriculums more frequently as vocational courses rather than as practical arts courses. Frequently it has been difficult to determine from the content of the instruction whether the objectives of the course were vocational or nonvocational. The following discussion is an attempt to trace briefly the development of these subjects as general education or practical arts subjects.

GENERAL AGRICULTURE

Organized instruction in agriculture in elementary and secondary schools has had nonvocational as well as vocational objectives since its beginnings in the nineteenth century. An agricultural reader for general school use was published in Vermont in 1824. The work-study schools of this era offered courses in agriculture as a means of acquiring general knowledge as well as for farming. The courses in agriculture in some of the academies were said to have some disciplinary values. A few high schools offered courses in academic agriculture which usually meant textbook study and lectures.

The Country Life Movement had its beginnings in the 1890s and this stimulated the further development of general agriculture in the elementary schools. General agriculture was frequently substituted for such required subjects as nature study and natural philosophy. During the first decade of the twentieth century courses in elementary agriculture were prescribed by law in 17 states. These states adopted textbooks in general agriculture for use in the elementary schools. General agriculture was one of the subjects required in the examination for teachers certificates in 26 states. Normal schools in less populous states offered courses in general agriculture for teachers who were preparing for careers in rural schools.

The enactment of the Smith-Hughes law in 1917 in which Federal funds were appropriated for vocational agriculture brought about

City Children are Educated for Life on the Farm. These city farmers are harvesting tomatoes at Philadelphia's High School of Agriculture and Horticulture. (Wide World)

a shift in emphasis in agriculture from general to vocational, and from the elementary to the secondary school level. States which required by law the teaching of agriculture made amendments and interpretations to permit vocational agriculture to meet the legal requirements of the law. Some public schools have continued to offer courses in general agriculture. The U.S. Office of Education estimated that about 38,000 students were enrolled in general agriculture in public secondary schools in 1961. This was about 7 percent of the total enrollment in agriculture for that year and indicates that general agriculture as such is seldom found in public secondary school curriculums. However, some students who apparently are not interested in entering agricultural occupations are enrolled in vocational agriculture curriculums in the secondary schools. Agriculture for these individuals is a nonvocational practical arts course.

GENERAL BUSINESS EDUCATION

The English grammar schools and academies in the United States offered courses in arithmetic, handwriting, and bookkeeping in the eighteenth and early nineteenth centuries. These courses were said to be designed to prepare students for "life" as well as college entrance. Bookkeeping was including in the curriculum of the English High School of Boston in 1823. Massachusetts enacted a law in 1827 in which instruction in bookkeeping among other subjects was specified for certain high schools. Some of the high schools offered commercial courses in the nineteenth century. Business education courses in these various schools were included for general education as well as practical usage.

Business education received less emphasis in public schools during the latter part of the nineteenth century because of the rise of private business colleges. Renewed interest in business education in the public schools occurred early in the twentieth century. Committees of the National Education Association in 1903 and again in 1919 pointed to the need for business education not only for vocational usage but for mental discipline and general education. Business education was introduced into the junior high school curriculum at this time for general knowledge, exploratory values, and as a means of reducing school dropouts. The specialized courses in commercial subjects were used at first, but later unified courses in business education were introduced.

In recent years, especially since World War II, attention has been given to education for life adjustment. The purpose of this movement was to provide an educational program for secondary school youth who were not enrolled in vocational curriculums and were not planning to attend college. Many of the objectives of the life adjustment curriculums are also the objectives of general business education, and courses in general business were suggested as a part of these curriculums. The personal-use objective for courses in general business is currently emphasized. Special courses designed to meet this objective have been organized in some schools. However, the usual practice is to use introductory courses in bookkeeping, typewriting, and clerical practice to meet personal-use objectives for students who desire knowledge and skill about business but do not plan to enter office occupations.

QUESTIONS FOR STUDY AND DISCUSSION

1. What is the meaning of the term *practical arts*? When and under what conditions did the term come into common usage?
2. Discuss the origins of drawing and its relationship to the fine arts in Italy, France, England and Germany.

3. What developments in art education occurred in the United States during the nineteenth century?
4. Discuss the early development of drawing courses in general education in the United States.
5. When and where was manual training introduced into the secondary school curriculum? What subjects and activities were included in the curriculum of the manual training high school?
6. What objections were raised to manual training in the secondary school, and how were these objections answered?
7. Discuss the different patterns of organization used by the various manual training high schools of the nineteenth century.
8. What was the origin and curriculum content of manual training in the elementary schools?
9. Discuss the various movements, and the characteristics of each, that influenced manual training during the transition from manual training to industrial arts.
10. What change in point of view came about as a result of the use of the term *industrial arts*?
11. What contributions did the Lake Placid conferences make to home-making education in the public schools?
12. Discuss the development of practical arts courses in agriculture and business education.

SOURCE REFERENCES

Anderson, Lewis F., *History of Manual and Industrial School Education*, Appleton-Century-Crofts, New York, 1926.
Bennett, Charles A., *History of Manual and Industrial Education up to 1870*, Manual Arts, Peoria, 1926.
Bennett, Charles A., *History of Manual and Industrial Education, 1870 to 1917*, Manual Arts, Peoria, 1937.
Bennett, Charles A., *The Manual Arts*, Manual Arts, Peoria, 1917.
Bevier, Isabel, *Home Economics in Education*, Lippincott, Philadelphia, 1924.
Bevier, Isabel, and Susannah Usher, *The Home Economics Movement*, Whitcomb and Barrows, Boston, 1906.
Branegan, Gladys A., *Home Economics Teacher Training Under the Smith-Hughes Act*, Contributions to Education, No. 350, Bureau of Publications, Teachers College, Columbia University, New York, 1929.
Cooley, Anna M., and others, *Teaching Home Economics*, Macmillan, New York, 1919.
Craig, Hazel T., *The History of Home Economics*, Practical Home Economics, New York, 1945.
Federal Board for Vocational Education, *Second Annual Report*, Washington, D.C., 1918.
Haynes, Benjamin R., and Harry P. Jackson, *A History of Business Educa-*

tion in the United States, Monograph 25, South-Western, Cincinnati, 1935.

Leavitt, Frank M., *Examples of Industrial Education,* Ginn, New York, 1912.

Mays, Arthur B., *Principles and Practices of Vocational Education,* McGraw-Hill, New York, 1948.

Monroe, Paul, *A Cyclopedia of Education,* Volume I, Macmillan, New York, 1928.

Stimson, Rufus W., *History of Agricultural Education,* Vocational Division Bulletin 217, Office of Education, U.S. Federal Security Agency, Washington, D.C., 1942.

Stombaugh, Ray M., *A Survey of the Movements Culminating in Industrial Arts Education in Secondary Schools,* Contributions to Education, No. 670, Bureau of Publications, Teachers College, Columbia University, New York, 1936.

CHAPTER FOUR

VOCATIONAL SCHOOLS AND CLASSES IN THE NINETEENTH CENTURY

The nineteenth century is characterized by the development of many new types of vocational schools and programs. These new programs had their origins in the movements and philosophies that grew out of the revival of learning during the fifteenth and sixteenth centuries. The humanistic movement of this time placed emphasis on the individual and his privileges and responsibilities. A shift in emphasis occurred in the sixteenth and seventeenth centuries when the movement for realism took form. This movement, as expressed by John A. Comenius (1592–1670) and John Locke (1632–1704), was responsible for the introduction into the curriculum of science and practical arts. The eighteenth century or Age of Reason, as it was called, was an age of democratic liberalism, benevolence, and tolerance. Among the noted exponents of these ideas were Jean Jacques Rousseau (1712–1778), Johann Bernhard Basedow (1724–1790), and Johann Heinrich Pestalozzi (1746–1827).

The characteristics such as self-education, importance of environmental factors, student participation in learning and universal education as advocated by educational leaders of the eighteenth century, led to the organization of new schools and programs in the nineteenth century. The increased interest in human welfare was responsible for the development of schools for poor and delinquent children. The desire for more learning by adults brought about the adult education program. The increased demands for labor and the decline in the apprenticeship system led to school substitutes for apprenticeship. The emphasis on mass education and the need for trained workers made necessary the organization of schools and curriculums for workers and prospective workers.

Vocational Education for Poor and Delinquent Children

The emphasis on individual welfare generated as a result of the Renaissance and further expanded during the seventeenth and eighteenth centuries, together with the widespread poverty and the increasing incidence of crime and delinquency, was responsible for the development in the nineteenth century of industrial schools for poor and delinquent children. Some of these schools were for orphans, paupers, and destitute children who were in need of a practical education and the moral and social influence of the home. Others were for children and youth who had violated a law or custom and who as a result had been committed to an institution for correction. The schools for the poor were referred to as hospitals or orphans' homes, and the schools for delinquents were called reform schools, houses of refuge, farm schools, and colonies. Because of the nature of instruction both types of schools were referred to as industrial schools, a name frequently associated with present-day schools of correction for children and youth.

EARLY SCHOOLS FOR UNDERPRIVILEGED CHILDREN

The nineteenth century industrial schools for poor and delinquent children were influenced by various types of institutions that had their beginnings in the preceding centuries. Among the first of these was the Christ's Hospital or Blue-Coat School of London organized in 1553 for orphans and foundlings. The boys from this school were apprenticed to craftsmen when they became old enough to work at a trade. William Blake of London was the originator of a charity school movement about 1685. The children in the charity schools were taught reading, arithmetic, religious teachings, and a trade.

The Francke Institute of Halle, Germany, organized in 1694, was instrumental in the development of the German *realschule*. This institution was organized primarily for the purpose of giving religious education to children from poor families. The institution grew to include a Latin school for well-to-do students, a teachers' seminary and a publishing house. The orphanage became the most important part of the institution. Manual arts were included in addition to religious teachings. The orphans were taught to spin, sew, and knit both for economic purposes and as a means of mental development. The students in the Latin school were provided with turning lathes and instruments for cutting glass, largely for purposes of recreation to prevent idleness and "childish amusements."

Some of the teachers who worked in the institute recognized the need for a new type of secondary school giving emphasis to science, art and the trades and industries. They therefore organized a curriculum which included mathematics, natural science, mechanics, and handicrafts. Johann Julius Hecker, one of the teachers in the Francke Institute, established an institute in Berlin in 1747 known as the *Royal Realschule*. The purpose of this school was to use models and plans and useful subjects as a basis for teaching children and youth. The curriculum of the school included drawing, mathematics, science, history, modern languages, and Latin. Instruction was given in manual skills such as turning, pasting, glass cutting, finishing, and others. This was the beginning of the German nonclassical secondary school curriculum.

Schools of industry were developed in Germany and England during the last quarter of the eighteenth century. These schools combined industrial work for wages with classroom study. The industrial work was provided to enable the students to earn money to pay school tuition. The various kinds of industrial work included spinning, knitting, furniture making, and wood carving for boys. There was little or no connection between the industrial work and the schooling. The usual practice in the English schools of industry was to provide one hour of instruction per day in reading and writing, and the remainder of the day was spent in industry. The school and industry day was from 6 A.M. to 6 P.M. in the summer and during the daylight hours in the winter. These schools did not get much public support, and the industrial work disappeared in a short time. They did, however, instill in German children a desire for work that later enabled many of them to achieve material prosperity, and these schools enabled many children in England to attend school who otherwise would have been unable to do so.

THE SCHOOLS OF PESTALOZZI AND FELLENBERG

Schools for underprivileged children were established by two educational philosophers—Johann Heinrich Pestalozzi and Philip Emanuel von Fellenberg—near the close of the eighteenth century. The schools of these two educational leaders not only had a profound influence on the nineteenth century industrial schools but also on present-day schools, both vocational and general. Pestalozzi brought a new method of instruction to the educational world. This method, known as the psychological method, proceeded from "things to words" rather than from "words to things," as in the traditional method of the times. Pestalozzi was among the first to organize hand work as a part of general school work, and as a consequence he is sometimes referred to as the father of manual training.

Pestalozzi's belief that intellectual and moral degradation was responsible for material poverty led him to establish a number of schools for children of the poor of Switzerland. The first of these, the Neuhof School, was established in 1774 when he brought about 20 underprivileged children to his home, gave them religious training and taught them to work in the fields. He used objects and manual labor as a means of teaching the traditional school subjects. The school was an educational success but a financial failure. The children were unable to provide the work required to cultivate the fields, and the school was closed in 1780.

Pestalozzi's belief in the use of the tools of the environment as a basis for educational practice was not lessened by this failure, and he established other schools to demonstrate his theories. Among these were the schools at Stanz (1794), Burgdorf (1799), and Yverdun (1805). The school at Yverdun became famous, and teachers from many countries came to it to study Pestalozzian methods of teaching. Drawing was an important subject at Yverdun, and Pestalozzi developed a special method known as the alphabet of form to use in teaching this subject. Drawing was taught as a means of assisting students to observe and evaluate things seen in order that they might better describe them. The school at Yverdun was obliged to close in 1824 because of mismanagement and internal difficulties.

Fellenberg demonstrated the importance of school organization and business management in the operation of a school system. The chief characteristic of this system was manual labor; and Fellenberg proved that manual activities, when properly organized and directed, could contribute both financially and educationally to the success of a school system. Fellenberg believed in the separation of people of different social levels and organized a series of schools and classes for these various social levels at Hofwyl, Switzerland, beginning in 1800. Among these were the academy for boys of the higher social class, the school of applied science for young men from the middle-class families and the farm and trade school for infants and boys from poor families. A school for underprivileged girls was organized as a part of the farm and trade school, and a normal school was organized for the training of teachers.

The farm and trade school, which started in 1807, was a most important feature of the Hofwyl school program. This school was designed to provide instruction in elementary subjects along with agriculture and a trade. The daily program of the school consisted of lessons and farm work with about 3 to 5 hours of instruction and 7 to 12 hours of labor per day, depending on the season. The instruction was omitted during the harvest season. Students were taught to sew, and they had responsibility for all housework. The Pestalozzian method of growth through natural processes rather than through artificial conditions was employed. Manual labor provided a natural environment for growth, and as many connections as possible between work and study were made.

Fellenberg employed mechanics representing several different trades to supply the needs of his institution. Among the skilled trades represented were those of blacksmith, wheelwright, cabinet maker, carpenter, shoemaker, harness maker, tailor, turner, brass worker, and bookbinder. When a student was old enough to become an apprentice he was allowed to select a trade as a part of his work experience at the school. Boys who selected a trade and were not financially able to pay tuition were bound to the school to remain until they were 21 years of age. When the boy left school, he was a practical farmer and had acquired a trade and a general education. The Fellenberg farm and trade school, characterized by its emphasis on manual labor, gave impetus to other types of industrial schools, including those for orphans and delinquent children.

ORPHANAGES AND INDUSTRIAL REFORM SCHOOLS IN EUROPE

One of the early industrial schools for orphans that developed from the experience of Pestalozzi and Fellenberg was established in Germany by John Daniel Falk in 1818. Falk provided in his home for 300 children. He later constructed an orphanage with the help of the children. Instruction in elementary subjects and manual labor was provided in the orphanages. An orphanage was established at Potsdam in 1824 for the maintenance and education of orphans of soldiers. Attempts were made without success to introduce industrial work for profit-making purposes at the orphanage. The orphans were taught a number of trades including blacksmithing, saddlery, shoemaking, and lithography. The usual practice was to permit each boy to select his trade. Some boys were permitted to work in town at trades not taught in school as a means of learning that trade. An orphans' home at Frankfort-on-the-Main provided instruction in handicrafts two hours each day. The instruction included such manual operations as making baskets and mats, cord turning, bookbinding, working with iron and brass, shoemaking, and tailoring.

The results achieved in industrial schools for poor and neglected children suggested that schools of this type might be used as a means of rehabilitating juvenile criminals and as a result return a large number of them to respectability and usefulness. This practice required that young offenders be separated from adult criminals and placed in schools or reformatories. Many of these reform schools were established in Europe during the latter part of the eighteenth and first half of the nineteenth centuries. Among these were St. Georges Fields, established in 1788 near London, England; Redemption Institute, established in 1833 near Hamburg, Germany; an agricultural colony, established in 1839 at Mettray, France; and Red Hill Farm, established in 1849 in Surrey, England.

The institution known as St. Georges Fields was designed as a home for juvenile criminals and destitute children. Both boys and girls were admitted during the early years of its existence, but later only boys were admitted. A description of the school program written in 1818 indicated that the boys were placed in various workshops which were conducted by master workmen and journeymen. The principal

Fellenberg's Farm School at Hofwyl, Including the Barns and Class-room Building. (Reproduced from *A Cyclopedia of Education*, Volume I, by Paul Monroe, published by The Macmillan Company, by permission of Mrs. Jeannette Monroe Basset)

trades were printing, copperplate printing, bookbinding, shoemaking, tailoring, rope making, and twine spinning. All children received instruction in morals and religion.

The Redemption Institute provided religious teachings along with elementary education and manual labor. Boys were housed in small or family-style units, and each received some money in addition to lodgings. The agricultural colony at Mettray was established to demonstrate the feasibility of rehabilitating juvenile criminals. Instruction in farming and gardening, together with trade training, was provided. Graduates of the colony were encouraged to settle in small towns or in rural areas, and the trades suitable for these areas, such as those of wheelwright, harness maker, shoemaker, and blacksmith, were taught.

The reform school known as Red Hill Farm, in which farm labor was the principal occupation and trades and handicrafts a secondary occupation, was established near Reigate in Surrey, England. This institution had at one time accommodations for 300 boys. The boys spent about 3 hours on alternate days in study and the remainder of the time in industrial occupations. About two-thirds of the occupants were assigned to field work and the remainder to various industries about the school. Boys were organized into crews with a foreman or trainer. Each boy's account was credited with a small sum of money each week which he might spend for such items as postage stamps, periodicals and entertainment. This school, like the others of its type, was credited with reforming many young offenders and reducing the incidence of crime by juveniles.

THE RAGGED AND REFORM SCHOOLS OF ENGLAND AND SCOTLAND

A number of individuals in England and Scotland initiated a movement known as the "ragged school" movement designed to combat the rising tide of lawlessness brought about largely because of poverty. The first of these schools was started in 1819 in a cobbler's shop in Portsmouth. Children were enticed into the shop by the promise of food, and they were taught how to read and write and earn an honest living. The term *ragged school* was adopted because it had an appeal to the public in the solicitation of funds for the school. A ragged school union was founded in 1844 to promote these schools. It was estimated that in 1855 the city of London had 50 of these schools with industrial classes enrolling about 2000 children.

The teachers of the ragged schools were volunteer workers who served without pay. Religious training was provided, and the Bible was the principal textbook. Some elementary subjects were taught, the number and kind varying with the school and the qualifications of the instructors. The usual practice was to attend school during the morning hours and engage in industrial work during the afternoon. The workers were divided into small groups or bands, each group performing some designated type of work. Such jobs as assorting bristles, making paper and canvas bags, making clogs, tailoring, printing, and making clothes were followed. The industrial work was considered valuable, but there was little effort to organize and coordinate it with the classroom work. The good results of the ragged schools were evident in the reduction of juvenile crime in London. These schools also helped to prepare the public mind for the free compulsory education that started in England with the passage of the Education Act of 1870.

INDUSTRIAL SCHOOLS FOR UNDERPRIVILEGED CHILDREN IN THE UNITED STATES

The United States from colonial times accepted the principle that all children should receive an education at public expense, and there was less need for special institutions for poor children in the United States than in Europe. There were, however, a number of institutions maintained for underprivileged children. In general, two types of institutions of this nature were maintained by private individuals and organizations. These were schools for orphans and physically handi-

Sewing Class for Girls in a "Ragged School" in England. (From *History of Manual and Industrial Education Up to 1870*, Chas. A. Bennett, by permission of Chas. A. Bennett Co., Inc.)

capped children and reformatories or houses of refuge for juvenile delinquents. Children from these two groups were sometimes placed in the same institution, but this did not prove satisfactory, and the practice of separating them was usually followed. The industrial school idea of including some manual activity in the curriculum was present in these schools, and some of them have contributed materially to the development of vocational education in the United States.

One of the first of the schools for orphans was the De la Howe agricultural school established by an endowment in 1797 provided in the will of Dr. John de la Howe of Abbeville, South Carolina. This school was designed to provide food, lodging, and education for orphans or boys and girls from poor families. Instruction in general subjects, religion, and agricultural industries was provided. The state of South Carolina assumed management of the institution in 1917, and it is now used to care for indigent children of the state. Some have suggested that this school is the oldest agricultural school in the United States.

The Boston Farm and Trade School, established in 1814 by private philanthropy, was designed to provide instruction and opportunities for manual work for orphans of Boston. Girard College in Philadelphia was established from a grant by Stephen Girard as a home for white male orphans. This institution, which opened in 1848, provided special woodworking shops in 1859. Provision was made in 1864 for instruction in typesetting, printing, bookbinding, typefounding, stereotyping, turning, carpentry, photography, electroplating, and telegraphy. The trade training was given to selected students in accordance with their interests and aptitudes.

Reformatories for children who violated laws and required detention were established about the same time as the schools for orphans. The New York City institution for juvenile delinquents was started in 1824. Similar institutions were established in Boston in 1827 and in Philadelphia in 1828. These institutions were designed to reform delinquent youth by training their minds in morality and religion and by teaching each of them to earn a living. Frequently, the work in these institutions was difficult and provided little opportunity for any type of training. These institutions were primarily prisons.

Later institutions of this type had less of the prison atmosphere and provided more and better instruction in manual and industrial work. Since many of the inmates were less than 14 years of age, not all were taught a trade, but all were trained in the habits of industry. Various types of handicraft work were provided, including shoemaking, tailoring, sewing, basket making, brush making, chair making, blacksmithing, and farming. The time allotted to labor as compared to study varied among the institutions. In general 6 or 7 hours per day were spent in work and 3 to 4 hours per day in study. Some of the boys who left the school were apprenticed in order that they might acquire more competency in a trade. This new type of school was expected through work and education to create and improve desirable character traits in delinquent children.

The Adult Vocational Education Movement

The forces set in motion by the revival of learning in the Middle Ages were responsible for an increased interest in adult education, beginning with the organization of the Sunday schools of the eighteenth century. These schools were the first to offer opportunities for working youth and adults to continue their education after their elementary school days were over. These schools originated from the ancient practice of catechizing in church and at first were concerned only with religious teachings. In the year 1789 some teachers in the Sunday school at Birmingham, England, formed a Sunday Society to give instruction in writing and arithmetic to young men who had ceased to attend religious schools. Geography, bookkeeping, and drawing were later added, and lectures on mechanics and natural philosophy were given to workers employed in the foundries and manufacturing plants. The instruction was provided free to the workers, and it led to the establishment of a library for the working classes. The interest shown in the work of the Sunday Society led to the organization of mechanics institutes in Great Britain and the United States.

MECHANICS INSTITUTES IN GREAT BRITAIN

The first of the mechanics institutes in Great Britain was organized in Glasgow, Scotland, in 1800. This institute was conducted by Dr. George Birkbeck, a professor of natural philosophy and chemistry in Anderson's University of Glasgow. The institute consisted of a series of lectures on mechanics delivered to provide instruction in science to workers engaged in mechanical trades. Interest in these lectures was high, and attendance increased from 75 workers at the first lecture to about 500 at the fourth. Much of this interest was due to the fact that Professor Birkbeck was familiar with the practical problems of the workers. Professor Birkbeck left Glasgow in 1804, but the mechanics class at Anderson's University was continued for many years.

As a result of the success of the Glasgow institute a similar institution was established in London in 1824, largely through the efforts of Professor Birkbeck who had previously moved to that city. The London institute included instruction in the principles of the arts that were practiced by the members and in the various branches of science. School facilities included a library, a reading room, and a laboratory for the display of machines. Lectures were given on philosophy, practical mechanics, astronomy, chemistry, literature, and the arts. The institution was financed by annual fees and by gifts from wealthy individuals and was managed by 6 officers and 30 committee men. During the early years the institute enrollment often exceeded 1000 persons. The success of the first mechanics institutes was responsible for the organization of similar institutions in several other cities, including one in Manchester, where a building was erected for the various institutional activities.

The number of mechanics institutes in Great Britain increased to 216 with a combined membership of more than 25,000 persons in 1841. The institutes began to experience difficulties shortly after they were organized. The foremost objective of the institute was to teach the principles of science to workers who had little or no educational background. It was necessary to secure lecturers or instructors who could talk the language of the workingman and these were difficult to find. The inadequate educational background of workers in the mechanical trades made it difficult for them to understand the simplest of scientific principles. Then, too, it became evident that many manufacturers were giving financial support to the institutes in order that they might obtain better workmen. Frequently these contributors influenced the curriculum to such an extent that much of its scientific content was sacrificed to the development of certain mechanical skills.

These difficulties caused the attendance to drop off, and many of the institutes were closed. Some of them became reading rooms and lending libraries where an occasional lecture was given. A number of the institutes continued to function until the passage of the Education Act of 1870 which eventually resulted in an advance in technical education in Great Britain. The institutes demonstrated a need for a comprehensive program of elementary education available to all workers. Many of the institutes have developed into present-day technical colleges.

WORKINGMEN'S COLLEGES IN ENGLAND

A new type of institution for adult education was started in England near the middle of the nineteenth century. This institution, known as the workingman's college, was designed to correct the faults that had developed in the mechanics institute program and to provide studies of a higher range for working-class people. The first of these institutions was the People's College of Sheffield, established in 1842. This college established classes in Latin, Greek, French, German, mathematics, English literature, logic, elocution, and drawing, in addition to some elementary school subjects. The class sessions were held from 6:30 A.M. to 7:30 A.M. and from 7:30 P.M. to 9:30 P.M. Both men and women were admitted to the classes. Most of these classes were taught by one teacher, the founder of the college.

Attendance kept up for a few years, but it gradually decreased until in 1848 a reorganization was necessary. A committee of 12 students was formed to operate the college on a self-supporting and self-governing basis. The enrollment shortly after reorganization increased to 200 students, and day classes were established for youth who were not working. The curriculum in 1853 included lectures on chemistry in its application to the trades of Sheffield workers. All specific religious teaching was barred from the college.

The success of the People's College at Sheffield was responsible for the organization of other workingman's colleges, the most influential of which was the college established in London in 1854 by Frederick D. Maurice at the request of a group of workingmen and university scholars. Maurice had previously served as professor of divinity at Kings College, London, and was greatly concerned with the apparent gulf between the people of different social strata. He saw in the idea of a workingmen's college a means of reducing the impact of this difference.

The faculty of the college consisted of eminent scholars such as John Ruskin who taught drawing and developed an instruction manual on drawing, Charles Kingsley, the writer, Thomas Hughes who was the author of *Tom Brown's School Days*, and Frederick James Furnivall, noted Shakespearean scholar. The curriculum included, in addition to drawing, such classical studies as English literature, English grammar, history, geography, natural philosophy, geometry, astronomy, and law. The students had major responsibility for financing the college and were represented on the governing board. The workingmen's colleges of England were not designed for technical training and had no manual instruction other than drawing. They did, however, have a definite influence on industrial education in both Great Britain and America.

MECHANICS INSTITUTES IN THE UNITED STATES

The mechanics institute movement developed about the same time in the United States as in Great Britain. Fundamentally, the movements were the same. They were a part of an effort made by working people to improve their social and economic conditions. The details of the movements differed in accordance with the social conditions of the country in which they were developed. The movement in the United States was more flexible because of the newness of the country and the sparsity of population.

The first of the institutes organized in the United States was started in New York City in 1820 by the General Society of Mechanics and Tradesmen. This organization had been formed in 1785 for mutual aid, assistance in case of sickness, and care of widows and orphans. The Society established a library for apprentices and a school for children of mechanics. The school was organized to meet a need for elementary education for the children of indigent members. Later, other children were admitted for a small tuition fee. The school was necessary because the public school system had not developed and because of the scarcity of charity schools. The New York City public school system assumed responsibility for the Society's day school instruction in 1858. A free vocational evening school was established by the Society at this time and this evening school is still in operation.

The second and most noted of the mechanics schools was the Franklin Institute of Philadelphia, incorporated in 1824 for the purpose of extending a knowledge of mechanical science to its members. This was to be accomplished by popular lectures, a museum of models and minerals, and a library. The Institute maintained an elementary

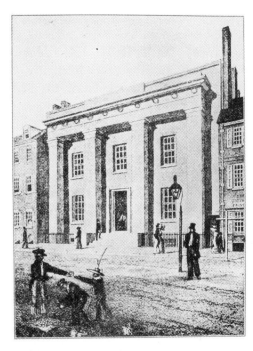

The Franklin Institute of Philadelphia Used the Building Pictured Above in 1825 for Providing Instruction to "Mechanics, Manufacturers and Others Friendly to the Useful Arts." (From *History of Manual and Industrial Education Up to 1870*, Chas. A. Bennett, by permission of Chas. A. Bennett Co., Inc.)

school to provide basic knowledge for the children of mechanics so that when they became adults they could better understand the scientific lectures. This elementary course covered three years of work and consisted of English, classical studies, modern language, mathematics, and practical science. The course in drawing which was given throughout the three-year course consisted of linear drawing, drawing of mechanical implements, maps, landscapes, models, machinery, and objects of natural history. Architectural drawing and drawing in perspective were included. The Institute provided instruction in the classics and other school subjects included in European technical and scientific schools. This Institute continued until 1832 and paved the way for the central high school of Philadelphia which opened in 1838.

Mechanics institutes were organized in Baltimore in 1825 and in Boston in 1827. The Boston institute required the instructors to deliver lectures in a "plain intelligent manner" in order that members who were lacking in educational background could understand them. The Ohio Mechanics Institute of Cincinnati was started in 1828. A course of lectures on mathematical and physical sciences was given two or three evenings each week during the winter months. Special classes in science and modern languages were organized on demand. These special classes were taught by the students themselves with some assistance from an experienced teacher.

THE AMERICAN LYCEUM

Mechanics institutes in the United States were organized in cities and provided adult education for city workers. The lyceum movement was designed to provide adult education to workers in small towns and in the country. Josiah Holbrook, a teacher and founder of an agricultural and manual labor school, published a handbook in 1826 providing for a comprehensive plan of popular education. This plan consisted of the organization of local lyceums, to be affiliated with state lyceums and these in turn with a national lyceum. Immediately after the plan was published, Holbrook succeeded in organizing 30 or 40 farmers and mechanics of Millbury, Massachusetts, into Millbury Lyceum No. 1, Branch of the American Lyceum. In a short time a number of towns in the vicinity of Millbury organized lyceums, and the Worcester County Lyceum was organized. The work of organization increased rapidly, and in 1830 a state lyceum was organized in Massachusetts. The lyceum movement spread throughout the country, and by 1833 there were about 1000 lyceums in the United States.

The plan of organization provided for meetings of local groups of farmers, mechanics, and other workers for the purpose of discussing selected subjects from the fields of natural philosophy such as mechanics, hydraulics, pneumatics, optics, chemistry, mineralogy, botany, mathematics, history, geography, astronomy, agriculture, morals, and domestic or political economy. Any person of good moral character was permitted to join the local upon the payment of the annual fee of $1. The monies collected could be used for the purchase of books, apparatus, and other supplies and equipment. The discussion leaders were selected from the membership. Among the advantages of the lyceums suggested by Holbrook was the general diffusion of practical knowledge in an economical manner. The lyceums were deemed to have good moral and political tendencies and were a means of improving the common schools. The lyceum movement, which lasted until near the middle of the nineteenth century, served as a means of building up useful knowledge in the natural sciences among people of the smaller towns of the United States.

School Substitutes for Apprenticeship

As a result of the Industrial Revolution the apprenticeship program lost its most important characteristic—the personal guidance and instruction by the master. This change in apprenticeship was due to the heavy increases in the demand for manufactured goods which were met by the use of machine operators who did not need a long period of apprenticeship to learn how to operate the machines. This fact, together with low wages, caused the apprenticeship program to decline and resulted in a decline in educational programs for young workers. The continued demand for goods resulted in a continued exploitation of workers, more especially child laborers. The wastefulness of an economic system that provided no opportunities for the children of the less favored classes to obtain an education was recognized, and educational leaders both in Europe and America began to seek substitutes for the educational opportunities formerly provided through apprenticeship.

THE ENGLISH HALF-TIME SCHOOLS

The decline of apprenticeship and the recognized evils of child labor under the factory system in England resulted in the organization of the English half-time schools. These schools were first organized in textile factories as a result of the child labor law of 1844. Under this act children could be employed for half-time work, beginning at 8 years of age, provided they spent the other half of their time in school. The law provided that children attend school for 5 hours between 8 A.M. and 6 P.M. on alternate work days. Children who were employed every day of the week were required to attend school two and one-half hours each working day. The usual practice was for half-time students to work in the factories from 6 A.M. to 12:30 P.M. with 30 minutes out for breakfast from 8 A.M. to 8:30 A.M. The lunch period extended from 12:30 P.M. to 2 P.M., after which the half-time worker was in school until 4:30 P.M. This schedule was reversed on alternate weeks, and the half-time student went to school in the mornings and to work in the afternoons. The employers were charged tuition to pay the cost of the instruction and were allowed to deduct a stated amount from the child's wages for the payment of this tuition. These schools provided instruction in reading, writing, and religion. The English half-time school plan was extended to all factories, and the beginning age of employment was increased to 10 years in 1874 and to 12 years in 1901. In the meantime, local schools and compulsory school attendance reduced the need for half-time schools, and the half-time school law was repealed in 1918.

The half-time system was subjected to both criticism and praise by English writers. In some instances the young workers attended day schools on alternate mornings and afternoons along with day school students who were in attendance each day for the entire day. The child worker had difficulty in keeping up with the all-day students. Then, too, reference has been made to the fact that the child workers constituted one social class apart from the other school students. As a result of this class distinction, they were not accorded the attention that all-day students were given. Other writers report that child workers who attended half-time schools made satisfactory progress and at the same time developed good work habits. It was also suggested in 1861 that the manual work feature of half-time schools be extended to all schools for children of the working class.

CONTINUATION SCHOOLS AND SHOPWORK INSTRUCTION IN GERMANY

Germany retained large numbers of small industries operated by craftsmen long after the Industrial Revolution, and the apprenticeship system did not decline in importance in Germany as in England. These craftsmen in small industries continued to take apprentices and develop journeymen. Large factories were operated in Germany after the Industrial Revolution, and beginning in 1853 stringent child labor laws were enacted to prevent exploitation of child labor. Children under 16 years of age who could not read and write were prohibited from working in factories. Children under 14 were limited to 6 hours of work per day and were required to attend school 3 hours per day. Children under 16 were permitted to work only between the hours of 5:30 A.M. and 6 P.M. Government inspectors were appointed to see that the regulations were enforced, and penalties were assessed for violating these regulations.

The German people established continuation schools for young workers near the beginning of the nineteenth century and provided for compulsory attendance at these schools. Some of these grew out of

Sunday schools and were a substitute for elementary school training for workers who could not attend school on week days. The compulsory attendance feature was dropped in 1859, but later in 1869 it was again required by law. Under this law employers were required to allow their workmen under 18 years of age to attend school, and the communes were empowered to require all workers under 18 years of age to attend continuation schools. Instruction in technical subjects was provided in some of these schools. Some difficulty was experienced in enforcing the law because of the limited number of continuation schools and the limited technical offerings in these schools.

Shopwork as a substitute for apprenticeship was introduced into some of the day schools of Germany. The Institute of Trades in Berlin provided this type of instruction in 1836. Theoretical instruction was given during the winter term and practical instruction during the summer. Four days a week were spent in the machine shop and two days in machine drawing and the study of machinery. The students constructed machines and tools in the shop for their own use as well as models for school use. This plan of shopwork was abandoned in 1852 because it was considered inadequate and inferior to apprenticeship. Instruction in drawing was continued, and evening classes were established after 1852 for providing instruction for employed workers. These classes met from 7 P.M. to 9 P.M three evenings each week and were taught by qualified craftsmen. The courses included practice in drawing, various kinds of arts and crafts, and the study of publications on industrial art. Many vocational schools were established by cities, employers and local authorities during the latter half of the nineteenth century. Shopwork was reinstated and instruction provided in a variety of occupations including commercial subjects and foremanship.

TECHNICAL AND ART SCHOOLS IN FRANCE

Apprenticeship in France declined rapidly after 1791, at which time the guilds of France were abolished by law. The leaders of France realized early that some substitutes for apprenticeship were needed, and they began to develop public elementary schools for basic learning and technical and art schools for occupational competency in industry. It was suggested that provisions be made in these technical and art schools for Sunday classes and evening classes. The first of the technical and art schools was established in 1788 as a private institution. It was converted into a state institution and transferred to Compiègne in 1799. Eight-year-old students were first admitted, but the age of admission was raised, and the beginning students were required to know how to read and write. Other schools were established early in the nineteenth century.

The technical schools provided shopwork for students. Special shops were maintained for the teaching of such trades as those of blacksmith, machinist, metal turner, foundryman, carpenter, joiner, cabinet maker, wood turner, and wheelwright. Two-thirds of each school day was spent in shopwork and one-third in theoretical studies. There was some question as to the value of shopwork as trade training, and the objectives of shopwork were frequently stated as means of providing the student with an opportunity to apply his theoretical knowledge rather than to develop skills in arts and crafts. These schools were designed to develop foremen and superintendents, and the shopwork provided these prospective technicians with some principles of manual operations. These schools gradually increased their entrance requirements and standards of completion and eventually became colleges for the education of engineers and technicians.

THE AMERICAN PUBLIC SCHOOLS

The apprenticeship program in the United States provided opportunities for elementary education and trade training for young workers for a period of about 200 years. The Industrial Revolution and the beginnings of the factory system in the nineteenth century caused a decline in apprenticeship and a corresponding loss of educational opportunities for these young workers. With the loss of educational opportunities, the hours of labor increased, and working conditions became more unsatisfactory. A recognition of the evils of child labor gradually emerged, and the need for a means of replacing the educational opportunities lost through apprenticeship became apparent. This need was met by the organization of the American public school system which started largely as an elementary school program and has developed into a comprehensive program of general and vocational education extending from the kindergarten through the senior college.

The present-day public school program had its origin in the compulsory education laws for children and apprentices enacted during the colonial era. These laws required parents and masters to provide educational opportunities and children and apprentices to take advantage of them. Legislation regulating child labor and compulsory school attendance made relatively slow progress during the nineteenth century, but a number of states enacted child labor laws during the latter part of that century. Compulsory school attendance laws were enacted in about half of the states between 1870 and 1890, and by 1920 all states had some type of compulsory school attendance laws. The general trend of legislation during these years was to strengthen both the compulsory attendance laws and the means of enforcement.

The child labor and compulsory attendance laws had the effect of greatly increasing the public school population, and this influx of students required more teachers and schools. The varying needs and interests of these students caused some educators to insist that curriculums be broadened to include manual and vocational subjects. As a result, manual training and other types of practical arts were introduced into the curriculum in the last quarter of the nineteenth century.

The Development of the Full-Time Vocational School in the United States

The various full-time schools previously described in this chapter were organized for purposes other than vocational education. These schools offered courses of a vocational nature, but these vocational courses were incidental or supplementary to the primary function of the school. The orphanages and correctional institutions, for example, provided various kinds of vocational courses incidental to the maintenance and correctional functions of these institutions. There were, however, some schools organized in the nineteenth century whose primary function was vocational preparation. Among these were the technical institutes and schools for special groups, the trade and business schools and the secondary schools of agriculture.

TECHNICAL INSTITUTES AND SPECIAL SCHOOLS

The technical schools came into prominence during the first quarter of the nineteenth century. These schools had objectives somewhat similar to those of the mechanics institutes and lyceums. They were designed to provide education in the practical applications of science and mathematics. The first of these schools was the Gardiner Lyceum established at Gardiner, Maine, in 1821. This institution has been classified by some writers as a manual labor school in which classical studies were combined with manual labor so that students could earn part of the cost of their education. However, the Gardiner Lyceum, which was operated with partial support from the state for a period of 10 years, was a full-time technical and scientific school with considerable emphasis on liberal or cultural subjects.

The second and most important of the technical institutes was the Rensselaer School established at Troy, New York, in 1824. The name of the institution was changed to Rensselaer Institute in 1833 and to Rensselaer Polytechnic Institute in 1850. This school was established specifically to give instruction to the sons and daughters of farmers and mechanics in the applications of experimental chemistry, philosophy, and natural history to agriculture, domestic economy, the arts, and manufactures. This school was the first institution to offer a curriculum in agriculture leading to a degree and to provide for the scientific education of women.

The first course of study at the Rensselaer School included land surveying, mensuration, and measurements of the velocity of flow of water, together with chemistry, experimental philosophy, astronomy, and geology. Hydrostatics and hydrodynamics were added in 1826. Civil engineering was added in 1828, and the first class in civil engineering was graduated in 1835. Arrangements were made with the proprietors of "well-cultivated farms and workshops in the vicinity of the school" to use their property as laboratories where the application of scientific principles might be taught. The Rensselaer Polytechnic Institute established departments of electrical engineering (1907) and chemical engineering (1913) and is presently one of the leading graduate schools of engineering in the nation.

General Samuel Chapman Armstrong, an officer in the Freedmen's Bureau, recognized a need for a special school for the education of Negroes. As a result of the efforts of General Armstrong, the Hampton (Virginia) Institute was established in 1868. The school operated a farm where students worked in squads or groups, each group working two days a week and spending the other four days in school. A plan of rotation of work and school was followed to provide continuous labor for the farm. The earnings of the students were credited to their board and tuition. Night classes were provided for students who found it necessary to work during the day. In addition to learning to farm, opportunities were provided for students to learn such trades as carpentry, house painting, shoemaking and blacksmithing, brickmaking, and janitorial work. New trades have been added from time to time, and these together with the scientific studies have made Hampton Institute one of the nation's outstanding schools.

Other institutes and special schools which emphasized the practical application of scientific facts and principles were Worcester, Massachusetts, Polytechnic Institute, established in 1868; Case School of Applied Science of Cleveland, Ohio, organized in 1881; Rose Polytechnic Institute of Terre Haute, Indiana, established in 1883; The

Hebrew Technical Institute of New York City, started in 1883; Armour Institute of Technology, established at Chicago, Illinois, in 1893; and California School of Mechanical Arts of San Francisco, organized in 1895. These schools and others of a similar nature have played an important part in the development of vocational education in the United States.

SCHOOLS FOR TRADES AND INDUSTRY

Many trade schools for employed and prospective workers in industrial vocations were organized during the last quarter of the nineteenth century. These included corporation schools, proprietary schools and endowed schools. These private and philanthropic schools were the forerunners of the public trade school which came into prominence early in the twentieth century. Some of these were designed to supplement and strengthen the apprenticeship program, and others were of a prevocational or preservice nature.

Among the first of these schools was the corporation school. This school was maintained by a business concern independently of outside control for the purpose of fitting its new employees for efficient service and for the further training of its older employees to fit them for positions of greater responsibility. Among the first corporation schools in the United States was the one developed in 1875 by the R. Hoe Printing Press Company of New York City.

The idea for this school doubtless came from the corporation school started in 1863 by the Chaix Printing Company of Paris, France. The school maintained by the R. Hoe Printing Press Company offered a class two evenings each week in which mechanical drawing, arithmetic, algebra, and geometry were taught.

Corporation schools were organized by the Baltimore and Ohio Railroad Company in 1885, by the Westinghouse Machine Company in 1888, and by the General Electric Company in 1901. Shortly after the turn of the century many other corporations organized these types of schools, and early in the twentieth century a national association for corporation schools was organized to improve the standards of corporation schools. The corporation schools followed various types of school organization. Some schools required the employee to spend the entire time in school, while others required him to divide his time between work and school. Some companies organized continuation schools which provided opportunities for the employees to study general education subjects.

Many of the trade schools were supported by endowments provided by individuals and organizations. Some of the endowed schools provided related instruction to supplement the work of apprentices, and others trained students to become journeymen in established trades. One of the best known of the endowed schools was the New York Trade School established in 1881. This institution in 1897 provided training in such trades as painting, bricklaying, plastering, stone-cutting, electrical work, steam and hot water fitting, blacksmithing, carpentry, printing, sheet metal cornice work, and plumbing. Students were taught the best procedures in each of the trades and the scientific principles upon which these procedures were based. The usual length of this day course leading to a certificate was six months.

The Williamson Free School of Mechanical Trades near Philadelphia, another endowed institution, was founded in 1891. This school was designed to take the place of the old system of apprenticeship. Students between the ages of 16 and 18 years were admitted and bound as indentured apprentices to the trustees of the school for 3 years. The apprentice was given a 6 months' preparatory course in woodworking and then placed at a woodworking or mechanical trade for the remainder of the time. While working at the trade, the apprentice received related training at the school.

During the latter years of the nineteenth century it was generally assumed that the teaching of trades should not be done at public expense, and many were of the opinion that this cost should be borne by the industry. There were, however, some persons who expressed the view that public funds should be used to provide trade education to boys and girls who did not expect to go to college. Some educators were among this latter group, and one of them, Thomas M. Balliet, superintendent of Springfield, Massachusetts, schools, established a public evening school of trades to provide opportunities for employed workers to increase their vocational efficiency. The work of this school attracted state-wide attention and paved the way for the establishment of other publicly supported trade schools for new and employed workers.

COMMERCIAL AND BUSINESS SCHOOLS

Private commercial schools or colleges flourished in the United States between the years 1852 and 1893. These schools had their origins in the commercial subjects taught during the colonial era. Cost accounting was taught as early as 1635 in the Plymouth Colony and in 1751 in the Franklin Academy. Stenography entered the curriculum about 1860. The first of the business colleges was established in 1818 by James A. Bennett, an accountant, in New York City. About 1850 the first of the chain schools of business appeared in Cincinnati and Cleveland. The Bryan-Stratton chain started in Cleveland in 1852, and by 1865 the chain included 50 schools. These schools provided training in penmanship, bookkeeping, business arithmetic, commercial law, and related subjects. The U.S. Bureau of Education indicated that there were 373 private schools for the teaching of commercial and business subjects in operation at the beginning of the twentieth century.

Commercial courses found their way into public high schools about 1890 through popular demand. The curriculums were borrowed from the private business colleges, and the principal courses were bookkeeping, shorthand, and typewriting. The public schools were slow to accept these subjects, and frequently the commercial courses were used for the placement of slow learners. Because of this fact, the public schools were unable to compete with the private business colleges, especially in the quality of output. However, the popular demand for this type of program increased, and by 1893 it was estimated that about 15,000 students were enrolled in commercial education courses in the public high schools of the nation.

SECONDARY SCHOOLS OF AGRICULTURE

Colleges and technical institutes for the study of agriculture were established early in the nineteenth century, but it was not until late in the century that agricultural high schools and other schools for the teaching of agriculture were developed. The first of the agricultural high schools was established at the University of Minnesota in 1888. Previous to the establishment of this school, an institution first known as the Storrs Agricultural School was established at Mansfield, Connecticut, in 1881. This institution, which had some of the characteristics of an institute as well as a secondary school of agriculture, has developed into the University of Connecticut.

The aim of the University of Minnesota agricultural school was to educate persons to become good farmers and housewives as well as useful citizens. The two-year course of study included English, arithmetic, algebra, accounts, physical geography, botany, physics, woodworking, mechanical drawing, horticulture, farm management, farm architecture, animal physiology, soils, fertilizer, livestock, dairying, and veterinary science. The lecture by the teacher was the most common method of instruction, and each student was required to engage in some work during the summer months. The course was extended to three years in 1892, and new buildings and equipment were added from time to time so that the work of this secondary school became more noted than that of the college. After a time, however, secondary schools of agriculture became more common throughout the state, and this school became less important.

Alabama in 1889 established two congressional district agricultural schools and started a movement that shortly spread to many states in the South. These schools, together with others established at a later date, provided practical instruction in science and agriculture. Each of the schools operated a demonstration farm which was used jointly by the schools and the state agricultural extension service. These schools were placed entirely under local control in 1935 when it was determined that congressional district schools were no longer needed. Secondary schools of agriculture were also established at the University of Nebraska and the University of Wisconsin. The Baron de Hirsch Agricultural and Industrial School at Woodbine, New Jersey, established in 1894, and the National Farm School, Doylestown, Pennsylvania, provided some opportunities for secondary school agriculture. There were only ten agricultural high schools in the country in 1898 and very few courses in agriculture in the elementary schools. The 1899 yearbook of the U.S. Department of Agriculture summarized the situation as follows: "There are a few private schools in which agriculture subjects are taught. There is some agitation in favor of the introduction of agriculture in the public schools but no definite movement in the direction has as yet been attempted."[1]

QUESTIONS FOR STUDY AND DISCUSSION

1. Discuss the organization and curriculum of some of the early schools for underprivileged children.
2. What were the characteristics of the Fellenberg schools?
3. What was the purpose of the ragged and reform schools of England and Scotland?
4. What types of schools for underprivileged children were organized in the United States?
5. Discuss the origin and development of mechanics institutes in England and in the United States.
6. What were the objectives and the type of organization of the American lyceum?

[1] Alfred C. True, "Agricultural Education in the United States," *Yearbook of the Department of Agriculture, 1899*, Washington, D.C., 1900, p. 188.

7. What school substitutes for apprenticeship were organized in England? In France? In Germany?
8. What effect did child labor laws have on public education in the United States?
9. Discuss the organization and development of the technical schools of agriculture and industry in the United States.
10. What types of schools were organized for trade training in the United States?
11. Discuss the origin and development of, commercial and business schools in the United States during the nineteenth century.
12. Indicate the names of some of the secondary schools of agriculture organized in the United States in the nineteenth century.

SOURCE REFERENCES

Anderson, Lewis F., *History of Manual and Industrial School Education,* Appleton-Century-Crofts, New York, 1926.

Bennett, Charles A., *History of Manual and Industrial Education up to 1870,* Manual Arts, Peoria, 1926.

Bennett, Charles A., *History of Manual and Industrial Education, 1870 to 1917,* Manual Arts, Peoria, 1937.

Leavitt, Frank M., *Examples of Industrial Education,* Ginn, New York, 1912.

McCarthy, John A., *Vocational Education: America's Greatest Resource,* American Technical Society, Chicago, 1952.

Mays, Arthur B., *Principles and Practices of Vocational Education,* McGraw-Hill, New York, 1948.

Prosser, Charles A., and Thomas H. Quigley, *Vocational Education in a Democracy,* American Technical Society, Chicago, 1950.

Sadler, Michael E., *Continuation Schools in England and Elsewhere,* Manchester, England, 1908.

Stombaugh, Ray M., *A Survey of the Movements Culminating in Industrial Arts Education in Secondary Schools,* Contributions to Education, No. 670, Bureau of Publications, Teachers College, Columbia University, New York, 1936.

CHAPTER FIVE

FEDERAL AID FOR VOCATIONAL EDUCATION

New developments in public school courses in vocational education came early in the twentieth century. In 1900 a few schools reported classes in "farm and garden" and "sewing and cooking." By 1910, a total of 965 schools reported an enrollment of 20,000 pupils in agriculture and in the same year there were 591 schools in which 32,870 students were enrolled in domestic economy. Enrollments in commercial education increased from 68,890 pupils to 110,925 in this same period.[1] Many of the private and endowed trade schools were converted into public schools early in the new century. Among these were the Manhattan Trade School for Girls, the Milwaukee School of Trades, and the Boston Trade School for Girls.

[1] U.S. Department of the Interior, Bureau of Education, *Reports of Commissioner of Education, 1901*, Vol. II, p. 2231, and *1911*, Vol. II, p. 1194, Washington, D. C.

The increasing demands for vocational education, as evidenced by the increase in the number of public school programs, stimulated the organization or further development of new types of vocational schools and classes in the public schools. Among these were the prevocational school, the continuation school, and the part-time cooperative school. The prevocational school was designed to provide education with an industrial bias for youth between the ages of 14 and 16, with 1 hour each day for industrial shopwork that conformed to actual industrial work. The continuation school was designed to enable students who had left the full-time school to continue their general education by attending school either in the evening or at times when they could leave their work. The part-time cooperative school was one in which the students spent alternate weeks, days or half-days in school and at work. The full-time trade school under public administration began to give more time to technical and related subject matter and to education for citizenship.

During the early years of the twentieth century the demand for vocational education at public expense became more pronounced. It was suggested that Federal aid for vocational education of less than college grade would stimulate the public schools to provide this type of training. This stimulation had proved effective in establishing the agricultural and mechanical programs of the land-grant colleges. Consequently, as a result of the activities of interested organizations, the movement for Federal aid which resulted in the passage of the Smith-Hughes Act and subsequent vocational education laws had its beginning. Some of the activities of the interested associations, some state-aid legislation, the early Federal-aid bills, and the laws enacted for vocational education of less than baccalaureate degree level are described in this chapter.

The Influence of National Agencies and Organizations

A number of Federal agencies and national organizations expressed an interest in providing additional opportunities for vocational education at the turn of the century. These groups engaged in studies, passed resolutions, and petitioned legislative bodies to provide financial assistance in establishing programs of vocational education at public expense. Among the first of these interested groups were the agricultural societies and organizations which expressed their interest through divisions of the U.S. Department of Agriculture and related organizations.

THE ACTIVITIES OF AGRICULTURAL AGENCIES

The Office of Experiment Stations of the U.S. Department of Agriculture in 1893 began to show a definite interest in agricultural education of less than college grade. This Office, through its publications and by means of addresses made by members of its staff, called attention to the need for publicly supported programs of agricultural education of less than college grade. The Office in 1902 began the publication of a section in its annual report on the progress of secondary education in agriculture, and an appropriation was made available to the Office for further studies of this nature. The Office of Experiment Stations became a clearing house for information and advice regarding problems of agricultural instruction in secondary schools.

The Association of Agricultural Colleges and Experiment Stations in 1902 recommended that the teaching of agriculture be introduced into the public schools and also in special agricultural high schools. In 1907 the Association published a syllabus for a course in agronomy for use in secondary schools and advocated the use of special agricultural high schools for the training of vocational teachers. At the 1909 meeting of the Association there was some disapproval expressed of the plan for separate agricultural high schools on the grounds that such schools would tend to become too narrowly vocational. The opinion was expressed that courses in vocational agriculture should be placed within walking or riding distance of every farm boy. Supervised home projects were suggested by a member of the Association in 1910. The Association in 1911 declared itself in favor of Federal aid for public secondary schools providing education in agriculture, in home economics, in trades and industries, and in manual training.

THE NATIONAL SOCIETY FOR THE PROMOTION OF INDUSTRIAL EDUCATION

Leaders in practical arts and vocational education realized early in the twentieth century that some type of organization was needed to stimulate the states to provide additional opportunities in vocational education. Two of these leaders, Charles R. Richards, professor of manual training, Teachers College, Columbia University, and James

P. Haney, director of art and manual training in the New York City schools, took responsibility in 1906 for leading this organization movement. These two leaders called a meeting at the Engineers Club in New York City, and, as a result of this meeting, the National Society for the Promotion of Industrial Education was organized on November 16, 1906.

The members of the Society consisted of educators, manufacturers, mechanics, businessmen, and representatives of other occupations. The purpose of the Society was to bring to public attention the importance of industrial education, to provide opportunities for the study and discussion of this problem and to promote the establishment of institutions for industrial training.

The Society attempted to accomplish its purpose by issuing bulletins containing information about the progress and problems of industrial education and holding conferences and conventions on problems involved in establishing programs of industrial education. One of the first publications of the Society was a bulletin entitled *A Symposium on Industrial Education.* The symposium consisted of answers to eleven questions concerning industrial education sent to leaders in labor and management. Both management and labor were favorable towards industrial education, and both considered trade schools a just charge on the public treasury. The two groups differed in matters of control of industrial education. One of the tasks of the Society was to harmonize these points of view with reference to control.

A bulletin entitled *Legislation upon Industrial Education* was issued in 1910. Bulletins issued in 1910 and 1911 were concerned with types and kinds of industrial programs and their social significance. The Society sponsored a number of vocational education surveys, and the findings and recommendations of each survey became the basis for a convention program. The Society was also obliged to promote industrial education among educators. The deep-seated prejudice against practical or vocational education was pronounced at this time. The Society gathered facts concerning the needs, types of organization, and kinds of industrial education.

The annual conventions of the Society during the years 1908 to 1916 were concerned primarily with state and Federal legislation relating to the organization and financing of vocational education in agriculture, in trades and industry, and in homemaking. Dr. C. A. Prosser became secretary of the Society in 1912 and began an active movement for Federal aid for vocational education. The Society was influential in securing the appointment in 1914 of a national commission on Federal aid to vocational education.

THE NATIONAL EDUCATION ASSOCIATION

A committee was appointed in 1903 at the Boston meeting of the National Education Association to investigate and report on industrial education in rural communities. The committee suggested that the larger, consolidated rural schools should teach nature study, elementary agriculture, and hand work, and the agricultural colleges should prepare teaching materials on industrial education for use in elementary and secondary schools. The committee also suggested that boys' and girls' clubs, reading courses and farmers' institutes should be promoted as a means of providing industrial education.

As a result of the interest in vocational education, a department of rural and agricultural education was organized in the National Education Association in 1908. The first meeting of the department concerned itself with values to be obtained from a study of agricultural subjects in rural schools. The NEA conventions of 1908 and 1909 centered attention on agricultural high schools. Some leaders contended that separate agricultural high schools would have a tendency to become too narrowly vocational, while others contended that special high schools of agriculture had the advantage of a greater breadth and thoroughness of agricultural instruction for mature youth.

A report in 1910 of an NEA subcommittee on industrial and technical education in the secondary schools provoked discussions on the advantages and disadvantages of special industrial schools administered by boards other than the boards of control of public secondary schools. Some educators objected to the dual system, while others insisted it was needed to maintain high standards in vocational education. The NEA in 1912 appointed a committee of educators, employers, employees, and social workers to study the needs of adolescent youth for vocational guidance and education. The committee objected to some of the early bills providing Federal aid for vocational education on the grounds that they were neither based on a study of needs nor framed in conference with school superintendents.

THE AMERICAN FEDERATION OF LABOR

The American Federation of Labor joined the movement to obtain Federal aid for vocational education early in the present century. The Federation at its annual convention in 1907 passed resolutions favorable to industrial education and in 1908 authorized the appointment of a special committee on industrial education. This committee, reporting in 1909, favored the establishment of public industrial schools. The committee suggested that the curriculum of these schools should include shop instruction for particular trades, English, mathematics, physics, chemistry, mechanics, and drawing applicable to each trade. It was also suggested that a history of the trade and a sound system of economics, including the philosophy of collective bargaining, should be included.

The 1912 convention of the Federation gave approval to the Page bill providing Federal aid for vocational education. A representative of the American Federation of Labor, speaking in 1914 to the Commission on National Aid for Vocational Education of the U.S. Congress, stated that the American Federation of Labor believed that the United States should cooperate with the states in establishing a system of vocational education.

ATTITUDES OF OTHER ORGANIZATIONS

The National Association of Manufacturers in 1912 adopted a series of resolutions setting forth the deficiencies of the public school program and suggestions for its improvement. The resolutions pointed out the need for vocational programs for employed youth and adults and for pre-employment training. The resolutions included the establishment of "independent state and local boards of industrial education consisting of one-third each professional educators, employers, and employees, thereby insuring as in the more successful European countries the proper correlation of the schools and the industries."[2] The NAM also pointed out the need for vocational guidance so that children who enter industry at 14 would enter properly advised.

The Chamber of Commerce of the United States in 1916 submitted a referendum to its member organizations concerned with the use of Federal funds for vocational education. The replies to the referendum indicated that chambers of commerce in the United States favored (1) Federal appropriations for the promotion of vocational education, (2) the allocation of these funds to the states on a uniform basis, (3) the creation of a paid representative Federal board to administer the funds, and (4) the use of advisory committees representing industry, commerce, labor, agriculture, homemaking, and general or

[2] L. S. Hawkins, C. A. Prosser, and J. C. Wright, *Development of Vocational Education*, American Technical Society, Chicago, 1951, p. 52.

vocational education to counsel with the officials of the proposed program of vocational education.

Commissions and Study Committees on Vocational Education

The growing interest in vocational education and practical arts in the first decade of the twentieth century led to the appointment of state commissions and study committees in a number of states. These commissions and committees were directed to investigate the present facilities and needs for vocational education. A number of state programs of vocational education were established as a result of the activities of these commissions and committees. Among the first and most influential of these was the commission appointed by Governor Douglas of Massachusetts.

THE DOUGLAS COMMISSION

Some writers have suggested that the present vocational education program had its beginning in Massachusetts with the report of the Douglas Commission. This Commission was appointed by Governor Douglas, in compliance with a Massachusetts law passed in 1905, to "investigate the needs for education in the different grades of skill and responsibility in the various industries in the Commonwealth. They shall investigate how far the needs are met by existing institutions and shall consider what new forms of educational effort may be advisable, and shall make such investigations as may be practicable through printed reports and the testimony of experts as to similar work done by other states, by the United States government, and foreign governments."[3]

The Commission consisted of nine persons representing manufacturing, agriculture, labor and education. It was given power to secure the services of experts and to employ a clerical staff. Carroll D. Wright, formerly United States Commissioner of Labor, was selected as chairman of the Commission. An important activity of the Commission was the several public hearings held throughout the state. The report of the Commission indicated that the following impressions were gained at these hearings:

[3] Massachusetts Commission on Industrial and Technical Education, *Report of the Commission*, Boston, 1906, pp. 1–2.

1. There was a widespread interest in special training for vocations by manufacturers, workmen, and educators.

2. There was a lack of skilled workmen in the industries, more especially workers with industrial intelligence.

3. The public schools were considered too exclusively literary and were not fully meeting the needs of modern industry and social conditions.

4. With minor exceptions, no remedial measures were suggested.

5. Many of the labor unions showed suspicion and hostility, because they feared the Commission would formulate a plan of education that would affect the labor market.

6. Technical schools could not solve the vocational school problems.

7. The expense of industrial education should be borne wholly or in part by the state.[4]

One phase of the report consisted of a study of 25,000 children of school age who were not in school. About one-sixth of these children had completed the grammar grades. They were not in school primarily because they were dissatisfied with the school offerings or because their earnings were needed by their parents. It was estimated that the earnings of not more than one-third of these children were needed to help support the family.

THE RECOMMENDATIONS OF THE COMMISSION

The Douglas Commission made recommendations with reference to the growth and development of industrial education as follows:

1. That cities and towns so modify the work in the elementary schools as to include for boys and girls instruction and practice in the elements of productive industry, including agriculture and the mechanic and domestic arts, and that the instruction in mathematics, the sciences, and drawing should show the application and use of these subjects in industrial life.

2. That all towns and cities provide, by new elective industrial courses in high schools, instruction in the principles of agriculture and the domestic and mechanic arts; that, in addition to day courses, cities and towns provide evening courses for persons already employed in trades; and that provision be made for instruction in part-time day classes of children between the ages of 14 and 18 years who may be employed during the remainder of the day.[5]

The Douglas Commission suggested that the Massachusetts General Assembly enact legislation providing for a state commission on industrial education. This commission, which was to be appointed by the governor of the state, would have responsibility for establishing

---

[4] *Ibid.*, p. 307.
[5] *Ibid.*, p. 20.

industrial schools apart from the public school system. This proposal recognized the fact that the industrial education program should not interfere with the public school program in general education. The proposal also recognized the rights of any local board of public education to include industrial education courses with the general education program if the board so desired.

COMMISSIONS AND COMMITTEES IN OTHER STATES

A number of states other than Massachusetts established state commissions on vocational education during the period from 1903 to 1913. Among these were Connecticut, Maryland, New Jersey, Maine, Michigan, Wisconsin, Indiana, and Illinois. The reports of the Douglas Commission served as a guide for the commission reports of many of these states. Differences in the commission reports reflected differences in principles and practices among the states. Leaders in vocational education in most of the states agreed that the organization of state commissions had proved to be the best means of establishing a state program of vocational education. Some of the states did not appoint state commissions but obtained data for establishing a vocational program from other sources. For example, a report issued in 1909 by the New York State Department of Labor had an important bearing on the New York State program of vocational education.

The New York State Department of Labor in 1909 published a study of the supply and demand for skilled labor and the conditions of employment of youth in New York State. This study was based on statistics gathered in 1907 and 1908 by Charles R. Richards, one of the founders of the National Society for the Promotion of Industrial Education. Records from 1182 firms employing more than 300,000 persons, many of whom were minors, were obtained. The data of the report served to provide a basis for an understanding between management and labor with reference to industrial education. The New York State report indicated that both management and labor favored a general industrial or trade preparatory school for youth from 14 to 16 years of age. Such a school was not designed to teach a trade but to give better preparation for entering industry than was being given in the common schools.

The report indicated that there was general opposition on the part of labor to trade schools operated by industrial concerns but that labor was inclined to be more favorable to trade schools administered by public officials which would provide thorough training and practical experience after the completion of the trade preparatory course. The report indicated that no trade school training can take the place of apprenticeship but that a properly organized, publicly administered trade school may, with the consent of the labor union, take the place of the first one or two years of apprenticeship and prepare the learner to gain a larger benefit from further years of experience. The industries in which the trade school system would seem to have the best possibilities include the machine and engine construction trades and the building trades.

State Legislation for Vocational Education

The report of the Douglas Commission, the activities of the other commissions and committees, and the work of the National Society for the Promotion of Industrial Education were effective in generating interest in public support for vocational education. During the 6 year period from 1906 to 1911 the following 5 states established state systems of vocational education: Massachusetts, New York, Connecticut, New Jersey, and Wisconsin. Differences were noted among these states in systems of control, but some degree of state support and control existed in each of the state systems. The state of Massachusetts established the first state system, and the Massachusetts plan with modifications was used in other states.

THE MASSACHUSETTS VOCATIONAL EDUCATION PROGRAM

The recommendations of the Douglas Commission with reference to the appointment of a state commission on vocational education were enacted into law in 1906 by the Massachusetts General Assembly. The Massachusetts Commission on Industrial and Technical Education, which was composed of 1 person from each of the following 5 occupational groups—education, business, labor, agriculture, and homemaking—was appointed to serve a 3-year term. This Commission employed Charles H. Morse, a manual training school administrator, as secretary of the Commission.

The new Commission had responsibility for putting into operation the principles established by the Douglas Commission. A survey of 900 plants was made by the Massachusetts Commission to determine the attitude of management and labor relative to the organization and administration of vocational education. It was concluded as a result of this study that it was the responsibility of the state to furnish

Federal Aid for Vocational Education Has Stimulated Many Public Schools to Establish and Maintain Effective Programs in Vocational Education. These vocational homemaking students are learning how to maintain happy and efficient homes. (Shelton from Monkmeyer)

the same type of elementary training for the industries as it was providing for the professions. It was also agreed that youth between the ages of 14 and 16 should be concerned with acquiring general mechanical knowledge.

During its 3 years of existence the Commission established, with the consent of local citizens, 16 evening schools and 4 day vocational schools. The day schools provided vocational education in agriculture, industry and homemaking. State aid equal to half of the local expenditures for these schools was supplied. The duties and responsibilities of the Commission were transferred to a reorganized State Board of Education in 1909. This Board employed C. A. Prosser as deputy commissioner in charge of vocational education.

A new idea of school and home farm cooperation became a part of the Massachusetts vocational program. This idea, referred to as the home project plan, was advocated in 1908 by Rufus W. Stimson, director of Smith's Agricultural School. The home project idea was designed to provide supervised farm experience for students who lived at home and attended day school classes. The home project replaced the compulsory farm labor which was commonly required of students in boarding schools at the beginning of the twentieth century. This idea was later incorporated in the Smith-Hughes vocational education law and is now referred to as the supervised farming program of the student in vocational agriculture engaged in the study of farming.

STATE VOCATIONAL EDUCATION LAWS IN WISCONSIN

A Wisconsin statute of 1907 granted permission for any city in the state to maintain a trade school for boys who had reached the age of 16 years (later reduced to 14 years). The law provided that the local school board might appoint an advisory committee composed of 5 citizens, each experienced in some trade, to assist in the administratration of the school. This committee had responsibility, subject to the approval of the local school board, for the preparation of courses of study, the employment and dismissal of teachers and the purchasing of supplies and equipment.

The state of Wisconsin in 1911 placed the control of vocational education on both the state and local levels in the hands of special boards of industrial education. The State Board of Industrial Education consisted of 3 skilled employees and 3 employers appointed by the governor, together with the state superintendent of education, the dean of the Extension Department, and the dean of the College of Engineering of the University of Wisconsin. The law provided for local industrial education boards for towns of 5000 or more inhabitants. These boards were composed of employers, employees, and superintendents of schools. These local boards had responsibility for employing vocational teachers and determining tax levies for industrial education.

The Wisconsin law also made provisions for apprentices and employed children. The law specified that these youth must attend school not less than five hours per week for such organized instruction as was required by the State Board of Industrial Education. All employers were required to allow youth between the ages of 14 and 16 a reduction in hours of work of not less than the number of hours the youth were required by law to attend school. This law gave to Wisconsin a system of vocational education that was controlled by boards consisting of representatives of both management and labor. Many leaders in general education objected to this type of control and referred to it as a dual system, because it divided the taxing power and control of education. Some vocational educators regarded this type of control with favor, because it was not possible for academicians to destroy the standards of instruction established by labor, industry, and the general public.

STATE PROGRAMS IN NEW YORK, CONNECTICUT, AND NEW JERSEY

The General Assembly of the state of New York, beginning in 1909, established a system of state-aided local public schools for the study of agriculture, mechanical arts and homemaking. General industrial schools were authorized for students who had completed the elementary grades or had reached the age of 14 years, and trade schools were established for persons who had reached the age of 16 years. Part-time and evening school classes as extensions of the day school program were authorized for employed workers. The vocational education program was administered by the State Board of Education and local school boards. State aid in amounts varying from about 25 to 40 percent of the cost was provided. Additional aid was given to some rural schools to enable these schools to employ instructors of agriculture during the summer months to supervise the farming activities of the students on the home farms. The law also provided for advisory boards of five members each representing local trades and industries to consult with the local school boards on matters relating to instruction in vocational subjects.

The state of Connecticut in 1909 made provisions for establishing state trade schools. These schools were administered directly by the State Board of Education, and no provision was made for local support. Appropriations for the support of these schools were made from the general treasury. These schools were open to all persons 14 years of age or older who were capable of receiving training. The scope of the vocational program was extended by legislative enactment in 1913. The school authorities in each local school district were authorized to establish all-day, part-time, and evening schools for instruction in trades and in other vocations. The local community was expected to supply the facilities and equipment. The State Board of Education provided state aid for the reimbursement of half the expenses of instruction, not to exceed a stated amount per student in attendance. Attendance at part-time and continuation classes was compulsory for all youth between 14 and 18 years of age who were not attending other schools. The State Board of Education and local school authorities were required to appoint representative advisory committees to provide counsel and guidance in the organization and operation of the vocational programs.

New Jersey in 1909 amended its laws to allow boards of education to establish schools for industrial education and provided state aid for these schools. A more comprehensive law was passed in 1913. This law authorized the State Board of Education to administer the program of industrial education. The organization of day school, continuation school and evening classes was authorized. State aid for approved schools or departments was provided in an amount equal to about half of the current cost of operating the program. The vocational departments were required to consist of courses, students, and teachers separate from those in general education.

Bills in the National Congress Providing Federal Aid for Vocational Education (1901 to 1916)

The National Congress prior to 1917 enacted a number of laws providing Federal aid for educational programs in or under the control of institutions of higher learning in the United States. Among these were the Morrill Acts of 1862 and 1890 and the Nelson Amendment of 1907, providing aid for land-grant colleges; the Hatch Act of 1887 and the Adams Act of 1906, allocating aid to agricultural experiment stations and the Smith-Lever Act of 1914 for cooperating with the states in agricultural extension programs.

During the 17-year period prior to the passage of the Smith-Hughes vocational education law, a number of bills concerned with some aspects of vocational education were introduced in the National Congress. The first of these, introduced in 1901, was designed to provide Federal aid to industrial institutes with state charters. It was not until the Davis bill of 1909 that the term *vocational education* appeared in these bills. These bills, some of which are summarized below, represent the varying points of view relative to the organization of vocational education. Their progress in Congress and final disposition indicate the difficulties encountered in reconciling the varying viewpoints of the leaders of the movement of Federal aid for vocational education.

THE POLLARD BILL

One of the early bills providing Federal aid to education was introduced on February 21, 1906, by Representative Ernest M. Pollard of Nebraska. A similar bill was introduced in the Senate the next day by Senator E. J. Burkett of Nebraska. The Pollard bill provided Federal funds to the normal schools of the states for training teachers of agriculture, manual training, domestic science, and related subjects. The bill provided that half of an annual appropriation which reached a maximum of $1 million was to be equally divided among the states, and the other half was to be allotted to the normal schools in proportion to the length of their terms and number of students. This bill was before Congress during the years 1906 to 1911. It was supported by the National Education Association. Although it failed to pass, it doubtless had some influence in making Federal funds included in the Nelson Amendment available for training teachers of agriculture and mechanical arts.

THE DAVIS AND DOLLIVER–DAVIS BILLS

In 1907 Representative Charles R. Davis of Minnesota introduced his first bill providing Federal aid for industrial education. This bill proposed to allocate Federal funds to district agricultural high schools for the teaching of agriculture and home economics and to secondary schools in urban communities for the teaching of mechanical arts and home economics. The bill also provided funds for branch agricultural experiment stations. The Secretary of Agriculture was designated in the bill as its administrator.

The Davis bill was amended in 1909 to include an appropriation for the teaching of agriculture, home economics, and domestic arts in public normal schools. This bill was approved by the National Grange, the Farmers National Congress, and the National League for Industrial Education. Some educators strongly opposed the bill because the administration of it was placed in the U.S. Department of Agriculture. These objectors were fearful that it would result in a dual system of education.

Senator Dolliver introduced a revised version of the Davis bill into the U.S. Senate in 1910. This revision, which had the approval of the American Federation of Labor, provided lump sums rather than per capita apportionments to the states. The Senate Committee on Agriculture and Forestry, of which Senator Dolliver was chairman, combined the Dolliver-Davis bill with the McLaughlin House bill providing Federal aid for agricultural extension, all to be administered by the Secretary of the Interior. This combination was made with the hope that all interested organizations would unite in the support of the bill. However, new opposition arose. The Association of American Agricultural Colleges and Experiment Stations gave its support to the original

McLaughlin extension bill, and the National Society for the Promotion of Industrial Education voiced objections to the Dolliver-Davis bill and insisted that it be amended to provide a clear definition of its purpose, a limitation on the amount of money appropriated for each purpose, the matching of Federal funds by states, state plans for vocational education and adequate Federal supervision. Senator Dolliver died in 1910, and friends of the bill did not seek its passage but concentrated on the Page bill of 1911.

THE PAGE BILLS

In March, 1911, Senator Carroll S. Page of Vermont introduced a bill proposing Federal appropriations to the states as follows: .

(1) $5,000,000 annually for instruction in the trades and industries, home economics, and agriculture in public schools of secondary grade in the States, Territories, and District of Columbia; (2) $4,000,000 annually for instruction in agriculture and home economics in State district agricultural schools of secondary grade; (3) $1,000,000 annually for branch agricultural experiment stations at the agricultural high schools; (4) $500,000 annually, with additional amounts increasing by $200,000 for five years, for extension departments of agriculture, trades and industries, home economics, and rural affairs, at the land-grant colleges, or State departments of agriculture, provided the States appropriated sums equal to the additional amounts; and (5) $1,000,000 annually for instruction in agriculture, trades and industries, and home economics at State and Territorial normal schools.[6]

The Page bill provided for a division of funds in states that maintained separate schools for Negroes in proportion to the population of the two races. The bill also provided for short continuation and evening schools and was to be administered by the Secretary of the Interior, with the cooperation of the Secretaries of Agriculture, Commerce, and Labor.

The Page bill was amended in the Senate in 1912 to provide funds for the preparation of teachers and to provide that the Secretary of Agriculture administer the funds allocated to extension departments and branch agricultural experiment stations. The states, under this amendment, were directed to provide a board for vocational education to control Federal funds for vocational instruction and teacher training in the states.

[6] Alfred C. True, *A History of Agricultural Education in the United States,* U.S. Department of Agriculture, Miscellaneous Publication No. 36, Washington, D.C., 1929, p. 364.

The Page bill was withdrawn after consultation with leaders in education and agriculture, and a substitute bill, approved by representatives of the American Federation of Labor and the National Society for the Promotion of Industrial Education, was introduced. The substitute bill carried no appropriation for branch agricultural experiment stations. The Congress could not agree on the provisions of the Page bill and adjourned without final action.

The Page bill was again introduced in Congress in 1913, but it soon became apparent that Congress would not approve the bill because of the strong opposition to combining appropriations for agricultural extension and vocational education in one bill. When it became evident that the Page bill would not pass, the National Society for the Promotion of Industrial Education and interested individuals suggested that the Congress, by joint resolution, establish a commission on national aid for vocational education. This joint resolution, which was in effect a substitute for the Page bill, passed both houses and was approved by President Wilson on January 20, 1914.

THE COMMISSION ON NATIONAL AID TO VOCATIONAL EDUCATION

The Commision on National Aid to Vocational Education consisted of four members from the National Congress and five leaders in the movement for vocational education. Senator Hoke Smith of Georgia was made chairman of the Commission, and Dr. C. A. Prosser, executive secretary of the National Society for the Promotion of Industrial Education, was included in the membership. The Commission had no members from organizations especially concerned with agricultural education.

The Commission held numerous conferences to determine (1) the need for vocational education, (2) the need for Federal grants, (3) the kinds of vocational education for which grants should be made, (4) the extent and conditions under which aid should be granted, and (5) proposed legislation. The Commission report, made in June, 1914, recommended Federal aid (1) for training teachers of agricultural, of trade and industrial, and of home economics subjects; (2) for paying part of the salaries of teachers of agricultural and of trade and industrial subjects; and (3) for studies and investigations.

The report specified that aid should be provided for day schools, part-time schools, and evening schools. Schools receiving aid should be supported and controlled by the public, should be of less than college grade and should be designed to prepare persons over 14 years of age for useful employment. The report contained suggestions on the amount of the grants, the administration of the program and the safeguarding of funds. The Commission report provided for state boards of vocational education designated by the several states and a Federal board composed of the Secretaries of the Interior, Agriculture, Commerce, and Labor, the Postmaster General and the Commissioner of Education who was designated as chairman. The report of the Commission was presented to Congress in 1914 and bills were introduced into the Senate by Senator Hoke Smith and into the House by Representative Dudley M. Hughes in 1915. Some amendments were added and the Smith-Hughes bill became a law when signed by President Wilson on February 23, 1917.

The National Vocational Education Laws[7]

During the time intervening between the passage of the Smith-Hughes Act in 1917 and the present, the Congress of the United States has passed a number of acts relative to some aspect of vocational education. These have included amendments and extensions of the Smith-Hughes Acts, acts concerned with vocational rehabilitation, surplus equipment, war training and reconversion, manpower development, and laws providing additional funds for vocational education. A discussion of the provisions of the Smith-Hughes Act and subsequent laws providing additional funds for vocational education is shown below.

THE SMITH–HUGHES ACT
(Public Law 347, 64th Congress)

The Smith-Hughes Act provided a continuing appropriation for vocational education in agriculture, in trades and industry, and in homemaking and for teacher training in each of these fields. Funds were appropriated for the administration of the program on the national level. The funds appropriated for the teaching of agriculture and of trades and industry increased annually from the fiscal year ending June 30, 1918, to the fiscal year ending June 30, 1926, at which time the appropriation reached the maximum of $3 million annually for each of the two services, and this amount has been appropriated an-

[7] The texts of the Smith-Hughes Act and of the Vocational Education Act of 1963 are included in the Appendix.

nually thereafter. The states, under the provisions of the law, were permitted to use an amount not to exceed 20 percent of the appropriation for trade and industrial education for salaries of teachers of home economics. The continuing appropriation for teacher training reached its maximum in 1921, at which time an annual appropriation of $1,000,000 was provided. A total of $200,000 annually was appropriated for the Federal administration, and sufficient additional funds were appropriated to insure that each state received a minimum of $10,000 each for the teaching of agriculture, of trades and industry, and of teacher training.

The Federal funds were appropriated as a reimbursement for the salaries of teachers, supervisors, and directors of agricultural subjects, and the funds so appropriated were allotted to each state in the proportion that its rural population bore to the rural population of the United States. The funds appropriated as a reimbursement for the salaries of teachers of trade and industrial and of home economics subjects were allocated to each state in the proportion that its urban population bore to the urban population of the United States. The law required that for each dollar of Federal money expended the state or local community or both must expend an equal amount.

The Smith-Hughes Act provided for a Federal Board for Vocational Education and a state board of not less than three members for each state. Each state was required to prepare a state plan for vocational education and to agree (1) that the Federally aided program of vocational education would be under public supervision and control, (2) that the controlling purpose would be to fit for useful employment, (3) that the vocational education would be of less than college grade and designed to meet the needs of persons over 14 years of age who had entered upon or who were preparing to enter the occupation for which they were receiving training, and (4) that the state or local community or both would provide the necessary plant and equipment.

Students in agricultural education were required to engage in a supervised practice program for a minimum of six months each year. Certain specifications with reference to length of term, use of funds for part-time classes and age of evening school students were made in the use of funds for trades and industry and for home economics education. The specifications for the use of teacher training funds limited the amount of funds for any one service and provided standards for the use of these funds. The Act also provided for the custody of the Federal funds and directed the Federal Board for Vocational Education to engage in the necessary studies and investigations to insure an efficient and productive program.

THE GEORGE–REED ACT
(Public Law 702, 70th Congress)

Congress recognized a need for additional Federal funds for vocational home economics education and vocational agricultural education and in 1929 passed the George-Reed Act. This Act authorized an annual appropriation for vocational agricultural education and vocational home economics education for a period of five years ending June 30, 1934. The sum of $500,000 was authorized for the first year, and this was increased by $500,000 each year until the total of $2,500,000 was reached. These amounts were divided equally between agricultural education and home economics education and were in addition to the appropriations in the Smith-Hughes Act.

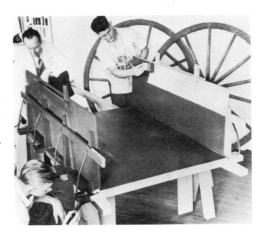

Future Farmers Learn Construction and Repair of Farm Machinery in the Agricultural Mechanics Shop. (U.S. Office of Education)

The organization and administration of agricultural education and home economics education under the George-Reed Act were similar to the provisions of the Smith-Hughes Act, with the following exceptions: (1) The allocation to the states of funds for agricultural education in the George-Reed Act was on the basis of farm population instead of rural population as provided in the Smith-Hughes Act. (2) The allocation to the states of funds for home economics was on the basis of rural instead of urban population. (3) The George-Reed Act was an authorization for funds whereas the Smith-Hughes Act was an appropriation. (4) Certain changes were made in the organization and administration of home economics education so that this service might be organized more nearly like the agricultural education program.

THE GEORGE–ELLZEY ACT
(Public Law 245, 73rd Congress)

As the time drew near for the expiration of the George-Reed Act, leaders in vocational education realized that Federal funds would be needed to insure the further promotion of the vocational education program. Accordingly, Congress was asked to provide additional funds and, in response to this request, enacted the George-Ellzey Act. This Act authorized an appropriation of $3 million annually for each of the fiscal years ending in 1935, 1936, and 1937. The amounts authorized were to be divided equally among vocational education in agriculture, and in home economics. The funds for agricultural education and home economics education were allocated to the states on the same basis as was provided in the George-Reed Act. The funds for trade and industrial education were allocated on the basis of nonfarm population. Funds for administration and for providing minimum allotments of $5,000 to each state for each field were provided. The Act in most particulars was administered in a manner similar to that of the Smith-Hughes and George-Reed laws.

THE GEORGE–DEEN ACT
(Public Law 673, 74th Congress)

Leaders in vocational education realized that the expiration of the George-Ellzey Act in 1937 would adversely affect the national program of vocational education and accordingly petitioned Congress, through the American Vocational Association, to provide additional supplementary funds for vocational education. Congress, in response to this need, passed the George-Deen Act which became effective July 1, 1937. This Act differed from the two preceding acts by authorizing a substantial increase in funds on a continuing basis and including distributive education in the Federally aided program. The Act authorized the sum of $12,000,000 annually, to be divided equally among agricultural education, home economics education, and trade and industrial education. An additional sum of $1,200,000 was provided for distributive education, and $1,000,000 was provided for teacher training. Funds were also provided for administration and for minimum allotments to the states, making an estimated total of $14,413,000. These funds were authorized for use in the states and territories.

The funds for agricultural education, homemaking education,

and trade and industrial education were allotted to the states on the same bases as were provided in the George-Ellzey Act. The funds for distributive education and for teacher training were allotted to each state in the ratio that the population of the state bore to the population of the United States and territories. A sliding scale of matching Federal funds was provided with half of the Federal appropriations matched for the first five years and an increase in amounts matched by 10 percent per year for the next 5 years until all Federal funds were matched for the fiscal year beginning July 1, 1946, and thereafter. Reimbursement for distributive education was limited to part-time and evening classes, and restrictions were placed on funds used for plant training. With these and one or two other exceptions, the authorizations of the George-Deen Act was subject to the same conditions and limitations as in the previous acts.

THE ADVISORY COMMITTEE ON EDUCATION

The President of the United States, in signing the George-Deen bill, stated that he did so with some reluctance and indicated that he would appoint an advisory committee on vocational education to make a study of Federal aid to vocational education and other matters. The committee was appointed and the scope of its activities extended to include Federal relationships to all education. This committee consisted of 24 persons, with Floyd W. Reeves as chairman. The committee prepared a number of staff studies on various aspects of education including one on vocational education. The report on vocational education made various references to the need for a revision of the laws concerned with Federal aid to vocational education to grant more authority to the local school administration. It was also suggested that Federal funds for vocational education of less than senior college grade should be consolidated into one fund and made available for such types of vocational education and vocational guidance as may be determined by the states. The report also emphasized the need for funds for general education and suggested that Federal appropriations for vocational education should not be increased until a relatively generous provision of Federal funds for general education was made.

THE GEORGE–BARDEN ACT
(Public Law 586, 79th Congress)

An amendment to the George-Deen Act became a law August 1, 1946. This law, referred to as the George-Barden Act, authorized increased appropriations for the programs of vocational education specified in the George-Deen Act and provided for more flexibility in the use of these funds. Annual authorizations were included in the amount of $10,000,000 for agricultural education, $8,000,000 each for home economics and trade and industrial education and $2,500,000 for distributive education. The authorizations included in the Act were available for vocational education programs in the United States, the territories of Alaska and Hawaii, the island of Puerto Rico, and the District of Columbia. The allocations to the states and territories were made in the same manner as were the allocations included in the George-Deen Act. Minimum allotments were provided annually in the Act to each state in the amount of $40,000 each for vocational education in agriculture, in home economics, and in trades and industry. The minimum allotment for distributive education was $15,000 annually.

The George-Barden Act made no specific allocation of funds for teacher training or for vocational guidance, but each state board for vocational education was permitted to use such amounts for these purposes as it deemed necessary. The George-Barden Act authorized the use of Federal funds for some items not specifically authorized in previous acts. Among these were funds for the salary and expenses of state directors of vocational education, for salaries and travel expenses of vocational counselors, for training and work experience training programs for out-of-school youth, for supervision of Future Farmer and New Farmer activities, and for the purchase or rent of equipment and supplies for vocational instruction. The Act provided that after June 30, 1951, not more than 10 percent of these funds could be used for the purchase or acquisition of equipment. The Act provided for more flexibility in the use of funds for administration, and, in general, the use of funds was subject to the conditions and limitations included in the previous vocational education laws.

THE VOCATIONAL EDUCATION ACT OF 1963
(Public Law 88–210, 88th Congress)

In 1963, Congress enacted legislation designed to (1) extend present programs and develop new programs of vocational education, (2) encourage research and experimentation, and (3) provide work-study programs to enable youth to continue vocational education. The 1963 Act also amended the Smith-Hughes, George-Barden and NDEA Acts.

Authorizations beginning at $60,000,000 for the fiscal year 1964 and increasing each year to a maximum of $225,000,000 for fiscal

1967 and thereafter were made for extension and development and for research and experimentation. Ninety percent of these sums are for extension and development programs and were distributed among the states by a formula based on population ratios and per capita income. The remaining 10 percent was reserved for grants to state boards and institutions by the U.S. Commissioner of Education to pay part of the cost of research and training programs, designed to meet the special vocational educational needs of youth.

The sums allocated to the states may be used for (1) vocational education programs for persons of various levels of achievement and various occupations except those requiring the baccalaureate degree; (2) for teacher education, administration, and other ancillary services; and (3) for the construction of area vocational education school facilities. Funds received for fiscal 1965 and thereafter must be matched on a dollar for dollar basis. One-third of each state's annual allotment prior to July 1, 1968 and 25 percent thereafter must be used for youth who have left school and/or for the construction of area schools. At least 3 percent of a state's allotment must be used for ancillary services.

The Act provided for administration by the state board for vocational education, for national and state advisory committees, and a state plan indicating the manner in which the state's program will be operated. The state plan must provide for cooperative arrangements with state public employment offices for occupational information regarding placement opportunities.

Special authorizations of $30 million for fiscal 1965, $50 million for 1966, and $35 million each for fiscal years 1967 and 1968 were made for work-study programs and residential vocational schools. Funds for the first 2 years do not require matching, but thereafter the Federal contribution will be 75 percent of the total amount expended. The U.S. Commissioner of Education had responsibility for determining the division of the funds between work-study and residential programs.

Funds for work-study programs were allocated to the states in proportion to the number of youth 15 to 20 years of age. Such programs must be furnished only to full-time students. Compensations may not exceed $45 per month or $350 per academic year except in special cases. Employment under the program shall be by the local educational agency or other public agency. The U.S. Commissioner may also make grants for the construction, equipment, and operation of residential schools to provide vocational education for youth between 15 and 20 years of age inclusive, who need full-time study on a residential basis. Special consideration in making grants will be given to the needs of areas having substantial school dropouts and unemployed youth.

AMENDMENTS TO SMITH–HUGHES AND GEORGE–BARDEN LAWS

The Smith-Hughes Act was amended in 1917 to permit the use of Federal funds for the purchase of books and periodicals and for printing, binding, and postage on foreign mail. The Act was extended to Hawaii in 1924 and to Puerto Rico in 1931. An annual authorization of $30,000 was made for the extension to Hawaii, and $105,000 for the extension to Puerto Rico. The funds in each of these extensions were made available under the same terms and conditions that applied to the states.

The George-Barden Act was extended to the Virgin Islands in 1950 with an annual authorization of $40,000. Three amendments to the George-Barden Act were made in 1956. These authorized annual appropriations as follows: (1) $5,000,000 to 1961 (later made permanent) for practical nurse education. (2) $375,000 for vocational education in the fishery trades and industry and distributive occupations therein. (3) $15,000,000 to 1962 (later made permanent) for area vocational education programs.

The Smith-Hughes and George-Barden Acts were amended in 1963 to (1) permit state boards for vocational education with the approval of the U.S. Commissioner of Education to transfer Federal and state matching funds formerly earmarked for a special service to another occupational category; (2) authorize the use of funds for agriculture for vocational education in any occupation involving knowledge and skills in agricultural subjects without directed or supervised practice; (3) permit funds earmarked for home economics to be used for training for gainful employment in any occupation involving knowledge and skills in home economics subjects; (4) require that at least 10 percent of funds earmarked for home economics be used to fit persons for gainful employment in occupations involving knowledge and skills in home economics subjects; (5) use George-Barden distributive education funds for pre-employment training in schools other than part-time or evening schools; (6) permit the use of funds earmarked for trade and industrial education for pre-employment training in schools and classes in session less than 9 months per year and 30 hours per week in single-skilled or semiskilled occupations without the requirement of 50 percent of the time to be given to shopwork; and (7) use less than one-third of funds earmarked for trade and industrial education for part-time classes.

QUESTIONS FOR STUDY AND DISCUSSION

1. In what ways did agricultural agencies and organizations assist in stimulating interest in vocational education?
2. When and for what purpose was the National Society for the Promotion of Industrial Education organized? Discuss some of the activities of this society.
3. What other organizations assisted in the movement for Federal aid to vocational education, and what was the nature of their contributions?
4. What were the recommendations of the Douglas Commission, and what effect did these have on the progress of vocational education?
5. What were the essential provisions of the Massachusetts law establishing a state program of vocational education?
6. In what respects did the Massachusetts state program of vocational education differ from that of Wisconsin?
7. What were the provisions of some of the bills introduced in the National Congress prior to 1917 that related to Federal aid for vocational education?
8. What was the National Commission on Vocational Education, and what were the recommendations of this Commission?
9. What are some of the principal provisions of the Smith-Hughes law?
10. In what way did the George-Reed, George-Ellzey, and George-Deen laws differ from the Smith-Hughes law?
11. What are the principal ways in which the George-Barden law differs from the Smith-Hughes law?
12. Discuss the provisions of the Vocational Education Act of 1963.

SOURCE REFERENCES

Bennett, Charles A., *History of Manual and Industrial Education, 1870 to 1917*, Manual Arts, Peoria, 1937.

Blauch, Lloyd E., *Federal Cooperation in Agricultural Extension Work, Vocational Education and Vocational Rehabilitation*, Federal Security Agency, Office of Education, Bulletin, 1933, No. 15, Washington, D.C., 1935.

Commission on National Aid to Vocational Education, *Report of Commission*, House of Representatives Document 1004, 63rd Congress, 2nd Session, Washington, D.C., 1914.

Hawkins, Layton S., Charles A. Prosser, and John C. Wright, *Development of Vocational Education*, American Technical Society, Chicago, 1951.

Mays, Arthur B., *The Concept of Vocational Education in the Thinking of the General Educator, 1845 to 1945,* University of Illinois Bulletin, Volume 43, No. 65, Univ. of Illinois, Urbana, 1946.

Stimson, Rufus W., and Frank W. Lathrop, *History of Agricultural Education of Less Than College Grade in the United States,* Federal Security Agency, Office of Education, Vocational Division Bulletin No. 217, Washington, D.C., 1942.

Struck, F. Theodore, *Foundations of Industrial Education,* Wiley, New York, 1930.

True, Alfred C., *A History of Agricultural Education in the United States,* U.S. Department of Agriculture, Miscellaneous Publication No. 36, Washington, D.C., 1929.

U.S. Department of Health, Education, and Welfare, Office of Education, *Digest of Annual Reports of State Boards for Vocational Education For Fiscal Year Ending June 30, 1962,* Washington, D.C., 1963.

U.S. Senate Committee on Labor and Public Welfare, *Selected Education Acts of 1963,* Washington, D.C., 1963.

CHAPTER SIX

ADMINISTRATION OF THE
FEDERALLY AIDED PROGRAM
OF VOCATIONAL EDUCATION

The U.S. Congress in 1917 provided for a Federally aided program of vocational education of less than college grade on the theory that vocational education is a matter of national interest and is essential to the national welfare and that Federal funds are necessary to stimulate and assist the states in making adequate provisions for the program. The Smith-Hughes Act, commonly referred to as the organic vocational education act, contained specifications for the organization and administration of the Federally aided vocational education program on national, state and local levels. This Act also recognized the fact that many of the policies and procedures necessitated cooperation between the Federal government and the states, and provisions for implementing this cooperation were made.

The program of vocational education has been developed through the years in accordance with the two basic ideas suggested above. The vocational divisions on both the Federal and state levels have cooperated in formulating policies and procedures designed to make effective the several laws providing Federal aid for vocational education. These cooperative agreements, which from time to time have required revisions, have been published in a U.S. Office of Education bulletin entitled *Administration of Vocational Education*. This publication, which is essentially one of administrative relationships between the Federal government and the states, has served through the years as a guide in the organization and administration of the vocational program on the Federal, state and local levels. Some of the more important administrative decisions, together with their resulting procedures, are set forth in this chapter.

Organization for Vocational Education

Leaders in vocational education recognized early in its history that publicly supported programs of vocational education functioned best when these programs were organized and directed by boards composed of laymen who had primary responsibility for approving polices suggested by professional educators who were in the employ of the respective lay boards. For this reason, in the beginning, the organization for vocational education was entrusted to boards of control on Federal, state, and local levels.

THE FEDERAL BOARD FOR VOCATIONAL EDUCATION

In accordance with recommendations of the Commission on National Aid to Vocational Education, the Smith-Hughes vocational education law made provisions for a Federal Board for Vocational Education. The provisions of the law, which differed somewhat from the Commission recommendations, provided for a Board consisting of four ex-officio members—the Secretaries of Agriculture, Commerce and Labor and the U.S. Commissioner of Education—and three citizens—one representing agriculture, one representing labor, and one representing manufacturing and commercial interests. The appointive members received their appointments from the President of the United

States, by and with the advice and consent of the U.S. Senate. The Federal Board for Vocational Education was an independent agency, responsible to the President and the Congress of the United States. The three appointive members were employed to devote full time to their duties as members of the Board.

The Federal Board organization consisted of a standing committee composed of the appointive members and the U.S. Commissioner of Education, a professional staff and the Board itself. The main function of the Board was to serve as a legislative body. The standing committee was made responsible for routine business, auditing, problems encountered in dealing with the states, and approval of state plans. The professional staff had responsibility for executing policies approved by the Board, administering the budget, recommending appointments, and engaging in other delegated responsibilities. The plan of organization also included a conference board composed of the members of the standing committee and the head officers of the professional staff. This conference board existed as an agency for the discussion of principles and practices operating on the Federal level.

The Federal Board for Vocational Education operated from July 1917 to October 10, 1933, free from undesirable political influences. The Board made no political appointments, and during its 16 years of existence it maintained cordial relations with agriculture, industry and labor. Some attempts were made during the years of its existence to transfer its duties to some agency of general education, ostensibly to unify control of education. In 1932 President Hoover recommended that the duties of the Board be transferred to the U.S. Office of Education, but Congress intervened and prevented the transfer. President Roosevelt, by executive order in 1933, transferred the functions of the Federal Board for Vocational Education to the U.S. Department of the Interior and provided that the Federal Board for Vocational Education serve in an advisory capacity without pay. The Secretary of the Interior placed the functions of the Board in the Office of Education.

The appointive members of the Federal Board for Vocational Education resigned in 1933, and no new appointments were made until 1935, at which time appointments were made to the Federal Advisory Board for Vocational Education. The appointive members served without pay until May 16, 1946, at which time President Truman, by executive order, abolished the Federal Board for Vocational Education. Thus by a series of executive orders the lay board, which Congress had decreed by law and vocational educators and

Apprentice Carpenters Receive Related Training in Organized Classes Conducted by Public Schools. (Board of Vocational Education and Rehabilitation, Illinois)

others interested in vocational education had insisted was necessary for the proper organization and administration of vocational education, was abolished.

ORGANIZATION OF THE FEDERAL DIVISION OF VOCATIONAL EDUCATION

The national vocational education acts place responsibility on the Federal authority for vocational education for making studies, investigations and reports, and for cooperating with the states in carrying out the provisions of the acts. The acts also authorize the employment of the personnel needed for meeting these responsibilities. The organization of the Federal staff personnel in vocational education has varied through the years. The first organization consisted, with some modifications, of a grouping of staff members according to the service fields of agricultural education, home economics education, and trade and industrial education. Each service was headed by a chief of service responsible to the Federal director of vocational education. The service fields of distributive and occupational information and guidance were added later. The staff members of each service made contacts with corresponding staff members on the state level.

This type of organization was continued until 1947, at which time a new plan of organization was put into effect. This plan involved the grouping of the personnel into three branches designated as Program Planning, Field Service, and Plans and Reports. The various specialists in the service fields were grouped under the Program Planning Branch, and their services were made available to the states by request. Responsibility for routine visits to the states was assigned to the Field Service Branch. This form of organization had the effect of changing the type of supervision from that of special or subject matter supervision to general or nonspecialized supervision.

The 1947 organization was changed in 1950 to the service branch type of organization of previous years. The Vocational Education Act of 1963 brought about another form of organization having some of the characteristics of the type of organization of 1947. The new organization which went into effect in 1964 consists of a Division of Vocational and Technical Education in the Bureau of Educational Assistance programs, Office of Education, U.S. Department of Health, Education, and Welfare. The division is administered by an assistant commissioner for vocational and technical education and is divided into the following three major program areas: Professional Resources, Field Administration, and Research and Development. The Field Administration area operates through nine regional offices in the cities of Boston, New York, Charlottesville, Atlanta, Chicago, Kansas City, Dallas, Denver, and San Francisco. A branch of the San Francisco office is located in Seattle.

STATE BOARDS FOR VOCATIONAL EDUCATION

The vocational education acts and related policy statements provide that each state shall create a state board for vocational education to cooperate with the Federal authority in the administration of the Federal vocational education acts. The Smith-Hughes Law directed that the board be created by legislative authority and that it consist of not less than three members.

Each of the 50 states, the District of Columbia, Puerto Rico, Guam, and the Virgin Islands have boards for vocational education.

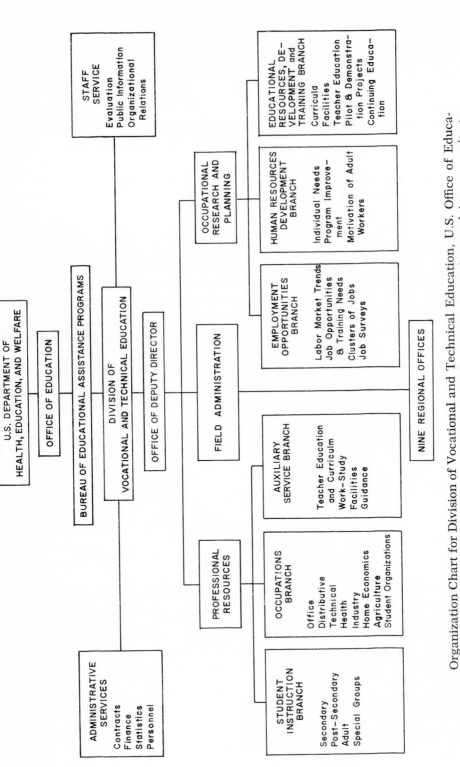

Organization Chart for Division of Vocational and Technical Education, U.S. Office of Education. The Division of Vocational and Technical Education operates in an advisory capacity to state and, through state, to local vocational services. (Adapted from *Tooling Up for the Future*, Volume 24, No. 7, American Vocational Journal, Washington, D.C., October, 1964)

The state board of education has been designated as the state board for vocational education in most of the states. Seven states do not have state boards of education and three states have state boards for vocational education that are not identical with the state board of education. These separate boards usually include members from industry, labor, and agriculture and are representative of management and labor. Separate boards afford some protection against any extreme emphasis on general or academic education that may tend to reduce the effectiveness of state and local programs of vocational education.

State boards for vocational education consist of an average of eight members each. In most of the states the governor appoints all or a major portion of these members. The chief state school officer is an ex-officio member of the state board for vocational education in four of the states that have a separate state board for vocational education. One state forms a state board for vocational education by adding representatives of management, labor, and/or agriculture to the existing state board of education. The chief state school officer has been designated as executive officer of the state board for vocational education in most of the states and territories of the United States.

ORGANIZATION OF STATE DIVISIONS OF VOCATIONAL EDUCATION

The state program of vocational education for public schools is organized as a separate division or bureau of the state department of education in most of the states. This program in a few states is in some other major division or bureau such as instructional services. The vocational division includes such services as agricultural education, distributive education, homemaking education, and trade and industrial education. Area vocational programs and practical nurse education are included either as separate services or under the trade and industrial education service. Vocational guidance and vocational rehabilitation were at one time in the vocational division. These programs in most states are in separate divisions responsible directly to the chief state school officer. Some states are revising the plan of organization of the state staff in vocational education to more nearly conform to the 1964 plan of the Federal Division of Vocational and Technical Education.

The vocational division in most states is headed by a state director of vocational education. The title of this position in some states is assistant commissioner, assistant division chief, or assistant superintendent. The state director of vocational education is responsible to the executive officer of the state board for vocational education for the general administration of the vocational education program. His duties are concerned with staff personnel relations, state plans, budgeting of funds, financial records, public relations, teacher training, and studies and investigations. The director in most of the states gives full time to vocational education. Other staff members of the division are state supervisors of the various services, assistant state supervisors, and district supervisors. The number of each depends upon the scope of the program for the service. Some states have subject matter specialists, itinerant teacher trainers, property supervisors, and finance officers. For the most part, the state vocational education staff serves in an advisory capacity to local vocational teachers to assist them to improve local programs of vocational education.

LOCAL ORGANIZATION FOR VOCATIONAL EDUCATION

The organization of a local program of vocational education is under the control of a local board of education. The size of the geographical area under the jurisdiction of this board varies from a small community to a county, which means that a local board may have jurisdiction over from 1 to more than 100 vocational teachers. These boards usually consist of from 3 to 7 members, and these members are charged with responsibility for organizing and operating the local public school systems. The principal duties of the local school board are to legislate and to approve policy, and an important function of the board is to employ a local school superintendent and delegate to him the policy executing and, in general, the policy planning functions.

Local teachers of vocational education have the same relationship to the local board of education and the local superintendent of schools as other teachers in the school system. This means that responsibility for employing, discharging, fixing salaries, and determining duties and responsibilities is vested in the local school authorities. However, if the local board of education receives a reimbursement from the state board for vocational education for a portion of the salary of the vocational teacher, certain standards with reference to the qualifications of the teacher and the use of his time must be observed to comply with Federal and state laws and regulations relative to the use of funds.

Local programs of vocational education in local school districts with relatively large student populations are frequently administered by a person known as a local supervisor, local director, or assistant superintendent for vocational education. This officer is responsible to the local superintendent of schools or his assistant for the organization and operation of the program in each of the vocational services represented in the school. This person frequently has responsibility for practical arts courses as well as vocational courses. His principal duties are concerned with improving instruction, recommending personnel, purchasing supplies and equipment, administering the budget, public relations, and planning and conducting studies and investigations.

ADVISORY COMMITTEES

Advisory committees are used to implement the organization and administration of the vocational education program on Federal, state, and local levels. A national committee, known as the Technical Advisory Committee on Trade and Industrial Education, was formed in 1936 to advise the U.S. Commissioner of Education and his staff on problems of plant training. This committee, which was composed of three representatives from employers, three from organized labor, and three from vocational education, was especially needed because of the change in the status of the Federal Board for Vocational Education. The Vocational Education Act of 1963 established an advisory committee for vocational education. This committee consists of the U.S. Commissioner of Education as chairman; 1 representative each from the U.S. Departments of Agriculture, Commerce, and Labor; and 12 members representative of management, labor, and education. The committee has responsibility for advising the Commissioner on policies and regulations concerned with vocational education.

The 1963 Vocational Education Act provided for the creation of a state advisory council, which included representatives of management and labor, junior colleges, technical institutes, or higher educational institutions offering programs of vocational or technical education, if the present state board for vocational education did not include such representation. This council has responsibility for consulting with the state board for vocational education in carrying out the state plan. Most of the states also provide advisory committees for each of the vocational services consisting of employers and employees from the occupations with which the service is concerned. The state supervisor of the service serves as ex-officio chairman of the committee. Both general advisory committees for vocational education and craft committees operate on the local level. The general committee is composed of representatives from the various occupational groups of the community, and the craft committees consist of representatives of management and labor from the occupational field concerned.

In general, the duties of advisory committees on the state and local levels are to advise the professional staff in vocational education on such matters as amount and type of training, equipment needed, qualifications of teaching personnel, content of subject matter, nature of work experience, number of trained workers needed, and general policies for vocational education. The committees usually consist of 6 to 12 members each, and these members are invited to serve by administrative officers of vocational education on state and local levels. The committees meet at the call of the chairmen and receive no pay other than the necessary travel expenses incurred in attending the meetings.

State Plans for Vocational Education

Each state is required under the provisions of the Federal vocational education acts to prepare and submit to the Federal authority a plan for the use of the Federal funds provided for vocational education. This plan is necessary to insure adequate standards, because the grants to the states are made under broad conditions and are intended to meet certain specific needs within a state that are not common to all the states. The state plan, when approved by the Federal authority, becomes a contract of agreement between a state and the Federal government.

PURPOSES OF STATE PLANS

The idea for a state plan for vocational education originated when attempts were being made in 1911 to pass the Page bill, prior to the passage of the Smith-Hughes Act. An amendment to the Page bill contained reference to a state plan for vocational education. The Commission on National Aid to Vocational Education suggested that provision for a state plan be incorporated in the bill providing Federal aid for vocational education. It was suggested that each state formulate plans for the administration of the grants in conformity with the provisions of a Federal statute and establish minimum requirements with reference to qualifications of teachers and equipment used in the schools.

The state plan for vocational education enables the state to exercise broad powers in determining the kind and characteristics of the state program in vocational education needed to meet conditions within the state. The plan is not only a contract between the state and the Federal government, but it also contains a description of the kinds of programs the state expects to carry out. The plan supplies the facts used in interpreting the Federal vocational education acts. It serves as a basis of understanding for cooperation between the state and Federal governments. A state in the process of preparing the plan benefits from the analysis it makes of its state program for vocational education. The state plan furnishes information to local school officials relative to the organization of local vocational programs in which Federal and state funds are used. It insures a continuous state program despite changes in state education administrations.

INFORMATION INCLUDED IN STATE PLANS

The Smith-Hughes and George-Barden Acts specified that the state plan shall state the kinds of vocational education for which it is proposed that the appropriation shall be used, the kinds of schools and equipment, courses of study, methods of instruction, qualifications of teachers, plans for the training of teachers, and plans for the administration and supervision of the vocational program. The acts did not provide detailed outlines for the plan, but the staff of the Vocational and Technical Division of the U.S. Office of Education has prepared from time to time topical outlines to guide the states in the preparation of their plans.

The topical outline for the state plan for Vocational Education under the provisions of the Vocational Education Act of 1963 consists of the following ten sections: (1) *Administration and Supervision* including such items as qualifications of personnel, cooperative arrangements with other agencies, and vocational education in special areas; (2) *State Fiscal and Accounting Procedures* with specific procedures for custody, allocation, and transfer of funds, and expenditures for salaries, equipment, and fees; (3) *Program of Instruction* with procedures for supervision and control to insure efficient instruction for gainful employment; (4) *Vocational Guidance and Counseling Services* to insure adequate occupational information and consultative services; (5) *Teacher Training* including standards and procedures for various teacher training services; (6) *Research, Demonstration, and Experimental Programs* concerned primarily with descriptions and plans for evaluation of programs; (7) *Construction* having to do with policies and procedures for approval of area vocational education school facil-

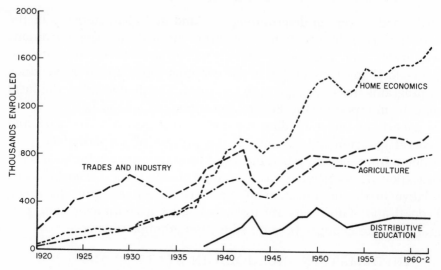

Enrollments in Vocational Classes by Type of Program in the States and Territories, 1920 to 1962. The enrollment in vocational home economics has exceeded the enrollments in each of the other services since 1940. (U.S. Department of Health, Education, and Welfare, Office of Education, *Digest of Annual Reports of State Boards for Vocational Education to the Office of Education, Fiscal Year Ended June 30, 1962*, Government Printing Office, 1963)

ities; (8) *Work-Study Programs* consisting of a supplement to the state plan containing the provisions for these programs; (9) *Vocational Education Fields* concerned with provisions for vocational education under the Smith-Hughes and George-Barden Acts; (10) *Interrelationship Among the Various Vocational Program Fields* with emphasis on procedures for developing programs that draw knowledge and skill from one or more vocational fields.

THE PREPARATION OF PLANS

State plans were prepared annually during the 5-year period from 1917 to 1922. In 1922 the Federal Board for Vocational Education suggested to the states that they prepare and submit plans for a 5-year period with the understanding that any state could propose amendments to its plan at any time and that these amendments would be acted upon immediately. The states complied with this suggestion, and this practice was followed until the close of the 5-year period 1948 to 1952. The 1948–1952 plan with such amendments as were needed was used until 1960 at which time the states were requested to prepare a new plan with such modifications as were required by new vocational education laws and regulations. The Vocational Education Act of 1963 necessitated a new state plan for vocational education.

The state plan is prepared by the professional workers on the state staff. The staff workers in each service usually take responsibility for preparing the first draft of the plan for their respective service. These drafts are reviewed by the state director and other staff members, and the completed plan is read and discussed before it is presented to the executive officer for review and transmission to the state board for vocational education. When the state board for vocational education has approved the plan, it is sent by its executive officer to the U.S. Commissioner of Education for his approval. The U.S. Commissioner of Education reserves the right to approve or disapprove state plans, but this authority does not imply authority to dictate or initiate plans in any state. This authority is concerned primarily with determining whether the plan meets the conditions for reimbursement under the Federal acts. Plans that do not violate these conditions are approved. The U.S. Office of Education has prepared, and revised from time to time, various publications concerned with standards, policies, and recommendations for the organization and administration of vocational education. These publications are useful in preparing state plans.

Many amendments to state plans have been submitted through the years. Some amendments have been suggested by the Federal Board for Vocational Education or its successor, the U.S. Commissioner of Education. For example, in 1938 the Commissioner authorized the use of Federal funds for vocational education for partial maintenance of state services in occupational information and guidance. However, before a state was permitted to use funds for this purpose it was necessary that a plan be prepared or that the existing state plan be amended, showing the conditions under which the Federal funds were to be used. Most of the amendments to state plans through the years have been initiated by state boards for vocational education to meet changing conditions within the state.

VARIATIONS IN STATE PLANS

In general, state plans for vocational education are similar. There are, however, some differences designed to meet the needs and problems of the several states. Differences are observed in the qualifications and duties of personnel. Staff members are expected to have a master's degree or the equivalent. Some states specify a bachelor's degree and 30 semester hours of graduate courses. A few states permit some staff members to be employed even if they possess only a bachelor's degree.

States differ in the number of years of experience required of the state staff prior to accepting the staff position. In general, both occupational and teaching or administrative experience is required. Job experience requirements among the states vary from about 2 to 6 years. Most staff members devote full time to the administration and supervision of vocational education, but some plans permit supervisors and other personnel to devote a portion of their time to nonvocational practical arts courses.

Local vocational agriculture and homemaking teachers, as a rule, are required to have a bachelor's degree with some job experience when they enter the teaching field. A bachelor's degree is not required of a teacher of vocational industrial or of vocational distributive education in most states, but this difference in educational requirement is usually made up by an increased requirement in trade experience. States differ in the specific course requirements for the certification of vocational teachers. Some teacher education curriculums contain a number of general education courses, while others do not include as many courses of this nature. In general, about 18 semester hours of professional education courses are required, with a few states requiring less than 18 and a few requiring more.

Some state plans specify a maximum and a minimum age for a beginning teacher. For example, in one state a teacher who enters the program for the first time is required to be between 21 and 40 years of age. Some states specify a minimum number of students per class. In one state this is 10 per class. States differ in requirements for supplies and equipment. Some states specify amounts per student, while others make no mention of specific amounts for this purpose.

IMPROPER USES OF PLANS

State plans through the years have provided the means of cooperation between the Federal government and the states, and, in general, they have served the purposes for which they were designed. Occasionally, however, state plans have been used in an improper manner, or have been improperly interpreted, in an attempt to justify some procedure or decision not within the scope of the plan. In some instances the qualifications of personnel have been written around an individual to insure his tenure in the job specified. Then, too, qualifications are sometimes written in such a manner that only the person for whom they are written can qualify. This procedure is sometimes followed in submitting amendments to existing plans to justify the employment of a specific individual.

Plans and amendments to plans sometimes contain too many qualifying or equivalent phrases in connection with fundamental standards. This practice permits individuals to make interpretations not contemplated in the original plan and not in conformity with the best practices or established standards. This practice is especially noticed with reference to qualifications and duties of personnel. The plan is sometimes used as a detailed course of study and list of requirements imposed upon a local school. Such a use prevents local initiative and local application, both of which are contemplated in the vocational education acts.

Staff personnel in some states occasionally leave the inference with local school authorities that the Federal government, through the state plan, prohibits certain practices, when in fact the state staff originated the regulations concerning these practices, and these regulations were simply approved by the Federal authorities. This practice has led many general educators to conclude that the Federal government was dominating the program when just the opposite was true. This improper usage has been noted in qualifications and duties of personnel; in facilities, supplies, and equipment for vocational classes; and in organization and content of courses. The state staff should be willing to assume its share of the responsibility for the operation of procedures and standards in vocational education.

Newly appointed officials in vocational education sometimes fail to become informed about the provisions of the state plan, and, when violations of the plan are called to their attention, they excuse themselves by referring to the plan as a scheme imposed upon them. Carelessness in preparing and submitting amendments sometimes leads to undesirable provisions. The failure to publicize properly and to make available copies of the state plan may lead to misunderstandings with reference to the nature and content of the plan. Local school authorities are likely to become suspicious of a document continually referred to but never available. The state plan for vocational education should be readily available to all citizens who desire to see it.

Teacher Education and Supervision

The Smith-Hughes law recognized the need for an adequate supply of competent teachers by providing specific funds for the education of teachers and by requiring each state to expend at least a minimum amount of funds for teacher education. A detailed plan for the teacher education program in vocational education is included in the state plan for vocational education. The state plan also contains a description of the program of supervision of vocational education, the primary purpose of which is the improvement of instruction. The similarity of teacher education and supervisory responsibilities was recognized early in the Federally aided vocational education program, when the Federal Board for Vocational Education permitted the use of funds earmarked for teacher education for state supervision. The responsibility for both teacher education and supervision in the Federally aided program of vocational education rests with the state board for vocational education. The state board usually delegates the preservice teacher education functions to an established institution approved for vocational teacher education and retains controls of the supervisory functions and, in many instances, the in-service teacher education functions.

TEACHER EDUCATION FUNCTIONS

Teacher education in vocational education includes those activities needed for assisting teachers or prospective teachers to secure the professional knowledge, abilities, understandings, and appreciations which will enable them to qualify for employment or advancement in vocational education. A complete program of vocational teacher education includes plans for the performance of the following six functions: (1) recruitment, counseling, selection, pre-employment training, and placement of new teachers; (2) the preparation of instructional aids for teachers in service; (3) the organization of educational programs, both institutional and on-the-job, for in-service teachers; (4) the follow-up of teachers through field contacts, for the purpose of both evaluating the teacher education program and assisting the teacher to improve his instructional program; (5) the improvement of professional and technical college teaching through the application of objectives established for vocational education; and (6) the conduct of studies and investigations that contribute to the development of the vocational program of the state.

The functions of teacher education are carried out in such activities as teaching organized courses at an institution or extension center; supervising student teachers; conducting follow-up studies of vocational teachers; writing and publishing teaching aids; conducting research studies concerned with selection, training, and duties of vocational teachers; organizing short, intensive technical courses for teachers and staff personnel; and coordinating the work of the teacher education staff.

The teacher education functions are carried out in teacher education programs organized in institutions of higher learning under public supervision and control and by representatives of the state board for vocational education or a local school board responsible for vocational education. The state board, in the first instance, delegates functions to a selected institution. The state board for vocational education uses such criteria as the following in designating these institutions: (1) the institution or agency has the facilities and personnel to provide the education; (2) qualified persons will enroll in the program; (3) the proposed plan provides adequate training; and (4) the number of teachers to be educated meets the probable needs. Approval of the work of an institution is an indication that it meets the standards of the state plan. Reimbursement from Federal funds for vocational education may be allowed only to institutions under public supervision and control.

THE ORGANIZATION OF VOCATIONAL TEACHER EDUCATION

The state board for vocational education usually delegates teacher education functions in vocational agricultural education and vocational home economics education to designated institutions of higher learning. In some instances, the education of coordinators, trade teachers, and counselors is also delegated. More frequently, teacher education for part-time and adult teachers in trades and industry and in distributive occupations is carried on by representatives of the state board for vocational education by means of conferences and short, intensive courses. Some local school boards maintain teacher educators for vocational teachers of out-of-school classes and other teachers who are in need of professional preparation.

The teacher education program in a higher institution is usually placed in the college of education, either as a coordinated department or division responsible for all fields of vocational education or as a separate department or field for each service. In some institutions, usually those whose major emphases are on agriculture, home economics, and engineering, the teacher education program is placed under the administration of the technical college concerned. This is especially true in land-grant colleges that are organized independently of state universities.

The organization of all vocational teacher education services in a single department or division of a teacher education institution has a number of advantages. This integrated type of organization facilitates the organization of courses designed for students in two or more vocational fields. Some courses, for example, history and principles of vocational education, may well be taken by students in each of the vocational fields of agriculture, distributive education, homemaking, trade and industrial education, and vocational guidance. This means that one course adapted to the needs of students in all fields may be offered in one educational institution.

The organization of all vocational services as an integrated department makes less difficult such activities as preparing course outlines, arranging class schedules and advising students. This type of organization is especially desirable in smaller institutions where class size in vocational courses is small. The integrated organization is also useful in conducting graduate programs in vocational education, where it is neither desirable nor economical to offer a large number of courses, each especially organized for students in only one vocational field. This type of organization also simplifies many administrative problems such as budgeting, billing, purchasing supplies and equipment, and planning cooperative activities.

Preservice teachers are required to engage in supervised student teaching as a part of the teacher education curriculum. This activity is usually an off-campus one, conducted in an established department in a local public school, usually for a period of from six to eighteen weeks. A representative of the teacher education institution visits and counsels with the student teacher during this period. Arrangements are made at the college or university for the student teacher to be absent from classes during this period. Preservice teachers in some institutions schedule all or most of the professional vocational education courses in one semester of the senior year. This practice simplifies the scheduling of off-campus activities by concentrating one semester's work in one department of the institution. Some institutions have organized a five-year program which, in general, provides for four years of academic and technical education and one year of professional education and cadet teaching at a local public school. The student teacher in this case may receive a stipend for his work.

THE DEVELOPMENT OF SUPERVISION

The states were permitted to use Federal funds for paying salaries of supervisors of agricultural education under the provisions of the Smith-Hughes Act. This Act made no such provision for supervisors of trade and industrial education nor were Federal funds authorized for use in paying for travel, supplies and other expenses of supervisors. Supervisors of agricultural education were provided from the beginning in some of the states, while in others directors of vocational education and teacher trainers supplied supervisory services. Many of the directors were not sufficiently familiar with the requirements in some of the services to serve in a supervisory capacity. Then, too, they were occupied in administrative duties and had little time for supervision. Teacher trainers were concerned primarily with preservice teacher education programs and had little time for supervision of in-service teachers. It soon became apparent that qualified supervisors were needed in each service as a means of improving local programs of vocational education.

In 1918 the Federal Board for Vocational Education authorized the states to use a portion of the Federal funds allocated for teacher training to pay salaries and other expenses of supervision. This authorization was designed to stimulate the states to provide state supervision in all three vocational education services. The procedure was justified on the grounds that supervision was primarily a teacher education function designed to improve in-service teachers. The authorization limited the amount of teacher training funds that could be used for supervision to 25 percent of the maximum available for teacher training in any one of the three services. Since the funds allocated for teacher training were used for salaries, clerical service, travel, communications, and supplies, that portion of the funds allocated for supervision was also available for these types of expenditures. All subsequent vocational education acts recognized the importance of supervision by providing that Federal funds could be used for this purpose.

The need for local supervision, especially in the field of trade and industrial education, became evident, and a survey was made in 1922 to determine the status of teacher training and supervision. The results of this survey indicated a need for local supervisors because of difficulties and inadequacies in state supervision and teacher training. Most of the trade and industrial teachers were selected from local industries, and it was frequently not feasible for state supervisors and teacher trainers to provide the necessary professional training for these teachers at the time training was needed. As a result of these and other facts, in December, 1925, the Federal Board for Vocational Education authorized the use of Federal teacher training funds in reimbursement for salaries of local supervisors of agricultural, of trade and industrial, and of home economics education. The use of these funds was contingent upon the approval of a plan for local supervision.

SUPERVISORY FUNCTIONS

The term *supervision* usually refers to those activities that are needed in the promotion, development, maintenance, and improvement of instruction. Specific activities in which supervisors engage include assisting in the planning of state and local programs, assisting teachers in improving methods of instruction and planning instructional material, securing adequate facilities, organizing and improving activities of student organizations in vocational education, and evaluating the results of the instructional program conducted by the local teacher. These activities involve the keeping and making of records and reports and the use of evaluative criteria and devices. Many of these activities may be classed as on-the-job teacher education for inservice teachers. This makes it necessary that supervisors of vocational programs be experienced in teaching vocational programs.

The supervisory staff in most states conducts studies and investigations in the promotion of vocational education and in the improvement of instruction. Such items as types of classes, instructional methods, and evaluation of local programs are frequently included in these research programs. The state supervisor has responsibility for organizing and supervising the teacher education program for his respective service when this program is retained as a function of the state board for vocational education and not delegated to some institution of higher learning. Close cooperation between the state supervisor and teacher educator is required when the teacher education program is delegated.

LOCAL SUPERVISION AND TEACHER EDUCATION

Local supervisors, when employed by local or county boards of education, have duties and responsibilities similar to those of state personnel with similar titles, except that local personnel are confined to supervision and teacher education at the local level. The local director of vocational education, who in many instances is the local supervisor and teacher educator, has responsibility for determining the number and kind of vocational schools and classes, duties and assignments of local teachers, local promotional programs, and plans for improving vocational teachers on the local level. Special supervisors and teacher educators are often provided in schools located in the larger cities. These individuals are directly responsible to the local director.

Some vocational teachers, especially those in vocational distributive education and vocational industrial education, learn their trade by experience and frequently are employed in the vocational program with little or no professional preparation in methods of teaching. It becomes necessary for local supervisors to provide opportunities for these teachers to acquire some knowledge of teaching methods and principles. There are many ways in which local teachers may engage in professional improvement. Among these are short, intensive advisory conferences, observations and demonstrations, visits to other departments, correspondence and extension courses, and courses at teacher education institutions. The local teacher educator will use these and other devices and activities to upgrade the teachers in the local school. In addition to professional courses, vocational teachers need frequent refresher courses in their trade or occupation. Frequently, the best opportunity for this type of teacher improvement is by employment in the trade or occupation. Local supervisors and teacher educators are usually in a position to organize these types of programs.

Financing Vocational Education

Vocational education of less than baccalaureate degree level is financed by Federal, state, and local funds. The amount of local funds has been greater than either state or Federal funds since the beginning of the program, and local funds have increased more rapidly than either state or Federal funds. Federal funds, before 1964, were earmarked for specific services and could not be expended for other services. Many states make lump-sum appropriations of state funds for vocational education and fix responsibility on the state board for vocational education to allocate among the several services such funds as are not needed for matching purposes. This practice, together with the growth of the program and the policy of increasing support from local sources, has brought about a number of problems concerned with the financing of vocational education. Some of these problems are discussed in this section.

THE NEED FOR FEDERAL FUNDS

The vocational education acts provide Federal funds for the purpose of stimulating the states to organize programs of vocational education and to assist them in the further development of these programs. Some persons have suggested that the states no longer need assistance in either the promotion or development of vocational education, and as a consequence Federal aid should be curtailed, leaving to the states and local communities responsibility for financing this program. During recent years, many attempts have been made to reduce Federal appropriations. Thus far none of these attempts has succeeded, although the annual appropriations under the George-Barden Act were less than the authorizations included in the Act prior to the fiscal year beginning July 1, 1956.

Vocational educators, on the other hand, contend that vocational education is so vital to the national welfare that its development cannot be left to the states working independently of each other. The mobility of the population and the constant need for high standards for workers in the various socially useful occupations call for national leadership. The validity of the argument that vocational education is necessary for the national welfare was demonstrated during World War II. At that time there was a need for large numbers of specially trained workers to produce war materials, and the vocational educators were called upon to train these workers. It was generally agreed that it would not have been possible to convert to a war economy as quickly as was done if the Federally aided program of vocational education had not been in operation.

There is a tendency for many individuals who have completed the public school course and attained a working age to move from the rural areas to urban areas in search of work. This is made necessary because of the high birth rate and the limited number of job opportunities in the rural areas. The states having large rural populations not only have a higher ratio of children to adults, but, for the most part, they also have less wealth per child, which tends to increase the burden on the local community and the state for the support of educational programs. Then, too, statistics indicate that many of those who leave when young return to the states with large rural populations when they reach the age of retirement. The Federal vocational aid provides needed assistance for these less wealthy states.

Federal aid for vocational education enables the several states to maintain certain standards that might prove extremely difficult, if not impossible, to maintain if state and local funds alone were available for vocational education. Such standards as are concerned with qualifications and responsibilities of teachers; types of schools and classes, including out-of-school as well as in-school classes; vocational school facilities and equipment; supervision and teacher education; and materials and methods of instruction are agreed upon by local, state, and

Federal authorities in vocational education. Federal vocational education funds are granted upon the condition that these acceptable standards be maintained. In the absence of such a condition, it is quite possible that standards would not be maintained, and the vocational program would likely lose some of its vocational aspects. This would be brought about in the less wealthy states by the pressure of general education to reduce or at least not to increase expenditures for vocational education. This condition would likely lead to general courses in such subjects as agriculture, homemaking, and industrial education, rather than the approved vocational program now in operation for in-school and out-of-school youth and adults.

TRENDS IN EXPENDITURES FOR VOCATIONAL EDUCATION

The Smith-Hughes Vocational Education Act appropriated $1,-655,587 for vocational education in 1918. The Federal allotments under the provisions of the Smith-Hughes Act increased until 1926, at which time the allotment was $7,184,901. Since the Smith-Hughes Act contains a permanent appropriation, an amount approximately equal to the above figure for 1926 has been allotted under the provisions of this Act each year since 1926. Additional funds have been provided for vocational education under other vocational education acts. The George-Reed Act authorized an increase in vocational funds for a 5-year period ending June 30, 1934. The maximum increase during these years was in 1932, at which time the combined Federal allotment from the Smith-Hughes and George-Reed Acts was $8,732,978.

The George-Ellzey Act resulted in an increase in Federal aid for vocational education for a 3-year period ending June 30, 1937. The annual Federal allotment from the Smith-Hughes and George-Ellzey Acts for the 3-year period was $10,377,531. The George-Deen Act of 1938 was responsible for an increase in Federal funds for the years from 1939 to 1947. During these years, the annual allotment from the two acts was about $21,768,000. The George-Barden Act authorized additional funds beginning July 1, 1946. However, no additional funds were appropriated under this Act until 1948, at which time the annual allotments from the Smith-Hughes and George-Barden Acts were $27,-127,000. Appropriations under the provisions of the George-Barden Act have been increased since 1948, and the total allotments from the Smith-Hughes and George-Barden Acts for the fiscal year ending June 30, 1962 were $53,619,000.

Congress appropriated a total of $872,779,000 in Federal funds

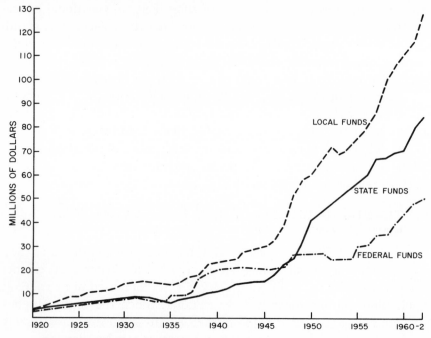

The Expenditures for Vocational Education by Source of Funds in the States and Territories, 1920 to 1962. Local communities are providing increasing amounts of money for financing local programs of vocational education. (U.S. Department of Health, Education, and Welfare, Office of Education, *Digest of Annual Reports of State Boards for Vocational Education to the Office of Education, Fiscal Year Ended June 30, 1962*, Government Printing Office, 1963)

to the states and subdivisions to carry out the provisions of the various national vocational education acts during the 45-year period 1918 to 1962. The states and territories have expended about 95 percent of this amount through the years for the purposes stated in the acts, leaving about 5 percent as an unexpended allotment. This unexpended allotment has been due to the inability of some states to utilize all the Federal funds for vocational education allotted to those states. The percentage of allotment unexpended has varied through the years. The unexpended allotment was 18 percent of the total during 1918 to 1922, the first 5 years of the national program. This relatively large, unexpended allotment was due to the newness of the program and the problems arising in establishing vocational education of less than college grade. The unexpended allotment represented about 5 percent of the total during the 5 years from 1958 to 1962. Increases of short duration in the unexpended allotment have occurred from time to time, due to changes in the vocational education laws and uncertainties in the provision of funds for certain services.

A short time after the passage of the Smith-Hughes Act, some educators expressed concern that Federal funds would be used to transfer the financial burden from local communities to the Federal government. These persons felt that any increase in Federal funds would be accompanied by a corresponding decrease in state and local funds. This transfer of funds, it was said, would defeat the purposes of stimulation and further development stated in the Federal acts. The facts indicate that these fears were groundless. Expenditures of Federal, state, and local funds for vocational education have totaled $3,748,-665,000 during the 45-year period 1918 to 1962. Federal funds account for 23 percent of this amount; state funds, 31 percent; and local funds, 46 percent. For each dollar of Federal funds expended for vocational education the states and local school districts have expended $3.51. The ratio of state and local funds to each dollar of Federal funds was $2.63 for the period from 1918 to 1922 and $4.40 for the period 1958 to 1962.

REIMBURSEMENT POLICIES

The national vocational education acts require that Federal funds be used as a reimbursement for authorized expenditures previously incurred. Accordingly, state boards for vocational education use Federal funds and any state vocational funds provided by the state as a reimbursement to local school boards for a proportionate part of the salaries and, in some instances, travel and other expenses of vocational teachers. This reimbursement is usually paid to the local school board quarterly for the expenditures incurred during the preceding three months.

The amount of the reimbursement varies both among states and among vocational services within a state. In general, it is not more, and more frequently it is less, than 50 percent of the total expenditures for salaries and travel of the vocational teachers. Local school districts sometimes receive full reimbursement for some vocational services. For example, salaries of teachers of adult classes are sometimes reimbursed in full. The amount of reimbursement a local district receives is usually determined by a formula or policy established by the state board for vocational education. Some of the formulas are simple statements to the effect that local boards will be reimbursed for a stated percentage of the expenditures made for salaries and travel of the approved vocational teachers. Maximum limits for salaries and travel are usually stated with the provision that when these are exceeded the local school board will not receive reimbursement for the amount paid in excess of the maximum.

Some states follow the practice of allocating a stated amount of money to the local school board for each approved vocational teacher. This amount is arrived at simply by prorating the funds available for this purpose among the several vocational teachers in the state. These amounts in some states vary among the different vocational services, while in others the amount per vocational teacher is the same, regardless of service. Separate allowances, varying with the vocational service, are made for travel in some states. The maximum allowance for travel is paid only when it is used for authorized travel on a mileage basis.

Some states make use of comprehensive formulas for determining the amount of reimbursement a local school district may receive for conducting a vocational program. These formulas are designed to stimulate the local school board and vocational teacher to conduct a comprehensive vocational program by providing increased reimbursement for additional service. The amount of the reimbursement by these formulas is determined by such factors as number of in-school and out-of-school students, training and experience of the teacher, and area in square miles of the district. Some states make reimbursements on the basis of approved teaching units, student hours, and number of out-of-school classes.

A few states that have minimum foundation programs provide state and local funds for vocational education in the same manner as for other school subjects and use Federal funds which are matched by state funds largely for state administration and supervision, travel of vocational teachers, out-of-school classes, and summer work. In one or two states Federal funds are matched on a state-wide basis and used in newly organized local programs as a means of stimulating the development of these programs. This aid is gradually withdrawn as the program becomes established, until the amount of aid is the same as that for the established programs.

Most of the states provide considerably more money than is required for matching Federal funds for vocational education. Those funds that are not required for matching are frequently used by the state board for vocational education to strengthen programs which receive limited Federal funds. While nonmatching state funds may be used in any manner the state may determine, the usual practice is to follow the same procedure and standards in the use of these state funds as those followed in the use of Federal and state matching funds. This policy insures high standards and approved practices in the state's program of vocational education.

QUESTIONS FOR STUDY AND DISCUSSION

1. How was the Federal Board for Vocational Education organized to perform its functions?
2. When and for what reason was this Board abolished?
3. What is the present organization for vocational education on the national level? On the state and local levels?
4. What are the functions of advisory committees in vocational education?
5. What information is included in the state plan for vocational education?
6. Indicate some variations and improper uses of state plans.
7. What are the principal functions included in vocational teacher education programs?
8. How are institutional teacher education programs in vocational education organized?
9. What are the duties of state and local supervisors?
10. Indicate some evidences of a need for Federal funds for vocational education.
11. What are some trends in expenditures of Federal, state, and local funds for vocational education?
12. What differences in reimbursement policies in vocational education are observed among the states?

SOURCE REFERENCES

Ayer, Fred C., *Fundamentals of Instructional Supervision,* Harper & Row, New York, 1954.

Cooper, Shirley, and Charles O. Fitzwater, *County School Administration,* Harper & Row, New York, 1954.

Federal Board for Vocational Education, *Annual Reports,* 1918 to 1932 inclusive, Washington, D.C.

Hawkins, Layton S., Charles A. Prosser, and John C. Wright, *Development of Vocational Education,* American Technical Society, Chicago, 1951.

Mays, Arthur B., *Principles and Practices of Vocational Education,* McGraw-Hill, New York, 1948.

Struck, F. Theodore, *Vocational Education for a Changing World,* Wiley, New York, 1945.

U.S. Department of Health, Education, and Welfare, Office of Education, *Administration of Vocational Education,* Vocational Education Bulletin No. 1, revised 1958, Washington, D.C., 1958.

U.S. Office of Education, *Digest of Annual Reports of State Boards for Vocational Education* for fiscal years 1933 to 1962 inclusive. Washington, D.C.

U.S. Department of Health, Education, and Welfare, Office of Education, *Education for a Changing World of Work,* Report of the Panel of Consultants on Vocational Education, Washington, D.C., 1963.

U.S. Department of Health, Education, and Welfare, Office of Education, *The State and Education*, Miscellaneous Publication No. 23, Washington, D.C., 1955.

CHAPTER SEVEN

VOCATIONAL AGRICULTURAL EDUCATION

An agricultural revolution, having many of the characteristics of the Industrial Revolution of the nineteenth century, has been taking place in the United States during the past 40 years. This movement has been due to the mechanization of farming and the use of many improved farming practices discovered as a result of the extensive program of agricultural research and teaching conducted by various public and private agencies in the United States. The results achieved have enabled the present-day farmer to produce more food, feed, fiber, and oil per acre and per farm worker. This increased production has enabled the people of the United States to maintain ever increasing standards of living with relatively fewer farm workers. These changes in farming have resulted in larger farms, higher farm incomes, and greater capital investments on individual farms. Success in farming presently

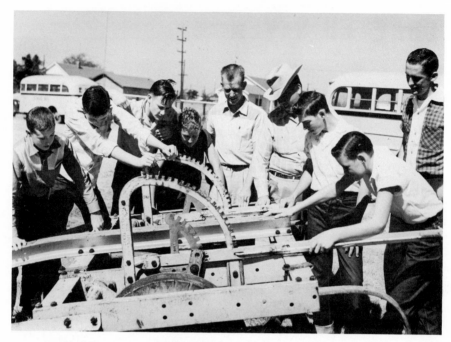

Students in Day School Classes in Vocational Agriculture Obtain Practical Instruction in the Care and Use of Farm Machinery. (J. E. Gray, East Texas State College)

requires knowledge and skill far beyond the requirements of the first two decades of the present century.

The science of agriculture not only includes the on-farm production of crops and livestock enterprises but also many nonfarm occupations that require knowledge and skill in agricultural subjects such as those in marketing agricultural products, producing farm supplies, processing farm products, and servicing the agricultural industry. Other nonfarm occupations requiring knowledge and skill in agricultural subjects are those concerned with agricultural research and agricultural education. Many facets of this expanding area of nonfarm agricultural occupations require persons with a background of training and experience in farming.

The Federally aided program of vocational agricultural education is one of the public programs having responsibility for providing the knowledge and skill needed for success in both on-farm and off-farm agricultural vocations. The aim of the program is to train present and prospective agricultural workers for proficiency in agricultural occupations. On the local level it is referred to as the local program of vocational agriculture. Vocational agricultural education came into prominence with the passage of the Smith-Hughes Vocational Education Act. This Act was designed to stimulate the development of schools and classes in vocational agriculture in the public secondary schools and area schools and in the communities served by these schools. This service which is operated by a public education authority for schools of less than baccalaureate degree level finds its origin in the agricultural problems of the community, and the methods and techniques employed in the various schools and classes in vocational agriculture are conditioned by this origin. This program and some of its conditioning factors are discussed in this chapter.

Agricultural Problems

Farmers, since the beginning of time, have encountered many troublesome problems. In early times farmers worked long hours with inadequate equipment. They endured physical discomforts and frequently were subject to attack from unfriendly peoples. Farm life has undergone many changes since those times. Modern machinery and appliances have taken much of the drudgery out of farming, and the farm home with modern facilities compares favorably with the city home in comforts of living. However, farming today is not without its problems. The growing population requires increasing amounts of food which must come from the land. Much of the plant food in the soil has been lost through erosion and must be replaced to maintain high yields. The increased use of power machinery has necessitated new skills and a larger capital investment. The processing, marketing, and servicing of agricultural enterprises and related vocations, at one time of small consequence, is now a major factor in agriculture. These and many other problems require constant study and various types of action programs to maintain agricultural production at a level sufficiently high to insure an acceptable standard of living to all people in the United States.

THE PRESSURE OF POPULATION

The land area of the world remains about the same, but the population is increasing at a rapid rate. The density of world population which was estimated at about 29 persons per square mile of land area in 1900 had increased to 57 persons per square mile in 1960. Wide variations in density are shown among the countries of the world, ranging from 3 per square mile in Australia to 885 in the Netherlands. The density of population in the United States increased from about 25 persons per square mile in 1900 to 50 per square mile in 1960. Future estimates indicate a population of about 214 million persons in the United States in 1970 or about 60 persons per square mile of land area.

The land area of the United States was estimated at 1,902 million acres in 1960. About 60 percent of this area was classified as land in farms. The land area in farms increased about 16 percent from 1920 to 1960, while the population increase was about 70 percent. The land area in farms includes crop land, pasture land, woodland, and other types of land. The crop land harvested represented about 20 percent of the land area of the United States in 1920 and about 16 percent in 1960. During this period, the crop land that was harvested decreased from 3.4 acres per capita in 1920 to 2 acres in 1960. These data indicate that the increased production on farms is due to factors other than increased acreage. The possibility of increasing the land area in farms in the United States is limited. The 40 percent of the total area of the United States not in farms consists of timber, grasslands, urban real estate, and waste land. Much of it is arid land high in elevation.

The U.S. Department of Agriculture has estimated that a net loss of 15 million acres of private agricultural land will occur in the 48 contiguous states during the 17-year period 1958 to 1975. This loss will be due to the fact that about 20 million acres of agricultural land will shift to urban and built-up areas and will be offset with only 5 million acres of Federal and other lands that will shift to private agricultural uses. It is expected that the domestic use of farm products will increase 40 to 50 percent during this 17-year period.

These facts indicate that, if the United States is to continue to enjoy high standards of living, it will be necessary to continue to increase the productivity of the present acreage in farms or seek other sources of production at much higher costs. Data supplied by the U.S. Department of Agriculture indicate that substantial increases in yields per acre of the principal crops grown in the United States have occurred during the past 40 years. These data also show that the average yields for the United States as a whole are below those of the better farms, indicating that additional increases in yields may be obtained when more farmers use better farm practices. The point of diminishing returns in yields obtained by the use of improved practices will eventually occur, and, with a continuous increase in population, it may be necessary to seek new sources of food. The alternative is a lower stand-ard of living.

As in the United States, the extent of land area available for food production in the rest of the world is limited. The United States Food and Agriculture Organization has estimated that about 30 percent of the world's land area is presently in fields and pastures. Since this per-centage is less than the corresponding figure of 60 percent for the United States, it would seem that much unused land is still available for food production, and the food supply of the United States could be increased by utilizing lands in other countries. However, it should be noted that the land area of the United States is more favorably situated for food production than is most of the land area in other parts of the world. Much of the food-producing land of the world has been ravaged by erosion, and that of other areas will require extensive drainage or irrigation practices to make it usable for food production. The present acreage of food-producing land in the world is used somewhat more intensively for food production than similar land in the United States. These data indicate that the problem of keeping the food supply apace with the growing population is not a simple one, and its solution will require new knowledge and skill that may be obtained from effective programs of agricultural education.

THE CONSERVATION OF SOIL

The necessity for producing increasing amounts of food and fiber has accelerated the rate of exhaustion of soil fertility. Much of this loss of fertility is due to mismanagement, and as a result the top layer of soil upon which man depends for his existence is being washed and blown away. When this topsoil leaves the land, an unproductive land and, in many instances, an uninhabited desert is left behind. The U.S. Soil Conservation Service estimates that it takes nature, under the most favorable climatic conditions, from 200 to 1000 years to form 1 inch of topsoil. On the average, the topsoil is about 7 inches deep, and when this layer is lost, its replacement will require from 1400 to 7000 years. History bears out the fact that soil losses bring about the decline and fall of civilizations. The classic examples are the civilizations of Babylonia and Assyria. The once fertile soils of the lands bordering the Mediterranean Sea, especially the one-time fertile plains of North Africa, were destroyed or severely damaged by erosion, with a resulting decline in the early civilizations in that area.

The loss of soil fertility in the United States, a relatively new nation, has become a matter of national concern. The U.S. Soil Con-

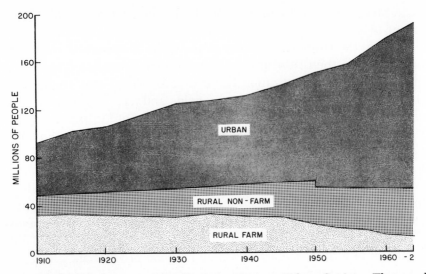

The United States is Rapidly Becoming an Urban Society. The rural farm population has decreased at an accelerated rate since 1945. (U.S. Department of Commerce, Bureau of the Census)

servation Service has estimated that approximately two-thirds of the privately owned cropland, grazing land and woodland in the 48 contiguous states are in need of some conservation treatment. The most dominant conservation problem is that of soil erosion. This occurs on about 53 percent of the cropland. Much of this land has secondary problems of excess water, unfavorable soil in the root zone, or adverse climate.

Experiments in soil conservation and land use have demonstrated that soil fertility can be maintained and improved even at a time when crops are growing on the land. Soil conservation practices, such as farm planning, the use of vegetation, mechanical control practices, upstream flood control, and forest and wildlife conservation, have resulted in an average increase of about 33 percent in yields per acre of all crops grown on the protected lands. The U.S. Soil Conservation Service, established by act of Congress in 1935 for the purpose of establishing a comprehensive soil and water conservation program, had extended its operations to include 2929 soil conservation districts in the United States as of June 30, 1962. These districts have initiated soil-conserving practices on more than 1705 million acres, including about 1044 million acres of land in farms. The U.S. Soil Conservation Service and the various soil erosion experiment stations are in constant search for new materials and practices designed to conserve and improve the thin layer of topsoil that is so important to the preservation of present-day civilization. Here again, however, the most important success factors in soil and water conservation are the knowledge, skill, and determination of the individual farmers who live on the land.

TECHNOLOGICAL CHANGES IN AGRICULTURE

During most of the years since man has been on earth, men and animals have provided the motive power for industry and agriculture. The extensive use of mechanical power in industry has contributed to the more recent change from men to machines in agriculture. The invention of the internal combustion engine made possible a shift in farm power from animals to machines, and by 1960 there were 4,770,-000 tractors on the farms of the United States, as compared to 920,000 in 1930. During this same period, the value of farm implements and machinery on farms in the United States increased more than sixfold, and the number of horses and mules decreased from 19,124,000 to 3,089,000 head.

New machinery on farms is mechanizing the production of agricultural commodities in much the same manner as the new machinery that was installed after the Industrial Revolution mechanized industrial production. Farm machinery such as cultivators that use flames to kill weeds; potato harvesters that dig, gather, grade, sack, weigh, and load; grain combines that harvest, thresh, and load; and portable irrigation systems that supply moisture where and when needed are but a few of these modern appliances. In addition, the farm home is replete with automatic time- and labor-saving devices for reducing the drudgery of farm life.

The use of modern equipment and appliances has greatly increased the total farm output and the farm output per man. A single-unit tractor combine operated by 1 man is capable of harvesting as much grain in 1 day as was previously harvested with 15 men and 27 horses. Modern cotton pickers can pick as much cotton per day as 40 or 50 skilled hand pickers. A 2-row corn picker operated by 1 man will harvest as much corn per day as 20 men harvesting by hand. The modern machines have enabled the farmer to increase total farm production by 50 percent since 1940 and reduce the number of farmers and farm workers about 30 percent since that time. The reduction in manpower on farms has been accompanied by a need for new knowledge and skills in farming. Then too the manpower reduction has presented a new problem of population adjustment for farm people who are not needed in the production phases of agriculture. All these needs require new and different types of educational programs for rural America.

DISTRIBUTION PROBLEMS

The increased output per man hour on farms during the past 20 years has reduced the number of persons required for the production of farm products. It is estimated that about 5 million persons were working as farmers, farm managers and farm laborers in 1962. These individuals were primarily concerned with the production of farm commodities. They were also concerned with the marketing or disposition of the products of the farm. This activity may consist of simply placing the product in a convenient place near the farm road where it may be transported to a processing plant for processing, packaging, and sale or to the delivery of products to the wholesale or retail markets. Farmers must obtain a fair price for the product when it leaves the farm in order to maintain acceptable standards of living for their families. Since farmers find it more difficult to curtail production than industrialists, agricultural production may remain at high levels during declining price trends. For this reason the Federal government has been obliged to use various types of agricultural programs to improve farm incomes during periods of declining prices.

The Federal government in the 1920s attempted to help agriculture by aiding cooperatives, providing credit, and creating a Federal Farm Board. This board attempted to stabilize the prices of some commodities by providing storage facilities to enable farmers to hold farm commodities for a more favorable price. Beginning in the 1930s, such agencies as the Agricultural Adjustment Administration for adjusting supply and demand, the Commodity Credit Corporation for providing loans to farmers, the Farm Security Administration for aiding low-income farmers, and the Soil Conservation Service for the promotion of soil conservation were created. Other Federal farm programs included lend-lease programs designed to expand agricultural exports, crop insurance programs of the Federal Crop Insurance Corporation, and the development of rural electrification under the Rural Electrification Administration.

The income of the farm family is affected not only by the efficiency of production but also by the efficiency with which farm products reach the ultimate consumer. Many individuals are engaged in supply and service industries some of which supply power, fuel, repair services, seed, feed, fertilizer, and other commodities without which the farmer would be unable to engage in profitable farming. Some workers are engaged in marketing and processing agencies which give sense and form value to farm products. Wholesale and retail sales of agricultural products provide necessary channels from the producer to the consumer. The U.S. Bureau of the Census in a report of the 1958 census of business estimated that almost 13 million people were engaged in these off-farm agricultural vocations. This number when added to the number of farmers and farm workers indicates that more than one-fourth of the employed civilian labor force is engaged in agricultural vocations.

Educational Objectives In Vocational Agriculture

Most of the problems of agriculture including those of the production and distribution of farm commodities and the servicing of the farm operations lend themselves to study and experimentation, and solutions to many of them have been found by the use of educational techniques. The continuous changes in agriculture make it necessary for all agriculturalists to engage in a constant study of agricultural problems and processes. Schools and classes in vocational agriculture have been established throughout the nation to provide teachers and facilities for this study. Objectives of these Federally aided programs have been established by students, teachers, and other workers in vocational agricultural education. These objectives give direction to educational programs in the various types of schools and classes in vocational agriculture.

Farming vocations. A committee on objectives in vocational agricultural education began its study of objectives in 1929. This committee, appointed by officials of the American Vocational Association, made its report in 1931. A second committee was appointed in 1938 by officials of the U.S. Office of Education and the American Vocational Association to review and revise the previous statement of objectives. This statement of objectives served as a guide in the formulation of specific objectives until 1955, at which time a revision of the 1938 report was made. The following statement of objectives is adapted from this report.[1]

[1] U.S. Department of Health, Education, and Welfare, Office of Education, *Educational Objectives in Vocational Agriculture*, Vocational Division Monograph No. 21, revised, 1955, Washington, D.C., 1955, pp. 4–13.

The aim of vocational agriculture is to train present and prospective farmers for proficiency in farming. Several abilities are needed by farmers and prospective farmers who expect to attain this aim. These abilities, commonly referred to as major objectives, include the ability to (1) make a beginning and advance in farming, (2) produce farm commodities efficiently, (3) market farm products advantageously, (4) conserve soil and other natural resources, (5) manage a farm business effectively, (6) maintain a favorable environment, and (7) participate in rural leadership activities.

These major objectives are designed primarily for secondary school students in vocational agriculture. They may be adapted to young and adult farmer instruction in vocational agriculture. These groups as a rule need abilities concerned primarily with the management and distribution phases of farming, new farming techniques, and supplies, and the operation of farm policies and programs.

Off-farm agricultural vocations.   The foregoing objectives were established primarily to prepare present and prospective farmers for proficiency in farming. This was the prevailing concept of agriculture stated in the Smith-Hughes Act. Present-day writers and Federal legislation suggest that although farming is still the principal concern of agriculture, other areas related to farming are also becoming increasingly important. These include the business and commercial aspects of modern agriculture such as off-farm service and supply for farmers and the broad fields of marketing and processing farm commodities. Students enrolled in vocational agriculture who are interested in these off-farm areas need certain knowledge and skills in addition to those suggested for the training of farmers. These additional objectives include (1) the development of scientific knowledge applicable to the agricultural occupations, and (2) educational experience in line with the scientific knowledge through work experience programs on farms and in the agricultural vocations.

The abilities needed to carry out these objectives depend upon the specific occupations in which training is desired. These abilities are determined by job analyses of specific vocations. These analyses indicate the work to be performed and the knowledge and skill necessary for its successful performance.

Technical and professional vocations in agriculture.   Special abilities are also needed by secondary school students in vocational agriculture who expect to continue their vocational education after graduating from high school by enrolling in post-high school or college courses in agriculture. Here again the objectives designed to prepare secondary school students for farming need some adaptations to include objectives for the desired goals. The general objectives for students who desire to continue their education beyond the secondary school level include (1) the development of an interest in and awareness of the occupational opportunities in technical and related fields of agriculture, (2) some knowledge of the scientific principles of agriculture, and (3) some experience in farming or agricultural business as a background for further study of technical agriculture.

A Committee of the American Vocational Association, appointed in 1964, is presently revising the objectives of vocational and technical education in agriculture. This committee suggests that the major objectives should include competencies needed by individuals engaged in or preparing to engage in farming and other agricultural occupations and that they should also include competencies designed to develop an understanding of career opportunities and requirements, satisfactory placement and advancement, the characteristics of success, and community leadership.

Types of Schools and Classes

The Vocational Education Act of 1963 recognizes the need for instruction in vocational education including instruction in agriculture for various groups of individuals. These groups include (1) persons attending high school, (2) persons who have completed or left high school and are available for full-time study in preparation for entering the labor market, (3) persons who have entered the labor market and who need training or retraining to achieve stability or advancement in employment, and (4) persons who have academic, socio-economic, or other handicaps that prevent them from succeeding in the regular vocational education program. Standards and specifications for the organization of instruction to meet the needs of the above groups of persons are left primarily to state boards of vocational education in the several states.

Instruction in vocational agriculture under the provisions of the Smith-Hughes and George-Barden Acts is organized for most of the above named groups of persons. The Acts and accompanying regulations specify three types of classes in vocational agriculture. These are (1) day school, or all-day classes for students who are regularly enrolled in school, (2) part-time classes for youth who are out of school and becoming established in agriculture, and (3) evening or adult classes for persons engaged in agriculture and who desire to improve their efficiency in their chosen occupation.

Day school classes. A day school class is organized in a secondary or post-secondary school for students who wish to prepare for farming or other agricultural occupations. Class instruction includes classroom, laboratory, and field activities; and agricultural mechanics. Day school instruction in the secondary school is usually offered in grades nine to twelve. These courses are frequently named Agriculture I, II, III, and IV. Some schools limit their offerings to 2 or 3 years. The day-school class meets 5 days a week during the school year, and from 5 to 7 clock hours a week. This class is a part of the regular secondary or post-secondary school program and appropriate units of credit are granted to each student who completes the course.

Part-time classes. A part-time class is designed to meet the needs of young persons who have left the full-time school and are becoming established in farming or other agricultural occupations. This class is referred to as a young farmer class when organized for young persons who are becoming established in farming. The part-time class instruction is flexible enough to meet the needs of students with varying levels of academic achievement. Some students are school dropouts and some have completed secondary school courses. The regulations for organizing this type of class under the provisions of the Smith-Hughes and George-Barden Acts require that each class meet a minimum of 30 clock hours per year.

Evening classes. Evening or adult classes are organized for farmers and persons in other agricultural occupations who are established in their occupation. The evening school course is designed to assist the enrollees to solve specific problems of agricultural occupations. The class instructor may be the local teacher of vocational agriculture, a special instructor employed by the state board of education or local school board, or some other qualified person. The instructor frequently uses the conference procedure technique for instructing the group. This technique utilizes the experiences of the adults in the class who have achieved success in some phase of the subject under class discussion. The evening class is frequently the focal point for community cooperation in various community activities. The regulations under the provisions of the Smith-Hughes and George-Barden

Acts require a minimum of 20 clock hours for each evening school class.

TRENDS IN ENROLLMENTS AND EXPENDITURES

The various schools and classes in vocational agriculture have had a total enrollment of 19,898,000 students during the 45-year period 1918 to 1962. These enrollments were in day school, part-time, and evening classes in the 50 states, Puerto Rico, Guam, and the Virgin Islands. The largest enrollment for the 45-year period was reported for day school classes. The enrollment in these classes was 58 percent of the total. Evening classes accounted for 36 percent of the total, and part-time classes 6 percent. Male and female enrollments were reported separately for all-day classes during the years 1918 to 1937. The female enrollment represented 3 percent of the total for the 20-year period reported. Female enrollments in evening classes represented about 7 percent of the total for the 15-year period from 1923 to 1937.

The average annual enrollment in day school classes for the 10-year period 1931 to 1940 was 206,833 students. The corresponding average for the 10-year period 1951 to 1960 was 446,880 students, an increase of 116 percent. Evening class enrollments increased 120 percent during this same period. The enrollment in part-time classes has shown wide fluctuation from year to year. For example, the total enrollment in part-time classes in 1940 was 62,489 persons. The 1945 total was 12,764 and the 1962 figure was 78,977.

The number of day school teachers of vocational agriculture increased from 895 in 1918 to 10,630 in 1962. The averages reported per year for the three 10-year periods ending in 1940, 1950 and 1960 were 5981, 8246 and 10,696, respectively. The average number of teachers reported for the 10-year period ending in 1960 was 3.4 times as large as the average reported for the 10-year period 1921 to 1930. During this same period the enrollment increased more than 7 times. A total of 30,800 persons qualified to teach vocational agriculture during the 20-year period, 1936 to 1955. This is an average of 1543 per year. This average is affected by the sharp drop during the war years 1943 to 1946, during which time an average of only 475 qualified per year.

Expenditures of Federal, state, and local funds for vocational agriculture for the 45-year period 1918 to 1962 inclusive were reported as 1141 million dollars. Federal funds represented 27 percent of this total, and state and local funds represented 73 percent. Local funds

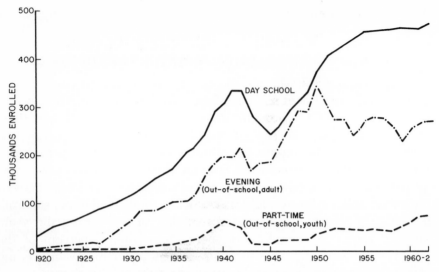

The Enrollments in Vocational Agriculture Classes by Type of Class in the States and Territories, 1920 to 1962. Enrollments in day school and adult classes in vocational agriculture have increased more rapidly than enrollments in part-time classes. (U.S. Department of Health, Education, and Welfare, Office of Education, *Digest of Annual Reports of State Boards for Vocational Education to the Office of Education, Fiscal Year Ended June 30, 1962,* Government Printing Office, 1963)

were 42 percent of the total, and state funds were 31 percent. For each dollar of Federal funds expended, state and local communities have expended $2.73. State and local funds have increased more than Federal funds since the beginning of the program. For example, during the 10-year period ending June 30, 1930, an average of $1.69 in state and local funds was expended for each dollar of Federal funds. The corresponding average for the 10-year period ending in 1940 was $1.54; for the 10-year period ending in 1950, the average was $2; and for the 10-year period ending June 30, 1960, the average was $3.63. These data indicate that the Federal funds are stimulating the states and local communities to make additional expenditures for vocational education and are not replacing state and local funds.

During the 10-year period 1951 to 1960 the expenditures for the administration of the program represented 1 percent of the total. The expenditures for supervision and teacher training represented 8 percent of the total, and the expenditures for instruction were 91 percent of the total. The average annual expenditure for vocational agricultural education for the 10-year period 1951 to 1960 varied from

$51,000 in Rhode Island to $6,208,000 in Texas. The following 8 states reported the highest expenditures: Texas, North Carolina, Illinois, Georgia, Oklahoma, California, Louisiana, and Pennsylvania. These 8 states, listed in descending order of expenditures, expended 40 percent of all funds spent for vocational agricultural education in the states and territories from 1951 to 1960.

The Instructional Program

The responsibilities of teachers of vocational agriculture include activities other than those involved in classroom teaching. Among the additional activities are those with reference to supervising the farming and other agricultural experience programs of students; engaging in community service; developing satisfactory public relations; maintaining adequate teaching facilities, materials and equipment; organizing and conducting FFA programs of work; and making records and reports. Success in carrying out these activities is conditioned by a number of factors, such as the qualifications of the teacher, the teaching techniques and materials available, the buildings and equipment, and the nature of the supervised agricultural experience programs. The instructional program in vocational agriculture provides opportunities for utilizing the services of instructors in other vocational fields to provide the necessary competencies for the various areas of agriculture. Cooperative programs in which the student receives instruction in farming from the agriculture teacher, instruction in distribution from the distributive education teacher, instruction in business from the business education teacher, and instruction in some farm mechanics jobs by the industrial education teacher, are examples of the team approach to the teaching of vocational agriculture.

THE QUALIFICATIONS OF THE TEACHER

The success of a local program of vocational agriculture is in a large measure dependent upon the technical, professional, and general education of the teacher. The many technological changes that are constantly occurring in agriculture require that a teacher of vocational agriculture possess a high degree of technical knowledge and skill acquired both in school and through experience. The technical requirement is generally met if the teacher is a graduate of a 4-year course in agriculture from a land-grant college or a college having equivalent staff and facilities. Special teachers of vocational agriculture responsible for teaching in agricultural areas other than farming should have the required technical knowledge and skill needed for the area in question.

Farm or other agricultural experience is an essential qualification for a teacher of vocational agriculture. The minimum requirement for teaching farming is 2 years acquired after the age of 14 years. Preferably, the teacher should be farm-reared and should have participated in the activities of the farm throughout his elementary and high school courses. This background of experience in farming enables the teacher to move with confidence among the patrons and students. A teacher of vocational agriculture who has previously had experience as a student in vocational agriculture possesses an added advantage.

Teachers of vocational agriculture need knowledge, skills, and attitudes in methods and techniques of teaching. These courses in professional education are given concurrently with the technical courses. Professional education courses are concerned with teaching techniques, materials and methods of instruction, supervised agricultural experience programs, and other duties and responsibilities of teachers. Practice in teaching is provided in off-campus cadet teaching centers under the direction of a superior local teacher of vocational agriculture and the staff of the teacher education institution.

The possession of a number of personal traits and characteristics, frequently acquired in formal education courses and through experience, contributes to the success of the teacher of vocational agriculture. Among these are leadership qualities, resourcefulness, industriousness, openmindedness, and dependability. The teacher of vocational agriculture is required to express himself in public and to participate intelligently in community affairs. A vocational teacher should possess an unquestionable character and should conduct himself at all times in a manner approved by the citizens of the community in which he is employed.

TEACHING TECHNIQUES AND MATERIALS

The nature and content of instruction in vocational agriculture are determined by the agricultural resources and needs of the community. These needs and resources are frequently arrived at by means of community and farm surveys.

The courses of study for teaching farming usually include 5 or 6 farm enterprises of importance to the community. For example, the enterprises selected may include *corn production* and *beef production*.

The enterprises are divided into five or six jobs each such as *planting corn* and *feeding beef cattle.*

Some changes are being made in the organization of the course content of day-school classes as a result of the increased need for instruction in nonfarming agricultural occupations. A *core* program is being used in many schools. The core consists of instructional units concerned with skills and information common to many agricultural

Student Teachers in Vocational Agriculture Engage in Frequent Conferences with the Vocational Agriculture Teacher of the Student Teaching Center. (College of Education, University of Tennessee)

occupations including farming. One pattern of the core program consists of two years of instruction in units such as agricultural occupations, soil science, plant science, animal science and agricultural mechanics. The occupations course is designed to supply information that will be helpful to the student in choosing a specific agricultural occupation. The agricultural science units provide knowledge and skill in the principles and practices common to many agricultural occupations.

The core program is followed by one or two years of more specialized courses designed to meet the occupational needs of students. Some of these specialized courses are organized for a cluster of related agricultural occupations. Among the course titles included in the advanced offerings are agricultural business, farming, ornamental horticulture, and agricultural mechanics. Usually one or two subject matter units together with agricultural mechanics are offered each year. Multiple teacher departments may offer a wider range of units from which students may make their selection.

The organization of instruction for adult classes in farming usually consists of farm enterprises common to the community together with farm management and farm mechanics. The enterprises for study are usually selected by the members of the class. Units of instruction for agricultural occupations other than farming are determined by the vocational interests of the class members. The technique of job analysis may be used to determine the specific content of the courses.

Success in teaching vocational agriculture requires the use of adequate teaching materials and facilities, including visual aids, reference books, experiment station bulletins, farm magazines, radio, television, local farms, and nearby agricultural industries. Students in vocational agriculture engage in laboratory demonstrations, field trips, and visits to processing plants. Day school students engage in a supervised study of various teaching materials that provide current information on agricultural problems. All these devices and activities provide, whenever possible, for instruction to be carried through the *doing* level, so that the student in vocational agriculture may put into practice the knowledge and skills acquired in the organized instructional program.

THE SUPERVISED AGRICULTURAL EXPERIENCE PROGRAM

It is desirable that each student who enrolls in any of the various types of schools and classes in vocational agriculture be required to engage in some form of supervised agricultural experience. Supervised farming is the usual requirement for students who are farming or preparing to farm. This program consists of various farming activities carried out under the supervision of the teacher of vocational agriculture. The program includes crop and livestock enterprises, such as corn production and egg production; improvement projects, such as constructing a dairy barn, controlling soil erosion and landscaping the home grounds; and supplementary farm jobs, such as culling hens, pruning grapevines, and testing soil. These activities are ordinarily carried out on the home farm of the enrollee, but some may be engaged in at the school shop, a neighboring farm, or a place other than the home farm.

The supervised farming program of the student in the day school class is used as a means of establishing this student in farming. The farming program is planned for a period of years, increasing in scope each year so that when the student completes his secondary school work his farming operations are of sufficient size to provide him with a full-time occupation. This long-time program of the student should include satisfactory business arrangements with his parents and others to insure him a share in the income and a voice in the management of his farming operations. The farming program of the student should be integrated with that of the home farm and should not consist of a "project" that has no relation to the type of farming engaged in on the home farm.

The planning of the long-time farming program involves cooperative endeavor on the part of the student, his parents, and his teacher. Properly made surveys of community farming practices, including uses of capital and farm machinery, are of assistance to the student in making an intelligent selection of the type of farming in which to engage. Supervised farming programs for young and adult farmers are related to the class instruction provided for these farmers. These supervised farming programs frequently include the organization and management of the entire farm when instruction is provided in farm organization and management.

Students enrolled in day school and adult classes in vocational agriculture may engage in various types of off-farm work experience related to the educational goal of the individual student. This experience may consist of part-time work or internship in agricultural industries such as milk plants, food processing plants, farm cooperatives, farm supply business, greenhouses, nurseries, forests, and various types of farm service agencies such as fertilizer factories, insecticide manufacturers and sales agencies, agricultural marketing agencies, and agricultural research and development institutions. The kind of work experience for the student will depend upon the needs of the student and the resources available in the community.

BUILDINGS AND EQUIPMENT

A complete program of vocational agriculture requires special housing facilities and equipment designed for the various activities included in the program. Many local departments of vocational agriculture are housed in separate buildings, conveniently located near the high school classroom building. These buildings include one or two classrooms, an agricultural mechanics shop, an office-conference room, a washroom, and storage rooms for laboratory apparatus, supplies, small tools and equipment. Some departments have community school facilities, such as food processing plants, included in the vocational agriculture unit. The separate building should fit into the general scheme of the school plant and should be carefully designed to meet the needs of the specific community for which it is intended.

Classrooms should be equipped with such items as blackboards, tables and chairs for students, cabinets for reference material and notebooks, bulletin boards, a teacher's desk, filing cabinets, and a table equipped with a sink and running water for use in performing class demonstrations. Agricultural classrooms that are used throughout the summer should be equipped with fans or air conditioning. Space should be provided and arranged for the use of audio-visual equipment, such as a motion picture projector, a slide projector, and an opaque projector. The teacher of vocational agriculture has many outside contacts and is required to keep and analyze farm and school records. His office should have a telephone, a typewriter, a calculating machine, a mimeograph and other equipment such as a stapling machine, a desk file and a paper punch.

Some laboratory equipment should be provided, such as a soil-testing outfit, a farm level, pruning tools, a sprayer, a microscope, a milk tester, and various types of glassware and chemicals. Equipment and supplies of this type should be purchased on the basis of need for use in teaching specific enterprises included in the course of study. These enterprises vary with the community, and, consequently, it is not advisable to formulate a standard list of laboratory equipment and supplies for all departments within a state. Lists of equipment compiled on an enterprise or unit basis have proved helpful in making a selection of laboratory equipment for a specific school. A land laboratory and a greenhouse are desirable for some units of instruction contemplated in the Vocational Education Act of 1963.

The increase in farm mechanization has brought about a need for special equipment for the agricultural mechanics shop. Some schools are teaching basic skills in areas such as drawing, tool fitting, woodwork, sheet metal, painting and glazing, electricity, concrete work, and welding. The skills taught are adapted for use in farm and nonfarm occupations. The shop should have necessary general purpose equipment such as work benches, tool cabinets, blackboards, and lumber racks. The safety factor is of first importance, and safe equipment properly arranged to lessen the chance of accidents is a basic consideration in planning the shop.

RURAL WAR PRODUCTION AND VETERANS FARM TRAINING PROGRAMS

Shortly before the beginning of World War II it became evident that the nation needed many additional workers for the war effort. Various types of training programs were organized including one known as the Rural War Production Training Program. This program which began in 1941 was first designed to provide pre-employment training in such courses as woodworking, metal working, machine shop, and auto mechanics. The need to maintain an adequate number of farm workers was also recognized and the objectives of the program in 1944 and 1945 were concerned with the production of agricultural products, the care of farm machinery and the production, processing, and conservation of food.

The Food Production War Training program was organized and conducted on Federal, state, and local levels by staff personnel and teachers of vocational agriculture. The local teacher was usually assigned responsibility for organizing and supervising the class and special teachers were employed to conduct the class. Most of the classes were held in the public high school buildings and Federal funds were made available for all costs of the program including equipment and supplies.

Enrollments in the Rural War Production Training program for the 5-year period ending May 31, 1945 totalled 4,188,000 persons. The total cost of the program all of which was paid by the Federal government was $48,475,000. About 23 percent of this was spent for equipment and rental of space and 77 percent for instruction and supervision. An appraisal of the program indicated that it had not only met the wartime needs but also demonstrated the value of vocational education to the nation's economy.

Provisions for the education and training of veterans of World War II were included in the G.I. bill which became a law in June 1944. Courses in agriculture were organized soon after its passage and the Veterans Administration in 1947 established minimum criteria for agricultural training. The law was amended to provide subsistence payments for veterans enrolled in on-farm courses. The Veterans Administration entered into contracts with state boards of education and local school boards. These contracts provided for the payment of salaries and travel of teachers, instructional supplies, and clerical service.

The training program consisted of organized group instruction of at least 200 clock hours per year at an educational institution and supervised work experience on a farm. Special teachers qualified in agriculture were engaged for the teaching and on-farm training. The program was under the supervision of the local teacher of vocational agriculture and was administered at state and national levels by staff personnel in agricultural education.

Students were taught proficiency in planning, producing and marketing farm commodities, farm management, conservation, and record keeping. Some veterans had control of the farm on which they secured work experience while others secured work experience as employees of other farmers.

Veterans farm training under the Korean G.I. law enacted in 1952 was similar to that of the World War II program except the cost of instruction was included in the Korean veteran's subsistence payment received from the Veterans Administration. The veteran paid tuition to the local training institution for all costs of instruction. A total of 785,000 farm veterans had entered training under the World War II and Korean G.I. laws by June 30, 1963. An all time high in enrollment was reached in May 1950 when nearly 362,000 were enrolled in on-farm training.

The Future Farmers of America

The Future Farmers of America, commonly referred to as the FFA, is the national organization of students and former students of vocational agriculture in the public schools that qualify for reimbursement under the provisions of the national vocational education laws. The FFA is considered an integral part of the public school curriculum in vocational agriculture and is used as a means of accomplishing some of the aims of vocational agriculture. The aims and purposes of the FFA are concerned with leadership and character development, cooperation, service, thrift, sportsmanship, scholarship, improved agriculture, patriotism, and citizenship. The members of the local FFA chapters engage in various activities designed to accomplish these objectives. The activities of the local chapter afford opportunities for members to learn how to conduct and take part in public meetings, to solve their own problems, and to assume civic responsibility.

THE ORIGIN OF THE FFA

The FFA originated in local organizations of students enrolled in day school classes in vocational agriculture. These local organizations, or clubs, first appeared shortly after the beginning of the Federally aided program of vocational education in 1917. These first clubs were organized primarily for recreation and leadership training. The Lincoln Aggie Club, for example, was organized at Bruno, Arkansas, on January 5, 1923, for leadership training and recreation. Local associations were formed in many states and, as the number of these increased and their possibilities became apparent, consideration was given to the formation of state associations. Walter S. Newman, then state supervisor of agricultural education in Virginia, proposed in 1925 that a state organization of farm boys be organized to give those boys who were enrolled in vocational agriculture a greater opportunity for self-expression and for the development of leadership. This idea was approved by a group of students in April 1926, and the Virginia state association was formed in the summer of 1926. The name Future Farmers of Virginia was suggested by Henry C. Groseclose, professor of agricultural education at Virginia Polytechnic Institute.

Many states formed similar state organizations of students enrolled in vocational agriculture, and the possibilities of a national organization soon became apparent. Special committees at regional conferences of supervisors and teacher trainers of agricultural education, working with a committee of the Agricultural Education Service of the Federal Board for Vocational Education, formulated a plan for a national organization. A tentative constitution was drawn up in the summer of 1928 by a special committee, and a call was made for a national convention to be held in Kansas City in November 1928. Eighteen states, 8 of which had state associations while the remainder had local chapters, responded to this call. These 18 states were Arizona, Arkansas, California, Colorado, Idaho, Iowa, Kansas, Michigan, Nebraska, New Jersey, North Dakota, Ohio, Oklahoma, Oregon, South Carolina, Utah, Virginia, and Wisconsin. Delegates from these states adopted a national constitution for the Future Farmers of America, elected national officers and conferred American Farmer degrees.

The FFA has developed into one of the most outstanding national organizations of secondary school students in America. It has grown from an active membership of 16,217 in 1929 to a membership of 395,812 members in 8368 local chapters in the United States, and Puerto Rico, as of June 30, 1962. The national association holds an annual convention in Kansas City, Missouri. There were about 12,000 persons in attendance at the 1963 convention. The national organization sponsors various types of national contests and maintains the FFA Foundation for financing its activities. The FFA has taken its place with other agencies interested in building up agriculture and improving country life.

THE FUTURE FARMERS ORGANIZATION

The FFA is composed of chartered state associations, including territorial and insular associations. These associations are composed of local chapters. Collegiate chapters are operated under the jurisdiction of the state association concerned. Each of the separate groups of Future Farmers has its own constitution. The local teacher of vocational agriculture serves as the adviser to the local chapter; the state supervisor of agricultural education is the state adviser; and the head of the Agricultural Education Branch, U.S. Office of Education, is the national adviser. A national advisory council composed of five representatives of the U.S. Office of Education and four state supervisors of vocational agriculture, one from each of the four regions of the United States, serves in an advisory capacity to the national officers.

There are four types of membership in the FFA. These are active, associate, collegiate, and honorary. Active members are school students not over 25 years of age who are enrolled in vocational agriculture classes. Associate members are persons who have terminated their active membership. Collegiate members include students in college who are preparing to teach vocational agriculture and all former FFA members enrolled in a collegiate chapter. Honorary members are persons who have rendered outstanding service to the FFA and who have been elected to this honor by active members.

There are four grades of active membership. These are Green Hand, Chapter Farmer, State Farmer, and American Farmer. The first two grades mentioned are conferred by local chapters, and the third is conferred by the state association. The American Farmer degree is conferred by the national organization. Advancement to each of these degrees is based on the accomplishments of the candidate as specified in the constitutions and bylaws. These accomplishments are concerned with earnings, investments, scholarship, and leadership. The number of candidates for the State Farmer degree and the American Farmer degree is dependent upon the number of members in the state Associations. Each year four American Farmers, one from each of the four regions, are designated as Star Farmers. One of these four is designated as the Star Farmer of America. These designations are made on the basis of the accomplishments of the individuals selected.

Each of the affiliated units is supported by dues collected from members. The national dues are 10¢ per member per year. The motto of the FFA is "Learning to Do, Doing to Learn, Earning to Live, Living to Serve." The FFA colors are national blue and corn gold. The national emblem is made up of five symbols—the owl, the plow, and the rising sun within the cross section of an ear of corn, which is surmounted by the American eagle. A Federal charter was granted to the FFA by the Congress of the United States on August 30, 1950.

THE FFA PROGRAM OF WORK

The FFA program of work is a written outline of activities and goals, and the ways and means of accomplishing them. The program of work covers a stated period of time, usually one year. Programs of work are formulated for the local, state, and national organizations. The state and national programs of work are based on the goals and accomplishments of the local chapters. The local program of work is based on the needs of the members and the organization as a whole. The program-of-work committee has responsibility for suggesting program-of-work activities to the local chapter.

The activities of the program of work are usually grouped into about nine divisions for convenience in reporting. The first of these is *supervised farming*, including plans for assisting members in getting started in farming, conducting tours and making contacts with parents. Another division is that of *cooperative activities*, in which Future Farmers learn cooperation by participating in cooperative activities. Plans for such activities as buying and selling cooperatively, conducting group projects, holding shows and sales, and cooperative advertising are included in this section. A division on *community service* is included, in which plans are made for services of educational value, such as beautifying the school ground, helping needy families, testing seeds for farmers of the community and conducting community safety campaigns. The plan also contains specifications for engaging in *leadership activities*, such as presiding at meetings, speaking and debating before groups, attending various meetings and participating in public speaking and parliamentary procedure contests.

Another division in the plan is concerned with *earnings and savings* received from supervised farming and cooperative projects. Such activities as thrift banks, chapter investments, individual investments in land and machinery, and the keeping of financial records are included in this division. Plans for the *conduct of meetings* are also included in the program of work. Such items as facilities, schedule of meetings, programs, and plans for officer training are in this division. A division on *scholarship* in the program is designed to encourage Future Farmers to maintain proper standards of classwork and to provide for counseling and supervised study. Wholesome *recreation* is

The American Farmer Degree is Awarded to Outstanding Future Farmers at the National Convention, Future Farmers of America. (National Association, Future Farmers of America)

important in the program of work. Activities of this nature include going on tours; attending state camps; sponsoring picnics, parties, banquets and camping trips; and holding joint meetings with other clubs.

Various other activities usually grouped as *general activities*, such as putting up FFA signs, giving assembly programs, holding demonstrations and buying equipment for the vocational agriculture department, are frequently included in the plan. Each chapter prepares an annual budget, showing the funds needed for the program of work, and includes in the program ways and means of financing these activities.

THE NEW FARMERS OF AMERICA

The New Farmers of America, or NFA, is a national association of Negro farm boys who are enrolled in vocational agriculture in some public schools throughout the United States. The organization was started at the suggestion of Dr. H. O. Sargent, Federal agent for agricultural education for Negroes, at about the time the FAA had its origin. The Virginia NFA was organized in May 1927, at which time a constitution written by G. W. Owens, teacher trainer at Virginia State College, was adopted. Other states organized state associations, and in 1935 the national organization known as the New Farmers of America was formed at Tuskegee Institute, Alabama. The NFA has become an important factor in the development of vocational agriculture throughout the nation.

The NFA was organized in a manner similar to that of the FFA. The grades of active membership are Farm Hand, Improved Farmer, Modern Farmer, and Superior Farmer, corresponding to the Green Hand, Chapter Farmer, State Farmer and American Farmer degrees of the FFA. The state associations were organized into three sections. The Booker T. Washington section included the states of Delaware, Maryland, North Carolina, South Carolina, and Virginia. The H. O. Sargent section comprised the states of Alabama, Florida, Georgia, Kentucky, and Tennessee. The Almmot section was composed of Arkansas, Louisiana, Mississippi, Oklahoma, and Texas. The NFA emblem is somewhat similar to that of the FFA except that the cross section of the ear of corn of the FFA is replaced by the cross section of a boll of cotton of the NFA. The annual program of work of the NFA contains activities similar to those of the FFA. The NFA had a total of 58,132 active members on June 30, 1963.

THE FFA FOUNDATION

The Future Farmers of America Foundation was incorporated under the laws of the District of Columbia on March 29, 1944. The Foundation was established to provide an agency for receiving and expending grants of money and property made by business, civic, and farm organizations for the purpose of furthering the programs of Future Farmers and New Farmers on local, state and national levels. The Foundation is governed by a board of trustees composed of 14 members, all of whom are employed in the state and Federal vocational education programs. The head of the Agricultural Education Branch, U.S. Office of Education, is chairman of the board. The funds received are expended by the board of trustees of the Foundation for such purposes as: (1) loans to young farmers who were formerly Future Farmers or New Farmers, (2) leadership training among students in vocational agriculture, (3) the development of public interest in vocational agriculture and farm mechanics, and (4) prizes and awards to Future Farmers and New Farmers. Donations are received with the understanding that they may be used without reservation or restriction by the donors, and donors are not identified with any specific award. Donors are not eligible to serve as members of the board of trustees of the Foundation.

The FFA Foundation makes a number of awards each year to assist Future Farmers to become established in farming. These awards are made for outstanding accomplishments in various activities. Included among these are awards made to Future Farmers who are designated as American Farmers, State Star Farmers, and the Star Farmer of America. Awards in this category are also given for outstanding accomplishments in farm mechanics, rural electrification, soil and water management, and dairy farming.

The Foundation makes farm safety awards to local chapters to stimulate them to engage in farm safety activities and campaigns. The Foundation provides annual awards to team and individual winners in the following five national judging contests: dairy cattle, dairy products, poultry, livestock, and meats. National public speaking contests are sponsored each year by the FFA. The Foundation provides cash awards for state and national winners of these contests. Foundation medals are provided for chapter award winners who show outstanding achievement in their farming programs and FFA activities as judged at the local chapter level. The Foundation also provides funds for state awards for improving agriculture and leadership.

QUESTIONS FOR STUDY AND DISCUSSION

1. Indicate some major problems of agriculture that suggest the need for a comprehensive program of agricultural education.
2. What are the objectives of vocational agriculture for students preparing for farming?
3. What objectives are suggested for students who are preparing for agricultural occupations other than farming?
4. Indicate some characteristics and practices in day-school classes in vocational agriculture.
5. What percentage of the total enrollment in vocational agriculture is represented by day-school students?
6. Federal funds represent what proportion of the total expenditures for vocational agricultural education?
7. What are the qualifications required of teachers of vocational agriculture?
8. What kinds of buildings and equipment are needed in vocational agricultural education?

9. What is the purpose of a supervised farming program, and what standards should be observed in establishing it?
10. What contribution has vocational agriculture made to war production and to farm veterans?
11. Discuss the history and purposes of the FFA and the NFA.
12. What are the grades of active membership in the FFA, and what factors govern the advancement from one degree to another?

SOURCE REFERENCES

Benedict, Murray R., *Farm Policies of the United States*, Twentieth Century Fund, New York, 1953.

Bennett, Hugh H., *Elements of Soil Conservation*, McGraw-Hill, New York, 1955.

Ekstrom, George F., and John B. McClelland, *Adult Education in Vocational Agriculture*, Interstate, Danville, Ill., 1952.

Federal Board for Vocational Education, *Annual Reports*, 1918 to 1932 inclusive, Washington, D.C.

Federal Security Agency, Office of Education, *The Advisory Council for a Department of Vocational Agriculture*, Vocational Division Bulletin No. 243, Washington, D.C., 1951.

Federal Security Agency, Office of Education, *Rural War Production Training Program, Final Report*, Bulletin 1946, No. 11, Washington, D.C., 1946.

Future Farmers of America, *Official Manual, Future Farmers of America*, Future Farmers Supply Service, Alexandria, Va., 1963.

Higbee, Edward, *American Agriculture*, Wiley, New York, 1958.

Hill, C. W., and J. P. Bail, *Objectives for Agricultural Education*, Agricultural Education Division, Cornell University, Ithaca, 1962.

Kreitlow, Burton W., *Rural Education*, Harper and Row, New York, 1954.

New Farmers of America, *NFA Guide*, The French-Bray Printing Company, Baltimore, 1960.

Nichols, Mark L., *Young Farmers, Their Problems, Activities, and Educational Program*, Interstate, Danville, Ill., 1952.

O'Kelley, George L., Jr., *Agricultural Education, The Preparation of Teachers*, Vocational Division Bulletin No. 295, Office of Education, Department of Health, Education, and Welfare, Washington, D.C., 1961.

Phipps, Lloyd J., *Handbook on Agricultural Education in Public Schools*, Interstate, Danville, Ill., 1965.

Tenney, A. Webster, *Practical Activities for Future Farmers*, Interstate, Danville, Ill., 1954.

U.S. Congress, *Laws Granting Education and Training and Other Benefits to Veterans*, Committee Print No. 308, 82nd Congress, 2nd Session, Washington, D.C., 1952.

U.S. Department of Commerce, Bureau of the Census, *Statistical Abstract of the United States, 1964*, Washington, D.C., 1964.

U.S. Department of Health, Education, and Welfare, Office of Education, *Administration of Vocational Education,* Vocational Education Bulletin No. 1, revised 1958, Washington, D.C., 1958.

U.S. Office of Education, *Digest of Annual Reports of State Boards for Vocational Education* for fiscal years 1933 to 1962 inclusive, Washington, D.C.

CHAPTER EIGHT

VOCATIONAL DISTRIBUTIVE EDUCATION

The first half of the twentieth century has been characterized as the age of production, and some persons have suggested that the second half of the century will be remembered for its accent on distribution. The increase in production, which has reached such proportions in the United States that the manufactured output equals that of the rest of the world, requires a vast army of persons to transfer these products from the farms, factories, stores, and offices to the consuming public. This is the task of distribution, and, because of the diversity of products and services, many people of widely different talents and training are needed in this occupational area. The field of distribution offers careers that are interesting and profitable, and, as is the case in most vocations, the best jobs go to those who are best prepared by education and training.

The Federally aided vocational distributive education program was established to provide opportunities for the education and training of the various kinds and types of workers required to distribute the output of goods and services. This program is a relatively recent addition to the Federally aided program of vocational education. It is designed for workers such as retailers, wholesalers, jobbers, commission men, and managers of cooperatives. Workers in large stores such as merchandising managers, salesmanagers, buyers, merchandise department heads, sales persons, section cashiers, demonstrators, floormen, adjusters, personal shoppers, and deliverymen are also in distributive occupations.

Services, both business and personal, are included in the field of distribution. These services are sold by workers engaged in advertising, financing, insuring, storing, warehousing, transporting, communicating, collecting, auctioneering, reporting, and employing. Personal service establishments in distribution include barber and beauty shops, laundries, cleaning and pressing shops, funeral parlors, and shoe shops. Some workers in hotels and places of amusement are classified as workers in distribution. Bookkeepers, stenographers, auditors, maintenance men, custodians, and other workers who are not in contact with customers are not classified as workers in distribution.

The Importance of Distribution

The importance of distribution has been increasing with the growth of the nation. Prior to the Industrial Revolution and the rise of large cities, distribution was of minor importance. The producer frequently used his products or disposed of them among his neighbors. Today distribution is one of the nation's three leading economic activities, along with industrial production and agriculture. The goods and services sold by persons in distribution provide jobs and purchasing power for many other persons. It is estimated that the goods sold by 1 sales person provide jobs for 33 other workers on farms, in factories, and in offices. The wages and payments to these persons increase their demand for goods and services and bring about an expansion in industry and agriculture. Distribution in some of its forms accounts for about two-thirds of the nation's business.

DISTRIBUTION ESTABLISHMENTS

Business establishments for the distribution of goods and services include retail businesses, wholesale establishments, and service agencies. The number of these three types of establishments increased from 2,610,000 in 1948 to 3,272,000 in 1962—an increase of about 25 percent during the 15-year period. The number of retail stores, which comprised about two-thirds of all the distribution establishments, increased 24 percent during this period. The number of wholesale establishments, which represented about 10 percent of the distribution establishments, increased 30 percent during this period. There were about 26 percent more service establishments in 1962 than in 1948.

Students in Cooperative Part-Time Classes in Vocational Distributive Education Learn the Techniques of Selling by Engaging in Part-Time Work in Business Establishments. (Chicago Public Schools)

While the increase in the number of retail stores was 24 percent, their aggregate sales receipts increased from $133 billion in 1948 to $235 billion in 1962—an increase of about 76 percent. The retail stores are divided into groups such as food, eating and drinking places, apparel, furniture, automotive, hardware, drug and proprietary, and second-hand stores. Sales receipts in food establishments represented about 25 percent and sales receipts in the automotive group about 18 percent of the total volume of sales of all retail stores in 1962. A survey made by the U.S. Bureau of the Census indicated that in 1958 about one-third of all retail stores had no paid employees but were operated by the owner and his family. About 4 percent of the stores had 20 or more paid employees, and these stores had 40 percent of the total sales.

The 332,000 wholesale establishments in the United States had sales receipts in excess of $156 billion in 1962. This was an increase of 73 percent over the volume reported for 1948. More than one-half of the total sales among wholesale establishments was made in stores located in the six states of New York, Illinois, California, Pennsylvania, Ohio, and Texas. Wholesale establishments are classified as merchant wholesalers, manufacturers' sales branches with stocks, manufacturers' sales offices without stocks, petroleum bulk stations, agents and brokers, and assemblers. The merchant wholesalers had the largest volume of business of wholesale establishments.

A total of 918,000 service establishments were in operation in the United States in 1962. The personal services group, which includes establishments such as barber and beauty shops, cleaning and pressing shops, laundries, and photographic studios, accounted for almost one-half the number of establishments and one-fourth of the total receipts of all service establishments in 1958.

These facts indicate that the distribution of goods and services is one of the nation's more important enterprises and one that employs large numbers of workers with a wide variety of competencies. The continuous changes in the number and size of these establishments require an ever changing personnel, and the intense competition among these establishments results in small margins of profit and demands a high degree of efficiency from the workers.

DISTRIBUTION COSTS AND SERVICES

Distribution costs, according to various estimates, account for from 50 to 60 percent of the consumer's dollar. This relatively high cost is due largely to consumer demands. Consumers demand commodities of all descriptions at nearby stores, packaged in a variety of sizes and processed for ready use—even commodities that must be collected from the far corners of the earth. In addition, consumers demand a variety of store services such as charge accounts, free deliveries, return privileges, and guarantees. These services add to the cost of distribution. Since consumers will likely continue their demands for more and more services, the only alternative to higher distribution costs is greater efficiency in distribution.

Distribution functions include all activities necessary to transfer goods and services from producers to consumers. Functions involved in this transfer of goods include assembling, transporting, buying, selling, grading and standardizing, processing, packaging, storing, financing, risk bearing and collecting, and using market information. Each of these functions adds time, place or ownership utility to the goods and involves various kinds of expense. Among these are expenses involved in direct selling, advertising and sales promotion, transportation, warehousing and handling, credit and collection, financing and general expense, including research and administration.

Consumer goods pass through various channels in going from producers to consumers. Some go directly from producer to consumer, some from producer to wholesaler to retailer to consumer. Industrial goods go from producer to user or from producer to wholesaler to user. Factors which influence the determination of the channels of distribution are: (1) the size of the producing concern; (2) the financial strength of the producer; (3) the nature and quantity of the commodity to be distributed; and (4) the number, location, and demands of the consumers. A producer may sell direct to consumers as a means of facilitating distribution and reducing costs, or he may find it more profitable to sell to a wholesaler.

The wholesaler is a middleman who is a specialist in distribution. He usually purchases goods in large quantities and resells them in smaller lots to retailers. Wholesalers perform services such as assembling, warehousing, delivering, financing, and advising. There are other wholesalers such as brokers, selling agents, manufacturers' agents, and commission men who do not handle goods. These distributors have developed special services to meet particular needs. The services of all these distributors are in demand by producers and consumers and involve a cost of distribution. The producer's problem is to select the combination of channels and agencies that will be most profitable. The problem of the distribution agency is to render the most service for the least cost, and agency personnel and methods are directed to this end.

WORKERS IN DISTRIBUTION

According to the U.S. Census more than 19 million sales persons were employed in retail and wholesale stores and service establishments in the United States in 1962. The 19 million workers in 1962 represented an increase of 33 percent over the corresponding figure for 1948 and was about 29 percent of the employed civilian labor force in 1962.

Most of the workers in distribution establishments are employed in retail stores. The number of retail store workers increased from 6,700,000 in 1948 to 8,500,000 in 1962, an increase of 25 percent. The wholesale establishment employed 2,800,000 workers in 1962, an increase of 12 percent more than the number in 1948. The number employed in service establishments increased 53 percent from 1948 to 1962. The U.S. Department of Labor has estimated that by 1975 the number of jobs in retail and wholesale establishments will increase by about one-third and the number in service establishments by about two-thirds.

Every year many young workers find their first employment in the distributive occupations, especially in retail selling. Relatively few of these young workers have had any vocational education for the jobs in which they are employed. Many have received little or no vocational guidance to help them determine their fitness for the jobs they have secured. These shortcomings have resulted in an unusually high turn-over of employees in retail stores.

DISTRIBUTION AND STANDARDS OF LIVING

The median income of families in the United States increased from $4400 in 1950 to $6840 in 1960. This represented an increase of 54 percent during this period. Much of the increase was due to the fact that more dollars were required to buy the same quantity of goods and services in 1960 than were required in 1950. However, a substantial amount of the family income represented an actual net increase in spendable wages that was available to buy additional goods and services for the family.

Data indicate that the net increase in spendable wages was used to purchase additional goods and services. For example, 1,580,000 room air conditioners were reported sold in 1960 as compared to 11,000 in 1940. The number of central gas heating units sold in 1960 was 1,173,000 and the corresponding number for 1940 was 117,000 units. The sale of washing machines increased from 1,455,000 units in 1940 to about 3,400,000 units in 1960. Passenger car and taxi registration increased from 1 for every 5 persons in 1940 to 1 for every 3 persons in 1960. The number of telephones per 100 persons increased from 17 to 48 during this period.

These additional purchases were made through the channels of distribution, and these purchases increased the standards of living of the families. Since a constantly rising standard of living is essential for a prosperous people, it is important that more and more goods and services be made available through channels of distribution. It should be kept in mind that purchases, not purchasing power, bring about higher standards of living, and purchasing power is not ordinarily reduced until purchasing is reduced. A faulty system of distribution for a commodity will reduce purchasing, and this in turn will make it necessary to curtail production. An efficient system of distribution increases sales, jobs, and purchasing power and makes possible improved standards of living. These facts indicate the importance to the national welfare of an efficient system of distribution.

The Development of the Vocational Distributive Education Program

The changes in the relationship between production and distribution, the characteristics of the large labor force in distribution and the nature of its services and agencies suggested the need for a program of vocational education designed to upgrade and to prepare workers for careers in distribution. While no funds were appropriated by the Smith-Hughes Vocational Education Act to stimuate business education, definite provision was made for aiding the states in the solution of business education problems by means of studies, investigations, and reports. The Federal Board for Vocational Education in 1918 appointed an assistant director for commercial education to direct studies in the various phases of commercial education as an aid to the states in providing training programs in this field. The Board in 1919 employed a special agent for retail selling, and in that same year the National Retail Dry Goods Association passed a resolution approving the principle of including instruction in retail selling in public secondary school curriculums.

An interpretation made in 1919 of the Smith-Hughes law permitted workers over 14 years of age who were employed in stores to enroll in part-time general continuation classes under certain condition. Further modifications in the regulations were made in 1931 to permit the organization of cooperative part-time classes for store employees. The distributive education program was somewhat slow in developing, largely because Federal funds were not available at that time for the reimbursement of salaries of supervisors and teacher educators of distributive education. Cooperative training in retail selling was offered in public secondary schools in 43 cities of the United States during the year 1933. The total enrollment in those classes was 9500 students.

The passage of the George-Deen Act, authorizing Federal funds for vocational distributive education, resulted in the rapid development of this program. These funds were first made available for the fiscal year ending June 30, 1938, and during this first year 20 states employed 21 full-time and 6 part-time state supervisors and teacher educators in distributive education. By the close of the fiscal year ending June 30, 1939, 31 states had employed 31 full time and 9 part-time supervisors, assistant supervisors, and teacher educators in distributive education. The vocational distributive education program in states other than those included above was directed by supervisors of other vocational services. A Business Education Service was established in the Vocational Division, U.S. Office of Education in 1939 to administer the distributive education program and coordinate other business education activities. This was changed to the Distributive Education Service in 1951. The program is now administered by the Division of Vocational and Technical Education, Bureau of Educational Assistance Programs, Office of Education, U.S. Department of Health, Education, and Welfare.

CHARACTERISTICS OF VOCATIONAL DISTRIBUTIVE EDUCATION

Vocational distributive education is a program of instruction in marketing, merchandising, and management. The program is concerned with the education needed for purposes of updating, upgrading, career development, and operational management. The following goals have been established to enable distributive education to accomplish its general purpose: (1) to offer instruction in marketing, merchandising and management; (2) to aid in improving the techniques of distribution; and (3) to develop an understanding of the wide range of social and economic responsibilities which accompany the right to engage in distribution in a free competitive society. Distributive occupations are those followed by proprietors, managers, or employees engaged primarily in marketing or merchandising goods or services. Such occupations may be found in establishments engaged in retailing, wholesaling, manufacturing, storing, transporting, financing, and risk bearing.

Various types of abilities are needed to attain the objectives of vocational distributive education. These include (1) social abilities necessary for making business contacts, (2) salesmanship abilities to assist customers in securing the kinds of goods and services desired, (3) abilities concerned with a knowledge of goods and services offered by the distributor, and (4) store service abilities necessary for efficient merchandising.

Social abilities include those required for making correct appraisals of customers, employers and fellow workers; for speaking in a pleasing and correct manner; and for presenting a good appearance.

Salesmanship abilities include those concerned with selecting goods and services to meet customer needs and with showing customers how to use goods and services to an advantage. Store service abilities have to do with conforming to store policies and practices, making accurate records and reports, and handling goods effectively and safely.

The foregoing list of goals and abilities is suggested as a guide for use in planning courses of study and other activities included in a vocational distributive education program. The specific needs will vary with the nature of the job for which training is provided, the characteristics of the learners, the time available, and the personnel at hand. Some information may be obtained through an analysis of specific jobs. This analysis will be useful in selecting objectives and abilities and in determining the types of classes needed to accomplish the objectives.

TYPES OF SCHOOLS AND CLASSES

The organization for instruction in vocational distributive education is designed to accomplish the objectives of the distributive education program. These objectives contemplate instruction for various groupings of workers and prospective workers in distribution. The Vocational Education Act of 1963 authorizes the use of Federal funds for instruction in distributive and other gainful occupations for in-school and out-of-school youth and adults and special classes for disadvantaged youth.

Two types of distributive education classes are authorized in the regulations for the administration of the George-Barden Act. These are extension classes and part-time cooperative classes. The Vocational Education Act of 1963 contains an amendment to the George-Barden Act which authorizes the use of Federal funds for pre-employment classes in distributive education. Some characteristics and requirements of these three types of classes follow.

Extension classes. An extension or adult class in vocational distributive education is organized for persons who are employed in distributive occupations. The course is designed to increase or extend knowledge and skill in the occupation in which the enrollee is employed. The class may be held during the usual working hours or during the nonworking hours. Adult classes are especially designed for (1) selling and nonselling employees of retail stores, (2) executives of large stores and owners or managers of small ones, (3) wholesalers and wholesale salesmen, (4) outside salesmen, and (5) employees of service establishments who have customer contacts. Most of the extension classes are short courses. However, the trend in some states is for long range programs leading to proficiency in specific areas.

Part-time cooperative classes. A part-time cooperative class in distributive education is one that provides for alternation of study in school with supervised on-the-job training in a distributive occupation. The two experiences are planned and supervised by the school and the employer so that each makes a definite contribution to the development of the student in his chosen occupation. Work periods and school attendance are on alternate days, weeks or other periods of time, but the hours at work are required to equal or exceed the hours spent in school during the regular school year. The student in this program is regularly enrolled in a public secondary or post-secondary school and receives instruction in both vocational and general education subjects.

Pre-employment classes. A pre-employment or preparatory class in distributive education is one that provides instruction in the knowledge, skills, and attitudes needed by a person who is preparing to enter a position concerned with the sale of goods and services. These classes may be included in a pre-employment curriculum in distributive education comprising technical and general education courses designed to prepare a person for entry into a position in the field of distribution. Pre-employment classes in vocational distributive education under Federally aided programs are usually placed at the secondary school level. Some classes are on the post-high school or junior college level.

PLANNING THE DISTRIBUTIVE EDUCATION PROGRAM

A complete local program of vocational distributive education consists of extension, part-time cooperative, and pre-employment classes. Before any of these types of classes are organized, a survey or investigation should be made to determine the need for, and interest in, the class. Various groups should be contacted, such as students, parents, school officials, employees, and employers. Students and their parents need to know about opportunities for employment and advancement in distribution and need to express an interest or opinion relative to part-time employment in distribution. School officials need to understand the curriculum requirements, class schedule adjustments, and personnel needs of the cooperative program. The possibilities and requirements for adult classes should be explained to employees and employers, and, in addition, employers should understand the requirements of the cooperative program.

Extension, part-time cooperative, and pre-employment classes may be organized simultaneously but the usual practice is to establish the cooperative part-time or pre-employment classes and later develop the adult classes. This procedure makes it possible for the coordinator or distributive education teacher to assist in the promotion and organization. Some schools provide courses preparatory to the related training of the cooperative program. The extension program on the adult level usually starts with classes for sales people and others who have customer contacts. These are followed by classes for junior executives, buyers, and department heads. Adult programs for owners, managers, and executives usually constitute the third stage in the extension class series.

The organization and operation of the vocational distributive education program in the local community may be facilitated by the use of a steering committee and an advisory committee. The steering committee is usually selected by the coordinator and serves without formal appointment. This committee is sometimes used pending the appointment of an advisory committee. The committee consists of employers and employees in distributive occupations. It assists the teacher to become acquainted with the merchants and with the problems and relationships in the community. The advisory committee may offer advice on wage rates, training stations, types of training, and standards to be observed. This committee can strengthen the distributive education program by establishing satisfactory contacts, through the coordinator or instructor, between the school and the cooperating business establishments.

TRENDS IN ENROLLMENTS AND EXPENDITURES

The number of enrollees in vocational distributive education increased from 36,000 enrollees in 1938 to 321,065 in 1962. During this 25-year period, a total of 5,941,000 students enrolled in distributive education classes. The enrollments in vocational distributive education were about equally divided between male and female students. The enrollment in part-time cooperative classes consisted of about 60 percent female students.

The number of teachers of vocational distributive education classes increased from 922 in 1938 to 7365 in 1962. This represents an increase of about 700 percent over the 25-year period. The average number of distributive education cooperative students per coordinator for the 25-year period was 26. This figure has remained about the same each year of the period.

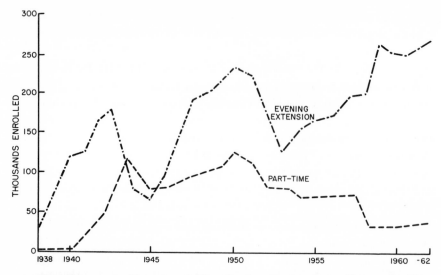

Enrollments in Vocational Distributive Occupations Classes by Type of Class in the States and Territories for the Years 1938 to 1962. The enrollments in evening extension classes have greatly exceeded the enrollments in other types of classes for most of the years since 1938. (U.S. Department of Health, Education, and Welfare, Office of Education, *Digest of Annual Reports of State Boards for Vocational Education to the Office of Education, Fiscal Year Ended June 30, 1962*, Government Printing Office, 1963)

Expenditures for vocational distributive education have totaled $123,055,000 for the 25-year period 1938 to 1962. Federal funds represented 28 percent of this amount, and state and local funds represented 72 percent. State and local funds were 35 percent and 37 percent respectively for the period. State and local communities have expended $2.59 for each dollar of Federal funds provided for vocational distributive education. The proportion of state and local funds is increasing. For example, during the first 5 years of the program from 1938 to 1942, state and local communities spent $.76 for each dollar of Federal funds. During the 5-year period ending June 30, 1962, the state and local communities expended $3.02 for each dollar of Federal funds received.

Expenditures for the cost of instruction in vocational distributive education classes represented 80 percent of the total cost for the 5-year period 1958 to 1962. Seventeen percent of the total cost was expended for supervision and teacher training, and 3 percent for administration of the vocational distributive education program.

Extension Classes

Extension classes are designed largely for workers who have acquired their vocational competencies by working on the job. Many of these workers are conscious of their limitations and recognize the need for additional training. They are willing to learn from other persons when these persons can demonstrate that they are competent. Most adult workers are eager to advance in their occupations, and when convinced that advancement may result from attending extension classes they are willing to attend these classes. These facts make it necessary that organizational, promotional, and teaching activities of vocational distributive education classes for adults be carefully planned and carried out.

ORGANIZATION AND ADMINISTRATION PRACTICES

The state board for vocational education is responsible for the state administration and supervision of extension classes in vocational distributive education. The state board may assume responsibility for conducting these classes or it may delegate this responsibility to local boards of education. State boards for vocational education employ state and district supervisors, teacher trainers, and itinerant teachers for promoting vocational distributive education programs. When the state board retains responsibility for teaching the classes, state itinerant teachers are usually assigned to these classes. These teachers, also referred to as circuit teachers, move from place to place about the state, and serve the smaller communities or other areas in which it is difficult to secure local persons qualified to serve as instructors. Itinerant instructors for retail selling and food service training are employed in many states throughout the nation.

Frequently, the state board for vocational education delegates responsibility to local boards of education to organize and administer extension classes in vocational distributive education. Local boards may employ persons to spend full time or part time in teaching these classes. Frequently, workers who currently work in the occupation in which instruction is needed are employed during their nonworking hours for this responsibility. When this type of organization is used, some school official, such as the local director of vocational education or the local coordinator, takes responsibility for promotional work and class organization. The class organizer, together with a representative advisory committee, selects the instructor and recommends to the local school authority that he be employed. These instructors usually receive pay on an hourly basis for their services.

PROMOTIONAL ACTIVITIES

The need for an extension class in vocational distributive education may be determined by an occupational survey. When the need for training is ascertained, it is usually necessary for the persons interested in sponsoring the class program to engage in some promotional activities. These activities are designed to acquaint various individuals and groups with the needs, as reflected in the survey, and the ways of meeting these needs. The promotion of the program is frequently referred to as "selling" and is carried out in much the same manner as that of selling goods and services.

Responsibility for promoting the program is assumed by various groups and individuals. Sometimes the state staff in vocational distributive education assists in promoting the program on the local level. Itinerant teachers assume charge of promotional activities in some instances. Responsibility for promotion of the program in the local community is often undertaken by the local director of vocational education or the local coordinator of distributive education. Local clubs, associations and chambers of commerce frequently cooperate in the promotional activities. Some classes are promoted by prospective students who see a need for additional technical information and recognize the fact that an adult extension class may supply this need.

The most effective promotion is by means of personal contacts with individuals and small groups. Other promotional devices include talks before interested groups, personal letters, posters, articles in newspapers, radio announcements, and field trips or visits to business establishments. Promotional information should include facts about the scope and extent of the distribution problem in the community, the need for extension classes, the nature of the program, and some results of previous class programs. Charts, graphs, illustrations, slides, motion pictures, and exhibits may be used to an advantage in presenting the data involved in the promotional activities.

COURSE CONTENT FOR EXTENSION CLASSES

The specific content of an extension course should be determined by a functional analysis of the occupation for which training is provided. General instruction in business subjects such as bookkeeping, business arithmetic, business law, and typewriting are not reimbursable from Federal funds, except that selected topics from subjects such as bookkeeping for retailers may be included in a reimbursable course.

Experience has shown that best results are obtained when the instruction is given in a series of related units. The units of the series are selected to constitute an integrated area in the field of distribution. For example, short units such as textiles, speech and personality, principles of retailing, economics of fashion, store organization, and sales promotion may be included in a comprehensive course in retailing. Each unit is complete within itself and is scheduled for 10 to 20 hours of instruction. These units, together with others, are scheduled in sequence so that a worker may take one or all of the short units. When all the short units in the sequence have been completed, the worker will have gained the essential information needed for advancement in the occupation of retailing.

TEACHING PRINCIPLES AND THEIR APPLICATION

Certain basic principles have proved helpful in selecting teaching procedures and materials for extension classes in vocational distributive education. Some of the more important principles include the following: (1) the learner should understand the goal; (2) the instructor should know his subject matter; (3) the learner should recognize successful accomplishment of objectives; (4) methods of instruction should be varied; (5) opportunities for learner participation should be provided; (6) experiences of the learner should be utilized; (7) opportunity for the progress of the learner, according to ability, should be provided; and (8) the physical environment should be conducive to learning.

The implications of these principles should be kept in mind in organizing subject matter for teaching and in presenting subject matter to learners. The use of short units with clear-cut statements of objectives and the relationship of these units and objectives to the problem should be emphasized. Advisory committees and school authorities responsible for the employment of instructors should make certain that instructors are qualified. Learners should be encouraged to evaluate their own progress and should be provided with the means and methods of so doing. Commendation by the instructor for successful accomplishment is an effective means of giving recognition to learners.

There is no one best method of teaching, and the use of various methods will tend to prevent learners from losing interest. The conference procedure which was developed by representatives of the Fed-

Employed Sales Persons Enrolled for Short-Unit Courses Designed to Improve Their Efficiency in Selling. (Arkansas State Department of Education, Vocational Division)

eral Board for Vocational Education for use in training foremen and supervisors is frequently used in extension classes. This procedure consists of informal and systematic group discussions carried out under the direction of a leader. The experiences of the learners are pooled, and the final conclusions are based on the combined experiences of the learners. The wide range of ability among adults makes it necessary that standards of accomplishment vary and that learners be allowed to progress independently of each other. The use of the unit method of teaching with directions for individual instruction will permit individual progress, and the use of maximum and minimum standards for each unit will prevent slow learners from holding back those who learn faster. Many teaching difficulties are caused by the fact that classes for adults are held in classrooms designed for youth. Instructors may lessen these difficulties by giving attention to temperature, ventilation, light, classroom arrangement, and outside noise and distraction.

Evaluation is an essential aspect of any instructional program. It includes testing but involves more than the conventional testing and examination techniques. Evaluation is designed to indicate whether the teacher has taught and whether the learner has learned. It helps to answer questions such as: Is the education program accomplishing its goals? Is it making actual changes in student behavior in the direction of the objectives? Among the devices used in an evaluation program are objective and subjective tests, self-rating scales, interviews, scales of judgments of students and teachers, check lists, diaries, observations, and student projects. The devices and techniques used will vary with the objectives desired. These devices should be carefully selected by qualified individuals to assure acceptable results from the evaluation program.

Part-Time Cooperative Classes

Part-time cooperative classes in vocational distributive education are designed to enlarge the vocational intelligence of workers 16 years of age or over who have entered upon employment. These classes are conducted on a schedule which combines organized vocational instruction in a public secondary school with occupational experience in a business establishment. Part-time cooperative classes in vocational distributive education have proved popular for many years as a means of enabling young persons employed in distributive occupations to obtain supervised experience in merchandising along with organized class instruction. This combination of education and experience has enabled competent youth to advance more rapidly to high-level positions in distribution.

ADMINISTRATION AND SUPERVISION

Part-time cooperative classes in vocational distributive education are administered on the state level in the same manner as are other Federally aided vocational programs. The vocational division of the state department of education has responsibility for assisting local boards of education in determining a need and in planning, organizing, and conducting these classes. Regulations concerning these classes are included in the state plan for vocational education. The plan provides that cooperative part-time students be employed at least half of the usual work week.

Three plans for providing part-time instruction based on the length of the cooperative program and the extent of organized in-school instruction are in general use. Plan A is a two-year program in which at least one regular class period per school day is assigned for organized instruction in vocational distributive education. Plan B is a one-year program which requires at least two regular class periods a day for vocational instruction. Plan C is a one-year program providing one class period per school day for vocational instruction for students who have previously acquired two high school credits in business education courses such as bookkeeping, salesmanship, and business economics.

The part-time cooperative program is conducted by a public school teacher, usually referred to as a coordinator. This individual is employed by the local board of education and has responsibility for teaching related classes and serving as a liaison officer between the school and the employer of the part-time cooperative student. Occupational experience in some field of distribution is an essential qualification for this position. This type of experience is needed to enable the coordinator to understand the problems and to speak the language of the workers in distribution.

The coordinator, in addition, should be a qualified teacher and should possess the personal characteristics pleasing to school and business personnel. Technical education on the college level in the field of distribution is a desirable qualification for a coordinator. Courses such as business finance, retail store management, salesmanship, accounting, labor relations, and business economics should be included in the technical requirements. The professional education of coordinators should include courses concerned with principles of vocational education and with principles, methods and materials of teaching, with special emphasis on teaching in vocational distributive education.

Since the cooperative program is designed for students who are employed in their chosen occupation, it is important that this fact be kept in mind in selecting students for this program. The program is not designed for the purpose of enabling students from low-income families to make money in order that they may remain in school, nor is it a course for students who have done poorly in other subjects. Only those students who have selected the occupation they expect to follow and who can profit from the instruction should be permitted to enroll in the cooperative program. Personal appearance, scholarship, health, enthusiasm, and maturity are important characteristics that should be considered in the selection of these students.

RELATED TRAINING

The organized class instruction provided for part-time cooperative students is referred to as related training. It consists of classroom and laboratory courses designed to increase knowledge, understanding, and ability to solve technical and theoretical problems concerned with a selected occupation. The course content selected for the related subjects depends upon student needs. In general, the various topics that are included in a course in retail store management may be grouped under the following headings: (1) topics concerned with retailing, (2) personal elements of retailing, (3) salesmanship factors, (4) commodity studies, and (5) advertising and sales promotion. Some of the information under each of these topics is of a general nature, while other information is specific and will vary with the type of commodity distributed. This means that coordinators must use both the group and individualized methods of teaching. The use of these two methods is especially necessary in smaller schools enrolling part-time cooperative students in a wide variety of distributive and sometimes diversified occupations.

Related Instruction is Provided in Public School Classes for Students Enrolled in Part-Time Cooperative Courses in Distributive Education. (Little Rock, Arkansas, Public Schools, Plegge)

The part-time cooperative program is usually placed in either the eleventh or twelfth grades, or both, depending upon whether the program is for one or two years. A part-time cooperative student who has only one class in related subjects each school day frequently enrolls for some high school subject in general education, such as English, social science, mathematics, or general science. Students who expect to enroll in cooperative classes are encouraged to plan their high school courses as early in their high school experience as possible, in order that the high school curriculum may include subjects and activities in grades nine and ten that will be of most value in the field of distribution. General courses such as elementary business training, business economics, record keeping, economic geography, and business arithmetic may be included among these preparatory courses.

Coordinators use various types of references and teaching materials in teaching related subjects. Books, bulletins, and pamphlets concerned with general principles of distribution and with facts about specific commodities are used. Such material as sales manuals, manufacturers' manuals, trade magazines, and fashion magazines may be obtained from manufacturers and distributors. Some coordinators use equipment and devices in the classroom such as cash registers, scales, counters, display windows, wrapping paper, price tickets, paper cutters, sales tickets, and telephones. These are used to enable students to acquire needed skills more rapidly and thereby give more efficient service to their employers. Some schools maintain a school store and assign responsibility for its management and operation to the coordinator and the part-time cooperative students. The value of each of these devices depends upon its need and its use in enabling students to acquire greater proficiency in their chosen field of distribution.

WORK EXPERIENCE EDUCATION

Work experience for students enrolled in part-time cooperative classes in vocational distributive education is part of the requirements of the course and is designed to provide supervised experience in the chosen occupation. Two general plans—the *alternate* and the *nonalternate*—are used for scheduling the work program. Under the alternate plan two students are paired, and one student works while the other is in school. At the end of a stated period—a month, term, or semester —the two students exchange places. Under the nonalternate plan students are not paired. Students attend school during stated hours and work at other hours. A plan frequently followed throughout the country is that of having students attend school during the morning hours and work during the afternoons. This plan makes it possible for students to enroll in regularly scheduled classes during the morning hours. The coordinator, under this plan, may teach related subjects each morning and visit students on the job each afternoon.

Responsibility for selecting the training stations is usually assigned to the coordinator. This selection is made on the basis of criteria approved by an advisory committee. Stores or places of business that have recognized prestige and adequate space, equipment, and personnel are selected. Students are placed in establishments that offer reasonable assurance of employment to the student at the close of the training period. These selected establishments usually enter into a written agreement with the school concerning such items as grade level of students to be accepted, work schedule, wages, plan of rotation, plan of evaluation of work, and responsibilities of coordinator and business establishment supervisor. The employer, as a rule, is also asked to agree not to offer the student full-time employment until he has completed his course of training.

The coordinator usually finds a place for the beginning student in the business establishment offering the type of work experience the student desires. Students sometimes find their own positions, and the coordinator then makes the necessary arrangements for carrying out the objectives of the cooperative program. When each student is assigned to a work station, he prepares, with the assistance of the store supervisor and coordinator, a training plan or schedule of work processes indicating the jobs or activities in which he will engage during the time he is at work, together with the kinds of information he will need to improve his performance of those jobs. The coordinator is expected to visit the student on the job at such times as may be agreed upon between the employer and the school authorities. These visits are for the purpose of lending encouragement to the student and conferring with the store supervisor concerning the progress of the student and his need for additional class instruction.

Pre-Employment Classes

Pre-employment classes in vocational distributive education are designed to prepare high school-age youth, youth with special needs, post-high school youth, and adults for positions in the field of distribution. Non-Federally aided pre-employment classes in distributive education of less than baccalaureate degree level have been offered in some high schools, post-high schools, community colleges, and technical institutes for a number of years. Recent Federal legislation providing Federal aid for these types of classes will bring about an expansion in this program.

DEVELOPMENT OF PRE–EMPLOYMENT PROGRAMS

The Vocational Education Act of 1963 authorized the use of Federal funds for pre-employment or preparatory classes. An amendment was enacted to the George-Barden Act to permit state boards of vocational education to use Federal funds for this purpose. This amendment specified that "any amounts allotted (or apportioned) under such Titles, Act, or Acts for distributive occupations may be used for vocational education for any person over 14 years of age who has entered

The Telephone is Becoming Increasingly Important in Business Transactions. Instructors from the Bell Telephone System are teaching these secondary school students the proper use of the telephone. (American Telephone and Telegraph Company)

upon or is preparing to enter upon such an occupation and such education need not be provided in part-time or evening schools."[1] The passage of this law has brought about a new interest in pre-employment classes for persons interested in preparing for positions in distribution.

Pre-employment classes may be useful in organizing combination programs among various vocational services. The vocational agriculture student who is interested in an agricultural business enterprise may take distributive education courses in marketing and management. Likewise distributive education students interested in entering food and housing industries may find that some courses in vocational homemaking will contribute to their efficiency as workers in distribution. Such a procedure involves the cooperative development of vocational curriculums by personnel in the various vocational fields.

CURRICULUM ORGANIZATION

The curriculum organization for pre-employment classes in distributive education varies with the type of school and objectives of the program. One curriculum pattern in the secondary school begins in

[1] Public Law 88–210, 88th Congress, Section 10-d, Washington, D.C., 1963.

grade nine with prerequisite courses in introduction to business along with appropriate academic subjects. This is followed in grade ten by business education courses such as typewriting and business arithmetic. The courses in distribution are offered in the eleventh and twelfth grades along with business law or other business subjects and academic subjects to meet graduation requirements.

Another curriculum pattern is designed to provide pre-employment classes in grades nine and ten to be followed by part-time cooperative classes in grades eleven and twelve for students who have completed the pre-employment classes and are eligible for participating in the part-time cooperative program. The pre-employment courses for grades nine and ten usually include units such as introduction to business, the nature of business, introduction to distribution, job interview, and occupational relations. These are followed by the general and technical related training of the cooperative program. Some pre-employment classes are designed to provide such information and skills as are feasible for use with occupationally handicapped students.

Pre-employment classes on the post-high school level are included in a two-year full-time day school curriculum including in some schools an internship program in marketing. Courses such as principles, salesmanship, business mathematics, economics, management, business law, and others are included. Such curriculums ordinarily do not include academic subjects except those such as psychology of human relations and communication skills that relate directly to the needs of the distributive education student.

WORK EXPERIENCE

Some form of supervised work experience is desirable in pre-employment classes. This may be met with some modifications in the present work experience programs of cooperative classes. Short periods of work during holidays or special sales or a special arrangement for work after school hours are provided in some programs. A form of internship in which pre-employment class students are placed in business establishments for a limited time under the guidance of qualified personnel is also used. Various types of activities in the classroom-laboratory are also suggested to provide work experience. These include arranging window and counter displays, using cash registers, wrapping packages, writing sales slips and credit tickets, making show cards, role playing, and viewing various kinds of visual aids depicting approved store and service establishment arrangements and marketing techniques. The school store may also provide a laboratory for many activities desirable in a pre-employment distributive education program.

The Distributive Education Clubs of America

The Distributive Education Clubs of America, commonly known as DECA, is a national organization, the active members of which are secondary school students enrolled in part-time cooperative classes in vocational distributive education. The national organization is composed of chartered state clubs which are made up of local clubs within the state. The organization was founded to provide school club activities for students who were unable to participate in many other high school clubs because of the time required for their supervised work experience. DECA is sponsored by an organization of adults, chartered under the name of DECA, Incorporated, which is responsible for the legal and financial activities of the student organization.

THE DEVELOPMENT OF DECA

The Distributive Education Clubs of America had its origin in local clubs organized during the years 1938 to 1942, at which time the vocational distributive education program was becoming established in the United States. These local clubs, known under various names such as Future Retailers, Future Merchants, Future Distributors, and Distributive Education Clubs, were organized to meet the need for social and professional growth and the common interests of students in cooperative classes. The number of these local clubs increased, and a number of states organized state clubs and state conventions between the years 1941 and 1944.

The various activities and programs of the local and state clubs suggested a need for a national organization to promote an interchange of ideas and information among states and to promote interest in and appreciation of the opportunities offered young people in vocational distributive education. Representatives of the U.S. Office of Education invited a committee of state supervisors of distributive education to meet in Washington in 1946 to explore the possibilities and develop plans for a national organization of part-time cooperative students. Plans were developed at this conference for a meeting to be held the following year in Memphis, Tennessee, to organize the national association.

The Memphis meeting, referred to as the first Interstate Conference of Distributive Education Clubs, was held in April 1947. Delegates from twelve states attended this meeting and adopted a resolution to form a national organization. At this same time, the organization was officially endorsed by the National Association of State Directors of Vocational Education which was in session at Chicago, Illinois. A committee was appointed to draft a charter and a constitution for consideration at the next annual meeting.

The second national convention was held in 1948 in St. Louis, Missouri, at which time the constitution was adopted and the official name of the organization became the Distributive Education Clubs of America. The following 17 states had representatives at this meeting and have been designated as charter member states: Georgia, Indiana, Kansas, Kentucky, Louisiana, Michigan, Mississippi, Missouri, North Carolina, Ohio, Oklahoma, South Carolina, Tennessee, Texas, Utah, Virginia, and Washington. A national advisory committee of adults was appointed to advise with the officers of the student organization, and in 1949 the adult organization of DECA, Incorporated, was established to serve as the legal body for the national student organization. DECA, Incorporated, was chartered under the laws of the state of Virginia in 1950, and the American Vocational Association became the official sponsor for DECA in that same year.

Many business firms have made financial contributions to DECA to pay for prizes for contest winners and other activities. The need for a special organization to receive and pay out these contributions became apparent, and the DECA Foundation was planned and organized for this purpose in 1951 and 1952. An executive secretary for DECA was employed in 1953 to coordinate the various activities of the organization. DECA in 1963 had a membership of 29,885 members in 1107 local chapters of 47 state associations. The official magazine, *The Distributor*, is published eight times a year, September through April, at the national headquarters. The national headquarters of DECA are located at 1510 H Street, N.W., Washington, D.C.

THE ORGANIZATION OF DECA

The structural pattern of DECA includes a student organization and an adult organization. The student organization is represented by a delegate body which meets annually at the national convention. The board of governors, composed of one student representative from each state, is the governing body of the student organization. The officers of this organization—consisting of a president, five vice-presidents, four associate vice-presidents, a secretary, a treasurer, a parliamentarian, and an historian—constitute the executive council. Much of the work of DECA is conducted by various committees—some of which are appointed by the national president and some of which are selected by the delegate assembly.

Membership in the adult organization, DECA, Incorporated, consists of one state supervisor or teacher trainer in vocational distributive education from each of the affiliated state clubs. The pattern of organization of this body includes a board of trustees responsible for the legal and financial affairs of DECA and of the DECA Foundation, a national advisory board, a national advisory committee, an advisory committee to the board of governors, and an advisory board to the executive council. These various groups and committees have specific responsibilities of an advisory nature to the student organization. The adult organization also includes a number of adult committees appointed by the national advisory council largely to assist in planning and conducting the national convention.

The state club organization is made up of chartered local clubs and is governed by a delegate body composed of representatives of local clubs. The delegate body usually meets in convention once each year. Each state club establishes its own pattern of organization not in conflict with the national constitution and bylaws. The usual pattern in a state includes an executive committee composed of the student officers of the state club; the state club sponsor, who is an adult; and the state club advisory committee. The local club organization resembles that of the state club. The local club is sponsored by the local coordinator of the part-time cooperative program in vocational distributive education.

Three grades of membership are included in the DECA organization. These are active, associate, and honorary. Active members, who are students enrolled in local cooperative programs in distributive education, have the privilege of voting in the elections. Associate members, who are graduates of the local programs, and honorary members, who are adults elected to this honor by active members, do not have voting privileges.

PROGRAMS AND ACTIVITIES OF DECA

DECA is primarily a leadership training organization, and the local, state and national clubs sponsor many activities of this nature. Local clubs prepare programs of work which include various types of chapter and committee meetings and other activities such as employer-employee banquets, special education tours, personality clinics, sales clinics, social and recreational gatherings, and local contests. The local club elects its officers, adopts its constitution and by-laws, selects its convention delegates and selects its entries in state contests.

Many of the local activities require the expenditure of money and one of the items included in the local program is that of a budget. Funds for some expenditures included in the budget are obtained from dues and special assessments and some are obtained by means of cooperative money-raising projects. These projects include concession stands at athletic games, amateur theatricals, the sale of windshield stickers showing the schedule of the school's athletic events, the sale of school calendars, and the sponsoring of school dances. Some local clubs operate a school store and are allowed a percentage of the profits for club use. This project not only provides funds for the budget, but also enables the members of the local club to gain experience in selling techniques and in managing a business.

The principal activities of the state club are conducted at the state convention. These include various types of contests, business meetings, election of officers, educational tours and recreation. The state contests are usually patterned after the national contests. These are of the following types: individual participation, group participation, and judging team participation. The individual participation contests include public speaking, individual student manual, job interview, ad layout, and copywriting and essay contests. The group participation contests include club activities manual, state newspaper, and state newsletter contests. Judging team participation includes window display and demonstration sales contests. Only active members of DECA are eligible for participation. Local clubs frequently designate the students who are winners of the local contests as their representatives at the state contests. These contest representatives may also be designated as official delegates.

As a rule, each state limits the number of official delegates that a local club may send to the state convention. This is considered advisable because of the difficulty of conducting a convention with a large delegate assembly and also because of the difficulties encountered in securing permission for a large number of cooperative students to be absent from school and from work. As a rule, each local club sends from two to four voting delegates, depending upon the number of local club members, to the state convention. The state club activities are usually financed by state dues paid by local club members. Each state club determines the amount of state dues each member is expected to pay. This amount, together with the amount of the national dues, is paid to the state treasurer. The state treasurer forwards the total amount collected as national dues to the national office.

The national convention serves a number of purposes. These include the development of the national program of work, the conducting of the national contests, the rewarding of club accomplishments, the election of officers, and other leadership training activities. The number of official, voting delegates from a state club is determined by the number of local clubs in the state club association. The conduct of delegates at the convention is regulated by a convention conduct committee and a student government council, each composed of one student representative from each state. The conduct committee drafts the specific rules of conduct, and the council is responsible for enforcing the rules. Awards for the winners of the various national contests are usually paid from funds provided by the DECA Foundation. The operating cost of the national organization is financed largely from membership dues paid through the state club associations.

QUESTIONS FOR STUDY AND DISCUSSION

1. Indicate some statistical evidence showing the importance of distribution.
2. What are the important services in distribution, and what changes are occurring in the demand for these services?
3. What is the relation of distribution to standards of living?
4. What are the objectives of vocational distributive education?
5. What is the trend in enrollments and expenditures in vocational distributive education?
6. What type of subject matter content is provided in extension classes in distributive education? Who is eligible for instruction in these classes?
7. Indicate some principles of teaching that should be observed in teaching extension classes.
8. How is the part-time cooperative program organized and administered?
9. Give some examples of related training in the part-time cooperative program in distributive education.
10. Discuss the important characteristics of the pre-employment class in distributive education.
11. Discuss the history and organization of DECA and DECA, Incorporated.
12. Indicate some of the activities in which members of DECA engage.

SOURCE REFERENCES

Beckman, Theodore N., and Nathanael H. Engle, *Wholesaling*, Ronald, New York, 1959.

Distributive Education Clubs of America, *The DECA Handbook*, Washington, D.C., 1962.

Federal Board for Vocational Education, *Annual Reports*, 1918 to 1932 inclusive, Washington, D.C.

Haas, Kenneth B., *Distributive Education*, Gregg, New York, 1949.

Heckert, J. Brooks, and Robert B. Miner, *Distribution Costs*, Ronald, New York, 1953.

Lebhar, G. M., *Chain Stores in America*, Chain Store Publishing, New York, 1952.

National Association of Manufacturers, *Your Opportunities in Distribution*, New York, 1954.

Robinson, O. Preston, and Norris B. Brisco, *Store Organization and Operation*, Prentice-Hall, Englewood Cliffs, N.J., 1957.

U.S. Department of Commerce, Bureau of the Census, *Statistical Abstract of the United States, 1964*, Washington, D.C., 1964.

U.S. Department of Health, Education, and Welfare, Office of Education, *Distributive Education Post High School Cooperative Programs*, OE82001, Washington, D.C., 1960.

U.S. Department of Health, Education, and Welfare, Office of Education, *The Role of Teacher Education in Distributive Education*, Vocational Bulletin No. 279, Washington, D.C., 1959.

U.S. Department of Health, Education, and Welfare, Office of Education, *Vocational Education in Distributive Occupations*, Vocational Division Bulletin No. 255, Washington, D.C., 1954.

U.S. Office of Education, *Digest of Annual Reports of State Boards for Vocational Education*, for fiscal years 1933 to 1962 inclusive, Washington, D.C.

CHAPTER NINE

BUSINESS EDUCATION FOR BOOKKEEPING, STENOGRAPHY, AND CLERICAL WORK

Business education has many facets. Its principles and techniques are needed by individuals in all walks of life. Individuals as citizens need knowledge and skill in keeping household accounts, in engaging in personal business transactions, in purchasing goods and services for the home, and in communicating with friends and business firms. Individuals as income producers need specialized types of business education, such as merchandising, bookkeeping, stenography, and office practice, to enable them to render more efficient service in their vocations. These needs suggest that business education has two major functions—first, to contribute to the general needs of all individuals and second, to supply the vocational needs of office and sales workers.

Business education for general needs is one of the nonvocational practical arts areas of general education. It is designed to assist individuals to develop a better understanding of the business system and to enable individuals to make more efficient use of the goods and services of industry, agriculture, and business. This type of business education has received more emphasis in recent years and has been responsible for the introduction of a number of new subjects such as general business, consumer business, business law and economics into the curriculums of the public secondary schools. The general business education emphasis has also resulted in some modifications in the objectives and techniques of teaching certain established subjects, such as bookkeeping, shorthand, and typewriting.

Vocational business education is designed to develop special competencies in marketable business skills and techniques. It includes specialized training for secretarial, stenographic, accounting, clerical, and sales or distributive occupations. The vocational emphasis in business education appeared several decades before the general education emphasis. Business courses of a vocational nature were first referred to as commercial courses, and this term is presently used in some schools. Changes in the needs of office and sales workers, as well as the emerging needs of individuals for business knowledge and skill, brought about a new emphasis, and the term *business education* has come into use as more descriptive of this new emphasis.

Business education is offered in private business colleges, technical institutes, area vocational schools, junior and senior colleges, and junior and senior high schools. The business education curriculums usually include offerings in stenography, typewriting, bookkeeping, clerical work, and distributive occupations. The distributive occupations program of less than the baccalaureate degree level is described in Chapter Eight of this volume. The public secondary school curriculums in bookkeeping, stenography, and clerical work are the primary concern of this chapter. Some aspects of post-secondary school business education programs are also included. Since the business education courses in these curriculums have both vocational and general education aims, a discussion of the contribution these courses make to the vocational and general education needs of students is included.

The Organization of Business Education

Business education came into the public schools in response to public demand and as a means of providing additional facilities for the train-

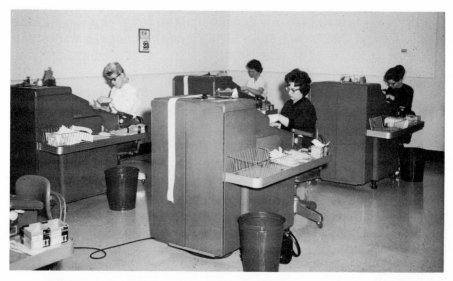

Many Types of Skills are Needed in Office Occupations. An important one is concerned with the use of data processing equipment. (Department of Education, Alaska)

ing of office and sales workers. The general public, since the early days of the secondary school, has insisted that this institution provide some vocational preparation for students who enter business or industry when they leave the secondary school. The business education curriculum has developed in response to this demand in the secondary and post-secondary schools, and its success has been due in no small part to the many sudents who have accepted office and sales positions after having completed it.

THE DEVELOPMENT OF BUSINESS EDUCATION

Vocational business education, like other forms of vocational education, had its origin in apprenticeship programs. When the apprenticeship agencies failed to meet the needs for bookkeepers and other clerical workers, preservice education programs for training these workers were organized in academies and proprietary schools. With the decline of the academies, the proprietary schools increased in number and scope and, during the latter years of the nineteenth century, these schools provided sufficient numbers of bookkeepers and clerical workers for business and industry. During this era a few public secondary schools organized commercial courses in response to a popular demand for practical courses to meet the needs of high school students, but most public school authorities saw little need for commercial courses.

The rapid expansion of business in the early years of the twentieth century and its need for larger numbers of stenographic, bookkeeping, and clerical workers brought about an increased interest in commercial education. This interest and need, together with the demands of the public for a more practical education, resulted in an expansion of the commercial education curriculums and courses in the public secondary schools. Educators became more concerned about commercial courses early in the twentieth century, and, as a result of this interest, the National Education Association in 1901 appointed a committee on commercial education. This committee in 1903 recommended a four-year course in commercial education and suggested that separate commercial high schools be organized in the larger cities. The committee also recommended that a number of academic subjects be included in the commercial education curriculum as a means of providing a more enriched program than was commonly offered in the proprietary schools. A curriculum study committee of the National Education Association recommended in 1915 that secondary schools provide two curriculums in commercial education—one for bookkeeping and one for stenography. The National Education Association in 1919 emphasized the need for specific job objectives in commercial education and suggested that commercial education should be concerned with more than bookkeeping and stenography.

Commercial education in the secondary schools received an additional stimulus in 1917 with the passage of the Smith-Hughes vocational education law. This law, which provided Federal aid for specified areas of vocational education, authorized the Federal Board for Vocational Education to make studies and investigations "with particular reference to their use in aiding the states in the establishment of vocational schools and classes and in giving instruction . . . in commerce and commercial pursuits." The Board published bulletins in 1918 concerned with the teaching of retail selling and of foreign trade and shipping. A bulletin was published in 1919 concerned with the organization and administration of commercial education.

The commercial education activities of the Federal Board were combined with the Business Education Service when this service was organized in 1937 to administer the distributive education program. The Vocational Education Act of 1963 authorizes the use of Federal funds for all gainful occupations of less than baccalaureate degree level including such types of schools and classes in business education as the state board for vocational education may designate in its state plan for vocational education.

Enrollments in the commercial courses of bookkeeping, shorthand, and typewriting in the public secondary schools increased from an estimated 15,000 students in 1893 to 743,900 in 1922. During this thirty-year period the public secondary school enrollment increased more than tenfold. Enrollments continued to increase in the 1920s and 1930s despite the facts that few states had special staff personnel for commercial education and that Federal funds were not available for training in office occupations. The estimated enrollment in 1934 was more than 1,600,000 students in the three courses of typewriting, shorthand, and bookkeeping, with typewriting representing about 47 percent of the total. In 1949, 2,100,000 students were enrolled in bookkeeping, shorthand, and typewriting of which 58 percent were in typewriting.[1] A total of 3,034,000 students were enrolled in bookkeeping, shorthand, and typewriting courses in public secondary schools in 1961.[2] About 60 percent of these were enrolled in typewriting. An additional 1,634,000 students were enrolled in courses such as general business, office practice, office machines, business arithmetic, business law and related courses. The number of pupils enrolled in business education was 40 percent of the total number enrolled in the public secondary schools.

The business education curriculums have been influenced through the years by many organizations and agencies, both public and private. These organizations and agencies have held meetings, published monographs and yearbooks, constituted policy forming committees, and established standards in business education courses and curriculums. Among the more important national organizations are the National Business Education Association, a department of the National Education Association; the National Association for Business Teacher Education, a division of the National Business Education Association; and the Business Education Division of the American Vocational Association. In addition to the national organizations there are a number of regional and state organizations for business educators, most of which are affiliated with one of the national organizations.

[1] U.S. Department of Health, Education, and Welfare, Office of Education, *Statistical Summary of Education, Biennial Survey of Education in the United States,* 1948–1950, Washington, D.C., Chapter I.

[2] Grace S. Wright, *Summary of Offerings and Enrollments in High School Subjects, 1960–1961* (Preliminary Report), U.S. Department of Health, Education, and Welfare, Office of Education, OE240101, Washington, D.C., 1964, pp. 11–12.

THE NEED FOR VOCATIONAL BUSINESS EDUCATION

Some indication of the need for vocational business education and the relative needs in the various areas of business education may be obtained by examining the changes in the number of workers in business occupations. The number of workers classified by the U.S. Bureau of the Census as clerical and kindred workers represented about 8 percent of the gainful labor force in 1930, 10 percent of the employed labor force in 1940, 12 percent of the employed labor force in 1950 and 15 percent in 1960. This was about 7,632,000 workers in 1960, of which 33 percent were classified as bookkeepers, stenographers, typists, and secretaries. The remaining workers were employed in clerical or office practice occupations of a different nature.

When commercial education was first introduced into the secondary school curriculum, the need for workers was greatest in the areas of bookkeeping, shorthand, and typewriting, and the early commercial courses were limited to these subjects. However, the need for clerical workers other than bookkeepers and stenographers became apparent early in the twentieth century. The Federal Board for Vocational Education called attention to this need in 1919, and business education authorities have suggested it from time to time. As a result of these influences some emphasis is now being given to courses in general office practice, clerical practice, business law, commercial geography, consumer education, and economics as well as the established courses in bookkeeping, shorthand, and typewriting.

The increase in purchasing power which has occurred in recent years has enabled the people of the United States to purchase larger quantities of goods and services. This has occasioned a need for more business education for consumers and citizens to prevent waste and extravagance in spending and to enable all individuals to gain an appreciation of the contributions that business and industry are making to American life. Students and educators in recent years have observed that business education courses, with some minor adjustments in content and teaching techniques, can provide business competencies for nonvocational as well as vocational usages. These courses, as a consequence, are now included in both vocational and general education curriculums.

ORGANIZING THE INSTRUCTIONAL PROGRAM

The business education curriculum has evolved through a series of stages, the first of which was the introduction of bookkeeping as a

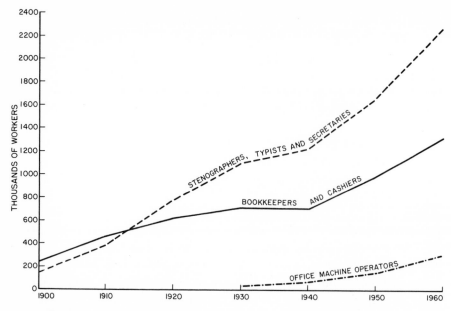

The Increasing Volume of Business Accounting and Communications has Resulted in Substantial Increases in Office Occupations. The number of stenographers and secretaries increased from about 134,-200 in 1900 to 2,256,000 in 1960. (U.S. Department of Commerce, *Historical Statistics, Colonial Times to 1957,* and *Decennial Censuses, 1950 and 1960,* Government Printing Office)

special subject in the secondary school. Other commercial education subjects such as shorthand and typewriting were later added, frequently as electives in the academic curriculum. Subsequently, a partial business curriculum was organized, and this was followed by a one-year business curriculum. This curriculum was increased to two years; then an optional third year was added which was followed by a four-year combination business curriculum. The combination curriculum included a variety of commercial courses such as bookkeeping, shorthand, typewriting, penmanship, commercial geography, and economics.

The combination curriculum was altered to provide for specialization in grades eleven and twelve in bookkeeping, shorthand, typewriting, merchandising, and salesmanship. The increasing demand for commercial subjects and the need for specialized vocational preparation resulted in another type of curriculum organization which consisted of separate four-year curriculums for stenography, bookkeeping, general clerical work, and merchandising. Each of these curriculums contained general education courses, general business education courses, and specialized business education courses for vocational preparation.

The single or combination business curriculum is offered in some of the smaller schools to train a student for both stenographic and bookkeeping positions, but the practice in this curriculum of substituting a relatively large number of technical commercial courses for needed general education courses is questionable. If the school is too small to justify the offering of one or more specialized commercial curriculums perhaps the best alternative is to offer one or two years of business education, including such units as business law, business organization, marketing, and insurance. When a larger program is desired, some technical courses in bookkeeping, stenography, and office practice may be offered upon the completion of the two years of business education.

The specialized curriculums of stenography, bookkeeping, general clerical work, and merchandising may consist of four-year curriculums with the first two years devoted to general business subjects that are needed by all individuals and the last two years given to vocational specialization with some academic subjects, such as English, social science and physical education, included in one or more of the four years.

Post-secondary school curriculums in business education are usually more specialized than secondary school curriculums. The post-secondary school curriculums have more courses of a technical nature such as accounting and the use of business machines. The general education courses in these curriculums are frequently limited to communication skills, social science, and physical education.

THE ADMINISTRATION OF BUSINESS EDUCATION

An important consideration in the administration of business education is the qualifications of the teaching and supervisory personnel. The teacher of business education subjects should possess the knowledge, skills, and attitudes desired of all educated persons, the technical competencies required in one or more areas of business education, a knowledge of the principles and methods of teaching and some practical experience in one of the business occupations. The education requirements are usually met by graduation from a four-year college or university course in business education leading to the bachelor's degree. Some teacher education institutions make provision for business experience as a part of the curriculum in business education.

The teacher education curriculum includes general education courses, which ordinarily constitute from one-third to one-half of the 4-year curriculum; business courses in the amount of 42 to 64 semester hours; and 12 to 18 semester hours of professional education courses. Most teachers of business subjects are required to teach in two or more areas of business education, and some teachers, especially those in small high schools, may be required to teach subjects other than business. Graduate teacher education programs should be organized to provide an opportunity for business education teachers to specialize in some specific area of business education. This is especially important when business education in a number of areas is included in the undergraduate curriculum.

Some supervisory activities designed to stimulate the improvement of instruction should be included in the plan of local administration. These activities may include class visitations, demonstration teaching, lesson planning, organizing testing programs, evaluating teaching materials and equipment, coordinating school and business, and planning, placement and follow-up services. The responsibility for supervision may be assigned to the school principal, the head of the business education department, or a special supervisor. The school principal usually has this responsibility in the smaller schools that do not have a business education department head or in which the department head is primarily a teacher. Very few local schools in the United States employ full-time local supervisors of business education. Some authorities suggest that a full-time supervisor should be appointed in all schools located in cities of 50,000 or more population.

The secondary or post-secondary school is frequently called upon to provide business education for the employed office and store personnel of the community, and plans for in-service training should be included in the public school program. The evening business school is one means of providing this training, and some cities have instituted four-year evening courses in business education. Speed-building courses in typewriting and stenography, special courses in the operation of office machines, and advanced courses in accounting and in bookkeeping machine operation are popular evening school offerings. Short, intensive courses organized on a unit basis are preferable in evening classes. The school program should be adjusted to fit work schedules, busy seasons and seasonal preferences. Some states make special provisions for extension and home study courses in business subjects conducted jointly by the local public school and some extension or home study agency. These various types of in-service programs provide opportunities for many individuals who cannot attend day school to acquire proficiency in business education.

Bookkeeping

The keeping of financial records is becoming increasingly important to the businessman and the consumer alike. Federal and state income tax laws, together with the complexity of modern business, have brought about an accelerated need for business and personal records and accounts. Individuals responsible for the keeping, analyzing, and verifying of financial records are known as bookkeepers, accountants, and auditors. The bookkeeper records business transactions in books of original entry; the accountant reports, summarizes, prepares financial statements, and calculates unit costs; and the auditor reviews and verifies the work of the accountant.

Bookkeeping is classified as single entry or double entry and is kept by hand or by machine. Single-entry bookkeeping is used by consumers and a few small concerns. It is a method in which debts owing to and by an individual are the only facts recorded. Double-entry bookkeeping, which is used by most present-day business firms, is a method in which every transaction is recorded in two parts, in one place as a debit to one account and in another place as a credit to another account. Bookkeeping machines of various kinds are used to record business transactions, and the operators of these machines require special competencies as machine operators, as well as knowledge and skill in bookkeeping.

The secondary school, as a rule, limits its offerings in the area of record keeping to the training of bookkeepers skilled in elementary bookkeeping and simple bookkeeping duties and leaves to area schools and colleges the education of bookkeeping machine operators, accountants and auditors. Some secondary vocational schools in the large cities are offering courses in accounting and bookkeeping machine operation.

THE DEVELOPMENT OF BOOKKEEPING EDUCATION

Both single-entry and double-entry bookkeeping were invented long before the beginning of the Christian era and have continued in general use since their invention. Accounts were first kept on single tablets of clay, but later bound books were used. The modern development is in the direction of abandoning the bound book in favor of detached sheets or cards that may be arranged to suit the convenience or needs of the business.

Bookkeeping machines were invented more than a century ago, but they have not had extensive use until recent times. Modern machines can post to the customer's ledger, the customer's statement, and the control account. They can transfer balances and prepare trial balances. They can also render the complementary services for accounts payable. The use of microfilm as an aid in accounting is increasing. Statistical tabulating machines, using punched cards, are becoming increasingly important in the business office. These various machines and devices have increased the efficiency and extended the use of financial and other records in the business office.

The increased use of business records has created a need for an increasing number and a wide variety of record keepers who are replacing the general bookkeeper of the previous century. The present-day business office may have bookkeeping responsibilities assigned to the following types of clerks: accounting, accounts payable, accounts receivable, audit, balance, billing, budget, cost, discount and interest billing, entry, general ledger, inventory, journal, ledger, posting, recording, voucher, and others. Special school training is desirable for all of them and necessary for some. The secondary school can train for only a few of these specialized vocations at most. The post-secondary school is providing business education courses for many of these specialized areas of bookkeeping.

THE OBJECTIVES OF BOOKKEEPING EDUCATION

Bookkeeping, like other business subjects, was first introduced into the secondary school for its value as a vocational subject. The bookkeeping course or curriculum was offered for the purpose of providing general bookkeepers for business establishments. The desire on the part of educators of the early twentieth century to endow all vocational subjects, including bookkeeping, with cultural value brought about some changes in objectives, and bookkeeping was offered for both its cultural and disciplinary value, as well as its vocational value. The disciplinary and cultural values of bookkeeping are now considered relatively unimportant and have been succeeded by certain personal and social use values. The changing needs of business for specialized rather than general bookkeepers have brought about changes in the vocational objectives of bookkeeping. Bookkeeping is currently offered in the secondary and post-secondary school for the purpose of training bookkeepers and other clerical workers, for personal use and for obtaining knowledge and skill in analyzing and interpreting records of interest to consumers and businessmen.

The vocational aim continues to dominate business education in bookkeeping, and the bookkeeping course or curriculum is offered primarily for the purpose of pre-employment training for bookkeepers and office positions in which the principles of bookkeeping are used. The vocational objective in bookkeeping involves the development of occupational competency on the initial employment level, the development of occupational intelligence, and the provision for related technical knowledge. Vocational education in bookkeeping in the secondary

The Keeping of Financial Records is Becoming Increasingly Important. Special machines are designed for different kinds of record keeping. (Minneapolis Vocational High School and Technical Institute, Minneapolis, Minnesota)

school, as a rule, carries through the journal, posting to the ledger, taking a trial balance, preparing a work sheet with the financial statements, adjusting and closing the books and taking a post-closing trial balance. This type of training is designed for ledger clerks. Secondary and post-secondary schools in which training is provided for bookkeeping machine operators or specialized bookkeepers have established appropriate objectives for these courses.

The increasing number of personal records and accounts that each individual is presently keeping has led business educators to suggest that bookkeeping be offered for personal use as well as for vocational proficiency. The average individual with a checking account in a bank has a need for a variety of information concerning financial transactions. Among these are using checks, keeping a bankbook, calculating interest, keeping personal cost accounts, planning a budget, taking inventory, checking bills and statements, keeping social security records, calculating various types of tax payments, making records of family income and expenses, and calculating net worth. The bookkeeping curriculum or course in the secondary school is usually designed to meet some or all of these nonvocational personal needs.

A third objective of business education in bookkeeping is concerned with the interpretation of business records and reports. Skill in the interpretation of records and reports is needed by individuals as businessmen and as consumers. Among the desired competencies needed in this area are those involving the interpretation of financial statements, balance sheets, profit and loss statements and contingent liabilities. The business manager or executive who employs and supervises bookkeepers needs to know the devices and processes used in recording data and to what extent they need improving and can be improved. Many of the bookkeeping and recording abilities needed by management are beyond the scope of the secondary school, but a beginning in the study of these needed abilities may be made in the secondary school.

BOOKKEEPING CURRICULUMS

The organization for teaching bookkeeping in the secondary school may consist of a four-year curriculum, a three-year curriculum, a two-year major, special courses in bookkeeping that may be taken as electives or a combination of the foregoing. The curriculum organization and course content are determined by the desired objectives of the bookkeeping program. Some teachers of bookkeeping attempt to accomplish the three previously mentioned objectives in one course, and this may result in graduates who are not proficient in any area. Some business educators have suggested that, since students with different objectives are involved in each area, a curriculum for each area should be established in a school that can justify three types of bookkeeping curriculums. Some schools offer a clerical curriculum with the opportunity for the study of the fundamentals of bookkeeping, initial use training in bookkeeping and calculating machine operation.

The first course in bookkeeping is placed in the tenth grade in some schools and in the eleventh in others. A suggested four-year vocational curriculum in bookkeeping with the first course in bookkeeping placed in grade eleven is shown below.

Ninth grade: English, general business, basic mathematics, social science, general or biological science, and health and physical education.

Tenth grade: English, typewriting, commercial geography, business arithmetic, consumer economics, and health and physical education.

Eleventh grade: English, social science elective, bookkeeping, spelling and filing, and health and physical education.

Twelfth grade: Business correspondence, bookkeeping, commercial law, business organization, social science elective, and health and physical education.

The first course in bookkeeping, which may be offered in the tenth or the eleventh grade, should include a study of accounting principles and an opportunity for students to apply these principles to business problems and to personal finances. The greater part of the course should be concerned with large and small businesses, with single proprietors, with partnerships and corporations and with manufacturing and distributive businesses. The course should include opportunities for students to learn bookkeeping by doing as well as by discussing. The second year or advanced course in bookkeeping is designed to develop vocational proficiency. It deals with more complex books, more intricate transactions and more detailed financial statements. It usually applies the principles of bookkeeping to types of accounts not ordinarily included in the elementary course.

The post-secondary school curriculum for the education of individuals for the keeping of accounts is called the general business administration or accounting curriculum. The curriculum is a two-year program usually requiring a high school diploma as a prerequisite for entrance. The first year includes such required courses as accounting, business mathematics, business law, communications skills, psychology, and physical education. The second year courses are advanced accounting, tax accounting, cost accounting, tabulation machine accounting, machine bookkeeping, office machines, office and personnel management, and economics. The satisfactory completion of the courses leads to some type of associate degree or diploma.

METHODS AND MATERIALS OF INSTRUCTION

Surveys made by business educators indicate that bookkeeping instructors use many different methods and approaches and that there is no one best method. It is generally agreed that any established method may be used successfully by a qualified instructor who prefers that particular method. Some bookkeeping instructors advocate the teaching of theory as a basis for practice while others prefer to teach all bookkeeping abilities through practice. This difference of opinion has prevailed since the middle of the nineteenth century, and superior bookkeepers have been trained by each method. The first method used in teaching bookkeeping in the secondary school was the business college method. This method consisted of detailed text and practice set instructions. Supervision and individual assistance were provided on a need basis by the instructor. This method is still widely used and is frequently referred to as the *project* method. Class recitations, lecture, and progressive methods are also used.

Four approaches are used in the teaching of bookkeeping. These approaches, which are also referred to as methods, are: the journal approach, the account approach, the balance sheet approach, and the business equation approach. Combinations of the above approaches, such as the journal and account approach, or the balance sheet and equation approach, are also used.

The *business equation* is currently a popular approach to the teaching of bookkeeping. It starts with the idea that for every value received there is an equivalent value parted with. The problem is presented as a formula in which the assets equal the liabilities plus proprietorship. The equation is balanced, a principle is deduced, and the entry follows. This approach delays the teaching of the bookkeeping cycle until the student understands the reason for each entry. The *balance sheet* approach which is sometimes combined with the business equation, begins with the introduction of the balance sheet. The balance sheet forms the basis for the teaching of the accounts, journals, and bookkeeping principles.

Bookkeeping instructors, as a rule, use textbooks as guides in teaching bookkeeping, and there are many satisfactory texts on bookkeeping. Various criteria have been established for evaluating bookkeeping texts. These criteria usually involve validity and reliability of content, objectives, use and teaching value and provision for individual differences. Bookkeeping teachers often use syllabuses, instruction sheets, and supplementary references. Students also keep actual sets of books as a means of acquiring proficiency. Various types of visual aids are also used in teaching bookkeeping. These include posters, charts, blackboard illustrations, motion pictures, slide films, flannel graphs, and illustrations for opaque projectors. These devices stimulate interest, provide variety, facilitate retention, and save time in the teaching of bookkeeping.

Post-secondary programs for teaching machine accounting have need for a variety of machines and special equipment in addition to the items listed for secondary school programs. The special equipment needs for post-secondary school programs and advanced programs in some secondary schools are bookkeeping machines, adding-listing machines, calculators, and payroll machines. Some programs in which computers are used for accounting have a need for key-punch, sorter, and tabulator printers.

Stenography

Stenography is defined as the science of taking dictation and transcribing it into mailable copy. The person trained in stenography, referred to as a stenographer, differs from a secretary and from a typist. The secretary is not only proficient in stenography but also in many other office responsibilities, such as taking notes at conferences, arranging itineraries, replying to routine correspondence, arranging appointments, receiving visitors, and taking telephone calls. The typist does not take dictation but types manuscripts, invoices, statistical data, and other information from prepared copy. The stenographic curriculum or course is taken both for vocational and for personal use. The stenographic course includes shorthand and typewriting and other business and academic subjects needed by stenographers. Students who complete the stenographic curriculum may secure positions as stenographers, typists, or office workers. The stenographic curriculum provides many of the competencies needed by secretaries and places stenographers in a position to receive early promotion to secretarial positions.

THE DEVELOPMENT OF STENOGRAPHY

Revolutionary changes have occurred in methods of business communication in recent years. During the many centuries prior to 1900 most people could neither read nor write and had to depend on professional scribes for this service. Longhand was first used, but shorthand, which is the act of writing legibly and at a rapid rate by the use of brief signs, was probably not far behind. The date of the invention of shorthand is not known, but it was used to record the speeches of Cicero and other members of the Roman Senate shortly before the beginning of the Christian era.

The first published system of modern shorthand appeared in England in 1588. The system was invented by Timothy Bright and dedicated to Queen Elizabeth. The beginning of phonetic shorthand occurred in 1602 when John Willis of England invented a system of phonetic writing. The first American system was published by Thomas Lloyd in 1819. The development of the modern English language shorthand began in 1837 with the invention of a phonetic shorthand system by Isaac Pitman of England. It is estimated that more than a thousand English language systems of shorthand have been published since the invention of the Pitman system. Among the more important of the systems presently in use are Gregg, Pitman, Dewey Script, Thomas Natural, Graham, and Munson.

A number of aids to facilitate business communication have come into general use in modern times. These include the dictation machine, the shorthand machine, the teletype, and the microfilm. The dictation machine is one of the most widely used aids to communication. This machine, which records the human voice on a tape, cylinder, or disc for later transcription, is a time saver for the businessman. The shorthand machine, invented about 1880, is a device by which shorthand symbols are recorded on a tape. It has many uses but perhaps finds its best use in reporting court proceedings and convention speeches. Some experimentation is under way to perfect a machine that will automatically transcribe the spoken word into a written letter. All these aids are useful in the office. They will likely supplement rather than replace either shorthand or longhand.

The typewriter is one of the most important aids to communication. It was first patented in England in 1714 but did not come into general use until after 1868, at which time Christopher Latham Sholes and his associates of Milwaukee, Wisconsin, patented a *typewriter*. The machine was manufactured by E. Remington and Sons, and by 1886 it had become a commercial success. The first machine had many of the fundamental features of the modern typewriter including the universal keyboard which is used today. Attempts have been made to change the position of the various letters on the keyboard to increase typewriting efficiency, but thus far no appreciable change in the keyboard has been made. Typewriters have been improved, made portable and electrified, and at present they are used in homes and offices throughout the land.

The stenographic course entered the program of studies of the secondary school in the latter years of the nineteenth century when special instructors of shorthand and typewriting were employed to teach these two commercial courses. Some experiments have been made in the use of the typewriter in the elementary school. The aim of this activity was not to teach typewriting but to use it as an aid in teaching reading. Some teachers have reported that the use of the typewriter as a more efficient writing instrument than the pen or pencil has resulted in an improvement in the efficiency of learning other subjects, such as reading, arithmetic, language, and history. Experiments indicate that shorthand is less difficult or at least no more difficult to learn than longhand and can be mastered by students in the elementary grades. However, these two subjects—shorthand and typewriting—find their most frequent use in the secondary and post-secondary schools.

THE STENOGRAPHIC CURRICULUM

Both shorthand and typewriting are studied for vocational and for general-use purposes. When taken for vocational purposes, it is expected that students will meet the standards of speed and accuracy established for certain types of stenographic duties. A business executive dictates at from 60 to 120 words per minute; he repeats and corrects himself and expects the stenographer to know when he is dictating and when he is correcting. The business executive is frequently interrupted, and when he resumes dictation he expects the stenographer to review the statements previously dictated. All this means that provision should be made in the stenographic curriculum for students to learn to take dictation under the conditions in which it will be used. The stenographer is required to transcribe the stenographic notes with reasonable speed and accuracy, whether they be taken by hand or with a shorthand machine. She may also be required to transcribe dictation machine copy from discs, cylinders, or other recording materials. The typist is expected to spell correctly, punctuate properly, space and form letters and sentences attractively, hyphenate and divide words and syllables according to best usage and make corrections neatly. She must know how to change the ribbon, clean the type, make carbon copies, use tabulating keys, and care for the machine. This suggests that if the prospective stenographer is deficient in these items, some of which are normally included in other courses, the stenographic course must make provision for them.

Typewriting has many possibilities for use in personal communication. The portable typewriter is inexpensive and readily adapted for home use. While requirements for personal typewriting are less exacting than those for business use, they are quite similar. Speed, accuracy, and attractiveness are as desirable for personal letters as for business office correspondence. Secondary and post-secondary schools, as a rule, make no distinction in first-year typewriting for business office use or for personal use. Schools that offer only one year of typewriting may provide some variations in the second semester, depending upon the objectives of the student. Shorthand is not generally used for purposes other than office work, but some business educators have suggested that it has undeveloped possibilities as a means of communication and other personal use.

The stenographic program, like that of other business subjects, is offered in the secondary school as a curriculum, as a major or as an elective. Provision is made for shorthand and typewriting to be taken together or separately in the academic curriculums. This has made typewriting one of the most popular subjects. Many schools offer a four-year stenographic or secretarial curriculum. The curriculums offered in the various schools differ in accordance with varying community needs, but in general they are about as follows:

Ninth grade: English, general business, social science, one elective unit in general or biological science, and health and physical education.

Tenth grade: English, bookkeeping, business arithmetic, typewriting, health and physical education, and one elective unit.

Eleventh grade: English, United States history, shorthand, typewriting and filing, and health and physical education.

Twelfth grade: Business correspondence, commercial law, shorthand, transcription and secretarial training, health and physical education, and a social science elective.

Shorthand and typewriting are offered in the eleventh and twelfth grades only in some secondary schools. This enables the student to elect academic or general business courses in the ninth and tenth grades to meet individual needs and desires. Some schools offer only one year of typewriting and shorthand. Secretarial science is gaining in popularity as a finishing course for stenography. This course, usually offered in the twelfth grade, is given as nearly as possible under job conditions.

Post-secondary schools and senior high schools that offer advanced curriculums in secretarial science require the following or similar courses for secretarial science majors. The first year includes introduction to business, business communications, business mathematics, shorthand, typewriting, machine calculations, applied psychology, and health and physical education. The second year consists of elements of accounting, secretarial office practice, office machines and appliances, advanced shorthand, dictation and transcription, filing systems, social science, and health and physical education. These courses provide a proper balance between the secretarial skills and special knowledge needed by a secretary.

TEACHING SHORTHAND

Speed and accuracy are the principal aims of instruction in shorthand. The symbols, the one or more meanings of each symbol, the word signs and special phrase patterns are referred to as the specific objectives. Various methods are used by teachers of shorthand to accomplish these objectives. Most of the methods are adaptations, variations, or combinations of the manual method or of the functional method. The manual method was the first devised, and this method, or some of its variations, is frequently used in today's schools. The manual method requires the immediate learning of the shorthand alphabet through a letter-by-letter stage. The sound units are joined to form word and phrase outlines through prearranged problem-rule sequences. The manual method emphasizes the early learning of the basic principles of shorthand. The functional method, devised by Louis A. Leslie, is based on a reading approach to the learning of shorthand. Students first read shorthand and later write it. The functional method suggests that shorthand is one of the language arts and should first be heard and seen before it is written or before any rules for writing are learned. This method is designed to enable the learner to see the shorthand symbols as a message or thought without a conscious interpretation of each curve or line in the symbol. The student is encouraged to read rapidly and then write rapidly with the idea that the errors will disappear in a short time, and the student will then have acquired both speed and accuracy.

Each method has its advocates and its critics. Some instructors object to the functional method because the student is not permitted to write shorthand until he has made considerable progress in reading shorthand. Other instructors object to the manual method because of the wide time span it may permit between learning and application. Each of these methods has proved efficient in the training of stenographers, which again suggests that there is no one best method, but that the method which suits the instructor and gets results is the best for that instructor. Many variations of these two general methods are in use throughout the nation and these, too, are proving successful in the education of stenographers.

A multiple channel magnetic tape system is used in some schools to facilitate the learning of shorthand. This system is designed to provide for individual differences among students in the rates in which they take dictation. The system, by means of 3 or 4 dictating machines connected by wires to each student's desk, provides dictated material at 3 or 4 speed ranges. The speed ranges vary from a low of 60 words per minute to a high of 120 words per minute. Each student may select the speed level he desires by using an individual control switch. The student receives dictated material from prerecorded reels of tape for practice in shorthand writing. This system enables each student to transpose dictation to shorthand at his own speed level.

TEACHING TYPEWRITING

The teaching of typewriting requires the cooperation of the teacher and the student, and one of the most important functions of the teacher is to demonstrate correct techniques before the student has acquired incorrect ones. Such beginning techniques as paper insertion and removal, stroking, carriage return, relaxation, shifting for capitals, and stroke and word level typing should be demonstrated by the teacher. These techniques should be demonstrated when first needed and repeated when it seems desirable. The student response to the demonstration should not be long delayed.

Among the first learning activities of the student typist is the mastery of the keyboard. Three methods of teaching the keyboard are in general use. One starts with the home row, another begins with the first fingers only, and the third skips around the keyboard. Studies do not indicate universal superiority for any one of the three methods. Practice copy for the typist may consist of words, sentences, and paragraphs, or it may consist of letter combinations and individual finger action. The first alternative referred to as teaching by the *whole* method is generally considered more effective. The whole method enables the student to acquire meaningful information while he types. Students seem to learn the keyboard as easily by sight as by touch. The student typist should learn the basic machine parts and the keyboard, as well as correct posture and touch and proper insertion and removal of paper in less than one month's schooling.

The right kind of practice is necessary for acquiring proficiency in typewriting. The practice must be regular and frequent and planned to provide a measure of satisfaction to the learner. This suggests that the learner should understand the purpose of each practice and the ultimate goal of the course. The learner should also be made aware of the progress he is making, as well as his recurring errors. These items suggest that the teacher has a responsibility for planning, encouraging, testing, and suggesting remedial work. Some instructors request beginning students not to make erasures in typed copy during a portion of their first semester of typewriting in order that errors may be observed and remedial measures planned.

Errors in typewriting may be overcome by the use of the technique of *locomotion*. This technique consists of writing the phrase containing the error five or six times, increasing the speed of writing each time. The last writing should be at top speed. Standards on erasing in typewriting should conform to business office standards. No business can afford to have a typist start over and waste letter paper when a correctible error is made. The business office, on the other hand, cannot afford to send out a letter showing careless erasures.

Clerical Work

Some secondary and post-secondary schools in recent years have instituted a business education curriculum or course of study for clerical workers. This curriculum differs according to local needs and practices and is variously referred to as the clerical curriculum, the clerical practice curriculum, the general business curriculum, the general office training curriculum or the office practice curriculum. This curriculum is designed for the training of office workers who are not classified as bookkeepers, accountants, sales persons, stenographers, secretaries, or managers. A difference of opinion exists among business educators relative to the desirability of including general clerical courses in the secondary school. Some educators insist that most of these types of competencies can best be learned on the job, and some suggest that a course of this nature should be offered on the post-secondary school level. However, many business educators realize the limited possibilities for employment in the traditional business education courses and are suggesting special secondary school curriculums for clerical workers to meet the needs of present-day business establishments.

DESCRIPTION AND OBJECTIVES OF CLERICAL WORK

Clerical workers are sometimes referred to as general clerks, although most of them are highly specialized employees who are responsible for a limited number of duties. Clerical workers are listed on the payroll by a wide variety of titles. Among these are agent, appraiser,

Many Secondary School Students Learn Typewriting for Business or Personal Use. (Department of Education, Hawaii)

checker, cash boy, dispatcher, file clerk, inspector, mail clerk, route clerk, office machine operator, payroll clerk, shipping clerk, stock clerk, telephone operator, and timekeeper. Some of these jobs are limited to the performance of six or eight different duties while others may involve many more. Some of the jobs require a knowledge of bookkeeping and typewriting, while others do not. The duties of some of these jobs are fairly uniform among different firms while others are peculiar to a single firm.

General clerical workers engage in a variety of office activities. The classifying and sorting of papers and the checking of data are among the most frequently assigned duties. Office clerks are required to fill in various forms, fill and seal envelopes, staple pads of paper, handle mail, answer and direct telephone calls, and audit and verify sales slips. Office clerks provide information to visitors, engage in shipping and receiving goods, prepare and handle orders, take inventory and proofread copy. Clerical workers also operate various types of office machines.

The general clerical curriculum was introduced into the secondary school primarily as a pre-employment course for young people. The objectives of the curriculum vary with the school, but in general the objectives are concerned with the development of desirable attitudes with reference to the duties of the clerical worker, such as accuracy in office work, dependability to see a job through, ability to turn out production at a reasonable rate and at an approved standard, ability to follow instructions, initiative and resourcefulness in office work, appreciation of time, judgment in attacking a job, pride of workmanship, good office deportment, and desirable personal traits. The objectives also include an understanding of how business is organized, the use of various business forms and office machines, the methods of recording business data, and the improvement of handwriting. These objectives may be used as guides in formulating objectives for a specified curriculum.

SKILLS NEEDED IN CLERICAL WORK

The many types of duties assigned to clerical workers require the use of a number of skills, many of which of necessity must be learned on the job. The school can, however, provide training in some of the basic skills most frequently used. Business educators have suggested that clerical workers are in special need of skills in arithmetic, communications, bookkeeping, typewriting, and filing. Most of these skills needed for initial contact positions in office work may be supplied by the secondary and post-secondary school. Some of these skills are included in the business education curriculums and others in the academic curriculums.

Office managers and supervisors frequently criticize office workers because of their inability to make the necessary arithmetical calculations required in the office. The prospective clerical worker must be more proficient in addition, subtraction, multiplication, and division than the average student. The office clerk may also need skill in the solution of the more complicated business problems. Individual needs differ, and the business education instructor should assist the student to determine and meet these individual needs. The instructor should point out that nothing short of 100 percent accuracy will be long tolerated in the business office.

Clerical workers are in constant communication with other individuals and should possess competency in the fundamentals of English to enable them to write and speak correctly. This suggests a need for drill in spelling, sentence structure, vocabulary, and penmanship. Most of the fundamentals of the communications subjects will be acquired before the student enters the business education course or curriculum. However, because of wide variations in the abilities of students, some business education students will need additional drill in the subject matter area of communications.

The clerical worker is usually required to keep some records and to type various forms. The skills needed for these duties may be acquired.

in bookkeeping and typewriting courses. The first course in bookkeeping with emphasis on business forms and the newer techniques in record keeping should provide the needed skills in this area. The general clerk, as a rule, spends much time in typing various forms with numerous carbon copies of each form. Many of these forms require special spacing and aligning and must be carefully proofread. General clerks also are required to prepare billings, stencils, and business forms and to type from rough drafts and direct dictation. Some of these skills are included in the first course in typewriting, but others will require additional demonstration and drill.

One of the major activities of the general clerk is that of filing. Filing involves an understanding of what to file, the preparation of materials for filing, an understanding of filing systems and techniques and the ability to find records quickly after they have been filed. Such abilities as sorting, coding, indexing, and preparing cross references are as important as alphabetizing. The abilities needed in filing are usually developed in an office practice or filing course.

THE USE OF OFFICE MACHINES

Most clerks are required to use some office machines such as the typewriter, mimeograph, liquid and offset duplicators, photocopy machine, varityper, addressograph, rotary, key-driven and printing tabulators, data-processing equipment, check protector, postage meter, and bookkeeping and accounting machines. Very few clerks use any of these machines on a full-time basis, and most of the machines are used only occasionally by clerical workers. The limited use of the machines does not justify extensive instruction in their use in the secondary school. However, clerical workers who are trained in the secondary school should be acquainted with some of them such as the adding, calculating, addressing, and duplicating machines.

Some secondary and post-secondary schools offer a special office machines course in which training is provided in a variety of office machines. This course, as a rule, is not required of all students in the clerical curriculum but only of those who are interested in achieving vocational proficiency in special types of office machines. Some schools follow the practice of including in the office practice course, or some other business course, some elementary instruction or acquaintanceship with a few of the machines more commonly used by office clerks in the community. Business educators advocate the use of a survey to determine the kinds of machines most frequently used in the community and the practice of selecting from the list of machines most frequently used those that may be properly taught in the school.

Business educators use various plans for teaching acquaintance-ship and for teaching speed and accuracy in operation. The *rotation* plan, which involves the rotation at stated intervals of groups of class members among the different machines, is especially useful in acquainting students with the machines. The *battery* plan, which is adapted to specialized training, requires that each student be provided with her own machine. A third plan, referred to as the *integrated office plan,* involves the arrangement of the classroom to simulate the arrangement of the office and the assignment of students to positions in the "office."

CURRICULUMS AND TEACHING PROCEDURES

Secondary school programs of instruction in clerical work, like those of other business subjects, are offered as curriculums, majors in a general business curriculum and as electives in academic or other types of curriculums. The wide diversity of duties, both general and specialized, makes for difficulty in arranging curriculums in this area of business education, and most schools provide for majors and electives. Schools that offer four-year curriculums in clerical work follow a pattern somewhat similar to the one shown below:

Ninth grade: English, general business and health and physical education; and two elective units selected from the social science, mathematics or science fields of study.

Tenth grade: English, commercial geography, business arithmetic, typewriting, health and physical education and one elective from the general education field.

Eleventh grade: English, American history, bookkeeping, health and physical education and one elective unit from the vocational or general education fields.

Twelfth grade: English, business law and economics, clerical and office practice, health and physical education and one elective unit from the general or vocational education fields.

Secondary schools that do not offer four-year curriculums in clerical work usually permit students in other curriculums who are preparing for this work to elect such courses as general business, clerical and office practice, typewriting, bookkeeping, and business organization.

Post-secondary school curriculums in clerical work are referred to as clerical, office, office clerical, and various other titles. Some schools offer specialized clerical curriculums in office machines, data processing, and systems analysis. The following courses are frequently required in the first year of the office clerical curriculum: introduction to business, business English, business mathematics, typing, filing, machine calculation, personal finance, applied psychology, and health and physical education. The second year includes elements of accounting, advanced typing, office machines, office practices, business law, psychology, and health and physical education. This curriculum, which is terminal in nature, provides semi-professional training for clerical occupations.

The varied nature of the clerical training program requires the use of individualized instruction, and various types of instruction sheets and individual laboratory activities are frequently included in this area. Clerical training requires the use of many skills which may be developed by job instruction training. This method involves demonstration, explanation, and practice. The development of skills in clerical work may require the use of many types of equipment and supplies. Since funds for the purchase of equipment are limited in most schools, the efficient use of equipment requires careful teacher planning and scheduling.

A number of secondary and post-secondary schools have developed cooperative office training programs that permit students in clerical work to gain actual experience in business offices while they are taking courses in the school. These on-the-job courses are organized and operated in somewhat the same manner as the cooperative part-time program in vocational distributive education. This type of organization permits the student to learn on the job the many skills required of clerical workers and frequently leads to the placement of the student in the position or firm in which he received his job training.

QUESTIONS FOR STUDY AND DISCUSSION

1. What is meant by the term *business education,* and what are some of the characteristics of this type of education?
2. Discuss the development of commercial and business education.
3. What are some of the indications of a need for business education in the secondary schools? In post-secondary schools?
4. What kinds of business education curriculums are offered in the public secondary and post-secondary schools?
5. How is the business education program organized and administered in the public secondary and post-secondary schools?
6. Discuss the development and objectives of business education in bookkeeping.
7. What subjects are included in bookkeeping education curriculums, and what methods and approaches are used in the teaching of bookkeeping?

8. Discuss the development and objectives of stenography in the secondary and post-secondary schools.
9. What subjects are included in the stenographic curriculums of public secondary and post-secondary schools?
10. What methods and techniques are used in teaching shorthand and typewriting?
11. What are the characteristics of clerical training and the evidences of the need for this type of training in the public secondary and post-secondary schools?
12. Discuss the skills needed, curriculum organization, and teaching techniques in the public secondary and post-secondary school program for training clerical workers.

SOURCE REFERENCES

American Business Education, *The Clerical Program in Business Education*, Yearbook, Vol. 16, New York University Bookstore, New York, 1959.

Blackstone, E. G., and S. L. Smith, *Improvement of Instruction in Typewriting*, Prentice-Hall, Englewood Cliffs, N.J., 1949.

Business Education Research Associates, *General Office Training*, Series II, Report No. 1, McGraw-Hill, New York, 1952.

Douglas, Lloyd V., James T. Blanford, and Ruth I. Anderson, *Teaching Business Subjects*, Prentice-Hall, Englewood Cliffs, N.J., 1958.

Eastern Business Teachers Association, *Business Education Facilities, Supplies, and Aids*, Yearbook, Vol. 36, Somerset, Somerville, N.J., 1963.

Harms, Harm, and B. W. Stehr, *Methods in Vocational Business Education*, South-Western, Cincinnati, 1963.

Knepper, Edwin G., *History of Business Education in the United States*, Edwards, Ann Arbor, 1941.

Leslie, Louis A., *Methods of Teaching Gregg Shorthand*, McGraw-Hill, New York, 1953.

Musselman, Vernon A., and J. Marshall Hanna, *Teaching Bookkeeping and Accounting*, McGraw-Hill, New York, 1960.

Nichols, Frederick G., *Commercial Education in the High School*, Appleton-Century-Crofts, New York, 1933.

Super, Donald E., *Appraising Vocational Fitness*, Harper & Row, New York, 1962.

Tonne, Herbert A., *Principles of Business Education*, McGraw-Hill, New York, 1960.

Tonne, Herbert A., Estelle L. Popham, and M. Herbert Freeman, *Methods of Teaching Business Subjects*, McGraw-Hill, New York, 1957.

Turille, Stephen J., *Principles and Methods in Business Education*, McClure, Staunton, 1949.

Walters, Rea G., and Carroll A. Nolan, *Principles and Problems of Business Education*, South-Western, Cincinnati, 1950.

CHAPTER TEN

VOCATIONAL HOMEMAKING EDUCATION

Social and economic changes that have occurred in American life since the Colonial era have resulted in concomitant changes in home and family life. The American family during the eighteenth and much of the nineteenth century was for the most part a complete, self-subsistent social unit. The family not only provided food, clothing, and shelter, largely from the products of its home and farm, but also reared, educated and employed its members. The changes that have occurred in agriculture and industry during the twentieth century have had their impact on family life. The rise of the cities, the decreased manpower needs on farms, the increased output per worker, the invention and discovery of new processes and products, and the rising standards of living have resulted in a decreased emphasis on homemaking problems involving manipulative skills and an increased emphasis on others, such as those involving personal relations.

The many new problems and the increased store of knowledge accumulated by modern research in home and family living have made it difficult for the family to provide, within itself, for the education of its members. This has necessitated that other agencies enter the educational field, and foremost among these agencies has been the public school. Public school programs of homemaking education were organized in the latter years of the nineteenth century but received their greatest emphasis after the passage of the Smith-Hughes Vocational Education Act of 1917. This law provided Federal aid for vocational homemaking education in the public schools. Vocational homemaking education under the provisions of this Act is centered on home activities. The Vocational Education Act of 1963 suggests that home economics education should give consideration to some activities outside the home. Techniques for increasing efficiency in home economics in and outside the home are determined by problems that confront present-day homemakers.

Present-Day Home and Family Life Problems

Public and private agencies have contributed much research to the many problems of today's homemaker, and research information of this nature is increasing daily. The problem is now one of utilizing the new ideas, discoveries, and inventions as a means of improving home and family living. The vocational homemaking course is one important means of making available new ideas and practices and stimulating their use. Homemaking teachers and others responsible for organizing the course of study in homemaking need some facts concerning the problems of homemaking as a basis for selecting the content of the courses. Some of these problems concerned with foods and nutrition, clothing and textiles, home planning and household equipment, and family relationships are indicated below.

FOODS AND NUTRITION

Man's survival through the ages has been due in a large measure to his choice of foods. During this span of time he has consciously or unconsciously selected the kind and quantity of food that has provided the proper nutrients for his growth and development. Some people

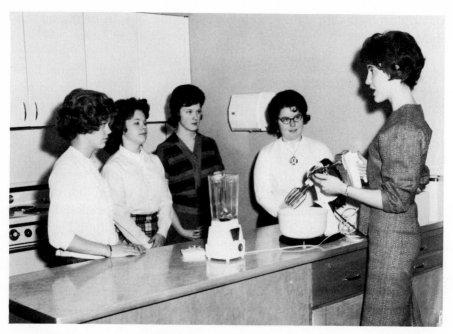

Students in Day School Homemaking Classes Engage in a Variety of Homemaking Activities Under the Supervision of the Homemaking Teacher. (Department of Education, Alaska)

through the centuries have been less fortunate than others and have chosen or been forced to accept food that was lacking in some of the essential elements. These people have contracted dietary-deficiency diseases. Some well-known examples of these are scurvy and beriberi which have been cured by the use of a proper diet. History indicates that human beings do not instinctively choose their food in accordance with the principles of nutrition, but they must learn the kinds of foods that are needed, the methods of producing those foods and the techniques of preparing the food for consumption.

Much progress has been made since the beginning of the present century in understanding the relationship of food and health. Scientists have discovered that more than 50 known nutrients found in food are necessary for the normal operation of the body. When any of these are lacking, some difficulty may arise. Nutrients frequently act as a group, and, if one nutrient is missing, the entire group is handicapped. Present-day diets, in general, are superior to those of the previous century, but some food nutrients are lost in milling, processing, and refining some of the more common foods presently consumed. However, scientists have found ways of replacing these losses. Foods of many kinds and in many different forms are available for the family. New methods of preparing and serving food are appearing daily, and many books, bulletins, magazine articles, and newspaper stories concerned with foods and nutrition have appeared in recent years.

Far more is known about foods and nutrition than is put into practical use. Statistics show that nutritional deficiencies are commonly found among people in the higher as well as the lower income levels. They are also found among people who produce food as well as those who purchase it. Studies show that food is distributed unequally among income groups, among regions of the nation, and in seasons of the year. Unequal distributions frequently result in problem areas even when national averages are normal. Statistics accumulated during both World War I and World War II indicated that large numbers of registrants for war service had defects specifically and almost solely due to nutritional deficiencies. The present-day family is spending about one-fourth of its income for food and is eating better than the family of World War II. The use of partially prepared foods has reduced the time required in meal preparation but has increased the need for knowledge about food.

Much of the responsibility for a proper diet falls to the lot of the homemaker. Studies show that some infirmities are due to the cumulative effects of improper diets over a long period of years, rather than to short periods of deficient diets. The right kind of food does far more than keep the family well. It adds enjoyment and happiness to life. These facts suggest that the homemaker needs to know what kinds of food are needed and how these foods should be prepared and served to make them more attractive, more tasty, and more nutritious. Homemakers need to know how to purchase suitable food within their financial means. This suggests that a knowledge of diets and food patterns and their relationship to economic and social backgrounds should be included in homemaking education.

SELECTION AND CARE OF CLOTHING AND TEXTILES

Studies indicate that the families of the United States spend from 8 to 12 percent of the family income for clothing and accessories. This expenditure in 1961 amounted to $32 billion. Expenditures vary among members of the family with about 47 percent of the expenditures for women's and children's clothing, 28 percent for men's and boys' clothing, 15 percent for footwear, and 10 percent for other items. Variations in the size of the family, the age and occupation of family members, and the family income result in variations in these percentages, as well as variations in the proportion of total income expended for clothing and accessories. The increasing trend of buying more ready-made clothes and the ever mounting prices of clothing and piece goods call for more careful planning in the purchase, construction and care of clothing and textiles for the family.

The homemaker has many decisions to make with reference to clothing and textiles. In the first place, a decision must be made whether to construct in the home or to buy ready-made. Prior to World War II, about 75 percent of the household linens and 60 percent of the wearing apparel were made in the home. The present-day trend is for the purchase of most of these items in retail stores. The purchase of apparel requires such decisions as how, when and where to shop; how to determine the quality, suitability and becomingness; and how to finance the purchase—cash or installment.

The matter of determining quality requires extensive knowledge and skill. Both natural and artificial textile fibers are available. Natural fibers are either vegetable, such as cotton, hemp and pineapple; animal, such as silk, wool and hair; or mineral, such as asbestos. Synthetic fibers are those chemically made by man and include many types, such as rayon, nylon, vinyon, orlon, dacron, lanitol, glass, and tinsel threads. Each of these varies in certain characteristics and optimum uses. There is continued research in fiber and fabric production which necessitates great skill in the selection and use of fabrics on the part of consumers. In the absence of dependable labels, the homemaker must rely on her own skill and knowledge to select the fiber and fabric suited to her needs. Even when labels are adequate it takes intelligent understanding to interpret them.

Many homemakers have sewing equipment and engage in some clothing construction in the home. Recent studies indicate that about 70 percent of the homes in the United States have sewing machines, most of which are powered by electricity. Sewing practices vary from simple repair to the construction of complete wardrobes. The art of clothing construction involves more than the operation of a treadle or an electric switch. Foremost among the requirements for successful clothing construction is a knowledge of the principles of design. Then, too, there is pattern making and alteration, cutting, hand and machine sewing, and fitting. Also involved is the construction of belts, collars, cuffs, hems, fastenings, buttonholes, and facings, as well as gatherings, pleats, godets, plackets, darts, pockets, and seams.

Present-day society requires that members of the family be well groomed, but present-day budgets require strict economy in the grooming process. This makes it necessary for homemakers to engage in the cleaning, storing, and repair of clothing. In 1960, 3 out of 4 homes had a clothes washer and 1 out of 6 a clothes dryer. Home cleaning has its hazards and limitations as well as its advantages. Different fabrics require different treatments, small tears have a habit of becoming larger, and fasteners must be properly attached. All this adds up to the fact that extensive knowledge, skills, and attitudes are required to insure good grooming for the family.

HOME PLANNING AND HOUSEHOLD EQUIPMENT

The American homemaker encounters many problems in planning new homes and in adapting old ones to family use. Some of these problems are due to the fact that many of the occupied dwellings were not planned by and for the families residing therein. The U.S. Bureau of the Census reports that 38 percent of the housing units in use in 1960 were renter-occupied. About 20 percent of the population moved to a different house from March 1961 to March 1962. Forty percent of the housing units had from 1 to 4 rooms and 12 percent averaged more than 1 person per room. The overcrowding that exists in many homes and the problems of moving to a different house in a different neighborhood frequently result in conflicts and frustrations that may have a serious effect on the physical or mental health of the family.

The problem of housing is more than one of providing space. The space must be divided into rooms and the rooms arranged in proper relationship to each other to promote safety and efficiency in the performance of household tasks. The increasing number of older persons in the population, many of whom must make their home with the younger generation, presents special housing problems of room and space arrangements to provide the desired privacy for each of the family units. Studies indicate that about one-half of the accidental injuries occur in the home. These injuries—more than 4 million in 1962—have resulted in many deaths and permanent injuries. Not all of these, but many, could have been prevented by proper planning to give adequate light; sufficient storage space; properly arranged halls, stairways, windows and balconies; and proper safeguards for hazardous equipment.

Human health and efficiency are influenced by the way in which the homes are heated and ventilated, as well as by the provisions for home sanitation. Data indicated that about 26 percent of the housing units had one or more plumbing facilities that were deteriorated or lacking in 1960. About 7 million units had no running water. Standards have been established to assist the homemaker in planning for proper heating, ventilation, illumination, and sanitation for the protection of the health of the family. More and more homemakers each year are purchasing equipment and devices to facilitate the tasks of food preparation, house cleaning, laundry work, and child care. The number of homes with mechanical refrigeration increased from 44 percent of the total number of homes reporting in 1940 to 95 percent of the total in 1960. The number of homes using either gas or electricity as a cooking fuel increased from 54 percent of the total in 1940 to 94 percent in 1960. More and more home appliances are being purchased, but frequently they are purchased and installed with little regard for need and convenience. Standards for determining the needed capacity of refrigerators, size of stoves, and height of sinks are available. Standards are also available for the selection, purchase and location of washing machines, dryers, ironers, and other appliances. The proper use of these standards will bring an added measure of health and happiness to American homes.

FAMILY RELATIONSHIPS

The family, which is the smallest unit of our social structure, provides the biological means of perpetuating the race and protecting and socializing the new generations. The family provides for its members —father, mother, and children—outlets for the love and affection considered essential in the emotional development of the individual. The family is the basis of the social structure and the means of control over all social relations. Society, in turn, recognizes the fundamental importance of the family and attempts through tradition, education, and regulation to promote and uphold family stability. Society by law and custom regulates practices involving courtship and marriage, modes of family living, child care, and kinship obligations.

Significant changes have occurred through the years in the structure and function of the family. These changes, more especially those that have occurred in recent times, have given rise to many perplexing problems of home and family relationships. An understanding of these changes is essential in planning an attack on these problems. One of these changes has to do with the size of the family. The average number of persons per household in the United States decreased from 5.3 persons in 1860 to 3.3 persons in 1960. Childless marriages, late marriages, and an aging population have reduced family size. These changes in family size affect the influence of the family as a social institution as well as the education, training, protective and recreational aspects of family life.

In 1890 about 17 percent of all women 20 to 64 years of age were employed. This figure was 29 percent in 1940, and it is estimated that it will be 43 percent by 1975. Women constituted 17 percent of the total labor force in 1890 and 33 percent in 1960. About 60 percent of the women in the labor force in 1960 were married as contrasted to 14 percent in 1890.

Changes in the average ages of the members of the family present family problems that require special treatment. The number of persons 65 years of age and older increased from 2.6 percent of the population in 1850 to 9.2 percent in 1960, and the number of children

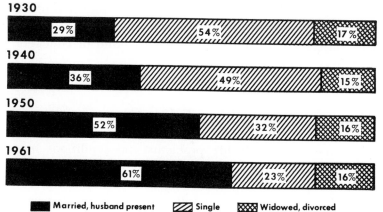

1930
29% 54% 17%

1940
36% 49% 15%

1950
52% 32% 16%

1961
61% 23% 16%

■ Married, husband present ▨ Single ▨ Widowed, divorced

More than 60 Percent of the Women in the Labor Force are Married. The percentage of married women in the labor force increased from 29 percent in 1930 to 61 percent in 1961. (Agricultural Research Service, U.S. Department of Agriculture)

under 5 years of age decreased from 15 percent of the population to 11 percent during the same period. Americans, in general, marry early and have their children relatively soon after marriage. Child development has taken on new meaning due to social changes such as women working and the extended use of communication facilities such as radio and television. The child, for the most part, has little opportunity to learn from his parents as was the custom in previous years when the father worked and the mother remained at home. The present-day trend is for both parents to be away from home during the day, and children are left to learn from other adults, who frequently are not selected with care, or from other children. Fifty percent of the women who marry are married before they are 21 years old. Statistics show that early marriages—under 20 years of age—are more likely to result in divorce than those contracted in later years.

Family instability seems to be a continuing and increasing problem for present-day society. The divorce rate in 1867 was .3 per 1000 population. This figure had increased to 1.0 per 1000 by 1914 and 1.7 per 1000 by 1929. Divorce rates decreased during the depression but reached the peak of 4.3 per 1000 population in 1946. The divorce rate in 1962 was 2.2 per 1000 population. It was estimated that 1 divorce for every 4 new marriages occurred in 1962. Twice as many marriages are dissolved by desertion or separation as by divorce. Some of these are permanent dissolutions, while others are temporary. The institution of marriage has contributed much to the advancement of civilization, and, therefore, every effort should be made to resolve the conflicts that arise in home and family life. This task will be less difficult when the individuals concerned participate in the right kind of education for home and family living.

Organization of Homemaking Education

The foregoing home and family life problems and conditions have stimulated the organization of various kinds and types of homemaking programs. These programs are sponsored by both public and private agencies and are for public school and college students and for youth and adults who are not enrolled in schools and colleges. Technical courses in homemaking on the college level are usually referred to as *home economics courses*. These courses are designed to prepare college students for home and family living and for positions in the areas of homemaking, such as homemaking teacher, dietitian, home demonstration agent, homemaking specialist, nursery school teacher, institutional manager, and other similar vocations.

Homemaking education in the secondary school may be classified as general or vocational. The purpose of general homemaking education, frequently referred to as a nonvocational practical arts subject area, is to interpret those aspects of modern life which have to do with the problems and activities of the home, without reference to their vocational significance. These courses may be placed on various grade levels in the junior and senior high schools and are designed for all students, regardless of their vocational choices. Vocational homemaking education is centered on home activities and relationships and is designed to enable school students and adults of both sexes to assume the responsibilities of making a home and of improving home and family living. Because of the similarity of course content it has been suggested by some educators that no distinction be made between general and vocational homemaking and all courses of this nature be classified as homemaking education courses.

OBJECTIVES OF VOCATIONAL HOMEMAKING EDUCATION

The aim of vocational education is to educate present and prospective workers for proficiency in their chosen, socially useful occupations. When applied to vocational homemaking education, this aim is one of educating present and prospective homemakers for the efficient and effective performance of the occupation of homemaking. The primary purposes of vocational homemaking education are those concerned with assisting the student of homemaking to (1) determine worth-while values for immediate personal and home living, (2) achieve a wholesome personality and satisfactory personal and social relationship, (3) discover her needs, interests, and capabilities as related to home and family life, and (4) use individual and family resources to achieve the desired goals in home and family living.

These objectives suggest that vocational homemaking programs should provide instruction in the following areas of homemaking: (1) child development; (2) family relationships; (3) food and nutrition; (4) clothing and textiles; (5) family economics and home management; (6) housing; (7) home furnishings and equipment; and (8) family health.[1]

The increasing number of married women who are gainfully employed outside the home has occasioned a greater emphasis on the management phases of the foregoing areas of homemaking and the addition of some new areas such as (1) deciding about working outside the home, (2) dividing responsibility for homemaking among members of the family, (3) management of time and energy, (4) management of money, and (5) family attitudes.[2]

The Vocational Education Act of 1963 provides that Federal funds may be used for gainful employment in teaching any occupation

---

[1] American Vocational Association, *Definitions of Terms in Vocational Technical, and Practical Arts Education*, Committee on Publications, Washington, D.C., 1964, p. 11.

[2] Adapted from W. W. Wood, Alberta Hill, and Edna P. Amidon, *Management Problems of Homemakers Employed Outside the Home*, Vocational Division Bulletin 289, U.S. Department of Health, Education, and Welfare, Office of Education, Washington, D.C., 1962, pp. 1–4.

involving knowledge and skills in home economics subjects. Some occupations in this category include (1) a child day-care worker, (2) a management aide for Federal or other housing projects, (3) a visiting homemaker, (4) a hotel and motel housekeeping aide, (5) a supervising food service worker, (6) a personal wardrobe maintenance specialist, (7) a companion to elderly persons, (8) a family dinner service specialist, and (9) a homemaker's assistant.

The homemaking teacher may cooperate with other teachers by providing knowledge and skills in home economics subjects needed by individuals who are preparing for or seeking advancement in other occupations. Homemaking teachers have provided instruction in such areas as good grooming, clothing and textiles, foods and nutrition, home furnishing and decoration, and family relationships which may be included in agricultural, distributive, and industrial occupations.

The major objectives and areas of homemaking may be used as a guide for establishing objectives for a specific local program for the homemaking teacher. The specific objectives may be stated in terms of interests, attitudes, appreciations, understandings, and abilities which should be acquired or developed by students. The formulation of specific objectives involves a number of steps, the first of which is determining community needs in the area of homemaking. This may be accomplished by home visits, community surveys, and group discussion. The homemaking teacher may then establish tentative objectives to serve as a basis for student-teacher planning of objectives for the designated school or class.

TYPES OF SCHOOLS AND CLASSES

Vocational home economics courses are organized to meet the needs of various groups of individuals in the community. These groups include (1) high school and post-high school students enrolled for full-time instruction; (2) out-of-school youth who have recently become established in homemaking or other home economics occupations, or who are planning for these vocations and are available for instruction part of the time, (3) adult homemakers, and (4) other adults who are in need of knowledge and skill in home economics, and are available for less than full-time instruction. Two types of classes for these groups are included in the vocational home economics program. These are the day school or in-school class for students who are regularly enrolled in school, and the out-of-school class for youth and adults who are available for instruction part of the time, and are in need of knowledge and skills in homemaking or some of its aspects.

Classes for in-school groups. The vocational homemaking curriculum for in-school youth is usually in the secondary school in grades nine through twelve. It is included in not less than two of these years and more frequently in three of them. The homemaking courses are usually referred to as Homemaking I, Homemaking II, and Homemaking III. The usual practice is for each high school class to meet a minimum of as many hours per week as is required for a full unit of credit for other school subjects in the school. This usually requires two class periods per day in schools where the length of the class period is 45 minutes and one class period per day in schools having 60-minute class periods. High school credit in the amount of one unit per year is provided if the minimum requirements for such credit are met.

The subjects included in the homemaking curriculum for day school students vary among the secondary schools and among different students in the same school. Each student in each grade usually takes four or five subjects in addition to the homemaking course. Among the general education subjects more frequently assigned to, or elected by, ninth-grade students in Homemaking I are English, algebra, community civics, general science, and health and physical education. The general education subjects more frequently elected by, or assigned to, tenth-grade students in the homemaking course are English, world history, plane geometry, biology, and health and physical education. Eleventh- and twelfth-grade students in homemaking take such general education courses as English, American history or another social science, typewriting or other business subjects, and health and physical education.

Special classes are organized for in-school youth not enrolled in homemaking but preparing for other vocations requiring knowledge and skills in home economics subjects. These vary in content with the needs of the group. Some are organized as short unit courses and others extend for one or two semesters. Some are units included in another curriculum. For example, the homemaking teacher may provide technical information in clothing and textiles for students in the field of distribution. In some schools the practice of exchanging classes is followed. For instance, the homemaking teacher may provide instruction in clothing selection and good grooming for the students in vocational agriculture. The agriculture teacher at the same time may instruct homemaking students in home gardening or flower growing.

Classes for out-of-school groups. The increasing interest of adults in continuing their education has led to the organization of classes for out-of-school youth and adults. Adults differ from school students in their maturity, needs, and interests, responsibility for homemaking, and time available for educational programs. Classes for out-of-school youth and adults should provide instruction and directed home experiences in the several aspects of home economics and for gainful employment in occupations involving knowledge and skill in home economics subjects. This instruction may be organized as short units of 5 to 10 hours each or as a single unit extending throughout the year. Some communities plan programs that extend over 3 or 4 years for out-of-school classes. The class for the out-of-school group may be scheduled to meet at a time of day convenient for the class members. The class is usually taught by the homemaking teacher employed to teach in the secondary school. Qualified homemakers and specialists in home economics may also be employed to teach these classes.

A separate class, sometimes referred to as a part-time class, is organized for out-of-school youth who are homemakers or prospective homemakers. The members of this group, as a rule, have not established families, and their interests are somewhat different from those of established homemakers. The part-time class usually extends over a longer period of time than the adult class. Frequently, the youth organize as a group and meet one night a week throughout the school year.

Many communities, more especially in rural areas, are developing a community program of adult education. This program is designed for all members of the family. The usual procedure for a class meeting is for the members of the various families in the community to meet first as a group for the discussion of matters of common interest, or for entertainment, then to divide into special interest groups for a discussion period and to reconvene for an evaluation and refreshment session. In the special group sessions, the homemaking teacher usually takes responsibility for sponsoring the women's discussion group and the other teachers have responsibility for discussion groups in their various teaching fields.

Homemaking teachers engage in many informal adult education activities. Among these are home visits to members of the adult class for the purpose of discussing individual and community problems with the homemakers; school visitation days, at which time adults are invited to the school to view exhibits and discuss homemaking problems with the homemaking teacher; surveys and studies of home and family life problems to be used as a basis for planning homemaking classes for adults and assisting in the organization of homemakers' clubs in which programs concerned with special homemaking problems are prepared and presented by the members. Other activities of a similar nature include educational tours of nearby schools and communities for the purpose of observing some activity or project of interest to homemakers; homemakers' clinics where the homemaking teacher makes her time available for consultation with homemakers; and radio and television programs designed to provide suggestions for the solution of problems of home and family life. Homemaking teachers may also arrange for family discussion groups as a supplement to organized adult class instruction.

TRENDS IN ENROLLMENTS AND EXPENDITURES

A total of 34,180,000 persons enrolled in various classes in vocational homemaking education in the United States and territories during the 45-year period 1918 to 1962 inclusive. The trend of enrollment has been upward through the years. The average enrollment per year for the 10-year period 1931 to 1940 was almost three times the corresponding average for the period 1921 to 1930, and the average for the period 1951 to 1960 was one and one-third times the average for the 1941 to 1950 period. Ninety-seven percent of the total enrollment through the 45-year period were female students and about 3 percent male students. This ratio has changed very little through the years. For example, about 3 percent of the enrollment for the 10-year period 1951 to 1960 were male students.

The largest enrollment for the 45-year period was in day school classes, representing 55 percent of the total. The enrollment in evening classes was 38 percent of the total, and the part-time class enrollment was 7 percent. These percentages are about the same for the various 10-year periods, except the period 1921 to 1930 when the day school class enrollment represented only 26 percent of the total.

During the 10-year period 1951 to 1960, the following states reported highest enrollments in vocational homemaking education: Texas, California, New York, Georgia, Florida, North Carolina, Michigan, South Carolina, Illinois, and Tennessee. Enrollments in these 10 states for the above period represented 57 percent of the total enrollment in vocational homemaking education for the states and territories of the United States.

The number of day-school teachers in vocational homemaking education increased from 398 in 1918 to 14,797 in 1962. The average number of these teachers reported for the 10-year period ending in

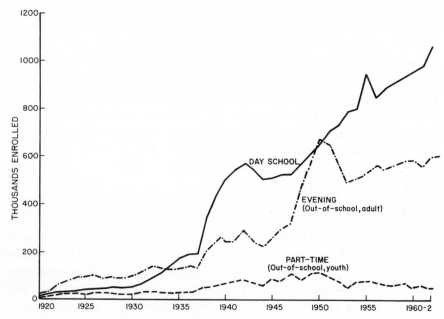

Enrollments in Vocational Homemaking Classes by Type of Class in the States and Territories for the Years 1920 to 1962. The trend of enrollments in the various types of homemaking classes resembles the trend of enrollments in similar types of classes in vocational agriculture. (U.S. Department of Health, Education, and Welfare, Office of Education, *Digest of Annual Reports of State Boards for Vocational Education to the Office of Education, for the Fiscal Year Ended June 30, 1962*, Government Printing Office, 1963)

1960 was 9.3 times larger than the average reported for the 10-year period 1921 to 1930. During this same period the average enrollment in day school classes increased almost twice as rapidly as the number of teachers. During the first 15 years that the vocational homemaking education program was in operation, an average of about 25 men teachers per year was reported for the entire national program. The number of day school students per teacher has increased from an average of 27 for the 10-year period 1921 to 1930 to 57 for the 10-year period ending in 1960. An average of 34 students per teacher was enrolled annually in vocational evening classes for homemakers during the period from 1921 to 1930. The corresponding average for the 10-year period 1951 to 1960 was 46 students per teacher.

Total expenditures for vocational homemaking education for the 45-year period 1918 to 1962 inclusive were reported as $1,022,150,-000. Annual expenditures during this period increased from $641,812 in 1918 to $79,898,000 in 1962. The 1962 amount is 125 times larger than the 1918 figure. Total expenditures have increased at an increasing rate. Total expenditures for the 10-year period 1931 to 1940 were about 2 times the total expenditures for the 10-year period 1921 to 1930. The corresponding figure for the period from 1951 to 1960 was about 2.5 times that of the preceding decade.

Federal funds represented 18 percent of the total expenditures for the 45-year period, and state and local funds represented 82 percent. State funds were 34 percent and local funds 48 percent. State and local communities have expended $4.62 for each dollar of Federal funds expended throughout the 45-year period. The ratio between expenditures of local and state funds and Federal funds has varied through the years. State and local communities expended $4.26 for each dollar of Federal funds expended during the 10-year period 1921 to 1930; $3.15 for each dollar of Federal funds expended from 1941 to 1950; and $5.88 for each dollar of Federal funds expended from 1951 to 1960. The expenditures for the administration of the vocational homemaking education program for the period from 1951 to 1960 inclusive represented about 1 percent of the total expenditures. The expenditures for supervision and teacher training were 8 percent of the total and for instruction 91 percent.

It should be kept in mind that the above statistics do not include data for non-Federally aided programs. The U.S. Office of Education estimated that 2,914,000 students were enrolled in homemaking courses in public junior and senior high schools in 1961. This represents one-fourth of the total secondary school enrollment. About one-half of the homemaking students were in grades seven and eight, and one-third in Federally aided vocational homemaking programs.

The Instructional Program

Teachers of vocational homemaking education have responsibility for teaching homemaking classes, supervising the directed work experiences of students and directing activities of student organizations. They are also required to hold conferences with individual students on directed experiences in home and community living and often to direct a child development laboratory as an integral part of the homemaking program. Homemaking teachers also make studies of home and community conditions and engage in follow-up activities of students who have completed the curriculum in homemaking. They also keep records, make reports and keep the school and community informed concerning the problems and achievements of the homemaking program. These various activities make it necessary for a homemaking teacher to work beyond the school year, and many school boards employ these teachers for 10 to 12 months annually. Teachers in vocational homemaking education need to possess all the qualifications of teachers of academic subjects and many additional qualifications in order that they may effectively perform the duties and responsibilities expected of homemaking teachers.

THE QUALIFICATIONS OF TEACHERS OF VOCATIONAL HOMEMAKING EDUCATION

Teacher qualifications in vocational homemaking education are expressed in terms of personal characteristics; academic education, including professional education; and homemaking experience. Many studies indicate the relationship between success in teaching and the possession of certain personality traits that are difficult to define. Superior teachers have broad interests, are cooperative with community groups and other school departments, are enthusiastic about teaching, and maintain student confidence. Superior teachers know their subject matter and know how to stimulate their students to acquire the desired knowledge, skills and attitudes. Superior teachers develop a philosophy of education and of vocational homemaking education, including understandings and attitudes relative to the function of homemaking education in the total school program and the relationship of homemaking education to other subject matter areas. Superior homemaking teachers develop satisfactory personal relationships with students and with other individuals in the school community.

State plans for vocational education specify the minimum educational experience required of teachers of vocational homemaking education. This varies from state to state, but in general it consists of the satisfacory completion of a four-year undergraduate course from an institution approved by the state board for vocational education for training vocational homemaking teachers. The four-year curriculum includes general education subjects, subject matter in technical home economics, and professional education subjects. The curriculum usually provides for a variety of experiences, including some practical homemaking activities, participation in community activities, work experience to help students develop skills, participation in student organizations, such as the FHA, and experience in caring for children.

Supervised experience in a total school program is also provided, and this includes directed teaching and other responsibilities usually associated with vocational homemaking education.

Homemaking teachers need special courses and some experience in organizing a child development laboratory. Actual experience in church, nursery, or play school programs for preschool children is desirable. Homemaking experience is an essential qualification of a homemaking teacher. Homemaking experience includes activities of interest and importance to the family well-being both inside and outside

Student Teachers in Vocational Homemaking Education Confer with Their Supervisor on Problems They Encounter While Engaged in Student Teaching. (College of Education, University of Tennessee)

the home. Girls who complete preservice teacher education programs usually have some home experience. They have at least grown up in a home and have been responsible for some homemaking duties. When these are not sufficient, other homemaking experiences may be obtained while in college or during the vacation period. Some colleges provide for summer projects which enable the prospective teacher to acquire knowledge and skill in food selection and preparation, clothing construction and other homemaking activities. The home management house maintained under the supervision of the college also provides opportunities for various types of experience in homemaking.

HOMEMAKING CURRICULUMS AND TEACHING TECHNIQUES

The content of the homemaking curriculum is determined by its objectives and consists of the learning experiences in home and family living for which the school is responsible. These experiences are selected by teachers and students and include directed home experience, club and group activities, and course content. Some plan of unit organization is commonly used in grouping or organizing the selected experiences for instructional purposes. Each unit consists of a group of worth-while experiences related to some central theme of homemaking. The time required for the completion of a unit usually varies from three or four days to six or eight weeks.

Various types of units are used in curriculum making in homemaking education. One type commonly used is the problem unit. A series of problems constitutes the unit. For example, such problems as the following are included in the unit Managing the Family Income: What is the income of the family? What are the family's needs? Can the needs be met with the income? What plans should be made for spending the family income? Some homemaking teachers use projects as a means of organizing units of instruction. Such projects as improving the homemaking laboratory or cottage, maintaining a day nursery, serving a father-and-son banquet, and landscaping the school grounds are examples of this plan of organization. These projects provide purposeful activity and opportunity for independent thinking. Short units concerned with a single phase of homemaking are frequently used in out-of-school classes.

The homemaking teacher who guides the learning experiences of youth and adults in organized classes needs to know about the students, their needs and interests, their home and family life, and their relationships with the community. Most of this information may be obtained in informal conversations with students and in visits to their homes. Other information of this nature may be obtained by various types of community leadership activities. The teacher may use this information in guiding students into and through educative experiences that promote growth. The homemaking teacher may lead students into educative experiences by using the personal problems of the students as they suggest them, by inviting suggestions from students and by suggesting activities and experiences for students. Various techniques may be used by the teacher to guide students through experiences. These include group discussions, panel discussions, role playing, directed study, laboratory activities, demonstrations, field trips, and problem-solving procedures. A single unit of instruction may offer possibilities for using a number of the above techniques. Many types of visual aids are also available, such as motion pictures, slides, film strips, illustrations, models, samples, posters, and charts. These techniques and devices, when suppemented with books, bulletins, magazines, leaflets, and newspapers, provide a wide variety of interesting materials and methods for use in homemaking classes.

DIRECTED HOME OR OTHER WORK EXPERIENCE

Home experience, also referred to as home projects, is defined as "learning activities related to personal and family problems, which are planned, carried out, and evaluated by the pupils in their homes, under the guidance of the teacher and parents, for the purpose of personal development and improvement of home life."[3]

Home experience is a necessary part of the vocational homemaking program just as farm, shop and business experiences are necessary parts of other vocational programs. The best schools cannot provide all the facilities and activities of the home. An appropriate type of directed home or other work experience should be provided for students enrolled in courses organized for gainful employment in occupations involving knowledge and skills in home economics subjects. This may involve some form of internship or supervised work experience in the home, health unit, day nursery, or housing facility.

A desirable type of directed home experience has a number of distinguishing characteristics. It should be undertaken by the student who is interested in acquiring the experience. The experience should meet a need and grow out of a problem recognized by the student. It should be carried out in the home with the cooperation of the parents. Desirable home experience should enable the student to acquire new abilities, and it should challenge and not discourage the student. A plan for the directed home experience should be carefully made and properly executed. The homemaking teacher should provide counsel and assistance as needed and should recognize superior accomplishments.

The term *home practice* is used to define one form of home experience. It is defined as "the practical application of specific school learning to home activities for the purpose of developing skill in, and appreciation of, sound homemaking procedures."[4] Home practice is of less scope than home projects. Examples are preparing a meat dish for dinner, cleaning one's room, waxing the dining room floor, and hanging draperies.

Home experience or home projects properly planned and carried out will help the student to plan, to work with others, to be more interested in home and family life and to develop certain skills of value in homemaking. Many homemaking teachers help day school students

[3] American Vocational Association, *Definitions of Terms in Vocational, Technical, and Practical Arts Education*, Committee on Publications, Washington, D.C., 1964, p. 11.
[4] *Ibid.*, p. 11

plan summer projects to be carried out when school is not in session. Summer projects, as a rule, are larger in scope than those undertaken during the school year. Group as well as individual projects are also carried out during the summer months. Home experience is also a part of the adult education program in homemaking, and adult homemakers, especially young adults, are acquiring greater efficiency in homemaking through directed home experience.

FACILITIES AND EQUIPMENT

Various kinds of facilities are used for housing the vocational homemaking department in the public schools. Some schools use a one-room, all-purpose laboratory that is equipped for all phases of homemaking. Furnishings and equipment in the all-purpose laboratory are of the movable type to permit flexible arrangements. The class may work as a single group, or it may be divided into smaller groups. Some departments are housed in two or more rooms in the main school building. One room, under this arrangement, may be equipped for a foods laboratory and the other room arranged as a clothing laboratory. If a third room is available, it may be used as a living room. A class may move from one room to another as the daily program requires. Here again, the room arrangement should be made as flexible as possible to permit a wide variety of homemaking activities.

Some homemaking departments are housed in separate buildings and in home economics cottages. The cottage resembles a home except that extra space for laboratory activities is provided. The cottage is more homelike and offers many desirable homemaking opportunities, especially in home management, room arrangement, cooperative group living and home furnishing. The living room of the cottage is frequently used as a social center for small group conferences and social affairs and as a study room. Comfortable, informal arrangements in the cottage or department are more conducive to ease and relaxation than more formal ones.

The kind and quantity of equipment and furnishings depend on the needs of the school community. The equipment and furnishings should be suited to the ages of the students and should be similar in quality to those in the more desirable homes of the community. Unit kitchens are provided in which the necessary equipment for cooking and serving food is arranged in a manner similar to that found in the homes of the student. Homemaking departments in some schools are equipped with unit kitchens with various types of stoves and other kitchen appliances at various cost levels. This arrangement has some value in teaching the factors to consider in selecting kitchen equipment and in teaching an appreciation of various types of equipment. Problems of clothing construction require sewing machines, tables, ironing boards and fitting space. Standards have been established for determining the number of unit kitchens and other items of equipment needed in the homemaking department. Frequently, these standards are included in state plans for vocational education.

The Future Homemakers of America

The Future Homemakers of America, commonly known as the FHA, is a national youth organization for homemaking students enrolled in secondary schools throughout the nation. The FHA is an incorporated, nonprofit youth organization. It is sponsored by the Division of Vocational and Technical Education, U.S. Office of Education, and by the American Home Economics Association. Cooperating groups include the American Vocational Association and the National Education Association.

The organization provides opportunities for members to share in problems of family life, to work for better homes and home living, to develop leadership and intelligent participation in a democratic society and to engage in wholesome individual and group recreation. The activities of the FHA are considered an integral part of the total homemaking program in the secondary schools. They are not designed to replace class activities but to supplement and extend them as a means of developing leadership and as a device for improving home and family life.

THE ORIGIN AND DEVELOPMENT OF THE FUTURE HOMEMAKERS OF AMERICA

The Future Homemakers of America had its origin in the various student clubs and local organizations of youth studying homemaking. These local clubs increased in numbers soon after the passage of the Smith-Hughes Vocational Education Act in 1917. By 1938 membership in these clubs located in schools and colleges was estimated at 90,000 members. The clubs were usually sponsored by local homemaking instructors and members of the state staff in vocational home economics education. The American Home Economics Association, through its department of student clubs, also encouraged the organization of local clubs and provided for their national affiliation with the

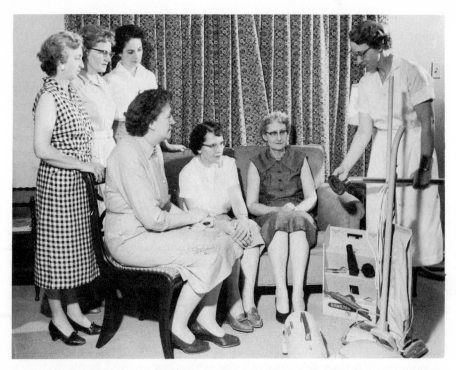

Adult Homemakers Receive Instruction in Evening Classes in Skills Designed to Improve Home and Family Living. (Milwaukee Vocational and Adult Schools, Milwaukee, Wisconsin)

AHEA. State clubs or associations, consisting for the most part of federated local chapters, were also organized during this period.

The possibilities of a national organization became apparent, and in December, 1943, a committee was appointed by the AHEA to study the feasibility of a national organization. As a result of the committee's recommendation, a national meeting was held in Chicago in March, 1944, at which time plans for a national organization of High School Home Economics Clubs were discussed. The organization, which was started in June, 1944, adopted a provisional constitution on June 11, 1945, and selected the name Future Homemakers of America as its official name.

The FHA functioned under a provisional constitution for 3 years, and, on July 9, 1948, at its first national meeting, the national constitution was ratified. The FHA had a membership of 540,872 individuals at the end of the 1963 fiscal year. These members were in 10,715 local chapters located in 50 states, Puerto Rico, and the Virgin Islands. The national office is located in the Home Economics Education

Branch, Vocational Division, U.S. Office of Education, Washington, D.C.

THE ORGANIZATION OF THE FHA

The FHA consists of local chapters, state associations and the national organization. These groups have active, associate and honorary members. Active members consist of students who are regularly enrolled in homemaking classes in junior and senior high schools. Associate members are former active members who have graduated from, or left, high school and are associated with an FHA chapter. Honorary members are individuals who have rendered outstanding service to the FHA by advancing its purposes. Honorary members are elected by a majority vote at any regular meeting of the national executive council and the national advisory board. Associate and honorary members may attend meetings of the organization but are not eligible to vote or hold office in the FHA.

The FHA has three degrees of achievement designed to promote growth of members who engage in specified activities. These are Junior Homemaker, Chapter Homemaker, and State Homemaker. Originally a National Homemaker degree was authorized but the awarding of this degree was discontinued by the National Advisory Board in 1950. Junior and Chapter Homemaker degrees are awarded by the local chapter, and the State Homemaker degree is awarded by the state association. Each of these degrees is awarded to candidates who have met established standards for the respective degrees. These standards of achievement are based on individual planning; participation; leadership; and growth in home, school and community activities related to homemaking.

The local homemaking teacher serves as the adviser to the local chapter. Many local chapters also have an advisory committee consisting of the adviser and other adults selected by members of the local chapter. The adviser to the state association is designated by the state supervisor of vocational home economics education in cooperation with the state advisory board. The national adviser is the administrative officer of the association and is selected by the national advisory board. This board is composed of 14 persons from the following organizations: state and Federal vocational home economics education services, American Home Economics Association, American Vocational Association, and the National Education Association. The national executive council of the FHA is composed of the 12 elected national officers. The national adviser and assistant national adviser serve as official advisers to the council. The executive council, with the advice of the advisory board, has authority and control of the national organization within the framework of the national constitution and bylaws.

Four regions, each consisting of three subregions, are included in the FHA plan of organization. Regional and subregional meetings are held from time to time. The present plan provides for a national convention once every three years, a regional meeting once every three years and a national leadership meeting once every three years. Officers are elected at these meetings. Each region provides specified officers according to an established plan of rotation that is arranged so that the regions take their turns in providing the national president, secretary, treasurer, parliamentarian, and historian.

FUTURE HOMEMAKERS' PROGRAM OF WORK

FHA members engage in many activities which contribute to better family living. These include caring for children, accepting home responsibilities, participating in family recreation, working with adults on civil defense, conducting nutritional campaigns, and sponsoring national projects, such as FHA Week, Families Together, United Nations Day, and World Christmas Festival. These and other activities are included in the chapter program of work, usually compiled by the program-of-work committee. The local program of work as a rule follows the state and national programs of work insofar as they are applicable locally.

The local program of work is based on the purposes of the organization, the needs of the group and the homemaking goals. Various types of activities, such as social, educational, service and financial, are included in the plan, and an attempt is made to attain a balance among these activities. The number of activities varies with the number of members. A sufficient number is selected to provide a challenge rather than a burdensome task. Activities that afford opportunities for cooperating with other agencies interested in home and family life are planned. Special attention is given to providing some activities in which all members may participate.

The program of work is developed by the membership as a whole under the guidance of a program-of-work committee. The program-of-work committee discusses homemaking goals, examines state and national programs of work and studies needs of the members as bases for planning the program of work. A tentative program of work is presented to the entire membership of the chapter for suggestions and approval. The committee then prepares a revised copy of the program of work and a calendar for the various activities. Subcommittees are made responsible for major activities or points of emphasis.

Among the more important activities in which FHA members engage for the purpose of financing their other chapter activities are cake, candy, egg, and hot dog sales, barbecues, catering services, hobo days, pancake breakfasts, luncheons for service clubs and other agencies, sale of magazines and cards, staging plays, revues and athletic games, and sponsoring concession stands. Activities for improving the homemaking department of the local school include making draperies, selecting and hanging pictures, decorating walls and making furniture for the cottage, and landscaping and growing flowers for the grounds. Recreational activities included in the program of work are mother-and-daughter banquets, bunking parties, faculty teas, daddy date nights, school guest nights, picnics, play parties, dances, treasure hunts, FHA camps and school carnivals. Other activities include assisting in children's clinics, operating nursery schools, assisting in "Keep the City Clean" campaigns, preparing scrapbooks for children of other nations and conducting style shows.

THE NEW HOMEMAKERS OF AMERICA

The New Homemakers of America is a national organization of Negro students studying homemaking in junior and senior high schools in some states throughout the nation. The New Homemakers of America, or NHA, like the Future Homemakers of America, had its origin in local homemaking clubs and state associations. These state associations recognized that a national organization would strengthen and broaden the opportunities of the local and state associations. The staff of the Home Economics Education Service, Vocational Division, U.S. Office of Education, together with other agencies, made plans in 1944 for the organization of the national association. Three sectional meetings were held in the spring of 1945, at which time candidates for national offices were selected and plans for the national organization were discussed. These meetings were held at Pine Bluff, Arkansas, Atlanta, Georgia, and Washington, D.C. The chairmen of the sectional meetings and the candidates for national offices met at Nashville, Tennessee, and completed the national organization on June 19, 1945.

The organization of the NHA was quite similar to that of the FHA. The three degrees of achievement were referred to as Featherweight Homemaker, Apprentice Homemaker, and Advanced Homemaker. The emblem, colors, flowers, and motto differed from those of the FHA, but the plan of organization, involving advisers, advisory committees and executive councils, was similar in make-up and function. The various state associations were combined into two groups or sections. Section I consisted of state associations in Alabama, Arkansas, Louisiana, Mississippi, Oklahoma, and Texas. Section II consisted of state associations in Delaware, Florida, Georgia, Kentucky, North Carolina, Tennessee, and Virginia. The NHA had a membership of 73,981 individuals on June 1, 1963. These members, through their 1386 local chapters, have contributed materially to the progress of homemaking in the several states in which NHA organizations are maintained.

QUESTIONS FOR STUDY AND DISCUSSION

1. What are some important problems that influence the need for homemaking education?
2. What progress has been made in the solution of these problems by the use of educational techniques?
3. What aspects of homemaking are included in the objectives of vocational homemaking education?
4. What types of classes are available to secondary school students and adults who desire to engage in the study of vocational homemaking?
5. Discuss the organization of a community program of vocational homemaking education for adults.
6. Distinguish among vocational homemaking education, general homemaking education, and home economics.
7. What are the trends in enrollment and expenditures for the vocational homemaking education program in the United States?
8. What are the qualifications required of teachers of vocational homemaking education?
9. What are some desirable characteristics and types of directed home experience?
10. What facilities and equipment are needed in vocational homemaking education?
11. Discuss the historical development of the FHA and the NHA.
12. Indicate how the FHA is organized for work, and discuss the various types of activities in which this organization is engaged.

SOURCE REFERENCES

American Public Health Association, Committee on the Hygiene of Housing, *Construction and Equipment of the Home*, Public Administration Service Bulletin, Chicago, 1951.

American Public Health Association, Committee on the Hygiene of Housing, *Housing an Aging Population,* New York, 1953.

Barclay, Marion S., and Frances Champion, *Teen Guide to Homemaking,* McGraw-Hill, New York, 1961.

Federal Board for Vocational Education, *Annual Reports,* 1918 to 1932 inclusive, Washington, D.C.

Future Homemakers of America, *Advisers Handbook,* Washington, D.C., 1962.

Future Homemakers of America, *A Guide to Help You Grow as a Future Homemaker of America,* Washington, D.C., 1962.

Hall, Olive A., and Beatrice Paolucci, *Teaching Home Economics,* Wiley, New York, 1961.

Hawley, Estelle E., Grace Carden, and Elizabeth D. Munves, *The Art and Science of Nutrition,* Mosby, St. Louis, 1955.

Justin, Margaret M., Lucille O. Rust, and Gladys E. Vail, *Foods,* Lippincott, Philadelphia, 1956.

Landis, Judson T., and Mary G. Landis, *Personal Adjustment, Marriage and Family Living,* Prentice-Hall, Englewood Cliffs, N.J., 1960.

Leverton, Ruth M., *Food Becomes You,* Iowa State University Press, Ames, 1960.

National Safety Council, *Accident Facts* (1962 edition), Washington, D.C., 1962.

New Homemakers of America, *Official Guide for New Homemakers of America,* Washington, D.C., 1960.

Sirjamaki, John, *The American Family in the Twentieth Century,* Harvard, Cambridge, 1953.

Sturm, Mary M., and Edwina H. Grieser, *Guide to Modern Clothing,* McGraw-Hill, New York, 1962.

U.S. Department of Commerce, Bureau of the Census, *Statistical Abstract of the United States, 1964,* Washington, D.C., 1964.

U.S. Office of Education, *Digest of Annual Reports of State Boards for Vocational Education* for fiscal years 1933 to 1962 inclusive, Washington, D.C.

U.S. President's Commission on the Status of Women, *American Women,* Washington, D.C., 1963.

Williamson, Maude, and Mary S. Lyle, *Homemaking Education in the High School,* Appleton-Century-Crofts, New York, 1954.

CHAPTER ELEVEN

VOCATIONAL INDUSTRIAL EDUCATION

The vast scope of American industry, together with its changing nature, has required programs of education and training of various kinds and types for its ever increasing labor force. Since the beginning of American industry, programs of education and training have been provided by apprenticeship; by corporations; and by proprietary, endowed, and public schools. The combined efforts of all these agencies and institutions are presently required to supply workers with needed competencies for efficient production in industry. The public school program, which is the newest of the industrial education programs, has had its greatest expansion since the passage of the Smith-Hughes Vocational Education Act of 1917. This law has stimulated the development of industrial education programs in times of peace and in times of war. This program, which was termed the trade and industrial education program, is now also known as the vocational industrial education program.

Vocational industrial education is defined as instruction which is planned for the purpose of developing basic manipulative skills, safety judgments, technical knowledge, and related occupational information for the purpose of fitting young persons for initial employment in industrial occupations and of upgrading or retraining workers employed in industry. Vocational industrial education, together with general industrial education or industrial arts, and vocational technical education constitute the broad field of industrial education. Vocational industrial education courses are given in trade schools, in technical schools, in general-purpose secondary schools and in factories and industrial plants. The present-day apprenticeship program, in which the school cooperates with industry and labor, is included in vocational industrial education.

Vocational educators have experienced some difficulty in differentiating between the various groups of occupations in vocational industrial, technical, and professional occupations in industry. The Vocational and Technical Division, Office of Education, U.S. Department of Health, Education, and Welfare, has defined vocational industrial occupations to include "(a) Any industrial craft, skilled trade, or semi-skilled occupation which directly functions in the designing, producing, processing, assemblying, maintaining, servicing, or repairing of any product or commodity; (b) other occupations including service occupations which are not covered in subsection (a), but which are usually considered technical or trade and industrial in nature." [1] Most of the occupations listed in the U.S. census under headings related to manufacturing, construction, mining, transportation and public utilities and some of the occupations listed under forestry and fishing and under domestic and personal services are classed as vocational industrial pursuits.

A functioning program in vocational industrial education is constantly undergoing changes to meet new needs. This means that the program must not only cover existing occupations but must also contemplate new ones growing out of technological developments. This requires that educators in charge of vocational industrial education programs maintain close relationships with workers in industry and be on the alert for changes in industry that affect programs in voca-

[1] U.S. Department of Health, Education, and Welfare, Office of Education, *Administration of Vocational Education*, tentative rules and regulations, Washington, D.C., 1964, article 102.68.

The Apparel Trades Provide Opportunities for Employment in Fashion Design, Pattern Making, Tailoring, and Dry Cleaning. (Los Angeles Trade-Technical College)

tional education. Industry also has an interest in this program to be assured that workers in vocational industrial education are properly trained for their responsibilities.

The Resources and Needs of American Industry

Programs of vocational education reflect the changes that take place in the economic well-being of the people. Therefore, any attempt to give direction to a program of vocational industrial education should take into account the economic and social trends affecting the people who are employed in industrial pursuits. Among the more important data concerned with the social and economic factors that have a bearing on vocational industrial education programs are those concerned with the nature of the labor force, the changes in industrial establishments, sources and extent of power and new industrial products and processes. A discussion of these factors is presented below.

WORKERS IN INDUSTRY

The U.S. Bureau of the Census estimated that 62,657,000 persons were employed in nonagricultural occupations in 1962. This is an increase of 20 percent over the 1950 figure. The principal nonagricultural industries are classified as manufacturing; wholesale and retail trade; government; service; transportation and public utilities; finance, insurance and real estate; contract construction; and mining. About one-third of the nonagricultural workers were classified as craftsmen, foremen, operatives, and kindred workers, most of whom were employed in industry. The relative number of these workers increased 5 percent from 1950 to 1962. About 3 percent of the craftsmen, foremen, and kindred workers and 28 percent of the operatives and kindred workers were female employees in 1962.

Relatively large numbers of craftsmen are employed as mechanics and repairmen, carpenters, machinists, painters, electricians, plumbers, linemen, and stationary engineers. Among the operatives and kindred workers are a number of apprentices engaged in learning such trades as those of machinist and toolmaker, printer, carpenter, plumber, and electrician. Large numbers of operatives and kindred workers are employed in the manufacture of both durable and nondurable goods and as truck and tractor drivers and mine operatives.

The manufacturing industries employed about 26 percent of the employed civilian labor force in 1950 and about 25 percent in 1962. About 43 percent of all workers in manufacturing establishments in 1958 were employed in plants and factories in which fewer than 250 workers per plant were employed. About one-half of all workers employed in manufacturing in the United States were in the following 6 states listed in the order of highest to lowest number employed: New York, Pennsylvania, California, Ohio, Illinois, and Michigan.

Workers employed in the construction industry represented about 4 percent of the employed civilian labor force in both 1950 and 1962. The number of workers in the transportation and public utilities establishments represented 7 percent of the employed civilian labor in 1950 and 6 percent in 1962. Many industrial workers are employed by state and local governments in public service occupations. Workers in these occupations include firemen, policemen, local utility workers, parks and recreation workers, housing and community development workers, and public health and sanitation workers.

These statistics indicate that industry is in need of increasing numbers of workers for various types and sizes of industrial establishments. These workers are engaged in various trades and are required to possess a variety of knowledge and skills, some of which may be obtained in industrial establishments, and some of which must be secured from institutions outside of industry.

INDUSTRIAL ESTABLISHMENTS

The number of manufacturing establishments in the United States increased from 241,000 in 1947 to 310,000 in 1962. This increase is for separate plants and factories employing one or more persons. This was an increase of 28 percent for the 16-year period. The value added by manufacturing increased from $74 billion in 1947 to $179 billion in 1962. Relatively high increases during this period occurred in industries engaged in the fabrication of transportation equipment, machinery, primary metal and fabricated metal products, chemicals and allied products, and food and kindred products.

Some indication of the changes that are occurring in the manufacturing industries may be gained by noting the increased expenditures for new plants and equipment. These expenditures for manufacturing establishments in the United States in 1950 were about $8 billion. The corresponding expenditures in 1962 were $15 billion. Expenditures for new machinery and equipment during this period have greatly exceeded expenditures for new structures and additions to plants. Much of this new equipment has been used to replace equipment made obsolescent by the discovery of new processes and techniques in manufacturing.

Vast increases have occurred in the construction industry. A total of 1,396,000 nonfarm dwelling units were started in 1950. This number had increased to 1,458,000 dwelling units started in 1962. About two-thirds of these were one-family units. The estimated construction cost of the residential units started in 1962 was more than $18 billion which is about 57 percent more than the estimated cost for 1950. The volume of domestic intercity freight traffic increased 22 percent and the value of mineral production 58 percent from 1950 to 1962.

SOURCE AND EXTENT OF POWER

Vast quantities of energy are required for present-day living. Energy is required to turn the wheels of industry, to light, heat, and cool the houses of the people, and to reduce the amount of hand labor required in the homes and on the farms of the nation. Energy has become so essential to present-day living that producing power or the raw materials for power is an industry in itself. Energy or power is derived from coal, oil, water, natural gas, wood and waste, wind, the rays of the sun, and certain basic chemical and physical reactions.

The production of energy from mineral fuels and water power for use in performing the various tasks of mankind has increased about 500 percent since 1900 and about 30 percent during the 12-year period 1950 to 1962. The sources of energy have also changed from time to time. Eighty-nine percent of the energy was supplied by coal in 1900 and 26 percent in 1962. Petroleum and natural gas supplied about 8 percent of the energy in 1900 and 69 percent in 1962. Water power supplied about 3 percent of the energy in 1900 and 4 percent in 1962.

The nation has substantial reserves of coal, petroleum, natural gas, and hydroelectric resources that may be used in the production of energy. Recent experiments in the use of atomic energy have demonstrated that vastly greater amounts of controlled atomic energy may be obtained in the future by the use of new processes.

More and more energy is being converted into electrical power for use by man and his machines. Electrical power is easier and more convenient to use than most other sources of power. The production of electrical energy increased from 389 billion kilowatt-hours during the fiscal year 1950 to 970 billion kilowatt-hours in fiscal 1963—an increase of 150 percent. About 90 percent of this power in 1963 was produced and distributed by electric utility companies for public use. The Federal Power Commission has estimated that about 2,139 billion kilowatt-hours will be needed by 1975—an increase of 120 percent over the 1963 production.

The use of electricity has enabled industrial concerns to establish plants, both large and small, throughout the nation. These plants are continually producing new types of products for improving the standard of living of the people of the United States. The production and distribution of power requires increasing numbers of professional, technical, skilled, and semiskilled workers, many of whom are required to have special knowledge and skills in order that they may manufacture and distribute power safely and efficiently. These workers must not only possess certain knowledge and skills at the time they begin employment, but they must also learn new techniques and processes while they are employed because of the constant changes and improvements that are being made in the power industry.

NEW PRODUCTS AND PROCESSES

The discovery, invention, and development of new materials, processes, and products that have come within the past two or three decades have brought about extensive changes in the way of living in America. Among these new developments are synthetic rubber for tires and tubes, synthetic resin for insulation and moldings, synthetic fibers for more suitable and economical clothing and textiles, titanium alloys for high tensile strength, toughness, and resistance to elevated temperatures, fluorescent dyes and brighteners for more suitable coloring materials, and new plastics for improved optical elements in periscopes. Many new products have been obtained from existing materials. New developments in hydrocarbon technology have produced chemicals formerly obtained from other sources. Petroleum now supplies glycerine and various alcohols, acetic acid, nylon, synthetic rubber, and benzine. Liquid fuels are now being manufactured from coal and other nonpetroleum sources.

These and other developments have been responsible for a new era known as the "era of automation." Automatic machines are rapidly replacing hand-operated machines and processes. Computers are keeping books and making complicated calculations. Special machines are calculating wages, making deductions and writing pay checks. Automobiles and aircraft parts are made in automatic, high-powered milling machines controlled by a magnetic tape. The tape starts the machine, directs the various operations, and stops the machine. Automation is used on automobile engine assembly lines where mechanical hands place the blocks of metal in the proper position for milling and boring. The transistor, a new type of circuit element, is extending the use of electronic control or amplification to new fields.

These various processes and machines have had a far-reaching effect on the number and qualifications of workers in industry. Fewer workers are required in automatic factories, and the work in these factories is more pleasant and less monotonous than the hand-operated, mass-production assembly lines. The use of automatic machines has greatly increased the output per worker, which means that fewer workers are required for a given volume of production. It is expected that automation will continue, and some scientists are suggesting the output per man-hour will be increased three or four times in the foreseeable future. Some writers have expressed the fear that automatic machines may lead to mass unemployment which in turn will reduce purchasing power and curtail production. However, past experience does not bear out this fear. The employed labor force is numerically greater at present than at any previous time. The increased production per unit in past years has enabled more of the population to maintain higher standards of living.

It is estimated by some economists that the anticipated increases in population and the rising standard of living will produce employment for all the expected increase in the labor force. Automation may bring about a reduction in the number of hours in the work week and may cause temporary periods of unemployment for some workers during the changeover periods. The problems involved will include the retraining of some workers to design, manufacture, maintain, and operate the new machines, and the redirection of other workers into other activity. Government and industry will need to plan for anticipated changes to prevent distress among industrial workers during these periods.

The Development of Vocational Industrial Education

Few industrial education programs had been developed in the public schools of the nation prior to the passage of the Smith-Hughes Vocational Education Act. This law resulted in the organization of vocational industrial education programs of some nature in every state during its first year of operation. These programs have expanded in scope and variety during the years since 1918. They have been characterized by flexibilty to meet changing conditions, high standards to provide superior workmen and adaptability to meet the needs of the various kinds and grades of workers. These characteristics are implied in the purposes or objectives which have served as guides in the development of the vocational industrial education program.

THE OBJECTIVES OF VOCATIONAL INDUSTRIAL EDUCATION

Modern industry finds a need for training unskilled workers, semiskilled operators, skilled mechanics, foremen, junior technical workers, engineers, and other high-level technical workers and executives. The training of engineers and executives is usually assigned to the colleges. High-level technicians are usually educated in colleges and special schools, and other technicians are educated in trade schools. Skilled and semiskilled workers receive education and training on the job and in vocational industrial education schools and classes. It is usually to the advantage of both the employer and the employee to provide training for the unskilled worker necessary for efficient production and for safety in plant operation. This training should be given by a competent individual, either the foreman or a

Students in Day Trade Classes Learn Machine Shop Skills in the School Shop. (Board of Education, Columbus, Ohio)

qualified instructor who has had foremanship or instructors' training courses.

The semiskilled worker usually has responsibility for operating production machines. No extensive training is needed since most of these machines are automatic, but a short period of instruction and practice is necessary. The skilled mechanic requires extensive knowledge and skill commonly acquired in apprenticeship programs, trade schools, extension classes, and corporation schools. The necessity for training foremen and supervisors is becoming more apparent in industry. These employees need to know about company policies, efficient production methods and how to deal effectively with employees.

The various kinds of workers and the differences in the training requirements of these workers suggest a need for a statement of principles to serve as a guide in the development of the various kinds of training programs needed. Guiding principles in terms of major objectives have been established for the vocational industrial education program. These major objectives are as follows:

1. To provide instruction of an extension or supplemental type for the further development of performance skills, technical knowledge, related industrial education, safety, and job judgment for persons already employed in trade and industrial pursuits.

2. To provide instruction of a preparatory type in the development of basic manipulative skills, safety judgment, technical knowledge and related industrial information for the purpose of fitting persons for useful employment in trade and industrial pursuits.

The major objectives are useful as a guide in overall planning, but more specific statements of objectives are required in local vocational industrial education programs. These specific objectives should be based on local needs. Various methods are used to determine local needs. Among these are questionnaires to be filled out by workers or employers, personal interviews, spot checks, employment service information, advisory committees and information from social, civic, and religious groups in the community. The information provided from these sources together with the statement of major objectives will enable the vocational industrial educator and his interested committee to determine the kinds of schools and classes needed in the local program of vocational industrial education.

TYPES OF SCHOOLS AND CLASSES

A complete program of vocational industrial education includes various types of schools and classes structured to accomplish the objectives of the program. The Vocational Education Act of 1963 does not identify specific classes for industrial education but does specify, as indicated in previous chapters, the types of individuals for which instruction designed for vocational efficiency in gainful occupations may be provided. These classifications include instruction for full-time secondary and post-secondary school students, instruction for persons who have left school and need training or retraining, and instruction for disadvantaged youth. The standards and specifications for such schools and classes necessary to accomplish these objectives are left largely to the discretion of the state and are included in the state plan for vocational education.

Federal funds available under the provisions of the Smith-Hughes and George-Barden Acts are used in specified schools and classes. The standards and specifications for these classes are indicated in the Acts and in the regulations. These classes include evening classes for extending the knowledge of the trades of employed workers, part-time classes for employed workers who may attend classes for a part of the usual work period, and day trade classes for full-time students regularly enrolled in day schools. A description of these classes is shown below.

Evening classes. An evening class is one conducted during the nonworking hours of the enrollees. Eligible students are required to be 16 years of age or older and instruction is such that will increase the skill or knowledge of the worker in the trade or industrial occupation in which he is employed. Class instruction may include manipulative skills, technical knowledge, safety, first aid, and economics of the occupation. The instructor is frequently a worker in the trade he is teaching and is paid on an hourly basis for teaching the class. Some instructors are employed by a state board for vocational education or a local school board on a full time basis for teaching these classes.

Part-time classes. Part-time classes are conducted for employed workers who have left the full-time day school. These classes are scheduled to meet during the usual working hours of the enrollees. All part-time classes reimbursed from funds appropriated in the Smith-Hughes Act must provide for not less than 144 hours of classroom instruction per year and students must be over 14 years of age. Enrollment in part-time classes under the provisions of the George-Barden Act is limited to workers 16 years of age or older.

Two types of part-time classes are authorized. They are (1) part-time extension classes, and (2) part-time general continuation classes. Part-time extension classes provide instruction which is supplemental to the daily employment of the worker. The instruction in part-time general continuation classes is designed to increase the civic intelligence of the enrollees rather than to develop specific occupational competencies. Enrollees in general continuation classes are required to be under 18 years of age.

Cooperative classes. A cooperative class, also referred to as a diversified occupations (DO) class, is one in which the student who is regularly enrolled in school spends part-time in on-the-job training. The job training is provided by means of a cooperative arrangement between the school and the employer. The agreement with the employer provides for the legal employment of the student-learner in conformity to state and Federal laws and regulations. Such employment must not result in the exploitation of student learners for private gain. Students are employed for an average of not less than 15 hours per week during the school year. These students are required to spend at least one class period per day in related instruction in vocational education. The related instruction is in a class limited to the enrollees in the cooperative program.

Day trade classes.   Day trade or all-day trade classes are designed for students who have not entered upon employment and are regularly enrolled in a full-time day school. Three types of day trade classes are in operation. These are Type A, Type B, and Type C. The related instruction in Type A classes is given as separate units outside the practical work in the shop. The related instruction in Type B classes is included as an integral part of the shop or laboratory work rather than as separate units. Type A and B classes extend for 9 or more months per year and are in session not less than 30 hours per week except that this schedule may be modified in communities of less than 25,000 population. At least one-half the time in Type A and B day trade classes must be given to work on a useful or productive basis. The instruction in related subjects is in addition to and an extension of the instruction in the school shop. Related instruction must have a functional value in the trade or occupation for which training is given.

Type C day-trade classes are a special type of pre-employment trade training offered in the day school. The courses may be scheduled for less than 9 months per year and less than 30 hours per week, and without the requirement that one-half of the school time be given to shopwork on a useful or productive basis. Type C classes under the provisions of the George-Barden Act may be organized for persons over 18 years of age or persons over 14 years of age who have left full time school. Under the provisions of the Smith-Hughes Act and the Vocational Education Act of 1963 such classes may be organized for persons over 14 years of age who are regularly enrolled in a full-time day school and are preparing to enter some type of semi-skilled occupation.

Classes for apprentices.   Special classes to provide technical and other related instruction may be organized for apprentices who are learning a recognized apprenticeable trade. The instruction is supplemental to the job training and usually extends for a minimum of 144 clock hours per year. Classes for apprentices must comply with the recognized standards for apprenticeship. Apprentices may enroll in part-time and evening classes for other workers in communities where

The School Foundry Provides Facilities for Instruction in Casting and Molding. (Edison Technical and Industrial School, Rochester, New York)

there is an insufficient number of apprentices to justify a separate class. Provision may be made for individualized instruction for apprentices through correspondence or other types of home study courses.

VOCATIONAL EDUCATION IN FISHERY OCCUPATIONS

The George-Barden Act was amended in 1956 by providing an authorization of $375,000 annually for vocational education in the fishery trades and industry and distributive occupations therein. This authorization was the result of a need for knowledge and skills to better utilize new equipment, new processes, and new techniques in the location of fish, in shipboard refrigeration and preservation, in processing on shore and afloat, and in packaging for distribution. The efficient use of these modern devices and techniques is necessary to meet competition in the international market.

The yield of commercial fisheries in the United States increased from 4 billion pounds in 1940 to 5 billion pounds in 1962. The 1962 catch was valued at $381 million, an increase of 285 percent over the value of the 1940 catch. About 500,000 persons, one-fourth of whom were fishermen, have been employed in the fisheries industries during the past few years. The number of motor driven fishing vessels is increasing and the number of small fishing boats decreasing. Fishermen, processors and distributors have an investment of over a billion dollars in boats, fishing gear, freezing and processing plants, and other facilities.

The enrollment in Federally aided vocational education classes in fishery occupations for the 5-year period 1958 to 1962 was about 12,000 students. About 75 percent of these students were enrolled in classes in Louisiana, New York, Florida, North Carolina, and Maine. A total of $900,000 was expended for classes in fishery occupations in the United States during the above mentioned 5-year period. About 42 percent of this amount was Federal funds. Most of the students were employed fishermen enrolled for part of the time in vocational industrial education classes. The more popular courses were in navigation, radio operation, diesel mechanics, visual communications, electronics, and boat operation and maintenance. There is an increasing trend in the number of pre-employment courses. Some technical schools use a fishing vessel as a laboratory. This vessel is complete with electronic navigational and depth sounding gear, marine life and ocean studies facilities, nets, and power facilities found on modern fishing vessels.

ENROLLMENT AND ENROLLMENT TRENDS

The rapid development of vocational industrial education is evidenced by the increase in enrollments and expenditures since the passage of the Smith-Hughes law. The various classes and schools in vocational industrial education in the United States and its territories have had a total enrollment of 28,537,000 persons during the 45-year period 1918 to 1962 inclusive. The evening class enrollment was 32 percent of the total and the day trade class enrollment 25 percent of the total. The part-time extension and other part-time class enrollments were 20 and 23 percent respectively for the 45-year period. Female students comprised about one-fourth of the total enrollment, the highest percentage of them being in part-time general continuation classes. Substantial increases in the enrollments in part-time

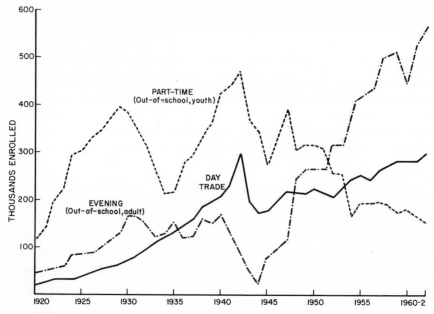

Enrollments in Vocational Industrial Education Classes by Type of Class in the States and Territories for the Years 1920 to 1962. Evening class enrollments have increased markedly since 1945. (U.S. Department of Health, Education, and Welfare, Office of Education, *Digest of Annual Reports of State Boards for Vocational Education to the Office of Education, Fiscal Year Ended June 30, 1962*, Government Printing Office, 1963)

trade extension classes and day trade classes have been noted in recent years.

The average number of vocational industrial education teachers reported per year for the 45-year period 1918 to 1962 was 18,390. This average has increased from 9148 annually for the 10-year period 1921 to 1930 to 34,350 annually for the 5-year period 1958 to 1962.

A total of $1,625,819,000 has been expended for vocational industrial education during the 45-year period 1918 to 1962 inclusive. About 50 percent of this amount was local funds, 28 percent state funds and 22 percent Federal funds. These percentages indicate that local communities are spending as much as both the state and Federal governments combined on vocational industrial education. The total expenditures have increased through the years, with an accelerated percentage of increase in recent years. For example, total expenditures for the 10-year period ending June 30, 1940, were 63 percent greater than for the 10-year period ending June 30, 1930. The corresponding increase for the 10-year period ending June 30, 1960, was 88 percent above the previous decade ending June 30, 1950. About 6 percent of the total expenditures—Federal, state, and local—for vocational industrial education were spent for teacher education in vocational industrial education during the 30-year period from 1918 to 1947. These data include costs of all teacher education, including programs conducted by colleges and universities, state departments of education, and local school boards. Local funds accounted for 12 percent of the expenditures, state funds 43 percent, and Federal funds 45 percent.

WAR PRODUCTION AND VETERANS TRAINING

Vocational industrial educators participated in training programs for war industries and for war veterans. The Federal Board for Vocational Education in 1918 made studies of war training needs and authorized evening class instruction for draftees. The Board prepared basic courses of study in various trades for use in these classes. National Army Training Detachments were established in 157 educational institutions and other agencies with assistance from the Federal Board. Training programs in ship-building and employment management were also organized. About 250,000 persons received training for various positions in war industries as a result of these programs.

Two major types of training were developed to meet the needs of war production industries for World War II. These were pre-employment and supplementary training and were conducted in schools and industrial plants largely by personnel trained in industrial education. Federal funds under the provisions of the Vocational Education for National Defense (VEND) program were provided and chief responsibility for operating the program was placed in the various state boards for vocational education. About 7,500,000 workers were trained in the VEND program at an average cost of about $40 per enrollee.

Vocational industrial educators have cooperated in education and training programs for veterans of World War II and the Korean conflict. Institutional programs of less than college level were operated in public and private schools and on-the-job-training was provided in industry. Most of these programs were by contract with the Veterans Administration and the sponsoring agency. The contracts included the cost of supervision, instruction, and books and supplies. Enrollees received a subsistence allowance from the Veterans Administration. About 4,337,000 veterans entered training in schools of less than college level and 1,622,000 entered on-the-job-training by June 30, 1963.

Establishing the Local Program

The local program of vocational industrial education usually includes classes for in-school youth and for out-of-school youth and adults. The responsibility for determining the nature and scope of the local program is vested in the local school board. This board usually looks to the superintendent of schools for advice and counsel in establishing the local program. A number of considerations are involved in establishing and maintaining the local program of vocational industrial education. Among these are the planning of the local program to meet community needs, the acquisition and maintenance of adequate facilities and equipment, the employment and advancement of competent personnel and the planning of appropriate supervisory techniques for the improvement of instructional programs and procedures in vocational industrial education.

PLANNING THE LOCAL PROGRAM

Planning is necessary in establishing new programs and in adjusting present programs to meet community needs more satisfactorily. One of the first considerations in planning is the determination of needs both of prospective enrollees and of business establishments. Surveys and various other devices are used to determine these needs. The information from these surveys, interviews, and other devices is evaluated and used to make a tentative selection of the objectives that should be considered in the organization of the local program. These objectives should in turn govern the types and kinds of classes and courses required to meet the needs of the local community.

Few local schools can provide all of the facilities and equipment needed for training programs in any considerable number of industrial vocations. Cooperative programs involving on-the-job training and school experiences are operated as a means of overcoming this difficulty. In this type of program the kinds of training are limited only by the types of work opportunities available in the community. The interrelationship of various areas of vocational education should be considered in planning the local program. The distributive and business education teachers may be called upon to provide instruction in some phases of marketing and accounting of industrial products and services. Agricultural teachers may provide instruction in mechanics as it applies to agriculture and the biological science needed for instruction in agriculture.

One important success factor in planning is that of keeping the citizens of the community informed about the problems and achievements in the planning process and inviting their participation in solving the problems of planning. The cooperative solution of such problems as the selection of trainees, numbers to be trained, grade levels or ages affected, and the selection and equipping of facilities will tend to insure the success of the program. An overall advisory committee composed of representatives of various community groups will provide a means for securing participation from these groups. The use of the local press, radio, television, and various types of group meetings will provide desirable publicity for the program.

The operation of the vocational industrial education program in a local public school requires some adjustments in public school schedules and guidance procedures, and these adjustments should be considered in planning for the program. Emphasis in vocational industrial education is placed on selection of students, occupationally competent instructors, special facilities and equipment, coordination and supervision, credit for work experience, longer shop periods, and special classes for adults. The entire teaching staff of the public school should be informed about the vocational industrial education program. School authorities should plan and conduct a series of staff conferences for the purpose of acquainting the teaching staff with the vocational industrial education program.

FACILITIES AND EQUIPMENT FOR THE LOCAL PROGRAM

A self-contained central plant simplifies the operation, administration, and supervision of the vocational industrial education program. Such a plant may include shops and laboratories for pre-employment training for youth and adults in the community. The number and kinds of shops should be determined by the needs of the community and justified by the number of workers employed in the vocations for which training is provided. The plant should also include classrooms and laboratories for related training. The plant should also have an auditorium, a library, general-purpose rooms for conferences, study, or other purposes, supply rooms, and offices and space for the administrative, supervisory, coordinating and guidance staff. Other space requirements for physical education, health, and sanitary purposes

Trade Schools Provide Vocational Industrial and Vocational Technical Education to Students Who Desire to Prepare for Occupations of This Nature. This school serves students in three parishes. (Louisiana State Department of Education, Vocational Division)

should be provided. Installations, such as hallways, stairways, elevators, heating, lighting, and ventilating systems, and student lockers, should be adequate. The location of the building should be accessible from the industries and to the student population. Single-story buildings are preferable if space is available.

Modern programs of vocational industrial education need modern equipment comparable to that found in industry. Equipment should be selected after the courses are planned and the needs for equipment are known. Less expensive equipment may be used in school shops if the principles of operation of the machines are the same as those used in industry. The school may be justified in using some equipment not of the modern type if the trainees are to be placed in plants in which modern equipment is not used. When modern equipment is installed in these industrial plants the workers will need additional training in the use of the new equipment.

The equipment should be located and installed in a manner that will insure safety and efficiency of operation and that will facilitate good housekeeping in the shop. Safety guards and devices should be installed, and students should be required to make use of them. Consideration should be given to the nature of equipment in selecting on-the-job training stations in industry in order that student learners may acquire proficiency in the use of suitable equipment.

The planning of facilities and the selection and installation of equipment for vocational industrial education require the advice and counsel of vocational educators and the services of architects and designers qualified in planning school plants. Representative advisory committees can also provide valuable advice and assistance in planning structures and selecting and installing equipment for instruction in vocational industrial education.

PERSONNEL FOR THE LOCAL PROGRAM

The administration of the local program of vocational industrial education in the larger cities is usually delegated by the local school superintendent to an assistant superintendent for vocational education or a director of vocational education. This individual usually has responsibility for all programs of vocational education and practical arts. In the smaller communities some of the administrative duties may be delegated to a supervisor of industrial education, a school principal, a coordinator, or a head teacher. Administrative responsibilities in vocational industrial education include such activities as program objectives, policies and plans for program development and operation, school and industry relationships, types of classes, facilities, and personnel administration. The administrative officer should possess qualifications which include education and experience in vocational education.

The supervisor of vocational industrial education, who may also be the director of vocational education, the school principal or the head of the vocational industrial education department, has responsibility for the improvement of instruction in vocational industrial education. The person responsible for supervision should possess educational qualifications comparable to those of other instructional supervisors and educational and occupational experience in the trade which he is supervising. This occupational experience will enable him to gain the confidence of the occupationally competent instructors he is supervising.

Many kinds of coordinators and instructors are employed in a local program of vocational industrial education. The coordinator who serves as an instructor and supervisor of student learners is a liaison officer between the school and industry. He must have qualifications that will enable him to work and plan with school administrators, advisory committees, employers, and civic organizations. Instructors of both in-school and out-of-school classes in vocational industrial education should be occupationally competent and educationally proficient. Teachers of in-school classes must maintain contacts with students, teachers, and procedures in general education, and this requires academic preparation. Teachers of adult classes need special skills for maintaining the interest of adults and for instructing them. Occupational competency is especially necessary for these instructors. Vocational teachers, as a rule, engage in some guidance activities, and they need some knowledge and skill in counseling, placement and follow-up. The duties and responsibilities of the teacher of vocational industrial education are manifold, and his success as a teacher is determined by how well his students perform on the jobs in which they are employed.

THE SUPERVISION OF THE LOCAL PROGRAM

Supervision of vocational industrial education usually involves recruiting and training teachers and assisting them to improve their teaching techniques. Frequently, instructors are recruited from local industries, and the local supervisor must maintain the necessary contacts for this recruitment program. The supervisor should be alert to recognize that some superior workmen can never develop into successful teachers, while others have the proper attitudes and interests and can acquire, with the help of the supervisor, the necessary teaching techniques. The supervisor should prepare lists of occupational competencies and personal characteristics needed for the teaching positions he is seeking to fill. He will need job descriptions, salary schedules, occupational experience equivalents for academic experience, and other information about school policies and procedures when he talks to prospective teachers from industry or from teacher education institutions.

The supervisor is usually responsible for the induction of new teachers and their training on the job. Proper induction procedures involve more than introducing the new teacher and providing him with the keys to his shop and classroom. A well-planned induction program, especially for a new teacher recruited from industry, includes a short induction course conducted preferably before the new teacher starts work or, if this is not possible, during his first month of teaching. This course should include facts about the school system and its operation. A teacher who has had no previous teaching experience should be given some instruction in methods of teaching in this induction course. The in-service professional training program may take the form of staff conferences, teachers' bulletins, individual conferences and formal courses. The formal courses may consist of extension classes or home study courses. They may be conducted by the local supervisor or by the staff of vocational teacher education institutions.

A major responsibility of the supervisor is to aid the teacher in the improvement of teaching and to give confidence and inspiration to the teacher who has doubts about his teaching ability. Frequently, the new teacher needs specific assistance in teaching techniques. The first step in providing this assistance is for the supervisor to gain the confidence of the teacher. The supervisor should approach the teacher as a co-worker rather than as an inspector and should encourage him to think his own thoughts and express them frankly. The supervisor should stimulate the teacher to engage in self-analysis, self-study, and self-appraisal. Teaching demonstrations and practice teaching are useful in the study of correct techniques of teaching.

The improvement of instruction often requires a reorganization of curriculums and courses of study. The supervisor should provide leadership for this activity. This involves cooperation with the teachers in the development of a plan for the production of courses of study. This plan should include the list of shop skills, related information, and general information for each trade or occupation to be taught. It is also necessary to develop a format for the production of individual instruction sheets. The curriculum revision program may be facilitated by organizing committees of teachers in one or more schools and assigning responsibility to each committee for the development of a different unit of instruction. The supervisor may also provide leadership in the construction of charts, models, cutaways, and other teaching aids for use in vocational industrial education.

Techniques and Procedures in Instruction

Instruction in vocational industrial education is given for the purpose of developing the knowledge, skills, and attitudes required in the successful performance of a selected occupation in industry. These three outcomes are not developed independently of each other but form inseparable parts of the instructional program. However, the usual practice in teaching is for the instructor to give special attention to each aspect, since a somewhat different teaching situation is involved in each outcome. In the process of developing each of these outcomes a number of practices and procedures are used to facilitate and evaluate instruction. Among these are techniques for organizing the instructional program, the use of appropriate teaching methods and materials, the sponsoring of student organizations for leadership development, and the use of evaluative devices and criteria.

ORGANIZING THE INSTRUCTIONAL PROGRAM

Instruction in vocational industrial education is given in various types of classes including extension, part-time and day trade classes. The extension class program provides instruction in various skilled trades such as auto mechanics, cabinet making, carpentry, electricity, foundry, machine shop, needle trades, plumbing, printing, radio service, sheet metal, shoemaking, and telegraphy. More recently, extension courses have been offered for public service employees such as firemen, food inspectors, park officials, policemen, public health workers, tax assessors, and water and sewage plant operators. A third type of course is concerned with the training of foremen, conference leaders, and plant instructors. Such topics as human relations, methods of leading a conference, and supervision of workers are offered in this type of course. The specific content of each of these courses is selected or approved by a craft advisory committee composed of experienced workers in the trade concerned. Many of the classes consist of short-unit courses ranging from 10 to 30 clock hours in length. Some courses extend for one or two years. Some classes meet each day or night during the week, and some are scheduled for two to three hours per day or night two or three times per week.

The courses of study for cooperative programs for secondary and post-secondary school students in vocational industrial education vary in accordance with the opportunities for employment of these students in the community. The course includes subject matter related to the trade and to industrial work in general for one or two periods daily and one or two other school subjects such as English, mathematics, or social science for one or two periods. The student is expected to spend one or two years in the cooperative program.

The curriculums for the day trade classes include both general and vocational courses together with shopwork in the school shop. As a rule, half of the school day is spent in the school shop. Shop practices are as near those followed in industry as is possible to give under school conditions. The remaining part of the school day is devoted to a study of related subjects and general education subjects. The courses selected in each of these areas depend upon the kind of trade for which the student is preparing and the needs of the student.

Day trade courses vary in length from two to four years depending on the policy of the school and the nature of the trade. The courses are usually placed in the upper high school grades. Short-unit courses may be organized in the form of day trade classes for youth and adults who have well-defined vocational needs. Among the more important trades, each requiring from two to four years for completion, included in the all-day trade program are machine shop, carpentry, electrical appliance servicing, millwork and cabinet making, radio servicing, sheet metal, auto mechanics, printing, air conditioning, barbering, bricklaying, practical nursing, foundry, needle trades, plastics, plumbing, upholstering, and watchmaking. Since most of these are apprenticeable trades, it is usually necessary for the student to enroll as an apprentice upon the completion of his day trade instruction. His time as an apprentice may be reduced as a result of his trade school instruction.

METHODS AND MATERIALS OF TEACHING

Since it is generally agreed that there is no one best method of teaching, it is desirable that each vocational industrial education instructor know something of the various instructional methods— their advantages and limitations. Among the more important methods of instruction are the conference procedure, the demonstration method, the field trip, the laboratory method, supervised study, the question and answer method, the problem or project method, the case method, and the lecture method. The selection of a method or combination of methods depends on the type of class, the nature of the instructional unit, the facilities available and the maturity, experience and interest of the students.

The use of the conference procedure in which various members of the class make contributions and effect a pooling of knowledge for the benefit of the entire group is especially valuable in trade extension classes. All classes require some demonstration and laboratory or shop practice to develop certain necessary skills. Since problem solving is a necessary technique, the problem method, in which individual problems are selected, studied, and carried to a conclusion, is frequently used in various types of classes. Supervised study, question and answer and lecture methods are useful in day trade classes. The effectiveness of different methods of instruction varies among instructors. Instructors should study and experiment with various methods of instruction, not with the idea of finding a single best method but for the purpose of determining which method or combination of methods is best suited to the instructor, the students, and the job or unit to be taught.

An important consideration in the instructional program in vocational industrial education is that of safety. Safety is a matter of understanding hazards, practicing proper work habits, and developing safety concepts. Safety hazards may be caused by improperly trained operators, faulty equipment, and poorly selected materials. Shop safety requires that workers understand the limitations of men and machines and involves the development of proper attitudes and under-standings concerning safety. Many shop accidents are caused by a lack of consideration for the welfare of others, and proper conduct in the shop is as important a safety factor as the mechanical arrange-ment and proper operation of equipment.

Effective teaching in industrial education requires the use of many types and kinds of teaching materials by the student and the teacher. Materials such as reference books, periodicals, catalogs, samples, models, mock-ups, charts, diagrams, blueprints, illustrations, films, and slides enable the instructor to teach more effectively and the students to learn more easily. Materials should be placed and arranged so that they are readily available. Students as a rule need some help in learning how to use these materials. The instructor is responsible for the selection of the materials, and these should be selected with the student's past experience and ability in mind so that each student will achieve some degree of success in his search for information.

Instructional material should indicate to the student the knowl-edge, skills, and attitudes he is expected to acquire. Instruction materials such as *job instruction sheets* or *operation sheets* may be used to an advantage in teaching skills on an individual basis. The use of study guides, supplemented by textbooks or reference books, is sug-gested for teaching technical information on an individual basis. When suitable textbooks or reference books are not available, *technical information units* that contain essential information about the jobs may be used together with job instruction sheets and study guides. Textbooks and other published information, supplemented by expla-nation, illustration, demonstration and discussion, may be used in organized classes.

STUDENT ORGANIZATIONS

Student organizations for persons enrolled in some types of trade and industrial education classes are functioning in some of the states. These organizations operate under such names as "T and I Clubs," "Future Craftsmen" or "Future Tradesmen." In most states member-ship is confined to day trade and part-time students who are enrolled in secondary school courses. Many states have state-wide organiza-tions with affiliated local units. The state organization in some states sponsors some form of competitive activities and an annual state meeting. Local clubs have such objectives as the development of leadership, recreational activities, scholarship, and cooperative attitudes. Local clubs sponsor field trips, exhibits of products of the school shop, initiation ceremonies, and special local programs.

An attempt was made in 1936 to form a national organization of students in vocational industrial education. This organization had its beginning in a trade school in Oregon. Other states expressed interest in the organization, and a meeting was held in Detroit to discuss the formation of a national organization of students in vocational industrial education. Some labor organizations expressed an objection to the formation of a national organization which included apprentices and other employed workers in the trades. In the face of this opposition, the idea of forming a national organization was dropped, and student organizations in vocational industrial education continue to be of state and local origin.

TESTING

One of the most important responsibilities of instructors in vocational industrial education is that of testing students and evaluating the effectiveness of training programs. It is especially important that both students and instructors know when the student has developed saleable skills in his occupation and is ready to take his place in industry. The testing of an individual involves a determination of such factors as acquaintance with modern tools and equipment, knowledge of current practices in the trade, ability to maintain high standards of workmanship and proper work habits, knowledge of safety measures and practices, cooperative attitude, and pride of workmanship. Other determinations that the teacher must make include the types of instruments to use in measuring these factors, the standards of performance, and the system of marking, grading, and reporting progress. This means that each teacher should have a well-established plan for appraising students.

Prior to 1900, learning was considered largely as an intangible substance that could be measured only by the individual teacher on a subjective basis. Standardized tests of intelligence and achievement came into prominence during World War I, and student scores were compared throughout the nation. After 1930 new tests of ability and aptitude were developed, and evaluative criteria were designed. These later merged into broad programs of evaluation designed for use in improving curriculums and school systems. Present programs for testing and evaluating programs of vocational industrial education include intelligence tests, aptitude and prognostic tests, achievement tests, and diagnostic and analytical tests.

One of the more important types of tests involving both subjective and objective measurement in vocational industrial education is the comprehensive trade test. This test includes oral questioning, written work, and practical performance. It is designed to measure the ability to handle tools and materials in a workman-like manner. Speed and accuracy are also measured. The oral part of the test is designed to reveal interests and attitudes towards the occupation. The written examination is used to measure the individual's familiarity with trade information. This test usually requires from one to two days for the completion of its various parts. The test is frequently used to determine an instructor's work experience qualifications for teacher certification. Rating scales are used to measure personality, character traits and interests. These traits are rated graphically by the teacher or the student. Some of these rating scales are used for judging the quality of workmanship in the shop.

QUESTIONS FOR STUDY AND DISCUSSION

1. Define vocational industrial education and indicate its relationship to industrial education and to vocational technical education.
2. Indicate the number of industrial workers in the labor force and the classification of these workers.
3. What changes are occurring in the number and kind of manufacturing establishments in the United States?
4. What effect has technological development had on the need for vocational industrial education?
5. What are the objectives of vocational industrial education, and how may statements of objectives be used in planning local programs?
6. What types of classes are available in programs of vocational industrial education?
7. Distinguish between the different kinds of part-time vocational industrial education classes, and illustrate each kind.
8. What are the trends in enrollments and expenditures in vocational industrial education?
9. What steps are involved in planning the local program of vocational industrial education?
10. What types and kinds of teaching methods and materials are used in vocational industrial education classes?

11. Discuss the development of student organizations in vocational industrial education.
12. What techniques are used in testing and evaluating vocational industrial education programs?

SOURCE REFERENCES

American Association for the Advancement of Science, Section on Industrial Science, *Industrial Science, Present and Future*, Washington, D.C., 1952.

Federal Board for Vocational Education, *Annual Reports*, 1918 to 1932 inclusive, Washington, D.C.

Federal Power Commission, *Annual Report, 1962*, Washington, D.C., 1963.

Hawkins, Layton S., Charles A. Prosser, and John C. Wright, *Development of Vocational Education*, American Technical Society, Chicago, 1951.

Mays, Arthur B., *Principles and Practices of Vocational Education*, McGraw-Hill, New York, 1948.

The Advisory Board, War Department Committee on Education and Special Training, *War Department Committee on Education and Special Training: A Review of Its Work During 1918*, Washington, D.C., 1919.

Traxler, Arthur E., and others, *Introduction to Testing and the Use of Test Results in Public Schools*, Harper & Row, New York, 1953.

U.S. Congress, *Laws Granting Education and Training and Other Benefits to Veterans*, House Committee Print No. 308, 82nd Congress, 2nd Session, Washington, D.C., 1952.

U.S. Department of Commerce, Bureau of the Census, *Statistical Abstract of the United States, 1964*, Washington, D.C., 1964.

U.S. Department of Health, Education, and Welfare, Office of Education, *Administration of Vocational Education*, Vocational Education Bulletin No. 1, revised 1958, Washington, D.C., 1958.

U.S. Department of Health, Education, and Welfare, Office of Education, *Curriculum Materials for Trade and Industrial Education*, OE84023, Washington, D.C., 1961.

U.S. Department of Health, Education, and Welfare, Office of Education, *Education for a Changing World of Work*, Report of the Panel of Consultants on Vocational Education, Washington, D.C., 1963.

U.S. Department of Health, Education, and Welfare, Office of Education, *The Operation of a Local Program of Trade and Industrial Education*, Vocational Division Bulletin No. 250, Washington, D.C., 1954.

U.S. Office of Education, *Digest of Annual Reports of State Boards of Vocational Education* for fiscal years 1933 to 1962 inclusive, Washington, D.C.

U.S. President, *Economic Report of the President, 1964*, Washington, D.C., 1964.

CHAPTER TWELVE

VOCATIONAL EDUCATION AND MANPOWER DEVELOPMENT

The rapid increase in the nation's population and the consequent expansion of the labor force, the persistent problems of unemployment and their impact on the nation's concept of full employment, the critical need for more and better trained workers in many vital job classifications, automation and its resultant need for retraining workers—all these and others have directed attention to the nation's manpower problem.

The manpower goal as expressed in the President's manpower report is "to enable and motivate every individual to develop his maximum potential and to give him an opportunity to use this potential fully on his own and in the national interest."[1] It is recognized that the

[1] U.S. Department of Labor, *Manpower Report of the President*, Washington, D.C., 1963, p. 117.

achievement of this objective is no easy task and a number of Federal-state programs have been established that are designed to facilitate the achievement of this goal. This chapter is concerned with some facts about the manpower problem and a description of four programs providing Federal aid for manpower development. These are area vocational schools, practical nurse education, and manpower development under the Area Redevelopment Act and the Manpower Development and Training Act.

Electronics Technology is a Popular Course in Many Area Vocational Schools. (Joe U. Davenport, Monroe Community College, Rochester, New York)

The Manpower Problem

A recognition of the fact that manpower is a basic national resource has occasioned a more intensive study of the factors affecting unemployment and ways and means of achieving full employment. For example, the rapid expansion of the labor force has required a corresponding expansion in new job opportunities. The nature of many new jobs has required new types of information and skill not previously provided in training programs of workers. Interstate movements of both workers and industry and automation in both farm and factory have resulted in the abolition or shifting of many jobs. These and other factors have contributed to the difficulty of finding a solution to the manpower problem of the nation.

THE CHANGING LABOR FORCE

Growth and change have characterized the population of the United States since the landing of the Pilgrims. About 4 million people were reported in the census of 1790. By 1960 this figure had grown to more than 178 million—an increase of 4350 percent. The rate of increase during the 20-year period from 1940 to 1960 was about 1.78 per cent per year. This rapid increase in population has resulted in corresponding increases in the labor force—the number of persons 14 years of age or older who are working or seeking work. The total labor force, including persons in the armed services, was estimated at 73,126,000 in 1960. This was an increase of about 13 percent since 1950. It is estimated that the labor force will total 87 million by 1970, an increase of about 2 percent per year for the 10-year period 1960 to 1970. The 1970 labor force will consist of 58 million workers who were in the 1960 labor force, 26 million young workers entering the labor force during the 1960 to 1970 decade, and 3 million women who will enter or re-enter the labor force during this decade.

The number of women in the labor force increased at the rate of about 6.7 percent per year from 1950 to 1960 as compared to an average increase for men of about 1.7 percent. Although the women in the labor force in 1960 constituted about one-third of the nation's workers they accounted for more than one-half of the increase in the labor force during the years 1950 to 1960. The increase in the number of women in the labor force started during the years of World War II and, contrary to what many persons predicted, did not prove to be a temporary attachment.

The increase in the number of women in the labor force is due to such factors as the shifts in population from rural to urban areas where more jobs are available for women and the introduction of labor-saving devices, packaged and precooked foods, and the availability of various homemaking services that may be purchased. In addition, the rising levels of education have qualified more women for work outside the home and they have been motivated by a desire to obtain funds to use in securing a better education for their children.

Married women have accounted for most of the recent rise in women's employment. The number of married women in the labor force increased 7,300,000 from 1947 to 1962. This was 56 percent of the total increase in the labor force during that period. There was little change in the number of unmarried women workers during the period. The extent of women's work is related to their family responsibilities.

Labor force participation is high in the late teens and early twenties. Participation drops off as the responsibilities of marriage and motherhood bring about withdrawals from the labor force. After the age of 35 and when children reach school age, women again seek employment outside the home. A new peak is reached at 45 to 54 and then employment tends to drop off because women retire at a younger age than men.

AGE OF WORKERS IN THE LABOR FORCE

The number of persons in the United States in the age groups 14 to 19 and 65 or over has increased in recent years while the relative number of jobs for these age-groups has declined. The proportion of workers among boys 14 to 19 years of age dropped from 54 percent in 1947 to 44 percent in 1962. Much of this decline was due to the migration of families from rural to urban areas and the increasing requirements of industry and business that beginning workers have a minimum of a high school education.

A slight decline has been noted in recent years in the labor force participation rate of men 60 to 64 and a marked decline in men 65 years of age and older. Earlier retirement made possible by social security and other pension plans, and the tendency for business and industry to favor younger workers in employment and re-employment has brought about this decline. There has been little change in the rate of participation in the labor force for men 25 to 54 years of age. Most men in this age group, which constitutes 64 percent of the labor force, are either working or looking for work.

EDUCATION OF THE LABOR FORCE

A significant rise in the educational level of workers in the United States has been noted in recent years. The relative number of college graduates in the labor force 18 years of age or older increased from 8 percent in 1952 to 11 percent in 1962. The relative number of workers who had at least a high school education increased from 43 percent in 1952 to 64 percent in 1962, a gain of about 20 percent. The proportion of workers with less than 5 years of schooling declined from 7.3 percent to 4.6 percent during this same period. However, this 4.6 percent represents more than 3 million workers who by educational standards are considered below the minimum required for functional literacy.

Changes have also occurred in the educational levels of white and nonwhite workers. During the period 1952 to 1962 the proportion of nonwhite workers with at least a high school education increased from 17 percent to 32 percent. The corresponding increase for white workers was from 46 percent to 57 percent. The proportion of nonwhite workers who had completed 8 years of school or less declined 20 percent during this same period.

In a variety of occupations, relatively high levels of education are now the rule. The educational level of professional and technical workers including workers in some job classifications that normally do not require college graduation as a prerequisite for employment, exceeds 4 years of college. Proprietors, managers, officials, clerks, and kindred workers average better than 12 years of schooling. Skilled workers average slightly over 11 years of schooling with operatives and kindred workers not far behind. The average level of schooling for farm workers, laborers, and private household workers is an eighth grade education.

FULL EMPLOYMENT

About 5.6 percent of the civilian labor force was unemployed and looking for work at the time of the 1960 census. The trend in unemployment has risen from an average rate of 4 percent in the immediate post-World War II years to 5.6 percent in 1962. There was a gain of 21 percent in the labor force during the 15-year period 1947 to 1962 and a gain of 17 percent in employment during this same period. This suggests that the nation's economy is not providing a sufficient number of the kinds of jobs necessary for the employment of all the labor force.

The rate of employment has declined in goods producing industries such as agriculture, mining, manufacturing, and construction, and increased in the service industries such as transportation, trade, finance, insurance, real estate, and government. Farm employment declined from an average of 8 million in 1947 to 5 million in 1962. The number of hired farm workers was about the same in 1947 as in 1962. Employment has grown much faster in white-collar than in blue-collar occupations. The professional, managerial, clerical, and sales employees numbered 30 million workers in 1962, an increase of 48 percent over the corresponding figure for 1947. This increase accounted for almost all of the total increase in the employed labor force in all fields of work for the 15-year period. Employment in blue-collar occupations was only 3 percent higher in 1962 than in 1947.

Unemployment varies among workers of different age groups, different educational levels, and in different regions of the United States. The rate of unemployment is relatively higher among young people, older workers, nonwhite workers, workers attached to declining and unstable industries and unskilled workers. Some areas of the United States have had persistent employment problems for a number of years due to the decline or disappearance of major industries.

The achievement of the goal of full employment will require the cooperation of all groups in our society—government, industry, labor, education, community organizations, the family, and the individual. All groups will need to be receptive to technological and economic changes and to make conscientious efforts to adjust to these changes. This will require that workers have broad educational backgrounds and frequent opportunities for upgrading and retraining. These factors are necessary to secure the fullest utilization of the nation's human resources. Success in this area will not only enhance the economic and military strength of the nation but also strengthen its influence as a leader in a democratic society.

Area Vocational Education Programs

The critical shortage of technicians and skilled workers in many occupations has been evident for some time. The number of technicians working with engineers and scientists was estimated at 775,000 in 1960. It is estimated that two to three times this number will be needed by 1975. There is also an increasing need for technicians in professions other than engineering such as agriculture, business, health sciences, and government. Craftsmen and kindred workers in occupations such as the building trades, the automotive industry, the metal trades, and communications will increase by 30 percent by 1975.

The Congress in 1958 recognized the need for additional technical and skilled workers and provided Federal aid for training in occupations necessary for national defense. This training was made possible by aid to area vocational education programs, referred to in some states as area vocational schools and classes. These programs are designed to serve the vocational needs of students who reside in an area larger than a single community or local school district. A description of the development, types of programs, operation and accomplishments of the area vocational education programs is shown below.

THE DEVELOPMENT OF AREA VOCATIONAL EDUCATION PROGRAMS

The idea for area vocational programs is not new. Many of the early vocational schools were organized to provide instruction for students from outside the immediate community in which the school was located. The congressional district agricultural schools established in Alabama in 1889 and in other states thereafter served a geographical area comprising a number of counties. In the early years of the present century some of the states enacted legislation to promote area vocational schools. New Jersey in 1913 established county vocational schools and today the Essex County, New Jersey, system includes five separate schools, a complete central office facility, and a number of programs located in various industrial and community centers.

Area programs were established on a regional basis in Connecticut and North Dakota in the decade 1910 to 1920. Data indicate that 21 area vocational education programs were started during this 10-year period. The state of Louisiana in 1934 established a state wide program of area vocational schools under the jurisdiction of the state board for vocational education. These schools, 31 in number, provide vocational and technical instruction for youth and adults in various geographic areas of the state.

A recent survey of area vocational schools indicated that nearly one-half million students were enrolled in more than 300 area schools in 33 states and the District of Columbia.[2] Seventy-one new area vocational schools were opened in 1963 and 37 were under construction. In addition, 53 area schools were planning to expand their offerings in technologies and many were adding new facilities. The area vocational schools are administered by various kinds of boards of control. Eleven states reported that area schools were administered by local boards of control. Area schools in 13 states were administered by the state board for vocational education or some other state board. Two states reported that area schools were administered by regional boards of control, and one state by a county board. Three states had both local

---

[2] American Vocational Association, "States Expand Area Schools and Programs," *The American Vocational Journal*, Volume 38, No. 6, September 1963, pp. 13–17.

and state boards, and 5 states had both local and regional boards, for the administration of area vocational schools.

FEDERAL AID FOR AREA VOCATIONAL EDUCATION PROGRAMS

The Smith-Hughes and George-Barden laws made no specific reference to area vocational programs nor did the language of these laws prohibit the use of Federal funds for these programs. Some Federal funds have been used for area programs when the conditions of the Acts were met. However, most of the Federal funds for vocational education under the provisions of these Acts were used to finance vocational education in public secondary schools.

The launching of the first Russian satellite in the fall of 1957 caused the nation to take a more critical look at its deficiencies in education and vocational education. The National Defense Education Act of 1958 was introduced early in 1958. This measure, which became a law (Public Law 864, 85th Congress) in September, 1958, included a provision for area vocational education programs.

Title VIII of the National Defense Education Act of 1958 is titled Area Vocational Education Programs. It is an amendment to the Vocational Education Act of 1946 (George-Barden), and is referred to as Title III of the 1946 Act. The amendment authorized $15 million annually until June 1962. This authorization was made permanent in 1963. The funds authorized are to be used in area vocational programs for the training of highly skilled technicians in occupations necessary for national defense. An area program consists of one or more less-than-college-grade courses conducted under public supervision and control on an organized systematic class basis. The program is available to residents of the state or an area designated and approved by the state board for vocational education.

The funds made available under the provisions of the area vocational education programs law must be matched on a dollar for dollar basis. The funds may be used for (1) salaries and travel of administrators, supervisors, teacher educators, teachers, coordinators, vocational guidance counselors, and others; (2) purchase, rental, and maintenance, and repair of instructional equipment; (3) purchase of instructional supplies and teaching aids; (4) cost of transportation of students; (5) determining needs for and planning and developing area vocational education programs; (6) travel expense of state board and advisory committee meetings; (7) training and work experience training programs for out-of-school youth; and (8) related instruction for apprentices. It is further provided that equipment and teaching aids purchased with the funds shall become the property of the state. The Act prohibits a state from using area vocational education funds as a replacement for services financed previously from Smith-Hughes and George-Barden vocational education funds.

The Vocational Education Act of 1963 (Public Law 88-210, 88th Congress) provides additional funds for area vocational programs. The Act permits state boards of education to use Federal funds appropriated under the provisions of the Act for the construction and operation of area vocational schools. The Act requires the state boards of vocational education to use at least one-third of the Federal funds in the state's allotment prior to July 1, 1968 and one-fourth thereafter for construction of area schools and/or for the education of persons who have completed or left school and are available for full-time study in preparation for entering the labor market. The funds for construction of area schools must be matched on a dollar for dollar basis. Both the amendment to the George-Barden Act and the Vocational Education Act of 1963 require that each state submit a state plan showing the manner in which the programs will be operated.

OPERATION OF THE AREA VOCATIONAL EDUCATION PROGRAM

The area vocational education program was defined in the National Defense Act of 1958 as a program for highly skilled technicians in vocations necessary for the national defense. The Vocational Education Act of 1963 permits the state boards of education to use a broader definition. Most of the states are using a more inclusive definition for the area programs they are conducting. This definition suggests that, "the term area vocational education program means a program consisting of one or more less-than-college-grade courses conducted under public supervision and control and on an organized systematic class basis, which is designed to fit individuals for useful employment in recognized occupations, and which is made available to residents of the state or an area thereof designated and approved by the state board for vocational education who either have completed junior high school or, regardless of their school credits, are at least 16 years of age and can reasonably be expected to profit by the instruction offered."[3] When this definition is used Federal funds

[3] American Vocational Association, *Area Vocational Education Programs*, Washington, D.C., 1959, p. 9.

are used only in those courses that qualify under the Acts, and other courses offered in the area programs are financed with state or other funds.

The area vocational education programs are conducted in a number of different types of institutions. Among these are vocational or trade schools, comprehensive high schools, community or junior colleges, technical institutes, technical high schools, area vocational technical schools, four-year colleges, and by state boards for vocational education. During the year 1960, 78 percent of the 598 programs were conducted in vocational or trade schools, comprehensive high schools, and junior colleges. Preparatory curriculums were established for high school students in the upper levels of secondary school, and for high school graduates who desired to pursue technical courses. Extension courses were organized for workers in a technical occupation to enable them to advance in their vocation, and for upgrading workers into new or more difficult jobs.

Area programs have a variety of course offerings in trade and technical subjects. Among the more frequent trade courses offered are auto mechanics, carpentry, cooking and baking, machine shop, sheet metal, electricity, and welding. Popular courses for technicians include aircraft hydraulics, computer programming, electronics, cosmetology, drafting, jet engines, nuclear energy, practical nursing, radio and television, industrial technology, medical technology, and petroleum technology. Courses available in some schools for agricultural technicians include farm management, insect and disease control, farm mechanics, dairy herd improvement, and landscaping. Courses in tax accounting, banking, business law, business machines, insurance, secretarial sciences, and public speaking are available for business technicians in some area vocational programs.

Area vocational education programs require facilities, faculties, and curriculums that meet acceptable standards. An advisory committee composed of representatives of labor, management, and education should be constituted in the early planning stages and continue to function during the life of the school. The buildings, whether they be new or remodeled, should be designed for the courses to be offered. Personnel for administration, supervision, teaching, and guidance should be technically and professionally qualified. Modern equipment and instructional materials suitable for the course offerings should be provided. Curriculums should be designed to meet the specific employment requirements of the area served and should be determined from an occupational survey. General education courses should

Modern Industry Requires Skilled Man and Woman Power. These technicians are assembling microwave ferrite switches. (Roy W. Roberts, Jr., MELABS, Palo Alto, California)

be offered where they are needed and high standards should be maintained in both technical and general courses.

The enrollment in Federally aided area vocational education programs increased from 48,500 students in 1959 to 149,000 in 1962. This represents an increase of about 208 percent. The extension class enrollment was two-thirds of the total. As more funds are made available and more programs started, the enrollment will increase. Electronics and mechanical programs including drafting and design account for almost three-fourths of the total enrollment. Expenditure of Federal funds for area vocational education programs have totaled about $63,857,000 from the beginning of the program to June 30, 1962. The percentage distribution of Federal, state, and local funds for this period was 43 percent, 22 percent, and 35 percent respectively. It should be kept in mind that these data are for Federally aided programs under the provisions of the George-Barden Act. Enrollment and expenditures for non-Federally aided programs are equal to if not greater than those of Federally aided programs. The data indicate that the demand for graduates of area vocational education programs continue to increase and this should stimulate the development of more programs to meet the growing needs of the nation's economy.

Practical Nurse Education

The number of practical nurses increased from 145,000 in 1950 to 217,000 in 1960, an increase of about 50 percent. During the same period the number of professional nurses increased 46 percent but the number of student professional nurses decreased 25 percent. The number of persons completing practical nurse training courses has increased markedly since the passage in 1956 of legislation authoriz-

Approved Courses in Practical Nursing Provide Opportunities for Students to Learn About Nursing Arts, Nutrition, Food Preparation, Home Management, Child Care, and Occupational Therapy. (Chicago Public Schools, Chicago, Illinois)

ing Federal aid for practical nurse education. The enrollment in these Federally aided programs increased from 3,388 persons in the preparatory program in 1955 to 30,966 in 1962. It is estimated that future needs for practical nurses will be accelerated because of the increase in population, the longer life span, and better medical care. It is expected that the Federally aided practical nurse education program will make significant contributions to the manpower needs in this area. A description of this program together with its relation to the problem of medical care is shown below.

DEVELOPMENT OF PRACTICAL NURSE EDUCATION

Man has required nursing care for his many afflictions since the beginning of time. In the early years of civilization he or members of his family or tribe provided what little medical care he received.

Then came medicine men, sorcerers, and later physicians to assist in the healing of the sick. During the Golden Age of Greece in the fifth century B.C., Hippocrates, the father of medicine, introduced the application of the scientific method in diagnosis and treatment of disease. The physicians of this age placed little emphasis on home care and nursing. With the advent of Christianity more attention was given to nursing care. Paul the Apostle brought Phoebe of Cenchreae, an ordained deaconess and practical nurse, to Rome about A.D. 60 to administer to the spiritual and medical needs of the Romans. Florence Nightingale provided nursing care for English soldiers in the Crimea and was responsible for the establishment of schools of nursing throughout the world. Among the early schools of nursing were the Saint Thomas Hospital school in London (1860), the Bellevue Hospital school in New York (1873), and the Columbia University, New York City, college level nursing course in 1907. The states of North Carolina, New Jersey, New York, and Virginia enacted laws requiring the licensing of nurses in 1903. The need for nursing care increased especially during World Wars I and II and the states established higher qualifications for entry into the vocation of professional nursing.

Near the latter part of the nineteenth century when the movement for the training of professional nurses was gaining momentum, physicians and laymen recognized other needs for the patient in the sickroom. One of these was for an assistant to the physician or professional nurse to perform some of the less technical procedures and make for a better utilization of the services of the professional nurse. Consequently, classes were organized in the Brooklyn YWCA in 1892 to care for "chronic invalids, elderly persons, and small children." Similar schools were organized by the New York City YWCA (The Ballard School) in 1893 and the Thompson practical nursing school of Brattleboro, Vermont, in 1907. These schools offered short courses of less than one year's duration emphasizing nursing care in the home.

The first practical nursing schools were private institutions. Public funds were first used for practical nurse education in 1919 in the Girls Vocational High School in Minneapolis, Minnesota. Practical nurse education in private and public schools continued to expand and by 1943 there were 14 practical nurse education programs in 6 states in Federally aided vocational education schools and classes. This number had grown to 80 programs in 30 states by 1950. During the 5-year period 1955 to 1959 the number of state approved programs of practical nurse education increased from 395 to 832 of which two-thirds were operated in public vocational education schools and classes. By 1962 the enrollment in practical nurse education had increased to almost 49,000 students in Federally aided schools in 54 states and territories of the United States.

LEGISLATION FOR PRACTICAL NURSE EDUCATION

The state of Virginia in 1918 enacted a law providing for the training and licensing of practical or attendant nurses. The administration of the Act was placed under the Virginia State Board of Examiners of Graduate Nurses. Legislation in other states came rather slowly. The majority of the states began to license practical nurses in the 1940s but it was not until 1960 that all states and territories of the United States authorized by law the licensing of practical nurses. In some states all persons who engage in practical nursing are required to have a license while in others the license is optional. Each state has its own legal requirements for licensing which usually include specific academic preparation, work experience, and the satisfactory completion of an examination under the direction of the state board of nursing.

The Smith-Hughes Act of 1918 and subsequent vocational education laws permitted the use of Federal funds for practical nurse education. Under the interpretation of these acts practical nursing was defined as one of the trades for which Federal funds for trade and industrial education were provided. The competition among the other trades for funds limited the number of practical nurse education programs. The apparent need for increasing the supply of practical nurses led to the passage of new legislation in 1956. This legislation was included in Title III of the Health Amendments Act (Public Law 911, 84th Congress) which amends the Vocational Education Act of 1946 (George-Barden) by adding Title II to extend and improve practical nurse training.

The 1956 Act authorized an annual appropriation of $5 million each year until June 30, 1961. The authorization was made permanent in 1963. The funds were apportioned among the states on the basis of the ratio of the amount the state received from the George-Barden Act to the amount all states received from this Act. Matching for the first 2 years was 75 percent Federal funds and 25 percent state and local funds, and dollar for dollar thereafter. States were required to specify in the state plan for vocational education the manner in which the funds would be used.

CONCEPTS AND DEFINITIONS

Many persons of varying qualifications provide nursing care for sick people. The professional nurse (R.N.) provides leadership and is usually the first in command among personnel who have responsibility for nursing care. The duties and qualifications of professional nurses have changed from time to time. Before Florence Nightingale, a nurse was any person who could be persuaded to remain in a sick room. The present day concept as expressed by the American Nurses Association is a person who has met the legal requirements for registration and has the technical knowledge and practical ability to engage in the art of nursing.

The role of the practical nurse has varied from that of a housekeeper-valet or companion with little or no knowledge concerning nursing techniques to a person qualified by training and experience to perform many nursing techniques. The present concept of the practical nurse is that of:

A person trained to care for selected convalescent, subacutely, and chronically ill patients and to assist the professional nurse in a team relationship especially in the care of the more acutely ill. She provides nursing services in institutions and in private homes where she is prepared to give household assistance when necessary. She may be employed by a private individual, a hospital, or a health agency. A practical nurse works only under the direct orders of a licensed physician or the supervision of a registered professional nurse.[4]

A further clarification of the concept of practical nursing is contained in the following statement of function of the practical nurse:

The fundamental role of the licensed practical nurse is nursing care of patients in those instances where the nursing needs do not require the constant attention of the professional nurse. The ultimate responsibility for evaluating the nursing needs of patients, for developing nursing care plans, and for delegating appropriate nursing functions rests with the professional nurse. . . . It is recognized that in their care of patients, the licensed practical nurse sometimes works under the direction of the licensed physician without professional nurse supervision. The essential contribution of the licensed practical nurse in today's health services can best be made where sound professional direction is provided. . . . In any situation, the licensed practical nurse should perform only those acts for which he or she has been prepared, bearing in mind the individual's personal responsibility under the law.[5]

[4] Kathryn Osmond Brownell and Vivian M. Culver, *The Practical Nurse*, Saunders, Philadelphia, 1959, p. 23.
[5] *Ibid.*, pp. 23–24.

Other persons who render direct and indirect patient care are orderlies, aides, attendants, floor clerks, receptionists, and secretaries. Aides and orderlies who are sometimes referred to as attendants are employed to relieve registered nurses and practical nurses of some of the semiskilled responsibilities of nursing care. Such duties as assisting the professional and practical nurse with the admission and discharge of patients, caring for hospital equipment and the patients surroundings, collecting simple specimens, assisting in personal hygiene, and taking temperatures may be assigned to these persons. Clerical and secretarial personnel serve as receptionists and floor clerks and assist in paper and desk work. The qualifications of these various aides and assistants vary and their duties are assigned in accordance with their qualifications. In general they are employed to enable the nurses to spend more time with their patients.

OPERATION OF THE PRACTICAL NURSE EDUCATION PROGRAM

Practical nurse education courses vary in length but the most common pattern is a 12-month course which combines classroomwork with supervised hospital experience. The foundation or preclinical area covers the first 4 months of basic instruction and is usually conducted in a classroom setting. The remainder of the time consists of supervised hospital experience with some classroom work. The class instruction includes courses or topics in community health, conditions of illness, family life, first aid, the human body, and personal hygiene, geriatric nursing, needs of children, and nursing acts such as medications and treatments, nutrition, and personal relationships. The supervised experience includes patient care in hospitals and outpatient departments. Extension courses for upgrading practical nurses are available in some centers.

The practical nurse who has completed the required course in an approved school and passed the state board examination may use the initials L.P.N. (Licensed Practical Nurse) after her name. In some states the initials L.V.N. (Licensed Vocational Nurse) are used. Prior to the completion of the state board examination but after graduation from the course the practical nurse is referred to as a graduate practical nurse. Student nurses frequently use the initials S.P.N. (Student Practical Nurse). The license is a legal permit to the practical nurse to allow her to practice nursing under the laws of a specific state. A license issued in one state may or may not be valid in another state. A license is not necessarily a permanent right, but can be revoked and may need to be renewed in accordance with the regulations under which it was issued.

Many professional organizations are available to persons engaged in practical nursing. The official organization for licensed practical nurses in the United States is the National Federation of Licensed Practical Nurses (NFLPN). Individual states have their own associations affiliated with the national federation. An organization known as the National Association for Practical Nurse Education and Service (NAPNES) is interested in improving standards for educational programs in this area. Membership in the organization includes licensed practical nurses, faculty members from practical nursing schools, interested citizens, and members from other health agencies. Active participation in one or more of these associations will not only improve the work of the individual nurse but also the group as a whole.

Manpower Development and Training

Congress recently enacted two laws designed to reduce unemployment and underemployment. One of these established the Area Redevelopment Administration (ARA) to help create new jobs and stimulate private investment in areas economically depressed by chronic unemployment or underemployment. The other act was known as the Manpower Development and Training Act (MDTA). This law established a program of training for unemployed and underemployed workers and a broad program of research in the area of manpower problems in the United States. A description of the operation of these two programs and their impact on vocational education is shown below.

THE AREA REDEVELOPMENT ACT
(Public Law 87–27, 87th Congress)

The Area Redevelopment Act was enacted to enable the Federal Government together with the states to help areas of substantial and persistent unemployment and underemployment to better plan and finance their redevelopment. Federal assistance is provided for (1) low interest, long-term loans to assist new industrial or commercial enterprises to get started or to help existing firms to expand, (2) loans and grants to communities to help provide public facilities for new or existing firms; (3) technical assistance to assist communities to plan and develop a program of economic development; and (4) programs to retain workers and to pay them subsistence allowances while in training in order to equip them with new skills needed for new industries or the expansion of existing ones.

The ARA law authorizes an annual appropriation of $4½ million for occupational training and $10 million for trainee subsistence payments. The occupational training or retraining needs of unemployed and underemployed workers are determined by the Secretary of Labor in consultation with the Secretary of Commerce and the Secretary of Agriculture. The Secretary of Labor is authorized to make payments to states either in advance or by way of reimbursement for the purpose of enabling the states as agents of the United States to make weekly subsistence payments to eligible trainees. The Secretary of Labor and the Secretary of Commerce are authorized to make the rules and regulations necessary for carrying out the section of the law concerned with subsistence payments.

The ARA law authorizes the use of funds for facilities as well as services in the event a need exists for facilities. If a state vocational agency is unable to provide the services and facilities required, the Secretary of Health, Education, and Welfare may contract with public or private educational institutions for services and facilities. The Secretary of Labor may provide any necessary assistance for setting up apprenticeships and to promote journeyman and other on-the-job training. The Act provides that special consideration be given to agricultural workers and other workers engaged in seasonal occupations.

THE OPERATION OF THE ARA TRAINING PROGRAM

The overall administration for the ARA program is placed in the Area Redevelopment Administration of the U.S. Department of Commerce. The responsibilities for training assigned to the Department of Labor are carried out through local and state employment-security offices. These offices select the trainees, determine the occupation for which training is needed and together with the state vocational education division personnel develop the training programs for submission to the Washington office of the U.S. Department of Labor for approval. The actual training including employing personnel for teaching, purchasing equipment and supplies, and recording attendance and competence of trainees is done by the personnel of the state vocational education division. In most cases local public school authorities have responsibility for conducting the classes.

The course titles are determined by employment-security authorities on the basis of needs and opportunities in the specific community in which the course is offered. Among the more popular courses are auto mechanics and related trades, carpentry and related trades, drafting, farm equipment repair and maintenance, heavy equipment operation, sewing machine operation and related needle trades, stenography, upholstering, and welding. Courses are usually set up for a 16-week period.

Individuals who are certified to be undergoing training or retraining may receive subsistence payments for the period the individual is in training, but not to exceed 16 weeks. The amount of the subsistence payment for a week of training is equal to the average weekly unemployment compensation payment for a week of total unemployment in the state making such payments. Subsistence payments are made directly to the trainee by the employment-security division of the state labor department. The vocational division of the state department of education has responsibility for indicating when the payment starts and ends. Individuals in training may not legally receive unemployment compensation and retraining subsistence payments for the same period of time.

A total of 145 projects authorizing the training of more than 5312 persons were approved for the fiscal year 1964 up to February 7, 1964. Some of these trainees had been unemployed for 5 years or longer. More than 6000 workers completed the training courses in 1963 of which 65 percent had been placed on jobs related to their training by the end of the fiscal year.

THE MANPOWER DEVELOPMENT AND TRAINING ACT
(Public Law 87–415, 87th Congress)

The Manpower Development and Training Act is designed to reduce unemployment by training and upgrading workers for vocations in need of qualified personnel. Title I of the law directs the Secretary of Labor to study the problems in the field of manpower requirements, development and utilization, and report to the President who will in turn report the findings with recommendations to Congress. The Act as amended authorizes an appropriation of $2 million for the fiscal year 1963 and $3 million for each of the fiscal years 1964, 1965, and 1966 for this title.

Title II authorizes a program of training workers for job opportunities that have been found through the research program. This title as amended authorizes an appropriation of $97 million for the fiscal year 1963, $161 million for fiscal 1964, $407 million for fiscal 1965 and $281 million for fiscal 1966. The Act as amended requires each state to pay one-third of its cost for Title II for the fiscal years 1965 and 1966. Title III of the Act authorizes an annual appropriation of $1 million for administrative purposes.

The Secretary of Labor is responsible for the administration of the Act and the Secretary of Health, Education, and Welfare for the operation of the training program. Training is conducted both in the schools and in on-the-job facilities. The Act is designed for persons who are unemployed or underemployed and who cannot reasonably be expected to secure appropriate full time employment without training. A special program is authorized for youths 16 years of age or older who are in need of occupational training or further schooling. Workers in farm families with less than $1200 annual net family income are considered unemployed for the purpose of the Act.

Training allowances are authorized for trainees who are legally enrolled and in attendance at the schools or classes. The amount of the training allowance does not exceed $10 more than the average weekly unemployment compensation payment. Such payments are made not to exceed a period of 52 weeks except that 20 additional weeks may be added for certain eligible persons who need basic education. The law provides that training allowances will be paid to unemployed persons who have had at least 2 years of experience in gainful employment and are either heads of families or heads of households, or who are members of a household in which the head is unemployed.

Training allowances may be paid to youths 17 years of age or older who require a training allowance in order to undertake training. The training allowance for these youths is at the rate of $20 a week. Youths must be properly certified and not eligible for training allowances under other parts of the Act. Other provisions of the Act require that youths be high school graduates or have failed to attend school for a period of not less than one year. Not more than 25 percent of the persons who are receiving training allowances may be under the age of 22.

THE OPERATION OF THE MDTA

The MDTA is operated in much the same manner as the ARA. Differences occur in overall administration, length of period for subsistence payments, amount of subsistence for youth, and areas from

NDEA Funds Have Provided Training in Many Trade and Technical Occupations. (Chicago Public Schools, Chicago, Illinois)

which trainees are selected. The local community or labor market is the focus of the MDTA program. The procedure for project approval requires the preparation of a training proposal. This proposal includes the following items: (1) survey of skills required, (2) referral of persons for training, (3) planning and development of the training program, (4) conduct of the program, and (5) placement and follow-up of those persons who have completed training. The development of the proposal is a joint undertaking of the representatives of the state department of employment-security and state division of vocational education.

When the state division of vocational education receives the results of the labor market survey showing a need for training, the division determines whether or not appropriate facilities are available and what additional facilities are needed to conduct the training program. The vocational division then prepares a detailed analysis of the training project to include: (1) course content of the curriculum, (2) location and description of the facilities to be used, (3) analysis of available instructional staff, (4) description of existing equipment and needs for additional equipment, and (5) statement of cost of program.

Each application for a training program is evaluated by representatives of state and Federal agencies responsible for the training. An important factor considered in this evaluation is that of placement. Selection and referral for training will not be made unless there is some evidence to indicate that the trainee may secure employment, either in the area in which he resides or outside the area, in the occupation for which he is trained.

Federal funds for both training costs and support of trainees are apportioned to the states under a formula based on the following factors: (1) the proportion which the labor force of a state bears to the total labor force of the United States, (2) the proportion which the unemployed in a state during the preceding calendar year bears to the total number of unemployed in the United States in that year, (3) the lack of appropriate full time employment in a state, (4) the proportion which the insured unemployed within a state bear to the total number of insured employed within the state, and (5) the average weekly unemployment compensation benefits paid by the state.

A total of 1191 training projects for 64,740 trainees were approved between July 1, 1963 and January 31, 1964. The projects were located in communities in 51 states and territories. By the end of 1963 a total of 40,683 persons were enrolled in training and had completed a training course. The estimated cost per trainee for the projects approved was $679 and the average training allowance was about $35 per week. The average duration of training was 31 weeks per trainee.

QUESTIONS FOR STUDY AND DISCUSSION

1. What changes have occurred in the number and characteristics of the labor force?
2. What percentage of the labor force is unemployed and what are the characteristics of the unemployed labor force?
3. How may the goal of full employment be achieved?
4. What is an area vocational education program? What is an area school?
5. What Federal funds are available for area vocational schools?
6. How are area vocational programs established, administered, and operated?
7. Discuss the history of practical nurse education.

8. What Federal aid is provided for practical nurse education?
9. How are practical nurse education programs operated?
10. What are the training provisions of the ARA Act?
11. What is the purpose and function of the MDTA?
12. Discuss the operation of the MDTA program.

SOURCE REFERENCES

Brownell, Kathryn O., and Vivian M. Culver, *The Practical Nurse*, Saunders, Philadelphia, 1959.

Powers, Helen K., *Practical Nursing*, International Altrusan, 1961. Reprinted by U.S. Department of Health, Education, and Welfare, Office of Education, Washington, D.C.

Ross, Carmen F., *Personal and Vocational Relationships in Practical Nursing*, Lippincott, Philadelphia, 1961.

U.S. Department of Commerce, Area Redevelopment Administration, *Annual Report for 1962*, Washington, D.C., 1963.

U.S. Department of Commerce, Bureau of the Census, *Statistical Abstract of the United States, 1964*.

U.S. Department of Health, Education, and Welfare, Office of Education, *Area Vocational Education Programs*, Misc. No. 3560, reprinted 1962, Washington, D.C., 1962.

U.S. Department of Health, Education, and Welfare, Office of Education, *Guides for Developing Curricula for the Education of Practical Nurses*, Vocational Division Bulletin 274, Washington, D.C., 1962.

U.S. Department of Health, Education, and Welfare, Office of Education, *Training Activities under the Manpower Development and Training Act*, Circular 706, Washington, D.C., 1963.

U.S. Department of Labor, *Manpower Report of the President and A Report on Manpower Requirements Resources, Utilization and Training*, Washington, D.C., 1963.

CHAPTER THIRTEEN

VOCATIONAL GUIDANCE

Vocational guidance is concerned with the problems and techniques involved in choosing an occupation and in becoming adjusted in it. Vocational guidance, like vocational education, had its origins in the changing nature of work and has developed concurrently with, but independently of, vocational education. The development of vocational guidance has been due to the efforts of individuals and organizations interested in the problems of workers and prospective workers who were struggling with occupational choices or were dissatisfied with choices previously made. Vocational educators learned early in the history of vocational education that the choice of an occupation and the adjustment thereto were important factors in the efficient production of the worker.

The relationship of vocational guidance to the efficiency of work stimulated vocational educators to acquire some proficiency in vocational guidance to enable them to counsel more intelligently with vocational students. The need for more extensive knowledge and skill in vocational guidance led vocational educators to seek an expansion of guidance services and, as a result, Federal funds were made available as a reimbursement for certain vocational guidance services. The use of Federal funds and the parallel development of vocational education and vocational guidance have led to some differences in point of view in the relationship of vocational guidance and vocational education. Some changes have occurred in the administration of the public school guidance programs as a result of the National Defense Education Act of 1958 which authorized Federal funds for guidance services. This chapter is concerned with various aspects of the vocational guidance program.

The Development of the Guidance Movement

Man's choice of an occupation prior to the Industrial Revolution was influenced by such forces as heredity, tradition, and superstition. The usual procedure during this period of time was for the son to learn the trade or profession of his father. Little consideration was given to such factors as aptitude, interest, and personal preference. With the advent of the machine age, however, the number of vocations increased markedly, and workers had more and more opportunities for occupational choices. These occupational choices were first conditioned by pseudoscience and superstition and later by the application of scientific method. An examination of the literature of education shows the changes that have occurred in the forces that have influenced the guidance movement.

EARLY BEGINNINGS

The writings of the philosophers of ancient times indicate that some of these persons were concerned about occupational choices. Plato, the Athenian philosopher who lived from 429 B.C. to 347 B.C., in his writings on the ideal society suggested that each worker should be assigned to the one occupation for which he was naturally fitted. Cicero (106 B.C. to 43 B.C.) in his essay On Duties stated, "We must decide what manner of men we wish to be and what calling in life we would follow; and this is the most difficult problem in the world." Cicero assumed self-determination for the individual, which suggests that some individuals of that age were concerned with occupational choices.

The French philosopher Blaise Pascal (1623–1662) discussed

the importance of a wise choice of an occupation in his writings. Some efforts were made about this time to teach the importance of the proper selection of an occupation to the children in Padre Orpheus, an orphans' home in Spain. John Locke in 1695 suggested that children's natures and aptitudes should be studied as a means of determining their capabilities for learning and the extent to which improvement might be secured.

The practice of phrenology came into prominence early in the nineteenth century. Phrenology taught that certain mental and moral characteristics could be determined by an inspection of the head, scalp, and face. Predictions for success in occupations and in other life activities were made on the basis of the findings of these examinations. Charles Dickens in his novel *Bleak House,* published in 1853, depicted a youth who was in need of vocational guidance to find out what his natural bent was. In 1859 Samuel Smiles of London published a vol-

Counseling is the Process of Helping an Individual Through Interviews and Other Relationships to Solve His Problems and Improve His Planning. (Southern State College, Magnolia, Arkansas)

ume entitled *Self-Help* which was designed to assist an individual in developing habits of industry. Lysander S. Richards, a New England writer, published a book called *Vocophy* in 1881. This volume indicated a system by means of which an individual could find the occupation for which he was best suited and suggested a new profession for enabling persons to find their right vocations. In 1884 President Andrew D. White of Cornell University prepared a booklet entitled *What Profession Shall I Choose and How Shall I Fit Myself for It?*

This pamphlet was written to assist students in selecting courses required for various vocational curriculums on the college level. George J. Manson of New York published a book for boys in 1889 entitled *Ready for Business or Choosing an Occupation*. It was written to answer such questions as a boy would ask about an occupation in which he was interested.

George A. Merrill organized the California School of Mechanic Arts in 1894, in which many of the elements of a plan for vocational guidance were present. Jesse B. Davis, principal of the Central High School of Detroit, Michigan, served as the counselor to students during the years 1898 to 1907. He was concerned primarily with the educational problems and vocational careers of the high school students. Mrs. Ogilvie Gordon of Aberdeen, Scotland, presented a plan in 1904 for guiding boys and girls into employment and in 1908 issued a handbook of employment. Two important books concerning requirements and other information on vocations were published in Massachusetts early in the twentieth century. One of these, *Starting in Life*, by Nathaniel C. Fowler, gave information on advantages, disadvantages and requirements for success in each of 32 occupations. The other publication, *What Can a Young Man Do?* by Frank W. Rollins, gave such information as qualifications, opportunities, salaries, and names of schools where training could be obtained for 53 vocations. These references indicated that the need for counseling, placement, and follow-up was recognized but that little response on the part of the school had been made to this need prior to 1907.

THE WORK OF FRANK PARSONS

Present-day programs in vocational guidance developed as a result of the work of Frank Parsons, the director and one of the founders of the Civic Service House, Boston. Dr. Parsons in 1907 gave an address on choosing an occupation to the members of the graduating class in one of the evening high schools in Boston. At the close of the address some members of the class asked for personal interviews with Dr. Parsons to discuss individual problems involved in choosing an occupation. The need for a guidance and counseling service became apparent from these interviews, and as a result Dr. Parsons organized the Vocation Bureau which formally opened in January 1908 in the Boston Civic Service House. Dr. Parsons stated that a large number of men and women from 15 to 72 years of age came for consultation during the first few months the Bureau was in operation. Among these persons were college students, young men in commercial and business life, boys and girls from the high schools and working boys and girls. The Bureau did not attempt to select the one occupation a counselee should follow but aimed to help the counselee investigate and come to his own conclusions. A vocation department was established in 1908 at the Boston YMCA, and a school for training counselors was among the activities engaged in by this department.

Dr. Parsons outlined the work of the vocation counselor in his volume, *Choosing a Vocation,* published in May, 1909, shortly after his death, which occurred in September, 1908. This volume suggested that the method of the vocation counselor involved the following considerations: (1) personal data, (2) self-analysis, (3) the person's own choice and decision, (4) counselor's analysis, (5) outlook in the vocational field, (6) induction and advice, and (7) general helpfulness in fitting into the chosen work. The counselee was expected to record on paper the personal data and self-analysis. The counselor was instructed to test the counselee's choice of an occupation and to provide him with occupational information.[1]

Dr. Parsons is said to have been the first person to use the term *vocational guidance,* and he paved the way for organizing vocational guidance programs in public schools by suggesting that educational institutions should undertake this responsibility. He organized the work of the Boston Vocation Bureau for the collection and study of information about occupations and workers. He recognized the importance of publicity and enlisted the assistance of friends and co-workers to carry on the work. He was succeeded as director of the Vocation Bureau by David S. Wheeler who, together with Ralph Albertson and Meyer Bloomfield, carried forward the guidance movement. Mrs. Quincy A. Shaw, Lincoln Filene, and other Boston philanthropists provided funds for maintaining the Bureau. Paul H. Hanus, chairman of the board of the Bureau, arranged for summer session courses in vocational guidance at Harvard University in 1911, and a Department of Vocational Guidance was established at Boston University in 1914. Thus, the vocational guidance movement in the United States had its origin in voluntary, educational, civic, and social work in the city of Boston.

VOCATIONAL GUIDANCE IN THE PUBLIC SCHOOLS

A vocational guidance program was organized in the Boston public schools in 1909. This program was planned by the director of

[1] Frank Parsons, *Choosing a Vocation,* Houghton Mifflin, Boston, 1909, p. 45.

The Work of the Vocation Bureau Established by Dr. Frank Parsons in the Civic Service House, Boston, led to the Development of the Present-Day Program of Vocational Guidance. (From *History of Vocational Guidance* by John M. Brewer, by permission of Harper & Row, Copyright 1942 by Harper & Row)

the Boston Vocation Bureau at the request of the superintendent of schools of Boston. The plan included a committee on vocational direction, a number of counselors, and a counselor training program under the direction of the Vocation Bureau. A short time prior to this, Eli W. Weaver, chairman of the students' aid committee of the New York City High School Teachers' Association, developed a vocational guidance program in the evening high schools. The guidance activities were conducted by teachers on a voluntary basis. The first national conference on vocational guidance was held in Boston in 1910, at which time it was suggested that vocational guidance was a public school responsibility. Grand Rapids, Michigan, in 1912 organized the first city-wide public school system of vocational guidance in the United States. Many other cities organized vocational guidance programs between 1914 and 1918, including Cincinnati, Lincoln, Minneapolis, Philadelphia, Oakland, Seattle, Pittsburgh, Atlanta, and Providence.

Interest in state-wide programs of vocational guidance came early in the history of the movement. The National Vocational Guidance Association was organized in 1913 to promote the organization of vocational guidance services throughout the United States. The Connecticut General Assembly in 1913 authorized local school boards to employ vocational counselors. The Vermont Legislature in 1915 directed the State Board of Education to arrange for a course of study on vocational opportunities to be given in all junior high schools. The Boston Vocation Bureau was transferred to Harvard University in 1917, at which time it became the Bureau of Vocational Guidance of the Harvard University, Division of Education. L. H. Dennis, director of agricultural education, Pennsylvania State Department of Education, appointed H. L. Holbrook to the position of field secretary in vocational guidance in 1918 with responsibility for promoting secondary school programs of vocational guidance. In 1929 New York State authorized state support for salaries of counselors and established the position of state supervisor of vocational and educational guidance. Michigan, Wisconsin, Virginia, and Ohio were among other states that expressed an interest in vocational guidance during this period by developing some type of state activity in guidance.

The local teacher of vocational education has occupied an important position in youth and adult counseling and guidance services through the years. The vocational teacher was the only source of occupational information during the early years of the guidance program. Students in the smaller schools of the present time rely upon the advice and counsel of vocational teachers in job placement and adjustment. Many vocational teachers assist school counselors in compiling occupational information about various occupations, and provide vocational counseling services to individual students. Vocational teachers have also assisted in providing counseling services for out-of-school youth and adults who need assistance in solving personal and vocational problems.

CHANGING CONCEPTS OF GUIDANCE

A review of the literature describing the development of the twentieth century program of vocational guidance indicates that concepts of the meanings and implications of vocational guidance have changed since the beginning of the program. While Dr. Parsons emphasized the importance of encouraging each counselee to arrive at his own decision relative to the choice of an occupation, he employed more direct techniques than are suggested by present-day standards. Parsons used such devices as rating sheets, interview techniques, and specific assignments. Standardized tests were not available at that time. Truman L. Kelley, a graduate student at Teachers College, Columbia University, used the term *educational guidance* in 1914 to describe the help given to students in the choice of school studies and in making other school adjustments. During the World War I period, a number of tests of intelligence and aptitudes were suggested as an aid to vocational placement and adjustment, and by 1929 considerable confidence in the validity and reliability of these tests was expressed.

These facts doubtless had a bearing on the definition of vocational guidance proposed in 1921 and revised in 1924 by the National Vocational Guidance Association in which the Association stated that "Vocational guidance is the giving of information, experience, and advice in regard to choosing an occupation, preparing for it, entering it, and progressing in it."[2] This definition suggests that guidance is a method rather than a process; it is giving rather than assisting. This definition may have caused some writers to regard vocational education as a part of the vocational guidance program because of the reference to giving information relative to preparing for and progressing in an occupation.

A somewhat different concept of vocational guidance was suggested by the National Vocational Guidance Association in 1937. The Association defined vocational guidance as "The process of assisting the individual to choose an occupation, prepare for it, enter upon and progress in it."[3] This definition suggests that vocational guidance is a process with emphasis on *assistance* rather than advising. Again the reference to assisting in preparing for an occupation and progressing in it has led to some misunderstandings, since these activities are included in the functions of vocational education. However, the emphasis in vocational guidance is on planning the program of instruction, which may also involve replanning, rather than carrying the instructional program to completion. Thus, vocational guidance under this concept is concerned primarily with helping individuals make decisions and choices involved in planning and engaging in a career.

A more recent concept quite similar to the last one mentioned is the definition suggested in 1954 by the Committee on Research and

[2] George E. Myers, "A Quarter Century of Vocational Guidance," *Occupations*, May, 1934, p. 35.
[3] National Vocational Guidance Association, "The Principles and Practices of Educational and Vocational Guidance," *Occupations*, May, 1937, p. 772.

Publications of the American Vocational Association. This committee suggested that "Vocational guidance is the process of assisting individuals to understand their capabilities and interests, to choose a suitable vocation, and to prepare for, enter, and make successful progress in it."[4] Here the emphasis is on assisting individuals to understand their capabilities in order that they may make wise choices.

These present-day concepts suggest that vocational guidance is not a device for finding the one job an individual can best do. Experience has shown that almost every person can achieve success in a number of occupations. These concepts recognize the fact that a single individual may have occasion to make a number of occupational choices and adjustments throughout his life span, and therefore vocational guidance becomes a continuous process of assisting individuals to understand themselves better as a basis for making decisions concerning their careers.

OBJECTIVES OF VOCATIONAL GUIDANCE

The purpose of the program of vocational guidance is to provide individuals with the information and skills needed to make wise decisions concerning problems of vocational adjustment. An efficient program of vocational guidance should improve the chances of the individual for progress and satisfaction in his occupation. The program should also result in increased efficiency in the organization and operation of the instructional program within the school.

The foregoing statements suggest that the major purpose of vocational guidance is that of providing assistance to individuals. Information is made available to the individual, referred to as the counselee, concerning his interests, aptitudes and abilities. Vocational guidance serves as a means of making available information about occupations and employment opportunities and sets up means for aiding in the placement and adjustment of the counselee. Vocational guidance also provides assistance to the counselee in the interpretation of information and encourages him to attempt to find solutions to his problems.

Another important purpose of vocational guidance is to help teachers to become more proficient in carrying out their responsibilities. Counselors may provide teachers with information about students and occupations and, on request, assist them in planning curriculums

[4] American Vocational Association, *Definitions of Terms in Vocational, Technical, and Practical Arts Education*, Committee on Publications, Washington, D.C., 1964, p. 10.

and teaching activities. Teachers are also aided through vocational guidance programs to handle difficult behavior problems better, to provide for individual differences and to help students who seek assistance. A third function of vocational guidance is that of encouraging new activities. The guidance program should encourage the school staff to engage in the study and research needed for a continuous reorganization and improvement of the school system.

The vocational guidance program is a part of the total educational program, but it is not a new form of instruction in the accepted sense of classroom activities. The guidance program contributes to the efficiency of the instructional, administrative and supervisory functions of the school, but the guidance service is not designed as an agency of recruitment for a department or as a student accounting office for the administration of the school. The lines between guidance and the services of instruction, supervision, and administration are not well defined and must be considered by each school in terms of its aims, personnel and school organization. This makes it necessary for each school system to formulate its own plan of vocational guidance and to assign responsibilities to its personnel on the basis of the foregoing considerations.

The Development of Federally Aided Guidance Programs

Federal funds authorized in the George-Barden Act of 1946 and in Title V of the National Defense Education Act of 1958 may be used as a reimbursement to the states for local programs of guidance, counseling, and testing and for state administration, supervision, and counselor education programs. The George-Barden funds are authorized to provide individuals with the information needed and to develop the understanding necessary to make wise decisions in matters affecting vocational choices and adjustments. Federal funds under NDEA guidance, counseling, and testing programs are designed to promote better guidance programs and for the identification and encouragement of able students.

VOCATIONAL GUIDANCE UNDER THE VOCATIONAL EDUCATION ACTS

A report made in 1933 by a committee of the National Vocational Guidance Association and published by the U.S. Office of Education indicated that nine states had state vocational guidance programs in operation at that time. The President's Advisory Committee on Education emphasized the need for vocational guidance in the 1938 report of the Committee. The U.S. Commissioner of Education in 1938, by interpretation of the Smith-Hughes and George-Deen laws, authorized the states to use Federal teacher training funds provided in these laws for paying salaries and travel expenses incurred in the supervision of occupational information and guidance services. The Commissioner in that same year established an Occupational Information and Guidance Service in the Vocational Division, U.S. Office of Education.

By 1944 a total of 30 states, the District of Columbia, Hawaii, and Puerto Rico had established state supervision of vocational guidance programs. The George-Barden Act of 1946 was responsible for a further expansion of vocational guidance and by 1950 Federal vocational education funds were being used to reimburse salaries of local guidance counselors in 15 states and territories, and for state supervision and counselor training in 34 states and territories. The relative number of states using George-Barden funds remained about the same until 1958 at which time NDEA funds brought about a rapid expansion of the guidance counseling and testing programs and eventually a reduction in the use of George-Barden funds for vocational guidance.

The U.S. Commissioner of Education discontinued the Occupational Information and Guidance Service of the Vocational Division, U.S. Office of Education in 1951. A Guidance and Pupil Personnel Section was established in the Division of State and Local School Systems of the Office of Education in 1953.

GUIDANCE COUNSELING AND TESTING UNDER THE NDEA

The National Defense Education Act of 1958 authorized Federal funds for aid to the states for guidance, counseling, and testing programs in public secondary schools. Provision was also made for the payment of the cost of testing of students in private schools. The states were required to match the funds on a dollar for dollar basis. The Act also authorized $6,500,000 annually to enable the U.S. Commissioner of Education to contract with institutions of higher education for conducting counselor training institutes in which institutions received Federal funds for conducting institutes and trainees received allowances for necessary expenses. The NDEA guidance, counseling, and testing program is administered by the Division of

State Grants and the counselor training institutes program by the Division of College and University Assistance of the U.S. Office of Education.

ORGANIZATION OF STATE AND LOCAL GUIDANCE SERVICES

Each state desiring Federal funds for guidance is required to prepare a state plan for vocational guidance. The plan for use of George-Barden funds becomes a part of the state plan for vocational education. The plan for NDEA funds is a separate plan and not a part of the state plan for vocational education. The plan for the use of George-Barden funds indicates the purposes for which Federal funds are to be used, the limitations of the use of these funds, and provides for necessary fiscal procedures and reports. The organization of the programs of state supervision and counselor education are included in the plan. Federal funds may be used for reimbursing counselor education courses in which persons are enrolled who are qualifying as vocational counselors, teacher-counselors, and supervisors or administrators of vocational guidance.

Supervisors of vocational guidance have responsibility for promoting, developing, and supervising the guidance program; for assisting local administrators in organizing guidance programs; for making studies and investigations of the needs and requirements of the program; for developing counselor training programs; and for recommending physical facilities needed in local programs of vocational guidance. These duties require that supervisors possess special qualifications for the supervision of the program. At least a year of graduate work in such areas as counseling, individual analysis, educational and occupational information, and the organization of vocational guidance is desirable. Supervisors should also have both teaching and counseling experience and other work experience, in addition to such personal characteristics as are required for professions of this type.

Local counselors are employed by local boards of education and are responsible to the local school authority in the same manner as other teachers and staff members. Local counselors are employed for full-time or part-time counseling duties depending upon the school enrollment. Part-time counselors, sometimes referred to as teacher counselors, spend a portion of their time in counseling and part of their time in teaching high school subjects. Duties and responsibilities of local counselors include: (1) securing and using the individual inventory and other informational services, (2) counseling with the individual, (3) assisting in the organization of placement and follow-up procedures including contacts with employment and referral agencies, (4) providing leadership in curriculum study, (5) assisting teachers with student problems, (6) conducting surveys and investigations of students and their problems, (7) assisting teachers in securing and utilizing educational and occupational information, and (8) evaluating guidance services.

The local counselor responsible for carrying out these various duties and responsibilities should possess desirable personal characteristics; experience, both in education and in business, and professional knowledge, skills, and understandings. The specific qualifications for counselors vary among the states. In general, local counselors are expected to be graduates of an approved four-year teacher education institution with some graduate work in counselor education, including principles and practices of vocational guidance, counseling techniques, occupational and educational information, individual analysis, supervised practice, and the organization of the program.

Some special facilities are needed for the counseling program. An office or conference room for conducting private interviews with students or adults is essential. The counselor must have access to many records, and space and equipment for these should be provided in the office or conference room. The guidance suite should also include a reception room and a room for conducting tests. The vocational guidance program requires an occupational information library which should be located either in the guidance suite or in the school library. The counselor must make many contacts with business firms, civic organizations, and parents, and it is highly desirable that he have a telephone in his office. Other items of equipment and furnishings needed include audiovisual equipment such as projectors, recorders, record players, and radios; office furnishings such as a desk, chairs, a typewriter, an adding machine, a reading table, and a magazine rack; and various kinds of charts and illustrative material concerning occupational opportunities for youth and adults.

SCOPE AND COST OF PROGRAM

Eleven states reported that Federal vocational education funds (George-Barden) were used for reimbursing salaries of local guidance counselors in 1948. These 11 states reported a total of 249 local counselors serving full time or part time. Maryland with 124 counselors and Arkansas with 27 accounted for about 60 percent of the total number reported. The largest number of Federally aided (George-

Barden) counselors reported in the United States since the beginning of the Federally aided program in 1948 was 721 counselors in the fiscal year ended June 30, 1950. The total number of counselors reported for the fiscal year ended June 30, 1962 was 408. A total of $17,763,000 was expended for the vocational guidance program under the George-Barden Act for the 13-year period 1948 to 1960. About 28 percent of this amount was Federal funds.

A total of 21,572 guidance counselors, the equivalent of 13,307 full-time counselors was employed in public secondary schools in 1959 under the provisions of the NDEA guidance, counseling, and testing program. This number had increased to 36,446 counselors or the equivalent of 24,497 full-time counselors by 1962. This represents an increase of about 84 percent in the full-time equivalent. These counselors are in about 7800 schools of which 58 percent are schools with a secondary school enrollment of less than 350 pupils. The student counselor ratio has decreased from 862 students per counselor in 1959 to 545 in 1962. The total expenditures for the 4-year period for the NDEA guidance counseling and testing program was $353,248,000 of which 3.9 percent was Federal funds, 13.5 percent state funds and 82.6 local funds. It is estimated that 70 percent of the secondary school population attend schools in which NDEA funds are used for guidance services.

During the 4-year period, 1959 to 1962 more than 22 million scholastic aptitude and achievement tests were administered to students in public secondary schools under the NDEA guidance, counseling, and testing program. In addition about 1,700,000 tests were administered to students in nonpublic schools. This represents about 30 percent of all tests administered. In 1962 a total of 19,800,000 tests were administered to public secondary school students of which about 7 million or 35 percent were under the provisions of the NDEA program.

A total of 11,524 trainees attended counseling and guidance training institutes supported by NDEA funds during the 4-year period 1959 to 1962. The enrollees were either high school counselors or teachers preparing to be high school counselors. More than 2000 of these enrollees attended regular session institutes providing a year of graduate study, and the remaining enrollees were in short term courses usually conducted during the summer sessions. The institutes were supported entirely from Federal funds and a total of $22,500,000 was expended of which one-half was spent in regular session institutes.

About 60 percent of the cost of the program was for stipends for enrollees and allowances for their dependents.

Guidance Services and Procedures

Certain activities usually referred to as guidance services are engaged in as a means of carrying out the objectives of the vocational guidance program in the local school. These services are: (1) making available to the individual cumulative evidence about his abilities, interests, and attitudes; (2) supplying comprehensive factual information about educational and occupational opportunities; (3) providing for the counseling of individuals; and (4) providing means for aiding the placement and adjustment in the individual's career. The procedures and techniques established for carrying out these services are indicated below.

THE INDIVIDUAL INVENTORY

The individual or personal inventory is used as a means of securing a variety of information in terms of an individual's interests, mental ability, verbal and manual skills, special aptitudes, limitations, personality patterns, health and physical condition, educational history, and home and community background. This information is secured by means of reports, records, tests and measurements, and personal interviews. School records usually provide general data helpful in locating the individual and in making contacts with those who have responsibility for him. These records also provide data on school progress and health and physical characteristics.

Properly selected tests and measurements provide various kinds of information for use in vocational guidance. Intelligence is an important success factor in most occupations, and individual and group intelligence tests, well chosen and properly administered, provide a better measure of intelligence than personal judgment. The intelligence quotient, or IQ, is useful in assisting an individual to determine how far he is likely to be able to go with his education. The degree of intelligence one possesses has some relation to the efficiency and satisfaction one obtains in certain occupations.

Tests of special aptitudes and interests are useful in assisting an individual in his choice of an occupational group and often of a specific occupation within the group. Some of these tests cover broad

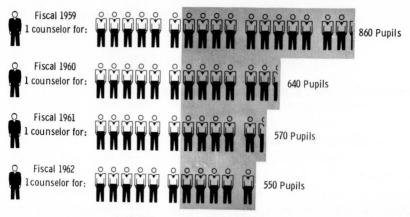

Fiscal 1959 1 counselor for:		860 Pupils
Fiscal 1960 1 counselor for:		640 Pupils
Fiscal 1961 1 counselor for:		570 Pupils
Fiscal 1962 1 counselor for:		550 Pupils

The Relative Number of Pupils per Counselor in Public Secondary Schools is Decreasing. The number of pupils per counselor decreased from 860 in 1959 to 550 in 1962. (U.S. Department of Health, Education, and Welfare, Office of Education, *Report on the National Defense Education Act, Fiscal Years 1961 and 1962*, Government Printing Office)

fields, such as mechanical and clerical occupations, while others cover single occupations. Interest inventories designed to compare the interests of the individual with the patterns of interests which characterize successful workers in different occupations are used along with aptitude tests. Achievement or scholastic proficiency tests are often used for diagnostic survey and administrative purposes. Personality tests and teacher- and self-rating scales are also used to provide information needed in the individual inventory.

Tests and rating scales, like other devices for obtaining information, have their limitations; this should be kept in mind in their use. Other devices that may be used along with school records and tests are biographies, self-inventories, questionnaires, diaries, graphic scales, and check lists. Data about the individual gathered over a period of time are more reliable and have more diagnostic and predictive value than a cross section of data taken at one time. These data will provide the individual with cumulative evidence about his abilities, interests, and attitudes.

OCCUPATIONAL INFORMATION

A second important service in a program of vocational guidance is concerned with making available to the counselee usable information about jobs and occupations. The information needed includes data on the importance of the occupation, the nature of the work, working conditions, personal qualities needed, preparation needed, opportunities for advancement, rate of pay, and advantages and disadvantages. Individuals seeking occupational information need to know about the general requirements of a group of occupations and to have specific information concerning a few occupations in which they are interested. Information of this type is used in carrying out vocational counseling and advisement and in planning training courses and educational programs.

Some of the occupational information needed by individuals is obtained by students in organized classes on occupations. These courses, classified as a form of group guidance, are taught by the school counselor or some other qualified person and are usually offered on the high school level. Students are encouraged to gather information concerning occupations in which they are interested and to participate in class discussions and individual reports on their findings. Adults who have achieved success in business enterprises in the community are invited to talk to students in the occupations class. Visual-aid equipment also provides a medium for conveying occupational information to interested individuals.

Occupational information may be obtained from many sources. A number of textbooks containing occupational information have been published in recent years. Many books suitable for use as references deal with specific groups of occupations, such as those in engineering, advertising, and metal trades. The *Dictionary of Occupational Titles*, published by the Bureau of Employment Security, U.S. Department of Labor contains descriptive information about many thousands of jobs. The Standard Industrial Classification (SIC) Manual published by the Bureau of the Budget, Executive Office of the President of the United States, lists names of establishments by industry. The U.S. Bureau of the Census publishes data at 10-year intervals and between census periods on various occupations in specified fields. Periodicals provide information on occupations. The *Personnel and Guidance Journal*, published by the American Personnel and Guidance Association, and the *Vocational Guidance Quarterly*, published by the National Vocational Guidance Association, provide information on requirements and trends in occupations as well as information on the functions of guidance. *Monthly Trends*, published by the U.S. Department of Labor, and the *Statistical Abstract of the United States*, published annually by the U.S. Department of Commerce, are also sources of occupational information.

The community occupational survey is frequently used as a technique for securing occupational information. The survey is designed to provide such information as the number of individuals employed in the various occupations and industries in the local community and the labor turnover, pay rate, training required, hours and shifts, and qualifications of workers and how they are recruited. The survey requires careful planning and the cooperative activity of many individuals. Important steps in making the survey include preparation and trial of all blank forms, selection and training of interviewers, organization and completion of field work, and analysis and use of data.

The various kinds of occupational information indicated above are useful only to the extent that they are readily available to the counselor and counselee. This suggests that some standard procedure for filing this information should be provided. If the occupational information is kept in the school library the librarian should be encouraged to obtain additional information and to make it easily accessible to students. Bulletin board announcements, displays and other devices may be used to call attention to the information available.

COUNSELING

A third guidance service, sometimes referred to as the heart of the guidance program, is counseling. This service is the process of helping an individual, through interviews and other individual relationships, to solve his problems and improve his planning. Counseling implies a situation involving two persons in which one known as the counselor gives a certain kind of assistance to the other—the counselee. Counseling is engaged in for the purpose of (1) assisting the individual in the interpretation of his personal data; (2) helping the individual in the identification of his major problems—vocational, educational, and personal; (3) assisting the individual in the planning of possible solutions to the problems; (4) helping the individual make a start towards carrying out his plans; and (5) providing assistance in necessary modifications of the plans.

Vocational counseling in the high school should reach all students, which means that interviews between students and counselors should be scheduled. A minimum program should make provision for each secondary school student to spend at least one hour each semester discussing problems with the counselor. This requires that a counselor have one hour free for counseling each day for every 75 students assigned to him. While some counseling is carried on by all classroom teachers, the specially trained vocational counselor should have major responsibility for the counseling of the student relative to educational, vocational, and personal problems and plans.

The counseling interview should be conducted at a time and place, and in a manner, that will give the student a favorable impression of the guidance program. This means a quiet, private, homelike place and sufficient time to avoid the appearance of haste. Counselors should make special preparation in advance for the interview. This requires that all the pertinent information about the counselee and his problem should be assembled or be readily available.

When the counselee appears for the interview, the first objective of the counselor should be to establish rapport. The friendliness of the counselor and his ability to use and understand the counselee's language will do much to establish this rapport. The counselee should be given a chance to talk and the counselor should listen attentively. As the counselee talks, the problem unfolds, and the solution is worked out by the counselee with such assistance in the nature of educational and occupational information as the counselor can provide. The interview should be terminated when it has reached a logical conclusion. The counselor should summarize the situation as it stands, should encourage the counselee to work towards the solution of the problem and should see to it that the individual feels that he is welcome to return to the counselor. This latter statement suggests that vocational counseling is not completed in one interview but may extend beyond the school into the adult life of the individual.

PLACEMENT AND FOLLOW-UP

A fourth essential service in a complete vocational guidance program is placement and follow-up. While there is some difference of opinion among educators relative to the extent of responsibility of the school, most persons agree that the service should be provided either by the school or some other agency such as the U.S. Employment Service. When other placement agencies are available, it is agreed that the school should cooperate with these agencies in the placement of school dropouts.

Placement is a process involving (1) preparation in which the individual is conditioned for the job, (2) induction into the new situation, and (3) encouragement on the job. This suggests that placement is not merely finding a job for an individual but is essentially an educational service concerned with making sure that youth are so placed that they will continue to develop on the job as they developed in school.

Preparation for placement involves conferences between the youth and the counselor in which information about the job is given, visits or contacts made with the employer, and reports made by the youth and the prospective employer to the placement officer. When youths are inducted into jobs, it is important that they consider themselves parts of the new situations from the outset and that they have successful experiences from the first. Good induction procedures involve a friendly reception, introduction to other workers and a clear assignment of duties, so that new employees know what is expected of them. Efficient plant or store supervisors give special attention to new employees from time to time during the early period of employment and encourage the worker and let him know how he is getting along. This process is continued until the worker is properly adjusted in his new environment.

Follow-up services are designed to help the youth make adjustments to his new environment and to take advantage of opportunities for advancement that may come his way. These adjustments are needed in connection with later placements, in connection with removing causes of dissatisfaction, for obtaining additional vocational preparation and during periods of prolonged unemployment. School counselors provide some of these services to youth, and civic organizations in some localities concern themselves with follow-up service to youth.

Some school systems conduct systematic follow-up studies of graduates and school dropouts. This is usually done by sending out questionnaires or interviewers to dropouts and employers. Information is secured at intervals of 1, 3, and 5 years. Some schools use prepared forms, such as those of the National Association of Secondary School Principals, for this purpose. Consideration should be given to the basic purpose of the study, the method of collection of data, the time of year, and the interpretation and use of data. Many educators realize that follow-up studies not only provide help for youth seeking jobs but also for staff members of the school in their efforts to discover youth needs and to maintain desirable contacts with the business world.

Vocational Guidance for Adults

When Dr. Parsons established the Vocation Bureau in 1908, many adults who had entered employment came to him for assistance in making life adjustments. A few years later responsibility for vocational guidance was for the most part shifted to local boards of education and incorporated in public school programs. This caused more public school students and fewer adults to avail themselves of guidance services, and guidance programs were organized for students in school. Recent follow-up studies of youth and increased interest in adult education programs have evidenced a need for more emphasis on adult counseling. As a result many communities have organized adult counseling centers operated by local school systems, in cooperation with various civic agencies of the community. Public school counselors in some of the Federally aided programs have organized vocational guidance services for adults.

THE NEED FOR ADULT GUIDANCE

Each year thousands of youth leave school, either at graduation or before graduation, and seek employment in agriculture, business, and industry. Many of these individuals find employment in the unskilled trades and are in need of guidance to assist them in planning educational programs that will prepare them for better positions. Some youth who leave school fail to find employment and, as a result, develop a sense of insecurity which may lead to serious problems of mental health. These also are in need of guidance.

The technological changes in agriculture and industry require new knowledge and skill, and the worker who expects to achieve success must be constantly planning new programs of vocational education designed to provide him with new knowledge and skill. A study of adult interests made in 1947 indicated that more than 2 out of every 5 adults were interested in taking courses in adult education. A program of guidance is needed to insure that this apparent interest in adult education may be utilized to the best advantage.

Many young adults needed the services of a vocational counselor in leaving a job that has become undesirable. Some adults remain on a job when it would be to their advantage to change to another job that offers greater possibilities for advancement. Fear of a change, timidity, unwillingness to take a chance, and ignorance of how to make the change may prevent a capable individual from advancing to a more desirable position. A vocational counselor can provide the information and encouragement needed to help the individual make the desired change.

Young and adult workers sometimes develop real or imaginary grievances which interfere with their usefulness and which may result in an undesirable change of position. An experienced counselor may assist the worker to face the facts squarely and remove the causes of dissatisfaction. Adult workers need help in planning the use of leisure time. The shorter work day and week provide additional time for the adult to engage in recreational, cultural and community service activities. Many of these activities are related to the vocational success of the worker, and a helpful counselor may not only render a service to the individual but to the community as well.

GUIDANCE SERVICES NEEDED FOR ADULTS

Vocational guidance services needed for young adults and adults are similar to those needed for school students. Differences exist in some procedures, due to differences between in-school youth and adults. Adults need an opportunity to receive counsel and encouragement in dealing with problems of a personal, social or vocational nature. They also need access to complete and up-to-date information on occupational opportunities, educational requirements, and available opportunities for education and training.

The adult counseling program should include a testing clinic for adults who need and desire this service. The use of modern measuring devices, especially for young adults who did not have an opportunity to obtain this service in school, may lead to better motivation and adjustment. A central placement service is needed in the adult counseling program. Where other employment agencies are available, the principal function of the central placement service within the school may be that of cooperation with the other agencies. This service may also undertake follow-up studies of young workers as a means of providing information for occupational adjustment and for counseling other young workers.

An important service that may be undertaken by the staff of the vocational guidance agency for adults is that of sponsoring a vocational survey and a youth survey in the local community. These activities require cooperation among community agencies and provide information for better community planning. They also encourage the coordination of the activities of various community organizations interested in youth problems.

ORGANIZATIONS FOR ADULT GUIDANCE

The organizations for adult guidance have taken many forms since Parsons established the Boston Vocation Bureau. Vocation bureaus have been maintained in some cities. Pasadena, California, for example, organized a bureau in 1919 to provide vocational placement and counseling service, first for women and later for men and boys as well. The bureau was first supported by donations and voluntary memberships. The bureau from 1921 to 1938 was supported by the Pasadena Community Chest. In the meantime, as a result of Federal legislation, the vocation bureau, municipal employment office for men and municipal employment office for women merged to establish the Pasadena Employment and Vocations Bureau. This Bureau in 1938 affiliated with the California State Department of Employment of the U.S. Employment Service.

Adult Counseling is an Important Service of the State-Federal Employment Security Division. These applicants for jobs are taking a general aptitude test for use in counseling. (Arkansas Department of Labor, Employment Security Division)

The State-Federal Employment Security Agencies have maintained an extensive guidance counseling and testing program since the early 1930s. This program in the depression years of the 1930s was concerned primarily with a junior placement service for youth. Since World War II the various agencies have provided guidance services to all persons in the labor force who are in need of such services. The total number of counseling interviews increased from 1,311,000 in 1952 to 2,020,000 in 1962. The number of standard tests administered by these agencies increased from 250,000 in 1952 to 800,000 in 1962. The counseling program in 1962 included 3120 counselors in 1900 offices throughout the United States. The U.S. Veterans Administration, through its guidance centers, provides a large-scale guidance program for adults. During the 10-year period ending in 1953, the Veterans Administration furnished vocational guidance to about 2,300,-000 veterans of World War II and the Korean conflict. Demonstration centers sponsored by interested groups with funds supplied by private foundations, have further demonstrated the feasibility of adult counseling.

Much of the vocational guidance service for adults is provided in vocational evening and part-time classes. The class instructor usually serves as teacher and counselor. Frequently, because of a lack of time or training, the counseling is inadequate and unorganized. Individual data and occupational information are not available or not properly used. For this reason, some local boards of education are employing qualified counselors to supplement the guidance services provided by the vocational teachers. These counselors assist teachers in discovering the problems and needs of the adult students, in planning course content, in acquiring skills in counseling and in enrolling adults. The counselors assist adult students to secure needed information about occupations.

The public school system is in a good position among community agencies to provide services in vocational guidance to all interested adults. The public schools have personal data on many young adults, and many local schools have student counseling services that can be extended to include adult counseling. Then, too, the organization of public education affords a satisfactory method of financing adult guidance programs. The Baltimore, Maryland, public school system organized an adult guidance program in 1945. This program, known as the Information and Counseling Service for Adults, was first organized for war veterans but has been made available to any adult in the community. Counseling services for adults are provided 5 days a week throughout the year and variously from 2 to 4 evenings a week at 18 locations throughout the city during the school session. The counselor for adults offers counseling services in educational and occupational areas, and information about vocations, schools and colleges. Adults who come to the counselor with personal, financial, and social problems that are beyond the scope of the adult counseling service are referred to other community agencies that can meet their needs.

The duties of the adult counselor include counseling and advisement; collecting and organizing occupational information; and maintaining a reference library of college catalogues, educational directories, school bulletins, and recreational and cultural programs. He provides information about testing services and refers adults who desire to take aptitude, intelligence, or interests tests to testing bureaus maintained by the public schools and other community and state agencies. The counselor also maintains a cumulative record and a follow-up service for each counselee. The annual reports of the counselor indicate that for the period 1958 to 1963 the counselor conducted somewhat less than 1000 interviews annually. In addition, the adult counselor has made many telephone calls and has written a number of letters concerned with problems of vocational guidance for adults.[5]

ADVISORY COUNCILS

Local school authorities who have assumed responsibility for providing vocational counseling for the adults of the community have found it desirable to organize advisory councils to assist the professional staff of the guidance program. Such a council is especially needed where there are many community organizations engaged in some form of guidance and counseling and where the school is attempting to provide some form of coordination for the guidance services of the various agencies.

The Fort Smith, Arkansas, Community Advisory Committee provided an example of the organization and functions of an advisory council for adult guidance programs. This committee, organized in 1944, was composed of representatives from 34 community organizations, each of which was engaged in guidance activities of some form. The organization included civic clubs, luncheon clubs, church groups, veterans and war service organizations, welfare groups, women's clubs, and various youth organizations. Each of the organizations, at the request of the local superintendent of schools, appointed a representative to a community meeting called for the purpose of discussing problems involved in coordinating vocational guidance activities.[6]

The Baltimore Public schools had an advisory council in the early phases of the adult counseling program but in recent years the guidance and placement staff has been able to establish satisfactory relations with business, industry, and social and educational agencies and institutions without a formal council. The placement service has proved to be an effective means of communication between the school and the various cooperating agencies.

The advisory council for the vocational guidance program is a means not only of securing information and advice from the public,

[5] Baltimore Public Schools, *Annual Report of the Information and Counseling Service for Adults for the Fiscal Year Ending June 30, 1955*, supplemented by information from the director of the Division of Guidance and Placement, Baltimore Public Schools, 1963.

[6] J. Fred Patton, "The Community Adult Counseling Service of Fort Smith, Arkansas," *Occupations*, February, 1945, pp. 275–278.

but it also stimulates lay people to learn more about the organization and operation of the guidance program. Most educational reforms have originated with lay people, and because of the many unusual aspects of a vocational guidance program for adults it is essential that some means be maintained for securing advice and counsel from local citizens in effecting coordination of community guidance activities.

QUESTIONS FOR STUDY AND DISCUSSION

1. Describe the organization of the Boston Vocation Bureau.
2. Indicate the factors involved in vocational counseling suggested by Dr. Frank Parsons.
3. Describe some of the first programs of vocational guidance organized in the public schools of the United States.
4. What changes have occurred in concepts of vocational guidance since the beginning of the guidance program in 1908?
5. Discuss the organization and development of the NDEA guidance, counseling and testing program.
6. What are the requirements for and limitations on the use of Federal funds for reimbursing expenditures incurred in the guidance program on the state and local levels?
7. What are the educational, personal, and experience qualifications suggested for vocational counselors in the public schools?
8. What is the purpose of the individual inventory, and what kinds of information are included in the inventory?
9. What kinds of occupational information are needed by counselees, and how may the vocational counselors obtain this information?
10. What is the purpose of counseling, and what techniques are needed in conducting the interview?
11. What information is needed as a preparation for placement, and how may follow-up information be obtained?
12. Indicate some evidences of a need for vocational guidance for adults, and describe some types of organizations for adult counseling.

SOURCE REFERENCES

Baltimore Public Schools, Department of Guidance and Placement, *The Program of Guidance and Placement*, Baltimore, 1953.

Bloomfield, Meyer, *The Vocational Guidance of Youth*, Houghton Mifflin, Boston, 1911.

Brewer, John M., *History of Vocational Guidance*, Harper & Row, New York, 1942.

Humphreys, J. Anthony, and Arthur E. Traxler, *Guidance Services*, Science Research, Chicago, 1954.

Keller, Franklin J., *Principles of Vocational Education,* Boston, 1948.

Klein, Paul E., and Ruth E. Moffitt, *Counseling Techniques in Adult Education,* McGraw-Hill, New York, 1946.

Mathewson, Robert H., *Guidance Policy and Practice,* Harper & Row, New York, 1962.

Moser, Leslie E. and Ruth Small Moser, *Counseling and Guidance: An Exploration,* Prentice-Hall, Englewood Cliffs, N.J., 1963.

Parsons, Frank, *Choosing a Vocation,* Houghton Mifflin, Boston, 1909.

Robinson, Francis P., *Principles and Procedures in Student Counseling,* Harper & Row, New York, 1950.

Shartle, Carroll L., *Occupational Information,* Prentice-Hall, Englewood Cliffs, N.J., 1952.

Traxler, Arthur E., *Techniques of Guidance,* Harper & Row, New York, 1957.

U.S. Department of Health, Education, and Welfare, Office of Education, *Report on the National Defense Education Act, Fiscal Years 1961 and 1962,* Washington, D.C.

U.S. Department of the Interior, Bureau of Education, *Vocational Guidance,* Bulletin 1914, No. 14, Washington, D.C., 1914.

Zeran, Franklin R. and Anthony C. Riccio, *Organization and Administration of Guidance Services,* Rand McNally, Chicago, 1962.

CHAPTER FOURTEEN

TECHNICAL EDUCATION

The higher institutions for many years have educated engineers, doctors, lawyers, agriculturalists, home economists, and other workers for the professions. The public vocational schools during the past forty years have provided workers for industry, farming, wholesale and retail selling, homemaking, and other occupations. In more recent times a need has developed for workers educated in occupations that require both technical knowledge and skills of a different nature from those needed by either tradesmen, professional engineers, scientists, or other professional workers. This area of work is known as technical occupations and workers in these occupations are termed technicians, laboratory assistants, production supervisors and other similar titles.

The demand for workers educated for technical occupations has increased greatly during the past few years, and educational programs in schools, colleges, and industry have been developed to meet this need. The programs take the form of full-time pre-employment training, supplementary training in evening and part-time classes, part-time cooperative programs, on-the-job training, and home study courses. These programs are offered in various occupational fields such as agriculture, business, health, homemaking, industry, and public service. Most of these programs that are under public supervision and control and are of less than baccalaureate degree level meet the requirements for Federal aid under the provisions of the national vocational education acts. A discussion of some of the more important aspects of technical education is included in this chapter.

Characteristics of and Need for Technical Education

The term *technical education* is not generally understood nor is it easily defined. It is used in some areas and in some nations to designate vocational industrial education at various grade levels ranging from elementary to college and at various degrees of skill from semi-skilled occupations to vocations classified as professions. The recent changes in the industrial economy and Federal legislation concerned with vocational education has brought about some uniformity in the understanding of technical education among vocational educators in the United States. Some definitions have appeared and some of its characteristics have been delineated both of which are designed to bring about a common understanding of technical education.

Community Colleges are Increasing their Offerings in Technical Education. This electronics technology student is troubleshooting a modular frequency standard. (Joe U. Davenport, Monroe Community College, Rochester, New York)

CHARACTERISTICS OF TECHNICAL EDUCATION

All occupations require the use of some manipulative skills and the application of some technical knowledge. The quantity and quality of each vary with the specific occupation. The professions, for example, require the extensive use of technical knowledge as well as some manipulative skill. Some occupations, especially those concerned with the design, manufacture, sale, installation, and servicing of a wide variety of products, require more manipulative skill and less technical knowledge than are required in the professions. These occupations are found in industry, business, agriculture, research, and service occupations. They are referred to as technical occupations and these workers are called technicians.

Most definitions of technicians include a listing of characteristics and duties of the workers. Dr. Lynn A. Emerson suggests that the technician is "A person who works at a job which requires applied technical knowledge and applied technical skill. His work in this respect is somewhat akin to that of the engineer, but usually the scope is narrower. His job also requires some manipulative skills—those necessary to handle properly the tools and instruments needed to perform the technical tasks.

"In his special field he has considerable technical knowledge of industrial processes and in this field he knows how to apply the necessary principles of the physical sciences and of mathematics. In general he uses instruments in contrast with tools. His contribution is mainly through mental effort in contrast with muscular exertion."[1]

This definition suggests that technical education is designed to prepare persons for, or upgrade them in, occupations for which graduation from a 4-year college is not required. Jobs that require specific knowledge and skill in such job operations as planning and control, operation and maintenance, testing and production, and supervision are in the technical area. A technical education program is a terminal program not preparatory to a college degree but geared to meet the needs of industry, business, agriculture, homemaking, and other vocations. Technical education programs vary in length from a single unit course of a few weeks to an integrated program operating on a part-time basis for several years. Pre-employment programs are usually from one to three years in length. These programs are available at various grade levels ranging from grade ten to grade fourteen with most programs at the junior college or grades thirteen and fourteen levels.

Technical education programs are especially effective for young adults and most other technical education students are quite mature

[1] Lynn A. Emerson, *Industrial Education in a Changing Democratic Society*, New York State College of Industrial and Labor Relations, Cornell University, Ithaca, 1955, p. 91.

in attitudes. Admission and graduation requirements in these programs are less formal than general educational programs although most pre-employment programs, as well as some in-service programs of technical education, require high school graduation as a prerequisite for entrance into the program.

Methods of teaching technical education courses emphasize shop and laboratory skills, field work and actual performance on the job, as well as book study. Individualized instruction, home study, and small classes with extended opportunities for individual progress are important characteristics of the program. Teachers of technical education programs are chosen primarily on the basis of practical experience and technical knowledge. Many teachers of technical education courses are taken directly from industry on a part-time basis. In-service teacher education programs are developed to upgrade these teachers in teaching methods and materials.

FACTORS AFFECTING TECHNICAL EDUCATION

Many factors have been responsible for the development of technical education. Among these are technological developments in industry, impacts of war, increases in the initial employment age, larger high school enrollments, and increasing interest in adult education. Technological development is on the increase. Scientists, engineers, technicians, and skilled workers have been developing new materials, processes, and products during the years. These discoveries and inventions have improved levels of living and reduced by mechanization much of the drudgery of hand work. The manufacture and use of many of these new processes and products have required workers and operators with new knowledges and skills somewhat different from those obtained heretofore in either trade or professional courses. These new knowledges and skills have been in the area of technical education.

Industry and business are requiring that youth begin their first employment at a more advanced age. This trend has been observed for several decades. It was interrupted during the last war due to a shortage of manpower, but the trend has been resumed now that war needs have been met. Many industries that formerly employed 16- to 18-year olds now have a minimum age of 19 or 20. Inquiries among employers and labor leaders have revealed that it is becoming increasingly difficult for a youth to secure any type of position except in a messenger service or other juvenile occupation before he has reached

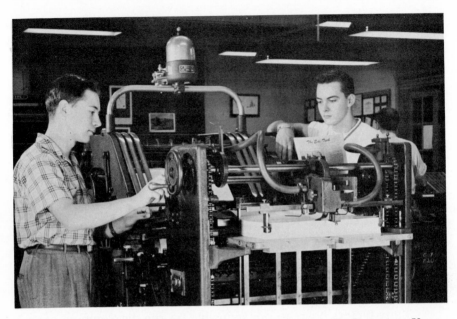

Modern Industry Requires the Services of Many Technicians. Vocational schools throughout the nation are preparing young workers for many positions in the graphic arts. (Edison Technical and Industrial High School, Rochester, New York)

the age of 20 or 21. Many employers will employ only those younger workers who are above the average in maturity for their age. These and other factors have caused youth who do not attend college to enroll in post-high school technical courses as a means of increasing their employability and insuring progress in their occupation.

Adults are becoming more interested in educational programs. Recent studies have shown that adults are interested in both vocational and general education. This increased interest is partly due to changes in the requirements of the occupations in which adults are employed. New technological developments require new skills. Ordinarily these must be acquired by employed workers, especially if the new content is not so extensive as to make training on the job impractical. The rising trend in the educational level of all citizens, especially noticeable in recent years, has made adults more conscious of the need for both general and vocational courses. Many men and women attended some type of courses while in the armed services, and these courses generated an interest in further training when they returned to civilian life. All these influences have brought about an increased interest among adults in technical training.

THE NEED FOR TECHNICAL EDUCATION

The need for technicians, laboratory assistants, testers, supervisors, inspectors, and other technical workers is evident in many occupational fields. The more important areas of need are in industry, business, agriculture, health, home economics and public service. A brief discussion of the important needs in each of these fields is presented below.

Industry. The need for technical workers is more evident in industry than in other occupational fields. A recent study made by the Bureau of Labor Statistics for the National Science Foundation indicated that there were about 594,000 technicians in American industry in 1960.[2] This was an increase of 8 percent over the comparable figure for 1959. The study indicates that about 1 million technicians will be needed in industry by 1970. The ratio of technicians to scientists and engineers is difficult to determine because of differences of definition. Variations in this ratio also occur among different industries. In general it is estimated that there will be a need for about two technicians for each scientist or engineer in the immediate future.

Industry uses some workers with professional engineering degrees for jobs that normally require workers with technical training. Professional engineers are used for these jobs because technicians are not available and engineers more nearly meet the requirements of the positions than other workers. Since the technician may be educated in about one-half the time required for engineers it is evident that this is not an efficient use of manpower. Some of the more important industrial occupations in which technical workers are needed include: (1) engineering aides and science aides requiring one or two years of pre-employment training; (2) inspectors, who may be trained in relatively short pre-employment courses; (3) production and maintenance supervisors who need background experience and technical training on the job; and (4) technical salesmen and factory accountants, who need technical training along with other vocational or professional training.

Business. Many business occupations require supplementary technical knowledge of the industry and its products in addition to special business information. The sale and distribution of building

[2] U.S. Department of Health, Education, and Welfare, Office of Education, *Education For a Changing World of Work, Appendix I, Technical Training in the United States,* Washington, D.C., 1963, p. 30.

materials, fuels, clothing, household appliances, farm products, and many other items require technical information for effective selling. Accountants and auditors frequently must have a knowledge of the plant and its products if they are to be successful in their occupation. The business field also needs a type of technical training for advanced secretarial positions requiring specialized knowledge of related fields such as law, medicine, insurance, transportation and communications.

Semiprofessional or technical education is needed in retail and wholesale operations, including such specialized fields as advertising and display, unit control, credit and collections, and in the management of service businesses such as laundries, hotels, and restaurants. In the general business field a specialized knowledge of modern business appliances and practices is needed. The operation of specialized office machines, such as the teletype, the key punch machine, and the card tabulating machine, requires special knowledge and skill. Accounting in specialized fields, such as insurance, banking, taxation and manufacturing, also requires technical knowledge.

Agriculture. Technological advances in agriculture have brought about an increasing need for technical workers. Many agricultural occupations for which little or no training was formerly needed now require workers with special knowledge and skill. Agricultural technicians are needed for managing specialized farming operations such as dairy farms, poultry farms, commercial orchards, and vegetable farms. They are needed for specialized occupations in these operations, such as that of herd superintendent, livestock breeder, broiler plant operator, hatchery manager, supervisor of processing plant, plant breeder, machinery operator, and plant and animal protection technologist. Various government agencies concerned with agricultural adjustment, soil conservation, agricultural marketing, food and feed inspection, livestock sanitation, animal disease and insect control, and farm credit require the services of many inspectors, estimators, surveyors, crops reporters and forecasters, laboratory technicians, classifiers and supervisors.

A number of technicians are needed in agricultural industries such as feed manufacturing plants, dairy supply houses, milk plants, commercial hatcheries, meat packing plants, canning plants, fertilizer manufacturing plants, farm supply and equipment houses, frozen food industries, refrigeration and storage plants, fungicide and insecticide manufacturing plants, plant nurseries, and landscape service firms. Studies indicate that there are very few institutions and agencies engaged in the education of technical workers in agricultural occupations and that the demand for agricultural technicians will continue to increase.

Health. Many technicians are needed to protect and improve the health of the people of the nation. Among these are medical technicians, dental technicians, physical therapy aides, laboratory technicians, x-ray technicians, practical nurses, nurses' aides, and hospital and clinic assistants. These technicians assist in making various kinds of medical and health tests, in keeping medical and health records, in assisting professional workers in the hospitals, clinics and public health centers, and in caring for indigent and disabled persons in the homes of the patients.

The people of the nation have become more conscious of the need for improved health services in recent years. This increased interest has resulted in more extensive public health and sanitation programs, as well as improved services by physicians, surgeons, dentists, and other medical personnel. Physicians and other health workers are realizing that their efficiency and extent of service may be increased by the use of properly qualified technicians to perform many of the services formerly undertaken by these professional workers. This increased use of technicians, together with the increase in the population of the nation, indicates that increasing numbers of technical health workers will be needed in the future.

Home economics. The vocation of homemaking, together with the other occupations related to and necessary for successful home and family living, requires the services of large numbers of technical workers. These workers are needed in the areas of home management, food preparation and preservation, family relations, and child care. Special knowledge and skill are needed in the selection of home furnishings, interior decoration; selection, preparation, and serving of food for various numbers of people on various occasions; the counseling of youth and adults, and the proper guidance of children.

Successful homemaking requires that the husband and wife make many joint decisions. For example, the management of the family income, the selection of food and clothing, the maintenance of family health, family recreation and home improvement are types of problems that require joint decisions. Some of these decisions are more intelligently made if the husband and wife possess technical information concerned with the problem. Present-day vocational education programs are providing some of this information. There is an evident need for more technical information than can be provided with the present personnel and facilities in the vocational education program. Some consideration in planning future programs should be given to this need in homemaking education.

Public service. Public service occupations are those maintained at public expense for the benefit of the general public. Among the more important are those concerned with public administration, education, health protection and safety, fire prevention and fire protection, crime prevention and law enforcement, correctional work, licensing, recording, tax collecting, public utility operation, public works development, conservation, and public welfare. Some of the occupations listed in public service are classified as professional and some as trades. However, many of them have the characteristics of technical occupations in that they require some technical information and limited trade skills. It is expected that all these occupations will require more and more technical knowledge as time goes on.

Public service workers have been offered few opportunities for vocational education when compared to workers in other occupational fields. Most of the programs of vocational education for public service workers have been those concerned with fire prevention. Some few programs have been established in law enforcement, public utility operation, custodial work, and health services. These programs for the most part have been short courses for employed workers rather than pre-employment courses for prospective employees. These programs are as a rule confined to the larger cities and frequently even in the cities are limited to a small number of vocations. There is a need for technical education programs for a variety of public service occupations. An expansion of technical education programs for public service will provide more efficient workers for the many public service occupations supported by public taxation.

Present Programs and Facilities
for Technical Education

A variety of institutions provide education for technical occupations, but the range of courses and the number of students enrolled fall short of the needs in this field. Technical courses are offered in junior colleges, technical institutes, engineering schools, state and area schools, and technical high schools. Some of these institutions, together with other special schools, offer correspondence courses in technical education. Technical education programs are also offered through trade associations and in industry. These courses are offered in both public and private institutions. Brief descriptions of the organization and programs of technical education in some of the more important institutions under public supervision and control are given below.

JUNIOR COLLEGE PROGRAMS

Three types of curriculums are usually provided in junior colleges. These are (1) curriculums that follow the first 2 years of a 4-year college program; (2) general education curriculums of a terminal nature; and (3) vocational education of a terminal nature, including technical education curriculums. The terminal curriculums are widely used in junior colleges, and their use is increasing as more and more high school graduates desire to continue their education before entering employment. These curriculums in junior colleges are designed primarily for pre-employment training, and most of them are full-time, 2-year programs. Junior colleges frequently award a degree or diploma referred to as the Associate in Science or the Associate in Arts upon the satisfactory completion of the curriculum requirements.

Junior colleges of both public and private types are a recent innovation in the United States. The number of junior colleges increased from 52 in 1920 to 509 in 1960. The junior colleges in 1960 had an enrollment of 403,000 students, of which 86 percent were in publicly controlled colleges and 14 percent in private institutions. Some of the public junior colleges are organized as branches of state universities or state colleges and some as state-operated, independent colleges. Local school districts or municipalities operate a considerable number of the junior colleges, and some are operated by two or more school districts for the benefit of the students in these districts. Some of the junior colleges operated as a part of the public school system are organized on the basis of four years of instruction, two of which are on the eleventh- and twelfth-grade levels. Other junior colleges as a rule require high school graduation as a prerequisite to entrance.

Most of the technical education curriculums in junior colleges are in the industrial fields. Some of the more common pre-employment technical education curriculums in industrial education offered in junior colleges include petroleum technology, electrical technology, radio and television, mechanical drafting, hotel and restaurant management, industrial technology, and aviation technology. Some vocational technical courses are offered by junior colleges in other occupational fields, and there is an indication of an increased trend in junior college offerings in technical education.

TECHNICAL INSTITUTE PROGRAMS

The technical institute is perhaps more directly concerned with technical education than any of the other institutions in which technical curriculums are offered. The technical institute is usually operated as a separate school, but sometimes it is administered by the board of control of a public school system. The technical institute usually operates at the post-high school level with some institutes providing specialized training in grades eleven and twelve. The principal objective of the technical institute is to educate men and women for occupations that require specialized knowledge supplemented by a broad understanding of operational procedures. Some technical institutes operate day school programs only and some operate evening programs only, but most of the institutes offer both day and evening programs.

The technical institute program differs from the technical education program in the junior college in a number of respects. The admission and graduation requirements of the technical institute are less formal and the methods of instruction are more direct than those of the junior college. The scheme of instruction of the technical institute follows more closely the actual usage of industry and agriculture than that of the other technical education institutions. There is greater variation in the lengths of the courses in the institutes than in the colleges, with most of the institute day courses extending for shorter periods.

AREA VOCATIONAL SCHOOLS

Many technical curriculums are included in the emerging area vocational schools. These schools as a rule are located in the less populous areas. They serve an attendance area larger than the traditional high school and the larger area enables these schools to offer a variety of specialized curriculums. The area schools have a diversity of administrative control, financial structure, and course offerings. The course offerings usually include vocational industrial as well as technical courses. The schools offer both day school and evening school classes for preservice and in-service students. Some area schools offer extension classes in nearby centers. Many area schools provide school transportation for enrollees and residence halls are included in the physical plant of some area schools.

TECHNICAL HIGH SCHOOL PROGRAMS

The technical high school is usually a dual purpose institution with both college preparatory and vocational objectives. Some so-called technical high schools offer little more than a general high school program with courses in industrial arts. Technical high school programs

Many Technical Students are Enrolled in Data Processing Courses. This student is learning to operate a key-punch machine. (Public Schools, Vocational Division, Little Rock, Arkansas)

are commonly three or four years in length, beginning at either the ninth- or tenth-grade level. Some four-year technical high schools provide four years of training beginning with the tenth grade. Students from these institutions who elect college preparatory courses may be admitted to advanced standing when they enter college. Some technical high schools operate as separate institutions, but most of them are organized as a part of the public school system.

Students are admitted to the technical high school usually upon the completion of either the eighth or ninth grade. Some technical high schools are highly selective and admit only a limited number of students each year. Factors involved in the selection of these students are scholastic record in previous school courses, recommendations of school officials and other citizens, entrance examinations, and aptitude tests. These selective institutions admit only students who show high promise of successful completion.

Most technical high schools operate classes for out-of-school youth and adults in addition to the day school classes. These out-of-school classes are organized primarily for employed workers, usually young adults who desire to increase their employability. Some of the classes are organized on the cooperative plan whereby enrollees work part time and attend classes part time during the working day, week, and month. The evening class courses are organized on a unit basis and are offered in a specified sequence to enable a student to qualify for a technical occupation upon the completion of the series of unit courses.

EXTENSION AND CORRESPONDENCE STUDY PROGRAMS

Extension and correspondence courses organized to assist persons to prepare for or progress in technical occupations are offered by public and private schools and colleges. Most of the universities have extension divisions that provide class instruction in various extension centers and public schools throughout a state. The extension centers are usually located in towns or cities some distance from the parent institution where the need for these courses is evident. The extension center facilities may include laboratories, a library, a dormitory, and conference and assembly rooms.

Technical courses offered in extension centers include machine design, structural design, heating and refrigeration, meteorology and navigation, blueprint reading, sheet metal drafting, fundamentals of electricity, alternating current theory, and electronic laboratory. Extension classes are also provided in agriculture, business, and other occupations such as animal husbandry, farm management, poultry keeping, and flower growing. Some of the courses are arranged in sequence to extend over a four-year period with class meetings scheduled for one or two evenings a week. A certificate of proficiency is usually given to each student who successfully completes the series.

Technical education appears to be especially suited to home study because much of the technical content involves basic sciences and applied technology which may be acquired from home study courses.

Many persons are unable because of economic and personal reasons to attend day school and extension classes. They are willing to engage in home study, and the wide variety of home study courses enables these persons to select a course or series of courses in which they are interested. Correspondence courses of a technical nature are available for industrial workers, social workers, agriculturalists, businessmen, and homemakers. Course offerings include a wide range of subject matter similar to the course offerings of the day schools. Some courses consist of relatively few lessons, while others may involve 1200 to 1500 hours of study. The maintenance of high standards of achievement is an especially important consideration in home study programs. The National Home Study Council, which was organized to promote high standards and ethical practices in this field, has been instrumental in improving home study programs.

Planning and Organizing the Technical Education Program

The success of any program of technical education is dependent in a large measure on the manner in which it is planned and organized. New or expanded programs have their beginnings in the minds of interested individuals. Frequently, these individuals are school administrators who through various other individuals are led to see a need and an opportunity. The first task of the educational leader is to secure the assistance of interested groups in the community or area. These groups should include representatives of industry, business, agriculture, homemaking, and education. The next step is the appointment of an advisory committee composed of some of the representatives of the above groups. The advisory committee, together with other interested leaders, should plan the other activities concerned with the organization of the technical education program. These include: (1) making industrial surveys to determine need, (2) making surveys of available educational facilities, (3) determining desirable administrative patterns, (4) constructing curriculums and determining plant and equipment needs, (5) establishing standards for personnel, and (6) obtaining financial support and initiating the program. The sequence in which these activities are undertaken may vary from that suggested above, and some of the suggested steps may be determined by circumstances. For example, it may be necessary to adapt a technical education program to a previously established administrative pattern. The selection of an advisory committee is usually the first step in planning the survey.

THE ORGANIZATION OF THE ADVISORY COMMITTEE

The planning and organization of a technical education program require that consideration be given to many factors which arise out of community needs and resources. Advisory committees consisting of representatives of management and labor from the various occupational fields concerned, together with educators, have increased the effectiveness of the planning and organizational procedures in technical education. Some communities may have a general vocational education advisory committee that may be used in planning and organizing technical education programs. It may be neceessary in other communities to establish a special advisory committee for technical education.

The advisory committee for technical education should have representatives from all vitally interested groups including labor, management, and education. The primary function of the advisory committee is counseling and advising school authorities responsible for planning and organizing the technical education program. The committee should make recommendations concerning such factors as (1) training needs and possibilities, including placement opportunities; (2) types and kinds of curriculums and course content; (3) qualifications of instructors and other personnel; (4) housing, equipment, and supply requirements; (5) production work in school shops; (6) public relations and publicity; (7) program evaluation; and (8) recruiting, counseling, and guidance of students.

The manner in which the members of the advisory committees are designated may have an important effect on the usefulness of the committee. One approved method of selecting the committee members is for the school authority to request in writing that each interested organization or association nominate several of its members to serve as representatives. The school authority may then select from these nominees the number of representatives needed. A representative of the school should be designated for each advisory committee. Some school authorities appoint alternates for each regular member to insure official representation at each meeting. The usual procedure is for the school authority to notify the members by official letter of their appointment.

The school authority should preside at the first meeting of the committee, at which time the duties and responsibilities of the advisory committee should be discussed and agreed upon. The fact that advisory committees do not have administrative authority should be stressed. A permanent chairman and a secretary should be elected by the members of the committee. The school representative may serve as secretary for the purpose of keeping the minutes and preparing agenda for the meetings. The agenda should be sent to each member far enough in advance of the meeting to permit consideration and study of the topics to be discussed. This will enable the members to secure pertinent information and advice and to be better prepared to participate in the committee discussions. It is important to acquaint the members of the committee with the technical education program as a whole and its relation to other educational and community programs.

DETERMINING COMMUNITY NEEDS

The specific needs for technical education vary among different communities, and it is necessary to determine the specific needs of each community. Occupational surveys are frequently used to determine these needs. A community occupational survey is defined as an organized method of obtaining a comprehensive body of information concerning the occupational life of the region. It involves a listing of the various jobs, the qualifications and needs of the workers, the training facilities, and the employment opportunities. Surveys may be made of all industries or of a single industry. They may include all cases or a sampling. No one pattern or method is best for all communities. Specific objectives, community size, and facilities available determine the particular method to use.

All occupational surveys require that some data be collected, tabulated, studied, and interpreted. The usefulness of the survey may be limited by the techniques and methods used in collecting and interpreting the data. While no one procedure may be used in all situations, it is possible to outline some general procedures for making the survey. These general procedures involve the following: (1) the selection of a person for organizing and directing the study, (2) the determination of the kinds of information needed, (3) the collection of the facts, (4) the selection of the facts that have an important bearing on the problem, (5) the interpretation of the facts, and (6) the development of the report including recommendations brought out in the survey.

Community or area occupational surveys are planned by the local school authority with the assistance of the advisory committee. Frequently, community organizations such as the chamber of commerce, trade associations, or luncheon clubs are called upon to serve with the community educational institutions as sponsors of the survey. Their principal function is to assist in keeping the public informed concerning the plans and the progress of the survey. Various types of special committees selected by the school authority with the assistance of the advisory committee provide effective leadership in making the survey. Leadership in determining the general survey policies and in initiating the action program should be delegated to a general steering committee. Working committees should be appointed with responsibility for following the survey procedures and techniques outlined by the steering committee for collecting and interpreting the data. A committee for tabulating the data and a publicity committee should be appointed. The results of the survey should be made available in report form to all interested persons. The results should be used by the school authority with the advice and counsel of the advisory committee to arrive at decisions and procedures concerning types of programs and curriculums in technical education.

When it is not feasible to make a comprehensive occupational survey, the school authority may obtain some information necessary for planning a technical education program from an informal survey. This type of survey consists of a variety of devices or techniques for determining whether or not training is needed in a specific occupation. These include such items as complaints from employers relative to shortcomings of employees, rapid expansion of a special industry, help-wanted advertisements for certain types of skilled workers, and conferences with employers and others relative to needs. When some indications of need are manifested, the school authority should present these to the advisory committee and with their help devise a technical education program to meet these needs.

PLANNING PROGRAMS AND FACILITIES

The occupational survey will reveal the occupations in which training is needed and the type of training—pre-employment or supplementary—required. An educational survey is then made to determine the present facilities available for giving the training. The data of these two surveys are used to determine the types of programs needed and the patterns of organization and administration required to establish and conduct the technical education program. The educational survey may suggest two or three feasible plans for the organization and administration of the program. For example, the program may be organized within the administrative framework of the local public school system, as a separate technical institute or as a junior college.

Technical education in small communities is expensive and often difficult to justify. It may be feasible to develop some technical curriculums in nearby secondary schools at grade levels thirteen and fourteen. Area vocational schools with technical curriculums are frequently located to serve rural areas. If the transportation facilities are adequate the students who attend the area schools may live at home; otherwise, it will be necessary to provide residence halls for the technical education students who reside in nearby rural areas. Business and industrial concerns may assist in financing technical schools or may provide scholarships to enable rural youth to become technicians.

The plant and equipment needs for programs of technical education should be determined by the types of curriculums and courses of study. This suggests that courses should first be planned, and then the equipment and facilities needed should be selected to meet the needs of the courses. Special care should be taken in the selection of equipment. Some types of equipment retain their usefulness for many years. This is especially true of equipment needed in teaching basic sciences. Specialized equipment may become obsolete in a relatively short time. Provision should be made for periodic replacement of equipment that has become obsolete. Frequently, the student load on equipment used in technical education programs is relatively low, and this means high unit costs, a fact which should be taken into account in planning these programs.

PERSONNEL FOR TECHNICAL EDUCATION

The most important factor affecting the success of a technical education program is the personnel employed to administer, supervise, and teach in the program. Well-qualified personnel can overcome many plant and equipment deficiencies, but the best of plants and equipment can never make up for inefficient teachers and other staff members. The number and qualifications of the personnel for technical education programs depend upon the administrative organization and the scope of the program. A large program operated as a separate institution or as an integral part of another educational institution requires the services of an administrator and a number of supervisors and teachers.

Frequently, the administrator of a technical education program in a public school system is designated as a principal or as an associate or assistant superintendent of schools. Administrative officers of technical institutes and technical junior colleges are frequently referred to as directors or as deans. The chief administrative officer of the technical education program should possess practical experience, technical training, and administrative competency. New administrators are usually selected from the staff of the technical school and given training in administrative procedures.

Competent supervision is especially necessary for the efficient operation of the technical education program. The supervisor is primarily concerned with the improvement of instruction and has little administrative responsibility. Separate supervisors are usually provided for the various departments. Some technical educators suggest that a supervisor should be designated for each vocational field in which 3 or more instructors are employed. The supervisor is responsible for stimulating instructors to use approved methods. One important qualification a supervisor should possess is successful teaching experience in a technical education program. Supervisors should also possess the required technical education at least equivalent to completion of a technical course with additional education in the techniques of supervision and in the basic principles of administration. Both administrators and supervisors should have a clear understanding of their duties and responsibilities. Job descriptions and organization charts are useful devices in accomplishing this objective.

The most important responsibility of administrators and supervisors is that of selecting and recommending to boards of education competent teachers for the technical education program. The members of the teaching staff have responsibility for shop, laboratory, and classroom activities, and, since all of these activities are closely related to industrial, business, and agricultural processes, the instructor responsible for each should have occupational experience in the field in which he is teaching. In addition to occupational experience in technical education, the instructor should have a knowledge of the basic sciences that govern the technical processes involved in the occupation he is teaching. The instructor should also be familiar with accepted educational techniques for presenting subject matter and instructing in skills. No less important are such personal qualifications as safety consciousness, patience, high standards of performance, personality, and other personal factors that superior teachers possess.

Curriculum Making in Technical Education

The term *curriculum* has many meanings in educational literature. These vary from the concept of the curriculum as simply a group of subjects to the concept that includes all the elements of directed experience in which the learner engages. The latter concept is used in this volume. The curriculum in technical education includes classroom, laboratory, shop, study trips, student organizations, and other activities engaged in by the learner for the purpose of meeting an occupational objective. The content of the curriculum includes both technical and general education activities, and these activities are arranged or grouped into subjects or other categories for instructional purposes. The general education content, such as health, English, and social studies, is usually included in pre-employment technical education curriculums and frequently omitted in in-service programs. The technical content of the curriculum is designed to provide occupational competency. This content is usually determined by means of occupational analysis.

OCCUPATIONAL ANALYSIS

An occupational analysis is essentially a technique for finding out what a worker in a specific occupation does and what he needs to know to perform his job efficiently. This technique has been used for many years as a means of determining teaching content in trade and industrial education and is equally applicable to technical education. The desired information may be obtained from workers and supervisors currently employed in the occupation and from instructors and other persons who are occupationally qualified. The information should be secured by a qualified analyst. Various types of blank forms are used in tabulating the information. The use of the occupational analysis technique requires the cooperation of persons in industry, business, and agriculture who are thoroughly familiar with the various operations and aspects of the occupation for which teaching content is to be prepared. The opinions of several persons are required for best results, including those from the occupation and those from the field of education. The analysis of occupations requires considerable time and attention and should be undertaken with this fact in mind.

When the analyst has determined what the worker does and what he needs to know, he must then classify this information so that it may be arranged in courses of study or teaching units. Various ways of grouping technical education content have been suggested, including the following: (1) basic technical information, (2) specialized technical information, (3) basic technical skills, (4) specialized technical skills, (5) technical judgment, (6) supervisory skills and knowledge, (7) industrial organization practices, and (8) human relationships. The important facts and appropriate questions should be included under the information categories. The technical content is frequently grouped and listed under the occupational title of the course. For example, the technical content of a two-year technical education course in electrical technology may be listed in the curriculum as *electrical trade*, which may be given daily during the two years. The jobs in this course are determined by occupational analysis, and the activities may include classwork, shopwork, laboratory work, and field trips.

Occupational analysis is sometimes used to determine the general education content of the technical education curriculum. This involves an analysis of life activities outside the place of employment. Health, recreation, home life, civic life, cultural appreciations, and many other aspects of home and family living must be considered in this analysis. The kind and amount of information of this type to include in the technical curriculum depend upon many factors. As a rule students who attend a technical education institution are more interested in the technical content than the general education content. If these programs are too heavily weighted with general education, students may seek schools with more technical and less general education, a pattern usually followed in proprietary schools. The curriculum maker should include only such general education content as can be made to appeal to the student and to function effectively in his life.

CHARACTERISTICS OF TECHNICAL EDUCATION CURRICULUMS

Wide variations are observed in the curriculums in various technical education programs. These differences are to be expected because of the variations in grade level from high school through junior college and because of the differences in needs of different localities. The technical curriculums as a rule are planned for specialized occupations rather than for broad occupational objectives. Some of these curriculums are less specialized than others. For example, some technical school curriculums are designed for junior engineers without special reference to a specific industrial field. A single technical education curriculum should not be expected to meet the needs of students who plan to continue their education in a higher institution and, at the same time, meet the needs of those students who expect to qualify for a technical occupation. The two objectives are quite different, and foundation courses for advanced education usually contain very little content essential to the efficient performance of industrial, business or agricultural occupations.

Some technical institutions offer a relatively large number of curriculums with a relatively small number of courses. These curriculums provide for an unusually large number of elective courses in each curriculum which reduces the specialized content and increases the general content. This type of curriculum organization is usually found in the smaller institutions, more especially the small junior colleges. There is some question as to the effectiveness of this type of organization. It is suggested that the number of curriculums be limited to those for which adequate courses and facilities can be provided. This means that small schools should, as a rule, offer only curriculums in keeping with their respective enrollments. The extent to which elective courses are provided depends upon such factors as degree of specialization, range of offerings possible, and maturity of students. Electives are sometimes provided in the final term of school to take care of the more common specializations. Elective courses in technical curriculums should be carefully examined to make sure that these courses meet definite needs and are not included simply to reduce the cost of instruction or to provide a wide variety of course offerings.

Various policies with reference to course credit are found in technical education institutions. The junior college usually measures credit in terms of semester hours. A semester hour of credit is allowed for each hour of class recitation per week for the duration of the semester. A course that meets for a 1-hour class period 5 times each week during the semester is allowed 5 semester hours of credit. Two hours of laboratory work or 3 hours of shopwork are considered equivalent to 1 hour of class recitation in measuring credit. Technical high schools sometimes use the term *unit* to measure credit. As a rule, about 4 or 5 units constitute a year's work. Some technical education institutions do not concern themselves with course credit. The course content is outlined in terms of clock hours of school work, and certificates of proficiency are given upon the satisfactory completion of the required number of clock hours. Most proprietary schools use this method for the organization of the curriculum content.

The technical curriculum should be arranged so that a student who finds it necessary to leave school before the completion of the curriculum may obtain as much education of direct benefit to his employment as is possible. The technical education curriculum should be continuously revised. This revision should not be limited to the adding or taking away of courses but should recognize the fact that technological changes are continually occurring, and these changes require changes in the content and method of teaching.

THREE TECHNICAL EDUCATION CURRICULUMS

Because of the wide variations in curriculums of technical institutions it is not feasible to suggest typical curriculums in technical education programs. As previously suggested, the needs of specific occupations as determined by occupational analysis should determine the content of the curriculum. Therefore, the curriculums suggested below are not intended as typical curriculums but may be useful as guides to curriculum making in the 3 types of technical education institutions represented.

Data processing systems and procedures analyst. The data processing curriculum shown below is offered in the San Joaquin Delta College, Stockton, California.[3] The currriculum is a 2-year program leading to the Associate in Arts degree. Students who complete this curriculum are prepared for employment in data processing work leading to positions of programmer, systems analyst, methods specialist, systems designer, computer specialist, and other positions in computer installations. Beginning positions may include computer console operator, high speed printer operator, programmer trainee, junior systems analyst, and systems and procedure trainee.

The data processing curriculum comprises 62½ units of course work of which 34 units or 54 percent consists of technical content and the remaining 46 percent consists of general education subjects. The program is arranged so that a minimum of additional lower-division courses will be required for final completion of a bachelor's degree at a four-year college or university. Students who are admitted to this

---

[3] San Joaquin Delta College, *Catalogue, 1963–1964*, Stockton, California, pp. 46–47.

DATA PROCESSING

First Year		Second Year	
Data Processing Fundamentals	3	Data Processing Systems	3
Punch Card Machines	2	Computer Programming	3
Principles of Accounting	8	Business Mathematics	3
Introduction to Business	3	Business Communications	3
Intermediate Algebra	3	Business Law	3
Written Communications	3	Computer Mathematics	3
Fundamentals of Speech	3	Introduction to Statistics	3
American Government and Institutions	3	General Psychology	3
Health Education	2	Science Requirement	6
Introduction to College	½	Physical Education	1
Physical Education	1		
Total units	31½	Total units	31

curriculum must be high school graduates. Mature persons over the age of 18 who by reason of previous educational or employment experience are qualified to make satisfactory progress in this curriculum may be eligible for admission even though they are not high school graduates. All applicants for admission to the San Joaquin Junior College who are working towards the degree of Associate in Arts are required to take the guidance and placement test prior to counseling and registration.

Food processing technology. The food processing curriculum described below is offered by the Agricultural and Technical Institute at Farmingdale, New York, and is described in the catalogue of the institution.[4] The curriculum is concerned with various aspects of food processing. Employment opportunities for graduates include food processing, inspection of food products, food plant quality control, food research and development, food purchasing, frozen food sales and sales supervision, advertising, distribution and merchandising of food, government regulatory inspection, precooked frozen food production, and food plant management. The course is one of a series included in the Division of Agriculture and Ornamental Horticulture. The course is a two-year, full-time program in which high school

[4] State University of New York, Agricultural and Technical Institute at Farmingdale, *Catalogue and Announcement, 1964–1966,* Farmingdale, New York, 1964, p. 95.

Students in Food Technology Study Relationship of Microorganisms to Frozen Food. These students are making an analysis of precooked frozen foods. (State University Agricultural and Technical Institute, Farmingdale, New York)

graduation with some specified high school courses is required for admission. All applicants are required to take a series of tests administered by the Institute to determine student aptitudes, interests, and achievements. The school authorities use these and other types of information to select students for entrance into the Institute program. The names of courses, together with the units of credit for each semester, are shown.

The two-year technical education program is organized on the semester hour basis, two 18-week semesters per year. A total of 67 semester hours is required for completion of the course of which 36 hours, or 54 percent, consist of required courses in technical and business subjects. The curriculum requires an average of 9 clock hours of laboratory work and 14 clock hours of class recitation per week. Students who complete the requirements of this curriculum are eligible to receive the degree of Associate in Applied Science.

	Clock Hours per Week		Semester Hours
	Class	Lab.	of Credit
First Semester			
Chemistry I	2	2	3
English Composition	3	0	3
Physical Education	0	2	½
Mathematics	3	0	3
General Microbiology	2	2	3
Food Preservation or			
Milk and Food Processing	2	3	3
	12	9	15½
Second Semester			
Chemistry II	2	2	3
English	3	0	3
Physical Education	0	2	½
Microbiology of Foods	2	3	3
Physics I	3	0	3
Food Preservation or			
Milk and Food Processing	2	3	3
	12	10	15½
Third Semester			
Accounting	2	2	3
Dairy Products Manufac-			
turing I	2	3	3
Food Processing Machinery	2	3	3
Precooked and Specialty			
Frozen Foods	2	3	3
Social Science	6	0	6
	14	11	18
Fourth Semester			
Commercial Processing of			
Precooked and Specialty			
Frozen Foods	2	3	3
Dairy Products Manufac-			
turing II	2	3	3
Quality Control of Foods	2	2	3
Salesmanship	3	0	3
Social Science	3	0	3
Elective	3[a]	0[a]	3
	15	8	18

Total credits required: 67

[a] Approximate, depending on elective.

Chemical process control technician. The course shown below for the training of chemical technicians is offered as a correspondence course by the International Correspondence Schools of Scranton, Pennsylvania.[5] The chemical technician curriculum is designed for those responsible for the efficient operation and control of manufacturing processes in chemical and allied industries such as the petroleum, plastics, pharmaceutical and metallurgical industries.

CHEMICAL PROCESS CONTROL

	Units		Units
Practical Arithmetic	6	Process-Pressure Measuring and Control Instruments	2
Formulas	1	Liquid Level Measuring and Control Instruments	2
Practical Geometry and Trigonometry	1	Temperature Measuring and Control Instruments	2
Logarithms	1	A-C Circuits and Generators	1
Inorganic Chemistry	12	Transformers and Rectifiers	1
Basic Organic Chemistry	2	Practical Electrical Measuring	1
Physics	2	Electricity, Part 3 only	1
Hydraulics, Parts 1–3	3	Fundamentals of Electronic Instrumentation and Control	1
Elementary Electrical Principles	1	Electronic Instrumentation Methods and Circuits	1
Electrostatics and Magnetism	1	Electronic Control Circuits and Applications	1
Unit Operations and Equipment	1	Principles of Digital and Analog Computers	1
Principles of Automatic Process Control Instruments	2	Telemetering	1
Automatic Process Control Valves	1		

The course offerings include mathematics and basic science courses. These courses are followed by detailed instruction on the operation and process application of pneumatic, hydraulic, mechanical, and electronic instruments. The ICS supplies texts and instruction units or assignments which include directions for study, examination questions, and other forms of tests. Laboratory activities are also included and the kits and outfits for these activities may be purchased from ICS.

The course consists of 49 units of instruction and the ICS estimates that the average student can complete the course in about 850

[5] International Correspondence Schools, *ICS Vocational Guidance Manual,* Scranton, 1963, p. 201.

clock hours of study. In order to enroll an individual must have completed at least 6 years of formal schooling or be able to demonstrate competence in reading and writing. A diploma is awarded to the student who successfully completes the course.

QUESTIONS FOR STUDY AND DISCUSSION

1. Define technical education, and indicate some of its more important characteristics.
2. What are some indications of the need for technical education in each of the more important occupational fields?
3. What factors have affected the development of technical education programs?
4. Indicate some characteristics of present programs in technical education in junior colleges.
5. In what respects do present-day technical institute programs in technical education differ from junior college programs of this nature?
6. What are the characteristics of present-day technical education programs in technical high schools? In industry?
7. What are the duties of the technical education advisory committee, and how should this committee be organized?
8. How may the need for technical education be determined?
9. How may the data of the community survey be used in the planning of technical education programs?
10. What is an occupational analysis, and how is this technique used in determining course content in technical education?
11. What are some characteristics of technical education curriculums?
12. What subject matter areas are included in technical education curriculums in junior colleges and technical institutes? In technical education curriculums offered by correspondence?

SOURCE REFERENCES

Burtt, Harold E., *Principles of Employment Psychology,* Harper & Row, New York, 1942.

California State Department of Education, *A Study of Technical Education in California,* Bulletin Vol. XXVIII, No. 7, Sacramento, 1959.

California State Department of Education, Bureau of Industrial Education, *Technical Education in California Junior Colleges,* Report of Subcommittee on Technical Education to Committee on Vocational Education in the Junior College, Sacramento, 1953.

Dobinson, C. H., *Technical Education for Adolescents,* Harrap, London, 1951.

Emerson, Lynn A., *Vocational Technical Education for American Industry*, Circular 530, U.S. Department of Health, Education, and Welfare, Office of Education, Washington, D.C., 1958.

Employment Security Commission of North Carolina, *North Carolina Study of Technical and Skilled Manpower*, Bureau of Employment Security Research, Raleigh, 1962.

Federal Security Agency, Office of Education, *Vocational Technical Training For Industrial Occupations*, Report of the Consulting Committee on Vocational Technical Training, Vocational Division Bulletin No. 228, Washington, D.C., 1944.

Mays, Arthur B., *Principles and Practices of Vocational Education*, McGraw-Hill, New York, 1948.

Technician Education Yearbook 1963–1964, Prakken, Ann Arbor, Michigan, 1963.

U.S. Department of Health, Education, and Welfare, Office of Education, *Organization and Effective Use of Advisory Committees*, Vocational Division Bulletin No. 288, Washington, D.C., 1961.

U.S. Department of Health, Education, and Welfare, Office of Education, *Vocational Education for a Changing World of Work*, Appendix I, *Technical Training in the United States*, Report of Panel of Consultants on Vocational Education, Washington, D.C., 1963.

University of the State of New York, *The Organization and Administration of Vocational-Technical Courses in Secondary Schools*, Bulletin No. 1383, Albany, 1950.

CHAPTER FIFTEEN

VOCATIONAL EDUCATION IN INDUSTRY

Industry and business have always assumed some responsibility for the education and training of their workers. This responsibility began in early times with the informal parent and child relationship and developed into the extensive systems of apprenticeship of the Middle Ages. The Industrial Revolution brought about new problems in industry and necessitated new types of education and training programs. The corporation school came into prominence during the latter part of the nineteenth century. This type of school stimulated the development in the early part of the twentieth century of various types of technical institutes and trade schools supported by industry.

The advent of World War I brought about a need for additional industrial workers and new programs of training. The organized program of on-the-job training came into prominence as a result of this need, and the vestibule school established in industry provided trained

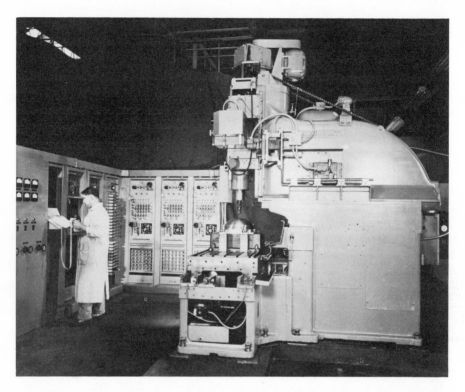

Machines of Modern Industry Require New Knowledge and Skills in Their Construction, Operation, and Maintenance. The numerically controlled milling machine pictured above operates by instructions transmitted to it on a paper tape. (Massachusetts Institute of Technology, Cambridge, Massachusetts)

workers for war industries. Technological changes in industry immediately after World War I brought about a need for better-trained foremen and supervisors, and the Federal Board for Vocational Education was largely responsible for the impetus given to training-in-industry programs for foremen and supervisors.

The depression of the 1930s stimulated some new developments in apprenticeship training and on-the-job training, especially in program organization and in standards of performance. World War II brought about a need for many new workers in a relatively short time, and programs of apprenticeship training, job training and supervisory training in industry were rapidly expanded to meet the needs of war industries. New developments in recent years have demonstrated a need for a new type of educational program in industry. This program, referred to as employee education, is designed to supply the employee with desired information about the company together with some basic economic information and to provide a means of recognizing the employee's contribution to the company's operations. A description of each of these four programs—modern apprenticeship, job training, supervisory training and employee education—is included in this chapter.

The Modern Apprenticeship System

Apprenticeship as a means of providing training in industry flourished during the Middle Ages and went into a decline in the nineteenth century. This decline in the United States, which extended into the twentieth century, was caused by the expansion of the factory system with its increasing division of labor together with the development of the public school system which provided the general education previously included in apprenticeship training. During the decline in apprenticeship the need for skilled craftsmen in America was met in part by immigrants from Europe and by private and public trade schools in the United States. Immigration restrictions and rapid increases in industrial production in the early part of the twentieth century caused some concern with reference to the supply of skilled craftsmen. However, no important changes were made in apprenticeship training during those years.

It should be recognized that some companies and craft organizations maintained satisfactory apprenticeship programs during the early years of the twentieth century. Three types of systems were in general use. The first or old type of apprenticeship, with little or no emphasis on related instruction, was used by some companies. A second type was one in which industry provided for the education of apprentices in both the classroom and the shop. For example, some companies provided "training rooms" in which a number of apprentices worked for a period of 2 years, after which they were placed in various departments of the company. In a third type of program the related instruction of apprentices was provided outside of working hours in organized evening classes.

Renewed interest in apprenticeship became apparent in the 1920s. This interest was occasioned by the growing emphasis upon manpower in industry. The need for skilled workers in mass-production industries was recognized. It was also evident that the needed skills could be developed efficiently in properly organized apprenticeship programs. The possibility of combining the best practices of the old system with new ideas was discussed. Inquiries were made relative to government participation in industrial education. The Federal Board for Vocational Education in 1923 issued a bulletin concerned with apprenticeship education. The Board sponsored conferences during this period for the discussion of apprenticeship training programs. Statistics gathered in the early 1930s indicated that a considerable portion of the skilled workmen of the country would reach retirement age within a few years, and there were too few replacements in training for these workers. These facts together with the extensive Federal works program of the 1930s stimulated the Federal government to interest itself in an apprenticeship program.

THE BUREAU OF APPRENTICESHIP

A Federal committee on apprentice training was created by executive order of the President of the United States in 1934 for the purpose of maintaining apprenticeship under the National Recovery Administration codes. The committee was administered by the U.S. Department of Labor in cooperation with the National Recovery Administration. This committee was primarily concerned with standards, wages and related training. The committee functions were transferred to the National Youth Administration in 1935 when the NRA was declared unconstitutional. The committee continued to operate in the U.S. Department of Labor with the full cooperation of the NYA. All functions of the committee were transferred to the U.S. Department of Labor in 1937 with the passage of the Fitzgerald Act (Public Law 308, 75th Congress). This Act authorized the Secretary of Labor to establish standards to guide industry in employing and training apprentices. The Act also provided plans to bring management and labor together to formulate programs for the training of apprentices, to appoint national committees and to promote acceptance of apprenticeship standards.

The Federal Committee on Apprenticeship was reorganized and enlarged under the Fitzgerald Act to include an equal number of representatives of management and labor in addition to one representative each from the U.S. Department of Labor and from the U.S. Office of Education. The Apprenticeship Training Service, now known as the Bureau of Apprenticeship, was established as the national administrative agency in the U.S. Department of Labor to carry out the objectives of the apprenticeship law and the policies of the Federal Committee on Apprenticeship. The United States Secretary of Labor in 1938 appointed the General Committee on Apprenticeship for the Construction Industry consisting of representatives of contractors and labor organizations to act as a coordinating body for apprenticeship training in the construction industry and to promote the development of national and local apprenticeship training programs in this industry. This special Committee was required because of the special need for skilled workers in the construction industry.

APPRENTICESHIP STANDARDS

The general policy of the Federal Committee on Apprenticeship is to encourage the development of programs for the employment and training of apprentices that are jointly established and mutually satisfactory to the employers and employees. As a means of implementing this general policy the Federal Committee on Apprenticeship has recommended certain standards to be used as guides by employers and employees for establishing standards in a specified trade. The following are the general standards suggested by the Committee:

1. A minimum of 16 years of age for the apprentice.
2. A schedule of work processes or operations in which experience is to be given the apprentice on the job.
3. A progressively increasing schedule of wages to be paid the apprentice which, as a minimum, should average over the period of apprenticeship approximately 50 percent of the rate paid journeymen during that period.
4. Related classroom instruction (144 hours per year is normally considered necessary).
5. Adequate supervision of the apprentice and the keeping of appropriate records concerning his progress.
6. Joint establishment of the apprenticeship program by the employer and the employees.
7. Indication that the number of apprentices to be employed conforms to the need in the community.
8. Review and registration of the written apprenticeship program, containing the terms and conditions of employment and training, by the Bureau of Apprenticeship or a state apprenticeship agency recognized by the Federal Committee on Apprenticeship.
9. Registration of the apprentice by the Bureau of Apprenticeship or a state apprenticeship agency recognized by the Federal Committee on Apprenticeship.[1]

This Committee agreed that the term *apprentice* meant a worker who learns, according to a written agreement, a recognized skilled

[1] U.S. Department of Labor, Bureau of Apprenticeship, *The National Apprenticeship Program*, Washington, D.C., 1953, p. 21.

trade requiring 2 or more years of work experience on the job, through employment supplemented by appropriate related training experience. The Committee also established criteria to assist in determining which trades should be recognized as apprenticeable. These criteria exclude occupations such as selling, retailing, managerial, clerical, professional and semiprofessional, and agricultural as apprenticeable trades. Other occupations which meet the criteria indicated below may be recognized as apprenticeable trades. An apprenticeable occupation is one:

1. Which customarily has been learned in a practical way through training and work experience on the job.
2. Which is clearly identified and commonly recognized throughout an industry.
3. Which requires 2 or more years (4000 or more hours) of work experience to learn.
4. Which requires related instruction to supplement the work experience.
5. Which is not merely part of an apprenticeable trade recognized by the Bureau of Apprenticeship as recommended by the Federal Committee on Apprenticeship.
6. Which involves the development of skill sufficiently broad to be applicable in like occupations throughout an industry, rather than of restricted application to the products of one company.[2]

STATE APPRENTICESHIP AGENCIES

Apprenticeship agencies composed of an equal number of representatives of employers and employees, and in some instances a representative of the state board for vocational education and a representative of the state department of labor, have been established in a number of states. These agencies, usually referred to as state apprenticeship councils, have responsibility for preparing and adopting a state plan for apprenticeship. This plan includes suggested standards and procedures for employers and employees to follow in conducting apprenticeship training.

Most state apprenticeship agencies derive authority through an apprenticeship law enacted by the state general assembly. However, some states without such a law have an approved state apprenticeship council that carries on these functions in about the same manner as does a council authorized by law. The state council functions within its borders in almost the same way that the U.S. Bureau of Apprenticeship functions throughout the United States. Its purpose is to provide the state with adequate skilled workers in all the recognized crafts.

[2] *Ibid.,* p. 3.

It endeavors to bring all the interested agencies, organizations, and functions together for the purpose of obtaining a satisfactory training program. The state apprenticeship council is usually designated by the Federal Committee on Apprenticeship as its official representative in the state. This designation places the state council in a position to carry out agreements with management and labor organizations made on a nation-wide basis.

TRADE JOINT APPRENTICESHIP COMMITTEES

Each apprenticeable trade or industry constitutes a unit in the national apprenticeship training program. This unit is governed by a series of trade joint apprenticeship committees on national and local levels. These committees are composed of an equal number of representatives from labor and management. The committee members are practical persons accustomed to dealing with the daily problems of the industry and manpower needs. The top national committee has responsibility for formulating national uniform standards of training for the industry it represents. National standards have been approved for trades such as bricklaying, carpentry, cement, asphalt and composition finishing, electrical, painting, photoengraving, plastering, plumbing, roofing, sheet metal, steam fitting, terrazzo work, and tile setting. The national committee also stimulates the formation of local joint labor-management apprenticeship committees for the trade or industry represented and assists them in establishing approved programs of apprenticeship training. The national trade joint apprenticeship committees are appointed by their own industries. They work on a voluntary basis with the U.S. Bureau of Apprenticeship. These committees advise the Bureau on the handling of general problems relating to or affecting training in their respective industries. The Bureau provides assistance to the national trade committees in the form of statistical reports and information about new programs, joint committees, and other items.

The employment and training of apprentices takes place in local communities under the direction and control of local committees. The national and state apprenticeship agencies direct their efforts toward maintaining standards and securing interest and action on the part of local employers and employees. Various types of joint committees are used in the organization and operation of the local apprenticeship program. A local joint apprenticeship committee for a particular trade is given responsibility for the apprenticeship program in that trade where both employers and employees maintain local organizations. This committee has responsibility for the actual training of apprentices. The committee adapts national and state apprenticeship standards to local conditions and establishes means and methods of training. Some of the more specific duties of joint committees are shown in the following list compiled by the New York State Apprenticeship Council to serve as a guide to local joint apprenticeship committees.

1. To determine, in accordance with the established ratio of apprentices to journeymen, the need for apprentices for the specific trade represented by the committee in a locality, taking into consideration the available facilities for acquiring the necessary experience on the job.

2. To establish minimum standards of education and experience required of apprentices and to pass on the qualifications of apprentice applicants.

3. To approve apprenticeship agreements between the employer and the apprentices, and to submit these apprenticeship agreements for registration with the New York State Apprenticeship Council.

4. To determine the quality and quantity of experience on the job which the apprentice must have and to be responsible for his obtaining it.

5. To hear and adjust all complaints of violations of apprenticeship agreements.

6. To arrange tests for determining the apprentice's progress in manipulative skills and technical knowledge.

7. To maintain a record of each apprentice, showing his related schooling, experience, and progress in the learning of the trade.

8. To make annual reports covering the work of the committee to the employer, the union, and the New York State Apprenticeship Council.

9. To recommend apprentices for advancement and for certificates of completion of apprenticeship.[3]

When it is not feasible for an employer to participate in a trade-wide apprenticeship program, the employer and his employees, if the latter have an organization, are encouraged to set up a plant joint committee to prepare a plan for an apprenticeship program. This plan is usually a written document defining the conditions of employment and training for apprentices in the plant. The plan usually contains a provision for a full-time or part-time supervisor of the apprenticeship program as well as an outline of the supervisor's functions in relation to those of the committee.

When employees in a plant do not have an organization or when the existing organization is not concerned with the training of apprentices, the employer may establish an apprenticeship system. If the system meets with the approval of the state apprenticeship agency it may

[3] New York State Department of Labor, New York State Apprenticeship Council, *Annual Report, January 1–December 31, 1946,* New York, 1947, p. 6.

be registered with the agency and is considered a part of the national apprenticeship program since it must meet acceptable standards to be registered.

Local apprenticeship programs provide for the registration of individual agreements between apprentices and their employers with the state apprenticeship agency. This registration serves as a public record of the fact that acceptable standards are observed in the training of the apprentice, acts as a safeguard for the interests of the apprentice and provides information about the apprentice for future employers. The registration also provides a basis for the issuance of certificates of completion of apprenticeship by the apprenticeship agency.

Joint apprenticeship committees have responsibility for determining the length of the apprenticeship period. These periods have been established on a national level for the apprenticeable trades. However, local joint committees may shorten or lengthen these for individual apprentices, depending on the individual qualifications of the apprentice. The usual length of apprenticeship for such trades as machine shop, carpentry, boiler making, and tailoring is 4 years. Trades such as cement finishing, lathe operation, and dressmaking usually require 2 to 3 years. Apprentice electricians, pressmen, and engravers spend 4 or 5 years in the program, and a die sinker goes through a 5- to 7-year apprenticeship program.

ON-THE-JOB AND RELATED TRAINING

The apprenticeship training programs are planned on the basis of what the apprentice must do and what he must know in order to perform the operation or the job in a safe and satisfactory manner. This involves actual participation in learning activities on the job and the study of related information in the classroom or shop. One of the first activities in planning on-the-job training is the preparation of a schedule of work processes. This schedule consists of a listing of the various types of jobs in which the apprentice will engage together with the approximate time that will be spent on the process. Work processes for an auto mechanics trade include such items as the separation and cleaning unit, lubrication, care and use of tools, gasoline motor, fuel system, exhaust system, cooling system, oiling system, and the transmission assembly. The schedule of work processes is not identical for the same trades in different shops, and the order in which the training is given need not necessarily follow the sequence of the work processes schedule.

The standards of the Federal Committee on Apprenticeship suggest that each apprentice spend a minimum of 144 hours per year in related instruction. Local trade joint apprenticeship committees in many cities have established standards above the minimum. Among the various types of arrangements for the time devoted to related training are: 1 day per week, 1 evening per week, two 3-hour sessions per week, an 8-hour day on alternate weeks, 1 day per week for 2 years of a 4-year apprenticeship program, two 3-hour sessions for 30 weeks per year, and others. The plan of related instruction involves classroom, laboratory and shop activities with the relative time for each of the three activities suggested in the plan.

The kind of related instruction varies with the trade. Related instruction for apprentice carpenters includes related mathematics, drafting, and blueprint reading. Apprentice cooks and chefs may study menu making, pricing, food buying, related chemistry, sanitation, color harmony, and food service. Apprentice plumbers may engage in the related study of the plumbing code, blueprint reading, and mathematics. Apprentice linemen in the electrical industry may study safety practices, the fundamentals of electricity, circuit work, maintenance of trolley wires, stop and go signals, street lights, alarms, and electronics.

Related instruction for apprentices is carried on by public and private vocational schools, by individual plants, and by labor unions. The public vocational school is, because of the training and experience of its personnel in teaching, usually in a better position to carry out this instruction. Related training conducted by any agency should be carried out in cooperation with labor and industry. Responsibility for supervising apprentices is ordinarily assumed by the foremen of the various departments in which apprentices are employed. In large apprenticeship programs an apprentice supervisor is usually appointed on a full-time basis and assigned responsibility for this part of the training program. Apprenticeship programs in some of the building trades such as bricklaying, carpentry, painting, plastering, plumbing, and others are supervised by apprentice coordinators, who are representatives of organized labor.

APPRENTICE STATISTICS

During the 22-year period 1941 to 1962 a cumulative total of 1,220,804 persons were enrolled in registered apprenticeship programs. During this period a total of 453,469 of these registered apprentices completed training, 608,719 left before completion and

158,616 were still in training at the close of the period. These data indicate that during this period there were 2 new registrants for each apprentice who left before completion and 1.3 apprentices who left before completion for each apprentice who completed the program. Studies have indicated that about half of the dropouts before completion obtained employment in the trade in which they were apprenticed. This suggests that greater efforts should be made to induce apprentices to remain in training until the completion of their period of apprenticeship.

Apprentices Receive Related Instruction in Interpreting Tool and Die Drawings in Public Vocational Schools. (Milwaukee Vocational and Adult Schools, Milwaukee, Wisconsin)

Prior to the post-World War II period there were fewer than 50,000 persons enrolled in registered apprenticeship programs. This number increased to 200,000 and above shortly after the war and declined after 1951 to about 160,000. The number increased to about 185,000 during the years 1955 to 1957 and turned downward thereafter. Apprentice completions were high in 1950 and 1951 but have remained steady at 25,000 to 30,000 since that time. The financial support associated with the G.I. Bill in earlier years contributed to the increase in the number of apprentices. The absence of this support and economic conditions have probably influenced the decline in the number of apprentices during the past few years.

More than 171,000 establishments were participating in registered apprenticeship programs in 1954, of which more than 60 percent were in the construction industry. Other industrial groups having a relatively large number of establishments engaged in registered apprenticeship training were printing and publishing, service industries, metal working industries, and retail trade. Most of the participating establishments in the construction and printing industries were in group apprenticeship systems involving more than one establishment. The service and retail industries were in individual apprenticeship

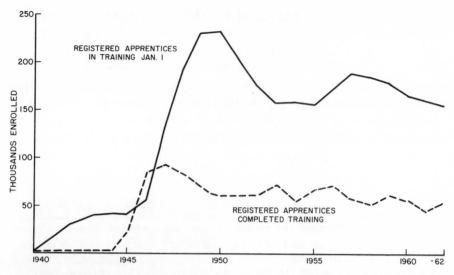

The Number of Registered Apprentices in Training Has Declined in Recent Years. The termination of the G.I. Bill and the increase in unemployment has resulted in a decrease in apprentice registrations. (U.S. Department of Labor, Bureau of Apprenticeship and Training, Division of Research)

systems. More than half of the registered apprentices were in the following states listed in descending order of number enrolled: New York, California, Ohio, Michigan, Illinois, Pennsylvania, Texas, Wisconsin, and Minnesota. The average age of the registered apprentice in the United States in 1954 was about 26 years, and as a rule the apprentice had responsibility for the support of a wife and family. It should be noted that the above data are for registered apprentices. There are in the United States considerable numbers of apprentices who are in nonregistered apprenticeship systems and who in time join the ranks of the craftsmen of the United States.

On-The-Job Training

The introduction of automatic machines and assembly-line processes in industry has created a need for a semiskilled worker having somewhat different training than that provided under the apprenticeship system. Industry found it necessary to organize special types of programs, designated as on-the-job training, for the training of these workers. The term *on-the-job training* has been defined to include various types of training programs in industry, but its use in this volume is limited to instruction in the performance of a job given to an employed worker during the usual working hours of his occupation, and for which wages are paid. It differs from apprenticeship training in that it requires less time and less organization for training. It differs from employee education programs in that it is primarily confined to the learning of job processes rather than related information or education of a general nature. Training of this type is needed when a new worker is employed, when an experienced worker is promoted, when a worker is temporarily replaced and when a new product or process is brought out by the company.

Prior to World War I there was little evidence of organized programs of on-the-job training. Training of this nature was conducted in an informal and sometimes trial-and-error manner. The increased demand for workers in war industries during World War I made it necessary that industry engage in an organized training program for these workers. Vestibule schools were organized in plants for the preliminary training of new employees. New workers were instructed on actual production jobs with actual materials and equipment but somewhat apart from the main production lines of the plant. Experienced workers shifted to new positions were frequently returned to the vestibule for training on the new job. An outgrowth of World War I training of this nature was the technique of job analysis for determining the skills and information that the new employee needed.

The expansion of industry as a result of World War II required a rapid and extensive expansion of on-the-job training. Method simplification and job breakdowns were combined with narrow, intensive training procedures to prepare persons without previous industrial experience for employment in industry. An intensive vocational training program for war production, in which on-the-job training was included, provided the required workers for war industries. The training methods and procedures that originated as a result of World War I and were further developed during World War II continue to be used in present-day, on-the-job training programs.

ORGANIZING ON–THE–JOB TRAINING

Job training begins with the employment manager who checks job specifications and attempts, insofar as is possible, to employ workers who more nearly meet the requirements of the jobs to be filled. Job training programs are not only designed for these beginning workers but also for employed persons who are in need of training because of changes in jobs and job specifications or because of production problems such as high cost of production, production-line accidents, and low-quality products.

The job training program is administered by the director of training or an executive of the company having this responsibility. The training director is responsible for planning the training program which includes ways in which the need for training may be met and the designation of personnel for conducting the training. Various ways are used in industry for providing on-the-job training. These include:

1. A training department apart from the production line to which trainees are assigned for training and reassigned to the production line upon the completion of the training.

2. A training department established to work on production jobs and manned by specially qualified workers. Trainees are first assigned to this line and reassigned to regular work upon the completion of training.

3. The use of qualified employees to work with trainees individually and assist them in the performance of the job assigned. Trainees are shifted to similar jobs in other departments when given the necessary instruction on the job.

4. The placing of trainees on practical jobs within the range of their abilities with the understanding that they are to work with experienced men who have been given responsibility to instruct the trainees.

5. The assigning of new or untrained workers to jobs, giving them brief instructions and letting them learn as best they can.

Each of these plans for training has its advantages and disadvantages. Separate training divisions are expensive, but they relieve the regular working force of the annoyance of trainees. Special training sections in the production division relieve the foremen and regular workers of training problems but may result in conflicts of authority. Training on the job with advisers brings trainees in direct contact with the work of the department but frequently requires an excessive amount of time of competent workers who serve as advisers. The plan of permitting new workers to learn as best they can is perhaps the most expensive to management and the most discouraging to workers.

An important consideration in job training is the selection of the instructor or adviser. It is important that the individual be occupationally competent, have some knowledge of how to teach and possess a well-balanced personality. Occupational competency may be indicated by such items as amount and nature of experience and ability as recognized by supervisors and associates. Ability to teach may be developed through training. A training course of 30 hours is frequently used for this type of training. A worker who has a well-balanced personality usually has abilities that enable him to deal successfully with things, ideas, other people and himself. This suggests that it is not always the expert worker but the well-balanced worker who makes the best instructor.

JOB TRAINING METHODS

When the need for training is agreed upon, the workers selected for the training course and the jobs in which training is needed determined, the next step is the process of training. This process varies among companies and jobs but in general it consists of two parts: (1) the preparation for instruction, and (2) the instruction of the trainee. The preparation for instruction involves a breakdown of the job, a timetable for each operation and the assembling of all the necessary tools and materials. The instruction process usually involves preparation of the trainee, presentation of the job or operation, tryout by the trainee and follow-up. A discussion of these steps is presented below.

The job breakdown consists of a step-by-step analysis of the job as it is performed by the operator. The breakdown should include the various steps in the handling of materials, machine processes, and hand work. The breakdown should be made on the job to make sure that all the small details are included. Such items as *take off face plate, put chuck on spindle nose, fasten work in chuck* illustrate the detail required in a job breakdown of a chucking operation on a lathe. The breakdown should be accompanied by a list of things the trainee needs to know about each step in the operation. A timetable is also prepared showing the length of time required for the trainee to perform the operation. The final step in preparation for the instruction is to assemble and try out the necessary equipment and supplies for teaching the job.

The first step in the instruction process consists of putting the trainee at ease, finding out what he knows and arousing his interest. Next, the job operation to be taught is presented by telling, demonstrating, and questioning to bring out important points. Each step is taken up one at a time. When each point has been mastered the trainee is allowed to perform each part of the job, illustrating the important points, and explaining the procedures. The instructor asks questions and corrects errors. When the trainee has mastered the operation he is put on his own with instructions on where to find additional assistance if it is needed.

New workers frequently receive some introductory training prior to or at the time the job training is given. This introductory training consists of information on items such as company organization and policies, company products, and employee benefits. This information is frequently given in four or five 2-hour class sessions during the first part of the training period. Employees receive an examination on this information when the course is completed.

TRAINING DEVICES AND MATERIALS

Various kinds of devices and materials have proved helpful in job training. Among these are job rating cards, time and motion studies, gauges, demonstrations, and visual aids. Job rating cards show the requirements of different occupations. They indicate such items as the needed amount of schooling, the length of the training period, the particular skills required, the responsibility that the worker must carry, the specific knowledge he must have, and the working conditions. Job ratings are used in determining wage scales in employing workers and in the training of workers. The job rating card constitutes a standard that may be used in matching workers with jobs and in determining what training should be emphasized.

Time and motion studies show the standard length of time that should be allowed for the performance of each operation in the job. This information is used as a guide in comparing the learner's effort with standard performance. If a learner does not come up to standard within a stated time, this fact is an indication that some further study of the course or the training process should be made. Another type of standard useful in training programs is the measuring gauge. The gauge not only indicates the quality of performance of the trainee to the supervisor, but it also indicates this to the worker as well.

The demonstration is a device frequently used in on-the-job training. It is an important part of the presentation step. The demonstration should be included for the actual purpose of instruction and not simply for a demonstration. The instructor should practice the demonstration before he attempts to give it to the trainees. Demonstrations are usually timed more slowly than the actual operation on the job, and this should be taken into account in the planning. It is more difficult to demonstrate and explain each step than it is to perform the actual operation on the production line. The instructor should demonstrate the correct method only. The trainee may be confused if several near-correct or incorrect methods are demonstrated. Visual aids are frequently used in explaining some phases of the demonstration. The various types of visual aids include diagrams, slides, slide films, motion pictures, models, and machines. Each of these has its optimum usage, and the instructor should know this in planning the instruction phase of the training program.

TESTING AND WORK REVIEW

An essential feature of an on-the-job training program is a means of testing or evaluating the outcomes of the training program. The results of this test not only indicate whether or not the trainee has learned but also whether or not the company can afford to continue his employment. It is recognized that testing is not a simple matter. Much of the information obtained in testing is subjective in nature and therefore influenced by personal factors. However, all workers are tested and rated either formally or informally, and this makes it necessary that every effort be made to obtain test data that are as reliable as possible.

Both objective and subjective tests are used in testing the results of job training. Factual information about what a worker knows may be determined by either of these types of tests. Work performance may be tested or rated by the use of rating scales. These scales involve judgments concerning such characteristics as accuracy, neatness, volume produced, use of equipment, and use of time. The quality of a production job may also be judged by expert opinion, various types of gauges, and measures of saleability of the product. The training program should include plans for testing, and tests appropriate to each skill or fact needed should be selected at the time the training program is planned.

Work review is a form of testing or evaluating the output of the worker. This review is made largely for the purpose of rating the worker for promotion or other recognition. The review is made at periodic intervals by one or more supervisors. Rating or work review sheets are used in the reviews. These are arranged to indicate varying degrees of quality of work, volume of work, knowledge of the job, attendance, and safety in work. The rating scale or work review sheet is arranged to provide a graphic representation of the worker's performance. Rating scales or review sheets are also used to evaluate the personal qualities of workers. The characteristics included in this type of scale are job interest, intelligence, leadership, planning ability, and follow-up. The terms used in the review sheets should be specific and not general. Review sheets should be constructed so that both the supervisor and the worker will understand the rating given. They should be designed to portray graphically the performance and personality of the worker.

Supervisory Training in Industry

Industrial concerns in recent years have shown an increasing interest in supervisory training programs. These programs are designed to improve the vocational efficiency of workers who have such titles as supervisor, foreman, general foreman, assistant foreman, forewoman, gang boss, overseer, section chief, and leadman. These persons serve as the connecting link between the workers and the management of the firm. The recent interest in the training of supervisors is due to a realization that a successful enterprise needs competent foremen and other types of supervisors for current operations and as candidates for future managerial positions.

THE DEVELOPMENT OF SUPERVISORY TRAINING

Attempts were made early in the twentieth century to provide vocational training for supervisors and foremen. Among the first of these was the Lowell School for Industrial Foremen organized by Massachusetts Institute of Technology in 1903. This school offered a few technical courses for foremen and supervisors. These were later supplemented with courses in business management, personnel organization, and production methods. All these courses involved the use of textbooks and lectures and required the passing of examinations. Little was accomplished in these early efforts largely because the academic nature of the courses had little appeal to employed craftsmen and supervisors.

A new approach to the problem of supervisory training was suggested in 1919 by the Federal Board for Vocational Education. This new approach consisted of an analysis of the supervisor's job in relation to his responsibilities. The first of these analyses was made in 1919 by Charles R. Allen, at that time an employee of the Federal Board for Vocational Education. A number of general and departmental foremen who were employed by the Du Pont Company assisted in this analysis. The discussions involved in identifying and discussing the responsibilities of the foreman led to the development of the technique known as the conference procedure. Representatives of the

Federal Board for Vocational Education conducted a series of regional conferences during the years 1919 and 1920 for the purpose of acquainting state supervisors of trade and industrial education with the new developments in the training of foremen. A series of conferences was held about this same time for training conference leaders, and many industries inaugurated foreman and supervisory training programs in which the job analysis and conference procedure techniques were used.

During the first few years after the supervisory training program was started special methods and procedures of conference work were developed and perfected by experimentation with groups of experienced foremen. During the period between 1919 and 1932 staff members of the Federal Board for Vocational Education conducted 70 conferences involving 1463 foremen in 35 states. The staff of the Federal Board for Vocational Education also conducted 43 courses in 25 states for the purpose of training personnel from industry and from state vocational education programs to serve as foremen conference leaders. The Federal Board also developed various bulletins and other material concerned with the training of supervisors and conference leaders.

The supervisory training program in industry was curtailed during the economic depression of the 1930s. During this period the Federal Board for Vocational Education encouraged the use of state and local conference leaders to provide training for foremen and supervisors employed by Federal agencies such as the Civilian Conservation Corps, the Forest Service, the National Youth Administration, the Soil Conservation Service, and the Works Progress Administration. Many of these conference leaders also provided related instruction as well as instruction on the job.

The increased manpower needs brought about by World War II required the use of many new supervisors and foremen, and supervisory training programs in industry were again conducted by state and local boards for vocational education in cooperation with the Vocational Division, U.S. Office of Education, and the War Manpower Commission. The states received war production training funds from the Federal government for the operation of supervisory training programs. A total of 986,000 persons were enrolled in the states in these programs from July 1, 1940, to June 30, 1945.

The change-over in industry from wartime to peacetime production increased the need for supervisory training, and many industrial firms instituted plant training programs at their own expense. A num-

Production Supervisors Instruct New Employees. This supervisor is explaining the function of a filter cavity of a multiplexer used to separate microwave signals. (Roy W. Roberts, Jr., MELABS, Palo Alto, California)

ber of private training agencies were organized to supply training services to industrial and business concerns. Some state boards for vocational education employed itinerant instructors to assist industry in establishing supervisory training. Industry is presently assuming more responsibility for organizing and financing supervisory training programs, and both large and small industries are conducting this type of program.

THE ORGANIZATION OF SUPERVISORY TRAINING

The supervisory training program in many industries is established as a section of the personnel department. Some large industries have established independent departments of education and training, and some small firms have assigned responsibility for the training program to the plant manager or superintendent. A director of training either on a part-time or full-time basis is assigned responsibility for administering the program. Before a training program is established the director of training usually consults with management with reference to who is to be trained and what kind of training is needed. Such information as job analyses, standards of performance, service ratings, company complaints, and safety records are helpful in making these determinations.

A decision must be made with reference to the grade or group of personnel to be trained and the size of the discussion groups. First consideration in supervisory training is usually given to supervisors and foremen in direct charge of the workers. Frequently, workers who have been selected as prospective supervisors are included. Small discussion groups of 15 to 25 persons are preferable. Discussion groups with fewer than 10 persons do not provide the desired diversity of experience. Supervisors from various trades are often included in one discussion group to provide variety in the discussion period. Voluntary rather than compulsory attendance is preferable from the standpoint of efficiency of instruction. In some cases, however, compulsory attendance may be justified, especially when supervisors who are in most need of training are unwilling to attend voluntarily.

Supervisory training meetings held on a voluntary attendance basis are usually scheduled immediately after work hours or in the evening. Meetings held on company time are often scheduled immediately before or after lunch. Once-a-week sessions throughout the year, from one and one-half to two hours in length, are also used in supervisory training. Intensive, off-the-job courses consisting of all-day sessions for one or two weeks are used by some companies. This schedule is especially recommended for preservice training of supervisors and for training programs for spot needs. Year-round courses include several types of units, some of short and some of longer duration.

The success of the course of instruction depends largely on the leadership qualifications of the conference leader. Some firms use staff personnel while others use line personnel as conference leaders. Staff personnel attached to the training division are usually better qualified in methods of teaching but less qualified in current operational procedures and problems. When a line supervisor is used as a conference leader the training department has responsibility for organizing and coordinating the program and training the leader in materials and methods of instruction. An alert, outstanding supervisor holding about the same rank as the trainee supervisor can more easily gain the interest and confidence of the group than some outside person. However, both staff personnel and individuals from outside sources have proved satisfactory in many plants.

Other important considerations in the organization of supervisory training programs include facilities for the classes and plans for the evaluation of the course. The physical comfort of the supervisors in training is an important consideration. A quiet, properly ventilated and lighted room equipped with tables and chairs is preferable for the training conferences. A U-shaped arrangement of the tables and chairs adds to the informality desired for the course. Some effort should be made to determine the effectiveness of each training course. This evaluation may be made from the point of view of the benefits derived by the firm or by the performance of the discussion leader. Evaluative devices include production records, operating data, cost analyses, records of class attendance, opinions of conferees, rating sheets and leadership rating scales. Each of these devices has advantages and limitations and requires information and skill in its administration. When properly used these devices provide valuable information for evaluating the training program.

COURSES OF STUDY FOR SUPERVISORY TRAINING

Supervisory training courses include a wide variety of topics or subjects concerned with the duties and responsibilities of supervisors together with other topics designed to provide a general background for managerial positions. Types of subjects or topics usually included in supervisory training programs are those concerned with (1) human relations, (2) principles of administration, (3) techniques of instruction, (4) economics, and (5) company information and policies. The specific topics included under each classification are determined on the basis of need and with the assistance of a planning committee from the supervisory and management groups.

A supervisory training program is frequently started with a course of instruction in human relations. This course is designed to develop a better understanding of people and of how to work with and stimulate them to a high point of efficiency in the production of goods and services. Some of the more important topics in a course in human relations include a study of responsibilities of supervisors, the giving and carrying out of orders, the use of time, working safely, maintaining discipline, job placement, handling grievances and complaints, promotion and commendation, worker security, and company loyalty.

The principles of administration or management involve such factors as leadership, responsibility, and authority, all of which are closely identified with human relations. Other topics included in this category are unity of command, which involves the authority of management; span of control, which has to do with the factors that affect the number of workers who report to a supervisor; delegation of authority; use of staff; function of management; and planning for the organization and management of personnel. The supervisor is an instructor of workers and as such must use various techniques of instruction. Topics usually classified in this category include recognizing the need for training, techniques in conducting a meeting, lesson planning, testing, and follow-up.

Workers are in need of basic economic information to help them understand and interpret many of the policies and procedures of management. Discussion topics such as the American system of free enterprise, prices and production, the profit motive, wages and hours, tariffs, taxes, factors affecting cost of production, and relationships of management and labor are included in this category. Supervisors need to have a thorough knowledge of the company and its personnel policies, agreements with labor unions, employee benefits, production controls, inventories, use and disposal of waste, and production costs. These and other similar topics are frequently used as a basis for the course content in company information and policies.

A number of firms have organized special courses for newly inducted supervisors, most of whom have been promoted from other jobs in the same firm. Two types of information are usually included in these courses. One type consists of acquainting the new supervisor with the executive and supervisory personnel, the company organization, the production materials and processes and the relationships of the various departments. This instruction is accomplished by arranging special conferences with the executives in their offices and by visits to the plant conducted by the director of training. About one week is used for this activity in the larger firms. The second phase of the training of new supervisors is concerned with human relations and personal development. Topics such as company policies, union contracts, job instruction, safety, and management development are included. Both individual study and group instruction are used, and classes and activities are arranged throughout the first year at times convenient to the new supervisor.

METHODS AND MATERIALS OF INSTRUCTION

The conference procedure continues to be the popular method of instruction in the training of supervisors. This method is used by both staff and line personnel. The conference procedure is primarily a group discussion directed by the leader along previously planned channels. An opportunity is provided for the members of the group to express different points of view and to arrive at conclusions based on the expression of the various members of the group. This method provides an opportunity for active participation of all group members, results in sustained interest in the problem under discussion, and stimulates cooperative effort in finding a solution for the problem.

The conference procedure is adapted to a study of problems on topics about which some or all members of the group have had some previous experience. The object of the conference is to pool the experiences of the group and use them in finding a solution to the problem. The steps in conference leading are (1) assembling experience, (2) selecting facts in the assembled experiences that have a bearing on the problem, (3) evaluating these facts or information, and (4) using these facts in arriving at a conclusion or suggesting a plan of action. The aim of this procedure is to develop more intelligent thinking so that when a supervisor is confronted with a similar situation in the future he may think the problem through in an intelligent manner.

The significant points developed in the conference should be recorded as they are developed by the members of the group. This information may be classified under various headings such as *errors— causes and remedies; situations or problems—causes, effects, and remedies;* and others selected by the members of the group. The facts brought out and recorded are used in drawing conclusions and suggesting plans of action. The group leader frequently uses various devices to direct and regulate the discussion. These devices include suggestive questions, specially prepared charts or other visual materials and the budgeting of time for each discussion topic. Some courses are arranged on a detailed time schedule with exact procedures for each activity indicated as a means of conserving time and eliminating useless discussion.

Various types of visual aids and teaching materials are used in supervisory training courses. Among these are wall charts, flannel boards, special charts, illustrations, slides, films, models, and mockups. These are useful in stimulating discussion, maintaining interest, and providing new information. The wall chart has proved superior to the blackboard for recording facts and data supplied by the conferees during the course of the discussion. This chart consists of a pad of several sheets of large (36 in. × 48 in.) white paper attached to the wall or an easel. A black marking crayon may be used as a pencil.

When one page is filled with data or notes it may be detached from the pad, leaving a new sheet exposed for recording other facts. The used sheets may be kept as a permanent record of the conference.

A flannel board may be used for displaying previously prepared data and illustrations. This device is especially useful in presenting facts new to the conferees. The flannel board enables the conference leader to present data and points for discussion in an attractive manner as each item comes up for discussion. The use of each of these devices requires extensive planning before the conference convenes to insure that it be used at the most appropriate time in the discussion. This suggests that all the various activities and procedures should, insofar as possible, be planned in advance to insure a successful supervisory training conference.

Employee Education

American industry is spending increasing sums of money for the development of employee education programs. The term *employee education* is defined in a number of ways, but in general it refers to educational and informational programs that deal with subjects or activities which are only indirectly related to the knowledge or skill needed by the employee in the performance of his job. Employee education programs include information about the company and its products, company health and retirement benefits, recreational services available to employees, the importance of the individual worker in the community, the American economic system and how it affects and is affected by industry and the technical processes and aspects of the company's operations. Employee education programs differ from on-the-job training programs in that the latter are concerned primarily with increasing the worker's ability to perform the machine operations directly concerned with his job, while the former are concerned with general information and education.

OBJECTIVES OF EMPLOYEE EDUCATION

Studies have shown that an employee is more responsive when his individual performance in a company is given some recognition and is more efficient in the performance of his job if he knows and understands what is occurring in the industry in which he is employed. Employee education is a means of affording this recognition and supplying this type of information. Surveys have indicated a wide variation among companies in the specific objectives of employee education programs. These vary from one of providing an opportunity for employees to express their opinions to one of broadening the employee's knowledge and understanding of company policies, practices, and procedures, and their effect on trends and future developments in industry. The more commonly used objectives may be classified into three categories of (1) company information, (2) individual recognition, and (3) economic education.

Employees need to know and are usually interested in a wide variety of information about the company. This includes the historical development and present organization of the company, the products— how they are made and their uses, the policies of the company and how they affect individuals, advance notice of changes in policy and reasons for such changes, facts about the earnings of the company and the future prospects for work, and advance information about layoffs or shutdowns and the reasons for these practices. The employee as a rule will receive this and similar information from some source. The choice so far as the company is concerned is whether the information is secured from rumors and unreliable sources or whether the company provides the facts in a properly organized program of employee education.

Many companies are beginning to realize the importance of individual recognition and are including objectives concerned with the individual's responsibility for company success, the importance of the individual and his contribution, the employee's feeling of belonging, his sense of ownership and the promotion of family spirit within the company. These objectives recognize the fact that workers not only want good pay and good working conditions but also desire to feel that they are a part of the company and to have the necessary facts to enable them to advance to higher positions and to achieve security. They want the satisfaction of respectful treatment and some recognition of satisfactory achievement.

Employees frequently need some knowledge of economic principles to understand company policies and procedures. Employees need to know something of the profit motive in business and its relationship to prices and costs. They also need to know the relationship of what they put into an industry and what they receive from it and the limitations on what a company can afford in wages and benefits. Employees need to have some understanding of the functions of management and its contribution to the success of the company. Information of this nature is needed to enable the worker to understand the system of free enterprise and its relation to the security and prosperity of the nation's business.

TYPES OF EMPLOYEE EDUCATION PROGRAMS

Industry is using a variety of employee education programs, most of which may be grouped under (1) activities on company time; (2) after-work-hours programs; (3) notices, pamphlets and other printed materials; and (4) public relations activities. The most frequently used type of program is the one conducted on company time. These include orientation programs, mass meetings, small discussion groups, advisory groups, plant tours, special programs, job rotation, exhibits, skits and plays, and counseling services. Orientation programs for both new employees and older employees are designed to demonstrate the company's interest in the workers. Mass meetings conducted by management provide opportunities for workers to become acquainted with company executives. Smaller group meetings are especially effective in encouraging employee participation. Plant tours give employees a chance to see what other employees contribute to the activities of the company. Special programs such as contests, quizzes, and special day programs provide additional opportunities for individual participation and self-expression.

Various types of printed or written materials are used in employee education and information programs. These include magazines and newspapers, handbooks, pay envelope inserts, bulletin boards, letters, films, and comic illustrations. Articles in employee magazines and newspapers of an educational nature should stimulate thought, raise questions, and provide some information for answering these questions. Brief messages relating to wages and deductions inserted in the pay envelope provide an inexpensive and effective means of communicating with employees. Posters and bulletin board notices are most effective when they are brief and in pictorial form. Some companies have found personal letters signed by the executive an effective means of communication. Topics such as collective bargaining developments, labor legislation, and production and sales problems are often included in these letters. The use of films and comic illustrations is effective in explaining difficult topics such as the operation of complex machines and some complex economic principles. Printed and visual media are usually less expensive than other types of employee education material and provide a means of reaching large numbers of workers.

Some companies recognize the importance of community relations and have organized education programs designed to keep the community informed about the company and its policies and problems. Various types of activity both of a formal and an informal nature are included in these programs. Among these are community study programs on economic facts and principles, open house at the factory, talks by company officials to local organizations, the organization of Junior Achievement Clubs in the schools and colleges, and cooperative efforts with local churches in the teaching of Christian ethics. All these activities are designed to provide basic information of a factual nature to the various members of the community who are not employees of the company in order that they may discuss community problems and policies more intelligently with company employees.

THE ORGANIZATION OF EMPLOYEE EDUCATION PROGRAMS

Employee education programs are referred to as voluntary or involuntary programs. Attendance at voluntary programs is optional but is required at involuntary programs. Employees who are required to attend and who have little or no choice in the content of the class nevertheless do have a choice as to whether they will listen, read, or believe. Therefore, a so-called involuntary program should be organized to provide employee interest and participation in planning. This may be done through special planning committees or small group discussions organized for the purpose of planning employee education programs.

Some person, preferably a high-ranking executive, should have responsibility for directing the employee education program. His duties should consist of overall planning and selecting the instructors or agencies that supply the instructional material. Instructors are more frequently taken from the supervisory personnel who have received supervisory training in employee education programs. This choice provides for the class a leader who is familiar with the company and its procedures and who can talk the language of the employees. Outside specialists are sometimes preferred for controversial subjects in the areas of economic theory and political systems. Vocational teachers and other personnel from public and private educational institutions are frequently called upon to teach courses or prepare teaching materials. These individuals are usually well qualified by training and experience for this responsibility.

Extension and correspondence courses sponsored by educational institutions are also used in employee education programs. These courses are conducted in the plant or at the college, usually under contract between the company and the institution. Some colleges provide a complete employee education program designed to meet the needs of a particular company. Local secondary schools, especially those having vocational programs, are sometimes called upon to provide education programs for industry, especially in areas where industry finds it difficult to obtain qualified assistance from other sources.

The success of an employee education program depends in part on the techniques used in organizing the program. One important technique is to find out what the employees want and include information concerning these wants in the educational program. This information may be obtained from a survey of all employees, through departmental meetings or through advisory committees. Such items as are concerned with security, advancement, proper treatment, useful work, and recognition are frequently included in the list of items employees want.

An important requirement for success is that of securing interest and confidence. This means that the materials and methods should be interesting and pertinent to the expressed wants of the workers. The use of illustrations, models, films, and conference discussions will increase interest and enthusiasm for the information presented. Accuracy in reporting factual information is essential in obtaining confidence. Workers are inclined to be suspicious of some types of information and any errors or half-truths will quickly destroy the confidence of the workers. If the worker does not have confidence in the company that employs him, any kind of employee education is likely to be interpreted as propaganda. This suggests that before any program of employee education is organized, management should know what the attitudes of the employees are towards the company and should include some activities designed to restore or improve confidence where such a need exists. The best educational program is said by many to be the day-to-day activities of a company that demonstrate the fact that the employees' needs and suggestions occupy an important place in the thinking of management.

QUESTIONS FOR STUDY AND DISCUSSION

1. What types of educational programs are financed and operated by industry?

2. What changes occurred in the apprenticeship program during the period 1930 to 1945?
3. What are the apprenticeship standards recommended by the Federal Committee on Apprenticeship?
4. How may an apprenticeship program be organized in a local industry?
5. Distinguish between on-the-job training and employee education.
6. What various ways are used in industry to provide for the organization of on-the-job training?
7. What training methods and procedures are used in on-the-job training?
8. Discuss the development of supervisory training programs.
9. What essentials are included in the organization of supervisory training programs?
10. What units are included in the course of study for the training of supervisors?
11. What are the types of employee education programs?
12. Discuss the characteristics of voluntary and involuntary employee education programs.

SOURCE REFERENCES

Amber, George H., and Paul S. Amber, *Anatomy of Automation*, Prentice-Hall, Englewood Cliffs, N.J., 1962.

Beckman, R. O., *How to Train Supervisors*, Harper & Row, New York, 1952.

Brophy, John M., *Training in New York State Industries*, Research Bulletin No. 1, New York State School of Industrial and Labor Relations, Cornell University, Ithaca, 1949.

Davis, Ralph C., *Industrial Organization and Management*, Harper & Row, New York, 1957.

Earl, Elmer W., Jr., *Employee Education*, Studies in Personnel Policy, No. 119, National Industrial Conference Board, New York, 1951.

Federal Board for Vocational Education, *Report of a Training Course for Foremen Conference Leaders*, Bulletin No. 164, Washington, D.C., 1932.

Fern, George H., *Training for Supervision in Industry*, McGraw-Hill, New York, 1945.

Form, William H., and Delbert C. Miller, *Industry, Labor, and Community*, Harper & Row, New York, 1960.

Gebhart, Carl, *Understanding American Industries*, McKnight, Bloomington, Ill., 1962.

Morgan, Howard K., *Industrial Training and Testing*, McGraw-Hill, New York, 1945.

Mussmann, William W., *Developments in Supervisory Training*, Studies in Personnel Policy, No. 124, National Industrial Conference Board, New York, 1952.

Peters, Raymond W., *Communication Within Industry*, Harper & Row, New York, 1950.

Petrill, Jack, *After the Whistle Blows: Recreation in Industry*, William-Frederick, New York, 1949.

Reitell, Charles E., *Training Workers and Supervisors*, Ronald, New York, 1941.

Schaefer, Vernon G., *Job Instruction*, McGraw-Hill, New York, 1943.

Spriegel, William R., and Edward Schulz, *Elements of Supervision*, Wiley, New York, 1957.

U.S. Department of Labor, Bureau of Apprenticeship, *Apprenticeship Past and Present*, Washington, D.C., 1952.

U.S. Department of Labor, Bureau of Apprenticeship, *Setting Up an Apprenticeship Program*, Washington, D.C., 1954.

U.S. Department of Labor, Bureau of Apprenticeship, *The National Apprenticeship Program*, Washington, D.C., 1953.

Wittich, Walter A., and Charles F. Schuller, *Audiovisual Materials*, Harper & Row, New York, 1962.

CHAPTER SIXTEEN

INDUSTRIAL ARTS

America in a few decades has changed from an agrarian to an industrial nation. This change has resulted in a higher standard of living, but at the same time it has given rise to many new social and economic problems whose solutions require an intelligent understanding of economic processes. The nation's ever increasing capacity to produce goods and services has resulted in a reduction in the hours per day and days per week of work, has postponed the entrance age of youth into employment and has shifted population from rural to urban areas. These changes in industry have brought and are continuing to bring about far-reaching changes in the way of living that require continuous adjustments on the part of the individual. A knowledge of the tools, materials, processes, productive capacity, and relationships of industry is needed to assist in making these adjustments. This is the function of industrial arts.

Industrial arts consists of instructional shopwork which provides general education experiences centered around present-day industrial and technical life. Those who participate in industrial arts programs receive orientation in the areas of appreciation, production, consumption, and recreation through actual experiences in planning, producing, servicing, and repairing various types of consumer goods in common usage. Industrial arts also provides opportunities for exploratory experiences which are helpful in the choice of a vocation. Industrial arts is one of the nonvocational practical arts subjects and consequently is not eligible for Federal aid under the vocational education laws. Industrial arts, unlike other practical arts subjects, is not designed to meet the objectives of both vocational and general education.

About 3,361,000 students were enrolled in industrial arts courses in public junior and senior high schools in 1961.[1] Forty-two percent of these students were in grades seven and eight. Course titles in which 100,000 or more students were enrolled include general shop, woodworking, drafting, metal working, electricity and electronics, handicraft, and graphic arts.

Objectives and Relationships

Industrial arts is often referred to as a curriculum rather than a course of study. It is presently available on various grade levels from the elementary school through the senior college. Industrial arts is available for both boys and girls and for adults who are not enrolled in school or college. The course includes shopwork in areas such as woods, metals, graphic arts, power mechanics, leather, plastics, and ceramics with general drawing and planning included in all of them.

OBJECTIVES OF INDUSTRIAL ARTS

Industrial arts is basically a shop or laboratory subject area, and its purpose is to foster the development of a strong foundation in skills, knowledge, and attitudes related to various aspects of American industry. This purpose is accomplished by planning the industrial arts curriculum to include many activities and experiences related to industrial problems and processes. This planning is facilitated by the use of a series of objectives to further define the purpose and assist in the selection of educational experiences for the curriculum. The selection of educational experiences for the curriculum is made on the basis of the needs of the learner, and youths and adults throughout the

[1] Grace S. Wright, *Summary of Offerings and Enrollments in High School Subjects 1960–1961* (Preliminary Report), U.S. Department of Health, Education, and Welfare, Office of Education, OE24010, Washington, D.C., pp. 9–10.

Senior High School Students Engage in Industrial Arts Experiences
That Are More Advanced and More Specialized Than Those on Other
Grade Levels. (Stoner Wood Products Company, Charleston, Illinois)

nation have many needs in common. This fact has made it possible
for industrial arts educators to prepare a suggested list of overall objectives for the industrial arts curriculum. Such a list was prepared
in 1953 by the Industrial Arts Policy and Planning Committee of the
American Vocational Association in cooperation with industrial arts
educators throughout the nation. The list of these objectives is given
below.

1. *Interest in Industry.* To develop in each pupil an active interest in
industrial life and in the methods and problems of production and exchange.

2. *Appreciation and Use.* To develop in each pupil the appreciation of
good design, materials, and workmanship, and the ability to select, care for,
and use industrial products wisely.

3. *Self-Realization and Initiative.* To develop in each pupil the habits
of self-reliance and resourcefulness in meeting practical problems.

4. *Cooperative Attitudes.* To develop in each pupil a readiness to
assist others and to join in socially accepted group undertakings.

5. *Health and Safety.* To develop in each pupil desirable attitudes and practices with respect to health and safety.

6. *Interest in Achievement.* To develop in each pupil a feeling of pride in his ability to do useful things and to develop certain worthy free-time interests particularly in the crafts.

7. *Habit of Orderly Performance.* To develop in each pupil the habit of an orderly and efficient performance of any task.

8. *Drawings and Design.* To develop in each pupil an understanding of all kinds of common graphic representations and the ability to express ideas by means of drawings and sketches.

9. *Shop Skills and Knowledge.* To develop in each pupil skill in the use of common tools and machines and an understanding of the problems involved in common types of construction and repair.[1]

The general objectives suggested above may be used as a guide in the selection of learning experiences for students in industrial arts. The use of objectives for this purpose is facilitated by first determining the desired behavior changes in the student that should result from accomplishing the objectives and, secondly, by selecting the learning experiences that may bring about the desired behavior changes. For example, when the objective *Interest in Industry* is accomplished the student will have some basic understandings of the industrial system, will be able to describe some of the basic industries, will know the sources of some of the raw materials and will associate industrial methods and activities with the experiences in the shop. The learning experiences that may be selected to accomplish these behavior changes include a study of the manufacture of common articles, a visit to a local industry, a discussion of new industries based upon new materials and the use of some of the raw materials of industry to construct useful projects in the school shop. The desired behavior changes, and more especially the learning activities, will vary among different industrial arts classes and different students in the same class. The industrial arts teacher should understand the techniques of using objectives and, with the assistance of the industrial arts students, select appropriate learning activities for the specific industrial arts class.

OUTCOMES AT DIFFERENT GRADE LEVELS

The foregoing list includes objectives for industrial arts courses on all grade levels. Some of these objectives are emphasized more at one grade level than at another, and some objectives are not applicable to some grade levels. The emphasis at any particular grade level is

[1] American Vocational Association, *A Guide to Improving Instruction in Industrial Arts*, Industrial Arts Policy and Planning Committee, Washington, D.C., 1953, pp. 19–28.

dependent on a number of factors, one of which is the maturity of the student which in turn affects his interests, needs and abilities. It is important that industrial arts educators select appropriate content to meet the objectives emphasized at various grade levels.

Industrial arts experiences in the first six grades are an integral part of the social studies programs. These activities help the children to understand the world in which they live. Emphasis is placed on resources in man's environment and the conversion of these resources into materials of value in improving standards of living. Handicrafts in the elementary school enable the student to develop many basic skills needed in the forming of raw materials into useful articles. The construction of these articles provides an opportunity for self-discovery and self-expression as well as an appreciation for the materials of the environment and the people who work with these materials.

Industrial arts in grades seven, eight, and nine is usually offered for the first time in the life of the student as a separate subject in a shop by a specialized instructor. This course plays an important role in assisting the student to make the adjustment from the elementary school with one teacher for all subjects to the departmentalized junior high school. A wide range of industrial arts experiences is provided to enable the youth to develop a broader understanding of industrial processes and to explore individual interests and aptitudes. Industrial arts in the junior high school provides an opportunity for the student to develop special interests and hobbies helpful in making a wise use of leisure time and such desirable traits and attitudes as pride of workmanship, respect for authority and property rights, and habits of safety. The student also develops skill in the use of common tools and equipment found in the home and school shop. He, or she, develops habits of orderly procedure, ability to do minor construction and repair jobs around the home, skill in the selection, care and use of the products of industry, and the ability to work effectively and pleasantly with others.

Industrial arts experiences in the senior high school are more advanced and more complex than those of the previous grade levels. The high school student is permitted to pursue his interest to the point of specialization in an area of industrial arts. This results in a high degree of accuracy in the use of tools and machines and the construction of projects. Special skill is developed in the use of power equipment, and the more advanced techniques in the use of this equipment result in the acquisition of skills and procedures approaching those used in industry. An extended opportunity is provided for creative work and experimentation which leads to attitudes and appreciations for exploration and discovery.

Industrial arts on the adult and college levels is offered primarily for such purposes as consumer education, recreation, use of leisure time, and general preparation for a vocation. Studies have shown that arts and crafts have therapeutic value for older persons in making adjustments to retirement from productive work. Many of them acquire new hopes and aspirations from arts and crafts hobbies. Industrial arts courses may also meet limited vocational needs for adults who need special skills that may be obtained through these courses. Industrial arts on the college level may become vocational for some students who are preparing to become teachers of industrial arts. Many of these persons enroll for industrial arts courses on the college level for the purpose of acquiring the special skills they will need in the profession of teaching.

RELATIONSHIP TO VOCATIONAL INDUSTRIAL EDUCATION

Some confusion has existed for many years with reference to the relationship between industrial arts and vocational industrial education. Some general educators maintain that there is little difference between industrial arts and vocational industrial education and that the trend is for these two subjects to become more and more alike. Vocational educators and industrial arts educators, on the other hand, insist that the two programs are different and should remain distinct and separate programs. These conflicting points of view are due to a number of causes. First, both types of courses use similar tools, equipment, and materials, and in the smaller schools the same shop is used for both programs. The use of similar materials and facilities has led some persons to make no distinction between the nonspecialized activities of industrial arts and the specialized activities and processes of vocational industrial education. Then, too, the fact that Federal aid is provided for vocational industrial education and not for industrial arts has led some educators to make less differentiation between the two courses than is justified in order to enroll larger numbers of students in the Federally aided courses.

Some misunderstandings with reference to the distinction between industrial arts and vocational industrial education are due to the use of certain terms in vocational industrial and practical arts education. For example, the term *industrial education* includes both industrial arts and vocational industrial education. This suggests to some individuals that the two areas are more similar than they actually are. Then, too, the terms *related information, project, job analysis,* and others are more or less common to both areas, and this adds to the difficulty of differentiating between industrial arts and vocational industrial education.

The distinction between industrial arts and vocational industrial education is one of purpose. Industrial arts is included in school curriculums primarily to serve the nonoccupational needs common to a majority of the students. The objectives of industrial arts are those of general education and are concerned with habits, attitudes, appreciations, leisure time, home mechanics, and consumer knowledge. While some skills useful in a vocation are frequently acquired in industrial arts, this acquisition is incidental and secondary to the major purposes of industrial arts. The purpose of vocational industrial education is to enable workers and prospective workers in industry to acquire vocational efficiency in a chosen occupation. Therefore, the problem of determining whether a specific course involving industrial shop activity is industrial arts or vocational industrial education is simply a matter of determining the major purpose of the shop activity. If it is designed to serve the needs held in common by a majority of school students or adults it is industrial arts insofar as these persons are concerned. If, on the other hand, the shop activity is organized to enable a student to prepare for or progress in a specific occupation of his choice the shop activity is classified as vocational industrial education.

INDUSTRIAL ARTS AND VOCATIONAL GUIDANCE

Some educators have suggested that industrial arts courses make a greater contribution to vocational guidance than any other school subject. This point of view is based on the following considerations. Industrial arts provides the best opportunity afforded by the school for the student to become acquainted with the tools, machines, materials, and processes of many industrial occupations. Industrial arts provides superior opportunities for each student to discover his own occupational interests and aptitudes. Industrial arts provides special opportunities for instructors to discover student attitudes and interests such as pride of workmanship, attention to detail, accuracy, and respect for rights of others, all of which are essential for success in industrial occupations. Industrial arts teachers as a rule are better qualified to counsel with students concerning industrial occupations and to follow them up on the job than are other teachers in the school system. These considerations indicate the possibility of a close relationship between industrial arts and vocational guidance, especially in senior high schools.

Industrial arts has guidance values, but, like other school subjects, it has some limitations in this respect. Industrial arts is primarily concerned with the tools, materials, problems, and occupational information of the mechanical trades. It is not concerned with occupational fields such as agriculture, business, homemaking, and many vocations in industry. The introduction into the industrial arts curriculum of a wide variety of divergent occupational information and activities will tend to reduce the effectiveness of industrial arts because of the time element. Industrial arts must compete with other subject matter areas for a place in the school curriculum, and the time allotted for this subject is limited. There simply is not sufficient time in an industrial arts course to include all the information and activities required for an effective program of vocational guidance. This means that industrial arts should be included in the curriculum because of its industrial arts values. The outcomes that may reasonably be expected to result from industrial arts teaching are sufficient justification for its place in the curriculum. Any guidance values are incidental to these other values.

The Organization of the Industrial Arts Program

The success of a program of industrial arts is influenced by the manner in which the program is organized and conducted. An important factor in the organization and operation of the program is the manner in which the industrial arts curriculum is organized. Then, too, the use of proper methods and materials of instruction is an important success factor. This involves the use of the materials of the environment and the choice of a method to fit a specific situation. Other important considerations involved in the organization of the industrial arts program are teacher qualifications and public relations. A discussion of these factors and procedures is presented below.

CURRICULUM ORGANIZATION IN INDUSTRIAL ARTS

Industrial arts is adaptable to each grade level in the elementary and secondary school and to junior and senior college levels. The industrial arts activities in grades one to six are usually integrated with the units of work in general education subjects and taught in the same room and by the same instructor as are these subjects. A few schools conduct industrial arts courses for grades four, five and six in school shops separate from the classroom. Special instructors are provided for these classes, and each grade group is scheduled to meet shop classes one or more times a week. Some schools have inaugurated a radio handicraft program for the upper elementary grades, in which lessons are broadcast to students in these grades.

Industrial arts courses in the junior and senior high schools are usually organized on three levels. These are exploratory courses, basic courses and intermediate or advanced courses. The exploratory and basic courses are offered in the junior high school and the basic and intermediate or advanced courses in the senior high school. The exploratory courses involve from four to six areas of industrial arts, selected to provide experiences of a handicraft nature on an exploratory level. The basic courses involve a concentration of industrial arts subject matter in one or two areas for one or two semesters. Some schools offer intermediate and advanced courses which provide concentration in one industrial arts area and some maintain research laboratories for talented students. Some schools make a practice of limiting instruction in any one area to three semesters for high school students enrolled in grades nine through twelve. This prevents excessive repetition and permits broadening a student's training to more than one industrial arts area.

The industrial arts classes in the junior and senior high schools are frequently taught in a general shop equipped for each of the areas included in the course. As a rule, one or two teachers have responsibility for teaching a number of areas simultaneously, and the students in one course are distributed among the areas included in the course. This procedure of distributing students among several areas requires the use of special techniques of class organization. In general, two methods of distribution are used. These are referred to as the rotation method and the integration method. The first method involves the rotation of students among the areas at designated intervals. Two plans of rotation are commonly followed. One requires that students spend a stated amount of time in each area, after which they are rotated. The usual practice is to divide students among the areas and rotate all students at the same time. The second method involves the rotation of individual students from one area to another upon the completion of a project.

The integration method of organization is one that permits the industrial arts student to work in one or more areas simultaneously, depending upon the requirements of his particular project. The integration method, as a rule, increases student interest and provides for individual differences. It requires special planning to prevent crowding at some work stations and may add to the difficulty of group instruction.

Industrial arts in the high school carries high school credit as a laboratory subject. Industrial arts classes must be in session the required number of hours per week for the credit allowed. The number of minutes required per week for 1 unit of high school credit in industrial arts varies among the states from 275 to 400 minutes. Some states allow preparation outside the organized classwork to count as part of the 400-minute per week requirement for 1 unit of high school credit.

TEACHING METHODS AND MATERIALS

The shop demonstration has long been the most important teaching method used in industrial arts. Other methods used include the lecture, problem-solving, conference, and textbook study methods. The demonstration consists of showing the student how to do something by actually doing it while he observes. This method is based on the theory of imitation. It is especially useful in teaching shop skills and operations in the industrial arts shop. Well-planned demonstrations involve step-by-step explanations and opportunities for the student to ask questions. Three types of demonstrations are commonly given. These are class demonstrations given to the entire group, small group demonstrations given to two or more students as needed and individual demonstrations given to individual students who need special help. Class demonstrations require careful preparation and review before they are presented to make sure that the desired results will be achieved.

Industrial arts teachers have long used visual aids in teaching. The demonstration method of teaching referred to above is a form of visual instruction. Illustrated lectures in which slides, motion pictures, illustrations, chalk talks and models are used have proved effective, especially in teaching related information. The use of mock-ups for illustrating working principles of devices, such as a telephone receiver, a carburetor, a radio hookup, and the controls of an airplane, have resulted in savings in time and effort in instruction. Visual aids

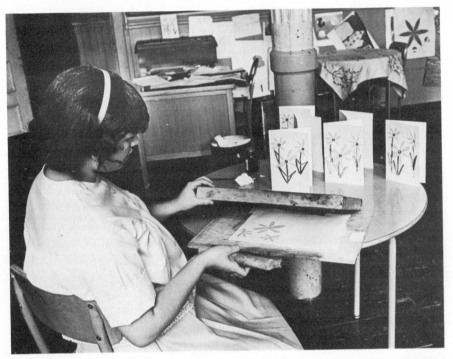

Industrial Arts Provides Many Opportunities for Self-Expression. This student is making silk-screen prints. (Wide World)

are not only useful in providing information, but the judicious use of pictures, charts, mock-ups, and models will add to the attractiveness of the school shop.

Various types of instruction sheets are used in industrial arts classes. Three of the most frequently used types are operation sheets, information sheets, and assignment sheets. Operation sheets are designed to give the learner a definite procedure for carrying out the various operations involved in the construction of an industrial arts project. The operation sheet usually lists the objectives, the tools needed, the materials to be used, and the procedure. Information sheets contain pertinent information the student needs to know about the job assignment or area of work. Assignment sheets are designed to provide directions to the student for the reading, study or experimental work in the industrial arts course. Industrial arts teachers in recent times have made use of student plan sheets. These consist of special blank forms on which each student indicates his own plans for study and construction. These sheets usually contain working drawings and lists of materials and operations.

The emphasis on planning in industrial arts suggests a need for a planning area other than the shop benches or the class recitation seats. The shop library, either in a separate planning room or in a space within the school shop, is coming into general use as a planning center. Most of the new shops have a planning center located as an integral part of the shop. This plan is preferable because it makes planning easier by providing a center in the place where the work is to be done. The planning center is equipped with reference books, bulletins, magazines, project sheets, illustrations, charts, special tables, drawing boards, and drawing instruments, and other devices to facilitate planning. A properly planned and equipped center suggests to the student that planning is an important and worthwhile function in industrial arts.

QUALIFICATIONS OF INDUSTRIAL ARTS TEACHERS

An industrial arts teacher should be qualified as a craftsman and as a teacher. As a craftsman he should possess the mechanical skill required to demonstrate all the craft and mechanical skills he expects students to learn. As a teacher he should have the general and professional education required of all other teachers. The possession of mechanical ability is especially important because students expect the instructor to perform the job operations required of them. Elementary school teachers who offer arts and crafts activities as a part of units of work should acquire the necessary skills either in preservice or in-service courses before attempting to teach these skills to young children. Teacher education institutions are recognizing this need, and more and more of them are organizing industrial arts courses for elementary teachers.

School administrators prefer that an industrial arts teacher have a degree in industrial arts from a four-year college with about one-third of the total graduation requirements in shop and drawing courses. The teacher should specialize in at least one shop area by completing about fifteen semester hours in this area. The remaining semester hours in shopwork should be spread over the other industrial arts areas. About one-sixth of the total graduation requirements should be in professional education courses including student teaching in industrial arts, methods of teaching, curriculum construction, and principles of industrial education. The remaining time should be spent in basic science and mathematics, social science and other general education courses. Craftsmen who are employed as teachers should be encouraged to qualify first in teaching methods and materials and then in general education subjects.

INDUSTRIAL ARTS AND PUBLIC RELATIONS

Industrial arts, together with other industrial education subjects, has a relatively high cost per pupil and is one of the newer additions to the public school curriculum. The general public is likely to question any activities they know little about and more especially the new activities. These facts make it necessary that the public be kept informed of the objectives and accomplishments of industrial arts to insure an intelligent evaluation of this program in times of decreasing school revenues when some groups of citizens are seeking ways of reducing total school costs. Experience indicates that a well-informed public that understands the objectives of industrial arts and its relationship to the total school program will reduce expenditures for this field as a last rather than a first resort. Public relations are also essential in times when school revenues are not declining to insure better support when such support is justified. A public relations program in industrial arts is not only beneficial to the course, but it may bring favorable benefits to the entire school program.

Planned public relations programs include exhibits, contests and sponsored projects, talks before luncheon clubs and community organizations, parent visitation days, newspaper publicity, school assemblies, bulletin boards and showcase exhibits, radio and television programs, and adult classes. Each of these devices has certain advantages and limitations. Exhibits, for example, may place too much emphasis on the completed project and may lead the teacher to do the more difficult operations of the student's work. On the other hand, when properly planned and conducted they provide visible evidence of accomplishments and have a strong appeal to most of the patrons of the school. Talks and addresses require extensive preparation, and not all teachers are proficient in this art. Well-chosen illustrations and visual aids add much to a talk and are essential for the teacher who is not talented in public speaking.

Desirable public relations may be achieved in ways other than planned activities. The day-to-day relationships between the instructor and the student have an important bearing on public relations in industrial arts. When the student reports that the school shop is well arranged and well kept, that the projects are carefully planned, that the instructor is friendly and sympathetic and that the students are acquiring new knowledge and skills, then good public relations are being formed. The attitudes formed by patrons as a result of student opinion are perhaps more important in promoting desirable public relations than are planned activities.

Courses of Study in Industrial Arts

Two types of content are included in the subject matter of industrial arts. These are manipulative skills and related information. The manipulative skills are usually taught by means of a construction project and some drill in the use of tools and materials. The related information is usually acquired by the learner in class or by individual instruction. It consists of information obtained by study and discussion such as the selection of materials and color combinations for projects, the principles of mechanics, the history of materials and the organization of industry. The content of industrial arts, whether it be manipulative or informational, should be selected to accomplish the objectives of industrial arts. Educators are in substantial agreement on the major objectives of industrial arts. The problem of the individual industrial arts teacher is to select the learning experiences for his particular class and school. Some suggestions for making this selection and some illustrations of subject matter content for the various grade levels are indicated below.

SELECTION OF PROJECTS

Most of the class time in industrial arts courses is spent in the making or doing of projects. The term *project* in industrial arts includes something to be made, such as a paper hat, a library table or a door knocker, and something or some job to be done, such as sharpening a plane bit or installing an electric light. The use of projects in industrial arts originated near the beginning of the present century from the use of models in sloyd classes. To the student, the project is the most important part of the industrial arts program. It provides objective evidence of accomplishment and meets an expressed need. To the teacher, the project is a means of accomplishing certain stated objectives of the course. The selection of a project from the standpoint of both the teacher and the pupil is an important industrial arts activity.

A number of factors should be considered in the selection of industrial arts projects. The instructor should evaluate each project that may be available for selection and determine whether or not the project offers an opportunity for the accomplishment of one or more of the objectives of industrial arts. Projects of a trivial nature that do not provide opportunities for accomplishing objectives should be discouraged. Projects should appeal to the interests of the student and should be within his ability. The student is especially interested in projects for his own use and projects for use as gifts to some member of his family. Projects that are beyond the ability of the student usually result in failure and discouragement. Group projects offer possibilities for cooperative action, and students should be encouraged to engage in these projects occasionally.

Industrial arts projects should provide opportunities for using approved construction practices and procedures. Selected projects should be well designed and should provide some new construction experiences for the students. Projects can be both pleasing in form and appearance and sturdy or adequate in details of construction. Since new skills and information are among the desired outcomes, each successive project should contribute something new to the knowledge, skill, and appreciation of the student. Economy is important in industry, and a project that permits the use of economical materials and does not require an excessive amount of time in its construction should be selected.

Teachers of industrial arts usually use a combination of methods for getting students to accept responsibility for projects. Some projects are assigned to students by instructors. Projects that afford opportunities for certain skills and information needed by all members of the group are in this category. Certain job operations for skill purposes are frequently assigned. This method does not permit student planning and frequently does not recognize student interests. Some instructors use a modified form of assignment of project by grouping a series of projects within each of the areas and permitting students to select projects within the designated groups. This method permits the student to exercise some choice and at the same time allows the instructor to include certain processes he considers necessary. In some industrial arts classes students are permitted free choice of projects. This may result in the selection of inconsequential projects or projects beyond the ability of the students. A combination of these methods will doubtless prove most desirable. This involves an assigned project, a group of projects from which individual selections may be made and some opportunity within reasonable limits for individual choice.

RELATED INFORMATION

Related information is included in the course of study in industrial arts for two purposes. These are to increase the student's efficiency in the performance of manual skills and operations and to provide information of a general nature about industrial materials and processes. Related information designed to increase performance and efficiency is frequently referred to as directly related information. By way of example, a student must know how to read an architect's scale before he can make a scale drawing; or he must know the kind of solder to use in constructing a funnel. The amount and kind of directly related information needed depend largely on the knowledge and ability of the student and the projects selected. This type of information is needed at the time the student is constructing the project or learning a process, and it should be taught at the time it is needed. Much of this information may be taught by the instructor at the time he is giving a demonstration. Directly related information may also be provided through individual instruction given as the need arises. Information assignment sheets are also used to provide suggestions and directions for the study of related information.

The second type of related information, given for nonspecific purposes, is often referred to as indirectly related information. Examples of indirectly related information include the study of period furniture, the operation of a factory, the principles of design, or how lumber is manufactured. Information of this nature is valuable in developing appreciations and in providing occupational information that may be useful to the student in making a choice of a future vocation. Related information of this nature should include such facts about the industry as the number of employees, opportunities for advancement, qualifications of workers, pay scale, and other similar data. When properly planned, indirectly related information is interesting enough to be presented to students for its own sake rather than to be hidden in demonstrations and directly related information.

It is not intended that related information, whether it be directly or indirectly related, shall occupy an undue amount of time in the industrial arts curriculum. The curriculum in most areas consists of shop activity, and related information is a supplementary activity. The usual practice in most of these areas is to spend from 75 to 80 percent of the time in manipulative activities and 20 to 25 percent in related information and activities other than tool work. Some industrial arts areas—electricity, for example—require as much or more time for related information as is required for manipulative work.

THE CONTENT OF INDUSTRIAL ARTS IN THE ELEMENTARY GRADES

The units of work in the primary grades one, two, and three provide opportunities for students to study and construct wagons, boats, automobiles, furniture, store counters, mailboxes, farm layouts, television sets, radios, and a host of other toy projects. These projects are constructed or cut out from wood, paper, textiles, clay, plastics, metals, and cardboard. The student in the elementary grades acquires skill in folding, cutting, pasting, and coloring paper; in cutting, sewing, cleaning, and pressing cloth; in shaping, forming, and decorating clay; in sawing, planing, sanding, shaping, and drilling wood; in beating, hammering, bending, shaping, and cutting metal; and in decorating, painting, carving, etching, printing, and dyeing various kinds of materials. Many of these projects are planned and constructed by a committee of students who in the process of planning and construction are learning to work together.

Students in grades four, five, and six learn to work with wood, textiles, plastics, metals, cardboard, and clay. They acquire many new skills such as curling, crimping, and painting paper; molding, forming, and glazing clay; hammering, finishing, and soldering metal; sewing and designing clothing; block printing, stenciling, and glass painting. Industrial arts projects suitable for grades four, five, and six include pull toys, game boards, cutting boards, and bird houses of wood; pin trays, bracelets, letter openers, coasters, and book ends of metal; handkerchiefs, scarfs, belts, hot-dish holders, pin cushions, and purses of textiles; buttons, bracelets, rings, key tags, trays, and bowls of plastic; fans, hats, place cards, pictures, and wastebaskets of paper; and bowls, vases, coasters, and trays of ceramic clay. Many of these and other projects provide opportunities in these grades for students to integrate shopwork with units of work in the classroom.

INDUSTRIAL ARTS COURSE CONTENT IN THE JUNIOR AND SENIOR HIGH SCHOOLS

Industrial arts in the junior and senior high schools usually consists of a series of units or areas designed to provide experience in a variety of industrial fields basic to everyday living. Exploratory courses, especially for junior high school grades, may include the areas of model making, cement craft, leather craft, metal craft, plastics, graphic arts, and electricity, with sketching and planning for each area. Courses offered on the senior high school level may include some of these together with mechanical drawing, auto mechanics, sheet-metal work, forging, foundry work, ceramics, and aeronautics.

Industrial arts courses for junior and senior high school students include many types of learning experiences concerned with planning, designing, and drawing projects in all industrial arts areas. Learning experiences in specific areas include sawing, planing, and fastening wood; layout, cutting, drilling, bending, smoothing, treating, and decorating metal; wiring, insulating, testing, and analyzing electrical circuits; lithoprinting, etching, photographing, and duplicating in the graphic arts; cutting, shaping, casting, assembling, and finishing plastics; tooling, stippling, embossing, fastening, and finishing leather; casting, firing, moulding, and decorating ceramic clay; and weaving, dyeing, knitting, and braiding textiles. The above are but a few of the skills that may be acquired in a few selected areas of industrial arts.

Industrial arts includes learning experiences other than those involving skills. Industrial arts students may acquire information both general and technical in each area. They learn about the sources of raw materials and how these sources have been developed. They acquire information about the characteristics, uses and limitations of these materials. They study the relationships of men and materials and of employers and employees in the industries that use raw materials. They learn about period design in furniture, how metals are refined, the nature of electrical phenomena, how paper is made, types of plastic materials, the care of leather products, the importance of ceramic products, and the care and selection of fabrics. These and many other similar experiences are used to develop understandings and appreciations of the products and problems of industry.

School Shop Management

The school shop is both the classroom and the laboratory of industrial arts education. It contains the tools, machines, and materials for work and study. Because of the wide diversity of experiences that students acquire in the shop it is important that shop facilities be properly organized and managed. A school shop properly arranged and conducted will increase the effectiveness of industrial arts instruction. A number of factors are involved in school shop organization and management. These include the planning of facilities to provide space for work stations and study; the selection and placement of equipment to insure safe and efficient work; the organization of shop personnel

Industrial Arts Students Acquire Knowledge, Skills, and Appreciation in Pottery Making. (Audio Visual Department, Berkeley Unified School District, Berkeley, California)

to provide efficiency in the care of shop facilities, tools, and machines; and the evaluation of shop projects and procedures as a means of maintaining desired standards of performance.

TYPES OF INDUSTRIAL ARTS SHOPS

The first school shops were referred to as manual training shops and, in most instances, were equipped with hand tools for woodworking and with some facilities and equipment for metal work. Emphasis in these shops was placed on the development of hand skills with less emphasis on planning and constructing completed projects. The changes in educational philosophy and practice that have occurred in recent years have brought about changes in school shops. Industrial arts areas other than woodworking and metal craft have been developed, and modern tools and power machines of various kinds have been installed. Present-day shops include arts and crafts work areas, and craft rooms and craft cottages for the elementary grades; general composite, general area, and unit shops for the junior and senior high schools; and mobile shops for small schools.

The handicraft activities carried on in the first three grades require space for a work bench with vises, a work table and cabinet, and shelf space for tools and materials. A corkboard should be provided for announcements and exhibits. The area should be equipped with the necessary hand tools for constructing the selected projects. A special craft room is occasionally provided for grades four, five, and six. This room should be somewhat larger than the classroom. It should include space for assembling the class for demonstrations and space for work in two or more areas such as woodwork, textiles, and art metal work. Storage facilities should be provided for supplies and materials. Some elementary schools have two or more craft cottages, each about 6 feet wide and 12 feet long. Work space for 10 students is provided in each cottage. Each cottage is used for one area, such as wood or metal, and a decorative sign indicates the area.

General composite shops, usually referred to as general shops, provide facilities in one room for instruction in more than one area at the same time. The general shop may serve the needs of smaller schools or schools that employ one or two industrial arts instructors. The general area shop is one in which the subject matter covers one field of industry. For example, a general metal shop may include facilities for welding, machine shop, and sheet-metal work. The general area shop is found in the large schools where more than one shop is needed. The unit shop has facilities for only one single activity of a division of industry. A machine shop, for example, in which instruction is offered in machine shopwork only, is a unit shop. The unit shop is most appropriate in the large senior high school where several shops are provided and advanced work in industrial arts is offered.

Factors to be considered in planning the shop include the area or areas of industrial arts, the nature of the equipment needed and the work space and other space required. The shape of the shop, especially the general shop, should be rectangular and should provide 60 to 80 square feet of floor space per student in addition to auxiliary areas. The shop should contain work stations, a demonstration and assembly area, a study and planning area, storage cabinets and rooms, and a finishing room. The use of small-scale, movable cutouts representing major items of equipment and facilities will be of help in preparing a floor plan for the shop. Attention should be given to heating, lighting, and ventilation, and provision should be made for dust collection especially from woodworking machines. Special consideration should be given in planning to provide safe working conditions. Color schemes, types of floors, spacing and location of machines, lighting and ventila-

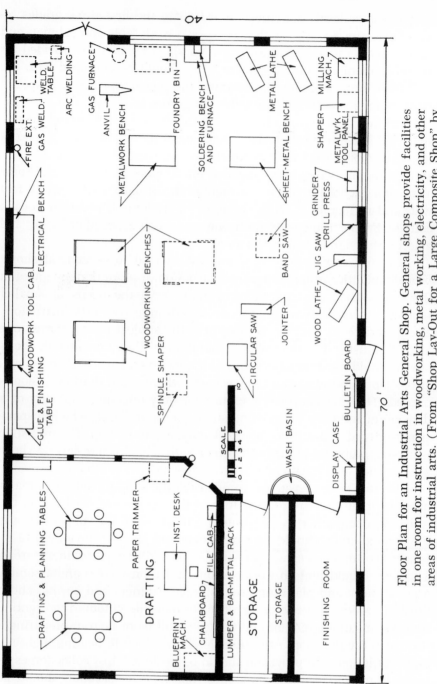

Floor Plan for an Industrial Arts General Shop. General shops provide facilities in one room for instruction in woodworking, metal working, electricity, and other areas of industrial arts. (From "Shop Lay-Out for a Large Composite Shop" by H. H. London, shown in *Industrial Arts and Vocational Education*, March, 1953, published by the Bruce Publishing Company)

tion, and power transmission facilities are important in planning for safety in the school shop.

SCHOOL SHOP EQUIPMENT

The type, amount, and characteristics of school shop equipment needed are determined by such factors as the nature of the course, the maturity of the students, the size and location of the shop space, and the funds available. These factors should be considered in selecting both hand tools and machine equipment. Hand tools are used in each of the areas of industrial arts. Hand tools of standard make and of diverse types and sizes to fit the maturity of the student should be purchased. Standard-make tools are slightly higher in price but are usually more lasting than tools of other brands. Small saws and hammers should be purchased for elementary school students. A wide variety of kinds

Industrial Arts Work Bench for Elementary Schools. This bench provides storage space for hand tools and small projects. (Brodhead–Garrett Company, Cleveland, Ohio)

and sizes of tools is especially needed in the general shop. Care should be taken to purchase only those tools that are needed for specific objectives. Lists of hand tools for specific objectives are included in many books and publications describing industrial arts projects and their construction.

Various systems are used for storing the hand tools. These are of three general types—the central tool room, the wall panel and the work bench storage area. The central tool room requires a tool checker to check tools and equipment in and out. The wall panel permits free access to the tools as needed. The storage of tools in the work bench eliminates wall boards and tool cabinets and reduces traffic in the shop. Each of these types has its advantages and limitations. Each system should be evaluated in terms of a specific situation and modified if necessary to meet the needs of a particular school or shop.

Various factors enter into the purchase of machine tools. Safety, maximum participation by students and type of construction are important considerations. Safe equipment has various types of guards, shields and enclosed housings, no projections such as set screws and knobs on moving parts, and electrical overload protective devices. Machines powered by individual motors with readily accessible starting and stopping switches add to the safety and efficiency of the industrial arts shop. Highly automatic machines are likely to discourage and reduce student participation. Machines designed for a single purpose or type of work rather than multipurpose machines are more satisfactory in industrial arts. Equipment designed for industrial arts rather than heavy, production-type equipment should be installed in the industrial arts general shop. The machines should be equipped with either ball or roller bearings and should have sufficient capacity to handle the work in the shop. These and other criteria which may be secured from textbooks and reference books concerned with industrial arts shops should be observed in securing school shop equipment.

Factors to consider in the installation of school shop equipment include the location of equipment, the preparation of footings and foundation structures, the fastening down of equipment, the installation of facilities for power transmission, the construction of sawdust or gas exhaust systems, and the location of racks and holders. Heavy machines require special foundations, and reinforced concrete is usually recommended for these foundations. Other machines are usually set on felt or rubber pads which are cemented to the machine and to the floor. Bolts and screws are used only on machines that are easily overturned. Acoustical material should be used in shops where it is essential that noise be kept to a minimum. Wiring diagrams and plans and specifications for installing equipment may be secured from equipment manufacturers. These should be followed to assure the efficient operation of power machines in the school shop.

SCHOOL SHOP PERSONNEL ORGANIZATION

The school shop should be organized to provide opportunities for students to conduct and control the shop. An organization of this nature not only saves the time of the instructor, but it provides leadership training and opportunity to learn how workers are organized in industry. Students are qualified to participate in many shop activities. A partial list includes acting as shop foreman, issuing tools and supplies, checking work stations, serving as librarian, supervising paint and finish rooms, lubricating tools and machines, and working on the cleanup committee. Other types of activities in which students may participate include keeping records of class attendance, checking on ventilation, heat and light, and giving out small supplies.

A personnel organization for a school shop should be planned by the instructor in cooperation with the students. The plan should include all items of school shop organization that can be assumed by students and a listing of specific duties and responsibilities for each item. Some method of assigning students and rotating them from one job to another should be agreed upon. Provision should be made for training the student workers for the tasks assigned, and these workers should be encouraged to assume full responsibility for the perform- ance of their tasks rather than to receive directions from the instructor for each activity.

The personnel organization for a general shop may consist of the instructor and several student foremen to assist with various shop activities. Student assistants may include a personnel foreman to check the roll and see that machines and tools are in order at the close of the period, a safety foreman to enforce safety rules, a supply fore- man to issue materials and keep records of materials used, and a pro- duction foreman to assist in planning and organizing group projects. Various other assistants may be selected to meet school shop needs. Some general shops also have a foreman for each area such as a wood- craft foreman, electrical work foreman, and a metal craft foreman. Each of these individuals is responsible for the care and use of the tools, benches, and machines in his area. These foremen see that ma- chines are in safe operating order and free from filings and shavings at the close of each period. When the assignments have been made an organization chart should be prepared showing the specific duties. Questions that arise with reference to assignments may be answered by referring the persons concerned to the charts. A properly managed personnel organization is one of the most valuable devices available for teaching responsibility, respect for rights of others, cooperation, and other attitudes desired of all students.

EVALUATING SHOP PROJECTS AND PROGRAMS

Industrial arts teachers use various types of tests and other meas- uring devices to determine the progress of students and to evaluate the efficiency of industrial arts instruction. Most of these tests are similar to those used in other industrial education areas. Manual skills are usually rated by judging the construction projects and processes. This judging is implemented by the use of gauges, rules, and other instruments for measuring accuracy of work. Progress charts are used to record the judgments made. The usual practice is to include the record of the class on the chart and place it so that it will be available for inspection at all times by all students. Another type of mechanical progress chart is sometimes used to record experiences acquired in the shop. When a student completes a practice such as squaring a board, using a bevel square and using a rip saw, a record of the completion is made on the chart. Some instructors allow each student to rate his own work, subject to review by the instructor.

Various types of teacher-made and standardized tests are used to determine progress and achievement in the acquisition of subject matter. Some tests are available for measuring skills and determining mechanical abilities. Teacher-made objective tests should permit of only one answer, cover many items and be within the comprehension of all students. The testing program should include a variety of tests such as true-false, multiple choice, completion, matching and comprehension tests.

The objectives of industrial arts include the acquisition of various kinds of attitudes. Progress and achievement in the development of desirable attitudes are difficult to measure. Some attempts have been made to devise objective tests for this purpose, but these have not come into general use. The best device presently in use is a subjective rating based on a variety of activities and responses. A day-to-day record of these activities and responses may be kept by the instructor. The information in this record may be used as a basis for arriving at a mark or a statement of progress or achievement in the acquisition of attitudes.

Evaluation is an important aspect of industrial arts programs. An evaluation of an industrial arts program is designed not only to reveal student progress but also to indicate the effectiveness of instruction. It includes various types of tests for students, evaluation sheets for self-evaluation of teaching by instructors, standards of achievement and performance in the shop, various anecdotal records of student experiences and reactions, and other devices designed to assist in the evaluation process. Each of the devices should be selected and used in terms of its validity in measuring one or more of the outcomes previously agreed upon. These outcomes in turn are derived from the objectives. This suggests that a plan of evaluation should be constructed as a result of a study of objectives and that the plan should include a variety of measuring devices, both subjective and objective. The use of such a plan should enable the industrial arts teacher to make continuing improvements in the industrial arts curriculum.

QUESTIONS FOR STUDY AND DISCUSSION

1. What are the objectives of industrial arts?
2. What are some expected outcomes of industrial arts at the elementary school level? At the high school level? At the adult level?
3. What is the relationship of industrial arts to vocational industrial education? To vocational guidance?
4. Suggest a plan of curriculum organization for industrial arts on the elementary and junior and senior high school levels.
5. Discuss the importance of the demonstration method of teaching industrial arts.
6. Outline an acceptable program of public relations for an industrial arts program including both planned and informal activities.
7. What are some characteristics of the industrial arts projects? How may students be led to accept responsibility for undertaking projects?
8. What are the two classifications or types of related information, and how may related information be organized for use in teaching?
9. Discuss the content of the industrial arts curriculum for the elementary school grades. For the junior and senior high school grades.
10. What shop facilities and equipment are needed for industrial arts in the elementary grades? For industrial arts in the junior and senior high school grades?
11. How should the school shop personnel be organized to provide for efficient shop management and opportunities for the development of desirable attitudes on the part of students?
12. Suggest a program of testing and evaluation for the industrial arts curriculum.

SOURCE REFERENCES

American Vocational Association, *A Guide to Improving Instruction in Industrial Arts,* Industrial Arts Policy and Planning Committee, Washington, D.C., 1953.

American Vocational Association, *Industrial Arts in Education* (pamphlet), Industrial Arts Policy and Planning Committee, Washington, D.C.

Bawden, W. T., and others, *Industrial Arts in Modern Education,* published in celebration of the 25th anniversary of the Manual Arts Conference of the Mississippi Valley, Manual Arts, Peoria, 1934.

Byram, Harold M., and Ralph C. Wenrich, *Vocational Education and Practical Arts in the Community Schools,* Macmillan, New York, 1956.

Feirer, John L., and John K. Lindbeck, *Industrial Arts Education*, The Center for Applied Research in Education, Inc., Washington, D.C., 1964.

Gerbracht, Carl, and Frank E. Robinson, *Understanding America's Industries*, McKnight, Bloomington, Ill., 1962.

Giachino, J. W., and Ralph O. Gallington, *Course Construction in Industrial Arts and Vocational Education*, American Technical Society, Chicago, 1954.

Jones, Walter B., *Problems in Teaching Industrial Arts and Vocational Education*, Bruce, Milwaukee, 1958.

Illinois Board for Vocational Education, *Industrial Arts in Grades Seven and Eight*, Series A, Bulletin 140, Springfield, 1953.

Leighbody, Gerald B., *Methods of Teaching Industrial Subjects*, Delmar, Albany, 1948.

Mays, Arthur B., and Carl H. Casberg, *School Shop Adiministration*, Bruce, Milwaukee, 1948.

Moore, Frank C., Carl H. Hamburger, and Anna-Laura Kingzett, *Handicrafts for Elementary Schools*, Heath, Boston, 1953.

Olson, Delmar W., *Industrial Arts for the General Shop*, Prentice-Hall, Englewood Cliffs, N.J., 1962.

Wilber, Gordon O., *Industrial Arts in General Education*, International Textbook, Scranton, 1954.

CHAPTER SEVENTEEN

VOCATIONAL REHABILITATION

Vocational rehabilitation is the process of preparing physically or mentally disabled persons for employment and placing them in suitable jobs. Many agencies in the United States, both public and private, have programs of various kinds for providing assistance to disabled persons. This chapter is concerned with a discussion of one of these programs referred to as the state-Federal vocational rehabilitation program, administered by the Vocational Rehabilitation Administration, U.S. Department of Health, Education, and Welfare. This program is designed for any man or woman of working age with a substantial job handicap due to a physical or mental impairment who has a reasonable chance of becoming employable. The rehabilitation services under the state-Federal program are conducted by the states with the cooperation of the Federal government. State responsibility for vocational rehabilitation in most states is assigned to the state board for vocational education. The Federal government provides leadership, technical assistance, and financial aid to the states.

Vocational rehabilitation is one of the conservation concepts developed in recent years along with those concerned with the conservation of resources. The expenditure of public funds for the conservation of both natural and human resources has become an established public policy. Expenditures for these purposes increase as society becomes more aware of the problems involved and the results that may be obtained. The Federally aided program of vocational rehabilitation has been able to make increasing gains as a result of these increased expenditures. Some facts concerning the growth and development of this program are indicated below.

Rehabilitation Concepts and Problems

The lot of the disabled has never been easy. In early times they were destroyed, abused, and neglected. In more recent years steps have been taken, first by private individuals and agencies and later by public institutions, to provide a more humane treatment for individuals who were so unfortunate as to be disabled. Steps were first taken to remedy some of the contributing causes of disability. Later, some recompense was provided for persons who became disabled in industry and, finally, plans for restoring these persons to employment status were developed.

CHANGING CONCEPTS OF VOCATIONAL REHABILITATION

Man in primitive society had a continual struggle for existence. The preservation of the tribe was of paramount importance, and, according to tribal custom, no individual had a right to live unless he was an asset to the group. The crippled, the blind, and the infirm were liabilities and were either put to death or abandoned to die of hunger and exposure. Defective children in Sparta and Athens were abandoned and allowed to die. Blind children in early Rome were trained to become beggars. Children in ancient Persia destroyed their weak and infirm parents.

During the early Middle Ages the crippled were ridiculed and held in contempt. Later, due to superstitious beliefs, they were suspected of possessing evil powers and punished accordingly. This intolerance persisted for many centuries. As late as the eighteenth century, for example, the English government classified its people into three groups, one of which was composed of "those whose defects make them an abomination." However, late in this same century the attitude toward disabled persons began to change, and in 1780 an English orthopedic surgeon stated that it was wise to educate and treat disabled persons. The first school for the blind in England was established at Liverpool in 1791.

The attitude of the people of the American Colonies was about the same as that of the people of England. The handicapped were first thought to be bewitched, and later they were simply neglected. The rise of modern orthopedic surgery in the nineteenth century resulted in the establishment of special institutions for crippled children. A school for the deaf was established in Hartford, Connecticut, in 1817.

A Physical Disability Need Not be an Occupational Handicap. This young person succeeded as a stenographer despite a disability caused by polio. (Arkansas Vocational Rehabilitation Service)

Between the years 1889 and 1910 the Congress of the United States made land grants to the states of Montana, North Dakota, South Dakota, Wyoming, Utah, New Mexico, and Arizona for special institutions for the care of deaf, dumb, and blind people. Boston, in 1893, established an industrial school for crippled and deformed children with vocational training as its object. Minnesota, in 1897, made the first direct state provision for medical care for crippled children.

Private social agencies in the large cities of the United States at the beginning of the twentieth century secured treatment and found employment for the disabled. Among these organizations were the New York Institute for the Crippled and Disabled, the Cleveland Association for Crippled and Disabled, and the Service League for the Handicapped in Chicago. With the increase in manufacturing, the number of accidents increased, and the problem became more acute. Beginning in 1911, the several states passed laws designed to compensate workmen for injury, and some attention was given to retraining. The need for conserving manpower became apparent in World War I, and a national program of rehabilitation of disabled veterans was established. This program had the effect of emphasizing the need for civilian vocational rehabilitation laws which would increase the manpower potential by returning to employment civilians who were unable to work because of disabilities.

Changes in industrial processes which began in the 1920s have brought about changing concepts of disability. During the first two decades of the twentieth century, a worker was either fit or unfit for work depending upon whether he was sound or unsound as a whole. Competence was measured in terms of anatomical perfection, and, if a man was handicapped for any part of a job, he was considered handicapped for all of it. This concept was justified because of the fact that jobs were not as specialized or subdivided as they have come to be during the last three decades.

The development of the assembly-line process and the increase in specialization have brought about new concepts of disability. A worker in a present-day industrial plant may work on part of a job. Experience has demonstrated that a disabled worker may be able to perform some jobs as well as, or better than, a worker who has no physical or mental disability. Many machines can be operated at maximum efficiency by sightless persons. Some jobs can be performed as well while sitting as while standing or moving, and these jobs can be easily done by some amputees or workers with heart or circulatory disabilities. These facts suggest that a handicap is a relative term. When a physical impairment no longer prevents an individual from doing efficient work, it ceases to be a handicap. Employers are slowly recognizing this fact, and many persons who have acquired disabilities are finding employment that enables them to live active lives and to enter the labor force as self-supporting citizens.

THE SCOPE OF THE REHABILITATION PROBLEM

It is estimated that 74 million persons in the United States (42 percent of the population) suffered from some chronic disease, orthopedic impairment, or serious defect of vision or hearing in 1961. Chronic conditions accounted for 88 percent of all disabling conditions, occupational accidents accounted for 5 percent, highway and other accidents 5 percent and congenital conditions 2 percent. About 9 million persons in the United States sustained work injuries in 1961 that required medical attention or caused restriction of activity for one or more working days. The National Safety Council estimated in 1962 that the annual loss in wages to workers who were injured was about $4400 million. Accidents cost the nation about 235 million man-days of labor in 1962, and about 350,000 persons received some type of permanent disability during that year.

Statistics indicate that there are about 2,150,000 persons in the United States who need and can benefit from vocational rehabilitation. About one-fifth of these persons are so severely disabled that comprehensive rehabilitation services at specialized facilities are considered necessary for their rehabilitation. This list of persons is increasing annually by 270,000 individuals. The disabled persons include 345,-000 persons who are sightless and about 1,500,000 who are blind in one eye. About 300,000 ocular injuries occur in industry each year.

There are in the United States about 200,000 amputees who require prosthetic appliances, and the number of amputees is increasing by from 25,000 to 35,000 persons each year. An estimated 150,000 persons in the United States over 15 years of age are deaf, and about 2,000,000 are hard of hearing. It is estimated that more than 40,000 of the deaf persons and 255,000 of the hard of hearing are in need of and can profit by vocational rehabilitation. The list of disabled persons, many of whom are in need of vocational rehabilitation, includes about 250,000 persons with tuberculosis, 1,500,000 persons with epilepsy and many hundreds of thousands with heart disease and other disabilities.

A report of the Task Force on the Handicapped indicates that the relative number of disabled citizens will probably increase for many years. This increase will be due to advances in medical science, the aging population, and changes in the nature of society. Advances in medical science are saving the lives of countless citizens, but many of them are left disabled. The average life expectancy of the population has increased from 50 years in 1900 to 70 years in 1960. During this period there has not been a corresponding reduction in the incidence of disability among the older people, and advanced age continues to take its toll in chronic illness and injury.

Many social and economic factors have operated to increase disability among the citizens of the nation. Mechanization of industry, urbanization, the increasing frequency and scale of wars, and changes in standards and methods of living have combined to produce a society subject to increasing incidences of disability. Programs of research and action are needed to reduce the causes of disability and rehabilitate the disabled as a means of avoiding waste of manpower and of conserving the human resources of the nation.

THE OBJECTIVES OF VOCATIONAL REHABILITATION

The vocational rehabilitation program is a service to a physically or mentally disabled individual. It assists him to overcome the limitations of his disability by preparing him for suitable employment in which he can earn a living for himself and those dependent on him. The handicapped worker must first be properly prepared physically, mentally, socially, and vocationally for the job he is to do. This suggests that vocational rehabilitation is an individual problem and varies not only with the disability but with the abilities, interests, and attitudes of the client to be rehabilitated. The extent of the handicap is not always in direct proportion to the degree of body impairment. The feeling of insecurity is in some cases a secondary handicap which interferes with rehabilitation.

A second objective in vocational rehabilitation is selective placement. Vocational rehabilitation is not complete until the individual is placed in a position suited to his capabilities and interests. Selective placement provides the opportunity for the disabled worker to use to the best advantage the functions and skills he possesses. The rehabilitated worker who is properly placed has no vocational handicap. The watch repairman must have two sensitive hands, but whether he has two legs or no legs makes little difference in his efficiency as a watch repairman. The experience of many organizations, both public and private, has proved that a combination of comprehensive rehabilitation services and selective placement can bring the disabled individual from a state of dependency to one of activity and productive work.

RESULTS ACHIEVED THROUGH VOCATIONAL REHABILITATION

Studies made through the years by the officials of the state-Federal vocational rehabilitation program have shown that the cost of vocational rehabilitation is repaid many times through increased income and other tax payments of persons rehabilitated. A study made in 1927, based on information from 6391 civilians who had received vocational rehabilitation, showed that their earnings after rehabilitation were in most cases as much as they were before they were disabled. During the period of disability before rehabilitation most of them were unemployed. A study of 66,000 persons who were rehabilitated in 1951 indicated that at the time rehabilitation started 76 percent were unemployed, and those who were employed earned about $16 million a year. After rehabilitation, the annual earnings of this group were estimated at $116 million, an increase of 625 percent. It is estimated that those who were rehabilitated during 1951 paid about $9,-200,000 in Federal income taxes for the first year after they re-entered employment. This represented about 44 percent of the cost of the program to the Federal government in 1951, and these persons will continue to pay income taxes year after year.

A total of 102,377 persons were rehabilitated in 1962 of which 74,000 were unemployed when they began to receive rehabilitation services. Those who had been working at the time they were accepted for services were earning at a rate of about $44 million a year. It is estimated that the entire number of rehabilitants will earn at the rate of $211 million during the first full year after rehabilitation. About 18,000 of the clients who were rehabilitated in 1962 were receiving welfare or other public assistance grants at the rate of $18 million annually at the time they were accepted for rehabilitation services. The conversion of these persons from tax consumers to productive citizens cost about $18 million in a one-time outlay. It is estimated that for every Federal dollar that was expended for their rehabilitation these persons will pay about $7 in Federal income taxes in addition to other taxes during the remainder of their lives.

All the gains from vocational rehabilitation are not measured in dollars and cents. Immeasurable benefits accrue to individuals who pass from relief rolls to payrolls. People who achieve this measure of security are happier and healthier. They develop into better citizens, interested in and contributing to the welfare of the nation. Vocational rehabilitation is an example of democracy at work. It affords the opportunity for disabled persons to get an education, work at a job, and enjoy a wholesome family life.

Vocational Rehabilitation Laws

Laws relative to vocational rehabilitation were enacted in a number of states prior to the passage of the first Federal vocational rehabilitation law. Massachusetts in 1918 became the first state to enact legislation providing for the training of persons who, because of accidents in industry, were unable to continue their occupations. Other states followed, and, at the time of the passage of the first national vocational rehabilitation law, the following twelve states had enacted legislation concerned with vocational rehabilitation: Massachusetts, Nevada,

Sightless Persons Receive Travel Training to Enable Them to Become Occupationally Competent. (Arkansas Vocational Rehabilitation Service)

North Dakota, New Jersey, Minnesota, Rhode Island, California, Illinois, Pennsylvania, Oregon, Virginia, and New York. Most of the state laws conformed in whole or in part to a model vocational rehabilitation law proposed in 1918 by the Red Cross Institute for Crippled and Disabled Men, an institution founded in New York City in 1917.

THE SMITH–FESS LAW
(Public Law 236, 66th Congress)

When Congress in 1918 enacted legislation for the rehabilitation of war veterans who were disabled as a result of service in World War I, there was some discussion concerning the advisability of including a provision in this law for the rehabilitation of persons disabled in industry. However, it was decided that the consideration of such a provision would delay passage of the veterans' rehabilitation bill, and it was agreed that a plan for the rehabilitation of persons disabled in industry would be considered at a later time. Bills for the rehabilitation of persons injured in industry were introduced in the U.S. Congress in September 1918. These bills failed to pass, but a similar bill, referred to as the Smith-Fess bill, became a law on June 2, 1920.

The Smith-Fess or Industrial Rehabilitation Act provided for the promotion of vocational rehabilitation of persons disabled in industry, or in any legitimate occupation, and their return to civilian employment. The Act made an appropriation of $750,000 for the year ending June 30, 1921, and $1,000,000 annually for the next three years. These sums were allotted to the states in the proportion which their population bore to the total population of the United States. The Federal Board for Vocational Education was made responsible for the administration of the law, and the procedure for establishing this program was similar to that proposed in the Smith-Hughes law for establishing programs of vocational education. This procedure involved acceptance of the law by the state, the allocation of responsibility for state administration to the state board for vocational education, the designation of the state treasurer as custodian of the funds, the matching of Federal funds on a dollar-for-dollar basis and the preparation of a state plan for vocational rehabilitation. The state plan was to indicate the kinds of vocational rehabilitation and schemes of placement, the types of instruction, the courses of study, the qualifications of teachers and officers, the provision for teacher training, and the plan of administration and supervision.

The state board for vocational education, under the provisions of this Act, was made responsible for determining the eligibility of persons who applied for training under the general principles established. The Act was made applicable to all persons of employable age who, by reason of a physical defect or infirmity, were incapacitated and who might become employable after receiving rehabilitation. No portion of the appropriations could be used by an institution for handicapped persons except for the special training of such individuals entitled to the benefits of the law.

SUPPLEMENTAL ACTS TO THE SMITH–FESS LAW

The appropriations in the Act of 1920 were operative for a period of 4 years, and supplemental acts carrying substantially the same provisions were enacted in 1924, 1930, and 1932. The Act of 1932 authorized funds for a 4-year period ending in 1937. Vocational reha-bilitation was extended by Congress to Hawaii in 1924, to the District of Columbia in 1929, and to Puerto Rico in 1931. Additional funds were made available by the Federal Emergency Relief Administration from October, 1933, to July, 1937. The use of relief funds was discon-tinued in July, 1937.

The Social Security Act of 1935 authorized an appropriation of $841,000 annually for vocational rehabilitation for the years 1936 and 1937. This amount was added to the appropriation made under the provisions of the Vocational Rehabilitation Act and resulted in a total appropriation of $1,938,000 for vocational rehabilitation for each of the 2 years. This amount was again authorized in 1938 and was in-creased to $3,500,000 in 1939. Meanwhile, Congress in 1936 enacted the Randolph-Sheppard law which authorized the placing of blind persons as operators of vending stands in Federal buildings. This pol-icy was enacted as a means of increasing the economic opportunities for the blind. This law also authorized the U.S. Office of Education to make surveys of employment opportunities for the blind.

THE BARDEN–LAFOLLETTE ACT
(Public Law 113, 78th Congress)

The Barden-LaFollette or Vocational Rehabilitation Act of 1943 amended the Industrial Rehabilitation Act of 1920. This law author-ized payments for physical restoration to reduce or eliminate the dis-ability, permitted service to the emotionally or mentaly ill and made new provisions for the rehabilitation of the blind. Under the provisions of this law, Federal funds were made available for the expense of voca-tional rehabilitation of war-disabled civilians and for the entire cost of state administration, including vocational guidance and placement. The law provided that other expenses were to be shared by the Federal government and the states on a dollar-for-dollar basis. These other costs included the cost of medical and psychiatric examinations, medi-cal treatment and hospital care, training and training supplies, living and certain travel expenses, and occupational tools, licenses and equip-ment.

The payments were made to the states in accordance with ap-proved state plans for vocational rehabilitation, and the funds neces-sary were authorized to be included in the appropriations for the Federal Security Agency. This Act changed the allocation of Federal funds to the states from a population-ratio basis to one of need as determined by the states and within the limits of the Federal appropriation for vocational rehabilitation.

THE VOCATIONAL REHABILITATION AMENDMENTS
(Public Law 565, 83rd Congress)

Congress in 1954 amended the 1943 vocational rehabilitation law to provide stated sums allocated to the states by formula for increased rehabilitation services and for new kinds of programs. The sums authorized increased from $30 million beginning in 1954 to $65 million in 1957 and thereafter as Congress should determine. These funds were available for grants to the states to assist them in meeting the cost of vocational rehabilitation services and for additional services not included in the 1943 Act, as follows: (1) hospitalization necessary in connection with surgery or treatment without the time limitation provided in the 1943 law; (2) tools, equipment, initial stock, and supplies for vending stands and small business enterprises for the severely handicapped; and (3) the establishment of special rehabilitation facilities for disabled persons and workshops for the severely disabled.

Three types of Federal grants were authorized in the vocational rehabilitation law of 1954. These were (1) grants to states to assist them in meeting the cost of vocational rehabilitation services; (2) grants to the states to assist them in initiating expansion and improvement projects; and (3) grants to the states and to public and private nonprofit organizations for research, demonstration, training and other special projects. The grants for rehabilitation services were allotted to the states by means of a special formula designed to provide relatively more unmatched Federal funds for the less wealthy states. The Federal share of these funds varied from a minimum of 50 percent of the cost of the program to a maximum of 70 percent. The grants for extension and improvement were allocated to the states on a population ratio. Grants for special projects were made by the Secretary of Health, Education, and Welfare when approved for aid by the National Advisory Council on Vocational Rehabilitation provided in the Act.

The new law also specified some requirements to be included in state plans for vocational rehabilitation; it required the Secretary to develop cooperative programs with other agencies to facilitate placement; it designated the state board for vocational education, or a state agency primarily concerned with rehabilitation, as the administrative agency; and it made provisions for studies and investigations of homebound physically handicapped individuals.

REHABILITATION OF DISABLED WAR VETERANS

Pensions to soldiers and sailors of the United States who became disabled in line of duty have been provided since 1776. The first home for disabled volunteer soldiers was established in 1865. Numerous laws granting pensions have been enacted but it was not until World War I that provisions for retraining disabled servicemen were made.

Congress in 1918 enacted the Smith-Sears Law (Public Law 236, 66th Congress) providing physical restoration and retraining for servicemen of World War I who were disabled in line of duty. Responsibility for the retraining was given to the Federal Board for Vocational Education, but in 1921 this responsibility along with other Federal government activities relating to war veterans was transferred to the Veterans Bureau. The rehabilitation program was operated until 1928 at which time all rehabilitation activities for World War I veterans ceased. During this 10-year period a total of 128,700 disabled veterans completed training at a cost of about 635 million.

Congress in 1943 enacted Public Law 16 providing for the rehabilitation of disabled veterans of World War II. The law was extended to disabled veterans of the Korean conflict by Public Law 894 of 1950. Provision was made for all neceessary expenses of rehabilitating disabled veterans including medical, educational and living costs. The Veterans Administration reported that a total of 680,000 disabled veterans of World War II and the Korean conflict had entered training under the provisions of these two laws by June 30, 1960. The Federal government expended about $2,400 million for subsistence, tuition, supplies and equipment for these programs.

Studies revealed that the average age of entering trainees was 27 years for World War II veterans and 24 years for Korean veterans. The average schooling was about 12 years Ninety percent of the veterans who were employed after rehabilitation were using skills acquired during training, and the average earnings of disabled veterans who completed training compared favorably with comparable groups in the total population.

Vocational Rehabilitation Services

The vocational rehabilitation of a handicapped person is a complex, specialized, personal service and must take form according to the peculiar difficulties and aptitudes of each person rehabilitated. This process of rehabilitation, as a rule, involves a number of services, some of which are provided at no cost to the individual and some at varying costs to the individual, depending upon his ability to pay. Among those provided at no cost are medical diagnostic services, individual counseling and guidance, vocational training and placement, and follow-up. Services provided on the basis of economic need are physical restoration, including hospitalization when needed; prosthetic appliances; maintenance and transportation while receiving service; and tools, equipment, and licenses. A discussion of these services is presented below.

MEDICAL EXAMINATION AND VOCATIONAL APPRAISAL

Every applicant who is considered eligible for vocational rehabilitation services receives without charge a general medical examination, including standard laboratory tests. Its purpose is to learn the extent of the disability, to discover possible hidden or secondary disabilities, to help determine how much work the client may be fitted to do, and to determine the applicant's eligibility for service and his need for further special examination. These examinations frequently indicate the need for physical restoration before training or other services are attempted. They provide the counselor with the needed information for counseling the client regarding his limitations and his capacities to follow specific training and to do particular jobs.

The personal appraisal made from the results of a personal interview gives the counselor a knowledge of the client's education, his work experience, and his home and family conditions. This helps the counselor and the client in deciding what work the client may do. Tests of aptitudes and interests are given to indicate possibilities of success in certain occupational fields. The information from the examinations, interviews and tests is used in preparing the vocational rehabilitation plan.

GUIDANCE AND COUNSELING

The guidance and counseling service is provided to coordinate the various parts of the rehabilitation process into an organized plan of rehabilitation for the individual concerned. The service begins at the first interview and extends through placement and follow-up on the job. Counseling helps the disabled person to understand his abilities and limitations and how to correct the difficulties he is encountering in the rehabilitation process. Proper counseling requires the services of specially qualified persons, and experience has shown that best results are obtained when the same counselor confers with a client throughout the rehabilitation program.

During the first phase of the counseling process the counselor considers such facts as the client's educational background and the availability of training and placement opportunities. A study is made of the social and economic environment of the client to determine to what extent his family and dependents are involved. Various standardized tests supply information that may be helpful in advisement. The counselor and the applicant use the medical diagnosis and prognosis together with the information obtained in the counseling interview to develop a complete rehabilitation plan.

Plans for fitting disabled persons for specific job objectives are always tentative. It is not infrequent for a plan to be revised several times before rehabilitation is finally accomplished. Rehabilitation plans for the same job objective will vary with persons or conditions. The preparation of a plan of rehabilitation is an individual matter, and group planning is not feasible. These facts make it necessary that guidance and counseling continue throughout the period of rehabilitation and placement.

The vocational rehabilitation laws provide for cooperation between the workmen's compensation agency and the rehabilitation services of a state. This cooperation consists largely of reporting the cases and adjusting compensation payments to facilitate rehabilitation. With proper guidance and job readjustment, many workers who are injured may be returned to the same or to other suitable jobs. In some cases the vocational service may recommend a lump-sum settlement to enable the injured person to go into business or take other steps in his vocational rehabilitation. In other cases the same procedures are followed as in the rehabilitation of persons disabled as a result of reasons other than those included in workmen's compensation regulations.

PHYSICAL RESTORATION

Physical restoration consists of any type of medical, surgical, psychiatric, or hospital care that is needed to remove or reduce the client's disability. This service or treatment is provided when it is determined that it will increase the vocational possibilities of the client. Included in these services are occupational therapy, hospitalization, dentistry, care in a convalescent or nursing home, drugs, and other medical supplies, and prosthetic appliances. Physical restoration services are provided by qualified physicians in approved hospitals and clinics.

Physical restoration is frequently a necessary antecedent to vocational rehabilitation. The physical restoration program is not a general medical care program but one designed to make definite contributions to improved job performance. The following conditions must be met if medical services beyond diagnosis are provided: disabling conditions must be stable, or relatively so; they must constitute substantial handicaps; they must be susceptible of substantial reduction or elimination as handicaps; and the time consumed in treatment must be reasonable.

The severely disabled frequently present a problem in vocational rehabilitation. These clients often require an integrated program of physical restoration and vocational training, and facilities of this type are limited. The rehabilitation center provides this type of service to the severely handicapped. These rehabilitation centers offer comprehensive programs for severely disabled persons following their medical or surgical treatment. Generally, the services comprise physical restoration, vocational counseling, psychological evaluation, social services, vocational training, and recreation. The physical restoration services include physical and occupational therapy.

In many instances, rehabilitation of the physically disabled is impossible without the supplying of appliances such as artificial arms, legs, eyes, braces, and hearing aids. These appliances are usually substitutes for missing members and are supplied for the purpose of restoring the individual to the greatest possible occupational efficiency. Sometimes an artificial appliance is needed for the sake of appearance and sometimes for the sake of morale. Merely providing an appliance does not necessarily increase the client's vocational skill, although it does add to his functional capacity. Frequently experience demonstrates that appliances have no practical value for certain types of disabilities. Proper fitting of the prosthetic appliance is most important, and specialists should be consulted for advice as to the type of appliance and other factors concerning the fitting of the appliance. Improper fitting may cause a disabled person to lay aside and never again use a prosthetic appliance.

VOCATIONAL TRAINING

Vocational training is designed to enable the client to acquire the knowledge, skills, and attitudes needed for the efficient performance of his chosen occupation. This may consist of helping the client to regain former skills or of assisting him to acquire new ones that are suited to his capabilities and interests. This training is usually provided after physical restoration, except that some severely disabled persons may receive training in rehabilitation centers while they are receiving physical restoration. The training is also provided in private or public schools and colleges, shops, factories, by correspondence, or other means. Instruction may be given on a part-time or full-time basis, in a group or by means of individual instruction techniques. Vocational training is provided for certain occupations at the client's home or farm. The extent of training is limited to the amount necessary to fit the client for the vocational objective set forth in the plan of vocational rehabilitation.

Supervision of both the client and the training agency is essential to the success of vocational training. The disabled person, the training agency, and all contributing agencies should be contacted at frequent intervals to determine the progress the client is making. Supervision also serves as a test of the success and efficiency of a program of rehabilitation. Supervision is accomplished through reports from training agencies, by personal visits and by conferences with individuals who know the disabled person and the work that he is doing. When the results of supervision show that the client is not making satisfactory progress, an attempt should be made to make any needed changes.

Disabled persons are not eligible for placement until they reach working age, but a large number of children are potential cases for rehabilitation when their difficulties constitute vocational handicaps. Provision is made in few states for the basic education of these children except in institutions for limited groups such as the blind and the deaf. The courses in most public schools are not properly arranged or adapted to these children. Much could be done to provide prevocational and basic education for disabled children, who eventually will be eligible for vocational rehabilitation, by establishing appropriate courses in public elementary and secondary schools.

MAINTENANCE AND TRANSPORTATION

Many disabled persons who have no means of support become serious problems for the state rehabilitation service. They must either be placed in employment immediately, usually below the level of their vocational capacities, or some means must be provided for their maintenance during their program of rehabilitation. Rural clients and clients in smaller communities are especially in need of this type of assistance, because training facilities are usually located in cities.

When clients do not have sufficient funds for maintenance and transportation to enable them to pursue a vocational rehabilitation program, funds may be supplied by the vocational rehabilitation service. Funds provided for maintenance and transportation are intended to supplement rather than replace resources or income available to the client, and a limit is usually placed on the period of time for which these funds are available.

Before aid is provided to a client for maintenance and transportation, the state agency makes a determination of the client's need for aid. A client is considered in financial need if he has insufficient resources to provide standard living requirements and to meet the cost of other necessary vocational rehabilitation services. Each state agency has a standard for measuring financial need. This standard is based on differences in cost of normal living requirements in different localities, on differences in cost of living due to different types of disabilities, and on differences due to special rehabilitation services to be provided. This standard is applied to the resources and needs of each particular client to determine the amount of financial aid that should be provided by the state rehabilitation agency and may be adjusted to short and long periods of training. Only those resources that are actually available to the client for use during the period of his rehabilitation are taken into account in the evaluation of the client's resources.

PLACEMENT AND FOLLOW-UP

A disabled person is not considered vocationally rehabilitated until he or she is placed in a remunerative occupation. Placement presents some difficulties largely occasioned by prejudice and fear of employing disabled persons. Experience has shown that when a properly trained person is placed in the occupation for which he was trained, his performance and safety record in employment equal or exceed those of other employees. The wide range of occupations for which disabled persons are adapted is illustrated by studies made by the U.S Vocational Rehabilitation Administration. These studies show that during the past few years about 30 percent of the rehabilitated persons were placed in skilled and semiskilled occupations, about 20 percent were placed in clerical and sales occupations, about 15 percent in service occupations, 10 percent in professional and managerial occupations, 10 percent were family workers and housewives, about 8 percent were in agriculture, and 7 percent in unskilled occupations.

The vocational rehabilitation agency shares responsibility for placement with other agencies such as the state employment service,

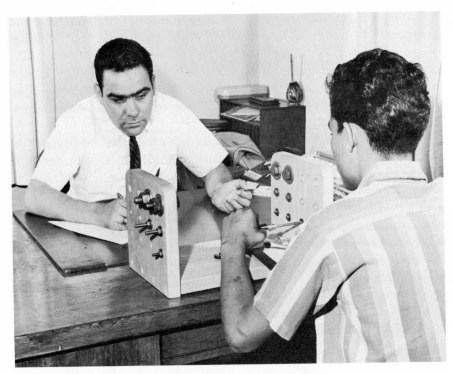

Vocational Rehabilitation Enables Many Disabled Persons To Become Self-Supporting Citizens. The disabled individual shown above is taking a mechanical aptitude test. (Fujihira from Monkmeyer)

private employment agencies, and various placement bureaus of educational institutions. The disabled person in many instances assumes responsibility for his own placement. Placement of disabled workers requires cooperation of employers. This cooperation is best secured when the employing agency has confidence in the efficiency of the training program. The employer should be able to rely on the recommendation of the rehabilitation counselor and should be conscious of the fact that he is not expected to provide work for a disabled person on a charitable basis.

The 1954 vocational rehabilitation law permitted the states to use a portion of the Federal vocational rehabilitation funds to remodel and equip workshops for the severely disabled. These workshops, in which manufacturing and hand work are carried on, are public or other nonprofit establishments. They are operated for the primary purpose of providing remunerative employment to severely disabled persons who cannot readily find employment in the competitive labor market.

The final phase of the rehabilitation program is that of follow-up. This service is performed by the rehabilitation counselor and consists of observing the disabled worker's job performance for a reasonable time. The function of follow-up is to ascertain whether the vocational handicaps have been removed, whether the client is able to engage in a remunerative occupation and whether he or she has the ability to satisfy the employer. The period of follow-up varies with the individual client. It may indicate that further medical, psychiatric, or surgical care is needed or that more training is required. In brief, the follow-up indicates whether or not the client and his employer are satisfied with one another—at no cost to either party.

The Organization of the Vocational Rehabilitation Program

The Industrial Rehabilitation Act of 1920 established the policy that the Federal government would share with the states the common responsibility for vocational rehabilitation. The Federal government under this policy assisted the states in financing the program but left to the states the responsibility for the operation of the program, and encouraged the states to develop standards of efficiency in this operation. The Federal government served as a clearing house for the states and made available to them the results of studies and investigations of vocational rehabilitation work. The Vocational Rehabilitation Act of 1943, as amended in 1954, made some changes in the basic plan of organization and administration of the state-Federal program of vocational rehabilitation.

THE FEDERAL ORGANIZATION

The Federal Board for Vocational Education assumed responsibility for the administration of the Smith-Fess law in 1920 and established a division of industrial rehabilitation on a coordinated basis with the two other divisions for which it was responsible—vocational education and vocational rehabilitation of disabled servicemen. The vocational rehabilitation division maintained a central office in Washington and district and local offices throughout the nation. The services rendered to the states included assistance in the training of new personnel, in organizing record systems, in improving case service, in reorganizing state programs, and in extending state programs into local communities. The vocational division also engaged in research and surveys for the purpose of improving programs of vocational rehabilitation.

When the functions of the Federal Board for Vocational Education were transferred to the Department of the Interior, the Secretary of the Interior placed the administration of the vocational rehabilitation program in the U.S. Office of Education under the Assistant Commissioner for Vocational Education. This arrangement continued until July, 1939, at which time a vocational rehabilitation division, with a director responsible directly to the U.S. Commissioner of Education, was created.

The program of vocational rehabilitation was reorganized as a result of the passage of the Vocational Rehabilitation Act of 1943. An Office of Vocational Rehabilitation was established in the Federal Security Agency. When the U.S. Department of Health, Education, and Welfare was created in 1953, the Office of Vocational Rehabilitation became a part of this Department. This Office became the Vocational Rehabilitation Administration in 1962. The principal sections of the office include administration, program planning and evaluation, rehabilitation services, management services, and state administrative development. The Office provides leadership for the program, establishes advisory standards, and furnishes technical assistance to the states. The rehabilitation of disabled persons involves the work of many agencies, and the Vocational Rehabilitation Administration serves as a clearing house for public and private organizations. The Administration has entered into agreements with many of these agencies to encourage the widest use of all community facilities needed for rehabilitating the disabled.

STATE ORGANIZATION FOR VOCATIONAL REHABILITATION

The Federal vocational rehabilitation acts, prior to the Act of 1954, designated the state board for vocational education as the administrative agency responsible for the state administration of vocational rehabilitation. Most of the states placed responsibility for the program of rehabilitation in the state board for vocational education, but in two states—New Jersey and Pennsylvania—the program was operated by some other agency. However, by agreement, the state boards for vocational education in these states were responsible to the Federal government for the administration of its policies concerned with the Federal vocational rehabilitation acts. The Vocational Rehabilitation Act of

1954 permitted an agency other than the state board for vocational education to administer the program.

The Vocational Rehabilitation Act of 1954 required that the head of the state program of vocational rehabilitation should be responsible only to the state rehabilitation agency or its executive officer. The usual practice under this law was to organize the vocational rehabilitation services as a division of the state department of education with a director of vocational rehabilitation responsible to the executive officer of the state board for vocational education. This meant that in most states the state director of vocational rehabilitation was responsible directly to the chief state school officer.

Few disabled persons apply for rehabilitation on their own initiative. Usually they are referred to the department by some interested agency or person. The agreements of cooperation between the state-Federal rehabilitation service and other state agencies are primarily for the purposes of locating cases and placing rehabilitated persons. Experience has shown that it is important to make prompt contact with the injured person to prevent him from becoming unduly affected by the idleness and hopelessness which often accompany physical or mental impairment.

Some vocational rehabilitation is conducted by the case method. It is a personal service for individuals, and the state organization needs a staff of officers to work with disabled persons. This staff has varied from 1 to 3 persons in some states to as many as 150 in other states. The state staff, in addition to the director, usually consists of officials in charge of rehabilitation, physical restoration, services for the blind, counselors and a medical advisory staff. The state staff has responsibility for purchasing from existing agencies and individuals the services needed in vocational rehabilitation.

The state division of vocational rehabilitation prepares the state plan for vocational rehabilitation for the approval of the state agency responsible for the administration of the program. The state staff is also required to maintain cooperative relations with the many other agencies in the state that are in a position to assist in the rehabilitation work. Among these other agencies are employment-security divisions; state departments of health, labor, and welfare; social agencies; physicians, hospitals and clinics; churches; and fraternal, civic, and business organizations. These cooperating agencies perform services such as reporting cases; providing social services for the disabled person and his family; and assisting in supervision, placement, follow-up, and the promotion of legislation for vocational rehabilitation.

SPECIAL SERVICES FOR THE BLIND

The blind constitute a special problem in vocational rehabilitation. This is due in part to the scarcity of modern rehabilitation centers, schools, and other facilities that offer vocational rehabilitation services to blind persons; and to the reluctance of many employers to hire qualified blind persons. The Federal government and the states have attempted to develop special facilities not only for the totally blind, but also for the partially sighted whose ability to see is so limited as to be a handicap to their employment. The services offered in these facilities include diagnosis, treatment, adjustment, vocational training, placement, and follow-up. The increase in the scope and nature of services to the blind reflects the changing concepts of vocational rehabilitation that have occurred in recent years.

The Federal government in 1879 created a perpetual fund to assist in the support of the American Printing House for the Blind. Since 1899 the Federal government has made special concessions on postage for literature for the blind. Since 1930, Congress has made special appropriations to the Library of Congress for the purchase and distribution of books for the blind. The Social Security Act of 1935 authorized Federal appropriations to enable the states to furnish financial assistance to needy blind individuals. The U.S. Treasury Department in 1929 granted blind persons the privilege of operating vending stands in Federal buildings. These stands were limited by regulation to the sale of newspapers and periodicals. The Randolph-Sheppard Act of 1936 permitted the sale of various articles in these stands in addition to newspapers and periodicals. The vocational rehabilitation amendments of 1954 authorized the state rehabilitation agency to use Federal funds to purchase equipment and initial stocks for vending stands for both the blind and the severely disabled.

Rehabilitation centers for the adult blind are in operation in some states. These centers are designed to assist the client in understanding his abilities and limitations, to restore his confidence in his ability to carry on certain work activities and to aid in the making of a vocational diagnosis. These centers are operated by public and private agencies usually in cooperation with state vocational rehabilitation services, state departments of public welfare, and private organizations interested in the rehabilitation of the blind. A center may serve the needs of one state or of a number of states in a region.

Two types of services are usually provided in these centers: diagnostic and adjustment. The diagnostic service is designed to enable the counselor in the center to obtain a thorough understanding of the client, and to provide the client with an understanding of his problems and an acceptance of his disability. The diagnostic service includes an analysis of intelligence, interests, aptitudes, motivation, social attitudes, habit patterns, and physical condition. Clients who are in need of vocational diagnosis engage in such activities as work tryouts, job samples, and exposure to occupational information.

The adjustment service which also may be a part of the diagnostic service is concerned with a personal acceptance on the part of the client of the reality of blindness, and with a plan for overcoming the problems growing out of this condition. The rehabilitation center uses various activities to promote better adjustment. Among these are personal grooming, table etiquette, use of the telephone and typewriter, script writing, Braille, learning to travel with a cane or a guide, and shopping and handling money. Clients also receive training in arts and crafts, general information, educational and vocational guidance, and physical conditioning. Various studies of clients who have completed training at rehabilitation centers have indicated that the center approach is meeting the needs of many sightless persons throughout the nation.

THE COST OF THE PROGRAM

Total expenditures for vocational rehabilitation for the 42-year period 1921 to 1962 inclusive were about $875 million. The Federal government expended about $557 million during this period, which represented about 64 percent of the total. The remaining 36 percent was expended by the several states. These data included expenditures by state boards for vocational education and state agencies for the blind. The total number of persons who took training and returned to employment during this 35-year period was 1,428,000 persons. The average expenditure per person for this period was about $612. Some states experienced difficulty prior to 1930 in matching all Federal funds appropriated, and legislation in 1930 provided that funds that were not used for this reason in one state could be transferred to another state if this other state would match the funds. The passage of this legislation resulted in the use of all the Federal funds appropriated.

The Vocational Rehabilitation Act of 1943 and the amendments of 1954 made Federal funds available for additional services and changed the method of appropriating funds. This resulted in a large increase in expenditures for rehabilitation. The total expenditures for vocational rehabilitation for the 19-year period 1944 to 1962 were

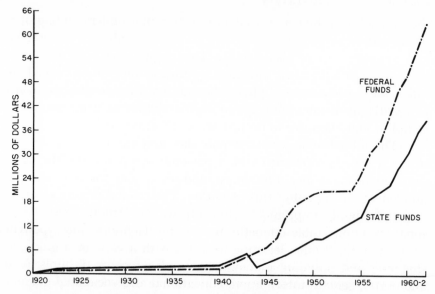

Expenditures for Vocational Rehabilitation by Source of Funds in the States and Territories, 1920 to 1962. Expenditures by the Federal government for vocational rehabilitation increased from about $6 million in 1944 to more than $60 million in 1962. (U. S. Department of Health, Education, and Welfare, Office of Vocational Rehabilitation, *Annual Report, 1954*, and *Departmental Report, 1962*, Government Printing Office)

$818 million. This amount represented 94 percent of the total expenditures for the 42-year period. The Federal government provided 65 percent of this 19-year total and the states 35 percent. A total of 1,217,900 persons were rehabilitated during this period at an average expenditure of $672 per client, as compared to an average of $268 per client for the 23-year period 1921 to 1943. These data indicate that the cost of rehabilitation is relatively inexpensive in terms of its social and economic values.

QUESTIONS FOR STUDY AND DISCUSSION

1. How is vocational rehabilitation defined, and what agencies are interested in vocational rehabilitation?
2. Discuss some of the changing concepts of vocational rehabilitation and some of their implications.
3. Indicate some of the problems involved in vocational rehabilitation and some of the results that have been achieved in vocational rehabilitation programs.

4. Discuss the provisions of the Smith-Fess law.
5. In what ways did the Barden-LaFollette law differ from the Smith-Fess law as amended?
6. What additional programs and services were provided in the vocational rehabilitation amendments of 1954?
7. Discuss the organization and scope of the rehabilitation program for war veterans.
8. What services are included in the state-Federal vocational rehabilitation program?
9. Discuss the importance of placement and follow-up and how these services are provided in the state-Federal vocational rehabilitation program.
10. Discuss the changes that have occurred in the Federal and state organizations for administering the state-Federal vocational rehabilitation laws.
11. What special services are provided for the blind in the state-Federal vocational rehabilitation program?
12. What has been the cost of the state-Federal vocational rehabilitation program through the years, and how has this cost been divided between the Federal government and the states?

SOURCE REFERENCES

Federal Board for Vocational Education, *Annual Reports,* 1920 to 1932 inclusive, Washington, D.C.

Federal Security Agency, Office of Vocational Rehabilitation, *The Vocational Rehabilitation Program, Facts in Brief* (monograph), Washington, D.C., 1952.

Federal Security Agency, Office of Vocational Rehabilitation, *Vocational Rehabilitation for Civilians* (pamphlet), Washington, D.C., 1952.

Hawkins, Layton S., Charles A. Prosser, and John C. Wright, *Development of Vocational Education,* American Technical Society, Chicago, 1951.

National Health Education Committee, *Facts On the Major Killing and Crippling Diseases in the United States Today,* New York, 1961.

U.S. Congress, *Laws Relating to the Physically Handicapped,* House Document No. 753, 79th Congress, 2nd Session, Washington, D.C., 1946.

U.S. Congress, *The Vocational Rehabilitation Amendments of 1954,* Public Law 565, 83rd Congress, Chapter 655, 2nd Session. Washington, D.C., 1954.

U.S. Department of Health, Education, and Welfare, *Annual Reports,* 1956 to 1962 inclusive, Washington. D.C.

U.S. Department of the Interior, Office of Education, *Vocational Rehabilitation of the Physically Handicapped,* Vocational Education Bulletin No. 190, Washington, D.C., 1936.

U.S. Office of Defense Mobilization, Manpower Policy Committee, *Report of the Task Force on the Handicapped to the Chairman, Manpower*

Policy Committee, Office of Defense Mobilization, Washington, D.C., 1952.

U.S. Office of Education, Digest of Annual Reports of State Boards for Vocational Education for fiscal years 1933 to 1943 inclusive, Washington, D.C.

U.S. Office of Vocational Rehabilitation, Annual Reports, 1944 to 1955 inclusive, Washington, D.C.

CHAPTER EIGHTEEN

VOCATIONAL EDUCATION IN OTHER NATIONS

The program of vocational education in the United States has been influenced by and has influenced vocational education programs in many lands. The early settlers brought the apprenticeship programs from Europe to colonial America. The schools of Pestalozzi and Fellenberg in Switzerland were used as patterns for the work-study schools of the United States in the early nineteenth century. Later in this century industrial education was influenced by the Russian system of manual training and the Scandinavian sloyd. France and Italy influenced instruction in the arts and crafts and Germany contributed the idea of continuation schools to the vocational education programs of the United States.

In recent years the program of vocational education in the United States has had an impact on many developing countries in Asia, Africa, and South America. Specialists from the United States have been employed by such agencies as the International Labor Organization (ILO) of the United Nations, the U.S. Agency for International Development (AID), the Peace Corps, and various private agencies. These specialists have assisted nations to establish apprenticeship programs, and schools and classes in vocational education in many lands. The ILO technical assistance program sent specialists from 50 nations to 102 countries during the 10-year period from 1951 to 1960. The AID has provided aid for organizing and establishing various types of agricultural and industrial schools and programs in the developing nations. A discussion of a few of the various programs of vocational education in nations that have influenced and been influenced by programs in the United States is included in this chapter.

Vocational Education in European Nations

Vocational education of less than college level in European countries is offered for the most part in separate vocational schools and institutes for students who have completed from 3 to 7 years of elementary school subjects. As a rule this vocational or prevocational training is followed by apprenticeship. The United Kingdom has recently engaged in a £140 million program designed to develop more comprehensive facilities in various types of special vocational schools and colleges for industry, commerce, agriculture, domestic service, and maritime trades.

Vocational education has expanded rapidly in Italy during the post-war years. In 1960 there were almost 1 million students in various types of vocational schools. The Ministry of National Education in the Republic of France has responsibility for the administration of national vocational secondary schools and technical secondary schools. Apprenticeship training centers financed by public funds provide training for youth 14 to 17 years of age who are not in full-time school attendance.

THE SCANDINAVIAN COUNTRIES

Education in Scandinavia is characterized by examinations, regulatory laws, and definite patterns for each type of school. Compulsory attendance begins at age 7 and ends at age 14 to 16. There is practically no illiteracy in Scandinavia. Many opportunities for vocational training are provided in day and night schools for students after they pass the age of compulsory school attendance. Responsibility for vocational education is divided among various ministries. For example, in Norway vocational schools of agriculture are under the Ministry of Agriculture. The Ministry of Fisheries is responsible for schools for fishermen. Schools for seamanship are controlled by the Ministry of Commerce and Shipping, and nursery schools by the Ministry of Family and Consumer Affairs.

Two national advisory councils have responsibility for planning supervision and examination programs for vocational schools in Norway. The 15-member State Council for Vocational and Technical Education appointed by the King is composed of representatives of management, labor, and government. This council has been especially active in establishing objectives for the vocational program. The 10-member State Apprenticeship Council, representative of employers and employees, administers and supervises the apprenticeship program.

The types of vocational schools in Denmark are similar to those of Norway. Apprenticeship schemes are used in Denmark to provide vocational education in various trades. Apprentices are required to attend special classes in general and technical education at local approved technical schools. A number of the *folk* high schools in Denmark have vocational curriculums in agriculture mostly for young adults who left day school when 14 years of age. These schools operate during the winter months. Denmark has more than 350 vocational schools, most of which offer 6-month courses with 8 to 10 hours of instruction weekly during the winter months.

Responsibility for much of the vocational education in Sweden is placed in a representative board of 15 members including management and labor in various vocational fields. This board known as the Board of Vocational Training is concerned with business schools, schools of domestic education, technical high schools, and trade schools. The Swedish Employer's Association and the Confederation of Swedish Trade Unions have established a joint council to deal with matters affecting training in industry.

The public school law of Finland enacted in 1958 provides for 6-year primary schools followed by a citizens' school of 2 years with curriculums in vocational and technical education. Graduates of the elementary schools may enter various types of vocational schools supervised by various ministries of the national government. Technical institutes with 4-year courses admit students who are 18 years of age or older. The communes receive 65 percent of the actual vocational school cost from the National Government and Federal aid is provided for other types of vocational schools.

Fundamental Education in Cambodia. A sewing class sponsored by
UNESCO. (United Nations)

THE SOVIET UNION

The USSR has established many types of vocational programs of
less than college level for the education of its workers. Four general
types of vocational schools are engaged in vocational industrial education. These are (1) basic elementary vocational schools, (2) 1- and
2-year vocational technical schools, (3) State and employer operated
schools and courses, and (4) formal and informal on-the-job and job
related training programs. Semiprofessional technicians for agriculture and industry are trained in *technicums*.

The basic elementary vocational schools for industry, popularly
known as labor reserve schools, train youth for semiskilled or skilled
work in industry. Many of the schools are financed and managed by
factories to which they are attached. Students enroll in some of the
basic courses with little previous education but most students have
completed 7 years of elementary education before enrolling. Curriculums range from 6 months to 2 years and stipends or payment for
work experience enable all eligible persons to attend.

The vocational technical schools are designed to train junior technical workers for employment in metallurgy, chemistry, construction, communications, mining, and other industries. Graduates of the 10-year secondary school between the ages of 17 and 25 who are not employed are admitted to these schools without examination. The curriculums are 1 to 2 years in length and students receive stipends to pay necessary expenses. Students receive basic instruction at the school and work experience on the job.

Soviet plants and factories provide on-the-job training for new employees. The program known as individual-brigade training is designed to train new and unskilled workers in the process of production. The instructor assigns the new worker to a variety of jobs and supervises him as he carries out his assignments. The course includes practical work and instruction in the technical aspects and theoretical principles relating to the job. Supervisors and foremen who are qualified for additional training are enrolled in advanced technical courses conducted at the plant after regular working hours. The courses vary in length from 2 to 3 years and include a research project of practical value.

Agricultural education has received special attention in the Soviet Union. Courses offered include: (1) 1- and 3-year agricultural management courses, (2) basic 1- and 3-year production courses for farmers and youth going into farming, (3) 3-year on-the-job training programs in agronomy and animal husbandry, (4) schools for the mechanization of agriculture, and (5) schools to train graduates of the 10-year schools for agricultural employment of a technical nature.

The Ministry of Higher Education has responsibility for the operation of semiprofessional programs for the training of technicians in industry and agriculture. The training programs are more advanced than the trade technical programs and less advanced than the professional programs for engineers and agriculturalists. The curriculums vary in length from 2 to 4 years and students are admitted from the 7- and 10-year general education programs. Some schools require specialty examinations in addition to entrance examinations. Students receive stipends and schools are in session about 36 weeks per year.

WEST AND EAST GERMANY

Vocational education in the Federal Republic of (West) Germany and the Soviet zone of East Germany have points of similarity and points of difference. The similarity is in the types of schools and technical content. The differences are in philosophy, administrative control, and nontechnical content of the curriculum.

The following three types of vocational schools are operated in West Germany: (1) part-time vocational schools, (2) technical trade schools, and (3) technical schools. The part-time vocational school is designed primarily for apprentices who must continue their general education until age 18. The curriculum consists of about two-thirds technical and one-third general education. Organized classes are in session 6 to 10 hours a week for 2 or 3 years. These schools in urban areas are frequently organized and supported by local industries and trade unions. Instruction in the part-time commercial trade school includes commercial, economic, and business subjects. The agricultural trade school is specialized according to the types of farming in the school community. About two-thirds of the schooling at the part-time agricultural trade school occurs during the winter months.

The technical trade school in West Germany is a full time vocational school. It is designed to replace all or part of the apprenticeship training. These schools may be organized and conducted by states, communities, vocational organizations, and private business concerns. The usual admission requirement is the completion of 8 or 10 years of general education. The school program is from 1 to 3 years in length. Some technical trade schools specialize in business or commercial subjects. The technical trade schools for women include curriculums in homemaking, training children's nurses and household assistants, and women's trades and crafts. Some technical trade schools specialize in the education of welfare and social workers, kindergarten teachers, and home economists.

The technical school in West Germany offers full time programs for the education of workers for technical occupations in such fields as building construction, chemistry, textiles, agriculture, commerce, and industry. The course of study combines practical training with theoretical instruction. The program of studies varies in length from 2 to 4 years, and the usual admission requirements are completion of the 10-year secondary school. The level of instruction is about equivalent to that offered in the post-high school technical institute in the United States.

Most of the vocational schools in East Germany are organized as an integral part of some socialistic factory or business enterprise. A few apprenticeship classes are in private industry. Full time general vocational classes also conducted by industry provide instruction in agriculture, industry, business, and minor trades. The plant manager appoints the director of education or training for the various schools and classes. The instructors must be technically competent and have satisfactory political and pedagogical qualifications.

Vocational technical schools of post-high school level in East Germany are under the control of the State Secretariat for Higher and Technical Education. Some schools are operated by industry and by county councils. The courses of study are prepared by the State Secretariat. Examinations and special projects are important aspects of the curriculum. Students who make outstanding records are eligible to receive diplomas which entitle them to special consideration in future work or study.

Vocational Education in the Far East

Vocational education in nations of the Far East is undergoing many changes in the aftermath of World War II. Gandhi's plan of a basic national education with emphasis on a socially useful activity like a craft is increasing in importance in India. The International Labor Organization in cooperation with the United Nations technical assistance program has assisted the Government of India to establish apprenticeship programs with acceptable apprenticeship standards and related instruction. The ILO has also assisted the faculties and staff in the reorganization of special institutes that provide training for craftsmen and instructors.

The Commission on National Education of the Government of Pakistan has recently recommended improvements in vocational schools, technical institutes, evening and part-time classes, management, industry and apprenticeship training, and in vocational guidance. The Commission also recommended the establishment of a central manpower committee to collect data and give information on the need for manpower training. Recommendations are included for training vocational teachers including short courses and 2- and 3-year courses.

The Ministry of Education along with other Ministries has responsibility for the various vocational schools in Indonesia. Technical schools for training in cottage industries offer 1- and 2-year courses for students who have completed the primary schools. Three-year junior technical schools offer a variety of trade courses to students who enter by examination. The 3-year senior technical school admits graduates of the junior high school for management training courses. Two- and four-year domestic science schools are available for girls.

Vocational education in Communist China is conducted in vocational schools attached to and operated by industrial and business enterprises, and in on-the-job training programs. More students are enrolled in on-the-job and spare-time training than in organized schools. The tendency is for all students to engage in some productive work and all workers to enroll in some type of school. Secondary vocational school curriculums in industrial education are 3 to 4 years in length. Three-year curriculums are offered in agriculture, forestry, and public health. The Ministry of Heavy Industry was operating some 30 vocational schools in 1955 with curriculums in such areas as oil well drilling, transportation, internal combustion engines, and the manufacture of farm machinery. It was estimated that about one million students were enrolled in secondary vocational schools in China in 1960.

JAPAN

The need for vocational education in Japan was recognized in 1871 by the establishment of a Bureau of Technical Education in the Department of Education. Vocational education in Japan prior to World War II specialized in job training and little general education was included in the program. Since World War II the program has been reorganized with the assistance of specialists from other countries. The present program is an outgrowth of the Vocational Education Promotion Law of 1951. This law provides funds at the national level for the improvement of vocational education and the organization of national and local advisory councils on vocational education. The national program is under the control of the Ministry of Education.

Vocational education in agriculture, fisheries, trade and industry, commerce, homemaking, and technical education is provided in lower secondary schools (grades 7, 8, and 9), upper secondary schools (grades 10, 11, and 12), special schools and in industry. Many of the upper secondary schools in rural districts are vocational schools with emphasis on vocational agriculture. These schools offer some general education courses. The agriculture curriculum is somewhat similar to that of vocational agriculture in the United States. The curriculum consists of farm enterprises common to the local community. Supervised farming is provided on school farms and in some instances on the home farms of students. Flower growing is an important enterprise in schools located near large urban centers. Leadership training is developed through the student organization the Future Farmers of Japan. Some schools are in session 6 days a week throughout the calendar year.

Trade and industrial education courses are offered in the upper secondary schools. The curriculums include from 12 to 16 hours per week of general education, 8 to 12 hours of vocational education, and 5 to 7 hours of electives mostly in science. Apprenticeship programs in small household industries and larger industries have constituted an important part of vocational training since the beginning of the present century. Students now have a high degree of freedom of choice in selecting a vocation and vocational counselors are employed in both the lower and upper secondary schools.

The homemaking curriculum for girls is a 2-year program in the upper secondary school with better home living as its basic purpose. The course content includes theory and practice in home economics departments equipped for cooking, sewing, and home management. Home projects and home practice are utilized in the teaching process. The tea ceremony and flower arrangements are also included in the curriculum. The Future Homemakers of Japan provides leadership training for girls enrolled in homemaking education curriculums.

Japan also maintains part-time and evening schools for employed youth and adults. Most part-time schools are administered by the secondary schools. Correspondence and extension courses are also offered by these institutions. Vocational technical education of a terminal nature is provided in some of the junior colleges. The national government makes grants of funds to some universities and colleges for teacher training in vocational education.

THE PHILIPPINE ISLANDS

The First Philippine Commission in 1901 created a trade school and an agricultural school. At the beginning of World War II there were 28 trade schools and 24 agricultural schools in the Philippines. Most of these were destroyed during the war. Funds received for war damage have been used to rebuild the facilities and replace the equipment. New materials and techniques have been introduced and enrollments in vocational schools have increased since World War II.

Three types of vocational schools are included in the present program of vocational education in the Philippines. These include 48 trades schools, 52 agricultural schools, and 13 schools of fishery administered by the Philippine Department of Education. Primarily these are secondary schools but some offer post-high school courses. The National Cottage Industry Development Administration has responsibility for the promotion of cottage industries for the training and employment of adults and out-of-school youth.

The trade schools are called schools of arts and trades, vocational high schools, technical schools, or trade schools. Most of the schools of arts and trades were formerly secondary trade schools and were converted to schools of arts and trades in recent years. Some schools offer technical courses such as electrical technology, building construction technology, automative technology, and cosmetology. These technical courses usually require 2 or 3 years beyond the 4-year secondary school curriculum. The vocational and technical high schools offer 4-year secondary school curriculums in various trades. About one-half time in the third and fourth years is given to shop and related training and somewhat less time to these subjects in the first and second years. Most of the schools provide a special 2-year course for youth and adults who cannot meet the usual entrance requirements.

Agricultural schools in the Philippines include regional agricultural schools, rural high schools, and agricultural high schools. Each of these schools offers a 4-year secondary school agricultural curriculum. Some of the schools offer a 1-year farm mechanics course for high school graduates. Special 5-month courses in swine production, poultry production, fruit growing, and other farm enterprises are offered in some schools to any applicant irrespective of his age and educational background. Teacher education curriculums for the training of agriculture teachers are included in some schools. Most rural high schools charge tuition. The 4-year curriculum in agricultural education includes general education, agricultural theory and practice, farm mechanics and farm practice, usually on the school farm. The Future Farmers of the Philippines provides training in leadership for youth in school.

The schools of fishery are administered by the Fishery Education Division of the Department of Education. They provide instruction in the areas of fish capture, fish culture, and fish preservation. Students enter the fishery school after graduation from the 6-year elementary school. The fishery schools offer a 4-year program of which about one-half time is devoted to technical and one-half to general education. Students specialize in one of the areas of fishery instruction at the beginning of the second year.

Home economics is first taught for girls in grades 5 and 6. It is also taught as a required subject for girls in the first and second years of the general secondary school and in all 4 years of the vocational schools. Home economics is offered as an elective subject in the third and fourth years of the secondary schools. Instruction in the various areas of family living is provided and some areas of specialization such as fabrics, food service, dressmaking, handicraft, home nursing, and tailoring are offered in the third and fourth year vocational curriculum of the secondary school. The Future Homemakers of the Philippines provides leadership training and recreation for girls in homemaking classes.

Apprenticeship has long been a means of education in the Philippines. A new apprenticeship law of 1957 provides for a Division of Apprenticeship in the Department of Labor and an apprenticeship unit in the Department of Education. These agencies work jointly with industry and youth to provide on-the-job training in industry and related training for apprentices in the vocational schools.

Vocational Education in Africa and the Middle East

Vocational education in the form of apprenticeship was practiced in Egypt long before the advent of the Christian Era. The oldest university in the world—the Al-Quara Wiyin University—was founded at Fez, Morocco in 859. Formal education in parts of Africa reached a high point in Timbuktu in the Sudan near the end of the fifteenth century A.D. Education went into decline during the Middle Ages and the tribal initiation ceremonies or bush schools were the usual means of preparing youth for the duties and responsibilities of adulthood. Significant changes are occurring in the development of vocational education in Africa and the Middle East. These countries are looking to the United Nations and the Western world for assistance in the development of vocational training programs. Illustrations of some of these new developments are shown below.

THE NEW NATIONS OF AFRICA

One of the pressing problems in African education is a reduction in the rate of illiteracy. The overall rate in Africa in 1960 was 80 to 85 percent. This figure is about twice that of the world average. Organized programs of education of all kinds are far from adequate to meet the needs of the people. The vocational schools are largely limited to urban areas. About three-fourths of the economy of Africa is based on agriculture, but agricultural education lags behind other types of voca-

Technical Education in Western Nigeria. These students are learning to operate a shaper at the Ibadan Technical College which receives technical assistance from USAID, Nigeria. (U.S. Agency for International Development)

tional education. The number of schools is increasing as the African nations recognize the importance of vocational education in their national economy and find the necessary resources to establish these programs.

The new nations of North and Central Africa are establishing vocational schools, most of which are for the education of workers for industry and business. Libya had 8 vocational schools with an enrollment of about 850 students in 1960. The ILO at that time was assisting in the operation of a vocational industrial and clerical training center in Tripoli for 300 students. Sudan had 22 vocational schools offering instruction in a variety of trades in 1960. A training center for diesel and petroleum mechanics, metalworkers, and plumbers was operated with ILO assistance at Khartoum from 1957 to 1962. Short courses of 3 to 6 months and longer courses of 1 year were included in the program. Schools for apprentices who have completed the primary grades are in operation in Morocco. The Moroccan Ministry of Agriculture has responsibility for national secondary schools of agriculture. Tunisia is operating specialized 6-year technical high schools and 3-year middle schools for practical training in basic vocational skills.

Some of the West African nations have made substantial progress in vocational education. The technical institutes at Kaduna, Enugu, and Yaba, Nigeria, offer 2- to 4-year courses in various trades for junior high school graduates. The Yaba Technical Institute offers courses alternating with work experience—1 year in school, 18 months at work. Homemaking courses are included in secondary schools in Nigeria. The government clerical school of Gambia offers commercial courses mostly for government workers. Ghana has technical schools for pre-apprentices, and two agricultural training centers operated by the Ministry of Agriculture. New secondary schools in Guinea provide technical training in nursing, social work, mining and agriculture. The National School of Rural Engineering at Dakar, Senegal, offers 3-year courses in plant and animal breeding, rural engineering, conservation and fisheries. Many African citizens are receiving training in vocational education in other nations by arrangement with the United Nations and special agencies in member nations. It is expected that these individuals will provide effective leadership in education and vocational education when they return to their native land.

THE UNITED ARAB REPUBLIC AND IRAQ

The United Arab Republic operates trade schools, agricultural schools, schools of commerce, and schools of applied arts and applied engineering for boys. Girls vocational schools offer instruction in homemaking, embroidery, dressmaking, and feminine culture. The 5-year trade schools admit boys who have completed the 4-year primary school. The program of studies includes instruction in sheet metal work, machine shop, carpentry, automobile mechanics, painting, decoration, and other fields of specialization. About three-fourths of the school time is spent on shopwork and one-fourth on language, mathematics, and science. Schools are in session 6 days each week. Some trade schools accept 3-year elementary school graduates and give them 3 years of training in carpet making, weaving, carpentry, decoration, and shoemaking.

Schools of commerce admit boys who hold the primary school certificate to prepare for clerical occupations. The first 2 years of the 5-year program consist of general education. Specialized work begins in the third year. Intermediate schools of agriculture offer a 5-year course in vocational agriculture. Specialization begins in the third year and the aim of the course is to train personnel for competency in crop and livestock production and agricultural industries. Various ministries of the United Arab Republic have responsibility for educational programs. The Ministry of Agriculture maintains a training center on its farm at Sakha. Several secondary agriculture schools in Syria are operated by the Ministry of Agriculture.

Iraq has 43 vocational schools enrolling about 8000 students who are preparing for mechanical, agricultural, homemaking, and commercial vocations. Four-year trade courses for boys who have passed the six-year primary school examination are offered in weaving, carpentry, automobile mechanics, electricity, and similar vocations. The home arts school in Baghdad provides instruction to girls in home and family life and in teacher education. The curriculum is 7 years in length and both general and vocational courses are offered. Vocational agriculture is offered in some secondary schools and in special schools. Students are admitted to these schools upon the completion of the primary grades. Frequent examinations are given for the purpose of determining the student's eligibilty for continuing the courses.

Courses in embroidery and needlework are offered in vocational schools which prepare girls for employment in these fields. The 4-year program includes religion, Arabic, French, and technical courses in sewing. Feminine culture schools are designed to prepare primary school graduates for the management of their homes. The curriculum includes domestic art and child care. The course is 6 years in length with about one-half time devoted to academic subjects and the other half to technical content in various areas of homemaking.

TURKEY, IRAN AND ISRAEL

The skilled craftsmen who were trained in the apprenticeship programs of the guilds brought prosperity to Turkey during the sixteenth and seventeenth centuries. With the decline of the guilds the prosperity of Turkey declined. A revival of education began after World War I and has accelerated since World War II. The Republic of Turkey now provides vocational education in some of the secondary and post-secondary schools. The Ministry of Education has authority over education in Turkey. Some special schools and adult education programs are directed by other ministries in cooperation with the Ministry of Education. A variety of vocational courses for boys and girls who have completed the 5-year elementary school is offered in the evening. These courses are designed for youth who are unable to continue their day school education.

Day school classes in post-primary trade schools offer a 5-year program of general and vocational education including instruction in such trades as auto mechanics, carpentry, and metal work. Girls' trade schools offer 5-year courses in home economics. Some post-secondary schools have 2- or 3-year curriculums for technicians and semiprofessional workers. These schools also offer 4-year vocational teacher training curriculums.

The Ministry of Education in cooperation with the U.S. Operations Mission to Iran has recently developed new emphases in vocational education in the Kingdom of Iran. A vocational teacher education department was established in Karaj Agricultural College and in the Teheran Vocational Industrial School. All the provinces now have vocational schools at the elementary or secondary school level. The secondary school program is designed to train prospective farmers for proficiency in farming, encourage farming as a desired vocation, and prepare workers for agriculturally related and industrial vocations. The vocational agricultural schools utilize school farms and home farms for demonstration and practice. Farm shop and adult education are also included.

Three-year secondary school curriculums in home economics are offered for girls in the second cycle (grades 10, 11, and 12) of some secondary schools. The curriculum includes both general and vocational subjects. The technical institutes, one of which is operated by the National Iranian Oil Company, provide curriculums for technicians and for the professions.

Vocational education in the State of Israel is provided in state and local schools, private schools, and by labor organizations. The Ministry of Education supervises vocational schools in various trades for boys and girls. The Ministry of Agriculture in cooperation with the Ministry of Education maintains secondary schools of agriculture for young and adult farmers. The Ministry of Labor, the trade unions and private agencies cooperate in maintaining apprenticeship training and adult classes for working people. Most of the organized vocational schools have local school boards with responsibility for local supervision and administration. State advisory committees, established by law and appointed by the Minister of Education, assist in making policies concerned with education and vocational education.

Trade and agricultural schools provide 2-, 3-, or 4-year secondary school curriculums including some general education subjects. These schools admit students after they have completed 8 years of primary school instruction. The curriculums in the vocational schools are designed to prepare students for employment, but students who make satisfactory grades on a college entrance examination may be admitted to an academic or professional college or university. Most vocational schools are coeducational and offer home economics courses for girls. The junior technical college and technical high school at Haifa are maintained for the training of technicians for employment in the various industries and commercial enterprises of the State.

Vocational Education in Other Nations of the Western Hemisphere

Organized programs of education and vocational education were in operation in the Western Hemisphere long before its discovery by Columbus. The Mayas, Aztecs, and Incas of the present-day Latin American countries maintained organized programs of education to prepare youth for priesthood and to work in the temples. A form of apprenticeship was used to train artisans who worked with metals and textiles. The early Spanish colonists operated courses in shoemaking, tailoring, carpentry, stonemasonry, and other trades in their mission schools. After the initial effort of the missionaries, education for work went into decline and the few general education schools were for the elite of the Latin American nations. Some increased activity in vocational education has been evident in the nations of the Western Hemisphere since 1920. The tempo has accelerated during the last two decades and new and improved programs are appearing throughout the hemisphere.

CANADA

Vocational education in Canada is conducted in various types of secondary schools, in trade and technical schools, by apprenticeship, and in correspondence courses. The public secondary schools are operated by local school boards with some financial assistance from the provincial governments. Trade and technical schools as a rule are operated by the provincial governments and the apprenticeship program is a joint undertaking of employers, labor organizations, and government.

Secondary schools offer 3- and 4-year courses in agriculture, service trades, industry, homemaking, forestry, and fisheries. Students spend a minimum of 50 percent of the school time in practical work and related subjects. Four of the ten provinces have secondary school programs in vocational agriculture and farm mechanics. Some schools offer evening school instruction for adult farmers. The Future Farmers of Canada provide opportunities for leadership training in some of the provinces. Agriculture is also offered in special vocational schools in diploma courses (two winter terms) and special short courses. Various trade and occupational schools operated by the provincial governments provide instruction in agricultural, mechanical, service, forestry, and other vocations. These schools offer full-time and part-time courses for pre-employment training, upgrading, and retraining. Prerequisites for entrance vary from completion of grade seven to high school graduation.

In 1962 about 20,000 apprentices were registered in eight provinces for apprenticeship programs in fifty skilled trades. In addition, there were many apprentices who were not registered. Programs in construction and in automotive trades are especially popular. Apprenticeship advisory boards on the provincial level composed of representatives of management, labor, and government have major responsibility for the control of these programs. Related training is carried on in either part-time classes, correspondence courses, or block-release classes of 4 to 12 weeks during each year of the apprenticeship. The Federal and provincial governments share the cost of these apprenticeship programs.

Post-secondary school programs are offered in institutes of technology operated by some of the provinces. Students who are high school graduates or the equivalent are admitted to these institutes. They offer 2- to 3-year curriculums for students who are preparing to enter such vocations as architectural, petroleum, electronic, metallurgical, and aeronautical technology. The programs are planned with the cooperation of industry and business. About 40 of these institutes were in operation with facilities for 20,000 to 25,000 students in 1963.

The passage of the Technical and Vocational Training Act of 1960 by the Federal Parliament of Canada has recently stimulated increased activity in vocational education. This Act is designed to upgrade present workers and educate new ones in the vocational and technical knowledge and skills needed for industry, business, and agriculture. Federal aid is provided to assist the several provinces of Canada to construct buildings and operate programs of vocational education. The funds are available on a matching basis for approved

Technical Institutes in Canada Offer a Variety of Technical Courses. Modern equipment for testing materials, Northern Alberta Institute of Technology. (Department of Industry and Development, Alberta Government, Edmonton, Alberta)

schools. The aid is for all vocational fields at the secondary and post-secondary school levels.

CENTRAL AMERICA AND THE CARIBBEAN

Vocational education in most of the Latin American countries is operated by the various ministries of the central governments. The governments as a rule finance the entire cost, select the teachers, and establish curriculums and courses of study. The national schools are frequently boarding schools and students receive scholarships in the equivalent of room, board, laundry, books, and often clothing. The schools of agriculture are controlled by the ministries of agriculture and the industrial schools as a rule are operated by other ministries. The number of schools is increasing but is still far short of the needs.

Programs of agricultural education have been maintained in the special schools of the United Mexican States since 1920. The present program administered by the Secretariat of Education is in operation in about 12 national schools of agriculture. The curriculum is 5 years in length beginning at the fifth grade level. The first and second cycles of the curriculum cover 2 years each and include some general and vocational subjects. Practical work on the school farm or laboratory is required of all students. During the final year of the 5-year curriculum the student is offered a differentiated program depending upon his interests. He may choose to specialize in agricultural mechanics, agricultural industry, or some phase of agricultural production. The students receive scholarships from the Federal Government of Mexico to defray expenses. The government also assists graduates to acquire land in agricultural colonies.

Three-year courses in business education subjects are offered in private schools for primary school graduates. Some 35 Federal and state trade schools offer courses in trade and technical subjects for youth over 15 years of age who have no trade experience, for persons employed in industry who need more vocational training, and for adult workers who wish to prepare for a different occupation. Some of the schools offer curriculums leading to subprofessional certificates for careers as technicians. Students are admitted to these curriculums who have completed 8 years of primary and secondary school courses. Mexico also has a number of private technical schools. The Technical Institute of Monterrey, for example, is financed by private funds and has facilities for about 2400 students.

The nations of the Caribbean affiliated with European countries have developed educational plans in cooperation with the Caribbean Commission to improve the economy of the area. In addition to the post-primary vocational and technical schools, which have been in existence for some time, some new technical institutes have been established. In Barbados a new technical institute was opened in 1955. This institute is now educating apprentices in trades and crafts on a daytime release plan and in evening classes. The institute also offers technical subjects for day-school students in secondary schools. Jamaica has three practical training centers located in rural areas for education in agriculture and one for education in home economics. Entrance is by examination on a selective basis and the curriculum is 3 years in length.

Regular vocational trade schools for boys in the Netherlands Antilles offer 3-year curriculums for students who have completed 6 years of elementary schooling. Schools supported by petroleum companies offer advanced technical curriculums. The Government of Martinique maintains a technical college which is a combination of a vocational secondary school and a center for the training of apprentices. Trade courses, seamanship, ceramics, jewelry making, and home economics are offered for boys and girls who have completed from 5 to 8 years of elementary schooling. The Caribbean Training Program afforded vocational training in the Commonwealth of Puerto Rico to more than 800 persons from British, Netherlands, and French Caribbean areas during the period 1955 to 1958. Fields of specialization include trade and industrial education, agriculture, home economics, community education, social science, and others.

THE NATIONS OF SOUTH AMERICA

South American nations have recently begun to improve their programs of vocational education. Uruguay in 1943, Bolivia in 1955, and Argentina in 1959 created national councils for the organization and development of vocational schools on the secondary level. Brazil has recently established two apprenticeship councils—the National Service of Industrial Apprenticeship (SENAI) and the National Service of Commercial Apprenticeship (SENAC). In 1958, Venezuela transferred vocational education at the secondary school level to a new Department of Technical, Industrial, and Commercial Education in the National Ministry of Education.

The Argentine Republic maintains public vocational schools for agriculture, business, and industry. Curriculums vary in length from 2 years in special agricultural schools to 6 years in some of the industrial education schools. Vocational schools for girls provide a 5-year program in various homemaking and related vocations. Some provincial industrial schools offer programs to boys and girls who have completed 3 years of elementary education. Schools known as popular vocational schools are coeducational for youths who are 14 years of age or have finished the 7-year elementary school program.

Vocational education was introduced into the educational system of the Republic of Bolivia in 1942. Elementary and secondary vocational training are being offered in the vocational trade schools for boys. The elementary curriculums are usually 2 years in length and are designed for various trades. Schools on the secondary level offer 4 years of training in the trades. Vocational schools for girls provide a 4-year curriculum in homemaking and related arts for girls who have completed 6 years of elementary schooling. Three of the universities offer 3 to 4 years of technical courses.

The United States of Brazil has various types of national vocational schools and classes and in addition the SENAI program which is essentially private in nature and supported by a payroll tax on Brazilian industries. The apprenticeship council maintains schools in the larger urban areas for youth and adults. Employed youth between the ages of 14 and 18 are selected by examinations for 3 years of day-school instruction in special SENAI schools. The students receive scholarships covering all necessary expenses and in some instances additional funds for miscellaneous purposes. The course of study includes some general education subjects and in some schools students are required to spend 41 clock hours per week in the classroom and laboratories. Advanced short courses are given for adult workers. A similar program is maintained by SENAC for students who desire to specialize in business education.

The Republic of Ecuador provides vocational education in public schools to students at least 12 years of age. Vocational education is also provided in special schools of agriculture, industry, and business. The agricultural schools offer 4- and 6-year courses leading to certification as skilled workers or technicians. Commercial schools offer 3-, 5-, and 6-year curriculums. Special 4-year schools in home economics lead to certification for teaching specialized courses such as cutting, sewing, and weaving.

The Oriental Republic of Uruguay provides free education from kindergarten through university. Each of the 19 states of Uruguay has at least one vocational school. The general entrance requirement is completion of 6 years of elementary school and the minimum age for admission is 13 years. Vocational curriculums are 2 years in length and include mathematics, drawing, and hygiene as required subjects for all students. Various private agricultural, commercial, and industrial schools, operated mostly by religious institutions, confer various types of diplomas on their graduates.

Most of the vocational programs in the Republic of Venezuela are apprenticeship programs. These programs are directed by a semi-autonomous official institution (INCE) composed of representatives of the Ministries of Education, Labor, and Development, employers' and workers' organizations, and of the national federation of teachers. INCE, which was established in 1959, is financed by a payroll tax, taxes levied on workers, and taxes from government sources. The educational activities of the agency range from literacy campaigns to apprenticeship training and on to formal vocational education programs. Venezuela also maintains some national schools under the direction of the Ministry of Education for vocational education in commercial and industrial vocations.

QUESTIONS FOR STUDY AND DISCUSSION

1. Discuss the characteristics of vocational education in the Scandinavian countries.
2. Indicate the types of vocational schools maintained by the Soviet Union.
3. Contrast vocational education in West and East Germany.
4. In what ways are vocational education programs in Japan similar to those of the United States?
5. What is the scope of vocational education in the Philippines?
6. What is the role of the United Nations in vocational education in Africa?
7. Discuss the vocational education programs for girls in the United Arab Republic.
8. What agencies are responsible for vocational education in Turkey? In Israel?
9. Discuss the provisions of the Technical and Vocational Training Act enacted by the Canadian Parliament in 1960.
10. What are the entrance requirements for the various vocational schools in Mexico?
11. What is the role of private agencies in the operation of vocational education programs in the Caribbean?
12. Discuss the organization and operation of apprenticeship programs in the South American nations.

SOURCE REFERENCES

"Africa—Its Educational Problems and Promises," *Phi Delta Kappan,* Volume XLI, No. 4, January, 1960.

Anderson, Ronald S., *Japan—Three Epochs of Modern Education,* Bulletin 1959, No. 11, U.S. Department of Health, Education, and Welfare, Office of Education, Washington, D.C.

Bodenman, Paul S., *Education in the Soviet Zone of Germany,* Bulletin 1959, No. 26, U.S. Department of Health, Education, and Welfare, Office of Education, Washington, D.C.

Canadian Department of Labor, *Vocational Training Programs in Canada,* 5A(1958), 5B(1959), 5C(1959), Ottawa.

Commission on National Education, *Report of the Commission*, Ministry of Education, Government of Pakistan, Government Press, Karachi, 1960.

Faust, A. F., *Brazil: Education in an Expanding Economy*, Bulletin 1959, No. 13, U.S. Department of Health, Education, and Welfare, Office of Education, Washington, D.C.

Ford, C. Ross, "Vocational Education in Canada," Volume 37, No. 10, *American Vocational Journal*, January, 1963.

Hauch, Charles C., *Educational Trends in the Caribbean*, Bulletin 1960, No. 26, U.S. Department of Health, Education, and Welfare, Office of Education, Washington, D.C.

Huus, Helen, *The Education of Children and Youth in Norway*, University of Pittsburg, Pittsburgh, 1960.

International Cooperation Administration of the United States and the National Economic Council of the Republic of the Philippines, *A Survey of the Public Schools of the Philippines—1960*, Carmelo and Bauermann, Manila, 1960.

International Labor Office, *Report to the Government of India on Apprenticeship Training*, (ILOTAP India R/13 1960); and *Report to the Government of the Republic of Sudan on the Establishment of the Vocational Training Centre, Khartoum*, (ILOTAP Sudan R/7 1962), Geneva.

Johnston, Marjorie C., *Education in Mexico*, Bulletin 1956, No. 1, U.S. Department of Health, Education, and Welfare, Office of Education, Washington, D.C.

Kerr, Anthony, *Schools of Europe*, Bowes, London, 1960.

Orleans, Leo A., *Professional Manpower and Education in Communist China, National Science Foundation*, Washington, D.C., 1961.

Sanchez, George I., *The Development of Education in Venezuela*, Bulletin 1963, No. 7, U.S. Department of Health, Education, and Welfare, Office of Education, Washington, D.C.

Sassani, A. H. K., *Education in Iran*, Bulletin 1963, No. 18, U.S. Department of Health, Education, and Welfare, Office of Education, Washington, D.C.

United Nations Educational, Scientific, and Cultural Organization, *World Survey of Education, III Secondary Education*, International Documents Service, Columbia, New York, 1961.

U.S. Department of Health, Education, and Welfare, Office of Education, Educational Data: Argentina (59); Bolivia (61); Ecuador (64); Federal Republic of Germany (35); Israel (29); Italy (39WE); Turkey (30); and Uruguay (62). Washington, D.C.

U.S. Department of Health, Education, and Welfare, Office of Education, *Education in the U.S.S.R.*, Bulletin 1957, No. 14, Washington, D.C., 1960.

CHAPTER NINETEEN

ORGANIZATIONS AND AGENCIES OF CONCERN TO VOCATIONAL EDUCATORS

Teachers and other workers in vocational education are frequently obliged to make contacts with various organizations and agencies in the course of their responsibilities as vocational educators. These contacts are primarily made for reasons such as the promotion of better public relations, the seeking of aid and counsel in the solution of special problems, and for purposes of self-improvement. This chapter is concerned with a discussion of some of these organizations and agencies. For convenience they are grouped under the following headings: professional, agricultural, labor, trade and management, and governmental. The discussion of each of the agencies and organiza-

498

Teachers of Vocational Education Seek Advice and Counsel from Many Organizations. The Farm Bureau provides leadership for many farm problems and programs. A meeting of the Board of Directors of the Arkansas Farm Bureau Federation is pictured. (Arkansas Farm Bureau Federation)

tions includes a brief account of its history, objectives, plan of organization, and program of work.

Professional Organizations

Vocational educators are indebted to a number of professional organizations for assistance in promoting vocational programs and educational legislation, for research and studies in the various fields of vocational education, and for providing facilities and services for mutual aid and counsel on problems involved in conducting vocational programs. A discussion of the following four of these organizations is presented below: the American Vocational Association, the American Home Economics Association, the National Vocational Guidance Association, and the National Education Association.

THE AMERICAN VOCATIONAL ASSOCIATION

The American Vocational Association (AVA) is a national professional organization of teachers, supervisors, teacher trainers, admin-

The House of Delegates for the First Meeting of the American Vocational Association. It was held December 2–4, 1926, at Louisville, Kentucky. (J. H. Moreau)

istrators, and others interested in the development of vocational and industrial arts education. The AVA had its origin in the National Society for the Promotion of Industrial Education, organized November 16, 1906, at Cooper Union, New York City. The Society made studies and investigations and was instrumental in directing attention to the need for Federal aid for vocational education. The name of the Society was changed to the National Society for Vocational Education in 1917 in recognition of the increased scope of the Society brought about by the introduction of the Smith-Hughes vocational education bill. In the meantime a vocational education association had developed in the western states having about the same purposes as the National Society for Vocational Education. The two organizations agreed to unite and the first convention of the new organization—the American Vocational Association—was held December 2–4, 1926, in Louisville, Kentucky.

The AVA is a federation of affiliated state associations of vocational and practical arts education. Vocational educators hold membership in both a state and the national association. The officers of the national association consist of a president, a past president, six vice-presidents, a treasurer, and an executive secretary. A professional

A Small Part of the AVA Membership That Participated in the House of Delegates Which Convened in Atlantic City, December 9–13, 1963. (Hess Commercial Studios, American Vocational Association)

staff is also employed by the Association. The business of the Association is transacted, except as otherwise provided in the constitution, in the House of Delegates which meets each year during the annual convention. The House of Delegates is composed of presidents of affiliated state associations and other delegates selected on the basis of membership of affiliated state associations. The AVA has the rights, powers, and privileges given to corporations by law.

The AVA has established the following divisions organized as professional units: Agricultural Education, Business Education, Distributive Education, Home Economics Education, Industrial Arts Education, Trade and Industrial Education, Vocational Guidance, and Vocational Rehabilitation. Each division of the AVA encourages sectional programs and activities for the varied interests within their respective divisions. Some of the divisions maintain special organizations for the professional improvement of vocational teachers, teacher educators, and supervisors. There are a number of other educational organizations closely associated with the AVA. These include the National Association of State Directors of Vocational Education, the National Council of Local Administrators of Vocational and Practical

Arts Education, the American Technical Education Association, and the Conference of Officers of Affiliated State and Territorial Associations.

The major objectives of the AVA include: (1) active national leadership in the promotion of vocational education, (2) service to members through promotion of professional interests, (3) provision of a national forum for the discussion of all questions involved in vocational education, and (4) union of all vocational education interests in the country. The AVA carries on a program of research and publications through various committees, serves as a spokesman for vocational educators in the promotion of national legislation for vocational education, cooperates with other associations and agencies which have an interest in vocational education, provides information and leadership in the life adjustment education program and gives support to state associations in their efforts to develop a state vocational education program. The AVA holds a convention each year and publishes the *American Vocational Journal* monthly, September through May, each year. The number of members in the AVA, on June 30, 1963, was 33,391. The AVA maintains a national headquarters at 1510 H Street, NW., Washington 5, D.C.

THE AMERICAN HOME ECONOMICS ASSOCIATION

The American Home Economics Association (AHEA) is a national organization of individuals and groups interested in promoting family well-being. The AHEA was organized January 1, 1909, in Washington D.C., during a meeting of the Teaching Section of the tenth Lake Placid Conference. Mrs. Ellen H. Richards was elected president, and the purpose of the Association was stated as the improvement of living conditions in the home, the institutional household, and the community. The Association recognized that at that time there were many critics of home economics in educational programs, and one task of the Association was to show the need for home economics in these programs. Prior to the organization of the AHEA, a number of other national organizations and movements concerned with homemaking had been established. The National Household Economic Association was organized in 1893. The work of this organization was merged with the General Federation of Women's Clubs in 1903. The Household Aid Company was organized in 1903 to study problems of household labor. This organization existed for two years.

The object of the AHEA is "to provide opportunities for professional home economists and members from other fields to cooperate in the attainment of the well-being of individuals and of families, the improvement of homes, and the preservation of values significant in home life."[1] The AHEA has exerted its influence to secure passage of the various Federal vocational education acts. The AHEA is organized into 6 subject matter sections and 9 professional sections. The subject matter sections, which are composed of members particularly interested in special phases of home economics subject matter, include Art, Family Economics—Home Management, Family Relations and Child Development, Food and Nutrition, Housing and Household Equipment, and Textiles and Clothing. The professional sections, which consist of members engaged in special areas of home economics, include Colleges and Universities; Elementary, Secondary, and Adult Education; Extension Service; Home Economists in Business; Institution Administration; Home Economists in Homemaking; Research; Health and Welfare; and College Chapters. These sections engage in various activities designed to accomplish the objectives of the Association, such as promoting education in home economics, recruiting prospective teachers in this field, making studies and investigations, and studying legislation designed to aid in improving home and family life.

The national Association consists of individual members and affiliated college chapters, homemaker groups, and foreign Associations. The officers consist of a president, three vice-presidents, a secretary, and a treasurer. Affiliated state home economics associations are organized in all states, the District of Columbia, and Puerto Rico. Membership in the AHEA and affiliated state associations is open to men and women trained in home economics or related fields who are engaged in professional programs concerned with home economics and family life. The Association publishes the Journal of Home Economics monthly, except in July and August. The AHEA had a total of 28,806 active members on July 31, 1963. There were also 419 affiliated college chapters and 212 groups of homemakers. The AHEA maintains a headquarters office at 1600 Twentieth Street, NW., Washington, D.C.

THE NATIONAL VOCATIONAL GUIDANCE ASSOCIATION

The National Vocational Guidance Association (NVGA) is a professional organization for counselors and other persons interested in vocational guidance. The NVGA was organized during a series of

[1] American Home Economics Association, Constitution and Bylaws of the Association, 1963, p. 1.

meetings held during the annual convention of the National Society for the Promotion of Industrial Education at Grand Rapids, Michigan, October 21–24, 1913. This meeting was the third national conference on vocational guidance, previous meetings having been held at Boston in 1910 and New York in 1912. A planning committee was appointed at the New York City meeting to prepare a plan for a permanent organization. It was suggested at the Grand Rapids meeting that there was a widespread demand for vocational guidance, and no existing organization was in a position to meet this demand. The 1913 constitution of the NVGA stated that: "The objects of this association shall be to promote intercourse between those who are interested in vocational guidance; to give a stronger and more general impulse and more systematic direction to the study and practice of vocational guidance; to establish a center or centers for the distribution of information concerning the study and practice of vocational guidance; and to cooperate with the public schools and other agencies in the furtherance of these objects."[2]

The NVGA functioned as an independent organization for almost 40 years, and during most of these years it published the magazine *Occupations*. This organization joined in 1952 with other groups and individuals interested in personnel and guidance work and formed the American Personnel and Guidance Association. The NVGA retains its identity as a division, along with four other divisions, of the APGA. The governing body of the APGA is an executive council. The NVGA is governed by a delegate assembly which meets each two years and in the interim by a board of trustees and the officers of the Association. The constitutions of the APGA and NVGA provide that a group of interested persons may be chartered either as a branch of the NVGA or as a branch of the APGA. A magazine, *The Personnel and Guidance Journal,* which is a successor to the journal *Occupations,* is published monthly, September through June each year. The NVGA publishes the *Vocational Guidance Quarterly* four times each year. The number of NVGA members reported as of August 31, 1963 was 7851. The Association maintains an office at 1605 New Hampshire Avenue, N.W., Washington, D.C.

THE NATIONAL EDUCATION ASSOCIATION

The National Education Association (NEA), a professional organization for teachers, supervisors, administrators, and others inter-

---

[2] U.S. Department of the Interior, Bureau of Education, *Vocational Guidance,* Bulletin 1914, No. 14, Washington, D.C., 1914, p. 7.

ested in education, had its origin in the National Teachers Association founded by 43 educators in Philadelphia on August 26, 1857. In 1870 the National Association of School Superintendents and the American Normal School Association united with the National Teachers Association to form the National Educational Association. The National Educational Association secured incorporation under laws of the District of Columbia in 1886. In 1906 it was chartered by Congress as the National Education Association of the United States.

The business of the Association is conducted by the officers; the executive committee of 11 members; the board of trustees of 5 members; and the board of directors composed of the president, first vice-president, treasurer, chairman of the board of trustees, former presidents of the Association elected prior to July 1, 1937, one state director from each state, territory, or district and the life directors of the National Education Association. States with 20,000 or more paid members as of May 31 are entitled to a second director. States with 40,000 or more paid members as of May 31 are entitled to 3 directors. The representative assembly is composed of delegates from affiliated state and local groups.

The National Education Association has 14 divisions including: Accounts, Adult Education Service, Audio-Visual Service, Business, Future Teachers of America, Legislation and Federal Relations, Membership, Office of the Executive Secretary, Press and Radio Relations, Publications, Records, Research, Rural Service and Travel Service.

The National Education Association also maintains a number of commissions and departments including: Educational Policies Commission, Legislative Commission, National Commission for the Defense of Democracy Through Education, National Commission on Safety Education, National Commission on Teacher Education and Professional Standards, National Council on Teacher Retirement, American Association for Health, Physical Education and Recreation, American Association of Colleges for Teacher Education, American Association of School Administrators, American Educational Research Association, American Industrial Arts Association, Association for Higher Education, Association for Supervision and Curriculum Development, Audio-Visual Instruction, Classroom Teachers, Elementary School Principals, Home Economics, International Council for Exceptional Children, Kindergarten—Primary Education, Music Educators National Conference, National Art Education Association, National Association of Deans of Women, National Association of Educational Secretaries, National Association of Journalism Directors of Secondary

Schools, National Association of Public School Adult Educators, National Association of Secondary School Principals, National Council for the Social Studies, National Council of Administrative Women in Education, National Council of Teachers of Mathematics, National Retired Teachers Association, National School Public Relations Association, National Science Teachers Association, Rural Education, Speech Association of America, United Business Education Association, and Vocational Education. Most of these divisions, departments, and commissions publish yearbooks and other volumes of interest to teachers. The National Education Association publishes the *NEA Journal* monthly, September through May.

The NEA has three kinds of active memberships. The regular membership entitles a member to nine issues of the *NEA Journal* and the privileges of attending association meetings, voting, holding office, and serving on committees and commissions. A special membership entitles the member to copies of the research bulletins and convention proceedings in addition to privileges of regular membership. All privileges of the special membership for life may be obtained by purchasing a life membership. The membership in the NEA reached a total of 903,384 members on June 1, 1964. The Association has maintained its headquarters at 1201 Sixteenth Street, N.W., Washington 6, D.C., since 1920.

Agricultural Organizations

Agricultural societies, which were both social and professional, were among the first organizations of farm leaders. The Philadelphia Agricultural Society was organized in 1785 and included among its members George Washington and Benjamin Franklin. Agricultural fairs became prominent early in the nineteenth century, and somewhat later farm journals such as the *American Farmer* (1819), the *Cultivator* (1834), and the *Prairie Farmer* (1840) began to appear.

The beginnings of a group consciousness among agricultural leaders emerged near the middle of the nineteenth century, and the need for farmers' organizations became apparent. This need was first expressed in the form of farmers' conventions. The first of these was the Centralia, Illinois, Convention held in September, 1858. This convention stressed the importance of producers and the need for cooperation between producers and consumers. These conventions were interrupted by the Civil War, but were resumed immediately thereafter, especially in the Midwest. Meanwhile, in the East a new organization for the protection of farmers began to take form. This was the Patrons of Husbandry or Grange, and this organization together with two others—the Farmers Union and the Farm Bureau Federation—is presently providing strong leadership in agriculture. A description of these three organizations is provided below. A number of other national organizations exerted influence on agricultural policies prior to 1900. One of these—the Farmers Alliance which in time included the Texas State Alliance, the Southern Alliance, the Colored Farmers Alliance, and the Northern Alliance—was especially active from 1875 to 1892. The Agricultural Wheel, which started in Arkansas in 1882, became a national organization in 1886 and consolidated with the Alliance in 1888. The Ancient Order of Gleaners was established in the central states about the beginning of the twentieth century and was instrumental in developing cooperative effort on a sound basis at a time when such development was greatly needed.

THE PATRONS OF HUSBANDRY

The Patrons of Husbandry, commonly referred to as the Grange, was the first important national organization of farmers. This organization came into being December 4, 1867, at Washington, D.C., largely through the efforts of O. H. Kelley, its first secretary. By 1873, there were granges in all but four states. The general objects of the National Grange as stated in the Declaration of Purposes adopted in 1874 are as follows: "(1) United by the strong and faithful tie of Agriculture, we mutually resolve to labor for the good of our Order, our country, and mankind. (2) We heartily endorse the motto: *In essentials, unity; in nonessentials, liberty; in all things, charity.*"[3]

The Grange is described as a fraternity and a representative legislative agency for rural people. The organization includes a subordinate grange in a local neighborhood; a Pomona grange in a county or district, composed of the subordinate granges; a state grange which is a delegate body; and the National Grange. The National Grange is composed of representatives or delegates from state granges. There is also the Juvenile Grange on the local level for children between the ages of 5 and 14 years. The Grange is a fraternity having seven degrees, which are conferred by the four types of granges. Four degrees are conferred by the subordinate grange and one each by the Pomona, state, and national granges.

[3] Charles M. Gardner, *The Grange, Friend of the Farmer*, National Grange, Washington, D.C., 1949, p. 517.

Through the years the Grange has sponsored or approved many kinds of farm legislation. The Grange, by resolution in 1878, suggested that the elementary principles of agriculture should be offered in the public schools and as a result lent its support to the Smith-Hughes Vocational Education Act of 1917. The Grange sponsored the Capper-Volstead Act of 1922; the export debenture plan of 1927; favored Federal aid to schools, better highways, an independent bipartisan board for farm credit, agricultural adjustment acts, rural health programs, reasonable tariff rates, and many others. The Grange maintains a mutual insurance program and sponsors cooperative marketing activities.

Membership in the Grange is on a voluntary basis. All members of the family over 14 years of age are eligible for membership, but each person seeking membership must make individual application, undergo examination, and be approved by ballot. Rural children who are interested in farm life are eligible for membership in the Juvenile Grange. The number of Grange members in the United States in 1963 was reported as 800,000 persons from 7000 local community units. About 50,000 boys and girls are members of 1500 Juvenile Granges. The National Grange and various state granges publish bulletins and periodicals of interest to the members. The headquarters of the National Grange is 1616 H Street, N.W., Washington, D.C.

THE FARMERS EDUCATIONAL AND COOPERATIVE UNION OF AMERICA

The first local of the Farmers Union was started September 2, 1902, at Point, Texas, by Newton Gresham, formerly an organizer for the Farmers Alliance. A national organization was formed in 1905 with representatives from seven cotton-producing states. In 1906, the Farmers Relief Organization, which was organized in 1900, merged with the Farmers Union. Two other farmers' organizations, the Farmers Mutual Benefit Association and the Farmers Social and Economic Union, joined with the Farmers Union in 1907, at which time the organization had locals in 20 states. The Producers Alliance and the American Society of Equity joined with the Farmers Union in the 1920s.

The Farmers Union is organized on a local, county, state, and national basis. Five or more local unions may form a county union. The state convention comprises delegates from local unions, and the national union consists of officers and delegates from the state unions. The purposes of the Farmers Union are: "To secure equity, establish justice and apply the Golden Rule; to discourage credit mortgage systems; assist members in buying and selling; educate the agricultural classes in scientific farming; teach farmers the classification of crops, domestic economy, and the process of marketing; systematize methods of production and marketing; to eliminate gambling in farm products; to bring farming up to the standards of other industries and business enterprises; to secure and maintain uniform prices for farm products; to strive for harmony and good will among all mankind and brotherly love among its members."[4]

Membership in the Farmers Union is limited to farmers and to persons employed by the Farmers Union or Farmers Union cooperatives, and to country mechanics, school teachers, physicians, and ministers of the gospel. Persons who apply for membership must be of sound mind, over 16 years of age, industrious, and must believe in a Supreme Being. The children of farm families between the ages of 8 and 14 years may become Farmers Union Reserves, and those 14 to 21 years of age may become junior members. Junior members over 16 years of age have full voting and participation rights, and after they become 21 years of age they pay dues to the Union.

The Farmers Union through the years has engaged in cooperative buying, selling, and manufacturing and has provided cooperative insurance for its members. The Union has favored a number of important policies that have been proposed from time to time, including Federal aid to education, especially rural education, strong organizations of both farmers and laborers, soil conservation measures, protection of agricultural products from foreign competition, crop insurance, the ever-normal granary, and the family-size farm idea. The National Farmers Union publishes a monthly paper, *The National Union Farmer*. The general office of the National Farmers Union is 1575 Sherman Street, Denver 3, Colorado. The Farmers Union in 1960 reported a membership of more than 250,000 family memberships in about 38 states.

THE AMERICAN FARM BUREAU FEDERATION

The American Farm Bureau Federation was officially organized March 3, 1920, at Chicago, Illinois, after two previous meetings held in 1919, one at Ithaca, New York, and one at Chicago. The national federation grew out of previously organized local and state farm bureaus sponsored by the agricultural extension services and other organized groups in the states. One of the first county farm bureaus

[4] Farmers Educational and Cooperative Union of America, *Constitution and By-Laws*, Denver, 1952, pp. 3–4.

was organized in Broome County, New York, in 1911, to provide assistance to and cooperation with the county agricultural agent. Missouri, in 1915, was the first state to form a state organization of its various county farm bureaus. The county farm bureau was defined in 1922 as "an association of people interested in rural affairs, which has for its object the development in a county of the most profitable and permanent systems of agriculture, the establishment of community ideals and the furtherance of the well-being, prosperity, and happiness of the rural people through cooperation with local, state, and national agencies in the development and execution of a program of extension work in agriculture and home economics."[5]

The Farm Bureau is organized on national, state, and county levels. Some counties also have township or community units. The national association consists of members and associate members. The affiliated state farm bureaus and agricultural associations are members, and the county farm bureaus and individual members are associate members. The Associated Women of the American Farm Bureau Federation was organized as an affiliated organization in 1934. This organization was incorporated into the AFBF as the Farm Bureau Women in 1954. The state farm bureaus consist of federations or associations of county farm bureaus.

A board of directors, consisting of representatives from each of the four regions, together with the national president, vice-president, and chairman of the American Farm Bureau Women's Committee, is the governing body between annual meetings. All county farm bureaus operate as county units with a county board of directors. Membership is on a family basis in all states. A single membership fee pays for all eligible members of the family. The qualifications for membership are established by each state, but only members of bona fide farm families are eligible for selection as voting delegates.

The Farm Bureau since its inception has worked for better farm to market roads, adequate rural credit facilities, maintenance of privately owned transportation agencies, solution of problems of irrigation, improvement of educational and rural health facilities, development of young members' programs, improvement of rural communities, and the organization of cooperative purchasing, marketing and bargaining agencies. Its program deals with a wide range of matters that affect farm people either as farmers or as citizens. These include foreign trade, international affairs, monetary and fiscal policies, labor-

[5] O. M. Kile, *The Farm Bureau Through Three Decades*, Waverly, Baltimore, 1948, p. 4.

management relations and the development of natural resources, as well as all public policies which relate more specifically to agriculture. The national organization reported a membership of 1,607,505 farm families in 1962. These members were in 2698 county farm bureaus and an estimated 20,000 community units. The Farm Bureau has special programs for out-of-school young people in most states. The organization publishes the *American Farm Bureau News Letter* each week, except the last week in December. A monthly magazine, *The Nation's Agriculture,* is published 11 times a year. The general headquarters of the American Farm Bureau Federation is in the Merchandise Mart, Chicago 54, Illinois.

Labor Unions

Organized labor is made up of autonomous national and international unions, which are composed of local organizations of workers in various crafts, trades, professions, and industries. Most of the national or international unions are affiliated with the recently organized AFL–CIO labor organization, which was formed in 1955 by consolidating the American Federation of Labor and the Congress of Industrial Organizations. A number of railroad and government workers' unions, as well as some others, have never become a part of a federated group. Some other unions at various times have belonged either to the AFL or the CIO but have withdrawn from these organizations. Unaffiliated unions are referred to as independent unions.

There are in the United States about 200 national and international unions, of which about 140 were affiliated in 1955 with the AFL–CIO. The number of local unions chartered by parent or national unions is estimated between 80,000 and 100,000. The combined membership in American labor unions was estimated at 18 million members in 1960. This estimate included about one million members in Canada.

EARLY ATTEMPTS AT ORGANIZATION

The first attempts at labor organization in the United States were made near the close of the eighteenth century. Local groups of workers in New York, Baltimore, and Philadelphia formed societies which engaged in activities such as strikes, picketing, boycotts, and the training of apprentices. Within a few years, trade unions composed of all the workers in a single city were formed. These groups held conventions and began to think in terms of larger groups of workmen, but the panic of 1837 brought about the collapse of the union movement. The trade union movement was revived during the Civil War, and the National Labor Union was formed in 1866. This union, which was the central unit of many local trade unions, engaged in political activity and social reforms. As a result of this activity and the depression of 1870, members began to withdraw, and employers began to blacklist and lock out union workers.

The action of employers in blacklisting resulted in secret societies of labor. The Philadelphia tailors organized the Knights of Labor, and this organization invited other labor groups to join. The movement soon included shoe workers, farmers, and some professional workers. The Knights of Labor in 1885 became the first labor group to meet with the management of a large corporation in the settlement of a grievance. This meeting, which resulted in the settlement of the railroad shopmen's strike, caused employers to organize an opposition movement. This opposition, together with the dissatisfaction of the skilled workers, who were included in the same organization with the semiskilled and unskilled workers, led to the dissolution of the Knights of Labor.

THE AMERICAN FEDERATION OF LABOR

The skilled workers who withdrew from the Knights of Labor formed a union in 1881 known as the Federation of Organized Trades and Labor Unions. This organization became known in 1886 as the American Federation of Labor. The AFL organization survived the depression of the 1890s. Most of the building and printing trades unions won the 8-hour day, collective bargaining began to achieve importance, and much progress was made for the cause of labor. The AFL in 1910 had organizations in the building, printing, mining, brewing, shoe manufacturing, and garment and textile trades.

The rapid growth of the AFL brought about increasing opposition from employer groups, and these groups formed organizations to discourage employees from joining unions. The conflict between management and labor was in part responsible for the organization in 1913 of the U.S. Department of Labor. Membership in the AFL increased during World War I, and the War Labor Board prohibited employers from interfering with the formation of unions and the practice of collective bargaining. AFL membership declined during the depression following 1929 but rose again after favorable Federal labor legislation was enacted beginning in 1933. During World War II the AFL, along with other unions, made substantial gains, and labor disputes were at a minimum. The postwar years have been characterized by a declining number of strikes, higher wages and greater emphasis on collective bargaining. The AFL has been influential in securing legislation establishing public schools, strengthening child labor laws and supporting compulsory school attendance laws. The AFL supported the Smith-Hughes Act and the subsequent acts providing Federal aid for vocational education.

THE CONGRESS OF INDUSTRIAL ORGANIZATIONS

The CIO was organized in November, 1935. This organization was the result of a difference of opinion among members of the AFL with reference to the organizational structure of the Federation. The presidents of eight AFL federated unions adopted a resolution favoring industrial organization as a policy. This type of organization was designed to permit all workers within one industry to be included in one union. The officials of the AFL favored a craft type rather than this industrial type of organization. This difference resulted in the suspension from the AFL of the unions that favored the industrial type of organization. The suspended unions immediately held a convention and formed a new organization including mine workers, typographical workers, smelter workers, and most of the workers in the garment and textile industries. The United Mine Workers, who were among the charter members of the CIO, withdrew from the CIO in 1942 because of political differences. The UMW applied for membership in the AFL, but the application was later withdrawn because of differences between the AFL and UMW. The UMW, with a membership of about 600,000, presently maintains an independent union.

THE AFL-CIO

A merger of the American Federation of Labor and the Congress of Industrial Organizations was effected in December, 1955. This organization, referred to as the AFL-CIO, is composed of the various affiliated groups of the two organizations. Each of the chartered or affiliated organizations retains its own membership and jurisdiction. The constitution of the new organization seeks to preserve the rights and privileges of each affiliated unit but encourages mergers and agreements among affiliates. The constitution provides for a president, a secretary-treasurer, and 27 vice-presidents. A 29-member executive council is empowered to make policy decisions between conventions, which are held biennially. An 8-member executive committee composed of the president, secretary-treasurer, and 6 vice-presidents, and a general board, are included in the policy-making organization.

The affiliates of the new organization include national and international unions, state federations of labor and state industrial union councils, local central bodies, Federal labor unions, and local industrial unions. The following departments are included in the new organization: Building and Construction Trades, Metal Trades, Union Label and Service Trades, Maritime Trades, Railway Employees, the Industrial Union Department, and the Organization Department. This merger of the two labor unions is designed to provide a more effective organization of working men and women and to secure for them higher standards of living and improved working conditions.

The AFL-CIO publishes the *AFL-CIO News* and various other publications relating to the labor movement. The AFL-CIO in 1960 had a membership estimated at more than 15 million members. The organization maintains an office at 815 Sixteenth Street, N.W., Washington, D.C.

INTERNATIONAL LABOR ORGANIZATION

The International Labor Organization (ILO) founded in 1919 is an international agency affiliated with the United Nations. Membership comprises 104 countries which send delegations representing government, management, and labor to conferences and meetings of the organization. The purpose of the organization is to promote the voluntary cooperation of nations to improve labor conditions and raise living standards thereby improving prospects of peace and fostering economic and social stability throughout the world. Technical assistance is an important activity of ILO and programs of technical assistance are conducted in cooperation with the United Nations in many countries. Since 1951 more than 2000 experts of 57 nationalities have undertaken more than 1500 assignments in 84 countries. These experts teach more efficient techniques for various industries and provide assistance in health, welfare, and educational programs. The headquarters of the ILO is Geneva, Switzerland, and an office is maintained at 917 Fifteenth Street, N.W., Washington, D.C.

STANDARD RAILWAY LABOR ORGANIZATIONS

Various labor unions whose members are for the most part employed by railway companies are referred to as standard railway labor organizations. The organizations include 23 unions associated together in the Railway Labor Executives Association (RLEA). The Railway

Labor Executives Association, organized in 1926, is an unincorporated and voluntary association of the chief executive officers of the various railway unions, representing most of the organized railway workers in the United States and Canada. Prior to the merger of the American Federation of Labor and the Congress of Industrial Organizations, 16 of the 18 unions in the RLEA were affiliated with the AFL, one was affiliated with the CIO and one was independent. The five train and engine service organizations include: Brotherhood of Locomotive Engineers, founded in 1863 after an early attempt in 1855; Order of Railway Conductors (1869); Brotherhood of Locomotive Firemen and Enginemen (1873); Switchmen's Union of North America (1877); and the Brotherhood of Railroad Trainmen (1883). These five unions were first organized for mutual aid. The first two have never affiliated with the AFL or the CIO, but all of them are now associated with RLEA. Membership in the five brotherhoods was estimated at about 250,000 workers in 1963.

During the past 75 years a system of handling labor disputes on the railways has been developed by a series of Federal laws. The first of these was the Arbitration Act of 1888. The Railway Labor Act of 1926, as amended, is the basic framework of the present laws. This Act provides for a Railroad Adjustment Board and a National Mediation Board. The railway workers are the beneficiaries of the Railroad Retirement Act of 1937 and the railway unemployment compensation systems. These Acts came as a result of collective bargaining by the companies and the railway unions. The Railway Labor Executives Association maintains an office at 10 Independence Avenue, S.W., Washington, D.C.

Trade and Management Associations

There are in the United States about 12,000 local, branch, state, and national trade associations, of which about 1800 are classed as national associations. About 800 of these are classed as manufacturers' associations, 400 are transportation associations, 300 are distributors' groups, and 300 are in other categories. These national associations have a membership of more than a million firms. A trade association is composed for the most part of employers and supervisors and is designed to assist its members and its industry in dealing with mutual problems primarily of concern to management. Most of the associations were formed after 1865, although some associations, such as the American Iron and Steel Institute, National Association of Cotton Manufacturers, and American Bureau of Shipping, were formed during the period between 1850 and 1865.

Association membership is usually open to any firm in the industry or part of the industry represented. Very large firms manufacturing many different types of commodities frequently hold membership in a number of national associations. Trade associations provide the membership with research data and information concerned with production, demand, and employment. Another major activity is that of cooperation with the Federal government in the issuing of statistical information. Trade associations and employers' associations also concern themselves with labor-management relations. Most of the associations issue bulletins and trade journals and hold annual conventions where matters of association policy are determined. A discussion of four trade associations is presented below.

THE NATIONAL ASSOCIATION OF MANUFACTURERS

The NAM is one of the two largest overall organizations representing American business. The NAM was organized January 22, 1895, at a convention held in Cincinnati, Ohio. As early as 1897 it adopted a resolution urging the promotion of vocational and other technical schools. A definite labor policy was formulated early in the twentieth century, in which opposition was expressed to the closed shop and to certain methods employed by labor unions in controversial matters. The NAM has favored pure food laws, the Federal Reserve System, and workmen's compensation. It has cooperated in war production, reconversion, and surveys of job possibilities.

The purposes of the NAM are "to promote industrial interest in the United States; to foster domestic and foreign commerce; to improve relations between employer and employee; to protect individual liberty and the rights of employer and employee; to disseminate information among the public with respect to the principles of individual liberty and ownership of property; and to support legislation in furtherance of these principles and oppose contrary legislation."[6] The board of directors is the governing body of the NAM. This board is composed of the officers of the Association, directors elected by the membership, ex-presidents, and representatives of affiliated associations. The officers of the association are elected by the board of direc-

[6] Federal Security Agency, Office of Education, *Educational Interests and Activities of 25 National Organizations*, prepared by The Citizens Federal Committee on Education, Washington, D.C., 1950, p. 83.

tors. The board of directors has full authority to make rules and regulations and to adopt policies when such do not conflict with the constitution of the Association. An executive committee appointed by the board of directors from its membership has responsibility for supervising the administration of the Association during the interim period between meetings of the board of directors.

The NAM has special policy committees on government finance, international economic relations, patents, labor-management relations, distribution, and other activities. A cooperating organization, the National Industrial Council, operates to bring about an understanding and sometimes common action between the two organizations. The NAM has a membership of about 21,000 companies located throughout the United States. About 385 trade associations, state associations, and local associations are affiliated with the NAM through the National Industrial Council. The NAM publishes a number of magazines and other volumes including *NAM News*. The NAM headquarters is 2 East 48th Street, New York 17, N.Y.

THE CHAMBER OF COMMERCE OF THE UNITED STATES

The Chamber of Commerce of the United States is a federation of businessmen, firms, and business organizations established to express the viewpoint of businessmen. It is one of the two largest organizations representing business and was founded April 22, 1912. The national organization had its origin in local chambers of commerce, the first of which was formed in New York City in 1768 and two years later was granted a charter by King George of England. Other cities followed New York in the organization of chambers of commerce, and by 1870 there were 40 active chambers of commerce in the United States. President Taft in 1911 expressed an interest in better cooperation between business and government and suggested some type of central organization to make this effective. Not long thereafter, a national commercial conference was held in Washington and the Chamber of Commerce of the United States was organized.

The National Chamber has always held to the principle that the general welfare is best served through free institutions, through freedom of opportunity, and through freedom of movement. As a consequence, it has consistently opposed public ownership and development of natural resources and government assistance except where absolutely necessary. The basic points of the National Chamber's current program are (1) government economy to eliminate unnecessary spending, (2) a fair and equitable tax system that will provide adequate revenue, (3) an expanding economy to absorb the growing labor force, (4) an improvement in the social security system, (5) sound labor legislation to bring greater harmony into the labor-management picture, (6) an economic understanding of the profit-and-loss system, and (7) a foreign policy designed to increase trade and promote world peace.

The Chamber of Commerce of the United States is made up of more than 25,000 business firms and individuals and more than 3600 local and state chambers of commerce and trade associations with an underlying membership of above 2,750,000 persons. The Chamber is governed by a board of directors of 58 businessmen, some of whom are the officers and former presidents of the Chamber. The Chamber carries on its work in four broad fields: research, policy forming, opinion development, and action getting. The organization maintains a national office in Washington, D.C., and division offices in New York, Atlanta, Chicago, Minneapolis, Dallas, and San Francisco. The Chamber publishes a monthly magazine, *Nation's Business,* and other periodicals in special fields. The national office is at 1615 H Street, N.W., Washington 6, D.C.

THE NATIONAL RETAIL MERCHANTS ASSOCIATION

The National Retail Merchants Association (NRMA) is the only national retail trade group specifically organized and functioning in behalf of the nation's department, chain, and specialty stores. From a small beginning the organization has grown to include a staff of more than a score of experts in specialized fields of retail endeavor. These persons provide personalized counsel and assistance to member stores in the solution of store operating problems. The purpose of the Association, in general, is to engage in any and all enterprises connected with the development of increased efficiency in all phases of retail operating procedures. The NRMA also functions in all areas in which the interests of the retail trade are at stake, particularly directing its efforts to matters which individual stores could not accomplish as well or economically as the Association.

The overall policies of the Association are determined by a Board of Directors consisting of management executives of member stores elected by the membership from each of the 50 states. The officers consist of a president, chairman of executive committee, executive vice-president, nine regional vice-presidents, treasurer, and secretary, all elected by the directors. The Association is divided into major groups and divisions, each staffed by specialists in a particular field and each functioning under its own board of directors. These groups are: (1) The Controllers' Congress, with responsibility for providing assistance to member stores on accounting, inventory, and other practices; (2) the Merchandising Division, with responsibility for member service and research in the 8 merchandising departments; (3) the Store Management Group, concerned with the physical operation and servicing of stores; (4) the Personnel Group, for the administration of personnel; (5) the Sales Promotion Division, concerned with advertising and member service in sales promotion; (6) the Credit Management Division, devoted to the study of credit and collection policies; (7) the Traffic Group, with responsibility for studying methods of transporting, receiving, and checking goods; (8) Visual Merchandising Group; (9) the Ready-to-Wear Group, concerned with ways of merchandising ready-to-wear clothing; (10) the Smaller Stores Division, which operates in the interest of stores with an annual volume of business under $2 million; (11) Employee Relations Service; (12) Home Furnishings and Major Appliance Group; (13) Accessories and Smallwares Group; (14) Retail Fur Council; (15) Vendor Relations; and (16) Piece Goods Executive Committee. The Association publishes a number of bulletins and special reports for the member stores, the Controllers' Congress, and the various other groups. This association was formerly (1958) the National Retail Dry Goods Association. The Association has a membership of over 9000 retail stores located in every state in the Union, Canada, and over 40 countries abroad. The office of the Association is located at 100 West 31st Street, New York 1, N.Y.

ASSOCIATION OF AMERICAN RAILROADS

The Association of American Railroads (AAR) is an organization of the operators of class I railroads (over 100 miles of track) in the United States. The AAR had its origin in a number of railroad organizations established to solve specific problems common to railway companies. The first of these organizations was the Master Car Builders Association, formed in 1867 for the purpose of reaching agreement on a standard gauge. The American Railway Master Mechanics Association was formed in 1868 to consider construction materials and problems. A Time Convention was held in 1875 to arrive at an agreement relative to uniform time belts for the operation of trains, and in 1891 this convention became the American Railway Association. This Association was broadened from time to time to include the first-mentioned and other organized groups. The present Association of American Railroads was formed in Chicago on September 21, 1934. Membership in the Association is by railroads, not individuals. All class I railroads in the United States are eligible for membership. The membership includes about 40 other railroads and some switching terminals. In addition, 5 railroads in Canada and 6 in Mexico are also members.

The work of the Association is carried on through the following 7 departments: Operations and Maintenance; Traffic; Finance, Accounting and Taxation; Law; Public Relations; Economics; and Competitive Transportation Research. The Association in 1950 had a membership of about 310 member facilities and maintained an office in the Transportation Building, Washington, D.C.

Federal Agencies

Teachers of vocational education have occasion to contact a number of Federal agencies for purposes of securing information concerning various Federal programs and activities related to vocational education. The more frequent contacts are made with the U.S. Departments of Agriculture; Commerce; Health, Education, and Welfare; and Labor. The following information, taken from the *United States Government Organization Manual*[7] includes a discussion of the organization and functions of each of these departments.

AGRICULTURE

The U.S. Department of Agriculture was created by an act of Congress approved May 15, 1862, and until 1889 it was administered by a Commissioner of Agriculture. The powers and duties of the Department were enlarged in 1889, and the Commissioner became a Secretary of Agriculture. The Department is directed by law to acquire and diffuse useful information on agricultural subjects. The Department performs functions relating to research, education, conservation, marketing, regulatory work, and agricultural adjustment. The Department administers the national forest and provides crop reports, commodity standards, Federal meat inspection service, and plant and

[7] General Service Administration, *United States Government Organization Manual, 1963–1964*, Federal Register Division, National Archives and Records Service, Washington, D.C., 1963, pp. 225–337.

animal disease controls. It promotes the efficient use of soils and helps farmers secure fair prices and stable markets. The Department provides agricultural credit and facilitates the maintenance of electric and telephone service in rural areas.

The principal work of the Department is organized in the following manner: (1) the Undersecretary has responsibility for Agricultural Research and Cooperative State Experiment Station Service, (2) the Foreign Agricultural Service is administered by the Assistant Secretary for International Affairs, (3) the Assistant Secretary for Marketing and Stabilization is responsible for the Agricultural Marketing Service; the Commodity Credit Corporation; the Agricultural Stabilization and Conservation Service; the Commodity Exchange Authority; the Federal Crop Insurance Program; and the Federal Extension Service, (4) the Assistant Secretary for Rural Development has charge of the Office of Rural Affairs Development; Farmer Cooperative Service; Farmers Home Administration; Forest Service; Rural Electrification Administration; and Soil Conservation Service, and (5) the Director of Agricultural Economics is responsible for the Economic Research Service and Statistical Reporting Service. The offices of the Department are at Fourteenth Street and Independence Avenue, S.W., Washington, D.C.

COMMERCE

A Department of Commerce and Labor was created by an act of Congress in 1903. The labor activities were transferred to a newly created Department of Labor in 1913, and the Department of Commerce was designated as such on March 4, 1913. The Department has responsibility for fostering, promoting and developing foreign and domestic commerce, the mining, manufacturing, fishing, and shipping industries, and the transportation facilities of the United States.

In addition to the general administrative duties, the Department is engaged in four major areas of service—transportation, economic affairs, domestic and international business, and science and technology. The area of transportation is concerned with the establishment of an integrated transportation program and the development of an overall transportation policy including the mobilization aspects. Within this area are the Maritime Administration concerned with the operation of the merchant marine, the Bureau of Public Roads for the development of Federal and Federal-aid highway construction, the Office of Emergency Transportation for the provision of centralized control of all modes of transportation in an emergency, and the Great Lakes Pilotage Administration for the establishment of an effective system of regulated pilotage on the Great Lakes.

The Assistant Secretary for Economic Affairs serves as principal adviser on economic programs and economic policy. The Bureau of the Census and the Office of Business Economics are included in this division. The Office of Domestic and International Business is concerned with industry, trade, and related economic activities. This division includes the Bureau of International Commerce to maintain a favorable trading climate overseas and stimulate trade, the Business and Defense Service Administrations, the Office of Trade Adjustment, the Office of Foreign Commercial Services, and the Office of Field Services.

The Assistant Secretary for Science and Technology has general supervision over the National Bureau of Standards concerned with accurate and uniform techniques of physical measurement, the Coast and Geodetic Survey, the Weather Bureau, the Patent Office, and the Office of Technical Services. The office of the Secretary of Commerce is on Fourteenth Street, between Constitution Avenue and E Street, N.W., Washington, D.C.

HEALTH, EDUCATION, AND WELFARE

The U.S. Department of Health, Education, and Welfare was created on April 11, 1953. The functions of this Department were performed by the Federal Security Agency prior to the above date. The Department was established for the purpose of improving the administration of those agencies of government the major responsibilities of which are to promote the general welfare in the fields of health, education, and economic security.

The Department is organized into six major areas of service. The Public Health Service, under the direction of the Surgeon General, has responsibility for protecting and improving the health of the people of the nation. This service includes the Office of the Surgeon General, the Bureau of Medical Services, the Bureau of State Services, and the National Institute of Health. The Office of Education is concerned with the collection of educational statistics and the making of reports, with providing counsel on educational matters and with the administration of the Federal vocational education acts. The Social Security Administration has responsibility for administering the social security law and has various divisions for managing this operation.

The Vocational Rehabilitation Administration has responsibility for administering the state-Federal vocational rehabilitation laws designed to return disabled persons with occupational handicaps to productive employment. The Food and Drug Administration has responsibility for protecting the public against unsafe foods and drugs. The Welfare Administration, which includes the Children's Bureau, has responsibility for programs for the aging, for prevention of juvenile delinquency and for youth development, refugees, and family service. The Department provides Federal assistance to Saint Elizabeth's Hospital, The American Printing House for the Blind, Gallaudet College, and Howard University. The Health, Education, and Welfare Building is located at Fourth Street and Independence Avenue, S.W., Washington, D.C.

LABOR

A Bureau of Labor was organized in the U.S. Department of the Interior in 1884. Later this Bureau became an independent department without executive rank. In 1903 it returned to bureau status in the U.S. Department of Commerce and Labor. The present U.S. Department of Labor was created March 4, 1913. The Department of Labor is charged with administering and enforcing statutes designed to advance the public interests by promoting the welfare of the wage earners of the United States, by improving their working conditions, and by advancing their opportunities for profitable employment.

In addition to the general administrative staff the Department is made up of the following five major divisions: Manpower Administration, Labor-Management Relations, International Affairs, Labor Standards, and Policy Planning and Research. The Manpower Administration has responsibility for a comprehensive manpower program which includes forecasting and research, development, distribution, utilization, administration, and program support. The Manpower Administration also has charge of the Bureau of Apprenticeship and Training and the Bureau of Employment Security.

The Labor-Management Relations activities of the Department include the regulation and reporting of information concerning welfare and pension plans, the reporting of certain transactions of labor organizations and employers, the assisting of war veterans to establish re-employment rights, and the establishment of standards for minimum wages, and child labor. The International Affairs section has responsibility for the functions of the Department of Labor in the international labor field. The Assistant Secretary of Labor Standards of the Department is concerned with the activities of the Women's

Bureau, the Bureau of Labor Standards, the Bureau of Employees Compensation, the Employees Compensation Appeals Board, and the President's Commission on the Status of Women. The Division of Policy Planning and Research has responsibility for reviewing programs, developing program projections for the future, and coordinating the research programs of the Department. The Department of Labor is located at Fourteenth Street and Constitution Avenue, N.W., Washington, D.C.

QUESTIONS FOR STUDY AND DISCUSSION

1. Discuss the origin, purposes, and accomplishments of the American Vocational Association.
2. What are the purposes of the American Home Economics Association? The National Vocational Guidance Association?
3. How is the National Education Association organized for the performance of its responsibilities?
4. Describe the history and development of farm organizations.
5. What are the purposes of the Grange? The Farmers Union? The Farm Bureau?
6. In what ways have these three organizations assisted in the development of vocational education?
7. Describe some of the early attempts at labor organization.
8. Discuss the history and functions of the AFL. The CIO. The railway unions. The AFL-CIO. The ILO.
9. What are trade and management associations, and what is the extent of development of these associations?
10. When and for what purpose was the National Association of Manufacturers organized? The Chamber of Commerce of the United States? The National Retail Merchants Association? The Association of American Railroads?
11. What contributions have these associations made to the development of the national program of vocational education?
12. Discuss the history and development of the U.S. Departments of Agriculture; Commerce; Health, Education, and Welfare; and Labor.

SOURCE REFERENCES

American Vocational Association, *The American Vocational Association, Your Professional Organization,* Washington, D.C., 1955.

Baldwin, Keturah E., *The AHEA Saga,* American Home Economics Association, Washington, D.C., 1949.

Benedict, Murray R., *Farm Policies of the United States,* Twentieth Century Fund, New York, 1953.

Bowyer, Carlton H., *The Directory of Education Associations*, Kansas State Teachers College, Emporia, 1962.

Chamber of Commerce of the United States, *The Chamber of Commerce of the United States, What It Is, What It Does, How It Works*, Washington, D.C., 1954.

Craig, Hazel T., *The History of Home Economics*, Practical Home Economics, New York, 1945.

Faricy, William T., *AAR, The Story Behind a Symbol*, The Newcomen Society in North America, New York, 1951.

Fisher, Commodore B., *The Farmers Union*, Studies in Economics and Sociology, No. 2, University of Kentucky, Lexington, 1920.

Gale Research Company, *National Organizations of the United States* (3rd edition), Detroit, 1961.

Gardner, Charles M., *The Grange, Friend of the Farmer*, National Grange, Washington, D.C., 1949.

General Services Administration, *United States Government Organization Manual, 1963–1964*, Federal Register Division, National Archives and Records Service, Washington, D.C., 1955.

Kile, Orville M., *The Farm Bureau Through Three Decades*, Waverly, Baltimore, 1948.

Lindstrom, David E., *American Farmers' and Rural Organizations*, Garrard, Champaign, Ill., 1948.

Peterson, Florence, *American Labor Unions*, Harper & Row, New York, 1963.

U.S. Department of Labor, Bureau of Labor Statistics, *Directory of National and International Labor Unions in the United States*, Bulletin No. 1320, Washington, D.C., 1962.

CHAPTER TWENTY

PRINCIPLES OF VOCATIONAL EDUCATION — A SUMMARY

A principle is defined as a fundamental consideration or basic rule which serves as a means of evaluating present practices or as a guide to future action. When established, principles constitute areas of general agreement among individuals qualified in the field with which the principles are concerned. Principles of vocational education are derived from past experiences and judgments that have proved to be satisfactory and efficient. Many of the accepted principles of vocational education grew out of the deliberations on Federal aid for vocational education conducted prior to the passage of the Smith-Hughes Act, and some of these are incorporated in the basic vocational education laws. Other principles have been derived from time to time as experience has demonstrated a need and established a pattern.

Some general principles of vocational education are included in this chapter. Most of them have been discussed to some extent in the previous chapters, but it is believed that a re-emphasis on some of them will serve a useful purpose in the determination of policies and procedures and in some measure constitute a summary of this volume. The principles selected for review are grouped for convenience into three divisions—organization, administration, and instruction. A discussion of each principle is included in an attempt to show its meanings and to suggest some ways of implementing it.

Organization

Principles of organization are concerned with definitions, functions, needs, and procedures. They may be used for the purpose of assisting in arriving at decisions concerning the advisability of establishing programs of vocational education. These principles may also constitute an effective means of evaluating the purposes and scope of existing programs, and they may be useful in locating some shortcomings, if such exist, in the organization of the vocational education programs.

The function of vocational education is to prepare persons for and enable them to progress in a gainful occupation. This principle suggests that vocational education is distinguished from other education by the purpose of the learner. If the learner participates in a course of instruction for the purpose of preparing for or progressing in an occupation, he is participating in vocational education. This interpretation suggests that vocational education cannot be defined by designating certain subjects as vocational subjects and others as nonvocational ones. Any subject, if studied by a learner for the purpose indicated above, becomes a vocational subject to that particular learner.

Some courses of study or school subjects are designed solely for students who have selected a vocation and are either preparing for it or are attempting to progress in it. These courses are designated as vocational courses. Secondary school courses of this nature usually include extensive activities and skills of a practical nature needed in the vocation. These courses frequently attract students who have not made a choice of an occupation. Since the course or subject is not designed for these students, they should not be permitted to enroll in it but should be encouraged to continue their general education until they have made a choice of an occupation.

This principle suggests that the Federally aided program in voca-

Employed Workers Improve Their Efficiency by Attending Short, Intensive Courses Directly Related to Their Occupations. (Arkansas State Department of Education, Vocational Division)

tional education does not represent all vocational education and that the subjects represented in the Federal laws are not vocational because of this designation but become vocational when the learner participates in them for the purpose indicated above. This also suggests that vocational courses are not designed for any and all students as exploratory courses but are designed for a special group—those who have made a choice of an occupation and are pursuing this study to enable them to prepare for or progress in this occupation.

Vocational education is a part of the total educational program. Vocational educators recognize that vocational education is not a substitute for general education but is a component part of the total educational program of those persons who have selected an occupation and who desire to prepare for it or progress in it. Both general education and vocational education have their useful functions, and these are related. A meager general education will not prepare a person for living and enjoying life any more than a meager vocational education will prepare him for success in his chosen occupation. This means that each individual should achieve some degree of balance between vocational and general education, in general devoting his early educational life to general education.

In view of the fact that many individuals terminate their formal education at the time of graduation from high school, it is apparent that if they are to acquire any preservice vocational education they must get it during their high school career. Here again unless the individual has made a choice of his occupation he should not enroll in a course designed to prepare persons for a specific occupation but rather should continue his general education until such time as he makes an occupational choice. This may mean that he will be obliged to delay vocational education until he enters an occupation and desires to progress in it. Post-high school vocational education courses are provided in some communities to enable students to complete high school before making a choice and preparing for entry into an occupation.

Federal aid for vocational education is justified as a means of stimulating the further development of vocational education and as a device for maintaining acceptable standards in vocational education throughout the nation. At the time of the passage of the national vocational education law in 1917, only 9 states had organized state programs of vocational education, and these programs provided educational opportunities for less than 1 percent of the workers. This situation existed despite the fact that vocational education was considered essential to the national welfare and recognized as a necessary part of public education. The states simply were not assuming responsibility for this program, and, as a consequence, the opportunity for vocational education was denied to many citizens of the nation.

Shortly after the passage of the Smith-Hughes Act of 1917, all states organized programs of vocational education in agriculture, industry, and homemaking, and these programs have increased in scope throughout the years. The increased scope of the programs has not been due entirely to increases in Federal funds. Each dollar of Federal funds expended throughout the 45-year period 1918 to 1962 has stimulated the states and local communities to spend $3.51. This ratio is widening, as indicated by the fact that for each dollar of Federal funds expended for vocational education for the 5-year period 1958 to 1962 state and local communities have expended $4.40, most of which has been provided by local communities. During some of the years, and for some Federally aided vocational programs, Federal funds have experienced a decline, and this decline in Federal funds has resulted in a decline in total expenditures for vocational education. These data indicate that Federal funds are stimulating the further development of vocational education.

Vocational education differs from general education in many aspects. Among these are types of schools and classes, teaching facilities, qualifications of teachers, standards of workmanship and organization for instruction. The tendency of school administrators to standardize all these aspects has operated to the disadvantage of vocational programs. Qualified teachers are difficult to find in many localities, and there is some tendency to sacrifice technical training for academic preparation. This is less likely to occur when Federal funds are used. These funds are granted on the condition that teachers with specified qualifications are employed and that other standards indicated in the state plan for vocational education are met. This procedure has enabled vocational educators to maintain acceptable standards in vocational education.

The need for vocational education in a specific area should be determined from the results of a community survey. Vocational education is based on individual and community needs, and some means of determining these needs must be used. A device frequently used for making these determinations is the community survey. The survey may be used to determine the nature and scope of vocational education needed, the subject matter required to meet these needs, the materials and processes that should be used, and the facilities and equipment that should be provided. The survey may also reveal the qualifications that students who are preparing for the occupation should possess and the opportunities that each occupation offers for employment and advancement. Surveys also reveal to community agencies the possibilities and limitations for new enterprises in the community.

Some of the more common techniques to use in making a survey include interviews, questionnaires, comparisons, rating scales and score cards, statistical techniques, judgments of experts, and research. Provision should be made for checking each technique used to avoid errors of omission or commission. The survey report should contain suggestions for interpretation and implementation, which may involve further study. Helpful suggestions may be obtained from a well-selected advisory committee to serve in such functions as advising upon objectives, policies, and procedures and for reviewing and interpreting the results of the survey. Qualified personnel are needed in planning, conducting, and interpreting the survey to be assured that the proper data are obtained and proper interpretations made so that the school authorities may establish vocational programs based on community and individual needs.

Vocational education is needed to insure an adequate and effi-

cient labor supply. The experiences of the nation in World War II demonstrated rather vividly the need for an adequate and efficient labor supply. There is general agreement that the national program of vocational education enabled this nation to convert from a peacetime to a wartime economy in a relatively short time. The vocational organization and facilities which had become well established as a result of many years of experience were quickly and easily adapted to war needs by the provision of additional personnel and facilities to supple-

The Results of a Community Survey Are Summarized to Serve as a Basis for Determining the Nature and Scope of the Public School Program in Vocational Agriculture. (J. K. Coggin, University of North Carolina, State College of Agriculture, Raleigh, North Carolina)

ment those of the regular program. Trained personnel were available as rapidly as industrial facilities were completed as a result of the long-time vocational education program.

An adequate and efficient labor supply is as necessary in peace as in war. The many and continuous technological changes that are designed to increase the efficiency of modern industry and business require an ever changing program of vocational education to meet these needs. Employed workers who are faced with a need for additional skill and information as a result of technological changes may find opportunities for acquiring these in vocational part-time and evening classes. The fact that these opportunities are present lends a feeling of security to the worker and makes him a better citizen. The use of the opportunities reduces the time required for learning the new techniques and consequently lessens the period of time he operates at less than normal efficiency.

Practical arts courses are designed for general culture rather than vocational efficiency. Practical arts courses in general agriculture, general business, general homemaking, and industrial arts are designed for such purposes as (1) providing recreational and avocational interest and skill, (2) supplying knowledge and skill needed by the consumer, (3) satisfying the students' desire for manual activity, and (4) contributing to intelligent vocational choices. During the first years of the present century, some educators suggested that a general course such as industrial arts would provide the vocational education needed in a trade or an industry. This point of view was rejected in the report of the Douglas Commission. Specific, rather than general, training was suggested for vocational education, and the practical arts were recommended as most worthwhile subjects for general culture.

Some educators at present are suggesting that a practical arts course, more particularly industrial arts because of its general nature, is more feasible for pre-employment training than a vocational industrial education course. This position is taken because of the multiplicity of occupations or trades and the difficulties and expenses of providing specific training in each of them. However, regardless of difficulty and expense, industrial arts is not a substitute for vocational industrial education, and this fact should be recognized. A school should have both industrial arts and vocational industrial education courses, the former for all students at various grade levels for the purposes indicated and the latter for those students who have selected a trade or occupation and who desire to prepare for work in the occupation selected. If school funds will not permit the operation of both programs, then the school authority should determine which of the two best meets the needs of the community, and it should be made clear that one is not a substitute for the other.

Occupational information and guidance should be provided for vocational students. Reference has been made to the fact that vocational education is designed for persons who have selected an occupation or gainful pursuit. Studies have shown that many individuals complete high school and even college before such a decision is made. Then, too, some individuals find that they have made an unwise or distasteful choice of an occupation, and, if they do not change, they are dissatisfied throughout their working lives. These facts point out the need for vocational guidance and counseling not only before the occupational choice is made but also during the period of preparation and throughout the early years of employment. Guidance and counseling contribute to an individual's well-being, and society in general benefits when individuals are properly placed.

A functioning vocational guidance program will supply an individual with an inventory of his abilities, aptitudes, and interests as they relate to occupations in which he is interested. The guidance service will supply the individual with information about the requirements of various occupations and will assist the individual in the process of matching his qualifications with the requirements of occupations available to him. The vocational counselor will also assist the individual to secure a position and will continue to counsel him concerning problems of adjustment, promotion, and retirement.

Vocational guidance and vocational education are two separate movements, distinct in organization and purpose, but rather closely related. Both guidance and vocational education are needed by every individual. They operate continuously throughout the individual's career, with guidance pointing out the need for vocational training, retraining or adjustment and serving to prevent errors that may prove costly both to the individual and to society in the selection of occupations and educational procedures.

Local initiative is essential for success in vocational education. The essential elements of a vocational education program have their origin in the local community. The needs to be met, the individuals to be served and the facilities to be used are local in origin. Vocational education functions best and is more likely to succeed when local rather than state or national interests are responsible for starting the program. This local interest may be generated in local organizations or agencies or by individual citizens who recognize a need and an opportunity. An approved procedure is for the interested agencies and individuals to create a community consciousness of the need. This in turn will stimulate local school superintendents and local school boards to investigate the need and plan a program of action. The state and Federal units may be called upon to provide some form of leadership and assistance in planning and executing the action program.

Local initiative and support are as essential for an established and going program of vocational education as for one in the initial or planning stage. Local industry, business, agriculture, and labor are in a position to know local needs and requirements and consequently may provide advice and counsel to vocational educators on programs, facilities, and personnel. Vocational educators need to keep local people informed on accomplishments, procedures, and needs. Local advisory committees are useful in maintaining community contacts.

It is not always feasible to provide all needed vocational services in the local community, and frequently the county or state is requested to provide some of these services. For example, in some vocational fields state education departments frequently employ itinerant instructors who go from place to place and teach courses for employed workers. The state unit is responsible for making known to local communities that this service is available, but here again local initiative should assume responsibility for determining the need for the course and for assisting in organizing and financing it.

Vocational education programs should be based on continuous research. A satisfactory research program should recognize three kinds of research activities. The first is concerned with planning new programs or the expansion of present programs. Various kinds of data are needed for this planning, including data concerned with kinds of occupations and manpower requirements in the state and area served, the probable number of enrollees and the possibilities of securing staff, facilities, and equipment. The research program should contemplate the means and method of interpreting these data.

The research program should include some activities concerned with the appraisal of programs of vocational education presently in operation. Some devices such as score cards, rating sheets, or evaluation techniques should be developed and applied to these programs to determine the extent to which they meet the objectives established for them. A research agency or staff, separate from the teaching or supervisory staff, is usually in a better position to make these evaluations because persons closely associated with a program are often unable to arrive at objective evaluations.

A third kind of research of importance in vocational education is that carried on for the purpose of discovering better ways of carrying out present educational practices and developing new ideas for new practices. This type of research requires the use of judgments of competent persons who are working in the field of vocational teaching. Frequently these persons must do this type of research as extra work for which the only pay they receive is recognition for their efforts. Effective research of this type requires cooperative effort, and the state research service may provide the leadership and stimulation necessary for this developmental research.

Administration

The efficient administration of a program of vocational education presents problems more complex than and quite different from those in general education. Some of the difference is occasioned by the fact that Federal funds are provided for certain designated programs, while other programs are financed by state and local funds only. Then, too, the cooperative nature of vocational education, involving the school, the home, and the industry or business, frequently involves procedures different from those of general education. These facts make it advisable to understand some principles of administration of vocational education, and those indicated below are concerned with the organization and administration of existing programs of vocational education. These principles have to do with boards of control, advisory committees, teacher education, supervision, qualifications of personnel, and efficiency of instruction.

Representative laymen and vocational educators should have primary responsibility for the administration of vocational education on the national level. Educational programs in colonial America were first administered directly by the people who met regularly in town meetings. These meetings provided opportunities for people of all occupational groups to offer advice and counsel on education matters. After a few years the problem became too complex to be handled in town meetings, and responsibility for the administration of educational programs was delegated to representative citizens. This type of school administration prevails at the present time. The lay board usually retains the policy-approving powers and delegates to the professional employees the policy-executing and, in general, the policy-planning powers.

In keeping with the long-established policy of lay control of education, a Federal Board for Vocational Education was created under the provisions of the Smith-Hughes Act. The law provided that the board be a representative board. The three appointive members were required to possess occupational qualifications—one was a representative of agriculture, one a representative of manufacturing and commerce, and one a representative of labor. This requirement was considered advisable because of the necessity for a degree of cooperation among the school, agriculture, and business not ordinarily required in general education programs. The Federal Board administered the vocational education program for 16 years after which its duties were transferred to the U.S. Commissioner of Education.

The Vocational Education Act of 1963 established the National Advisory Committee for Vocational Education. This committee, consisting of 12 members, is appointed by the U.S. Commissioner of Education who serves as ex-officio chairman. The committee has responsibility for advising with the Commissioner on regulations and policies for vocational education. The proper use of the advisory committee should result in some improvement in administrative relationships in vocational education. However, it leaves much to be desired in the administrative structure. A committee appointed by the Commissioner to advise with the Commissioner is somewhat removed from the vocational administrators who operate the vocational program on the national level.

Steps should be taken to improve the status position of vocational education on the national level. Most agencies of the Federal government with which vocational educators in the Office of Education confer contact officers on a higher administrative level. This adds to the difficulties of proper liaison between agencies. In the absence of the Federal Board for Vocational Education, the establishment of an Office of Vocational and Technical Education in the U.S. Department of Health, Education, and Welfare with a representative lay committee to share in some administrative functions concerned with policies and regulations, would improve the administrative structure of vocational education. Such an arrangement would enable vocational education to maintain standards and practices that are acceptable to industry, business, and agriculture with greater ease.

Some provision should be made for representative lay participation on state boards for vocational education.   Some states have established state boards for vocational education, separate from state boards of education, as a means of providing for representative lay participation in vocational education. State boards of education in the remaining states serve as state boards for vocational education, and these boards, in general, do not include designated representatives of agriculture, business, and labor. The usual policy in general education is for the state board of education to be appointed by the governor on the basis of state-wide or area representation. While a board so constituted is approved for general education, it does not have the advantages of the type of representative lay participation desired in vocational education.

The Vocational Education Act of 1963 requires that the states provide for representation of management, labor, and educational institutions on state boards or advisory committees for vocational education. The addition of representative laymen on legally constituted boards will insure administrative rather than advisory relationships. These representatives may be added to the existing state board of education to constitute the state board for vocational education. A state in which it does not appear feasible to organize or otherwise constitute a representative board for vocational education should consider the advisability of establishing by law a state advisory committee to advise with the state board for vocational education on matters concerning standards, qualifications of personnel, curriculums, and organizational patterns. The method of selection, duties, responsibilities, and limitations of this advisory committee should be specific and should be fixed by law. Final authority and responsibility should rest with the state board for vocational education with the advisory committee suggesting alternate plans when the original plans are not acceptable to the board.

Representative lay participation in organizing and planning the local vocational education program should be provided. Local boards for vocational education were established in a few states in the early years of the vocational education program. These boards were designed to provide the desirable type of representation referred to above. Most of these boards have been discontinued because of objections raised by general educators to so-called *dual control* of education. Local advisory committees are presently authorized for vocational programs, but these programs in many cases have been administered with little or no advice and counsel from their advisory committees. This has caused many vocational programs to lose some of their vocational aspects and take on those of general education. This is evidenced by a reduction in the length of some class periods in vocational education, less emphasis on out-of-school classes, less than full-time vocational programs in which vocational teachers are assigned to nonvocational subjects for a part of their teaching time and assigning students to vocational classes irrespective of their occupational interests.

It is suggested that some means be devised to stimulate all local boards in control of local vocational education programs to utilize the services of representative advisory committees on the local level. Some means for providing status for these representative advisory committees should be devised. This may be accomplished by legislation authorizing their appointment or by specific appointments made by the local school board president. Constant reference should be made in all types of publicity to the work of these advisory committees and their responsibilities. These committees should be especially helpful on the local level in maintaining acceptable standards for local programs of vocational education.

Each state should maintain a complete program of vocational teacher education. An adequate supply of competent teachers is an essential feature of a program in vocational education. This fact was recognized in the Smith-Hughes Act, which provided specific appropriations for vocational teacher education and required each state to expend the money for teacher education as a requisite for using the funds appropriated in the Act for salaries of teachers. Funds for vocational teacher education are not earmarked in the other vocational education acts, but state boards for vocational education are expected to use such amounts as they consider necessary for this purpose. Responsibility for vocational teacher education is assigned under the provisions of the vocational education laws to state boards for vocational education. The state boards may, and usually do, delegate to institutions of higher learning the task of providing some or all of the vocational teacher education services and functions, especially when the teacher education institution is in a position to provide the services more effectively than the state board for vocational education.

A complete program of vocational teacher education should be provided for the preparation and improvement of teachers in the several vocational services. Such a program should consist of (1) recruiting, preservice education, and placement; (2) in-service education; (3) follow-up; (4) preparation of instructional aids; (5) research and study; and (6) improvement of technical and general education courses required of vocational teachers. Such a program requires a staff professionally and technically qualified for providing these services. This means that as a rule the teacher education staff will consist of more persons than are usually provided for teacher education in general education. This increases the cost of vocational teacher education and makes it necessary that state and Federal funds for vocational education be used, together with institutional funds, to provide an adequate teacher education program. This procedure is contemplated in the Federal vocational education laws.

Institutions designated for teacher education in vocational education should have superior facilities and personnel to provide the teachers needed. This principle is suggested in the vocational educational policies of the U.S. Office of Education. It is designed to provide superior teachers for vocational education. The principle is needed because of competition among teacher education institutions in some of the states, especially in the vocational fields of agriculture and homemaking. Teachers qualifying in these fields require specialized courses of a technical nature in the field of preparation. The land-grant colleges or institutions having equal facilities are best equipped and staffed for providing this type of vocational teacher education. As a rule the facilities of these institutions are adequate to provide all the teachers needed in these fields.

The approval of a teacher education institution that does not measure up to desirable standards has a tendency to weaken the vocational teacher education in the approved institution, because, in this event, funds earmarked for vocational teacher education must be divided between two or more institutions to provide duplicate services. Since funds for vocational teacher education in most states are limited, a division of funds usually results in a reduction of teacher education services. In some instances the approval of a second or third teacher education institution results in a surplus of vocational teachers. If any considerable number of qualified trainees fail to secure positions in their field of training, the funds and efforts of the vocational teacher education staff are not efficiently used.

Supervision is essential for the improvement of instruction. The term *supervision* is used to include such activities as are concerned with assisting teachers in improving methods of instruction, planning and preparing instructional materials, securing facilities and conditions conducive to effective teaching, and evaluating the results of the instruction given. Much of the work of the supervisor is on-the-job teacher education. Vocational education presents many problems of a supervisory nature that are different from those encountered in general education. Among these are the promotion of schools and classes for out-of-school youth and adults, the use of materials of instruction based on community resources and problems, the organization of classes to resemble conditions in the occupation, and the application of standards used in industry and business to measure progress and achievement. These differences require specialized knowledge and skill, and supervisors must possess these if they are to be of assistance in the improvement of instruction. This means that the supervision of programs of vocational education should not be assigned to supervisors of general education subjects, who are not technically qualified in vocational education.

Supervisors use various devices and techniques in assisting in the improvement of instruction. Among these are conferences, demonstrations, rating sheets, visitations to superior programs, contests, exhibits, and professional courses. An improtant factor affecting the success of the supervisor's efforts is the attitude of the teacher. It is difficult, if not impossible, for a supervisor to help a teacher to improve instruction if the teacher has no desire for improvement, if the teacher has no confidence in the supervisor's ability to teach, or if the teacher thinks of the supervisor as an inspector rather than a helping teacher. This makes it important for supervisors to be master teachers and points out the difficulty of combining some of the administrative jobs, such as rating teachers, fixing of salaries, transfer of personnel, and records and reports, with the job of the improvement of instruction. Since the local supervisor is usually not burdened with administrative duties, and since he has fewer teachers to supervise, he is in a better position to obtain an improvement in the instructional program. Many programs are too small in scope to justify a local supervisor; therefore, area, district, and state supervisors are provided for the several vocational services. The farther away the supervisor is from the local teacher, the more difficult becomes the supervisory function, and much planning is needed to accomplish the principal objective of supervision —the improvement of instruction.

Vocational education personnel should be occupationally competent. State plans for vocational education specify that personnel in vocational education must possess extended occupational experience in the fields in which they are working. This occupational experience is needed to enable the teacher or staff member to acquire competency in his occupation. Occupational competency is necessary in vocational education because of the nature of the task and the individuals taught. Much of vocational education is devoted to the upgrading and retraining of employed workers. The student worker quickly loses respect for and confidence in the teacher who is inept at the trade or occupation. The vocational teacher must know the problems of the worker and the difficulties he will encounter. Such knowledge may be acquired through experience.

It is recognized that some workers do not acquire competency even with extended experience. This suggests that some means of determining the competency of prospective teachers must be found. Documentary evidence such as a certificate or union card is sometimes used, although in some instances documentary evidence is not readily available. The judgment of qualified specialists is another means of determining competency. In some occupations, such as agriculture and homemaking, experience coupled with technical knowledge acquired on the college level is considered a measure of competency. Prospective teachers in these and some other occupations may acquire experience during the period of time they are enrolled in preservice teacher education courses. These students may work at their occupations between college terms. All these and other means are used to enable prospective teachers to acquire competency and learn the language of the trade or occupation.

Vocational education personnel should be professionally qualified. The term *professional qualifications* is used in education literature to refer to courses and experiences concerned with the principles and practices of teaching. Professional education is as essential for vocational teachers as it is for teachers in general education. The teaching content in vocational education varies from area to area and from time to time. Constantly changing conditions require change in content and emphasis. Vocational teachers use job instruction sheets, evaluation techniques, course calendars, long-time programs, and other devices that require skill in their construction. Vocational teachers have expensive equipment that must be used by many students. Plans are needed for class and shop organization, purchase of supplies, and handling of small tools. Vocational teachers make field trips, home visits, and visits to local industry, and vocational teachers have responsibility for planning the work of student organizations in vocational education. All these are in the province of professional education.

The importance of professional education is recognized in state plans for vocational education which contain detailed outlines of professional courses for preservice and in-service teachers. Some form of off-campus or cadet teaching is usually included for vocational services such as agriculture and homemaking. Specialists in teacher education are employed by state boards for vocational education to bring professional education to teachers of part-time and evening classes who are occupationally qualified but who have not had an opportunity to secure professional education courses. All these activities emphasize the importance of professional qualifications for all vocational teachers.

Programs of vocational education should be operated efficiently. The efficient operation of a vocational program requires that value received be obtained for the funds expended. The determination of value received is no easy task. However, a number of factors are usually associated with efficiency of instruction. For example, qualified instructors are more likely to provide efficient instruction than those not qualified. Efficient instruction requires adequate space, equipment similar to that used in business and industry, sufficient supplies of the kind and quality needed, properly selected library materials, and laboratory and visual-aid equipment. The presence of all these does not guarantee efficient instruction but contributes to it.

Efficiency in vocational education requires that a reasonable number of trainees be enrolled in each class offered. This means that care should be exercised in starting a class to be sure that the probable enrollment will justify the cost of the course. Most states have suggested standards for maximum and minimum enrollments per teacher. Class size is not the only measure of the efficiency of operation. All enrollees should possess the qualifications necessary for entrance into the occupation for which they are preparing or the characteristics necessary for advancement when the course is completed. The satisfactory completion of the course is not alone sufficient. Trainees should actually be employed in jobs for which they prepared in the course. Since vocational education is largely supported by public funds it is important that the public know these factors concerned with efficiency, for in the last analysis they are the judges of efficiency in vocational education and have the authority to withdraw support from programs they consider inefficient.

Instruction

Materials and methods of instruction in vocational education differ from those in general education, due to such factors as the interests and purposes of the learner, the demands of the industry or business enterprise, the standards of achievement and performance and the technological changes that are constantly occurring in the economic order. The observance of some principles of instruction will enable the teacher to better serve the needs of individuals in a class in vocational education. Some important principles of this nature are indicated below.

Vocational instruction should be established and maintained on the basis of occupational needs.   The content of vocational education should consist of the knowledge, skills, and attitudes that the trainee will need to perform efficiently the job for which he is being educated. This means that the vocational educator must be familiar with what the worker does and what he must know. This information may be obtained from an occupational or job analysis—a technique developed by vocational educators under the direction of the Federal Board for Vocational Education. Job analysis identifies the nature and degree of skill needed on a specific job or type of work and also the related technical content, such as science, mathematics, and drawing, which applies to the job.

A job analysis should not be confused with a job description or job specification. A job analysis is a classified list or inventory of the learning units of a trade or occupation. The principal steps in making a job analysis consists of (1) making a list of the things a man must know and do in his trade or occupation, (2) listing specific directions for the performance of each of the above items, (3) preparing a list of topics concerning the information needed to carry out the directions on how to perform the job analyzed, and (4) making a list of related science or mathematics topics that will provide the information needed to master the topics listed under item 3 above. The use of the job analysis technique gives information and direction based on the specific needs of the occupation for which the trainee is preparing.

Vocational instruction should be available for those who need, want and can profit by it. A common misconception that has prevailed in preservice education for vocations is that certain individuals, who are not able to learn certain types of subject matter commonly associated with mental discipline, should be encouraged to pursue courses involving manual dexterity. Since most vocational courses, more especially those of less than college grade, include many activities of this nature, there is a tendency to associate vocational courses with those designed for dull students. Many students, when motivated by a desire to prepare for a chosen occupation, perform in class much better than students who are not so motivated—not necessarily because of superior or inferior mental capacity but because of a felt need which generates a motive.

There are some students, and for that matter some employees, who are limited in their capacity to learn and consequently can profit little from any course, whether it be one designated as vocational or one commonly designated as nonvocational. Techniques such as guidance and counseling are used to discover these shortcomings. No student should be encouraged to pursue a vocational program of studies regardless of his wants if it is evident that he cannot succeed because of deficiencies, whether they be mental, physical or social. Experience has demonstrated that, other things being equal, superior students perform better than inferior students, and superior students who make a choice of an occupation should be encouraged to prepare for that occupation.

Conditions under which vocational instruction is given should compare favorably with desirable conditions in the occupation concerned. "Conditions," as used in this principle, refers to such items as supplies and equipment used in instruction; the arrangement of the shop, laboratory, or classroom; the scope and sequence of the job; the organization for teaching; and the means of evaluation. Inadequate and poorly utilized space and poorly selected equipment in a school shop may make it difficult, if not impossible, for learners to achieve the speed and accuracy required by industry, agriculture, and business. Then, too, the use of poorly adapted equipment may discourage

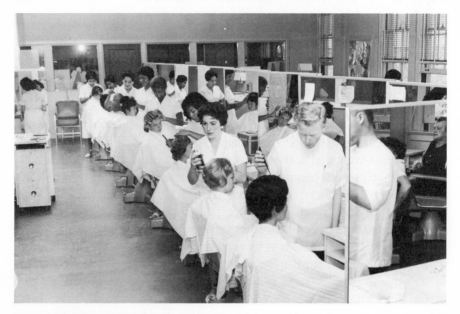

Vocational Education Should be Available for Those Who Need, Want, and Can Profit From It. These students are acquiring proficiency in cosmetology. (Los Angeles Trade-Technical College, Los Angeles, California)

the learner who recognizes the need for maintaining high standards but finds himself unable to do so because of conditions that do not compare favorably with the work-a-day world.

In some cases, sufficient time is not available for shop, laboratory, and field work, and the quality of the work suffers as a result of attempting to complete a job or unit of work in too little time. The organization of the school shop for work should, insofar as possible, resemble the organization in agriculture, industry, and business. Learners should work under a foreman or supervisor and should be responsible for planning the layout, for the care and upkeep of equipment and tools, and for the observance of safety rules and practices. Insofar as possible, learners should acquire attitudes, such as pride in work, a desire to increase one's efficiency and a sense of social responsibility, such as a good workman possesses. Devices and activities commonly used in the occupation should also be used in the teaching program. Such activities and devices as sales meetings, inspirational talks, quotas, competitive practices, employee organizations, cooperative activities, and visual aids have a place in the instructional program as ways and means of duplicating conditions in the industry concerned.

Real jobs provide the best laboratory for vocational education. Vocational education is best given through jobs that are real and essential. The use in vocational education of equipment and practices found in industry and business encourages the performance of real jobs. This practice carries out the slogan of vocational education, "We learn by doing." Real jobs present a challenge to the learner that cannot be provided in developing knowledge, skills or attitudes through the use of practicums or exercises.

Vocational educators recognize that it is more difficult to provide real jobs for day trade courses in some trades than in others. For example, it is more difficult to provide real jobs in carpentry and steam fitting than in printing, auto mechanics, and pattern making. This suggests that unless these difficulties can be overcome it is probably desirable to teach only those trades and occupations in which real jobs for learners can be provided.

Real jobs are essential in pre-employment education in agriculture and homemaking. This means that the supervised farming program should be sufficient in scope to justify the time and effort of the learner, and the nature of the program should be such that it has the possibilities of growing into a full-time farming program when the trainee has completed his vocational course. Likewise the home projects of the girls in homemaking should consist of such jobs and activities as are real and essential to successful homemaking.

The standards in vocational education should be as high or higher than the accepted standards in the occupation concerned. A standard is a device or technique for evaluating the output of the learner. This evaluation in vocational education is made in terms of what industry, agriculture, or business expects of its workers. The world of work expects its workers to turn out a saleable product that will be purchased by the consumer or user. When a worker is employed or engages in self-employment, his worth is determined by the saleability of his product, whether it be goods or services. Since vocational education has for its purpose the education of individuals for work, it is important that standards in education be as high or higher than those accepted as desirable in the world of work. This means that the output of the school shop or laboratory should match that of workers in agriculture, business, homemaking, and industry in quality and in speed and that the personal characteristics of students, such as appearance, honesty, fair-mindedness, and loyalty, should be up to the standards expected of superior workers in the occupation concerned.

Industry, agriculture, and business have various ways of evaluat-

The Local Food Store Is the Laboratory Where Students in Home-making Classes Learn About Quality and Cost of Food. (Bloom from Monkmeyer)

ing their products and services, and many of these same devices and techniques may be used in vocational education. A rule or caliper may be applied to a product in the shop, a score card or rating sheet to the performance of a service, a written or oral test to some activities involving a knowledge of subject matter, and the judgment of a qualified person may be used when objective measures are not available. The application of this principle or standard makes it necessary that the person responsible for the evaluation, which in most cases is the teacher, should know what standards are acceptable in the occupation and what devices should be used in making evaluations. This again illustrates the importance of a teacher's having both professional preparation and skill in his occupation in order that standards of performance may be maintained at a level acceptable to the trade or occupation.

Vocational education programs should include both short, intensive courses and long-term courses. Vocational education should be available for all persons who need, want, and can profit from it. Many persons who are in this category are employed and unable to attend full-time school because of the necessity for making a living. This means that these persons have a limited time available for attending vocational classes. In order to make the best use of this time, it is necessary to organize short, intensive courses at a time convenient for these workers. The content of these courses must be directly concerned with the important problems of the occupation, and little time is available for material or activities indirectly related to the occupation. Frequently these short courses are organized around single units or jobs for as little as ten clock hours of instruction. A coordinated series of these courses in one community will enable an individual to acquire a great deal of information over a period of time.

Courses of longer duration should be available in vocational education for pre-employment and retraining. Some cooperative courses of long-time duration should be available for employed workers who are seeking advancement. These courses offer opportunities for the study of related material, and time is frequently available for the study of subjects for recreation, personal satisfaction and other nonvocational purposes. Since courses of longer duration require more time, equipment, and money, there is a special need for the exercise of judgment in establishing them. Some factors to consider in making this determination are: (1) the degree to which a need exists; (2) the availability of qualified teachers, adequate space and proper equipment; and (3) the probability of securing employment when the trainees have finished the course.

Instructional programs in vocational education should be characterized by flexibility. Flexible programs are easily changed to meet changing conditions. This means that a minimum of restriction should be placed on local school authorities and vocational teachers in making such decisions as kinds of vocational education to establish in the community, the types of schools and classes, the lengths of the courses, the materials and methods of instruction, and the means of evaluating the programs. Any restrictions on the above items should be imposed only for the purpose of assuring that high standards are maintained and that value received is obtained from expenditures for vocational education. The Federal vocational education laws encourage this flexibility in permitting the states to establish the necessary standards for these items in the state plan for vocational education. The states in turn leave specific determinations, within the framework of established standards, to the local school authorities and teachers.

The acceptance of this principle of flexibility places responsibility on the local authorities and teachers for implementing it. Local people must use the best means available to determine the kinds of schools and classes needed, the lengths of the courses, and the means and methods of instruction. This suggests that occupational surveys should be made, qualified personnel should be employed and local advisory committees should be consulted to insure that only the best practices are used in the community programs of vocational education. A flexible program in vocational education may require some flexibility in phases of the general education program, and facts needed in making this determination should not be overlooked. Frequently local authorities will need to counsel with specialists from the state education department or the U.S. Office of Education. Such counsel should provide suggestions and techniques for obtaining the desired information needed to obtain a flexible program of vocational education.

More and more technical information is needed in socially useful occupations. Recent studies have shown that there is a growing need for workers who possess less operative skill and more technical knowledge than tradesmen. Such positions as are concerned with testing and production, planning and control and supervision of plant operation and maintenance are included in these technical occupations. There are at present relatively few programs of a vocational technical nature, and many more are needed for pre-employment, retraining, and for advancement in an occupation. The specific needs of a community for this type of training may be determined by a vocational survey.

Much of the technical training may be given at the post-high school level, and special technical institutes and junior colleges designed to offer terminal courses are institutions especially adapted to this type of vocational program. The technical institute caters principally to persons who have selected their occupation and who desire intensive preparation for this occupation. Because of the intensive nature of its offerings, the technical institute provides courses of shorter duration than those of the professional colleges. These short, intensive courses are terminal rather than college preparatory. In view of the increasing importance of technical education, the general public should give more attention to this need, especially to the desirability of using public funds to finance programs of technical education.

Vocational instruction should include information and activities designed to protect and conserve human life. Current literature is replete with statistical evidence showing the extent of loss, both in manpower and in money, due to accidents and sickness. There are many agencies, both private and governmental, that are working to prevent sickness and accidents in industry and business. It is especially important that vocational students be taught to work safely. Since many of the accidents are due to the improper use of machinery, special emphasis should be placed on safety practices while students are learning to operate machines. This applies not only to the operation of industrial machinery, but also to the operation of machines that are used in the home and on the farm. Accidents in the home and on the farm can be reduced by proper instruction in safe working practices.

Many Present-day Occupations Require the Use of Technical Information. (Public Schools, Detroit, Michigan)

Some vocational teachers make a practice of appointing a safety engineer for the school shop. This person, usually a student, has responsibility for checking clothing, aprons, goggles, guards, belts, tools, heat and power outlets, and other items that may become hazards. Sometimes, such duties are left to a committee of two or more students, and this responsibility is rotated among class members. While it is a good practice to develop resourcefulness in students, it is doubtful if full responsibility for safety education should be delegated to them. Certainly the instructor should at all times be aware of the shop and classroom practices that students in his classes observe.

Visual aids are used to teach safety in shops, classrooms, and homes. Posters, films, slides and models are used to supplement safety instruction in vocational education. These devices in general should show safe practices rather than unsafe practices and their results. Accidents sometimes occur because material is not properly stored, floor space not properly cleaned, machinery and equipment improperly placed, and facilities improperly lighted. The ultimate aim of safety education is the development of safety concepts that will serve to conserve human life.

QUESTIONS FOR STUDY AND DISCUSSION

1. Discuss the importance and use of principles in planning and evaluating programs of vocational education.
2. How may vocational education be differentiated from general education? From industrial arts? Why are the differences important?
3. Discuss the importance of determining community needs as a basis for programs of vocational education. What devices are used in making this determination?
4. What is the relation of vocational education and vocational guidance? When should vocational guidance be provided for workers and prospective workers?
5. Discuss the importance of representative lay boards for the administration of vocational education. What are the functions of advisory committees?
6. What factors should operate in determining whether or not a teacher education institution should be approved for educating vocational teachers? What are the characteristics of a complete program of vocational teacher education?
7. Discuss the various types of qualifications that personnel in vocational education should possess.
8. What considerations are involved in an efficient program of vocational education?
9. What is the relationship of occupational needs to vocational education? How may these needs be determined?
10. Discuss the importance of including both short- and long-term courses in vocational education. What is meant by flexibility in vocational education programs?
11. To what extent should high standards be maintained in vocational education?
12. What is the importance of technical information in vocational education? Why should safety be stressed in vocational programs?

SOURCE REFERENCES

Bayles, Ernest E., *Democratic Educational Theory*, Harper & Row, New York, 1960.

Burke, Arvid J., *Financing Public Schools in the United States*, Harper & Row, New York, 1957.

Byram, Harold M., and Ralph C. Wenrich, *Vocational Education and Practical Arts in the Community School*, Macmillan, New York, 1956.

Emerson, Lynn A., *Vocational Technical Education for American Industry,* Circular 530, Office of Education, U.S. Department of Health, Education, and Welfare, Washington, D.C., 1958.

Hawkins, Layton S., Charles A. Prosser, and John C. Wright, *Development of Vocational Education,* American Technical Society, Chicago, 1951.

Keller, Franklin J., *Principles of Vocational Education,* Heath, Boston, 1948.

Mays, Arthur B., *Principles and Practices of Vocational Education,* McGraw-Hill, New York, 1948.

Selvidge, Robert W., and Verne C. Fryklund, *Principles of Trade and Industrial Teaching,* Bennett, Peoria, 1946.

Struck, F. Theodore, *Vocational Education for a Changing World,* Wiley, New York, 1945.

Thomas, Lawrence Gregg, *The Occupational Structure and Education,* Prentice-Hall, Englewood Cliffs, N.J., 1956.

U.S. Department of Health, Education, and Welfare, Office of Education, *Administration of Vocational Education,* Vocational Education Bulletin No. 1, revised 1958, Washington, D.C., 1958.

U.S. Department of Health, Education, and Welfare, Office of Education, *Education for a Changing World of Work,* Report of the Panel of Consultants on Vocational Education, Washington, D.C., 1963.

U.S. Department of Health, Education, and Welfare, Office of Education, *Vocational Education in the Next Decade,* Washington, D.C., 1961.

APPENDIXES

STATISTICAL TABLES

TABLE 1

ENROLLMENT IN VOCATIONAL AGRICULTURE CLASSES BY TYPE OF CLASS IN
THE STATES AND TERRITORIES, 1918 TO 1962

Year	Total Enrollment	Enrollment in			
		Day-School Classes	Day Unit Classes	Part-Time Classes	Evening Classes
1918	15,450	15,450			
1919	19,933	19,933			
1920	31,301	31,301			
1921	43,347	40,763		1,445	1,139
1922	60,236	52,961		5,942	1,333
1923	71,298	57,978	1,911	2,090	9,319
1924	85,985	65,358	3,257	2,143	15,227
1925	93,125	70,958	4,002	2,330	15,835
1926	109,528	82,431	5,142	2,716	19,239
1927	124,937	89,390	5,698	3,622	26,227
1928	144,871	96,941	8,310	4,458	35,162
1929	168,444	106,111	9,922	5,128	47,283
1930	188,311	113,728	9,957	4,164	60,462
1931	235,153	131,619	11,361	6,485	85,688
1932	252,199	143,079	11,190	10,792	87,138
1933	264,105	159,858	10,000	12,558	81,689
1934	286,150	164,882	10,256	11,719	99,293
1935	325,685	183,394	11,238	21,083	109,970
1936	343,809	204,736	10,726	20,830	107,517
1937	386,302	224,678	11,902	29,096	120,626
1938	460,876	246,213	12,950	42,900	158,813
1939	538,586	291,653	13,378	51,593	181,962
1940	584,133	318,223	11,175	62,489	192,246
1941	596,033	332,612	9,730	59,460	194,231
1942	605,099	332,939	7,601	49,977	214,582
1943	491,967	286,229	18,439	19,360	167,939
1944	469,959	259,235	10,705	16,139	183,880
1945	446,953	243,200	7,918	12,764	183,071
1946	510,331	255,096	6,221	24,401	224,613
1947	584,533	293,684	4,017	23,714	263,118
1948	640,791	314,263	4,522	24,293	297,713
1949	651,604	330,356	3,654	27,319	290,275
1950	764,975	373,113	3,784	43,071	345,007
1951	771,028	405,371	3,936	42,625	319,096
1952	744,348	422,282	2,500	48,406	271,160
1953	755,292	429,381	2,968	47,835	275,108
1954	737,502	444,063		46,164	247,275
1955	776,138	456,964		46,811	272,363
1956	785,599	460,300		47,450	277,849
1957	774,850	458,242		46,478	270,130
1958	775,892	461,778		48,677	265,437
1959	757,223	466,450		55,507	235,266
1960	796,237	463,960		65,548	266,729
1961	805,322	462,756		73,406	269,160
1962	822,664	474,118		78,977	269,569

NOTE: The statistical data shown in Appendix Tables 1 to 8 were taken
from the *Annual Reports of the Federal Board for Vocational Education,* 1918
to 1932 inclusive, and from the *Digest of Annual Reports of State Boards of
Vocational Education* for fiscal years 1933 to 1962 inclusive.

TABLE 2

EXPENDITURES FOR VOCATIONAL AGRICULTURAL EDUCATION BY SOURCE OF
FUNDS IN THE STATES AND TERRITORIES, 1918 TO 1962 (IN DOLLARS)

Year	Total Expenditures	Federal Funds	State Funds	Local Funds
1918	861,177	329,925	273,737	257,515
1919	1,720,835	660,564	526,210	534,061
1920	2,993,865	1,140,721	910,837	942,307
1921	4,096,943	1,521,424	1,293,624	1,281,895
1922	4,798,491	1,773,065	1,348,593	1,676,833
1923	5,392,577	2,014,712	1,423,312	1,954,553
1924	6,009,851	2,239,740	1,517,375	2,252,736
1925	6,905,479	2,605,331	1,709,106	2,591,042
1926	7,961,704	3,002,998	1,926,260	3,032,346
1927	8,281,183	3,149,599	1,869,380	3,262,204
1928	8,420,678	3,196,680	1,898,752	3,325,246
1929	9,221,593	3,247,469	2,070,127	3,903,997
1930	9,569,826	3,526,260	2,152,140	3,891,426
1931	10,830,183	3,812,085	2,469,308	4,548,790
1932	11,016,522	4,024,075	2,489,239	4,503,208
1933	10,183,931	3,660,076	2,300,485	4,223,370
1934	8,998,444	3,290,416	1,921,941	3,786,087
1935	9,607,718	4,049,443	1,811,250	3,747,025
1936	11,083,566	4,197,989	2,366,294	4,519,283
1937	11,631,797	4,314,984	2,509,069	4,807,744
1938	14,803,212	6,678,231	2,685,422	5,439,559
1939	16,768,205	7,261,991	2,998,517	6,507,697
1940	18,372,724	7,346,146	3,570,962	7,455,616
1941	18,969,061	7,505,172	3,906,643	7,557,246
1942	19,718,779	7,539,210	4,304,785	7,874,784
1943	19,379,788	7,383,550	4,233,282	7,762,956
1944	19,817,907	7,247,483	4,674,552	7,895,872
1945	19,151,606	7,137,392	4,423,239	7,590,975
1946	21,293,344	7,270,563	5,192,795	8,829,986
1947	24,556,393	7,560,510	6,303,691	10,692,192
1948	30,545,440	9,877,067	6,844,943	13,823,430
1949	33,633,226	10,048,995	8,037,858	15,546,373
1950	38,523,072	10,086,847	12,658,580	15,777,645
1951	41,491,626	10,120,289	14,004,493	17,366,844
1952	45,496,180	10,148,314	15,335,887	20,011,979
1953	47,490,396	10,104,623	16,618,589	20,767,184
1954	49,976,160	10,116,565	17,684,335	22,175,260
1955	53,707,125	11,825,581	18,472,982	23,408,562
1956	56,658,154	12,667,686	19,554,736	24,435,732
1957	59,915,145	13,582,114	21,499,563	24,833,468
1958	64,542,476	13,644,019	22,632,441	28,265,986
1959	66,667,806	13,668,059	23,889,202	29,110,544
1960	67,302,240	13,687,975	24,575,958	29,038,307
1961	69,606,746	13,668,744	25,860,886	30,077,116
1962	73,291,897	13,644,907	28,589,744	31,057,246

TABLE 3

ENROLLMENT IN VOCATIONAL DISTRIBUTIVE OCCUPATIONS CLASSES BY TYPE
OF CLASS IN THE STATES AND TERRITORIES, 1938 TO 1962

		Enrollment in	
Year	Total Enrollment	Evening Classes	Part-Time Classes
1938	36,008	32,408	3,600
1939	88,429	83,143	5,286
1940	129,433	122,933	6,500
1941	156,617	126,328	30,289
1942	215,049	162,707	52,342
1943	297,534	180,038	117,496
1944	181,509	86,802	94,707
1945	152,781	71,134	81,647
1946	174,672	93,882	80,790
1947	235,141	140,996	94,145
1948	292,936	192,269	100,667
1949	313,475	207,621	105,854
1950	364,670	239,554	125,116
1951	341,440	228,173	113,267
1952	234,984	148,268	86,716
1953	209,012	127,734	81,278
1954	220,619	152,413	68,206
1955	235,355	164,591	70,764
1956	257,025	173,085	83,940
1957	279,903	203,795	76,108
1958	282,558	202,408	80,150
1959	310,591	274,135	36,456[a]
1960	303,784	264,106	39,678[a]
1961	306,083	262,904	43,179[a]
1962	321,065	276,948	44,117[a]

[a] Post-high school and high school cooperative.

TABLE 4

EXPENDITURES FOR VOCATIONAL DISTRIBUTIVE EDUCATION BY SOURCE OF
FUNDS IN THE STATES AND TERRITORIES, 1938 TO 1962 (IN DOLLARS)

Year	Total Expenditures	Expenditures of		
		Federal Funds	State Funds	Local Funds
1938	643,029	248,210	116,837	277,982
1939	817,639	487,052	144,721	186,866
1940	1,074,218	637,427	211,822	224,969
1941	1,328,442	782,795	311,174	234,473
1942	1,605,018	944,686	358,245	302,087
1943	1,639,152	893,551	409,279	336,322
1944	1,758,128	913,923	461,619	382,586
1945	1,932,775	941,836	562,281	428,658
1946	2,232,875	967,481	653,161	612,233
1947	2,623,491	1,035,939	841,772	745,780
1948	3,791,717	1,525,426	1,249,497	1,016,794
1949	4,676,978	1,550,935	1,443,705	1,682,338
1950	5,408,144	1,682,691	1,770,753	1,954,700
1951	5,795,856	1,649,282	2,046,345	2,100,229
1952	5,350,789	820,726	2,308,964	2,221,099
1953	4,838,999	410,983	2,355,317	2,072,699
1954	5,105,096	417,414	2,398,917	2,288,765
1955	6,032,663	825,254	2,602,545	2,604,864
1956	6,423,833	1,430,347	2,474,099	2,519,387
1957	8,172,519	2,438,561	2,661,100	3,072,848
1958	9,302,626	2,509,332	3,109,829	3,683,465
1959	9,602,409	2,505,856	3,240,064	3,856,489
1960	9,900,019	2,507,591	3,411,961	3,980,467
1961	10,593,143	2,556,886	3,697,390	4,338,867
1962	11,405,837	2,564,754	4,302,611	4,538,472

TABLE 5

ENROLLMENT IN VOCATIONAL HOMEMAKING CLASSES BY TYPE OF CLASS IN
THE STATES AND TERRITORIES, 1918 TO 1962

| Year | Total Enrollment | Enrollment in | | |
		Day-School Classes	Part-Time Classes	Evening Classes
1918	30,799	8,439		22,360
1919	39,414	12,445	4,278	22,691
1920	48,938	16,437	7,733	24,768
1921	63,395	22,561	8,878	31,956
1922	118,708	28,987	23,696	66,025
1923	139,341	30,936	29,706	78,699
1924	156,767	36,253	27,440	93,074
1925	154,491	40,341	21,228	92,922
1926	177,205	41,622	34,278	101,305
1927	164,420	44,261	31,583	88,576
1928	175,944	48,881	28,916	98,147
1929	154,890	41,089	20,351	93,450
1930	174,967	56,369	21,223	97,375
1931	220,248	67,471	33,823	118,954
1932	265,495	91,747	32,501	141,247
1933	278,398	109,131	31,730	137,537
1934	297,851	142,476	31,694	123,681
1935	349,346	176,321	38,634	134,391
1936	374,901	195,647	37,080	142,174
1937	377,437	194,781	48,526	134,130
1938	627,394	358,015	54,211	215,168
1939	741,503	439,877	65,592	236,034
1940	818,766	500,126	72,790	245,850
1941	871,891	545,408	81,737	244,746
1942	954,041	566,823	91,494	295,724
1943	873,771	542,920	78,827	252,024
1944	806,605	507,425	65,530	233,650
1945	890,464	512,933	93,112	284,419
1946	911,816	527,314	82,238	302,264
1947	968,846	530,287	105,403	333,156
1948	1,139,766	569,560	93,775	476,431
1949	1,328,521	614,308	107,275	606,938
1950	1,430,366	647,711	115,979	666,676
1951	1,458,605	701,726	97,328	659,551
1952	1,391,389	731,813	80,577	578,999
1953	1,327,285	782,492	58,620	486,173
1954	1,380,147	799,174	79,710	501,263
1955	1,555,846	942,214	82,907	530,725
1956	1,486,816	850,531	70,532	565,753
1957	1,507,940	890,050	65,137	552,753
1958	1,559,822	914,899	67,472	577,451
1959	1,585,860	928,398	75,810	581,652
1960	1,588,109	946,860	54,914	586,335
1961	1,610,334	981,109	62,815	566,410
1962	1,725,660	1,062,664	52,209	610,787

TABLE 6

EXPENDITURES FOR VOCATIONAL HOMEMAKING EDUCATION BY SOURCE OF
FUNDS IN THE STATES AND TERRITORIES, 1918 TO 1962 (IN DOLLARS)

Year	Total Expenditures	Expenditures of		
		Federal Funds	State Funds	Local Funds
1918	641,812	147,089	206,682	288,041
1919	966,463	291,971	318,270	356,222
1920	1,653,917	409,372	549,401	695,144
1921	2,572,443	525,331	906,718	1,140,394
1922	2,896,999	582,632	970,624	1,343,743
1923	3,530,122	627,134	955,083	1,947,905
1924	3,563,102	680,513	1,055,125	1,827,464
1925	3,722,101	709,383	1,187,482	1,825,236
1926	3,863,040	815,631	1,108,448	1,938,961
1927	4,155,391	817,141	1,224,679	2,113,571
1928	4,525,304	832,436	1,396,147	2,296,721
1929	4,748,789	826,698	1,476,055	2,446,036
1930	5,238,192	1,026,089	1,639,632	2,572,471
1931	5,651,553	1,230,063	1,758,515	2,662,975
1932	6,002,841	1,481,285	1,776,124	2,745,432
1933	5,481,534	1,443,006	1,599,401	2,439,127
1934	4,961,632	1,261,635	1,244,680	2,455,317
1935	5,806,546	1,709,414	1,448,634	2,648,498
1936	6,605,342	1,784,402	1,680,544	3,140,396
1937	6,688,833	1,793,277	1,872,152	3,023,404
1938	10,288,816	4,223,638	2,006,178	4,059,000
1939	12,864,193	4,730,522	2,624,389	5,509,282
1940	13,071,601	4,916,111	2,636,832	5,518,658
1941	14,014,482	5,031,690	2,978,433	6,004,359
1942	14,727,229	5,035,715	3,387,088	6,304,426
1943	16,501,240	5,068,847	3,698,422	7,733,971
1944	17,238,043	5,087,258	4,163,406	7,987,379
1945	18,217,859	5,097,063	4,396,867	8,723,929
1946	20,370,178	5,131,080	5,499,020	9,740,078
1947	22,459,839	5,186,095	6,358,733	10,915,011
1948	28,130,283	6,260,607	7,539,872	14,329,804
1949	32,354,308	6,243,033	8,729,534	17,381,741
1950	36,916,403	6,241,255	12,782,184	17,892,964
1951	39,339,124	6,267,092	13,708,179	19,363,853
1952	42,966,577	6,256,588	15,057,294	21,652,695
1953	43,114,330	6,278,782	16,060,118	20,775,430
1954	45,291,115	6,257,447	16,938,422	22,095,246
1955	49,461,352	7,700,881	18,036,243	23,724,228
1956	53,281,959	8,388,692	19,184,936	25,708,331
1957	57,177,777	8,906,532	21,124,660	27,146,585
1958	62,909,965	8,902,237	23,668,706	30,339,022
1959	67,001,071	8,906,541	25,688,582	32,405,948
1960	68,656,113	8,908,087	26,218,232	33,529,794
1961	72,622,267	8,937,696	27,744,801	35,939,770
1962	79,898,309	8,874,426	32,522,053	38,501,830

TABLE 7

ENROLLMENT IN VOCATIONAL INDUSTRIAL CLASSES BY TYPE OF CLASS IN THE STATES AND TERRITORIES, 1918 TO 1962

Year	Total Enrollment	Enrollment in			
		Evening Extension Classes	Part-Time Extension Classes	Other Part-Time Classes	Day Trade Classes
1918	117,934	46,333	53,005		18,596
1919	135,548	43,485	22,616	50,783	18,664
1920	184,819	48,354	17,159	98,082	21,224
1921	217,500	51,823	20,978	119,657	25,042
1922	296,884	66,477	33,106	165,911	31,390
1923	325,889	69,856	37,931	184,001	34,101
1924	409,843	84,973	35,475	256,133	33,262
1925	429,071	85,553	31,343	272,509	39,666
1926	466,685	89,694	41,834	290,358	44,799
1927	494,629	97,574	38,406	308,533	50,116
1928	537,611	114,629	42,531	323,012	57,439
1929	563,515	131,103	36,063	331,511	64,838
1930	620,422	165,317	47,349	336,297	71,459
1931	592,215	168,822	47,195	295,717	80,481
1932	560,150	151,042	44,476	271,232	93,400
1933	489,900	123,807	38,064	217,183	110,846
1934	466,999	130,901	37,995	174,618	123,485
1935	503,865	154,352	72,952	144,981	131,580
1936	537,151	120,216	125,961	145,343	145,631
1937	580,905	125,291	150,411	145,433	159,770
1938	685,804	163,319	183,591	154,691	184,203
1939	715,239	156,464	221,145	141,265	196,365
1940	758,409	167,908	241,098	142,481	206,922
1941	804,515	133,787	309,373	130,116	231,239
1942	850,597	85,207	349,738	118,201	297,451
1943	618,471	52,413	244,252	125,373	196,433
1944	543,080	27,717	210,707	134,270	170,386
1945	522,733	70,154	158,281	119,734	174,564
1946	630,844	94,503	240,346	97,359	198,636
1947	720,098	116,781	295,693	90,371	217,253
1948	762,628	243,203	178,110	125,114	216,201
1949	801,912	267,883	224,319	95,328	214,382
1950	804,602	266,647	216,648	98,568	222,739
1951	792,339	268,276	207,228	101,447	215,388
1952	793,213	327,478	162,589	96,389	206,757
1953	808,549	328,633	190,418	66,092	223,406
1954	826,583	411,776	121,460	46,168	247,179
1955	870,954	421,321	129,260	66,442	253,931
1956	883,716	439,640	148,597	45,591	246,698
1957	951,761	492,883	151,308	46,130	261,440
1958	983,644	520,182	146,766	44,687	272,009
1959	968,114	512,480	133,007	41,824	280,803
1960	938,490	485,020	139,185	41,964	272,321
1961	963,609	524,238	132,027	36,210	271,134
1962	1,005,385	557,604	122,625	30,773	294,383

TABLE 8

EXPENDITURES FOR VOCATIONAL INDUSTRIAL EDUCATION BY SOURCE OF FUNDS IN THE STATES AND TERRITORIES, 1918 TO 1962 (IN DOLLARS)

Year	Total Expenditures	Expenditures of		
		Federal Funds	State Funds	Local Funds
1918	1,618,225	346,374	534,242	737,609
1919	2,264,481	607,474	722,148	934,859
1920	3,887,381	926,410	1,210,046	1,750,925
1921	5,948,874	1,310,739	1,874,157	2,763,978
1922	7,117,498	1,494,421	2,204,722	3,418,355
1923	8,209,746	1,667,040	2,496,137	4,046,569
1924	9,272,397	1,912,626	2,602,332	4,757,439
1925	10,292,276	2,299,836	2,875,387	5,117,053
1926	11,357,055	2,730,029	3,114,373	5,512,653
1927	12,080,052	2,762,472	3,399,810	5,917,770
1928	12,763,765	2,792,336	3,728,073	6,243,356
1929	13,495,002	2,804,364	3,916,753	6,773,885
1930	15,050,882	2,851,876	4,441,377	7,757,629
1931	15,657,455	2,936,580	4,626,550	8,094,325
1932	16,281,083	2,911,473	4,766,857	8,602,753
1933	14,357,472	2,625,162	4,300,679	7,431,631
1934	14,020,738	2,398,894	3,921,979	7,699,865
1935	13,872,866	3,613,122	3,519,749	6,739,995
1936	15,737,269	3,766,543	4,557,897	7,412,829
1937	18,072,817	3,905,409	4,520,329	9,647,079
1938	19,259,479	6,587,038	4,638,315	8,034,126
1939	22,204,812	6,954,989	5,166,593	10,083,230
1940	22,561,482	7,104,548	5,315,259	10,141,675
1941	23,387,198	7,226,165	5,719,147	10,441,886
1942	22,966,092	7,237,253	5,992,595	9,736,244
1943	25,966,868	6,960,698	5,868,048	13,138,122
1944	25,484,573	6,709,641	5,715,996	13,058,936
1945	26,336,448	6,828,283	5,962,427	13,545,738
1946	28,910,435	7,258,948	7,192,876	14,458,611
1947	33,612,358	7,304,891	8,675,878	17,631,589
1948	40,871,957	8,537,268	10,199,607	22,135,082
1949	44,466,859	8,566,019	12,227,838	23,673,002
1950	47,869,435	8,611,835	13,322,257	25,935,343
1951	50,727,619	8,648,391	14,448,562	27,630,666
1952	52,652,137	8,637,340	15,116,271	28,898,526
1953	50,507,488	8,572,071	17,183,566	24,751,851
1954	50,916,359	8,627,467	17,528,017	24,760,875
1955	55,560,077	9,999,165	18,479,477	27,081,435
1956	59,521,628	10,693,640	20,607,603	28,220,385
1957	64,074,868	11,340,441	22,079,580	30,654,847
1958	69,423,215	11,394,299	22,355,802	35,673,114
1959	73,504,181	11,411,388	23,853,393	38,239,400
1960	72,860,158	11,482,347	23,778,177	37,599,634
1961	75,395,615	11,436,119	25,834,435	38,125,061
1962	85,087,009	11,476,867	30,847,949	42,762,193

PUBLIC LAWS FOR VOCATIONAL EDUCATION

THE SMITH–HUGHES ACT
(Public Law 347, 64th Congress)

An Act To provide for the promotion of vocational education; to provide for cooperation with the States in the promotion of such education in agriculture and the trades and industries; to provide for cooperation with the States in the preparation of teachers of vocational subjects; and to appropriate money and regulate its expenditure.

Be it enacted by the Senate and House of Representatives of the United States of America in Congress assembled, That there is hereby annually appropriated, out of any money in the Treasury not otherwise appropriated, the sums provided in sections two, three, and four of this Act, to be paid to the respective States for the purpose of cooperating with the States in paying the salaries of teachers, supervisors, and directors of agricultural subjects, and teachers of trade, home economics, and industrial subjects, and in the preparation of teachers of agricultural, trade, industrial, and home economics subjects; and the sum provided for in section seven for the use of the Federal Board for Vocational Education for the administration of this Act and for the purpose of making studies, investigations, and reports to aid in the organization and conduct of vocational education, which sums shall be expended as hereinafter provided.

SEC. 2.   That for the purpose of cooperating with the States in paying the salaries of teachers, supervisors, or directors of agricultural subjects there is hereby appropriated for the use of the States, subject to the provisions of this Act, for the fiscal year ending June thirtieth, nineteen hundred and eighteen, the sum of $500,000; for the fiscal year ending June thirtieth, nineteen hundred and nineteen, the sum of $750,000; for the fiscal year ending June thirtieth, nineteen hundred and twenty, the sum of $1,000,000; for the fiscal year ending June thirtieth, nineteen hundred and twenty-one, the sum of $1,250,000; for the fiscal year ending June thirtieth, nineteen hundred and twenty-two, the sum of $1,500,000; for the fiscal year ending June thirtieth, nineteen hundred and twenty-three, the sum of $1,750,000; for the fiscal year ending June thirtieth, nineteen hundred and twenty-four, the sum of $2,000,000; for the fiscal year ending June thirtieth, nineteen hundred and twenty-five, the sum of $2,500,000; for the fiscal year ending June thirtieth, nineteen hundred and twenty-six, and annually thereafter, the sum of $3,000,000. Said sums shall be allotted to the States in the proportion which their rural population bears to the total rural population in the United States, not including outlying possessions, according to the last preceding United States census: *Provided,* That the allotment of funds to any State shall be not less than a minimum of $5,000 for any fiscal year prior to and including the fiscal year ending June thirtieth, nineteen hundred and twenty-three, nor less than $10,000 for any fiscal year thereafter, and there is hereby appropriated the following sums, or so much thereof as may be necessary, which shall be used for the purpose of providing the minimum allotment to the States provided for in this section: For the fiscal year ending June thirtieth, nineteen hundred and eighteen, the sum of $48,000; for the fiscal year ending June thirtieth, nineteen hundred and nineteen, the sum of $34,000; for the fiscal year ending June thirtieth, nineteenth hundred and twenty, the sum of $24,000; for the fiscal year ending June thirtieth, nineteen hundred and twenty-one, the sum of $18,000; for the fiscal year ending June thirtieth, nineteen hundred and twenty-two, the sum of $14,000; for the fiscal year ending June thirtieth, nineteen hundred and twenty-three, the sum of $11,000; for the fiscal year ending June thirtieth, nineteen hundred and twenty-four, the sum of $9,000; for the fiscal year ending June thirtieth, nineteen hundred and twenty-five, the sum of $34,000; and annually thereafter the sum of $27,000.

SEC. 3.   That for the purpose of cooperating with the States in paying the salaries of teachers of trade, home economics, and industrial subjects there is hereby appropriated for the use of the States, for the fiscal year ending June thirtieth, nineteen hundred and eighteen, the sum of $500,000; for the fiscal year ending June thirtieth, nineteen hundred and nineteen, the sum of $750,000; for the fiscal year ending June thirtieth, nineteen hundred and twenty, the sum of $1,000,000; for the fiscal year ending June thirtieth, nineteen hundred and twenty-one, the sum of $1,250,000; for the fiscal year ending June thirtieth, nineteen hundred and twenty-two, the sum of $1,500,000; for the fiscal year ending June thirtieth, nineteen hundred and twenty-three, the sum of $1,750,000; for the fiscal year ending June thirtieth, nineteen hundred and twenty-four, the sum of $2,000,-000; for the fiscal year ending June thirtieth, nineteen hundred and twenty-five, the sum of $2,500,000; for the fiscal year ending June thirtieth, nineteen hundred and twenty-six, the sum of $3,000,000; and annually thereafter the sum of $3,000,000. Said sums shall be allotted to the States in the proportion which their urban population bears to the total urban population in the United States, not including outlying possessions, according to the last preceding United States census: *Provided,* That the allotment of funds to any State shall be not less than a minimum of $5,000 for any fiscal year prior to and including the fiscal year ending June thirtieth, nineteen hundred and twenty-three, nor less than $10,000 for any fiscal year thereafter, and there is hereby appropriated the following sums, or so much thereof as may be needed, which shall be used for the purpose of providing the minimum allotment to the States provided for in this section: For the fiscal year ending June thirtieth, nineteen hundred and eighteen, the sum of $66,000; for the fiscal year ending June thirtieth, nineteen hundred and nineteen, the sum of $46,000; for the fiscal year ending June thirtieth, nineteen hundred and twenty, the sum of $34,000; for the fiscal year ending June thirtieth, nineteen hundred and twenty-one, the sum of $28,000; for the fiscal year ending June thirtieth, nineteen hundred and twenty-two, the sum of $25,000; for the fiscal year ending June thirtieth, nineteen hundred and twenty-three, the sum of $22,000; for the fiscal year ending June thirtieth, nineteen hundred and twenty-four, the sum of $19,-000; for the fiscal year ending June thirtieth, nineteen hundred and twenty-five, the sum of $56,000; for the fiscal year ending June thirtieth, nineteen hundred and twenty-six, and annually thereafter, the sum of $50,000.

That not more than twenty per centum of the money appropriated under this Act for the payment of salaries of teachers of trade, home economics, and industrial subjects, for any year, shall be expended for the salaries of teachers of home economics subjects.

SEC. 4. That for the purpose of cooperating with the States in preparing teachers, supervisors, and directors of agricultural subjects and teachers of trade and industrial and home economics subjects there is hereby appropriated for the use of the States for the fiscal year ending June thirtieth, nineteen hundred and eighteen, the sum of $500,000; for the fiscal year ending June thirtieth, nineteen hundred and nineteen, the sum of $700,000; for the fiscal year ending June thirtieth, nineteen hundred and twenty, the sum of $900,000; for the fiscal year ending June thirtieth, nineteen hundred and twenty-one, and annually thereafter, the sum of $1,000,000. Said sums shall be allotted to the States in the proportion which their population bears to the total population of the United States, not including outlying possessions, according to the last preceding United States census: *Provided*, That the allotment of funds to any State shall be not less than a minimum of $5,000 for any fiscal year prior to and including the fiscal year ending June thirtieth, nineteen hundred and nineteen, nor less than $10,000 for any fiscal year thereafter. And there is hereby appropriated the following sums, or so much thereof as may be needed, which shall be used for the purpose of providing the minimum allotment provided for in this section: For the fiscal year ending June thirtieth, nineteen hundred and eighteen, the sum of $46,000; for the fiscal year ending June thirtieth, nineteen hundred and nineteen, the sum of $32,000; for the fiscal year ending June thirtieth, nineteen hundred and twenty, the sum of $24,000; for the fiscal year ending June thirtieth, nineteen hundred and twenty-one, and annually thereafter, the sum of $90,000.

SEC. 5. That in order to secure the benefits of the appropriations provided for in sections two, three, and four of this Act, any State shall, through the legislative authority thereof, accept the provisions of this Act and designate or create a State board, consisting of not less than three members, and having all necessary power to cooperate, as herein provided, with the Federal Board for Vocational Education in the administration of the provisions of this Act. The State board of education, or other board having charge of the administration of public education in the State, or any State board having charge of the administration of any kind of vocational education in the State may, if the State so elect, be designated as the State board, for the purposes of this Act.

In any State the legislature of which does not meet in nineteen hundred and seventeen, if the governor of that State, so far as he is authorized to do so, shall accept the provisions of this Act and designate or create a State board of not less than three members to act in cooperation with the Federal Board for Vocational Education, the Federal board shall recognize such local board for the purposes of this Act until the legislature of such State meets in due course and has been in session sixty days.

Any State may accept the benefits of any one or more of the respective funds herein appropriated, and it may defer the acceptance of the benefits of any one or more of such funds, and shall be required to meet only the conditions relative to the fund or funds the benefits of which it has accepted: *Provided,* That after June thirtieth, nineteen hundred and twenty, no State shall receive any appropriation for salaries of teachers, supervisors, or directors of agricultural subjects, until it shall have taken advantage of at least the minimum amount appropriated for the training of teachers, supervisors, or directors of agricultural subjects, as provided for in this Act, and that after said date no State shall receive any appropriation for the salaries of teachers of trade, home economics, and industrial subjects until it shall have taken advantage of at least the minimum amount appropriated for the training of teachers of trade, home economics, and industrial subjects, as provided for in this Act.

SEC. 6. That a Federal Board for Vocational Education is hereby created, to consist of the Secretary of Agriculture, the Secretary of Commerce, the Secretary of Labor, the United States Commissioner of Education, and three citizens of the United States to be appointed by the President, by and with the advice and consent of the Senate. One of said three citizens shall be a representative of the manufacturing and commercial interests, one a representative of the agricultural interests, and one a representative of labor. The board shall elect annually one of its members as chairman. In the first instance, one of the citizen members shall be appointed for one year, one for two years, and one for three years, and thereafter for three years each. The members of the board other than the members of the Cabinet and the United States Commissioner of Education shall receive a salary of $5,000 per annum.

The board shall have power to cooperate with State boards in carrying out the provisions of this Act. It shall be the duty of the Federal Board for Vocational Education to make, or cause to have made, studies, investigations, and reports, with particular reference to their use in aiding the States in the establishment of vocational schools and classes and in giving instruction in agriculture, trades and industries, commerce and commercial pursuits, and home economics. Such studies, investigations, and reports shall include agriculture and agricultural processes and requirements upon agricultural workers; trades, industries, and apprenticeships, trade and industrial requirements upon industrial workers, and classification of industrial processes and pursuits; commerce and commercial pursuits and requirements upon commercial workers; home management, domestic science, and the study of related facts and principles; and problems of administration of vocational schools and of courses of study and instruction in vocational subjects.

When the board deems it advisable such studies, investigations, and reports concerning agriculture, for the purposes of agricultural education, may be made in cooperation with or through the Department of Agriculture; such studies, investigations, and reports concerning trades and industries, for the purposes of trade and industrial education, may be made in cooperation with or through the Department of Labor; such studies, investigations, and reports concerning commerce and commercial pursuits, for the purposes of commercial education, may be made in cooperation with or through the Department of Commerce; such studies, investigations, and reports concerning the administration of vocational schools, courses of study, and instruction in vocational subjects may be made in cooperation with or through the Bureau of Education.

The Commissioner of Education may make such recommendations to the board relative to the administration of this Act as he may from time to time deem advisable. It shall be the duty of the chairman of the board to carry out the rules, regulations, and decisions which the board may adopt. The Federal Board for Vocational Education shall have power to employ such assistants as may be necessary to carry out the provisions of this Act.

Sec. 7. That there is hereby appropriated to the Federal Board for Vocational Education the sum of $200,000 annually, to be available from and after the passage of this Act, for the purpose of making or cooperating in making the studies, investigations, and reports provided for in section six of this Act, and for the purpose of paying the salaries of the officers, the assistants, and such office and other expenses as the board may deem necessary to the execution and administration of this Act.[1]

Sec. 8. That in order to secure the benefits of the appropriation for any purpose specified in this Act the State board shall prepare plans showing the kinds of vocational education for which it is proposed that the appropriation shall be used; the kinds of schools and equipment; courses of study; methods of instruction; qualifications of teachers; and, in the case of agricultural subjects, the qualifications of supervisors or directors; plans for the training of teachers; and, in the case of agricultural subjects, plans for the supervision of agricultural education, as provided for in section ten. Such plans shall be submitted by the State board to the Federal Board for Vocational Education, and if the Federal board finds the same to be in conformity with the provisions and purposes of this Act, the same shall be approved. The State board shall make an annual report to the Federal Board for Vocational Education, on or before September first of each year, on the work done in the State and the receipts and expenditures of money under the provisions of this Act.

Sec. 9. That the appropriation for the salaries of teachers, supervisors, or directors of agricultural subjects and of teachers of trade, home economics, and industrial subjects shall be devoted exclusively to the payment of salaries of such teachers, supervisors, or directors having the minimum qualifications set up for the State by the State board, with the approval of the Federal Board for Vocational Education. The cost of in-

---

[1] Sec. 7 was amended by Act, Public, No. 473, 73d Cong. approved June 26, 1934, so as to change the permanent appropriation to a permanent authorization.

struction supplementary to the instruction in agricultural and in trade, home economics, and industrial subjects provided for in this Act, necessary to build a well-rounded course of training, shall be borne by the State and local communities, and no part of the cost thereof shall be borne out of the appropriations herein made. The moneys expended under the provisions of this Act, in cooperation with the States, for the salaries of teachers, supervisors, or directors of agricultural subjects, or for the salaries of teachers of trade, home economics, and industrial subjects, shall be conditioned that for each dollar of Federal money expended for such salaries the State or local community, or both, shall expend an equal amount for such salaries; and that appropriations for the training of teachers of vocational subjects, as herein provided, shall be conditioned that such money be expended for maintenance of such training and that for each dollar of Federal money so expended for maintenance, the State or local community, or both, shall expend an equal amount for the maintenance of such training.

SEC. 10.   That any State may use the appropriation for agricultural purposes, or any part thereof allotted to it, under the provisions of this Act, for the salaries of teachers, supervisors, or directors of agricultural subjects, either for the salaries of teachers of such subjects in schools or classes or for the salaries of supervisors or directors of such subjects under a plan of supervision for the State to be set up by the State board, with the approval of the Federal Board for Vocational Education. That in order to receive the benefits of such appropriation for the salaries of teachers, supervisors, or directors of agricultural subjects the State board of any State shall provide in its plan for agricultural education that such education shall be that which is under public supervision or control; that the controlling purpose of such education shall be to fit for useful employment; that such education shall be of less than college grade and be designed to meet the needs of persons over fourteen years of age who have entered upon or who are preparing to enter upon the work of the farm or of the farm home; that the State or local community, or both, shall provide the necessary plant and equipment determined upon by the State board, with the approval of the Federal Board for Vocational Education, as the minimum requirement for such education in schools and classes in the State; that the amount expended for the maintenance of such education in any school or class receiving the benefit of such appropriation shall be not less annually than the amount fixed by the State board, with the approval of the Federal board, as the minimum for such schools or classes in the State; that such schools shall provide for directed or supervised practice in agriculture, either on a farm provided for by the school or other farm, for at least six months per year; that the teachers, supervisors, or directors of agricultural subjects shall have at least the minimum qualifications determined for the State by the State board, with the approval of the Federal Board for Vocational Education.

SEC. 11.   That in order to receive the benefits of the appropriation for the salaries of teachers of trade, home economics, and industrial subjects the State board of any State shall provide in its plan for trade, home economics, and industrial education that such education shall be given in schools or classes under public supervision or control; that the controlling purpose of such education shall be to fit for useful employment; that such education shall be of less than college grade and shall be designed to meet the needs of persons over fourteen years of age who are preparing for a trade or industrial pursuit or who have entered upon the work of a trade or industrial pursuit; that the State or local community, or both, shall provide the necessary plant and equipment determined upon by the State board, with the approval of the Federal Board for Vocational Education, as the minimum requirement in such State for education for any given trade or industrial pursuit; that the total amount expended for the maintenance of such education in any school or class receiving the benefit of such appropriation shall be not less annually than the amount fixed by the State board, with the approval of the Federal board, as the minimum for such schools or classes in the State; that such schools or classes giving instruction to persons who have not entered upon employment shall require that at least half of the time of such instruction be given to practical work on a useful or productive basis, such instruction to extend over not less than nine months per year and not less than thirty hours per week; that at least one-third of the sum appropriated to any State for the salaries of teachers of trade, home economics, and industrial subjects shall, if expended, be applied to part-time schools or classes for workers over fourteen years of age who have entered upon employment, and such subjects in a part-time school or class may mean any subject given to enlarge the civic or vocational intelligence of such workers over fourteen and less than eighteen years of age; that such part-time schools or classes shall provide for not less than one hundred and forty-four hours of classroom instruction per year; that evening industrial schools shall fix the age of sixteen years as a minimum entrance requirement and shall confine instruction to that which is supplemental to the daily employment; that the teachers of any trade or industrial subject in any State shall have at least the minimum qualifications for teachers of such subject determined upon for such State by the State board, with the approval of the Federal Board for Vocational Education: *Provided*, That for cities and towns of less than twenty-five thousand population, according to the last preceding United States census, the State board, with the approval of the Federal Board for Vocational Education, may modify the conditions as to the length of course and hours of instruction per week for schools and classes giving instruction to those who have not entered upon employment, in order to meet the particular needs of such cities and towns.

SEC. 12. That in order for any State to receive the benefits of the appropriation in this Act for the training of teachers, supervisors, or directors of agricultural subjects, or of teachers of trade, industrial, or home economics subjects, the State board of such State shall provide in its plan for such training that the same shall be carried out under the supervision of the State board; that such training shall be given in schools or classes under public supervision or control; that such training shall be given only to persons who have had adequate vocational experience or contact in the line of work for which they are preparing themselves as teachers, supervisors, or directors, or who are acquiring such experience or contact as a part of their training; and that the State board, with the approval of the Federal board, shall establish minimum requirements for such experience or contact for teachers, supervisors, or directors of agricultural subjects and for teachers of trade, industrial, and home economics subjects; that not more than sixty per centum nor less than twenty per centum of the money appropriated under this Act for the training of teachers of vocational subjects to any State for any year shall be expended for any one of the following purposes: For the preparation of teachers, supervisors, or directors of agricultural subjects, or the preparation of teachers of trade and industrial subjects, or the preparation of teachers of home economics subjects.

SEC. 13.   That in order to secure the benefits of the appropriations for the salaries of teachers, supervisors, or directors of agricultural subjects, or for the salaries of teachers of trade, home economics, and industrial subjects or for the training of teachers as herein provided, any State shall, through the legislative authority thereof, appoint as custodian for said appropriations its State treasurer, who shall receive and provide for the proper custody and disbursements of all money paid to the State from said appropriations.

SEC. 14.   That the Federal Board for Vocational Education shall annually ascertain whether the several States are using, or are prepared to use, the money received by them in accordance with the provisions of this Act. On or before the first day of January of each year the Federal Board for Vocational Education shall certify to the Secretary of the Treasury each State which has accepted the provisions of this Act and complied therewith, certifying the amounts which each State is entitled to receive under the provisions of this Act. Upon such certification the Secretary of the Treasury shall pay quarterly to the custodian for vocational education of each State the moneys to which it is entitled under the provisions of this Act. The moneys so received by the custodian for vocational education for any State shall be paid out on the requisition of the State board as reimbursement for expenditures already incurred to such schools as are approved by said State board and are entitled to receive such moneys under the provisions of this Act.

SEC. 15.   That whenever any portion of the fund annually allotted to any State has not been expended for the purpose provided for in this Act, a sum equal to such portion shall be deducted by the Federal board from the next succeeding annual allotment from such fund to such State.

SEC. 16.   That the Federal Board for Vocational Education may withhold the allotment of moneys to any State whenever it shall be determined that such moneys are not being expended for the purposes and under the conditions of this Act.

If any allotment is withheld from any State, the State board of such State may appeal to the Congress of the United States, and if the Congress shall not direct such sum to be paid it shall be covered into the Treasury.

SEC. 17.   That if any portion of the moneys received by the custodian for vocational education of any State under this Act, for any given purpose named in this Act, shall, by any action or contingency, be diminished or lost, it shall be replaced by such State, and until so replaced no subsequent appropriation for such education shall be paid to such State. No portion of any moneys appropriated under this Act for the benefit of the States shall be applied, directly or indirectly, to the purchase, erection, preservation, or repair of any building or buildings or equipment, or for the purchase or rental of lands, or for the support of any religious or privately owned or conducted school or college.

SEC. 18.   That the Federal Board for Vocational Education shall make an annual report to Congress, on or before December first, on the administration of this Act and shall include in such report the reports made by the State boards on the administration of this Act by each State and the expenditures of the money allotted to each State.—Approved, February 23, 1917.

VOCATIONAL EDUCATION ACT OF 1963
(Public Law 88–210, 88th Congress)

DECLARATION OF PURPOSE

SEC. 1.   It is the purpose of this part to authorize Federal grants to States to assist them to maintain, extend, and improve existing programs of vocational education, to develop new programs of vocational education, and to provide part-time employment for youths who need the earnings from such employment to continue their vocational training on a full-time basis, so that persons of all ages in all communities of the State—those in high school, those who have completed or discontinued their formal education and are preparing to enter the labor market, those who have already entered the labor market but need to upgrade their skills or learn new ones, and those with special educational handicaps—will have ready access to vocational training or retraining which is of high quality, which is realistic in the light of actual or anticipated opportunities for gainful employment, and which is suited to their needs, interests, and ability to benefit from such training.

AUTHORIZATION OF APPROPRIATIONS

SEC. 2.   There are hereby authorized to be appropriated for the fiscal year ending June 30, 1964, $60,000,000, for the fiscal year ending June 30, 1965, $118,500,000, for the fiscal year ending June 30, 1966, $177,-500,000, and for the fiscal year ending June 30, 1967, and each fiscal year thereafter, $225,000,000, for the purpose of making grants to States as provided in this part.

ALLOTMENTS TO STATES

SEC. 3.   (a) Ninety per centum of the sums appropriated pursuant to section 2 shall be allotted among the States on the basis of the number of persons in the various age groups needing vocational education and the per capita income in the respective States as follows: The Commissioner shall allot to each State for each fiscal year—

(1) An amount which bears the same ratio to 50 per centum of the sums so appropriated for such year, as the product of the population aged fifteen to nineteen, inclusive, in the State in the preceding fiscal year and the State's allotment ratio bears to the sum of the corresponding products for all the States; plus

(2) An amount which bears the same ratio to 20 per centum of the sums so appropriated for such year, as the product of the population aged twenty to twenty-four, inclusive, in the State in the preceding fiscal year and the State's allotment ratio bears to the sum of the corresponding products for all the States; plus

(3) An amount which bears the same ratio to 15 per centum of the sums so appropriated for such year, as the product of the population aged twenty-five to sixty-five, inclusive, in the State in the preceding fiscal year and the State's allotment ratio bears to the sum of the corresponding products for all the States; plus

(4) An amount which bears the same ratio to 5 per centum of the sums so appropriated for such year, as the sum of the amounts allotted to the State under paragraphs (1), (2), and (3) for such year bears to the sum of the amounts allotted to all the States under paragraphs (1), (2), and (3) for such year.

(b) The amount of any State's allotment under subsection (a) for any fiscal year which is less than $10,000 shall be increased to that amount, the total of the increases thereby required being derived by proportionately reducing the allotments to each of the remaining States under such subsection, but with such adjustments as may be necessary to prevent the allotment of any of such remaining States from being thereby reduced to less than that amount.

(c) The amount of any State's allotment under subsection (a) for any fiscal year which the Commissioner determines will not be required for such fiscal year for carrying out the State's plan approved under section 5 shall be available for reallotment from time to time, on such dates during such year as the Commissioner may fix, to other States in proportion to the original allotments to such States under such subsection for such year, but with such proportionate amount for any of such other States being reduced to the extent it exceeds the sum the Commissioner estimates such State needs and will be able to use under the approved plan of such State for such year and the total of such reductions shall be similarly reallotted among the States not suffering such a reduction. Any amount reallotted to a State under this subsection during such year shall be deemed part of its allotment under subsection (a) for such year.

(d) (1) The "allotment ratio" for any State shall be 1.00 less the product of (A) .50 and (B) the quotient obtained by dividing the per capita income for the State by the per capita income for all the States (exclusive of Puerto Rico, Guam, American Samoa, and the Virgin Islands), except that (i) the allotment ratio shall in no case be less than .40

or more than .60, and (ii) the allotment ratio for Puerto Rico, Guam, American Samoa, and the Virgin Islands shall be .60.

(2) The allotment ratios shall be promulgated by the Commissioner for each fiscal year, between July 1 and September 30 of the preceding fiscal year, except that for the fiscal year ending June 30, 1964, such allotment ratios shall be promulgated as soon as possible after the enactment of this part. Allotment ratios shall be computed on the basis of the average of the per capita incomes for a State and for all the States (exclusive of Puerto Rico, Guam, American Samoa, and the Virgin Islands) for the three most recent consecutive fiscal years for which satisfactory data is available from the Department of Commerce.

(3) The term "per capita income" for a State or for all the States (exclusive of Puerto Rico, Guam, American Samoa, and the Virgin Islands) for any fiscal year, means the total personal income for such State, and for all such States, respectively, in the calendar year ending in such fiscal year, divided by the population of such State, and of all such States, respectively, in such fiscal year.

(4) The total population and the population of particular age groups of a State or of all the States shall be determined by the Commissioner on the basis of the latest available estimates furnished by the Department of Commerce.

USES OF FEDERAL FUNDS

SEC. 4. (a) Except as otherwise provided in subsection (b), a State's allotment under section 3 may be used, in accordance with its approved State plan, for any or all of the following purposes:

(1) Vocational education for persons attending high school;

(2) Vocational education for persons who have completed or left high school and who are available for full-time study in preparation for entering the labor market;

(3) Vocational education for persons (other than persons who are receiving training allowances under the Manpower Development and Training Act of 1962 (Public Law 87–415), the Area Redevelopment Act (Public Law 87–27), or the Trade Expansion Act of 1962 (Public Law 87–794)) who have already entered the labor market and who need training or retraining to achieve stability or advancement in employment;

(4) Vocational education for persons who have academic, socioeconomic, or other handicaps that prevent them from succeeding in the regular vocational education program;

(5) Construction of area vocational education school facilities;

(6) Ancillary services and activities to assure quality in all vocational education programs, such as teacher training and supervision, program evaluation, special demonstration and experimental programs, development of instructional materials, and State administration and leadership, including periodic evaluation of State and local vocational education programs and services in light of infor-

mation regarding current and projected manpower needs and job opportunities.

(b) At least 33⅓ per centum of each State's allotment for any fiscal year ending prior to July 1, 1968, and at least 25 per centum of each State's allotment for any subsequent fiscal year shall be used only for the purposes set forth in paragraph (2) or (5), or both, of subsection (a), and at least 3 per centum of each State's allotment shall be used only for the purposes set forth in paragraph (6) of subsection (a), except that the Commissioner may, upon request of a State, permit such State to use a smaller percentage of its allotment for any year for the purposes specified above if he determines that such smaller percentage will adequately meet such purposes in such State.

(c) Ten per centum of the sums appropriated pursuant to section 2 for each fiscal year shall be used by the Commissioner to make grants to colleges and universities, and other public or nonprofit private agencies and institutions, to State boards, and with the approval of the appropriate State board, to local educational agencies, to pay part of the cost of research and training programs and of experimental, developmental, or pilot programs developed by such institutions, boards, or agencies, and designed to meet the special vocational education needs of youths, particularly youths in economically depressed communities who have academic, socioeconomic, or other handicaps that prevent them from succeeding in the regular vocational education programs.

STATE PLANS

SEC. 5. (a) A State which desires to receive its allotments of Federal funds under this part shall submit through its State board to the Commissioner a State plan, in such detail as the Commissioner deems necessary, which—

(1) designates the State board as the sole agency for administration of the State plan, or for supervision of the administration thereof by local educational agencies; and, if such State board does not include as members persons familiar with the vocational education needs of management and labor in the State, and a person or persons representative of junior colleges, technical institutes, or other institutions of higher education which provide programs of technical or vocational training meeting the definition of vocational education in section 8(1) of this Act, provides for the designation or creation of a State advisory council which shall include such persons, to consult with the State board in carrying out the State plan;

(2) sets forth the policies and procedures to be followed by the State in allocating each such allotment among the various uses set forth in paragraphs (1), (2), (3), (4), (5), and (6) of section 4(a), and in allocating Federal funds to local educational agencies in the State, which policies and procedures insure that due consideration will be given to the results of periodic evaluations of State and local vocational education programs and services in light

of information regarding current and projected manpower needs and job opportunities, and to the relative vocational education needs of all groups in all communities in the State, and that Federal funds made available under this part will be so used as to supplement, and, to the extent practical, increase the amounts of State or local funds that would in the absence of such Federal funds be made available for the uses set forth in section 4(a) so that all persons in all communities of the State will as soon as possible have ready access to vocational training suited to their needs, interests, and ability to benefit therefrom, and in no case supplant such State or local funds;

(3) provides minimum qualifications for teachers, teacher-trainers, supervisors, directors, and others having responsibilities under the State plan;

(4) provides for entering into cooperative arrangements with the system of public employment offices in the State, approved by the State board and by the State head of such system, looking toward such offices making available to the State board and local educational agencies occupational information regarding reasonable prospects of employment in the community and elsewhere, and toward consideration of such information by such board and agencies in providing vocational guidance and counseling to students and prospective students and in determining the occupations for which persons are to be trained; and looking toward guidance and counseling personnel of the State board and local educational agencies making available to public employment offices information regarding the occupational qualifications of persons leaving or completing vocational education courses or schools, and toward consideration of such information by such offices in the occupational guidance and placement of such persons;

(5) sets forth such fiscal control and fund accounting procedures as may be necessary to assure proper disbursement of, and accounting for, Federal funds paid to the State (including such funds paid by the State to local educational agencies) under this part;

(6) provides assurance that the requirements of section 7 will be complied with on all construction projects in the State assisted under this part; and

(7) provides for making such reports in such form and containing such information as the Commissioner may reasonably require to carry out his functions under this part, and for keeping such records and for affording such access thereto as the Commissioner may find necessary to assure the correctness and verification of such reports.

(b) The Commissioner shall approve a State plan which fulfills the conditions specified in subsection (a), and shall not finally disapprove a State plan except after reasonable notice and opportunity for a hearing to the State board designated pursuant to paragraph (1) of such subsection.

(c) Whenever the Commissioner, after reasonable notice and opportunity for hearing to the State board administering a State plan approved under subsection (b), finds that—

(1) the State plan has been so changed that it no longer complies with the provisions of subsection (a), or

(2) in the administration of the plan there is a failure to comply substantially with any such provision,

the Commissioner shall notify such State board that no further payments will be made to the State under this part (or, in his discretion, further payments to the State will be limited to programs under or portions of the State plan not affected by such failure) until he is satisfied that there will no longer be any failure to comply. Until he is so satisfied, the Commissioner shall make no further payments to such State under this part (or shall limit payments to programs under or portions of the State plan not affected by such failure).

(d) A State board which is dissatisfied with a final action of the Commissioner under subsection (b) or (c) may appeal to the United States court of appeals for the circuit in which the State is located, by filing a petition with such court within sixty days after such final action. A copy of the petition shall be forthwith transmitted by the clerk of the court to the Commissioner, or any officer designated by him for that purpose. The Commissioner thereupon shall file in the court the record of the proceedings on which he based his action, as provided in section 2112 of title 28, United States Code. Upon the filing of such petition, the court shall have jurisdiction to affirm the action of the Commissioner or to set it aside, in whole or in part, temporarily or permanently, but until the filing of the record the Commissioner may modify or set aside his action. The findings of the Commissioner as to the facts, if supported by substantial evidence, shall be conclusive, but the court, for good cause shown, may remand the case to the Commissioner to take further evidence, and the Commissioner may thereupon make new or modified findings of fact and may modify his previous action, and shall file in the court the record of the further proceedings. Such new or modified findings of fact shall likewise be conclusive if supported by substantial evidence. The judgment of the court affirming or setting aside, in whole or in part, any action of the Commissioner shall be final, subject to review by the Supreme Court of the United States upon certiorari or certification as provided in section 1254 of title 28, United States Code. The commencement of proceedings under this subsection shall not, unless so specifically ordered by the court, operate as a stay of the Commissioner's action.

PAYMENTS TO STATES

SEC. 6. (a) Any amount paid to a State from its allotment under section 3 for the fiscal year ending June 30, 1964, shall be paid on condition that there shall be expended for such year, in accordance with the State plan approved under section 5 or the State plan approved under the Vocational Education Act of 1946 and supplementary vocational education Acts, or both, an amount in State or local funds, or both, which at least equals the amount expended for vocational education during the fiscal year ending June 30, 1963, under the State plan approved under the Vocational Education Act of 1946 and supplementary vocational education Acts.

(b) Subject to the limitations in section 4(b), the portion of a State's allotment for the fiscal year ending June 30, 1965, and for each succeeding year, allocated under the approved State plan for each of the purposes set forth in paragraphs (1), (2), (3), (4), and (6) of section 4(a) shall be available for paying one-half of the State's expenditures under such plan for such year for each such purpose.

(c) The portion of a State's allotment for any fiscal year allocated under the approved State plan for the purpose set forth in paragraph (5) of section 4(a) shall be available for paying not to exceed one-half of the cost of construction of each area vocational education school facility project.

(d) Payments of Federal funds allotted to a State under section 3 to States which have State plans approved under section 5 (as adjusted on account of overpayments or underpayments previously made) shall be made by the Commissioner in advance on the basis of such estimates, in such installments, and at such times, as may be reasonably required for expenditures by the States of the funds so allotted.

LABOR STANDARDS

SEC. 7.   All laborers and mechanics employed by contractors or subcontractors on all construction projects assisted under this part shall be paid wages at rates not less than those prevailing as determined by the Secretary of Labor in accordance with the Davis-Bacon Act, as amended (40 U.S.C. 276a—276a–5). The Secretary of Labor shall have with respect to the labor standards specified in this section the authority and functions set forth in Reorganization Plan Numbered 14 of 1950 (15 F.R. 3176; 5 U.S.C. 133z–15) and section 2 of the Act of June 13, 1934, as amended (40 U.S.C. 276c).

DEFINITIONS

SEC. 8.   For the purposes of this part—

(1) The term "vocational education" means vocational or technical training or retraining which is given in schools or classes (including field or laboratory work incidental thereto) under public supervision and control or under contract with a State board or local educational agency, and is conducted as part of a program designed to fit individuals for gainful employment as semiskilled or skilled workers or technicians in recognized occupations (including any program designed to fit individuals for gainful employment in business and office occupations, and any program designed to fit individuals for gainful employment which may be assisted by Federal funds under the Vocational Education Act of 1946 and supplementary vocational education Acts, but excluding any program to fit individuals for employment in occupations which the Commissioner determines, and specifies in regulations, to be generally considered professional or as requiring a baccalaureate or higher degree). Such term includes vocational guidance

and counseling in connection with such training, instruction related to the occupation for which the student is being trained or necessary for him to benefit from such training, the training of persons engaged as, or preparing to become vocational education teachers, teacher-trainers, supervisors, and directors for such training, travel of students and vocational education personnel, and the acquisition and maintenance and repair of instructional supplies, teaching aids and equipment, but does not include the construction or initial equipment of buildings or the acquisition or rental of land.

(2) The term "area vocational education school" means—

(A) a specialized high school used exclusively or principally for the provision of vocational education to persons who are available for full-time study in preparation for entering the labor market, or

(B) the department of a high school exclusively or principally used for providing vocational education in no less than five different occupational fields to persons who are available for full-time study in preparation for entering the labor market, or

(C) a technical or vocational school used exclusively or principally for the provision of vocational education to persons who have completed or left high school and who are available for full-time study in preparation for entering the labor market, or

(D) the department or division of a junior college or community college or university which provides vocational education in no less than five different occupational fields, under the supervision of the State board, leading to immediate employment but not leading to a baccalaureate degree,

if it is available to all residents of the State or an area of the State designated and approved by the State Board, and if, in the case of a school, department, or division described in (C) or (D), it admits as regular students both persons who have completed high school and persons who have left high school.

(3) The term "school facilities" means classrooms and related facilities (including initial equipment) and interests in land on which such facilities are constructed. Such term shall not include any facility intended primarily for events for which admission is to be charged to the general public.

(4) The term "construction" includes construction of new buildings and expansion, remodeling, and alteration of existing buildings, and includes site grading and improvement and architect fees.

(5) The term "Commissioner" means the Commissioner of Education.

(6) The term "State" includes, in addition to the several States, the District of Columbia, the Commonwealth of Puerto Rico, the Virgin Islands, Guam, and American Samoa.

(7) The term "State board" means the State board designated or created pursuant to section 5 of the Smith-Hughes Act (that is, the Act approved February 23, 1917 (39 Stat. 929, ch. 114; 20 U.S.C. 11–15, 16–28)) to secure to the State the benefits of that Act.

(8) The term "local educational agency" means a board of education

or other legally constituted local school authority having administrative control and direction of public elementary or secondary schools in a city, county, township, school district, or political subdivision in a State, or any other public educational institution or agency having administrative control and direction of a vocational education program.

(9) The term "high school" does not include any grade beyond grade 12.

(10) The term "Vocational Education Act of 1946" means titles I, II, and III of the Act of June 8, 1936, as amended (20 U.S.C. 15i–15m, 150,–15q, 15aa–15jj, 15aaa–15ggg).

(11) The term "supplementary vocational education Acts" means section 1 of the Act of March 3, 1931 (20 U.S.C. 30) (relating to vocational education in Puerto Rico), the Act of March 18, 1950 (20 U.S.C. 31–33) (relating to vocational education in the Virgin Islands), and section 9 of the Act of August 1, 1956 (20 U.S.C. 34) (relating to vocational education in Guam).

ADVISORY COMMITTEE ON VOCATIONAL EDUCATION

SEC. 9. (a) There is hereby established in the Office of Education an Advisory Committee on Vocational Education (hereinafter referred to as the "Advisory Committee"), consisting of the Commissioner, who shall be chairman, one representative each of the Departments of Commerce, Agriculture, and Labor, and twelve members appointed, for staggered terms and without regard to the civil service laws, by the Commissioner with the approval of the Secretary of Health, Education, and Welfare (hereinafter referred to as the "Secretary"). Such twelve members shall, to the extent possible, include persons familiar with the vocational education needs of management and labor (in equal numbers), persons familiar with the administration of State and local vocational education programs, other persons with special knowledge, experience, or qualification with respect to vocational education, and persons representative of the general public, and not more than six of such members shall be professional educators. The Advisory Committee shall meet at the call of the chairman but not less often than twice a year.

(b) The Advisory Committee shall advise the Commissioner in the preparation of general regulations and with respect to policy matters arising in the administration of this part, the Vocational Education Act of 1946, and supplementary vocational education Acts, including policies and procedures governing the approval of State plans under section 5 and the approval of projects under section 4(c) and section 14.

(c) Members of the Advisory Committee shall, while serving on the business of the Advisory Committee, be entitled to receive compensation at rates fixed by the Secretary, but not exceeding $75 per day, including travel time; and, while so serving away from their homes or regular places of business, they may be allowed travel expenses, including per diem in lieu of subsistence, as authorized by section 5 of the Administrative Expenses Act of 1946 (5 U.S.C. 73b–2) for persons in the Government service employed intermittently.

AMENDMENTS TO GEORGE-BARDEN AND SMITH-HUGHES VOCATIONAL EDUCATION ACTS

SEC. 10. Notwithstanding anything to the contrary in title I, II, or III of the Vocational Education Act of 1946 (20 U.S.C. 15i–15m, 15o–15q, 15aa–15jj, 15aaa–15ggg), or in the Smith-Hughes Act (that is, the Act approved February 23, 1917, as amended (39 Stat. 929, ch. 114; 20 U.S.C. 11–15, 16–28)), or in supplementary vocational education Acts—

(a) any portion of any amount allotted (or apportioned) to any State for any purpose under such titles, Act, or Acts for the fiscal year ending June 30, 1964, or for any fiscal year thereafter, may be transferred to and combined with one or more of the other allotments (or apportionments) of such State for such fiscal year under such titles, Act, or Acts, or under section 3 of this part and used for the purposes for which, and subject to the conditions under which, such other allotment (or apportionment) may be used, if the State board requests, in accordance with regulations of the Commissioner, that such portion be transferred and shows to the satisfaction of the Commissioner that transfer of such portion in the manner requested will promote the purpose of this part;

(b) any amounts allotted (or apportioned) under such titles, Act, or Acts for agriculture may be used for vocational education in any occupation involving knowledge and skills in agricultural subjects, whether or not such occupation involves work of the farm or of the farm home, and such education may be provided without directed or supervised practice on a farm;

(c) (1) any amounts allotted (or apportioned) under such titles, Act, or Acts for home economics may be used for vocational education to fit individuals for gainful employment in any occupation involving knowledge and skills in home economics subjects;

(2) at least 10 per centum of any amount so allotted (or apportioned) to a State for each fiscal year beginning after June 30, 1965, may be used only for vocational education to fit persons for gainful employment in occupations involving knowledge and skills in home economics subjects, or transferred to another allotment under subsection (a), or both.

(d) any amounts allotted (or apportioned) under such titles, Act, or Acts for distributive occupations may be used for vocational education for any person over fourteen years of age who has entered upon or is preparing to enter upon such an occupation, and such education need not be provided in part-time or evening schools;

(e) any amounts allotted (or apportioned) under such titles, Act, or Acts for trade and industrial occupations may be used for preemployment schools and classes organized to fit for gainful employment in such occupations persons over fourteen years of age who are in school, and operated for less than nine months per year and less than thirty hours per week and without the requirement that a minimum of 50 per centum of the time be given to practical work on a useful or productive basis, if such preemployment schools and classes are for single-skilled or semiskilled occupations which do not require training or work of such duration or nature; and less than one-third of any amounts so allotted (or apportioned) need be applied to part-time schools or classes for workers who have entered upon employment.

EXTENSION OF PRACTICAL NURSE TRAINING AND AREA VOCATIONAL
EDUCATION PROGRAMS

SEC. 11. (a) (1) Section 201 of the Vocational Education Act of 1946 (20 U.S.C. 15aa) is amended by striking out "of the next eight fiscal years" and inserting in lieu thereof "succeeding fiscal year."

(2) Subsection (c) of section 202 of such Act is amended by striking out "of the next seven fiscal years" and inserting in lieu thereof "succeeding fiscal year."

(b) Section 301 of such Act (20 U.S.C. 15aaa) is amended by striking out "of the five succeeding fiscal years" and inserting in lieu thereof "succeeding fiscal year."

PERIODIC REVIEW OF VOCATIONAL EDUCATION PROGRAMS AND LAWS

SEC. 12. (a) The Secretary shall, during 1966, appoint an Advisory Council on Vocational Education for the purpose of reviewing the administration of the vocational education programs for which funds are appropriated pursuant to this Act and other vocational education Acts and making recommendations for improvement of such administration, and reviewing the status of and making recommendations with respect to such vocational education programs and the Acts under which funds are so appropriated.

(b) The Council shall be appointed by the Secretary without regard to the civil service laws and shall consist of twelve persons who shall, to the extent possible, include persons familiar with the vocational education needs of management and labor (in equal numbers), persons familiar with the administration of State and local vocational education programs, other persons with special knowledge, experience, or qualification with respect to vocational education, and persons representative of the general public.

(c) The Council is authorized to engage such technical assistance as may be required to carry out its functions, and the Secretary shall, in addition, make available to the Council such secretarial, clerical, and other assistance and such pertinent data prepared by the Department of Health, Education, and Welfare as it may require to carry out such functions.

(d) The Council shall make a report of its findings and recommendations (including recommendations for changes in the provisions of this part and other vocational education Acts) to the Secretary, such report to be submitted not later than January 1, 1968, after which date such Council shall cease to exist. The Secretary shall transmit such report to the President and the Congress.

(e) The Secretary shall also from time to time thereafter (but at intervals of not more than five years) appoint an Advisory Council on Vocational Education, with the same functions and constituted in the same manner as prescribed for the Advisory Council in the preceding subsections of this section. Each Council so appointed shall report its findings and recommendations, as prescribed in subsection (d), not later than July 1 of the second year after the year in which it is appointed, after which date such Council shall cease to exist.

(f) Members of the Council who are not regular full-time employees of the United States shall, while serving on business of the Council, be entitled to receive compensation at rates fixed by the Secretary, but not exceeding $75 per day, including travel time; and while so serving away from their homes or regular places of business, they may be allowed travel expenses, including per diem in lieu of subsistence, as authorized by section 5 of the Administrative Expenses Act of 1946 (5 U.S.C. 73b-2) for persons in Government service employed intermittently.

WORK-STUDY PROGRAMS FOR VOCATIONAL EDUCATION STUDENTS

SEC. 13. (a) (1) From the sums appropriated pursuant to section 15 and determined to be for the purposes of this section for each fiscal year, the Commissioner shall allot to each State an amount which bears the same ratio to the sums so determined for such year as the population aged fifteen to twenty, inclusive, of the State, in the preceding fiscal year bears to the population aged fifteen to twenty, inclusive, of all the States in such preceding year.

(2) The amount of any State's allotment under paragraph (1) for any fiscal year which the Commissioner determines will not be required for such fiscal year for carrying out the State's plan approved under subsection (b) shall be available for reallotment from time to time, on such dates during such year as the Commissioner may fix, to other States in proportion to the original allotments to such States under paragraph (1) for such year, but with such proportionate amount for any of such other States being reduced to the extent it exceeds the sum the Commissioner estimates such State needs and will be able to use for such year and the total of such reductions shall be similarly reallotted among the States not suffering such a reduction. Any amount reallotted to a State under this paragraph during such year shall be deemed part of its allotment for such year.

(b) To be eligible to participate in this section, a State must have in effect a plan approved under section 5 and must submit through its State board to the Commissioner a supplement to such plan (hereinafter referred to as a "supplementary plan"), in such detail as the Commissioner determines necessary, which—

(1) designates the State board as the sole agency for administration of the supplementary plan, or for supervision of the administration thereof by local educational agencies;

(2) sets forth the policies and procedures to be followed by the State in approving work-study programs, under which policies and

procedures funds paid to the State from its allotment under subsection (a) will be expended solely for the payment of compensation of students employed pursuant to work-study programs which meet the requirements of subsection (c), except that not to exceed 1 per centum of any such allotment, or $10,000, whichever is the greater, may be used to pay the cost of developing the State's supplementary plan and the cost of administering such supplementary plan after its approval under this section;

(3) sets forth principles for determining the priority to be accorded applications from local educational agencies for work-study programs, which principles shall give preference to applications submitted by local educational agencies serving communities having substantial numbers of youths who have dropped out of school or who are unemployed, and provides for undertaking such programs, insofar as financial resources available therefor make possible, in the order determined by the application of such principles;

(4) sets forth such fiscal control and fund accounting procedures as may be necessary to assure proper disbursement of, and accounting for, Federal funds paid to the State (including such funds paid by the State to local educational agencies) under this section;

(5) provides for making such reports in such form and containing such information as the Commissioner may reasonably require to carry out his functions under this section, and for keeping such records and for affording such access thereto as the Commissioner may find necessary to assure the correctness and verification of such reports.

(c) For the purposes of this section, a work-study program shall—

(1) be administered by the local educational agency and made reasonably available (to the extent of available funds) to all youths in the area served by such agency who are able to meet the requirements of paragraph (2);

(2) provide that employment under such work-study program shall be furnished only to a student who (A) has been accepted for enrollment as a full-time student in a vocational education program which meets the standards prescribed by the State board and the local educational agency for vocational education programs assisted under the preceding sections of this part, or in the case of a student already enrolled in such a program, is in good standing and in full-time attendance, (B) is in need of the earnings from such employment to commence or continue his vocational education program, and (C) is at least fifteen years of age and less than twenty-one years of age at the commencement of his employment, and is capable, in the opinion of the appropriate school authorities, of maintaining good standing in his vocational education program while employed under the work-study program;

(3) provide that no student shall be employed under such work-study program for more than fifteen hours in any week in which classes in which he is enrolled are in session, or for compensation which exceeds $45 in any month or $350 in any academic year or its equivalent, unless the student is attending a school which is not within reasonable commuting distance from his home, in which case his compensation may not exceed $60 in any month or $500 in any academic year or its equivalent;

(4) provide that employment under such work-study program shall be for the local educational agency or for some other public agency or institution;

(5) provide that, in each fiscal year during which such program remains in effect, such agency shall expend (from sources other than payments from Federal funds under this section) for the employment of its students (whether or not in employment eligible for assistance under this section) an amount that is not less than its average annual expenditure for work-study programs of a similar character during the three fiscal years preceding the fiscal year in which its work-study program under this section is approved.

(d) Subsections (b), (c), and (d) of section 5 (pertaining to the approval of State plans, the withholding of Federal payments in case of nonconformity after approval, and judicial review of the Commissioner's final actions in disapproving a State plan or withholding payments) shall be applicable to the Commissioner's actions with respect to supplementary plans under this section.

(e) From a State's allotment under this section for the fiscal year ending June 30, 1965, and for the fiscal year ending June 30, 1966, the Commissioner shall pay to such State an amount equal to the amount expended for compensation of students employed pursuant to work-study programs under the State's supplementary plan approved under this section, plus an amount, not to exceed 1 per centum of such allotment, or $10,000, whichever is the greater, expended for the development of the State's supplementary plan and for the administration of such plan after its approval by the Commissioner. From a State's allotment under this section for the fiscal year ending June 30, 1967, and for the next succeeding fiscal year, such payment shall equal 75 per centum of the amount so expended. No State shall receive payments under this section for any fiscal year in excess of its allotment under subsection (a) for such fiscal year.

(f) Such payments (adjusted on account of overpayments or underpayments previously made) shall be made by the Commissioner in advance on the basis of such estimates, in such installments, and at such times, as may be reasonably required for expenditures by the States of the funds allotted under subsection (a).

(g) Students employed in work-study programs under this section shall not by reason of such employment be deemed employees of the United States, or their service Federal service, for any purpose.

RESIDENTIAL VOCATIONAL EDUCATION SCHOOLS

SEC. 14. For the purpose of demonstrating the feasibility and desirability of residential vocational education schools for certain youths of high school age, the Commissioner is authorized to make grants, out of sums appropriated pursuant to section 15 to State boards, to colleges and universities, and with the approval of the appropriate State board, to public educational agencies, organizations, or institutions for the construction, equipment, and operation of residential schools to provide vocational education (including room, board, and other necessities) for youths, at least fifteen years of age and less than twenty-one years of age at the time of enrollment, who need full-time study on a residential basis in order to benefit fully from such education. In making such grants, the Commissioner shall give special consideration to the needs of large urban areas having substantial numbers of youths who have dropped out of school or are unemployed and shall seek to attain, as nearly as practicable in the light of the purposes of this section, an equitable geographical distribution of such schools.

AUTHORIZATION FOR SECTIONS 13 AND 14

SEC. 15. There is authorized to be appropriated for the purpose of carrying out the provisions of sections 13 and 14, $30,000,000 for the fiscal year ending June 30, 1965, $50,000,000 for the fiscal year ending June 30, 1966, and $35,000,000 for the fiscal year ending June 30, 1967, and the succeeding fiscal year. The Commissioner shall determine the portion of such sums for each such year which is to be used for the purposes of each such section.

FEDERAL CONTROL

SEC. 16. Nothing contained in this part shall be construed to authorize any department, agency, officer, or employee of the United States to exercise any direction, supervision, or control over the curriculum, program of instruction, administration, or personnel of any educational institution or school system.

SHORT TITLE

SEC. 17. This part may be cited as the "Vocational Education Act of 1963." Approved December 18, 1963.

INDEX